Mr. & Mrs. Robert Hotchkiss, Jr.
7005 NW Cross Road
Parkville, MO 64152

PATRIARCHS
OF THE
FAITH

PATRIARCHS

OF THE

FAITH

By
Rev. F. B. Meyer

AMG
PUBLISHERS
Chattanooga, TN 37422

Patriarchs
of the Faith

©1995 by AMG Publishers
All Rights Reserved.

Originally published by
the Fleming H. Revell Company in New York.

ISBN 0-89957-206-5

Printed in the United States of America

Contents

Foreword

F. B. Meyer's *Patriarchs of the Faith* is an inspiring collection of Scripture biographies of four Old Testament patriarchs—Abraham, Jacob, Joseph and Moses. In delineating the lives of these men of God, Meyer presents insightful homilies regarding the events of their lives and the roles they played in God's divine plan for His people.

We at AMG Publishers have compiled what were previously four separate volumes into this one work, and in doing so, we have made a few minor changes to the original works to help make their content more clear to modern readers: We have updated spelling and some archaic terms in accordance with how our language has changed over the years; in some cases, unusual forms of punctuation have been simplified in order to eliminate confusion. Readers should note that the points of current history mentioned by Meyer are from the latter half of nineteenth-century England.

It is our hope that readers will be moved by the wisdom in these chapters to seek a deeper knowledge and understanding of God's Word.

I
Abraham: The Obedience of Faith

Preface

In sending out from the Press these Studies in the Life of Abraham, I am very sensible of the inadequacy of my attempt to conceive, or portray, one of the greatest characters of History. And yet there is one thought pervading the entire narrative, which brings it near to the poorest limner of its noble outlines. Abraham was great through his faith. And that faith was at first but a silver thread, a tiny streak, an insignificant sinew—not stronger than that which trembles in the humblest and weakest reader of these lines.

But whatever faith is, it is the link with the Omnipotence; the channel for the Divine communications; the wire along which the Fire of Heaven may travel. And as it is used according to the promptings of the Divine Spirit, and in obedience to his commands, it will grow. It grew in Abraham. It will grow in us.

To trace the laws of that growth, and its gradual increase, for the encouragement of those who by faith are the children of Abraham, and who long with intense desire to emulate their great progenitor, until they can remove mountains of difficulty and achieve apparent impossibilities, has been the great principle on which these pages have been prepared.

F. B. Meyer.

1
The Hole of the Pit

The God of glory appeared unto our father Abraham, when he
was in Mesopotamia, before he dwelt in Charran; and said unto
him, Get thee out of thy country, and from thy kindred, and
come into the land which I shall show thee.
—Acts 7:2, 3

Look unto the rock whence you are hewn, and to the hole of the
pit whence ye are digged. Look unto Abraham your father.
—Isaiah 51:1, 2

In the grey dawn of history the first great character that arrests
our attention at any length is that of Abraham; who would command
out notice for this, if for nothing else, that he is spoken of
as the "Friend of God." Surely it must be well worthy of our devout
consideration to study the inner life, and outward carriage, of such a
man: that we, too, in our smaller measure, may become—not servants
only, but—"friends"; the favored confidants of God—from whom
He will not hide His secrets, to whom He will make known His will.

Many rays of interest focus in the story of Abraham. His portrait
is drawn with such detail, that it lives before us, with the same hopes
and fears, golden hours and hours of depression, that are familiar factors
in our lives. Then, also, his life is so constantly referred to in the
Old Testament, and in the New, that it would seem as if the right understanding
of it is necessary to give us the clue to many a difficult passage,
and many a sacred doctrine, in the succeeding pages of the
Bible. Nor can it fail to interest us to discover the reason why the wild
Bedouin of the desert and the modern Englishman—the conservative
East, and the progressive and swift-moving West; the Mohammedan
and the Christian—can find in the tent of the first Hebrew a common
meeting ground, and in himself a common origin.

Our story takes us back two thousand years before the birth of Christ, and to the ancient city of Ur. And it may be well, by the aid of modern discovery, to consider the earliest conditions amid which this life was cradled. We like to stand in that lone spot among the hills, where, amid the bracken and the gorse, or from some moss-grown basin of rock, there springs forth the river which drains a continent, and flows, laden with navies to the sea. We ask the biographer to tell us something of the scenes amid which a great life was nurtured, because we think that we can better understand its color, current, and drift. So would we thank modern discovery for having cast its lantern on the ruins of that old world city, which was the busy home of life when flocks browsed on the seven hills of Rome; and red deer, light of foot, roamed over the site of St. Paul's, or came down to drink the undefiled and pellucid waters of the Thames.

We must look for Ur, not in Upper Mesopotamia, where a mistaken tradition has fixed it, but in the ruins of Mugheir, in the near vicinity of the Persian Gulf. Forty centuries, slowly silting up the shore, have driven the sea back about a hundred miles. But at the time of which we speak it is probable[*] that Abraham's natal city stood upon the coast near the spot where the Euphrates poured the volume of its waters into the ocean waves.

"The present remains of the town consist of a series of low mounds disposed in an oval shape, measuring about two miles in extent, and commanded by a larger mound of seventy feet in height, on which are the remains of what must have been once a vast temple, dedicated to the Moon."[**] In olden days, it was a large and flourishing city, standing on the sea, and possessed of fleets of vessels, which coasted along the shores of the Indian Ocean, freighted with the products of the rich and fertile soil.

It would be foreign to our purpose to attempt a description of the luxuriance of that Chaldean land, watered by its two mighty streams,[†]

---

[*] The site of Ur is still a matter of discussion, into which I have no desire to enter. I have adopted the more recent suggestion because the distance from Charran seems to comport better with the narrative. The old site assigned to Ur was only a day or two's march from Charran, and surely Terah would not have broken up his home for so short a journey.

[**] Professor Rawlinson   [†] The Euphrates and the Tigris

and in which the corn crop was of marvelous abundance, and the date palm attained to an extraordinary growth, repaying richly the scanty labors of the people; and where pomegranates and apples, grapes and tamarisks grew wild. Suffice it to say, that it was a long green strip of garden land, sufficient to attract and maintain vast populations of men, and specially suitable for the settlement of those shepherd tribes which required extensive pasture lands for their herds and flocks.

These sons of Ham were grossly *idolatrous*. In that clear transparent atmosphere, the heavenly bodies blazed with extraordinary effulgence, beguiling the early Chaldeans into a system of Nature worship, which speedily became identified with rites of gross indulgence and impurity, such as those into which humanity always falls, when it refuses to retain God in its knowledge, and gives itself up to the dictates of its own carnal lusts. The race seemed verging again on the brink of those horrible and unnatural crimes which had already necessitated its almost total destruction; and it was evident that some expedient must be speedily adopted to arrest the progress of moral defilement, and to save mankind. This enterprise was undertaken by Him, whose delights have ever been with the sons of men, and who, in after days, could say, with majestic emphasis, "Before Abraham was, I AM." And He accomplished His purpose then, as so often since, by *separating* to Himself one man, that through him and his descendants, when they had been thoroughly purified and prepared, He might operate upon the fallen race of man, recalling it to Himself and elevating it by a moral lever, working on a pivot outside itself.

Four centuries had passed away since the Flood; and they must have been centuries abounding in emigrations. Population multiplied more rapidly than now, and all the world was open where to choose. Leaving the first seats of life, swarm after swarm must have hived off in every direction. Surging waves of men, pressed on by hunger, love of conquest, or stronger hordes behind, spread outwards over the world. The sons of Japheth pushed northwards, to colonize Europe and Asia, and to lay the foundations of the great Indo-European family. The sons of Ham pushed southwards, over the fertile plains of Chaldea, where, under the lead of the mighty Nimrod, they built towns of baked clay; reared temples, of which the ruins remain to this day; and cultivated the arts of civilized life to an extent unknown elsewhere. They are said to have been proficient in mathematics and astronomy; in weaving, metal working, and gem engraving; and to have preserved their thoughts by writing on clay tablets.

Now, it so happened, that into the midst of this Hamite colonization there had come a family of the sons of Shem. This clan, under the lead of Terah, had settled down on the rich pasture lands outside Ur. The walled cities, and civilized arts, and merchant traffic, had little attraction for them, as they were rather a race of shepherds, living in tents, or in villages of slightly constructed huts. And if Noah's prediction were verified (Gen. 9:26), we may believe that their religious life was sweeter and purer than that of the people among whom we find them.

But, alas! the moral virus soon began its work. The close association of this Shemite family with the idolatrous and abominable practices of the children of Ham, tainted the purity and simplicity of its early faith; and it is certain that a leveling down process was subtly at work, lowering its standard to that of its neighbors. Joshua (Josh. 24:15) says distinctly that the fathers of the children of Israel, who dwelt beyond the flood of the Euphrates, served other gods. And there are traces of the evil in the home of Laban, from which Rachel stole the images (*teraphim*), the loss of which so kindled her father's wrath (Gen. 31:19–35). It is a heavy responsibility for godly people to live amid scenes of notorious godlessness and sin. If they escape the snare, their children may be caught in it. What right have we heedlessly to expose young lives to foul miasma, which may taint and defile them for evermore! And if through the claims of duty we are compelled to live in any such baleful and noxious atmosphere, let us ask that the fire of Divine purity may extend like a cordon of defense around our home; and that our dear ones may dwell in the secret place of the Most High.

Amid such scenes ABRAHAM was born, and grew from youth to manhood. But, from the first, if we may credit the traditions which have lingered in the common talk of the unchanging East, he must have possessed no ordinary character. According to those stories, which, if not literally true, are no doubt based on a substratum of fact, as a young man Abraham offered an uncompromising opposition to the evil practices which were rife, not only in the land, but in his father's house. He employed the weapon of sarcasm, used so effectively afterwards by the prophets to his own descendants. He broke the helpless images to pieces. He refused to bow before the subtle element of fire at the bidding of the monarch, and under the penalty of martyrdom. Thus early was he being detached from the quarry of heathendom, dug from "the hole of the pit," preparatory to being shaped as a pillar in the house of the Lord.

There is nothing of all this in Scripture, but there is nothing inconsistent with it. On the contrary, as the peculiar movements of a planet suggest the presence of some celestial body of a definite size, which is yet hidden from view in the depths of space: so the mature character, the faith, and the ready obedience of this man, when he first comes under our notice, convince us that there must have been a long previous period of severe trial and testing. The mushroom is the child of a single night, but the oak, which is a match for the tempest, is the result of long years of sun and air, of breeze and storm.

At last, THE GOD OF GLORY APPEARED UNTO HIM. The light had been growing on his vision; and finally the sun broke out from the obscuring clouds. In what form of glory Jehovah revealed himself we cannot guess, but we must believe that there was some outward manifestation which dated an epoch in Abraham's life, and gave him unmistakable basis of belief for all his future. Probably the Son, who from all eternity has been the Word of God, arrayed Himself, as afterwards on the plains of Mamre, in an angel form; or spoke to him, as afterwards to Isaiah, from the midst of the burning seraphim (Is. 7). In any case, the celestial vision was accompanied by a call, like that which in all ages of the world has come to loyal hearts, summoning them to awake to their true destiny, and take their place in the regeneration of the world: "Get thee out of thy country, and from thy kindred, and from thy father's house, unto the land that I will show thee" (Gen. 12:1). If we live up to our light, we shall have more light. If we are faithful in a very little, we may have the opportunity of being faithful in much. If we are steadfast in Chaldea, we may be called out to play a great part in the history of the world. God's choice is never arbitrary, but is based on some previous traits in those whom He summons from among their fellows to His aid. "Whom He foreknew, He also did predestinate."

It is impossible to tell into whose hands these words may fall. Young men amid the godless tea planters of India, or in the wild bush life of Australia. Sailors on shipboard, and soldiers in camp. Lonely confessors of Christ in worldly and vicious societies; where there is everything to weaken, and nothing to reinforce the resistance of the brave but faltering spirit. Let all such take heart! They are treading a well-worn path, on which the noblest of mankind have preceded them; and which was much more difficult in days when few were found in it, and specially in that day, when a solitary man, the "father of many nations," trod it.

One symptom of being on that path is *loneliness*. "I called him alone" (Is. 51:2). It was a loneliness that pressed hard on the heart of Jesus. But it is a loneliness which is assured of the Divine companionship (see John 8:16, 29; 16:32). And though no eye seems to notice the struggles, and protests, and endeavors of the solitary spirit, they are watched with the sympathy of all heaven; and presently there will be heard a call, like that which started Abraham as a pilgrim, and opened before him the way into marvelous blessedness.

Despair not for the future of the world. Out of its heart will yet come those who shall lift it up to a new level. Sauls are being trained in the bosom of the Sanhedrin; Luthers in the cloisters of the Papal Church; Abrahams under the shadows of great heathen temples. God knows where to find them. And, when the times are darkest, they shall lead forth a host of pilgrim spirits, numberless as the sand on the seashore; or as the stardust, lying thick through the illimitable expanse of space.

2

The Divine Summons

Get thee out of thy country, and from thy
kindred, and from thy father's house, unto
the land that I will show thee: and I will
make of thee a great nation, and I will bless
thee, and make thy name great;
and thou shalt be a blessing.
—Genesis 12:1, 2

While Abraham was living quietly in Ur, protesting against the idolatry of his times, with all its attendant evils, and according to tradition, suffering bitter persecution, for conscience sake, "The God of glory appeared unto him, and said, Get thee out of thy country, and from thy kindred, and come into the land which I shall show thee" (Acts 7:2, 3).

This was the first of those marvelous appearances which anticipated the Incarnation; and marked the successive stages of God's manifestation of Himself to men.

When this Divine appearance came we do not know; it may have been in the still and solemn night, or in the evening hour of meditation; or amid the duties of his position: but suddenly there shone from heaven a great light round about him, and a visible form appeared in the heart of the glory, and a voice spake the message of heaven in his ear. Not thus does God now appear to us; and yet it is certain that He still speaks in the silence of the waiting spirit, impressively His will, and saying, "Get thee out." Listen for that voice in the inner shrine of thine heart.

This same voice has often spoken since. It called Elijah from Thisbe, and Amos from Tekoa; Peter from his fishing nets, and Matthew

11

from his toll booth; Cromwell from his farm in Huntingdon, and Luther from his cloister at Erfurt. It ever sounds the perpetual summons of God, "Come out from her, My people, that ye be not partakers of her sins, and that ye receive not of her plagues"; "Come out from among them, and be ye separate, saith the Lord, and touch not the unclean thing." Has it not come to you? Strange, if it has not. Yet, if it has, let nothing hinder your obedience; strike your tents, and follow where the God of glory beckons; and in that word COME, understand that He is moving on in front, and that if you would have His companionship, we must follow.

I. THIS CALL INVOLVED HARDSHIP. He was a childless man. He had sufficient for the supply of his needs. He was deeply attached to those who were united to him by the close ties of a common nature. It was no small matter for him to break up his camp, to tear himself from his nearest and dearest, and to start for a land which, as yet, he did not know.

And so must it always be. The summons of God will ever involve a wrench from much that nature holds dear. We must be prepared to take up our cross daily if we would follow where He points the way. Each step of real advance in the Divine life will involve an altar on which some dear fragment of the self life has been offered; or a cairn beneath which some cherished idol has been buried.

It is true that the blessedness which awaits us will more than compensate us for the sacrifices which we may have to make. And the prospect of the future may well allure us forward, but still, when it comes to the point, there is certain anguish as the last link is broken, the last farewell said, and the last look taken of the receding home of past happy years. And this is God's winnowing fan, which clearly separates chaff and wheat. Many cannot endure a test so severe and searching in its demands. Like Pliable, they get out of the slough by the side nearest to their home. Like the young man, they go away sorrowful from the One to whom they had come with haste. Shall this be the case with you? Will you hear the call of God and shrink back from its cost? Count the cost clearly indeed, but, having done so, go forward in the name and by the strength of Him in whom all things are possible and easy and safe. And in doing so you will approve yourself worthy to stand with Christ in the regeneration.

Nothing is more clear than that, in these critical days, God is summoning the whole Church to a great advance, not only in knowledge, and in spiritual experience, but also in the evangelization of the world. Blessed are they who are privileged to have a share in this sublime campaign!

II. BUT THIS CALL WAS EMINENTLY WISE. It was wise for *Abraham himself.* Nothing strengthens us so much as isolation and transplantation. Let a young man emigrate, or be put into a responsible position; let him be thrown on his own resources—and he will develop powers of which there would have been no trace, if he had always lived at home, dependent on others, and surrounded by luxury. Under the wholesome demand his soul will put forth all her native vigor.

But what is true of the natural qualities of the soul is preeminently true of faith. So long as we are quietly at rest amid favorable and undisturbed surroundings, faith sleeps as an undeveloped sinew within us; a thread, a germ, an idea. But when we are pushed out from all these surroundings, with nothing but God to look to, then faith grows suddenly into a cable, a monarch oak, a master principle of the life.

As long as the bird lingers by the nest, it will not know the luxury of flight. As long as the trembling boy holds to the bank, or toes the bottom, he will not learn the ecstasy of battling with the ocean wave. As long as men cling to the material, they cannot appreciate the reality of the promises of God. Abram could never have become Abraham, the father of the faithful, the mighty exemplar of faith, if he had always lived in Ur. No; he must quit his happy home, and journey forth into the untried and unknown, that faith may rise up to all its glorious proportions in his soul.

It may not be necessary for us to withdraw from home and friends, but we shall have to withdraw our heart's deepest dependence from all earthly props and supports, if ever we are to learn what it is to trust simply and absolutely on the eternal God. It may be that He is breaking away just now the shores on which we have been leaning, that the ship may glide down upon the ocean wave.

It was wise *for the world's sake.* On this one man rested the hope for the future of the world. Had he remained in Ur, it is impossible to say whether he would have continued true; or whether he might not have been seriously infected by the idolatry around. Or, even if he had been enabled to resist the adverse influences, his family, and, above all, his children, might have failed beneath the terrible ordeal. Was it not therefore, wise for the world's sake, and for the sake of the Divine purposes, that he should be taken right away from his home and early associations, to find a fresh religious starting point for the race, on new soil, and under new conditions?

Was it not thus that, in days of abounding vice and superstition, God led the Pilgrim Fathers to cross the seas and found a new world, on the inhospitable shores of New England? And has it not been the plan of the Divine government in all ages? It is impossible to move our times, so long as we live beneath their spell, but when once we have risen up, and gone, at the call of God, outside their pale, we are able to react on them with an irresistible power. Archimedes vaunted that he could lift the world, if only he could obtain, outside of it, a pivot on which to rest his lever. Do not be surprised then, if God calls you out to be a people to Himself, that by you He may react with blessed power on the great world of men.

Sometimes, indeed, He bids us stay where we are, to glorify Him there. But more often He bids us leave unhallowed companionships, irreligious associations, evil fellowships and partnerships, and at great cost to get ourselves away into the isolation of a land which He promises to reveal.

III. This Call was accompanied by Promise. God's commands are not always accompanied by reasons, but always by promises, expressed or understood. To give reasons would excite discussion, but to give a promise shows that the reason, though hidden, is all-sufficient. We can understand the promise, though the reason might baffle and confuse us. The reason is intellectual, metaphysical, spiritual, but a promise is practical, positive, literal. As a shell encloses a kernel, so do the Divine commands hide promises in their heart. If this is the command: "Believe on the Lord Jesus Christ"; this is the promise: "And thou shalt be saved." If this is the command: "Sell that thou hast and give to the poor"; this is the promise: "Thou shalt have treasure in heaven." If this is the command: "Leave father and mother, houses and land"; this is the promise: "Thou shalt have a hundredfold here, and everlasting life beyond." If this is the command: "Be ye separate"; this is the promise: "I will receive you and be a Father unto you." So in this case: Though thou art childless, I will make of thee a great nation: though thou art the youngest son, I will bless thee, and make thy name great: though thou art to be torn from thine own family, in thee shall all the families of the earth be blessed. And each of those promises has been literally fulfilled.

It may seem that the hardships involved in the summons to exile are too great to be borne; yet study well the promise which is attached. And as the "City which hath foundations" looms on the view, it will dwarf the proportions of the Ur in which you have been content to spend your days; and you will rise to be gone. Sometime, therefore, it seems easier not to dwell on the sacrifice involved, but on the contents of the Divine and gracious promise. Bid people take; and they will give up of themselves. Let men find in Jesus the living water, and, like the woman of Samaria, they will leave their waterpots. Fire the hearts of the young with all the beauty and blessedness of the service of Jesus; and they will not find it so hard to leave nets, and fishing boats, and friends, to forsake all and follow Him. "When it pleased God to reveal His Son in me . . . immediately I conferred not with flesh and blood."

St. Francis de Sales used to say, "When the house is on fire, men are ready to throw everything out of the window; and when the heart is full of God's true love, men are sure to count all else but worthless."

IV. This Call teaches us the Meaning of Election. Everywhere we find beings and things more loftily endowed than others of the same kind. This is markedly evident in the religious sphere. And there is at first a jarring wonder at the apparent inequality of the Divine arrangements; until we understand that the superior endowment of the few is intended to enable them the better to help and bless the rest. "I will bless thee, and thou shalt be a blessing."

A great thinker feels that his end is approaching; he has made grand discoveries, but he has not as yet given them to the world. He selects one of his most promising pupils, and carefully indoctrinates him with his system; he is very severe on any inaccuracies and mistakes; he is very careful to give line on line. Why does he take all this care? For the sake of the young man? Not exclusively for the pupil's benefit, but that he may be able to give to the world those thoughts which his dying master has confided to his care. The young disciple is blessed that he may pass the blessings on to others.

Is not this a glimpse into the intention of God, in selecting Abraham, and in him the whole family of Israel? It was not so much with a view to their personal salvation, though that was included, but that they might pass on the holy teachings and oracles with which they were entrusted. It would have been worse than useless to have given such jewels directly to mankind. As well put a gorgeous banquet before a hungry babe. To say the least, there was no language ready in which to enshrine the scared thoughts of God. The genius of truth required that the minds of men should be prepared to apprehend its sacred lessons. It was needful that definitions and methods of expression should be first well learned by the people, who, when they had learned them, might become the teachers of mankind.

The deep question is, whether election has not much more to do with our ministry than with our personal salvation. It brings less of rest, and peace, and joy, than it does of anguish, bitterness, and sorrow of heart. There is no need to envy God's elect ones. They are the exiles, the crossbearers, the martyrs among men, but careless of themselves, they are all the while learning God's deepest lessons, away from the ordinary haunts of men; and they return to them presently with discoveries that pass all human thought, and are invaluable for human life.

V. THIS CALL GIVES THE KEY TO ABRAHAM'S LIFE. It rang a clarion note at the very outset, which continued to vibrate through all his after-history. The key to Abraham's life is the word "Separation." He was from first to last a SEPARATED MAN. Separated from his fatherland and kinsfolk; separated from Lot; separated, as a pilgrim and stranger, from the people of the land; separated from his own methods of securing a fulfillment of the promises of God; separated from the rest of mankind by special sorrows, which brought him into closer fellowship with God than has ever been reached by man; separated to high and lofty fellowship in thoughts and plans, which God could not hide from him.

BUT IT WAS THE SEPARATION OF FAITH.

There is a form of separation known among men, in which the lonely soul goes apart, to secure uninterrupted leisure for devotion; spending the slow-passing hours in vigil, fasting, and prayer; hoping to win salvation as the guerdon of its austerities. This is not the separation to which God called Abraham, or to which we are summoned.

Abraham's separation is not like that of those who wish to be saved, but rather that of those who are saved. Not towards the Cross, but from it. Not to merit anything, but, because the heart has seen the Vision of God, and cannot now content itself with the things that once fascinated and entranced it; so that leaving them behind, it reaches out its hands in eager longing for eternal realities, and thus is led gradually and insensibly out and away from the seen to the unseen, and from the temporal to the eternal.

May such separation be ours! May we catch the Divine Call, irradiated by the Divine Promise! And as we hear of that fair land, of that glorious city, of those Divine delights which wait us, may we leave and relinquish those lesser and injurious things which have held us too long, spoiling our peace, and sapping our power; and striking our tents, obey our God's behest, though it may lead us whither we know not!

3

"He Obeyed"

By faith Abraham, when he was called to go
out into a place which he should after receive
for an inheritance, obeyed.
—Hebrews 11:8

A h, how much there is in those two words! Blessedness in heart, and home, and life; fulfilled promises; mighty opportunities of good—lie along the narrow thorn-set path of obedience to the word and will of God. If Abraham had permanently refused obedience to the voice that summoned him to sally forth on his long and lonely pilgrimage, he would have sunk back into the obscurity of an unknown grave in the land of Ur, like many an Eastern sheik before and since. So does the phosphorescent wave flash for a moment in the wake of the vessel plowing her way by night through the southern seas; and then it is lost to sight forever. But, thank God, Abraham obeyed, and in that act laid the foundation stone of the noble structure of his life.

It may be that some will read these words whose lives have been a disappointment, and a sad surprise; like some young fruit tree, laden in spring with blossom, but which, in the golden autumn stands barren and alone amid the abundant fruitage of the orchard. You have not done what you expected to so. You have not fulfilled the prognostications of your friends. You have failed to realize the early promise of your life. And may not the reason lie in this, that away back in your life, there rang out a command which summoned you to an act of self-sacrifice from which you shrank? And *that* has been your one fatal mistake. The worm at the root of the gourd. The little rot within the timber. The false step, which deflected the life course from the King's highway into a blind alley.

Would it not be well to ascertain if this be not so, and to hasten back to fulfill even now the long delayed obedience, supposing it to be possible? Oh, do not think that it is now too late to repair the error of the past; or that the Almighty God will not refuse, on account of your delay, that to which He once summoned you in the young, glad years, which have taken their flight forever. "He is merciful and gracious, slow to anger, and plenteous in goodness and truth." Do not use your long delay as an argument for longer delay, but as a reason for immediate action. "Why tarriest thou?"

Abraham, as the story shows, at first met the call of God with a mingled and partial obedience; and then for long years neglected it entirely. But the door stood still open for him to enter, and that gracious Hand still beckoned him; until he struck his tents, and started to cross the mighty desert with all that owned his sway. It was a partial failure, which is pregnant with invaluable lessons for ourselves.

I. AT FIRST, THEN, ABRAHAM'S OBEDIENCE WAS ONLY PARTIAL. *He took Terah with him;* indeed, it is said that "Terah took Abram his son, and Lot the son of Haran, and Sarai his daughter-in-law; and they went forth with them from Ur of the Chaldees" (Gen. 11:31). How Terah was induced to leave the land of his choice, and the graves of his dead, where his son Haran slept, we cannot tell. Was Abraham his favorite son, from whom he could not part? Was he dissatisfied with his camping grounds? Or, had he been brought to desire an opportunity of renouncing his idols, and beginning a better life amid healthier surroundings? We do not know. This, at least, is clear, that he was not wholehearted; nor were his motives unmixed; and his presence in the march had the disastrous effect of slackening Abraham's pace, and of interposing a parenthesis of years in an obedience which, at first, promised so well. Days which break in sunlight are not always bright throughout; mists, born of earth, ascend and veil the sky: but eventually the sun breaks out again, and, for the remaining hours of daylight, shines in a sky unflecked with cloud. It was so with Abraham.

The clan marched leisurely along the valley of the Euphrates, finding abundance of pasture in its broad alluvial plains, until at last Haran was reached; the point from which caravans for Canaan leave the Euphrates to strike off across the desert. There they halted, and there they stayed till Terah died. Was it that the old man was too weary for further journeyings? Did he like Haran too well to leave it? Did heart and flesh fail, as he looked out on that far expanse of level sand, behind which the sun set in lurid glory every night? In any case, he would go no farther on the pilgrimage, and probably for as many as fifteen years, Abraham's obedience was stayed; and for that period there were no further commands, no additional promises, no hallowed communings between God and His child.

It becomes us to be very careful as to whom we take with us in our pilgrimage. We may make a fair start from our Ur, but if we take Terah with us, we shall not go far. Take care, young pilgrim to eternity, to whom you mate yourself in the marriage bond. Beware, man of business, lest you find your Terah in the man with whom you are entering into partnership. Let us all beware of that fatal spirit of compromise, which tempts us to tarry where beloved ones bid us to stay. "Do not go to extremes," they cry; "we are willing to accompany you on your pilgrimage, if you will only go as far as Haran! Why think of going farther on a fool's errand—and whither you do not know?" Ah! this is hard to bear, harder far than outward opposition. Weakness and infirmity appeal to our feelings against our better judgment. The plains of Capua do for warriors what the arms of Rome failed to accomplish. And, tempted by the bewitching allurements, which hold out to us their siren attractions, we imitate the sailors of Ulysses, and vow we will go no farther in quest of our distant goal.

"When his father was dead, He removed him into this land" (Acts 7:4). Death had to interpose, to set him free from the deadly incubus which held him fast. Terah must die ere Abraham will resume the forsaken path. Here we may get a solution for mysteries in God's dealings with us, which have long puzzled us; and understand why our hopes have withered, our schemes have miscarried, our income has dwindled, our children have turned against us. All these things were hindering our true development; and, out of mercy to our best interests, God has been compelled to take the knife in hand, and set us at liberty. He loves us so much that He dares to bear the pain of inflicting pain. And thus Death opens the door to Life, and through the grave we pass into the glad world of Hope and Promise which lies upon its farther side.

> Glory to God, 'to God,' he saith,
> Knowledge by suffering entereth,
> And life is perfected through death.

II. ABRAHAM'S OBEDIENCE WAS RENDERED POSSIBLE BY HIS FAITH—"So Abram departed, as the Lord had spoken unto him. And he took Sarai his wife, and Lot, his brother's son, and all their substance that they had gathered, and the souls that they had gotten in Haran, and they went forth" (Gen. 12:5). No easy matter that! It was bitter to leave the kinsfolk that had gathered around him; for Nahor seems to have followed his old father and brother up the valley to their new settlement at Haran, and we find his family living there afterwards.[*] There was no overcrowding in those ample pastures. And to crown the whole, the pilgrim actually did not know his destination, as he proposed to turn his back on the Euphrates, and his face towards the great desert. Do you not suppose that Nahor would make this the one subject of his attack?

"What do you want more, my brother, which you cannot have here?"

"I want nothing but to do the will of God, wherever it may lead me."

"Look at the dangers: you cannot cross the desert, or go into a new country without arousing the jealousy of some, and the cupidity of others. You would be no match for a troop of robbers, or an army of freebooters."

"But He who bids me go must take all the responsibility of that upon Himself. He will care for us."

"Tell me, only, whither you are going, and where you propose to settle."

---

[*] Compare Gen. 11:29; 22:20–23; 24:10; 27:43.

"That is a question I cannot answer; for, indeed, you know as much about it as I do myself. But I am sure that if I take one day's march at a time, that will be made clear—and the next—and the next —until at last I am able to settle in the country which God has selected for me somewhere."

This surely was the spirit of many a conversation that must have taken place on the eve of that memorable departure. And the equivalents to our words, "Enthusiast," "Fanatic," "Fool," would be freely passed from mouth to mouth. But Abraham would quietly answer; "God has spoken; God has promised; God will do better for me than ever He has said." At night, as he walked to and fro beneath the stars, he may have sometimes been inclined to give up in despair, but then that sure promise came back again on his memory, and he braced himself to obey. "BY FAITH Abraham, when he was called to go out into a place which he should after receive for an inheritance, *obeyed*" (Heb. 11:8). Whither he went, he knew not; it was enough for him to know that he went with God. He leaned not so much upon the promise as upon the Promiser: he looked not on the difficulties of his lot—but on the King eternal, immortal, invisible, the only wise God; who had deigned to appoint his course, and would certainly vindicate Himself.

And so the caravan started forth. The camels, heavily laden, attended by their drivers. The vast flocks mingling their bleatings with their drovers' cries. The demonstrative sorrow of Eastern women mingling with the grave farewells of the men. The forebodings in many hearts of imminent danger and prospective disaster. Sarah may even have been broken down with bitter regrets. But Abraham faltered not. He staggered not through unbelief. He "knew whom he had believed, and was persuaded that He was able to keep that which he had committed to Him against that day." "He was fully persuaded that what God had promised, He was able also to perform."

Moreover, the sacred writer tells us that already some glimpses of the "city which hath foundations," and of the "better country, the heavenly," had loomed upon his vision; and that fair vision had loosened his hold upon much which otherwise would have fascinated and fastened him.

Ah, glorious faith! This is thy work, these are thy possibilities: contentment to sail with sealed orders, because of unwavering confidence in the love and wisdom of the Lord High Admiral; willinghood to arise up, leave all, and follow Christ, because of the glad assurance that earth's best cannot bear comparison with heaven's least.

III. ABRAHAM'S OBEDIENCE WAS FINALLY VERY COMPLETE—"They went forth to go into the land of Canaan, *and into the land of Canaan they came*" (Gen. 12:5). For many days after leaving Haran, the eye would sweep a vast monotonous waste, broken by the scantiest vegetation; the camels treading the soft sand beneath their spreading, spongy feet; and the flocks finding but scanty nutriment on the coarse, sparse grass.

At one point only would the travelers arrest their course. In the oasis, where Damascus stands today, it stood then, furnishing a welcome resting place to weary travelers over the waste. A village near Damascus is still called by the patriarch's name. And Josephus tells us that in his time a suburb of Damascus was called "the habitation of Abraham." And there is surely a trace of his slight sojourn there in the name of his favorite and most trusted servant, Eliezer of Damascus, of whom we shall read anon.

But Abraham would not stay here. The luxuriance and beauty of the place were very attractive, but he could not feel that it was God's choice for him. And, therefore, ere long he was again on the southern track, to reach Canaan as soon as he could. Our one aim in life must ever be to follow the will of God, and to walk in those ways in the which He has preordained for us to walk. Many a Damascus oasis, where ice cold waters descending from mountain ranges spread through the fevered air a delicious coolness, and temper the scorching heat by abundant verdure, tempts us to tarry. Many a Peter, well-meaning but mistaken, lays his hand on us, saying, "This shall not be unto thee: spare thyself." Many a conspirator within the heart counsels a general mutiny against the lonely desolate will. And it is well when the pilgrim of eternity refuses to stay short, in any particular, of perfect consecration and obedience to the extreme demands of God. When you go forth to go into the land of Canaan, do not rest until into the land of

Canaan you come. Anything short of complete obedience nullifi
that has been done. The Lord Jesus must have all or none; and Hi
mands must be fulfilled up to the hilt. But they are not grievous

What a glorious testimony was that which our Master utt
when He said, "The Father hath not left Me alone: for I do always tl
things that please Him." Would that it might be true of each of us!
us henceforth give to Christ our prompt and unlimited obedience; s
that, even if He bids us ride into the valley of death, it is through
blunder or mistake, but out of some sheer necessity, which forbids H
to treat us otherwise, and which He will ere long satisfactorily e
plain.

> Ours not to make reply,
> Ours not to reason why,
> Ours but to do and die.

4

The First
of the Pilgrim Fathers

Abram departed (v. 4). Abram went forth (v. 5). Abram passed
through (v. 6). Abram removed (v. 8). Abram journeyed (v. 9).
—Genesis 4:7–9

He went out, not knowing whither he went.
—Hebrews 11:8

All through the history of mankind there has been a little band of men, in a scared and unbroken succession, who have confessed that they were pilgrims and strangers upon earth. Not more certainly does the scallop shell on the monument of the cathedral aisle indicate that he whose dust lies beneath once went on a pilgrimage beyond the seas, than do certain indications, not difficult to note, betray the pilgrims of the Unseen and Eternal. Sometimes they are found afar from the haunts of men, wandering in deserts and in mountains, dwelling in the dens and caves of the earth—to which they have been driven by those who had no sympathy with their other-worldliness, and hated to have so strong a light thrown on their own absorption in the concerns of the earth, and time, and sense. But very often they are to be found in the marketplaces and homes of men, distinguished only by their simpler dress; their girded loins; their restrained and abstemious appetite; their loose hold on gold; their independence of the maxims and opinions and applause of the world around; and the faraway look which now and again gleams in their eyes, the certain evidence of affections centered, not on the transitory things

27

of time and earth, but on those eternal realities which, lying beneath the veil of the visible, are only revealed to faith.

These are the pilgrims. For them the annoyances and trials of life are not so crushing or so difficult to bear, because such things as these cannot touch their true treasure, or affect their real interest. For them the royalties and glories; the honors and rewards; the delights and indulgences of men—have no attraction. They are children of a sublimer realm, members of a grater commonwealth, burgesses of a nobler city than any upon which the sun has ever looked. Foreigners may mulct an Englishman of all his spending money, but he can well afford to lose it, if all his capital is safely invested at home, in the Bank of England. How can a dukedom in some petty principality present attractions to the scion of an empire, who is passing hastily through the tiny territory, as fast as stream and wealth can carry him, to assume the supreme authority of a mighty monarchy? The pilgrim has no other desire than to pass quickly over the appointed route to his home—a track well trodden through all ages—fulfilling the duties, meeting the claims, and discharging faithfully the responsibilities devolving upon him, but ever remembering that here he has no continuing city, and seeks one which is to come.

The immortal dreamer, who has told the story of the pilgrims in words which the world will never let die, gives three marks of their appearance:

First: "They were clothed with such kind of raiment as was diverse from the raiment of any that traded in that fair. The people, therefore, of the fair made a great gazing upon them; some said they were fools, some they were Bedlams; and some they were outlandish men."

Secondly: "Few could understand what they said, they naturally spoke the language of Canaan: but they that kept the fair were the men of this world; so that from one end of the fair to the other they seemed barbarians to each other."

Thirdly: "But that which did not a little amuse the merchandisers was, that these pilgrims set very light by all their wares; they cared not so much as to look upon them, and if they called on them to buy, they would put their fingers in their ears, and cry, *Turn away mine eyes from beholding vanity,* and look upwards, signifying that their trade and traffic was in heaven."

Evidently this type of man was well known when that great dreamer dreamed—and long before. For the Apostle Peter wrote to scattered strangers (1 Pet. 1:1), and reminded them *as strangers and pilgrims,* to abstain from fleshly lusts. And long before that day, in the sunniest period of Jewish prosperity, David, in the name of his people, confessed that they *were strangers and sojourners as were all their fathers,* and that their days on earth were as a shadow on the hills, now covering long leagues of landscape, and then hasting way, chased by glints of brilliant sun.

We left the patriarch moving leisurely southward; and thus he continued to journey forward through the land of promise, making no permanent halt, till he reached the place of Sichem, or Shechem, in the very heart of the land, where our Lord in after years sat weary by the well. There was no city or settlement there then. The country was sparsely populated. The only thing that marked the site was a venerable oak, whose spreading arms in later ages were to shadow the excesses of a shameful idolatry.[*] Beneath this oak on the plain of Sichem, the camp was pitched; and there, at last, the long silence was broken, which had lasted since the first summons was spoken in Chaldea, "And the Lord appeared unto Abram, and said, Unto thy seed will I give this land: and there built he an altar unto the Lord, who appeared unto him" (Gen. 12:7).

He did not, however, stay there permanently, but moved a little to the south, to a place between Bethel and Ai; where, according to Dr. Robinson, there is now a high and beautiful plain, presenting one of the finest tracts of pasturage in the whole country.

Three things then engage our thought: the Tent, the Altar, and the Promise.

I. THE TENT—When Abraham left Haran his age was seventy-five. When he died he was one hundred and seventy-five years old. And he spent that intervening century moving to and fro, dwelling in a frail and flimsy tent, probably of dark camel's hair, like that of the Bedouin

---

[*] See Judges 9:27–46; 1 Kings 7:25.

of the present day. And that tent was only a befitting symbol of the spirit of his life.

He held himself aloof from the people of the land. He was among them, but not of them. He did not attend their tribal gatherings. He carefully guarded against intermarriage with their children, sending to his own country to obtain a bride for his son. He would not take from the Canaanites a thread or a sandal thong. He insisted on paying full market value for all he received. He did not stay in any permanent location, but was ever on the move. The tent which had no foundations; which could be erected and struck in half-an-hour—this was the apt symbol of his life.

Frequently may the temptation have been presented to his mind of returning to Haran, where he could settle in the town identified with his family. Nor were opportunities to return wanting (Heb. 11:15). But he deliberately preferred the wandering life of Canaan to the settled home of Charran; and to the end he still dwelt in a tent. It was from a tent that he was carried to lie beside Sarah in Machpelah's rocky cave. And why? The question is fully answered in that majestic chapter which recounts the triumphs of faith. "Abraham dwelt in tents, because he looked for the City which hath the foundations" (Heb. 11:9, R.V.). Precisely so: and the tent life is the natural one for those who feel that their fatherland lies beyond the stars.

It is of the utmost importance that the children of God should live this detached life as a testimony to the world. How will people believe us, when we talk about our hope, if it does not wean us from excessive devotion to the things around us? If we are quite as eager, or careworn; quite as covetous or grasping; quite as dependent on the pleasures and fascinations of this passing world as themselves, may they not begin to question whether our profession be true on the one hand, or whether after all there be a real city yonder on the other.

We must not go on as we are. Professing Christians are too much taken up in business cares, in pleasure seeking, in luxury, and self-in-dulgence. There is a slight difference between the children of the kingdom and the children of this generation. The shrewdest observer could hardly detect any in their homes, or in the education of their children, in their dress, or in their methods of doing business. They eat, they drink; they buy, they sell; they plant, they build; they marry, they give in marriage—though the flood is already breaking through the crumbling barriers to sweep them all away.

Yet how is it to be altered? Shall we denounce the present practice? Shall we inveigh against the reckless worldliness of the times? This will not effect a permanent cure. Let us rather paint with glowing colors that City which John saw. Let us unfold the glories of that world to which we are bound. Let us teach that even here, the self-denying, resolute, and believing spirit may daily tread the golden pavement, and hear even the symphonies of angel harps; and surely there will come into many a life a separateness of heart and walk which shall impress men with the reality of the unseen, as no sermon could do, however learned or eloquent.

I. THE ALTAR—Wherever Abraham pitched his tent, he built an altar. Thus the Pilgrim Fathers, on the shores of the New World, set up their altars of worship even before they reared their homes. And long after the tent was shifted, the altar stood to show where the man of God had been.

Ah, it would be a blessed token of our religious fervor if we could set up altars in every house where we pass the night, and in every locality where it might be our hap to live, setting the example of private and family prayer, which would live long after we had passed away. If we would only dare to do it, the very Canaanites would come to revere the spot where we had knelt, and would hand on the sacred tradition, stirring coming generations to kneel there also, and call upon the name of the Lord.

Let us also remember that the altar means sacrifice, whole burnt offering, self-denial, and self-surrender. In this sense the altar and the tent must ever go together. We cannot live the detached tent life without some amount of pain and suffering, such as the altar bespeaks. But it is out of such a life that there springs the most intense devotions, the deepest fellowship, the happiest communion.

If your private prayer has been lately hindered, it may be that you have not been living enough in the tent. The tent life of separation is sure to produce the altar of self-denial and of heavenly fellowship.

Confess that you are a stranger and a pilgrim on the earth; and you will find it pleasant and natural to call on the name of the Lord. We do not read of Abraham building an altar, so long as he dwelt in Charran; he could not have fellowship with God while living in open disobedience to Him; or as long as he was ensconced comfortably in a settled life. But out of the heart of the real pilgrim life there sprang longings, desires, and aspirations, which could only be satisfied by the altars which marked his progress from place to place.

But Abraham's altar was not for himself alone. At certain periods the whole clan gathered there for common worship. A motley group that, in which slaves bought in Egypt or Ur mingled with those born in the camp; in which children and parents, young and old, stood in silent awe around the altar, where the patriarch stood to offer their common sacrifice and worship. "I know Abraham," said God, "that he will command his children and his household after him" (Gen. 18:19). He, in whom all families of the earth were to be blessed, practiced family religion; and in this he sets a striking example to many Christians whose homes are altarless. Would that Christians might be stirred by the example of the patriarch to erect the family altar, and to gather around it the daily circle of their children and dependents, for the sweetening and ennobling of their family life! Many an evil thing, like the gargoyles on the cathedral towers, would be driven forth before the hallowing influence of praise and prayer.

III. THE PROMISE—"Unto thy seed will I give this land" (Gen. 12:7). As soon as Abraham had fully obeyed, this new promise broke upon his ear. And it is ever thus, Disobey—and you tread a path unlit by a single star. Obey, live up to the claims of God—and successive promises beam out from heaven to light your steps, each one richer and fuller than the one before. Hitherto God had pledged Himself only to show the land: now He bound Himself to give it. The separated pilgrim life always obtains promises.

There was no natural probability of that promise being fulfilled. "The Canaanite was then in the land." Powerful chieftains like Mamre and Eshcol; flourishing towns like Sodom, Salem, and Hebron; the elements of civilization—all were there. The Canaanites were not wandering tribes. They had settled and taken root. They built towns, and tilled the land. They knew the use of money and writing; and administered justice in the gate. Every day built up their power, and made it more unlikely that they could ever be dispossessed by the descendants of a childless shepherd.

But God had said it; and so it came to pass. "The counsel of the Lord standeth fast forever; the thought of His heart to all generations" (Ps. 33:11). I know not what promise may be over-arching your life, my reader, with its bow of hope, but this is certain, that if you fulfill its conditions, and live up to its demands, it will be literally and gloriously fulfilled. Look not at the difficulties and improbabilities that block the path, but at the might and faithfulness of the Promiser. "Heaven and earth shall pass away, but His words shall not pass away." Not one jot or tittle shall fail (Matt. 5:18; Mark 13:31; Luke 16:17). And promise after promise shall light your life, like safety lighthouses at night along a rocky coast, which pass the vessel onward, till at last the rays of the rising sun shine full on the haven where the mariner would be.

5

Gone Down into Egypt

Abram went down into Egypt to sojourn
there; for the famine was grievous
in the land [of Canaan].
—Genesis 12:10

The path of the separated man can never be an easy one. He must be willing to stand alone; to go outside the camp; and to forego the aid of many of those supplied on which other men freely draw. It is a life, therefore, which is only possible to Faith. When Faith is strong, we dare cut ourselves adrift from the moorings which coupled us to the shore; and launch out into the deep, depending only on the character and word of Him at whose command we go. But when Faith is weak, we dare not do it; and, leaving the upland path, we herd with the men of the world, who have their portion in this life, and who are content with that alone. Ah, how can we say enough of His tender mercy, who, at such times, bends over us, with infinite compassion, waiting to lift us back into the old heroic life!

"AND THERE WAS A FAMINE IN THE LAND."—A famine? A famine in the Land of Promise? Yes, as afterwards, so then, the rains that usually fall in the latter part of the year had failed; the crops had become burned up with the sun's heat before the harvest; and the herbage, which should have carpeted the uplands with pasture for the flocks, was scanty, or altogether absent. If a similar calamity were to befall us now, we could still draw sufficient supplies for our support from abroad. But Abraham had no such resource. A stranger in a strange land; surrounded by suspicions and hostile peoples; weighted with the responsibility of vast flocks and herds—it was no trivial matter to stand face to face with the sudden devastation of famine.

Did it prove that he had made a mistake in coming to Canaan? Happily the promise which had lately come to him forbade his entertaining the thought. And this may have been one principal reason why it was given. It came, not only as a reward for the past, but as a preparation for the future; so that the man of God might not be tempted beyond what he was able to bear. Our Savior has His eye on our future, and sees from afar the enemy which is gathering its forces to attack us, or is laying its plans to beguile and entrap our feet. His heart is not more careless of us than, under similar circumstances, it was of Peter, in the darkening hour of his trial, when He prayed for him that his faith might not ail, and washed his feet with an inexpressible solemnity. And thus it often happens that a time of special trial is ushered in by the shining forth of the Divine presence, and the declaration of some unprecedented promise. Happy are they who gird themselves with these divine preparations, and so pass unhurt through circumstances which otherwise would crush them with their inevitable pressure.

How often do professing Christians adopt a hurt and injured tone in speaking of God's dealings with them! They look back upon a sunny past, and complain that it was better with them before they entered the wicket gate and commenced to tread the narrow way. They had no famines in Ur or Charran, but now, in the Land of Promise, they are put to sore straits and are driven to their wit's end. The trader had met with bad debts, which sorely embarrass him; the capitalist has been disappointed in several of his most promising investments; the farmer has been disheartened by a succession of bad seasons. And they complain that the service of God has brought them misfortune rather than a blessing.

But is not this the point to be borne in mind on the other side?—These misfortunes would probably have come in any case; and how much less tolerable would they have been had there not been the new sweet consciousness that God had now become the refuge of the soul! Besides this, God our Father does not undertake to repay His children in the base coin of this lower world. Spiritual grace will ever be its own reward. Purity, truth, gentleness, devotion, have no equivalent in the ore drawn from the mines of Peru, nor in the pearls of the sea, but in the happy consciousness of the heart at peace with God, and rejoicing in His smile. Had God pledged Himself to give His servants an unbroken run of prosperity, how many more counterfeit Christians would there be! Well is it that He has made no such promise; though it is certainly true that "godliness has the promise of the life that now is, and of that which is to come." Do not be surprised if a famine meets you. It is no proof of your Father's anger, but is permitted to come to test you—or to root you deeper, as the whirlwind makes the tree grapple its roots deeper into the soil.

"AND ABRAM WENT DOWN INTO EGYPT TO SOJOURN THERE."— What a marvelous history is that of Egypt, linking successive centuries. Full of mystery, wonder, and deep thinking on the destiny of man. The land of Pyramid and Sphinx, and mighty dynasties, and of the glorious Nile. We need not wonder that Egypt has ever been one of the granaries of the world, when we recall the periodic inundation of that marvelous river, which preserves the long narrow strip of green between far reaching wastes of sand. Thither in all ages all countries have come, as Joseph's brethren did, to buy corn. The ship in which the Apostle Paul was conveyed to Rome was a corn ship of Alexandria, bearing a freight of wheat for the consumption of Rome.

In the figurative language of Scripture, Egypt stands for alliance with the world, and dependence on an arm of flesh. "Woe to them that go down to Egypt for help; and stay on horses; and trust in chariots because they are many; and in horsemen because they are very strong, but they look not unto the Holy One of Israel, neither seek the Lord!" (Is. 31:1).

There were occasions in Jewish history when God Himself bade His servants seek a temporary asylum in Egypt. While Jacob was halting in indecision on the confines of Canaan, longing to go to Joseph, and yet reluctant to repeat the mistakes of the past, Jehovah said, "I am God, the God of thy father: fear not to go down into Egypt; for I will there

make of thee a great nation: I will go down with thee into Egypt" (Gen.
46:3, 4). And, in later days, the angel of the Lord appeared to Joseph
in a dream, saying, "Arise, and take the young child and his mother, and
flee into Egypt" (Matt. 2:13). There may be times in all our lives
when God may clearly indicate that it is His will for us to go out into
the world, with a view of accomplishing some Divine purpose with respect to it. "Go, shine as lights," He seems to say. "Arrest corruption,
even as salt does. Witness for Me where My name is daily blasphemed." And when God sends us, by the undoubted call of His
providence, He will be as sure to keep and deliver us as He did Jacob
and his seed, or the Holy Child.

But it does not appear that Abraham received any such Divine direction. He acted simply on his own judgment. He looked at his difficulties. He became paralyzed with fear. He grasped at the first means
of deliverance which suggested itself, much as a drowning man will
catch at a straw. And thus, without taking counsel of his heavenly Pro-
tector, he went down into Egypt.

Ah, fatal mistake! But how many make it still. They may be true
children of God: and yet, in a moment of panic, they will adopt
methods of delivering themselves which, to say the least, are ques-
tionable; and sow the seeds of sorrow and disaster in afterlife, to save
themselves from some minor embarrassment. Christian women plunge
into the marriage bond with those who are the enemies of God, in order
that they may be carried through some financial difficulty. Christian
merchants take ungodly partners into business for the sake of the
capital they introduce. To enable them to stave off the pressure of difficulties, and to maintain their respectability, Christian people of all
grades will court the help of the world. What is all this—but going
down to Egypt for help?

How much better would it have been for Abraham to have thrown
the responsibility back on God and to have said, "Thou hast brought me
here; and Thou must now bear the whole weight of providing for me and
mine: here will I stay till I clearly know what Thou wilt have me to do."
If any should read these lines who have come into positions of extreme
difficulty, through following the simple path of obedience, let them not
look at God through difficulties, as we see the sun shorn of splendor

through a fog, but let them look at difficulties through God. Let them put God between themselves and the disasters which threaten them. Let them cast the whole responsibility upon Him. Has He not thus brought you into difficulties, that He may have an opportunity of strengthening your faith, by giving some unexampled proof of His power? Wait only on the Lord, trust also in Him: His name is Jehovah-jireh; He will provide.

SEE HOW ONE SIN LEADS TO ANOTHER. When Abraham lost his faith, and went down into Egypt, he also lost his courage, and persuaded his wife to call herself his sister. He had heard of the licentiousness of the Egyptians, and feared that they might take his life, to get possession of Sarah; who, even at the age which she had reached, must have been possessed of very considerable charms.

There was an element of truth in the statement that Sarah was his half-sister, but it was meant as a lie; and it certainly misled the Egyptians, "for she was taken into Pharaoh's house." It was a mean and cowardly act on Abraham's part, which was utterly indefensible. It was a cruel wrong to one who had faithfully followed his fortunes for so long. And it endangered the promised seed. Yet so it happens; when we lose our faith, and are filled with panic for ourselves, we become regardless of all and every tie, and are prepared to sacrifice our nearest and dearest, if only we may escape.

The world may entreat us well (12:16), but that will be a poor compensation for our losses. There is no altar in Egypt, no fellowship with God, no new promises, but a desolated home, and a wretched sense of wrong. When the prodigal leaves his Father's house, though he may win a brief spell of forbidden pleasure; yet he loses all that makes life worth living, and brings himself down to the level of the swine. In such a case there is no resource, save to retrace the way that we have come, to "do the first works," and like Abraham to go up out of Egypt to the place of the altar where we are "at the first" (13:4). Abraham's failure in Egypt gives us an insight into the original nature of the patriarch, which was by no means heroic; and betrays a vein of duplicity and deceit, similar to that which has so often reappeared in his posterity.

How thankful should we be that the Bible does not shrink from recording the story of the sins of its noblest saints! What a proof of its veracity is here, and what encouragement there is for us! For if God was able to make His friend out of such material as this, may we not aspire to a like privilege, though we, too, have grievously violated the high calling of faith? The one thing that God requires of His saints is implicit obedience—entire surrender. Where these are present, He can still make Abrahams out of us, though, by nature, the soil of our being is prone to barrenness and weeds.

6

Separated from Lot

Is not the whole land before thee? separate
thyself, I pray thee, from me. If thou wilt
take the left hand, then I will go to
the right; or, if thou depart to the right
hand, then I will go to the left.
—Genesis 13:9

In our last, we saw something of the original stuff of which God makes His saints. By nature Abraham was not superior to the general run of Orientals, who do not hesitate to lie, in order to gain a point or to avert a disaster. Compared with an average Englishman, Abraham would have come off a bad second. The faith which one day was to do business in the ocean waves could not swim across a tiny creek. It is hard to imagine that such a man would ever arrive at a stature of moral greatness so commanding as to overtop all his contemporaries, and look across the ages to see the day of Christ. Yet so it was. And from that thought we may take courage.

Our God does not need noble characters, as the groundwork of His masterpieces. He can raise up stones as children. He can turn thorns into fir trees, briars into myrtle trees. He can take fishermen from their nets, and publicans from their toll booths, making them into evangelists, apostles, and martyrs. We are not much by nature—wild, bad blood may be flowing in our veins, but God will be the more magnified, if from such stones He can raise up children unto Abraham. The miracle of His grace and power will bring more conspicuous glory to His holy Name, in proportion to the unpromising character of the materials on which He works.

"Abram went up out of Egypt, he, and his wife, and all that he had, and Lot with him, into the south."

Very marvelous this! Judging as men, we might have thought that he would never recover from that sad mistake, that disastrous failure and sin. Surely he will reap as he has sown! He will never see his faithful wife again, but must bear forever on his conscience the brand of coward treachery! Or if, indeed, she be given again to him, he will never extricate himself from the meshes into which he has thrown himself! Irritated and deceived, Pharaoh will surely find some method of avenging the wrong with which the foreigner has repaid his generous hospitality!

But no. Contrary to all human anticipation, Jehovah appears on the behalf of his most unworthy servant. In after years the Psalmist gives us the very words which He uttered in the heart of the king: "Touch not Mine anointed, and do My prophets no harm" (Ps. 105:15). What a marvel of tenderness! God does not cast us away for our sin. "He hath not dealt with us after our sins; nor rewarded us according to our iniquities. For as the heaven is high above the earth, so great is His mercy toward them that fear Him" (Ps. 103:10, 11). And thus, notwithstanding repeated falls and shortcomings, He lovingly pursues His Divine purpose with the soul in which the "root of the matter"[*] is found, until He sets it free from its clinging evils, and lifts it into the life of faith, and power, and familiar friendship with Himself. "Rejoice not against me, O mine enemy: when I fall, I shall arise; when I sit in darkness, then the Lord shall be alight unto me" (Mic. 7:8).

Warned by this Divine voice, and restrained by a power which suffered him not to do God's servant harm, Pharaoh had commanded his men concerning him: and they had "sent him away, and his wife, and all that he had." This is how it comes to pass that we find them again traversing the uplands of Southern Palestine on their way back to Bethel, unto the place where they had halted on their first entrance into Palestine. So complete was the delivering power of God, that

---

[*] Job 19:28.

the Egyptian monarch did not even take back the gifts which he had bestowed as a dowry for Sarah. The "sheep, and oxen, and he-asses, and menservants, and maidservants, and she-asses, and camels," still remained in Abraham's possession. And we are, therefore, prepared to learn, that "Abram was very rich, in cattle, in silver, and in gold." That visit to Egypt beyond doubt laid the foundation of the immense wealth of the family in after time; and it was out of this that the next trouble sprang. A trouble it seemed at first, but God marvelously overruled it for drawing His child yet closer to Himself, and severing the metal to a further extent from the alloy which had clung to it too long. Hitherto, we have been told repeatedly, "and Lot went with him." This record will not be made again.

I. Who was Lot?—The son of Abraham's dead brother, Haran. He had probably succeeded to his father's inheritance. He may have come with his uncle across the desert in the secret hope of bettering his condition, but we will hope that he was prompted by worthier motives. He seems to have been one of those men who take right steps, not because they are prompted by obedience to God, but because their friends are taking them. Around him was the inspiration of a heroic faith, the fascination of the untried and unknown, the stir of a great religious movement: and Lot was swept into the current, and resolved to go too. He was the Pliable of the earliest Pilgrim's Progress. He may have thought that he was as much in earnest as Abraham, but it was a great mistake. He was simply an echo; a dim afterglow; a chip on the bosom of a mighty current.

In every great religious movement there always have been, and always will be a number of individuals who cast in their lot with it, without knowing the power which inspires it. Beware of them! They cannot stand the stress of the life of separation to God. The mere excitement will soon die away from them; and, having no principle to take its place, they will become hindrances and disturbers of the peace. As certainly as they are harbored in the camp, or their principles are allowed within the heart, they will lower the spiritual tone; allure to worldly policy; suggest methods which would not otherwise occur to us; and draw us towards the Egypt-world.

Nothing but supreme principle can carry anyone through the real, separated, and surrendered life of the child of God. If you are prompted by anything less, such as excitement, enthusiasm, fashion, contagious example—you will first be a hindrance, and end by being a failure. Examine yourselves, whether ye be in the faith. Prove your own selves. And, if you are consciously acting from a low and selfish motive, ask God to breathe into you His own pure love. Better act from an inferior motive, if only it be in the right direction, but covet earnestly the best.

II. THE NECESSITY OF SEPARATION. That recent failure in connection with Egypt may have been due, to a larger extent than we know, to the baneful influence of Lot. Had Abraham been left to himself, he might never have thought of going down to Egypt: and, in that case, there would have been another paragraph or passage in the Bible describing the exploits of a faith which dared to stand to God's promise, though threatened by disaster, and hemmed in by famine; waiting until God should bid it move, or make it possible to stay. There is something about that visit to Egypt which savors of the spirit of Lot's afterlife. In any case, the time had come, in the providence of God, when this lower and more worldly spirit must go its way; leaving Abraham to stand alone, without prop, or adviser, or ally; thrown back on the counsel and help of God alone.

The outward separation of the body from the world of the ungodly is incomplete, unless accompanied and supplemented by the inner separation of the spirit. It is not enough to leave Ur, Haran, and Egypt. We must be rid of Lot also. Though we lived in a monastery, shut away from the homes and haunts of men, with no sound to break upon the ear but the summoning bell of worship, and the solemn chant; yet so long as there as an alien principle in our breast, a Lot in our heart-life, there could not be that separation to God which is the condition of the growth of faith, and of all those higher forms of the true life which make earth most like heaven. Lot must go. "Know that the Lord hath set apart him that is godly for Himself" (Ps. 4:3). No other foot then must intrude within the enclosure of the Divine proprietorship.

O souls that sigh for saintliness as harts pant for waterbrooks, have ye counted the cost? Can ye bear the fiery ordeal? The manufacture of saints is no child's play. The block has to be entirely separated from the mountain bed, ere the Divine chisel can begin to fashion it. The gold must be plunged into the cleansing fire, ere it can be molded or hammered into an ornament of beauty for the King.

As Abraham was separated from one after another of nature's resources, so must it be with all aspirants for the inner chambers of the palace of God. We must be prepared to die to the world with its censure or praise; to the flesh, with its ambitions and schemes; to the delights of a friendship which is insidiously lowering the temperature of the spirit; to the self-life, in all its myriad subtle and overt manifestations; and even, if it be God's will, to the joys and consolations of religion.

All this is impossible to us of ourselves. But if we will surrender ourselves to God, willing that he should work in and for us that which we cannot do for ourselves, we shall find that he will gradually and effectually, and as tenderly as possible, begin to disentwine the clinging tendrils of the poisoning weed, and bring us into heart union with Himself.

It may be that Abraham had already felt for himself the ill effect of association with Lot, and may have longed to be free from him, without knowing how the emancipation could be effected. In any case, somewhat akin to this may be the condition of some who shall read these words. Entangled in an alliance which you seem powerless to break off, your only hope is to beat it quietly till God sets you at liberty. Meanwhile guard your will, by God's grace, from swinging round, as a boat with the tide. Declare to God continually your eager desire to be emancipated. By prayer and faith get honey out of the lion's carcass. Wait patiently till God's hour strikes, and His hand opens the fast-locked door, and bids you be free. That time will come at length; for God has a destiny in store for you, so great that neither He nor you can allow it to be forfeited for any light or trivial obstacle.

III. HOW THE SEPARATION WAS BROUGHT ABOUT. The valleys around Bethel, which had been quite adequate for their need when first they came to Canaan, were now altogether insufficient. The herdsmen were always wrangling for the first use of the wells, and the first crop of the pastures. The cattle were continually getting mixed. "The land was not able to bear them, that they might dwell together."

Quarrels between servants have a habit of traveling upwards, and embroiling their masters. And so Abraham and Lot would be told by their head men of what was happening; and each would be tempted to feel irritated with the other.

Abraham saw at once that such a state of things must not be allowed to go on: especially as "the Canaanite and the Perizzite dwelt then in the land." For if those warlike neighbors heard of the dissensions in the camp, they would take an early opportunity of falling upon it. United they stood; divided, they must fall. Besides, there was the scandal of the thing, which might work prejudicially on the name and worship of that God to whom Abraham was known to bow the knee. Would that the near presence of the world might have the same wholesome effect of checking dissension and dispute among the children of the same Father!

And so Abraham called Lot to him, and said, "Let there be no strife between me and thee, and between my herdmen and thy herdmen: for we be brethren. Is not the whole land before thee? Separate thyself, I pray thee, from me. If thou wilt take the left hand, then I will go to the right; or if thou depart to the right hand, then I will go to the left" (13:8, 9).

The proposal was very *wise*. He saw that there was a cause for the disturbance, which would lead to similar troubles continually. If he spoke sharply to Lot, Lot would answer in the same spirit, and a breach would be made at once. So he went to the root of the matter, and proposed their separation.

His line of action was very MAGNANIMOUS. As the elder and the leader of the expedition, he had the undoubted right to the first choice. But he waived his right in the interests of reconciliation. But, above all, it was BASED ON FAITH. His faith was beginning to realize its true position; and, like a fledgling, to spread its wings for further and still further flights. Had not God pledged Himself to take care of him, and to give him an inheritance? There was no fear, therefore, that

Lot could ever rob him of that which was guaranteed to him by the faithfulness of God. And he preferred, a thousand times over, that God should choose for him, than that he should choose for himself.

The man who is sure of God can afford to hold very lightly the things of this world. God Himself is his inalienable heritage; and, in having God, he has all. And, as we shall see, the man who "hedges" for himself does not do so well in the long run as the man who, having the right of choice, hands it back to God, saying: "Let others choose for themselves, if they please, but as for myself, Thou shalt choose mine inheritance for me."

> Not mine—not mine the choice
>   In things or great or small;
> Be Thou my Guide, my Guard, my
> Strength,
>   My Wisdom and my 'All.'

7

The Two Paths

Is not the whole land before thee? Separate thyself, I pray thee, from me. —Genesis 13:9

braham and Lot stood together on the heights of Bethel. The Land of Promise spread out before them as a map. On three sides at least there was not much to attract a shepherd's gaze. The eye wandered over the outlines of the hills which hid from view the fertile valleys nestling within their embrace. There was, however, an exception in this monotony of hill, towards the southeast, where the waters of the Jordan spread out in a broad valley, before they entered the Sea of the Plain.

Even from the distance the two men could discern the rich luxuriance, which may have recalled to them traditions of the garden once planted by the Lord God in Eden, and have reminded them of scenes which they had lately visited together in the valley of the Nile. This specially struck the eye of Lot; eager to do the best for himself, and determined to make the fullest use of the opportunity which the unexpected magnanimity of his uncle had thrown in his way. Did he count his relative a fool for surrendering the right of choice? Did he vow that he must allow no false feelings of delicacy to interfere with his doing what he could for himself? Did he feel strong in the keenness of his sight, and the quickness of his judgment? Perhaps so. For he had little sympathy with the pilgrim spirit.

But the time would come when he would bitterly rue his choice, and owe everything to the man of whom he was now prepared to take advantage.

"Lot lifted up his eyes, and beheld all the plain of Jordan, that it was well watered everywhere . . . as the garden of the Lord. . . . Then Lot chose him all the plain of Jordan" (13:10, 11). He did not ask what God had chosen for him. He did not consider the prejudicial effect which the morals of the place might exert upon his children and himself. His choice was entirely determined by the lust of the flesh, the lust of the eyes, and the pride of life. For the men of Sodom were "sinners before the Lord exceedingly."

How many have stood upon those Bethel heights, intent on the same errand as took Lot higher! Age after age had poured forth its crowds of young hearts, to stand upon an exceeding high mountain, while before them have been spread all the kingdoms of this world, and the glory of them; the tempter whispering, that for one act of obeisance all shall be theirs. In assurance and self-confidence; eager to do the very best for themselves, prepared to consider the moralities only insofar as these did not interfere with what they held to be the main chance of life—thus have succeeding generations looked towards the plains of Sodom from afar. And, alas! like Lot, they have tried to make stones into bread; they have cast themselves down from the mountainside for angels to catch; they have knelt before the tempter, to find his promise broken, the vision of power an illusion, and the soul beggared forever— while the tempter, with hollow laugh, has disappeared, leaving his dupe standing alone in the midst of a desolate wilderness.

Let us not condemn Lot too much because he chose without reference to the moral and religious conditions of the case; lest, in judging him, we pronounce sentence on ourselves. Lot did nothing more than is done by scores of professing Christians every day.

A Christian man asks you to go over and see the place which is about taking in the country. It is certainly a charming place: the house is spacious and well-situated; the air balmy; the garden and paddock large; the views enchanting. When you have gone over it, you ask how he will fare on Sunday. You put the question not from feelings of curiosity, but because you know that he needs strong religious influences to counteract the effect of absorbing business cars, from Monday morning till Saturday night; and because you know that his children are beginning to evidence a deepening interest in the things of God. "Well," says he, "I really have never thought of it." Or perhaps he answers, "I believe there is nothing here like we have been accustomed to, but one cannot have everything: and they say that the society here is extremely good." Is not this the spirit of Lot, who bartered the altar of Abraham's camp for the plains of Sodom, because the grass looks green and plentiful?

Have mothers, professing Christians, never gone into society where evangelical religion is held in contempt, for no other reason than to make a good match for their daughters, so far, at least, as the world is concerned? Ah, the world is full of breaking hearts and wrecked happiness, because so many persist in lifting up their eyes to choose for themselves, and with sole reference to the most sordid considerations.

If Abraham had remonstrated with Lot, suggesting the mistake he was making, do you not suppose that he would have answered petulantly: "Do you not think that we are as eager as you are to serve the Lord? Sodom needs just that witness which we shall be able to give. Is it not befitting that the light should shine in the darkness; and that the salt should be scattered where there is putrefaction?" Abraham might not be able to contest these assertions, and yet he would have an inner conviction that these were not the considerations which were determining his nephew's choice. Of course, if God sends a man to Sodom, He will keep him there; as Daniel was kept in Babylon: and nothing shall by any means hurt him. He shall be kept as the eye is kept: guarded in its bony socket from violence, and by its delicate veil of eyelid sheltered from the dust. But if God does not clearly send you to Sodom, it is a blunder, a crime, a peril to go.

Mark how Lot was swiftly swept into the vortex; first he saw; then he chose; then he separated himself from Abraham; then he journeyed east; then he pitched his tent toward Sodom; then he dwelt there; then he became an alderman of the place, and sat in the gate. His daughters married two of the men of Sodom; and they probably ranked among the most genteel and influential families of the neighborhood. But his power of witness-bearing was gone. Or if he lifted up his voice in protest against deeds of shameless vice, he was laughed at for his pains, or threatened with violence. His righteous soul might vex itself, but it met with no sympathy. He was carried captive by Chedorlaomer. His property was destroyed in the overthrow of the cities. His wife was turned into a pillar of salt. And the blight of Sodom left but too evident a brand upon his daughters. Wretched, indeed, must have been the last days of that hapless man, cowering in a cave, stripped of everything, face to face with the results of his own shameful sin.

It is, indeed, a terrible picture; and yet some such retribution is in store for everyone whose choice of home, and friends, and surroundings, is dictated by the lust of worldly gain, or fashion, or pleasure, rather than by the will of God. If such are saved at all, they will be saved as Lot was—so as by fire. Now, let us turn to a more inviting theme, and further consider the dealings of the Almighty God with Abraham, the one man who was being educated to hold fellowship with Jehovah as a friend.

I. GOD ALWAYS COMES NEAR TO HIS SEPARATED ONES. "And the Lord said unto Abram, *after that Lot was separated from him*." It may be that Abraham was feeling very lonely. Lot and he had been constant and close companions; and when the last of the camp followers had moved off, and Lot had disappeared into the long distance, a cold chill may have enveloped him, as a November fog does the man who has arisen before the dawn to see his friend away by the early mail. Then it was that God spake to him.

We all dread to be separated from companions and friends. It is hard to see them stand aloof, and drop away one by one; and to be compelled to take a course by oneself. The young girl finds it hard to refuse the evening at the theater, and to stay alone at home when her gay companions have gone off in high spirits. The young city clerk finds it hard to refuse to join in the "sweepstake," which is being got up on the occasion of some annual race. The merchant finds it hard to withdraw from the club or society with which he has long been identified, because there are practices creeping in which his conscience refuses to sanction. The Christian teacher finds it hard to adopt a course which isolates him from brethren with whom he has had sweet fellowship, but against whose views he is obliged to protest.

And yet, if we really wish to be only for God, it is inevitable that there should be many a link snapped; many a companionship forsaken; many a habit and conventionalism dropped: just as a savage must gradually and necessarily abjure most of his past, ere he can be admitted into the society and friendship of his European teacher.

But let us not stand looking on this aspect of it—the dark side of the cloud. Let us rather catch a glimpse of the other side, illuminated by the rainbow promise of God. And let this be understood, that, when once the spirit has dared to take up that life of consecration to the will of God to which we are called, there break upon it visions, voices, comfortable words, of which the heart could have formed no previous idea. For brass He brings gold, and for iron silver, and for wood brass, and for stone iron. Violence is no more heard, nor wasting, nor destruction. The sun is no more needed for the day, nor the moon for the night. Because the Lord has become the everlasting light of the surrendered and separate heart, and the days of its mourning have passed away forever.

"Come out from among them, and be ye separate, saith the Lord, and touch not the unclean thing: and I will receive you, and will be a Father unto you; and ye shall be My sons and daughters, saith the Lord Almighty. Having, therefore, these promises, dearly beloved, let us cleanse ourselves from all filthiness of the flesh and Spirit" (2 Cor. 6:7).

II. GOD WILL DO BETTER FOR THOSE WHO TRUST HIM THAN THEY COULD DO FOR THEMSELVES. Twice here in the context we meet the phrase, "lifting up the eyes." But how great the contrast! Lot lifted up his eyes, at the dictate of worldly prudence, to spy out his own advantage. Abraham lifted up his eyes, not to discern what would best make for his material interests, but to behold what God had prepared for him. How much better it is to keep the eye steadfastly fastened on God till He says to us, "Lift up now thine eyes, and look from the place where thou art—northward, and southward, and eastward, and westward: for all the land which thou seest, to thee will I give it, and to thy seed forever" (13:14, 15).

God honors them that honor Him. He withholds "no good thing from them that walk uprightly." He "meets him that rejoices and works righteousness." If only we will go on doing what is right, giving up the best to our neighbor to avoid dispute, considering God's interests first, and our own last, expending ourselves for the coming and glory of the kingdom of heaven, we shall find that God will charge Himself with our interests. And He will do infinitely better for us than we could. Lot had to ask the men of Sodom if he might sojourn among them, and he had no hold on the land, but it was all given unasked to Abraham, including that verdant circle on which Lot had set his heart. "Blessed are the meek, for they shall inherit the earth."

It is difficult to read these glowing words, *northward, and southward, and eastward, and westward,* without being reminded of "the length, and breadth, and depth, and height, of the love of Christ, that passeth knowledge." Much of the land of Canaan was hidden behind the ramparts of the hills, but enough was seen to ravish that faithful spirit. Similarly, we may not be able to comprehend the love of God in Christ, but the higher we climb the more we behold. The upper cliffs of the separated life command the fullest view of that measureless expanse.

In some parts of the Western Highland, the traveler's eye is delighted by the clear and sunlit waters of a loch—an arm of the sea, running far up into the hills. But as he climbs over the heathery slopes, and catches sight of the waters of the Atlantic, bathed in the light of the setting sun, he almost forgets the fair vision which had just arrested him. Thus do growing elevation and separation of character unfold ever richer conceptions of Christ's infinite love and character. God's promises are ever on the ascending scale. One leads up to another, fuller and more blessed than itself. In Mesopotamia, God said, "I will show thee the land." At Bethel, "This is the land." Here, "as I give thee all the land, and children innumerable as the grains of sand." And we shall find even these eclipsed. It is thus that God allures us to saintliness. Not giving anything till we have dared to act—that He may test us. Not giving everything at first—that He may not overwhelm us. And always keeping in hand an infinite reserve of blessing. Oh, the unexplored remainders of God! Whoever saw His last star?

III. GOD BIDS US APPROPRIATE HIS GIFTS. "Arise, walk through the land in the length of it and in the breadth of it." This surely means that God wished Abraham to feel as free in the land as if the title deeds were actually in his hands. He was to enjoy it; to travel through it; to look upon it as his. By faith he was to act towards it as if he were already in absolute possession.

There is a deep lesson here, as to the appropriation of faith. "Be strong and very courageous" was addressed six several times to Joshua. "Be strong" refers to the strength of the wrists to grasp. "Be every courageous" refers to the tenacity of the ankle joints to hold their ground. May our faith be strong in each of these particulars. Strong to lay hold, and strong to keep.

The difference between Christians consists in this. For us all there are equal stores of spiritual blessing laid up in our Lord, but some of us have learned more constantly and fully to appropriate them. We walk through the land in its lengths and breadths. We avail ourselves of the fullness of Jesus. Not content with what He is for us in the counsel of God, our constant appeal is to Him in every moment of need.

We need not be surprised to learn that Abraham removed to Hebron (which signifies fellowship), and built there an altar to the Lord. New mercies call us to deeper fellowship with our Almighty Friend, who never leaves or forsakes His own. And, as the result of his dealings with us, let us build fresh altars, and make a new dedication of ourselves and all we have to His blessed service.

8

Refreshment between the Battles

Four kings with five.
—Genesis 14:9

The strife recorded in Genesis 14 was no mere border foray. It was an expedition for chastisement and conquest. Chedorlaomer was the Attila, the Napoleon of his age. His capital city, Susa, lay across the desert, beyond the Tigris, in Elam. Years before Abraham had entered Canaan as a peaceful emigrant, this dreaded conqueror had swept southwards, subduing the towns which lay in the Jordan Valley, and thus possessing himself to the master key to the road between Damascus and Memphis. When Lot took up his residence towards Sodom, the cities of the plain were paying tribute to this mighty monarch.

At last the men of Sodom and Gomorrah, of Admah and Zeboiim, became weary of the Elamite yoke and rebelled, and Chedorlaomer was compelled to undertake a second expedition to chastise their revolt and regain his power. Combining his own forces with those of three vassal and friendly rulers in the Euphrates Valley, which lay in his way, he swept across the desert, and fell upon the wild tribes that harbored in the mountains of Bashan and Moab. His plan was evidently to ravage the whole country contiguous to those Jordan towns before actually investing them.

At last the allied forces concentrated in the neighborhood of Sodom, where they encountered fierce resistance. Encouraged by the pitchy nature of the soil, in which horseman and chariots would move with difficulty, the townsfolk risked an engagement in the open. In spite, however, of the bitumen pits, the day went against the effeminate and dissolute men of the plain, in whose case, as in many others, social corruption proved itself the harbinger of political overthrow. The defeat of the troops was followed by the capture and sack of those wealthy towns; and all who could not escape were manacled as slaves, and carried off in the train of the victorious army.

Sated at length with their success, their attention engrossed by their rich booty and their vast host of captives, the foreign host began slowly to return along the Jordan valley on its homeward march. "And they took Lot, Abram's brother's son, who dwelt in Sodom, and his goods, and departed." Then one of the survivors of that fatal day climbed the hills and made for Abraham's encampment, which he may have known in earlier days, when, as one of Lot's many servants, he lived there. "And when Abram heard that his brother was taken captive, he armed his trained servants, . . . and divided himself against them" (14:14, 15).

I. HERE IS THE UNSELFISH AND SUCCESSFUL INTERPOSITION OF A SEPARATED MAN, ON THE BEHALF OF OTHERS. Hidden in the configuration of the country, and confederate with his friends, Abraham had watched the movements of the devastators from afar. "But they had not come nigh him; only with his eyes had he beheld and seen the reward of the wicked" (Ps. 91:8). Common prudence would have urged him not to embroil himself. "Be thankful that you have escaped, and do not meddle further in the business; let you make these mighty kings your foes."

But true separation never argues thus. Granted that the separated one is set apart for God, yet he is set apart that he may react more efficiently on the great world over which God yearns, and towards which He has entertained great purposes of mercy, in the election of the few. Genuine separation—an unattachedness to the things of time and sense, because of an ardent devotion to the unseen and eternal—is the result of faith, which always works by love; and this love tenderly yearns for those who are entangled in the meshes of worldliness and sin. Faith makes us independent, but not indifferent. It is enough for it to hear that its brother is taken captive; and it will arm instantly to go in pursuit.

Ah, brothers and sisters, have there never come to you the tidings that your brothers are taken captive? How, then, is it that you have not started off long ago for their deliverance? Is this separation genuine, which stands unconcernedly by while there is such need for immediate an unselfish action?

But Abraham's interposition was as *successful* as it was unselfish and prompt. The force with which he set out was a very slender one, but his raw recruits moved quickly, and thus in four or five days they overtook the self-reliant and encumbered host amid the hills where the Jordan takes its rise. Adopting the tactics of a night attack, he fell suddenly on the unsuspecting host, and chased them in headlong panic, as far as the ancient city of Damascus. "And he brought back all the goods, and also brought again his brother Lot, and his goods, and the women also, and the people" (14:16).

Is it not always so? The men who live the life of separation and devotion towards God, are they who act with most promptness and success when the time for action comes. Lot being in Sodom could neither elevate its morals nor save it from attack. Abraham living among the hills is alone able to cope successfully with the might of the tyrant king. Oh, do not listen to those who say you must live on the level and in the midst of worldly men in order to elevate and save them; and advise you to go to the theater, the ballroom, the public house, in order to give them a higher tone. Did Lot save Sodom? Nor will a better fate than his befall any man, who, unbidden by God, settles down in the world for his own whim and pleasure. If you would lift me, you must stand above me. If Archimedes is to move the world, he must rest his lever on a point far enough outside the earth itself.

II. THE TIME OF A GREAT SUCCESS IS OFTEN THE SIGNAL FOR A GREAT TEMPTATION. The King of Sodom had not been among the prisoners. He had probably saved himself, by a timely flight to the hills, from the field of battle. When therefore he received tidings of the patriarch's gallant and successful expedition, he set out to meet and welcome him. He would ascend from the Jordan plain by one of the gorges into the hills, and would come out on the great central road, by which Abraham and his confederates were marching back to Hebron.

The two met at the King's Dale, a place to become memorable as the years went on; and situated near the city of Salem, a title which was destined to develop into the word—Jerusalem. A memorable meeting that: between the representatives of two races—the one destined to grow weaker and weaker still, until it was dispossessed by the children of that very man whose sword now saved it from utter extinction.

But more memorable than the place is the record of the spiritual encounter that took place there. Grateful for Abraham's succor and deliverance, the King of Sodom proposed to him to surrender only the persons of the captives, while he kept all the spoils to himself and his allies.

It must have been a very tempting offer. No slight matter for a shepherd to have the chance of appropriating all the spoils of settled townships, so large and opulent; especially when he seemed to have some claim on them.

But he would not hear of it for a moment. Indeed, he seems to have already undergone some exercise of soul on the matter, for speaking as of a past transaction, he said, "I have lift up mine hand unto the Lord, the Most High God, the Possessor of heaven and earth, that I will not take from a thread even to a shoe latchet; and that I will not take anything that is thine, lest thou should say, 'I have made Abram rich.' " What a magnificent contempt of specious offer! What a glorious outburst of the independence of a living faith!

There is a close parallel between this suggestion of the King of Sodom and the temptation of our Lord in the wilderness when Satan offered Him all the kingdoms of the world for one act of obeisance. And does not this temptation assail us all? Are we not all tempted to take the gilded wage of the world, which is so eager to lay us under obligation to itself, and to feel that we are in its pay and power? The world is aware that, if we will only accept its subsidies, we shall have surrendered our position of independence, and have stepped down to its level, no longer able to witness against it, shorn of the locks of our strength, and become weak as other men.

In theory it may be argued that we can turn to good account the wealth which has been ill gotten. But, practically, we shall not find it so. The wealth of Sodom will scorch the hand that handles it, and will blight every godly enterprise to which it may be put. Besides, what right have we to depend on the revenues of the world, we, who are heirs to the Possessor of heaven and earth, the children of the Great King: to whom, in giving us His Son, He has also pledged to give us all things? Better a thousand times be poor, until He make us rich with the gold that has passed through His cleansing furnace. Happy they who prefer to be pensioners on the daily providence of God to being dependent on the gold of Sodom—the wages of iniquity.

III. THE PREVENIENT GRACE OF GOD. It may be that Abraham would not have come off so grandly in the second conflict if he had not been prepared for it by the wondrous encounter with greater king than either we have named. After his defeat of Chedorlaomer, and before the advent of the King of Sodom, the Hebrew had met Melchizedek, the Priest-King of Salem.

We may not stay to speak now of all the interest that gathers around this sacred figure, sacred as the type of our blessed Lord. Of that more anon. We shall be satisfied to notice now that he brought bread and wine, and blessed the weary conqueror, and coined in his hearing a new name for God. For the first time God received the title, "Possessor of heaven and earth"—one which seems to have made a deep impression upon Abraham; for we find him using it in his encounter with the King of Sodom—and it was the talisman of victory. Why should he need to take aught from man, when this new revelation of God had just fallen upon his ear, and enriched his heart forever?

Is not this the work of the Lord Jesus still? He comes to us when wearily returning from the fight. He comes to us when He knows we are on the eve of a great temptation. He not only prays for us, as for Peter, but He prepares us for the conflict. Some new revelation; some fresh glimpse into His character; some holy thought—these are given to fill the memory and heart against the advent of the foe. Oh, matchless mercy! He forewarns and forearms us. He prevents us with the blessings of His goodness.

When next we are tempted with the bribes of an ungodly world, let us recall that name for God, which, in Abraham's case, was the talisman of victory; and let us think of him as the POSSESSOR of heaven and earth. Why should we soil our fingers will ill-gotten gains, even though they seem needful for our existence, when our Father is the Owner of all that flies in the air, treads on the land, swims in the water, or lies embedded in the rocks.

We have not infrequently been made sweet and strong, or have passed through some marked spiritual experience, for no other object than to fit us for coming peril. Let us avail ourselves of such occasions, whenever they occur, and let us ever be grateful to our Lord for victualing His castles before they are attacked, and for giving us His own new name, by which we may overcome all the wiles of men and evils.

O King of loyal hearts, may we meet Thee more often on life's highway, especially when some tempter is preparing to weave around us the meshes of evil; and bending beneath Thy blessing, may we be prepared by the communications of Thy grace for all that may await us in the unknown future!

9

Melchizedek

*This Melchizedec, King of Salem, priest
of the Most High God.*
—Hebrews 7:1

Christ is here! The passage is fragrant with the ointment of His name. Our hands drop with myrrh, and our fingers with sweet smelling myrrh, as we lay them upon the handles of this lock (Song. 5:5). Let us get aside from the busy rush of life, and think long, deep thoughts of Him who is the Alpha and Omega of Scripture, and of saintly hearts. And let us draw from the unsearchable depths of His nature, by the bucket of this mysterious record touching Melchizedec, the King of Salem.

There is a sense in which Christ was made *after the order of Melchizedec,* but there is a deeper sense in which Melchizedec was made *after the order of the Son of God.* The writer to the Hebrews tells us that Melchizedec was "made like unto the Son of God" (Heb. 7:3). Christ is the Archetype of all; and from all eternity has had those qualities which have made Him so much to us. It would seem as if they could not stay to be manifested in the fullness of the ages; they chafed for expression. From of old His delights were with the sons of men. And so this mysterious royal priest was constituted—reigning in his peaceful city, amid the storm and wreckage of his times—that there might be given among men some premonition, some anticipation, of that glorious life which was already being lived in Heaven on man's behalf, and which, in due course, would be manifested on our world, and at that very spot where Melchizedec lived his Christ-like life. Oh that we, too, might be priests after the order of Melchizedec in this respect, if in no other, that we are made as like as possible to the Son of God!

MELCHIZEDEC was a Priest. The spiral column of smoke climbing up into the clear air, in the fragrant morn, and at the dewy eve, told that there was one heart at least which was true in its allegiance to the Most High God: and which bore up before Him the sins and sorrows of the clans that clustered near. He seems to have had that quick sympathy with the needs of his times which is the true mark of the priestly heart (Heb. 4:15). And he had acquired thereby so great an influence over his neighbors that they spontaneously acknowledged the claims of his special and unique position. Man must have a priest. His nature shrinks from contact with the All Holy. What is there in common between vileness and purity, darkness and light, in all ages, men have selected from among their fellows one who should represent them to God, and God to them. It is a natural instinct. And it has been met in our glorious Lord, who, while He stands for us in the presence of God, face to face with uncreated Light, ever making intercession, at the same time is touched with the feeling of our infirmities, succors us in our temptations, and has compassion on our ignorance. Why need we travel farther afield? Why imitate Micah in setting up for ourselves a priest whom human hands have made? (*see* Judg. 17:10). Why permit any other to bear this sacred name, or to intrude on this holy office? None but Christ will satisfy or meet the requirements of God, or "become us" with unutterable needs (Heb. 7:26).

THIS PRIESTHOOD CAME OF GOD, AND WAS RATIFIED BY AN OATH. The priests of the house of Levi exercised their office after "the law of a carnal commandment" (Heb. 7:16). They assumed it, not because of any inherent fitness, or because specially summoned to the work by the voice of heaven, but because they had sprung from the special sacerdotal tribe. The Priesthood of Christ, on the other hand, is God's best gift to men—to thee, my reader, and to me; more necessary than spring flowers, or light, or air. Without it our souls would wander ever in a Sahara desert. "Christ glorified not Himself to be made a High Priest" (Heb. 5:5), but He was called of God to be a High Priest after the order of Melchizedec (v. 10). And such was the solemnity of His appointment, that it was ratified by "the word of the oath." "The Lord sware and will not repent, Thou art a Priest forever after the order of Melchizedec" (Heb. 7:21–28). Here is "strong consolation" indeed. No unfaithfulness or ingratitude can change this priesthood. The eternal God will never run back from that word and oath. "Eternity" is written upon the High Priest's brow: "forevermore" rings out, as He moves, from the chime of His golden bells: "an unchangeable Priesthood" is the law of His glorious being. Hallelujah! The heart may well sing, when, amid the fluctuation of earth's change, it touches at length the primeval rock of God's eternal purpose. He is "consecrated" Priest "forevermore."

THE PRIESTHOOD WAS ALSO CATHOLIC. Abraham was not yet circumcised. He was not a Jew, but a Gentile still. It was as the father of many nations that he stood and worshiped and received the benediction from Melchizedec's saintly hands. Not thus was it with the priesthood of Aaron's line. To share its benefit a man must needs become a Jew, submitting to the initial rite of Judaism. None but Jewish names shone in that breastplate. Only Jewish wants or sins were borne upon those consecrated lips. BUT CHRIST IS THE PRIEST OF MAN. He draws *all men* unto Himself. The one sufficient claim upon Him is that thou bear the nature which He has taken into irreversible union with His own—that thou art a sinner and a penitent pressed by conscious need. Then hast thou a right to Him, which cannot be disallowed. He is thy Priest—thine own; as if none other had claim on Him than thou. Tell Him all thy story, hiding nothing, extenuating, excusing nothing. All kindreds, and peoples, and nations, and tongues, converge in Him, and are welcome; and all their myriad needs are satisfactorily met.

THIS PRIESTHOOD WAS SUPERIOR TO ALL HUMAN ORDERS OF PRIESTS. If ever there were a priesthood which held undisputed supremacy among the priesthoods of the world, it was that of Aaron's line. It might not be as ancient as that which ministered at the shrines of Nineveh, or so learned as that which was exercised in the silent cloisters of Memphis and Thebes, but it had about it this unapproachable dignity—in that it emanated, as a whole, from the Word of God. Yet even the Aaronic must yield obeisance to the Melchizedec Priesthood. And it did. For Levi was yet in the loins of Abraham when Melchizedec met him; and he paid tithes in Abraham, and knelt in token of submission, in the person of the patriarch, beneath the blessing of this greater than himself (Heb. 7:4–10). Why then need we concern ourselves with the stars, when the sun has arise upon us? What have we to do with any other than with this mighty Mediator, this Daysman, who towers aloft above all rivals; Himself sacrifice and Priest, who has offered a solitary sacrifice, and fulfills a unique ministry!

THIS PRIESTHOOD PARTOOK OF THE MYSTERY OF ETERNITY. We need not suppose that this mystic being had literally no father, or mother, beginning of days, or end of life. The fact on which the inspired writer fixes is—that no information is afforded us on any of these points. There is an intention in the golden silence, as well as in the golden speech of Scripture. And these details were doubtless shrouded in obscurity, that there might be a still clearer approximation of the type to the glory of the Antitype, who abides continually. He is the Ancient of Days; the King of the Ages; the I AM. The Sun of His Being, like His Priesthood, knows nought of dawn, or decline from meridian zenith, or descent in the western sky. "He is made after the power of an endless life." "He ever liveth to make intercession." If, in the vision of Patmos, the hair of His head was white as snow, it was not the white of decay, but of incandescent fire. "He continueth ever, and hath an unchangeable priesthood." "He is the same yesterday, today, and forever." He does for us now what He did for the world's grey fathers, and what He will do for the last sinner who shall claim His aid.

THIS PRIESTHOOD WAS ROYAL. "Melchizedec, King of Salem, priest." Here again there is no analogy in the Levitical priesthood. The royal and priestly offices were carefully kept apart. Uzziah was struck with the white brand of leprosy when he tried to unite them. But how marvelously they blended in the earthly life of Jesus! As Priest, He pitied, and helped, and fed men: as King, He ruled the waves. As Priest, He uttered His sublime intercessory prayer: as King, He spoke the "I will" of royal prerogative. As Priest, He touched the ear of

Malchus: as the disowned King, to whom even Caesar was preferred, He was hounded to the death. As Priest, He pleaded for His murderers, and spake of Paradise to the dying thief: while His Kingship was attested by the proclamation affixed to His cross. As Priest, He breathed peace on His disciples: as King, He ascended to sit down upon His throne.

He was *first* "King of Righteousness," and after that also King of Salem, which is King of Peace (Heb. 7:2). Mark the order. Not first Peace at any price, or at the cost of Righteousness, but Righteousness first—the righteousness of His personal character; the righteous meeting, on our behalf, of the just demands of a Divine and holy law. And then founded on, and arising from, this solid and indestructible basis, there sprang the Temple of Peace, in which the souls of men may shelter from the shocks of time. "The work of righteousness shall be peace; and the effect of righteousness, quietness and assurance forever. And My people shall dwell in a peaceable habitation, and in sure dwellings, and in quiet resting places" (Is. 32:17, 18).

Ah, souls, what is your attitude towards Him? There be plenty who are willing enough to have Him as Priest, who refuse to accept Him as King. But it will not do. He must be King, or He will not be Priest. And He must be King in this order, first making thee right, then giving thee His peace that passeth all understanding. Waste not precious time in paltering, or arguing with Him; accept the situation as it is, and let thy heart be the Salem, the city of Peace, where He, the Priest-King, shall reign forever. And none is so fit to rule as He who stooped to die. "In the midst of the throne stood a Lamb as it had been slain" (Rev. 5:6). Exactly! The throne is the befitting place for the Man who loved us to the death.

THIS PRIESTHOOD RECEIVES TITHES OF ALL. "The patriarch Abraham gave a tenth of the spoils" (Heb. 7:4, R.V.). This ancient custom shames us Christians. The patriarch gave more to the representative of Christ than many of us give to Christ Himself. Come, if you have never done so before, resolve to give your Lord a tithe of your time, your income, you all. "Bring all the tithes into His storehouse." Nay, thou glorious One, we will not rest content with this; take all, for all is Thine. "Thine is the greatness, and the power, and the glory, and the victory, and the majesty: for all that is in the heaven and in the earth is Thine; Thine is the Kingdom, O Lord, and Thou art exalted as King above all. Now, therefore, we thank Thee and praise Thy glorious name."

10

The Firmness
of Abraham's Faith

*He staggered not at the promise of God
through unbelief, but was strong in
faith, giving glory to God.*
—Romans 4:20

In this chapter (Gen. 15), for the first time in Scripture, four striking phrases occur, but each of them is destined to be frequently repeated with many charming variations. We may speak then of this precious paragraph as of some upland vale where streamlets take their rise which are to flow seawards, making glad the lowland pasture lands on their way. Now, first, we meet the phrase, "the word of the Lord came." Here, first, we are told that "the Lord God is a shield." For the first time rings out the silver chime of that Divine assurance, "Fear not!" And now we first meet in human history that great, that mighty word, "believed." What higher glory is there for man than that he should reckon on the faithfulness of God? For this is the meaning of all true belief.

The "word of the Lord" came to Abraham about two distinct matters.

I. GOD SPOKE TO ABRAHAM ABOUT HIS FEAR. Abraham had just returned from the rout of Chedorlaomer and the confederate kings in the far north of Canaan; and there was a natural reaction from the long and unwonted strain as he settled down again into the placid and

69

uneventful course of a shepherd's life. In this state of mind he was most susceptible to rear; as the enfeebled constitution is most susceptible to disease.

And there was good reason for fear. He had defeated Chedorlaomer, it is true, but in doing so he had made him his bitter foe. The arm of the warrior king had been long enough to reach to Sodom; why should it not be long enough and strong enough to avenge his defeat upon that one lonely man? It could not be believed that the mighty monarch would settle down content until the memory of his disastrous defeat was wiped out with blood. There was every reason, therefore, to expect him back again to inflict condign punishment. And, besides all this, as a night wind in a desert land, there swept now and again over the heart of Abraham a feeling of lonely desolation, of disappointment, of hope deferred. More than ten years had passed since he had entered Canaan. Three successive promises had kindled his hopes, but they seemed as far from realization as ever. Not one inch of territory! Not a sign of a child! Nothing of all that God had foretold!

It was under such circumstances that the word of the Lord came unto him, saying, "Fear not, Abram: I am thy Shield, and thy exceeding great Reward." Ah, our God does not always wait for us to come to Him; He often comes to us; He draws near to us in the low dungeon; He sends His angel to prepare for us the cruse of water and the baked cakes, and on our souls break His tender assurances of comfort, more penetrating than the roar of the surge, "Be of good cheer; it is I; be not afraid."

But God does not content Himself with vague assurances. He gives us solid ground for comfort in some fresh revelation of Himself. And oftentimes the very circumstances of our need are chosen as a foil to set forth some special side of the Divine character, which is peculiarly appropriate. What could have been more reassuring at this moment to the defenseless pilgrim, with no stockade, or walled city in which to shelter, but whose flocks were scattered far and wide, than to hear that God Himself was around him and his, as a vast, impenetrable, though invisible shield. "I am thy Shield."

Mankind, when once that thought was given, eagerly caught at it; and it has never been allowed to die. Again and again it rings out in prophecy and psalms, in temple anthem and from retired musings. "The Lord God is a sun and shield." "Thou art my hiding place and my shied." "Behold, O God, our shield; and look upon the face of thine Anointed." "His truth shall be thy shield and buckler." It is a very helpful thought for some of us! We go every day into the midst of danger; men and devils strike at us; now it is the overt attack, and now the stab of the assassin; unkind insinuations, evil suggestions, taunts, gibes, threats; all these things are against us. But if we are doing God's will and trusting in God's care, ours is a charmed life, like that of the man who wears chain armor beneath his clothes. The Divine environment pours around us, rendering us impervious to attack, as the stream of electricity may surround a jewel case with an atmosphere before which the stoutest attack of the most resolute felon is foiled. "No weapon that is formed against thee shall prosper" (Is. 54:17). "Thou shalt not be afraid for the terror by night; nor for the arrow that flieth by day; nor for the pestilence that walketh in darkness; nor for the destruction that wasteth at noonday. A thousand shall fall at thy side, and ten thousand at thy right hand, but it shall not come nigh thee." Happy are they who have learned the art of abiding within the inviolable protection of the eternal God, on which all arrows are blunted, all swords turned aside, all sparks of malice extinguished with the hissing sound of a torch in the briny waters of the sea.

Nor does God only defend us from without, He is the *reward* and satisfaction of the lonely heart. It was as if He asked Abraham to consider how much he had in having Himself. "Come now, my child, and think; even if thou wert never to have one foot of soil, and thy tent were to stand silent, amid the merry laughter of childish voices all around— yet thou wouldst not have left thy land in vain, for thou hast Me. Am not I enough? I fill heaven and earth; cannot I fill one lonely soul? Am not I 'thy exceeding great reward'; able to compensate thee by My friendship, to which thou art called, for any sacrifice that thou mayest have made?"

Our God, who is love, and love in its purest, divinest essence, has given us much, and promised us more, but still His best and greatest gift is His own dear self; our reward, our great reward, our exceeding great reward. Hast thou nought? Is thy life bare? Have lover and friend forsaken thee? Art thou lonely and forsaken of all the companions of earlier, younger, days? Well, answer this one question more, Hast thou God? For if thou hast, thou hast all love and life, all sweetness and tenderness, all that can satisfy the heart, and delight the mind. All lovely things sleep in Him, as all colors hide in the sunbeam's ray, waiting to be unraveled. To have God is to have all, though bereft of everything. To be destitute of God is to be bereft of everything, though having all.

II. GOD SPOKE TO ABRAHAM ABOUT HIS CHILDLESSNESS. It was night, or perhaps the night was turning towards the morning, but as yet myriads of stars—the watchfires of the angels; the choristers of the spheres; the flocks on the wide pasture lands of space—were sparkling in the heavens. The patriarch was sleeping in his tent, when God came near him in a vision; and it was under the shadow of that vision that Abraham was able to tell God all that was in his heart. We can often say things in the dark which we dare not utter beneath the eye of day. And in that quiet watch of the night, Abraham poured out into the ear of God the bitter, bitter agony of his heart's life. He had probably long wanted to say something like this, but the opportunity had not come. But now there was no longer need for restraint; and so it all came right out into the ear of his Almighty Friend, "Behold, to me Thou hast given no seed: and, lo, one born in my house is mine heir." It was as if he said, "I promised for myself something more than this; I have conned Thy promises, and felt that they surely prognosticated a child of my own flesh and blood, but the slowly moving years have brought me no fulfillment of my hopes; and I suppose that I mistook Thee. Thou never intendest more than that my steward should inherit my name and goods. Ah, me! It is a bitter disappointment, but Thou has done it, and it is well."

So often we mistake God, and interpret His delays as denials. What a chapter might be written of God's delays! Was not the life of Jesus full of them, from the moment when He tarried behind in the Temple, to the moment when He abode two days still in the same place where He was, instead of hurrying across the Jordan in response to the sad and agonized entreaty of the sisters whom He loved. So He delays still. It is the mystery of the art of educating human spirits to the finest temper of which they are capable. What searchings of heart; what analyzing of motives; what testings of the Word of God; what upliftings of soul—searching what, or what manner of time, the Spirit of God signifies! All these are associated with those weary days of waiting, which are, nevertheless, big with spiritual destiny. But such delays are not God's final answer to the soul that trusts Him. They are but the winter before the burst of spring. "And, behold, the word of the Lord came unto him, saying, This shall not be thine heir, but thine own son shall be thine heir. Look now toward heaven, and tell the stars, if thou be able to number them. So shall thy seed be" (Gen. 15:4, 5). And from that moment the stars shone with new meaning for him, as the sacraments of Divine promise.

"AND HE BELIEVED IN THE LORD." What wonder that those words are so often quoted by inspired men in after ages; or that they lie as the foundation stone of some of the greatest arguments that have ever engaged the mind of man! (See Rom. 4:3; Gal. 3:6; James 2:23).

HE BELIEVED BEFORE HE UNDERWENT THE JEWISH RITE OF CIRCUMCISION. The Apostle Paul lays special emphasis on this, as showing that they who were not Jews might equally have faith, and be numbered among the spiritual children of the great father of the faithful (Rom. 4:9–21; Gal. 3:7–29). The promise that he should be the heir of the world was made to him, when as yet he was only the far-traveled pilgrim; and so it is sure to all the seed, not to that only which is of the law, but to that also which is of the faith of Abraham, who is the father of us all.

HE BELIEVED IN FACE OF STRONG NATURAL IMPROBABILITIES. Appearances were dead against such a thing as the birth of a child to that aged pair. The experience of many years said, "It cannot be." The nature and reason of the case said, "It cannot be." Any council of human friends and advisers would have instantly said, "It cannot be!" And Abraham quietly considered and weighed them all "without being weakened in faith" (Rom. 4:19, R.V.). Then he as carefully looked unto the promise of God. And, rising from his consideration of the comparative weight of the one and the other, he elected to venture everything on the word of the Eternal. Nay, that was not all; as shock followed shock, and wave succeeded wave, booming with crash of thunder on his soul, he staggered not; he did not budge an inch; he did not even tremble, as sometimes the wave-beat rock shivers to its base. He reckoned on the faithfulness of God. He gave glory to God. He relied implicitly on the utter trustworthiness of the Divine veracity. He was "fully assured that what He had promised He was able also to perform." Ah, child of God, for every look at the unlikelihood of the promise, take ten looks at the promise: this is the way in which faith waxes strong. "Looking unto the promise of God, he wavered not through unbelief, but waxed strong" (Rom. 4:20, R.V.).

HIS FAITH WAS DESTINED TO BE SEVERELY TRIED. If you take to the lapidary the stones which you have collected in your summer ramble, he will probably send the bulk of them home to you in a few days, with scanty marks of having passed through his hands. But some one or two of the number may be kept back, and when you inquire for them, he will reply: "Those stones which I returned are not worth much: there was nothing in them to warrant the expenditure of my time and skill, but with the others, the case is far otherwise: they are capable of taking a polish and of bearing a discipline which it may take months and even years to give, but their beauty, when the process is complete, will be all the compensation that can be wished."

Some men pass through life without much trial, because their natures are light and trivial, and incapable of bearing much, or of profiting by the severe discipline which, in the case of others, is all needed, and will yield a rich recompense, after it has had its perfect work. God will not let any one of us be tried beyond what we are able to bear. But when He has in hand a nature like Abraham's, which is capable of the loftiest results, we must not be surprised if the trial is long continued, almost to the last limit of endurance. The patriarch had to wait fifteen years more, making five-and-twenty years in all, between the first promise and its fulfillment in the birth of Isaac.

HIS FAITH WAS COUNTED TO HIM FOR RIGHTEOUSNESS. Faith is the seed germ of righteousness; and, when God sees us possessed of the seed, He counts us as also being in possession of the harvest which lies hidden in its heart. Faith is the tiny seed which contains all the rare perfumes and gorgeous hues of the Christian life, awaiting only the nurture and benediction of God. When a man believes, it is only a matter of education and time to develop that which is already in embryo within him; and God, to whom the future is already present, accounts the man of faith as dowered with the fruits of righteousness, which are to the glory and praise of God. But there is a deeper meaning still than this—in the possession through faith of a judicial righteousness in the sight of God.

The righteousness of Abraham resulted not from his works, but from his faith. "He believed God: and it was reckoned unto him for righteousness." "Now it was not written for his sake alone, that it was reckoned unto him, but for our sake also, unto whom it shall be reckoned, who believe on Him that raised Jesus our Lord from the dead" (Gal. 3:6; Rom. 4:23, 24, R.V.). Oh, miracle of grace! If we trust ever so simply in Jesus Christ our Lord, we shall be reckoned as righteous in the eye of the eternal God. We cannot realize all that is included in those marvelous words. This only is evident, that faith unites us so absolutely to the Son of God that we are ONE with Him forevermore; and all the glory of His character—not only what He is in the majesty of His risen nature—is reckoned unto us.

Some teach imputed righteousness as if it were something apart from Christ, found over the rags of the sinner. But it is truer and better to consider it as a matter of blessed identification with Him through faith; so that as He was one with us in being made sin, we are one with Him in being made the Righteousness of God. In the counsels of Eternity that which is true of the glorious Lord is accounted also true of us, who, by a living faith have become members of His body, of His flesh, and of His bones. Jesus Christ is made unto us Righteousness, and we are accepted in the Beloved. There is nothing in faith, considered in itself, which can account for this marvelous fact of imputation. Faith is only the link of union, but inasmuch as it unites us to the Son of God, it brings us into the enjoyment of all that he is as the Alpha and Omega, at the Beginning and the End, the First and the Last.

11
Watching with God

The vision is yet for an appointed time, but at the end it shall speak, and not lie. Though it tarry, wait for it: because it will surely come; it will not tarry—Habakkuk 2:3.

It is good that a man should both hope and quietly wait for the salvation of the Lord—Lamentations 3:26.

If we hope for that we see not, then do we with patience wait for it—Romans 8:25.

It is not easy to watch with God, or to wait for Him. The orbit of His providence is so vast. The stages of His progress are so wide apart. He holds on His way through the ages; we tire in a few short hours. And when His dealings with us are perplexing and mysterious, the heart that had boasted its unwavering loyalty begins to grow faint with misgivings, and to question—When shall we be able to trust absolutely, and not be afraid?

In human relationships, when once the heart has found its rest in another, it can bear the test of distance and delay. Years may pass without a word or sigh to break the sad monotony. Strange contradictions may baffle the understanding and confuse the mind. Officious friends may delight in putting unkind and false constructions on conduct confessedly hard to explain. But the trust never varies or abates. It knows that all is well. It is content to exist without a token, and to be quiet without attempting to explain or defend. Ah, when shall we treat God so? When shall we thus rest in him, where we cannot understand? Can any education be too hard which shall secure this as its final and crowning result? Surely that were heaven, when the heart of man could afford to wait for a millennium, unstaggered by delay, untinged by doubt.

At this stage, at least, of his education, Abraham had not learned this lesson. But in that grey dawn, as the stars which symbolized his posterity were beginning to fade in the sky, he answered the Divine assurance that he should inherit the land of which he as yet did not own a foot, by the sad complaint: "Lord God, whereby shall I know that I shall inherit it?"

How human this is! It was not that he was absolutely incredulous: but he yearned for some tangible evident token that it was to be as God had said; something he could see; something which should be an ever present sacrament of the coming heritage, as the stars were of the future seed. Do not wonder at him, but rather adore the love which bears with these human frailties, and stoops to give them stepping stones by which to cross the sands to the firm rock of an assured faith.

I. WATCHING BY THE SACRIFICE—In those early days, when a written agreement was very rare, if not quite unknown, men sought to bind one another to their word with the most solemn religious sanctions. The contracting party was required to bring certain animals, which were slaughtered and divided into pieces. These were laid on the ground in such a manner as to leave a narrow lane between; up and down which the covenanting party passed to ratify and confirm his solemn pledge.

It was to this ancient and solemn rite that Jehovah referred, when he said, "Take Me a heifer of three years old, and a she-goat of three years old, and a ram of three years old, and a turtledove, and a young pigeon. And he took unto him all these, and divided them in the midst, and laid each piece one against another" (Gen. 15:8, 10).

It was still the early morning. The day was young. And Abraham sat down to watch. Then there came a long pause. Hour after hour passed by, but God did not give a sign or utter a single word. Judging by appearances, there was neither voice, nor any to answer, nor any that regarded.

Higher and ever higher the sun drove his chariot up the sky, and shone with torrid heat on those pieces of flesh lying there exposed upon the sand, but still no voice of vision came. The unclean vultures, attracted by the scent of carrion, drew together as to a fast, and demanded incessant attention if they were to be kept away. Did Abraham ever permit himself to imagine that he was sitting there on a fool's mission? Did not the thought instill itself into his mind, that perhaps after all he had been led to arrange those pieces by a freak of his own fancy, and that God would not come at all? Did he shrink from the curious gaze of his servants, and of Sarah his wife, because half-conscious of having taken up a position he could not justify?

We cannot tell what passed through that much-tried heart during those long hours. But this, at least, we recognize; that this is in a line with the discipline through which we all have to pass. Hours of waiting for God! Days of watching! Nights of sleepless vigil! Looking for the outposts of the relief that tarries! Wondering why the Master comes not! Climbing the hill again and again, to return without the expected visions! Watching for some long expected letter, till the path to the Post Office is trodden down with constant passing to and fro, and wet with many tears! But all in vain! Nay, but it is not in vain. For these long waiting hours are building up the fabric of the spirit life, with gold, and silver, and precious stones, so as to become a thing of beauty, and a joy forevermore.

Only let us see to it that we never relax our attitude of patience, but wait to the end for the grace to be brought unto us. And let us give the unclean birds no quarter. We cannot help them sailing slowly through the air, or uttering dismal screams, or circling around us as if to pounce. Be we *can* help them settling down. And this we must do, in the name and by the help of God. "If the vision tarry, wait for it."

II. THE HORROR OF A GREAT DARKNESS. The sun at last went down, and the swift Eastern night cast its heavy veil over the scene. Worn out with the monumental conflict, the watchings, and the exertions of the day, Abraham fell into a deep sleep. And in that sleep his soul was oppressed with a dense and dreadful darkness; such as almost stifled him, and lay like a nightmare upon his heart. "Lo, a horror of great darkness fell upon him."

Do my readers understand something of the horror of that darkness? When one who has been brought up in a traditional belief, which fails to satisfy the instincts of maturer life, supposes that in letting go the creed, there must also be the renunciation of all faith and hope, not seeing that the form may go, while the essential substance may remain: when one, mistaking the nature of sin and the mercy of God, fears that there has been committed an unpardonable sin, or that the bounds of repentance have been overstepped forever: when some terrible sorrow which seems so hard to reconcile with perfect love, crushes down upon the soul, wringing from it all its peaceful rest in the pitifulness of God, and launching it on a sea unlit by a ray of hope: when un-kindness, and cruelty, and monstrous injustice browbeat, and mock, and maltreat the trusting heart, till it begins to doubt whether there be a God overhead who can see and still permit—these know some-thing of the horror of great darkness; and what weird and frightful vi-sions will in that darkness pass one after another before the spirit, like the phantoms of a drunkard's delirium or the apparitions of an un-healthy brain.

It was a long and dark prospect which unfolded itself before Abra-ham. He beheld the history of his people through coming centuries, strangers in a foreign land, enslaved and afflicted. Did he not see the anguish of their souls, and their cruel bondage beneath the taskmas-ter's whips? Did he not hear their groans, and see mothers weeping over their babes, doomed to the insatiable Nile? Did he not witness the building of Pyramid and Treasure city, cemented by blood and suf-fering? It was, indeed, enough to fill him with darkness that could be felt.

And yet the somber woof was crossed by the warp of silver threads. The enslaved were to come out, and to come out with great sub-stance, their oppressors being overwhelmed with crushing judgment. They were to come into that land again. While, as for himself, he should go to his fathers in peace, and be buried in a good old age.

It is thus that human life is made up: brightness and gloom; shadow and sun; long tracks of cloud, succeeded by brilliant glints of light. And amid all, Divine justice is working out its own schemes, affecting oth-ers equally with the individual soul which seems the subject of special discipline. The children of Abraham must not inherit the Land of Promise till the fourth generation has passed away, because the iniquity of the Amorites had not yet filled up the measure of their doom. Only then—when the reformation of that race was impossible; when their condition had become irremediable, and their existence was a menace to the peace and purity of mankind—was the order given for their extermination, and for the transference of their power to those who might hold it more worthily.

Oh, ye who are filled with the horror of great darkness because of God's dealings with mankind, learn to trust that infallible wisdom which is coassessor with immutable justice; and know that He who passed through the horror of the darkness of Calvary, with the cry of forsakenness, is ready to bear you company through the valley of the shadow of death, till you see the sun shining upon its further side. "Who is among you that walketh in darkness, and hath no light? Let him trust in the name of the Lord, and stay upon his God."

III. THE RATIFICATION OF THE COVENANT. When Abraham awoke, the sun was down. Darkness reigned supreme. "It was dark." A solemn stillness brooded over the world. Then came the awful act of ratification. For the first time since man left the gates of Eden there appeared the symbol of the glory of God; that awful light which was afterwards to shine in the pillar of cloud, and the Shekinah gleam.

In the thick darkness, that mysterious light—a lamp of fire— passed slowly and majestically between the divided pieces; and, as it did so, a voice said: "Unto thy seed have I given this land, from the river of Egypt unto the great river, the river Euphrates" (Gen. 15:18).

Remember that promises, made with the most solemn sanctions, never repealed since, and never perfectly fulfilled. For a few years during the reign of Solomon the dominions of Israel almost touched these limits, but only for a very brief period. The perfect fulfillment is yet in the future. Somehow the descendants of Abraham shall yet inherit their own land, secured to them by the covenant of God. Those rivers shall yet form their boundary lines: for "the mouth of the Lord hath spoken it."

A foreign power forbids their entrance yet; and Jerusalem is trodden down of the Gentiles. But we may be entering on a series of events, which shall shatter the decrepit empire of the unspeakable

Turk, and release Egypt and Palestine from his blighting sway, so that the land which awaits the people, and the people which awaits the land, may be reunited beneath the blessing of Him who, by word and oath, gave strong consolation to His much-tried servant Abraham.

As we turn from this scene—in which God bound Himself by such solemn sanctions, to strengthen the ground of His servant's faith—we may carry with us exalted conceptions of His great goodness, which will humble itself so low in order to secure the trust of one poor heart. By two immutable things, His word and oath, God has given strong assurance to us who are menaced by the storm, drawing us on to a rock-bound shore. Let us, by our Forerunner, send forward our anchor, Hope, within the veil that parts us from the unseen: where it will grapple in ground that will not yield, but hold until the day dawn, and we follow it into the haven guaranteed to us by God's immutable counsel (Heb. 6:19, 20).

12
Hagar, the Slave Girl

Now Sarai, Abram's wife, had a handmaid,
an Egyptian, whose name was Hagar.
—Genesis 16:1

N one of us knows all that is involved when we tear ourselves from the familiar scenes of our Harans to follow God into the lands of separation which lie beyond the river. The separated life cannot be an easy one. We may dimly guess this as we step out into the untried and unknown, but God graciously veils from our eyes that which would needlessly startle and daunt us; unfolding to us His requirements, only as we are able to bear them.

The difficulties of the separated life arise, not from any arbitrary appointments of Divine Providence, but from the persistent manifestation of the self-life in its many Protean forms. It is absurd to say that it dies once for all in some early stage of the Christian life; and it is perilous to lead men to think so. When men think or boast that it is dead, it peeps out in their very assertions, and laughs at the success of its efforts to blind them to its presence. This is the masterpiece of its art: to cajole its dupes into thinking that it is dead. Gangs of thieves always like to secure the insertion of a paragraph in the newspapers, announcing that they have left the neighborhood, because, in the false security which is induced by the announcement, they are more able to carry out their plans of pillage.

We say, in the first moments of consecration, that we are eager, not only to be reckoned dead in the sight of God, so far as our self-life is concerned, but to be dead. And if we really mean what we say, God undertakes the work, first of revealing the insidious presence of the self-life where we had least expected it, and then of nailing it in bitter sufferings to the cross of a painful death. O ye who know something of the analysis of your inner life, do not your hearts bear witness that, as the light of heaven breaks with glowing glory on your souls, it reveals unexpected glimpses into the insidious workings of self? So much so that you are driven to claim, with no bated breath; first, Divine forgiveness for harboring such a traitor; and then, the interposition of Divine grace to mete out that death which is the only condition of growth and blessedness.

There is here a very startling manifestation of the tenacity with which Abraham's self-life still survived. We might have expected that by this time it had been extinguished: the long waiting of ten slow-moving years: the repeated promises of God: the habit of contact with God Himself—all this had surely been enough to eradicate and burn out all confidence in the flesh; all trust in the activities of the self-life; all desire to help himself to the realization of the promises of God. Surely, now, this much-tried man will wait until, in His own time and way, God shall do as He has said. Abraham would not take a shoe latchet, or a thread, from the King of Sodom, because he was so sure that God would *give* him all the land. Nor was he disappointed: when God said, "I am thy exceeding great reward." And similarly we might have expected that he would have strenuously resisted every endeavor to induce him to realize for himself God's promise about his seed. Surely he will wait meekly and quietly for God to fulfill His own word, by means best known to Himself.

Instead of this he listened to *the reasoning of expediency,* which happened to chime in with his own thoughts, and sought to gratify the promptings of his spirit by doing something to secure the result of which God had spoken. Simple-hearted faith waits for God to unfold His purpose, sure that He will not fail. But mistrust, reacting on the self-life, leads us to take matters into our own hands—even as Saul did, when he took upon himself to offer sacrifice, without awaiting the arrival of Samuel.

I. THE QUARTER WHENCE THESE REASONINGS CAME. "Sarai said unto Abram." Poor Sarah! She had not had her husband's advantages. When he had been standing in fellowship with God, she had been quietly pursuing the routine of household duty, pondering many things.

It was clear that Abraham should have a son, but it was not definitely said by God that the child would be hers. Abraham was a strict monogamist, but the laxer notions of those days warranted the filling of the harem with others, who occupied an inferior rank to that of the principal wife, and whose children, according to common practice, were reckoned as if they were her own. Why should not her husband fall in with those laxer notions of the marriage vow? Why should he not marry the slave girl, whom they had either purchased in an Egyptian slave market, or acquired among the other gifts with which Pharaoh had sent them away?

It was a heroic sacrifice for her to make. She was willing to forego a woman's dearest prerogative; to put another in her own place; and to surrender a position to which she had a perfect right to cling, even though it seemed to clash with the direct promise of God. But her love to Abraham; her despair of having a child of her own, and her inability to conceive of God fulfilling His word by other than natural means— all these things combined to make the proposal from which, in another aspect, her wifely nature must have shrunk. Love in Sarah did violence to love.

No one else could have approached Abraham with such a proposition, with the slightest hope of success. But when Sarah made it, the case was altered. The suggestion might have flitted across his own mind, in his weaker moments, only to be instantly rejected and put aside, as doing a grievous wrong to his faithful wife. But now, as it emanated from here, there seemed less fear of it. It was supported by the susceptibilities of natural instinct. It was consistent with the whisperings of doubt. It seemed to be a likely expedient for realizing God's promise. And without demur, or reference to God, he fell in with the proposal. "Abram hearkened to the voice of Sarai."

It is always hard to resist temptation when it appeals to natural instinct or to distrusting fear. At such an hour, if the Savior be not our Keeper, there is small hope of our being able to resist the double assault. But the temptation is still more perilous when it is presented, not by some repellent fiend, but by some object of our love; who, like Sarah, has been the partner of our pilgrimage, and who is willing to sacrifice all in order to obtain a blessing which God has promised, but has not yet bestowed.

We should be exceedingly careful before acting on the suggestions of any who are not as advanced as we are in the Divine life. What may seem right to them may be terribly wrong for us. And we should be especially careful to criticize and weigh any proposals which harmonize completely with the tendencies of our self-life. "If the wife of thy bosom, or thy friend, which is as thine own soul, entice thee secretly, . . . thou shalt not consent unto him, nor hearken unto him; neither shall thine eye pity him neither shalt thou spare" (Deut. 13:6–8). But does not the response of the soul to such suggestions indicate how far the self-life is from being dead?

II. THE SORROWS TO WHICH THEY LED. As soon as the end was obtained, the results, like a crop of nettles, began to appear in that home, which had been the abode of purity and bliss, but which was now destined to be the scene of discord. Raised into a position of rivalry with Sarah, and expectant of giving the long-desired son to Abraham, and a young master to the camp, Hagar despised her childless mistress, and took no pains to conceal her contempt.

This was more than Sarah could endure. It was easier to make one heroic act of self-sacrifice, than to bear each day the insolent carriage of the maid whom she had herself exalted to this position. Nor was she reasonable in her irritation; instead of assuming the responsibility of having brought about the untoward event, so fraught with misery to herself, she passionately upbraided her husband, saying: "My wrong be upon thee: the Lord judge between me and thee" (Gen. 16:5).

How true this is to human nature! We take one false step, un-sanctioned by God; and when we begin to discover our mistake, we give way to outbursts of wounded pride. But instead of chiding ourselves, we turn upon others, whom we may have instigated to take the wrong course, and we bitterly reproach them for wrongs of which they at most were only instruments, while we were the final cause.

Out of this fleshly expedient sprang many sorrows. Sorrow to Sarah, who on this occasion, as afterwards, must have drunk to the dregs the cup of bitter gall; of jealousy and wounded pride; of hate and malice, which always destroy peace and joy in the nature, from which they stream as the fiery lava torrents from a volcanic crater. Sorrow to Hagar, driven forth as an exile from the home of which she had dreamed to become the mistress, and to which she had thought her-self essential. Ah, bitter disappointment! Sorrow to Abraham, loath to part with one who, to all human appearance, would not become the mother of the child who should bless his life: stung, moreover, as he was, by the unwonted bitterness of his wife's reproaches.

If any should read these words who are tempted to use any expe-dients of human devising for the attainment of ends, which in them-selves may be quite legitimate, let them stand still, and take to heart the teachings of this narrative. For, as surely as God reigns, shall every self-ish expedient involve us in unutterable and heartrending sorrow. "From this time shalt thou have wars."

III. The Victim whose Life course was so largely involved. We cannot be surprised at the insolent bearing of the untutored slave girl. It was only what might have been expected. But we mourn to see in her only one of myriads who have been sacrificed to the whim or pas-sion, to the expediency or selfishness, of men. Innocent and light-hearted, she might have been the devoted wife of some man in her own station and the mother of a happy family. But, taken as she was from her true station, and put into a position in which she was a mother without being a lawful wife, what could her lot be but misery in the home in which she had no proper status, and at last in the exiled and homeless wanderings to which Sarah's bitter jealousy twice drove her: once for a time—afterwards forever?

Abraham, for the sake of the peace of his home, dared not interpose between his wife and her slave. "Behold," said he, "thy maid is in thy hand; do to her as it pleaseth thee." Not slow to act upon this implied consent, the irate mistress dealt so bitterly with the girl that she fled from her face, and took the road, trodden by the caravans, towards her native land. "The angel of the Lord" (and here, for the first time, that significant expression is used, which is held by many to express some evident manifestation of the Son of God in angel guise) "found her by a well of water" which was familiarly known in the days of Moses. There, worn, and weary, and lonely, she sat down to rest. How often does the Angel of the Lord still find us in our extremity—when we are running away from the post which was assigned to us; when we are evading the cross. And what questions could be more pertinent, whether to Hagar or to us: "Whence camest thou? And whither wilt thou go?" Reader, answer those two questions, ere thou read further. What is thine origin? And what thy destiny?

Then there followed the distinct command, which applies to us evermore, "Return, and submit." The day would come when God Himself would open the door, and send Hagar out of that house (Gen. 21:12–14). But until that moment should come, after thirteen years had rolled away, she must return to the place which she had left, bearing her burden and fulfilling her duty as best she might. "Return and submit."

We are all prone to act as Hagar did. If our lot is hard, and our cross is heavy, we start off in a fit of impatience and wounded pride. We shirk the discipline; we evade the yoke; we make our own way out of the difficulty. Ah! We shall never get right thus. Never! We must retrace our steps; we must meekly bend our necks under the yoke. We must accept the lot which God has ordained for us, even though it be the result of the cruelty and sin of others. We shall conquer by yielding. We shall escape by returning. We shall become free by offering themselves to the bound. "Return and submit." By and by, when the lesson is perfectly learned, the prison door will open of its own accord.

Meanwhile the heart of the prodigal is cheered by promise (16:10). The Angel of the Lord unfolds all the blessed results of obedience. And as the spirit considers these, it finds the homeward way no longer lined by flints, but soft with flowers.

Nor is this all: but in addition to promise, there breaks on the soul the conception of One who lives and sees; who lives to avenge the wronged, and to defend the helpless; and who sees each tear and pang of the afflicted soul.

"Thou art a God that seeth." Not like those blind Egyptian idols that stare with stony gaze across the desert: having eyes, though they see not. It was a new thought to the untutored slave girl; it is familiar enough to us. And yet we might find new depths of meaning in life and duty, if every moment were spent in the habitual realization of these words. Let us look after Him that seeth us. Let us often stay the whir of life's shuttles to say softly to ourselves, "God is here; God is near; God sees—He will provide; He will defend; He will avenge." "The eyes of the Lord run to and fro throughout the whole earth, to show Himself strong in the behalf of them whose heart is perfect toward Him" (2 Chr. 16:9; Zech. 4:10).

13

"Be Thou Perfect"

I am the Almighty God: walk before
Me, and be thou perfect.
—Genesis 17:1

Thirteen long years passed slowly on after the return of Hagar to Abraham's camp. The child Ishmael was born, and grew up in the patriarch's house—the acknowledged heir of the camp, and yet showing symptoms of the wild ass nature of which the angel had spoken (16:12, R.V.). Not a little perplexed must Abraham have been with those strange manifestations; and yet the heart of the old man warmed to the lad, and clung to him, often asking that Ishmael might live before God.

And throughout that long period there was no fresh appearance, no new announcement. Never since God had spoken to him in Charran had there been so long a pause. And it must have been a terrible ordeal, driving him back on the promise which had been given, and searching his heart to ascertain if the cause lay within himself. Such silences have always exercised the hearts of God's saints, leading them to say with the Psalmist: "Be not silent to me; lest, if Thou be silent to me, I become like them that go down into the pit" (Ps. 28:1). And yet they are to the heart what the long silence of winter is to the world of nature, in preparing it for the outburst of spring.

Some people are ever on the outlook for Divine appearances, for special manifestations, for celestial voices. If these are withheld, they are almost ready to break their hearts. And their life tends to an incessant training after some startling evidence of the nearness and the love of God. This feverishness is unwholesome and mistaken. Such manifestations are, indeed, delightful, but they are meant as the bright surprises, and not as the rule of Christian life: they are flung into our lives as a holiday into the school routine of a child, awakening thrilling and unexpected emotions of joy. It is true that they are liable to be withheld when we are walking at a distance from God, or indulging in cold-heartedness and sin. But it is not always so. And when the child of God has lost these bright visitations for long and sad intervals—if, so far as can be ascertained, there is no sense of condemnation on the heart for known unfaithfulness—then it must be believed that they are withheld, not in consequence of palpable sin, but to test the inner life, and to teach the necessity of basing it on faith, rather than on feelings however gladsome, or experiences however divine.

At last, "when Abram was ninety years old and nine," the Lord appeared unto him again, and gave him a new revelation of Himself; unfolded the terms of His covenant; and addressed to him that memorable charge, which rings its summons in the ear and heart of every believer still: "Walk before Me, and be thou perfect."

I. THE DIVINE SUMMONS. "Walk before Me, and be thou perfect." Men have sadly stumbled over that word. They have not erred, when they have taught that there is an experience, denoted by the phrase, which is possible to men. But they have sadly erred in pressing their own significance into the word, and in then asserting that men are expected to fulfill it, or that they have themselves attained it.

"Perfection" is often supposed to denote sinlessness of moral character, which at the best is only a negative conception, and fails to bring out the positive force of this mighty word. Surely perfection means more than sinlessness. And if this be admitted, and the further admission be made, that it contains the thought of moral completeness, then it becomes yet more absurd for any mortal to assert it of himself. The very assertion shows the lack of any such thing, and reveals but slender knowledge of the inner life and of the nature of sin. *Absolute sinlessness* is surely impossible for us so long as we have not perfect knowledge; for as our light is growing constantly, so are we constantly discovering evil in things which once we allowed without compunction: and if those who assert their sinlessness live but a few years long, and continue to grow, they will be compelled to admit, if they are true to themselves, that there was evil in things which they now deem to be harmless. But whether they admit it or not, their shortcomings are not less sinful in the sight of the holy God, although undetected by their own fallible judgment. And as to *moral completeness*, it is enough to compare the best man whom we ever knew with the perfect beauty of God incarnate, to feel how monstrous such an assumption is. Surely the language of the Apostle Paul better becomes our lips, as he cries, "Not as though I had already attained, or were already perfect, but I follow after." Perhaps in the dateless noon of eternity such words will still best become our lips.

Besides all this, the word "perfect" bears very different renderings from those often given to it. For instance, when we are told that the man of God must be *perfect* (2 Tim. 3:17), the underlying thought, as any scholar would affirm, is that of a workman being "thoroughly equipped for his work," as when a carpenter comes to the house, bearing in his hand the bag in which all necessary tools are readily available. Again, when we join in the prayer that the God of Peace would make us *perfect* in every good work to do His will, we are, in fact, asking that we may be "put in joint" with the blessed Lord; so that the glorious Head may freely secure through us the doing of His will (Heb. 13:20, 21). Again, when our Lord bids us be *perfect* as our Father in heaven is perfect, He simply incites us to that "impartiality of mercy" which knows no distinctions of evil and good, of unjust and just, but distributes its favors with bountiful and equal hand (Matt. 5:48).

What, then, is the true force and significance of this word in that stirring command which lies before us here, "Walk before Me, and be thou perfect"? A comparison of the various passages where it occurs establishes its meaning beyond a doubt, and compels us to think into it the conception of "wholeheartedness." It denotes the entire surrender of the being; and may be fairly expressed in the well-known words of the sweet and gifted songstress of modern days:

> True-hearted, whole-hearted, faithful and loyal,
> King of our lives, by Thy grace will we be.

This quality of wholehearted devotion has ever been dear to God. It was this that He considered in Job, and loved in David. It is in favor of this that His eyes run to and fro to show Himself strong (2 Chr. 16:9). It is for this that He pleads with Abraham; and it was because He met with it to so large an extent in his character and obedience that He entered into eternal covenant bond with him and his.

Here let each reader turn from the printed page, to the record of the inner life lying, open to God alone, and ask, "Is my heart perfect with God? Am I wholehearted towards Him? Is He first in my schemes, pleasures, friendships, thoughts, and actions? Is His will my law, His love my light, His business my aim, His 'well-done!' my exceeding great reward? Do others share me with Him?" There is no life to be compared with that of which the undivided heart is the center and spring. Why not seek it now?—and, turning to God in holy reverie, ask Him to bring the whole inner realm under His government, and to hold it as His forevermore. "If thine eye be single, thy whole body shall be full of light" (Matt. 6:22).

And such an attitude can only be *maintained by a very careful walk*. "Walk before Me, and be thou perfect." We must seek to realize constantly the presence of God, becoming instantly aware when the fleeciest cloud draws its veil for a moment over His face, and asking whether the cause may not lie in some scarcely noticed sin. We must cultivate the habit of feeling Him near, and the Friend from whom we would never be separated, in work, in prayer, in recreation, in repose. We must guard against the restlessness and impetuosity, the excessive eagerness and impatience, which drown the accents of His still, small voice. We must abjure all expedients He does not inspire, all actions He does not promote. We must often turn from the friend, the poem, the landscape, or the task, to look up into His face with a smile of loving recognition. We must constantly have the watches which we carry next to our hearts synchronized by His eternal movements. All this must be. And yet we shall not live forced or unnatural lives. None so blithe or lighthearted as we. All the circles of our daily life will move on in unbroken order and beauty; just as each shining moon circles around its planet, because the planet obeys the law of gravitation to the sun. Would you walk before God? Then let there be nothing in heart or life which you would not open to the inspection of His holy and pitiful eye.

II. THE REVELATION ON WHICH THIS SUMMONS WAS BASED. "I am the Almighty God" ('EL-SHADDAI'). What a name is this! And what awful emotions it must have excited in the rapt heart of the listener! God had been known to him by other names, but not by this. And this was the first of a series of revelations of those depths of meaning which lay in the fathomless abyss of the Divine name, each disclosure marking an epoch in the history of the race.

In God's dealings with men you will invariably find that some transcendent revelation precedes the Divine summons to new and difficult duty; promise opens the door to precept: He gives what He commands, ere He commands what He wills. And on this principle God acted here. It was no child's play to which He called His servant. To walk always before Him—when heart was weak, and strength was frail, and the temptation strong to swerve to right or left. To be perfect in devotion and obedience, when so many crosslights distracted, and perplexed, and fascinated the soul. To forego all methods of self-help, however tempting. To be separated from all alliances that others permitted or followed. This was much. And it was only possible through the might of the Almighty. Abraham could only do all these things on the condition, on which the Apostle insisted in after days, that God should strengthen him. And, therefore, it was that which broke on him the assurance: "I am the Almighty God." It is as if He had said: "All power is Mine in Heaven, and upon earth. Of old I laid the foundations of the earth, and the heavens are the work of My hands. I sit upon the circle of the earth; and its inhabitants are as grasshoppers. I bring out the starry hosts by number, calling them all by names, by the greatness of My might, for that I am strong in power: not one faileth. Hast thou not known—hast thou not heard—that the everlasting God, the Lord, the Creator of the ends of the earth fainteth not, neither is weary?"

All this is as true today as ever. And if any will dare venture forth on the path of separation, cutting themselves aloof from all creature aid, and from all self-originated effort; content to walk alone with God, with no help from any but Him—such will find that all the resources of the Divine Almightiness will be placed at their disposal, and that the resources of Omnipotence must be exhausted ere their cause can fail for want of help. O children of God, why do we run to and fro for the help of man, when the power of God is within reach of the perfect heart? But this condition must be fulfilled ere that mighty power can be put in operation on our behalf. "To him that overcometh I will give a white stone, and in the stone a new name written." In Abraham's case, that name, graved on the glistening jewel, was "I am the Almighty God"; for Moses it was "Jehovah"; for us it is "the God and Father of our Lord Jesus Christ."

III. THE COVENANT WHICH WAS DIVINELY PROPOSED. "I will make My covenant between Me and thee." A covenant is a promise made under the most solemn sanctions, and binding the consenting parties in the most definite and impressive way. What mortal would not consent when the Almighty God proposed to enter into an everlasting covenant with His creature, ordered in all things and sure, and more stable than the everlasting hills!

It referred to the seed. And there was a marked advance. In Haran it ran thus, "I will make of thee a great nation." At Bethel, thus, "Thy seed shall be as the dust of the earth." At Mamre, thus, "Tell the stars; so shall thy seed be." But now, three times over, the patriarch is told that he should be the father of many nations, a phrase explained by the Apostle as including all, of every land, who share Abraham's faith, though not sprung from him in the line of natural descent (Gal. 3:7–29). In memory of that promise his name was slightly altered, so that it signified the "father of a great multitude." "Nations of thee, and kings of thee" (Gen. 17:6). *We* are included in the golden circle of those words, if we believe; and we may claim the spiritual part, at least, of this covenant, which was made with Abraham before he was circumcised.

It referred to the land. "I will give unto thee, and to thy seed after thee, the land wherein thou art a stranger, all the land of Canaan, for an everlasting possession." This promise waits for fulfillment. The word "everlasting" must mean something more than those few centuries of broken, fitful rule. The recent immigration of Jews to Palestine may be an initial stage to its realization. But there is a time, no doubt, at hand when our covenant-keeping God will build again the tabernacle of David, which is fallen down, and will repair the ruins thereof; and the land, which now sighs under the cruel despotism of the infidel, shall be again inhabited by the seed of Abraham His friend.

It referred to the coming world. Till then Abraham had no other thought than that Ishmael should be his heir. But this could not be: (1) because he was slave-born; and the slave abideth not in the house forever: (2) because he was a child of the flesh, and not the direct gift of God. Abraham had been left to wait till the hope of children had become as remote from him as it had been for years from his wife; so that the heir should be evidently the creation of the Almighty God, whose name was disclosed, ere this astounding announcement was made. This is why we are kept waiting till all human and natural hope has died from our hearts, so that God may be All in all. "And God said, Sarah, thy wife shall bear thee a son indeed; and thou shalt call his name Isaac" (v. 19).

For us there is yet a crowning sweetness in the words, "I will be a God unto thee, and to thy seed"; words repeated, in Hebrews 8:10, so as certainly to include us all, if we believe. Who can unfold all the wealth of meaning of these words? All light, and no darkness at all. All love, and no shadow of change. All strength, and no sign of weakness. Beauty, sweetness, glory, majesty, all are in God, and all these will be thine and mine, if God saith to us, "I will be a God unto thee."

Nor shall this heritage be ours only: it shall belong to our children also, if we exercise Abraham's faith. God pledges Himself to be the God of our seed. But it is for us to claim the fulfillment of His pledge. Not in heartrending cries, but in quiet, determined faith, let us ask Him to do as He has said.

14

The Sign
of the Covenant

*I will make My covenant between Me and
thee, and will multiply thee exceedingly.*
—Genesis 17:2

Three times over in Scripture Abraham is called "the friend of God." In that moment of agony, when tidings came to King Jehoshaphat of the great heathen alliance which had been formed against him, he stood in the Temple, and said, "Art not Thou our God, who didst drive out the inhabitants of this land, . . . and gavest it to the seed of Abraham, thy friend, forever?" (2 Chr. 20:7).

And the Apostle James, at the close of his argument about faith and works, tells us that when Abraham believed God, "it was imputed unto him for righteousness, and he was called the friend of God" (James 2:23).

But, better than all, Jehovah Himself uses the title of friendship, and acknowledges the sacred tie between this much tried spirit and Himself: "Thou Israel art my servant, Jacob whom I have chosen, the seed of Abraham My friend" (Is. 41:8).

And it would almost appear as if these two chapters, Genesis 17 and 18, had been written for this, among other things: to show the familiarity and intimacy which existed between the Eternal God and the man who was honored to be called His "friend." However, in reading them, we must not suppose that there was something altogether exceptional and unique in this marvelous story. Without doubt it is a true record of what happened more than three thousand years ago, but it is surely also intended as a specimen of the way in which the Eternal God is willing to deal with true-hearted saints in all ages. To hundreds, and perhaps thousands, of His saints, God has been all that He was to Abraham; and He is willing to be all that to us still.

Let us peruse these ancient lines beneath the flood of light shed on them by our Savior, when He said: "Henceforth I call you not servants; for the servant knoweth not what his lord doeth, but I have called you friends" (John 15:15).

The friendship of God is freely offered to us in Jesus Christ our Lord. We cannot merit it or deserve it. We cannot establish a prior claim to it. We are simply His bankrupt debtors forever, wondering at the heights and depths, the lengths and breadths, of the unsearchable riches of His grace. May we not say that one ultimate cause of this friendship is in the yearning of the heart of the Eternal for fellowship? But it must remain forever a mystery why He should seek it among ourselves; the fallen children of Adam; the tenants of bodies of dust; the aphids on the tiny leaf, called earth, amid the forest foliage of the universe.

Surely, if He had so desired it, He might have found—or if He could not have found, He might have created—a race more noble, more obedient, more sympathetic than ourselves. Or, at least, He might have secured one which should not cost Him so dearly, demanding of Him the anguish of Gethsemane, and the blood of the cross. So, perhaps, we are sometimes prone to think. And yet it could not be. That which is, and has been, must on the whole be the best that could be, since infinite love and wisdom have so ordered it. And perhaps none could be so perfectly the companions and fellows of the Son of God through all the ages as those who know the light, because they have dwelt in the darkness; who know the truth, because they have been ensnared in the meshes of the false; and who can appreciate love, because they have been in the far country, wasting their substance in riotous living, but have been redeemed by His blood.

But what a wondrous destiny there is within our reach! One to which the firstborn sons of light might aspire in vain! At the best they can only be ministers, flames of fire, hearts of love, excelling in strength, hearkening to His word. But we may be the FRIENDS of God; sons and daughters of the great King; members of the body of Christ; constituent parts of His Bride, in her peerless beauty and meetness for her Spouse. As one writes such words as these, the brain almost reels beneath the conception that flashes before it of the blessedness which awaits us, both in this world, and in those ages which rear their heads in the far distance, as lines on lines of snowy breakers rolling in from a sunlit sea.

Oh, FRIENDS OF GOD, why do you not make more of your transcendent privileges? Why do you not talk to Him about all that wearies and worries you, as freely as Abraham did, telling Him about your Ishmaels, your Lots, and His dealings? Why do you not fall on your faces while God talks with you (17:3)? Life should be one long talk between God and us. No day at least should close without our talking over its history with our patient and loving Lord; entering into His confessional; relieving our hearts of half their sorrow, and all their bitterness, in the act of telling Him all. And if only we get low enough, and be still enough, we shall hear His accents sweet and thrilling, soft and low, opening depths which eye hath not seen, nor ear heard, but which He has prepared for those who love and wait for Him.

There are, however, three conditions to be fulfilled by us if we would enjoy this blessed friendship: SEPARATION, PURITY, and OBEDIENCE, each of which was set forth in the rite of circumcision, which was given to Abraham for himself and his descendants at this time.

Circumcision seems to have been in vogue among the Egyptians and other nations, even before it was taken up and adopted as the seal of the sacred covenant between God and Abraham. It existed previously, but it had never borne the interpretation with which it was now invested; just as the immersion of new disciples had been long practiced both by the Baptist and the Jews, before our Lord appropriated it and gave a significance which opened up in it entirely fresh depths of meaning and beauty.

We are all of us more or less dependent on outward symbols and signs; and Abraham and his children were no exception to this rule; and it seemed good to God to carve in the flesh of His people an unmistakable reminder and sacrament of that holy relationship into which they had entered. A similar function, in the Christian Church, is met by the ordinances of Believers' Baptism and the Lord's Supper.

The rite of circumcision was rigorously maintained among the children of Abraham. Moses was not permitted to undertake his life work while his son was left uncircumcised. Nor were the people allowed to enter Canaan until they had rolled away the reproach of Canaan, and had submitted to this rite on the threshold of the Land of Promise. The sanctity of the Sabbath might at any time be invaded, rather than permit the eighth day of a child's life to pass without the act of circumcision being performed. It is said of the child Jesus that "eight days were fulfilled for circumcising Him" (Luke 1:21, R.V.). Paul noted the fact that in his own life, according to Jewish usage, he was "circumcised the eighth day" (Phil. 3:5). And no one could receive benefit through sin offering or sacrifice who had not passed through this initiatory rite. So strict was the line of demarcation, that the Jew counted the uncircumcised as unclean, and would not eat with them or go into their houses. It was a formidable charge against the Apostle Peter, on his return to Jerusalem from visiting in the house of Cornelius, "Thou wentest in to men uncircumcised, and didst eat with them" (Acts 11:3).

It was concerning this matter that controversy waxed so warm in the early Church. The Pharisee party were quite willing for Gentiles to meet with them in Church fellowship, if they were circumcised as Jews, but not otherwise. They went so far as to affirm, "Except ye be circumcised after the manner of Moses ye cannot be saved" (Acts 15:1, 24). And, not content with affirming this in Antioch and Jerusalem, they sent their emissaries far and wide, especially visiting the churches which had been recently founded by the Apostle Paul's assiduous care, and insisting upon the circumcision of the new converts so soon as he had turned his back.

There was no compromise possible in this matter; and both the Council at Jerusalem and the Apostle Paul, guided by the Spirit of God, made it abundantly clear, both by circular letter and epistle, that circumcision was part of the temporary ritual of Judaism, which was destined to pass away. "If ye be circumcised, Christ shall profit you nothing." "In the new man there is neither circumcision nor uncircumcision." "In Christ Jesus neither circumcision avails anything or uncircumcision, but a new creature" (Gal. 5:2, 6; 6:15; Col. 3:2). And thus this danger was averted from the Church, which had been in peril of becoming a Jewish institution, a kind of inner circle of the Judaistic commonwealth, but which henceforth became the common meeting ground for all who loved, trusted, and obeyed the Lord Jesus in sincerity.

At the same time, as in so many other Jewish rites, there was an inner spirit, which passed on into the Christian Church, and is our heritage today. St. Paul, the deadly foe of the outward rite, speaks of the spiritual circumcision, and says it is made without human hands, by the direct interposition of the Holy Spirit: and that it consists in "the putting off of the body of the sins of the flesh" (Col. 2:11). Oh, blessed High Priest, this is what we need: take the knife in hand; and, though it cost us blood, make haste to set us free from the dominion of evil, and to constitute us the true circumcision: "For we are the circumcision, which worship God in the Spirit, and rejoice in Christ Jesus, and have no confidence in the flesh" (Phil. 3:3).

It is only in proportion as we know the spiritual meaning of circumcision that we can enter into the joyous appropriation of the friendship of God. But if we are willing, our Lord and Savior is both able and willing to effect in us this blessed spiritual result.

I. SEPARATION. Abraham and his seed were marked out by this rite as a separated people. And it is only as such that any of us can be admitted into the friendship of God. Blood shedding and death—the cross and the grave—must lie between us and our own past life; yea, between us and all complicity with evil. The only trysting place for Christ and His followers is outside the camp, where the ground is still freshly trodden by the feet of the exiled King.

There are times when we may be expressly bidden to abide where we were originally called of God, but this will be for special purposes of ministry, and because the darkness needs light, and the carcass requires salt. For the most part the clarion note rings out to all who are wishful to know the sweets of Divine fellowship: "Come out from among them, and be ye separate, saith the Lord, and touch not the unclean thing; and I will receive you, and will be a Father unto you" (2 Cor. 6:17, 18).

This was the key to Abraham's life; and is the inner meaning of the rite of circumcision.

II. PURITY. "Putting off of the body of the flesh by the circumcision of Christ" (Col. 2:11, R.V.). There is hardly a single grace dearer to God than this—to keep lily white amid the defiling atmosphere: to walk with unspotted garments even in Sardis: to be as sensitive to the taint of impurity as the most delicate nostril to an evil odor. Ah, this is a condition of great price in the sight of God, and one to which He unveils Himself. "Blessed are the pure in heart, for they shall see God" (Matt. 5:8).

Purity can only be attained by the special grace of the Holy Spirit; and by doing two things: first, by our turning instantly from paragraphs in papers, or pictures on the walls, and all things else, which excite impure imaginations; secondly, by our seeking immediate forgiveness, when we are conscious of having yielded, even for a moment, to the deadly and insidious fascinations of the flesh.

There are some who sigh after the white rose of chastity, with a kind of despair that it should ever become their own. They forget that it is only possible to us by the grace of Christ, and through the Holy Spirit; whose temples we profess ourselves to be. Let us trust Him to keep His own property in the perfect loveliness of that purity and chastity which are so dear to God; this is the circumcision of Christ.

III. OBEDIENCE. For Abraham this rite might have seemed less necessary than for some in his camp. But no sooner was it commanded than it was undergone. "In the selfsame day was Abraham circumcised, and Ishmael his son." Does it not remind us of Him who said, "Ye are My friends, if ye do whatsoever I command you"? Instant obedience to known duty is an indispensable condition of all intimacy with

God: and if the duty be irksome and difficult, then remember to claim all the more of the Divine grace; for there is no duty, to which we are called, for the discharge of which there is not strength enough within reach, if only we will put forth our hands to take it.

We do not obey in order to become friends, but having become friends we hasten to obey. Love is more inexorable than law. And for the love of Him who calls us by so dear a title, we are glad to undertake and accomplish what Sinai with all its thunders would fail to nerve us to attempt.

Of the secrets which shall be revealed; of the delights which shall be experienced; of the blessings which shall accrue to ever widening circles, through the friendship of one man with God—we have not space to speak. This, however, is true, that the soul laughs to itself (v. 17), not with incredulity, but with the uncontrollable gladness of conscious acceptance and love.

15

The Divine Guest

The Lord appeared unto Abraham
in the plains of Mamre.
—Genesis 18:1

When, in the course of some royal progress, a sovereign deigns to sojourn in the homestead of one of the subjects of his realm, the event becomes at once the theme of chroniclers, and the family selected for so high an honor is held in deepened respect. But what shall we say in the presence of such an episode as this—in which the God of heaven became the guest of His servant Abraham!

There is no doubt as to the august character of one of the three who, on that memorable afternoon, when every living thing was seeking shelter during the heat of the day, visited the tent of the patriarch. In the first verse we are expressly told that Jehovah appeared unto him in the plains of Mamre, as he sat in the tent door in the heat of the day. And in the tenth verse there is the accent of Deity, who alone can create life, and to whom nothing is too hard, in the words of promise which tell how certainly Sarah should have a son. And, besides, we are told that two angels came to Sodom at even. Evidently they were two of the three who had sat as Abraham's guests beneath the tree which sheltered his tent in the blazing noon. But as for the other, who throughout the wondrous hours had been the only spokesman, His dignity is disclosed in the amazing colloquy which took place on the heights of Mamre, when Abraham stood yet before the Lord, and pleaded with Him as the Judge of all the earth.

It was thus that the Son of God anticipated His incarnation; and was found in fashion as a man before He became flesh. He loved to come *incognito* into the homes of those He cherished as His friends, even before He came across the slopes of Olivet to make His home in the favored cottage, where His spirit rested from the din of the great city, and girded itself for the cross and the tomb. "He rejoiced in the habitable part of the earth, and His delights were with the sons of men" (Prov. 8:31).

It is very marvelous! We may well ask with deepest reverence and awe the question of Solomon, when he felt the utter inadequacy of his splendid Temple as the abode of the eternal God: "Will God in very deed dwell on the earth? Behold, heaven and the heaven of heavens cannot contain Thee; how much less this house that I have built!" (1 Kgs. 8:27, R.V.). But this question has been forever settled by God Himself, in the majestic words: "Thus saith the high and lofty One that inhabiteth eternity, whose name is Holy; I dwell in the high and holy place; with him also that is of a contrite and humble spirit, to revive the spirit of the humble, and to revive the heart of the contrite ones" (Is. 57:15). And the life of our blessed Master is a delightful commentary on these mighty affirmations. He said to a publican, "Zaccheus, make haste and come down, for today I must abide at thy house." He went to the home of Peter, and was ministered to by one of the household, whom He had raised from the gates of death. And after His resurrection, He entered the humble lodging of the two disciples in whose company He had walked from Jerusalem, seeking to dry their tears as they went.

Nor is this all. There is no heart so lowly but that He will enter. There is no home so humble, but that He will make Himself a welcome inmate. There is no table so poorly provided, but that He will sit thereat, turning water into wine, multiplying the loaves and fishes, and converting the simple meal into a sacrament. When seated at meat with those He loves, He still takes bread, and blesses it and breaks, and gives to them (Luke 24:30). To each and all He says, as He stands laden with raiment, eyesalve, gold, and viands for the evening meal: "Behold, I stand at the door, and knock: if any man hear My voice, and open the door, I will come in to him, and will sup with him; and he with Me" (Rev. 3:20).

Abraham evidently, at the outset, did not realize the full meaning of the episode in which he was taking part. Even so do we often fail to value aright characters with whom we come in contact. It is only as they pass away from us forever, and we look back upon them, that we realize that we have been entertaining angels unawares. Let us so act always and everywhere, that as we review the past we may have nothing to regret; and may not have to reproach ourselves with having omitted to do something or other, which we would have inserted in our program had we only realized our opportunities.

ABRAHAM TREATED HIS VISITORS WITH TRUE EASTERN HOSPITALITY. He *ran* to meet them, and bowed himself toward the ground. He proposed water for their feet, and rest for their tired frames, beneath the spreading shadow. He started his wife to the immediate kneading of the meal for baking on the scorching stones. He ran to choose his tenderest calf, refusing to delegate the work to another's hand. He served his visitors himself, and stood as a servant by their side, under the tree, while they did eat. Christians have not much to boast of—and a good deal to learn—as they consider the action of this old-time saint, and his dealings with the three strangers who came to his tent. The faith which he had towards God had a very winsome aspect towards men. There was nothing in him which was austere or forbidding, but much that was exceedingly lovely, and brimming with the milk of human kindness.

MAY IT NOT BE THAT CHRIST COMES TO US OFTEN IN THE GUISE OF A STRANGER? But we are too busy, or too tired, or too much afraid of making a mistake; and, therefore, we either refuse Him altogether, or we treat Him so badly that He passes unobserved away, to carry to someone else the blessing which He would have left with us had we only shown ourselves worthy.

Does He not test us thus? Of course if He were to come in His manifested splendor as the Son of the Highest, everyone would receive

Him, and provide Him with sumptuous hospitality. But this would not reveal our true character. And so He comes to us as a wayfaring man, hungry and athirst; or as a stranger, naked and sick. Those that are akin to Him will show Him mercy, in whatsoever disguise He comes, though they recognized Him not, and will be surprised to learn that they ever ministered to Him. Those, on the other hand, who are not really His, will fail to discern Him; will let Him go unhelped away; and will wake up to find that "inasmuch as they did it not to one of the least of these, they did it not to Him" (Matt. 25:45).

There was much truth in the simplicity of the little German lad, who left the door open for the Lord to enter and sit with his mother and himself at their frugal supper table; and who, as a beggar stood within the portal, asking alms, remarked: "Perhaps the Lord could not come Himself, and had therefore sent this poor man as His representative."

BUT GOD NEVER LEAVES US IN HIS DEBT. He takes care to pay for His entertainment, royally and divinely. He uses Peter's fishing smack, and gives it back, nearly submerged by the weight of the fish which He had driven into the nets. He sits down with His friends to a country marriage feast, and pays for their simple fare by jars brimming with water turned to wine. He uses the five barley loaves and two small fishes, but He fills the lad with an ample meal. He sends His prophet to lodge with a widow, and provides meal and oil for him and her for many days. And Abraham was no loser by his ready hospitality; for, as they sat at meat, the Lord foretold the birth of Sarah's child: "I will certainly return unto thee; and Sarah thy wife shall have a son."

Sarah was sitting inside the flimsy curtain of camel's hair, secluded after the Eastern fashion for those of high rank; and as she heard the words, she laughed within herself the laugh of incredulity. That laugh was at once noticed by Him from whom nothing can be hid, and whose eyes are as a flame of fire. "And the Lord said unto Abraham, Wherefore did Sarah laugh, saying, Shall I of a surety bear a child, which am old? Is anything too hard for the Lord?" (Gen. 18:13, 14).

With strange simplicity she answered through the curtain, denying that she had laughed: for she was afraid. But her reply was met by the stern and uncompromising asseveration, which was altogether final, "Nay, but thou didst laugh." These were the only audible words which we know to have passed between God and Abraham's wife; and they reveal the superficiality and unbelief of her nature. But we must not judge her too harshly, for she had not had the opportunities of her husband. However, she seems to have been led by those words into a true faith; for it is said, "By faith also Sarah herself received strength to conceive seed, and was delivered of a child when she was past age, because she judged Him faithful who had promised" (Heb. 11:11).

THIS IS THE TRUE LAW OF FAITH. Do not look at your faith or at your feelings, but look away to the word of promise, and, above all, to the Promiser. Study the punctuality of His orderings in the starry firmament. Are planets ever overdue? Or do the seasons forget to revolve? Consider how accurately He has kept His word with the nations of the past, whose ruined cities attest His judgments! Has He ever failed to keep His word? Is there any conceivable reason why He should not keep it? His power is omnipotent; and would He ever have pledged Himself to do what He could not effect? "He is faithful that promised." Look from faith to the promise, and from the promise to the Promiser. And as we become conscious of possessing the power of vision while we look on any object to which we may direct our gaze, so we shall become conscious of the presence and growth of faith as we look away to our faithful God.

"IS ANYTHING TOO HARD FOR THE LORD?"—That is one of God's unanswered questions. It has lain there for three thousand years, perused by myriads, answered by none; unless, indeed, those words of Jeremiah are the only answer which mortal man can give: "Ah, Lord God! Behold, Thou has made the heaven and the earth by Thy great power and stretched-out arm; and there is nothing too hard for Thee" (Jer. 32:17).

It may seem to you hard to the verge of impossibility, that ever God should keep His word, in the conversion of that friend for whom you have a warrant to pray, according to 1 John 4:16. Hard to vindicate your character from the aspersions with which it is being befouled. Hard to keep your evil nature in the place of death; and to cast down your evil imaginings, bringing every thought into captivity to the obedience of Christ. Hard to make you sweet and gentle, forgiving and loving. Hard to produce from you the fruits of a lovely and holy nature. It may be hard, but it is not too hard for the Lord. "With God all things are possible." And, as Sarah found it, all things are possible to those who believe.

The one thing that hinders God is our unbelief. Sarah must believe, and Abraham also, ere the child of promise could be born. And so must it be with us. As soon as we believe, then, according to our faith it is done to us; yea, exceeding abundantly beyond all we had asked or thought.

It may seem hard that the sins of a life should be forgiven, but God will do it for any penitent and believing soul. "All that believe in Christ are justified from all things" (Acts 13:39). It may seem hard that our naked souls should be attired in vestments fit for the royal palace, but it shall be so, if we have faith; for the righteousness of Christ is imputed and reckoned to all who believe (Rom. 3:22). It may seem hard that rebels should become children; yet this, too, shall be; for to them that receive Him He gives the right to become children of God (John 1:12).

You ask how to obtain this faith. Remember that faith is the receptive attitude of the soul, begotten and maintained by the grace of God. Christ is the Author and Finisher of faith; not only in the abstract, but in the personal experience of the soul. Faith is the gift of God. If, then, you would receive it, put your will on the side of Christ; not a passing wish, but the whole will of your beings: will to believe patiently, persistently, yearningly; let your eyes be ever toward the Lord; study the promises of God; consider the nature of God; be prepared to be rid of everything that grieves His Holy Spirit; and it is as certain as the truth of Christ, that you will have begotten and maintained in you the faith that can move mountains, and laugh at impossibilities.

And to such faith God will come, not as a passing wayfarer, but to abide; to feast with the soul in holy strengthening fellowship; to fill it with the true laughter; and to leave behind promises soon to become accomplished facts. "Behold, the tabernacle of God is with men, and He will dwell with them; and they shall be His people, and God Himself shall be with them, and be their God" (Rev. 21:3).

16
Pleading for Sodom

And Abraham stood yet before the Lord;
and Abraham drew near.
—Genesis 18:22, 23

As the day wore on, Abraham's mysterious guests went off across the hills towards Sodom; and Abraham went with them to bring them on their way. But all three did not reach the guilty city, over which the thunder clouds had already commenced to gather. That evening two angels entered it alone. And where was their companion? Ah! He had stayed behind to talk yet further with His friend. Tradition still points out the spot on the hills at the head of a long steep ravine leading down to the sullen waters of the Dead Sea where the Lord tarried behind to tell Abraham all that was in His heart.

Why did not the Lord accompany His angels down to Sodom? Was it because vengeance is His strange work, in which He can take no pleasure? It surely befits the dignity of the sovereign Judge to delegate to other hands the execution of His decrees. "The Son of Man shall send forth His angels, and they shall gather out of His Kingdom all things that offend, and them that do iniquity" (Matt. 13:41).

But there was a deeper reason still. Abraham was the "friend of God"; and friendship constitutes a claim to be entrusted with secrets hidden from all beside. "The secret or the Lord is with them that fear

Him." "Henceforth," said the Master to His disciples, "I call you not servants; for the servant knoweth not what his lord doeth, but I have called you friends; for all things that I have heard of My Father I have made known unto you" (John 15:15). If we live near God, we shall have many things revealed to us which are hidden from the wise and prudent. The Septuagint version has well brought out he spirit of the Divine reverie, when it puts the question thus: "Shall I hide from Abraham, *my servant*, the thing which I do?" The Lord does nothing which He does not first reveal to His holy servants and prophets.

But the words which follow point to a yet further reason for the full disclosures that were made: "For I know Him, that he will command his children and his household after him; and they shall keep the way of the Lord, to do justice and judgment" (Gen. 18:19). Was there a fear lest Abraham and his children might doubt the justice and judgment of God if the righteous were summarily cut off with the wicked; and if the cities of the plain were destroyed without a revelation of their sin on the one hand, and the display of the Divine mercy on the other? Certainly it has placed the Divine character in an altogether different light, in that we have been permitted, in such a case as this, to understand some of the motives which have actuated God in His goodness or severity. And though His judgments must ever be a great deep, yet such a wondrous colloquy as this shines above them; as the rainbow trembles in its matchless beauty over the steamy depths of Niagara's plunge.

I. THE BURDEN OF THE DIVINE ANNOUNCEMENT. "The cry of Sodom and Gomorrah is great." What a marvelous expression is this! There, far down the valley, bathed in the radiance of the westering sun, lay the guilty cities, still and peaceful. No sound traveled to the patriarch's ear, not even the roar which aeronauts detect in the dizzy heights of air, through which they travel on their adventurous way, passing mighty cities far beneath, which betray their existence by their voice. Quiet though Sodom seemed in the far distance, and in the hush of the closing day; yet to God there was a cry. The cry of the earth compelled to carry such a scar. The cry of inanimate creation, groaning and travailing in pain. The cry of the oppressed, the downtrodden—the victims of human violence and lust. The cry of the maiden, the wife, and the child. These were the cries which had entered into the ears of the Lord God of Sabaoth. And each sin has a cry. "The voice of the brother's blood crieth unto Me." And it will go on crying; unless it is silenced by the yet greater voice of the blood of Christ, "which speaketh better things." And, if each sin has a cry, what must not be the volume of sound for a life, and for a city! Must not God still have to say of our great cities, one by one?—"Its cry is great; and its sin is very grievous."

"I will go down now, and see." God always narrowly investigates the true condition of the case, before He awards or executes His sentences. He comes seeking fruit for three years, before He gives the order for the cutting down of the tree that cumbered the vineyard soil. He walks our streets day and night. He patrols our thoroughfares, marking everything, missing nothing, He glides unasked into our most sacred privacy; for all things are naked and open unto the eyes of Him with whom we have to do. He is prepared, nay, eager to give us the benefit of any excuse. But flagrant sin, like that which broke out in Sodom that very night, is enough to settle forever the fate of a Godless community when standing at the bar of Him who is Judge and Witness both.

"And if not, I will know." There was something very ominous in all these words, which Abraham clearly understood to indicate the approaching destruction of the place; for in his prayer he again and again alludes to the imminence of its doom: "Wilt Thou, also, destroy the righteous with the wicked?" But what is there that God does not know? "The darkness and the light are both alike to Him." Yet He says, "I will know." Yes, ungodly man who mayest read this page: remember that from God no secrets can be hid. He will search out the most hidden ramifications of thy sin; bringing them out before the gaze of the universe; and justifying His righteous judgments which He will not spare.

II. THE IMPRESSION WHICH THIS ANNOUNCEMENT MADE ON ABRAHAM'S MIND. So soon as the angels had gone on, leaving Abraham alone with the Lord, he was thoroughly aroused by the revelation which had broken upon him; and his mind was filled with a tumult of emotion. He hardly dared expostulate with God: what was he, but "dust and ashes"? And yet he was impelled to make some attempt to avert the doom that threatened the cities of the plain.

The motives that prompted him were twofold: (1) *There was a natural anxiety about his kinsman, Lot.* Twenty years had passed since Lot had left him, but he never ceased to follow him with the most tender affection. He could not forget that he was the son of his dead brother Haran; or that he had been his ward; or that he had braved the hardships of the desert in his company. All this had been present to his mind, when, a few years before, he had made a heroic effort to extricate him from the hands of Chedorlaomer. And now the strong impulse of natural affection stirred him to make one strenuous effort to save Sodom, lest his nephew might be overwhelmed in its overthrow. Real religion tends not to destroy, but to fulfill all the impulses of true natural love.

(2) *There was also a fear lest the total destruction of the cities of the plain might prejudice the character of God in the minds of the neighboring peoples.* Abraham did not deny that the fate which was about to overtake them was deserved by many of the people of that enervating and luxuriant valley: but he could not bring his mind to suppose that the whole of the population was equally debased; and he feared that if all were summarily swept away, the surrounding nations would have a handle of reproach against the justice of his God, and would accuse Him of unrighteousness, inasmuch as He destroyed the righteous with the wicked.

The character of God has ever been dear to his true-hearted servants of every age. Moses was prepared to forego the honor of being the ancestor of the chosen people, rather than that the nations which had heard of the Divine fame should be able to say that God was not able to bring them into the Land of Promise.[*] And when the men of Israel fled before Ai, Joshua and the elders appear to have thought less of the danger of an immediate rising to cut them off than of what God would do for His great name. Oh for more of this chivalrous devotion to the interests and glory of our God! Would that we were so ab-

---

[*] See Exodus 32:10; Numbers 14:12.

sorbed in all that touches the honor of the Divine name among men, that this might be the supreme element in our anxiety, as we view the drift of human opinion concerning the enactments of Divine providence!

This passion for the glory of God burned with a clear strong flame in Abraham's heart; and it was out of this that there arose his wondrous intercession. And when we become as closely identified with the interests of God as he was, we shall come to feel as he did; and shall be eager that the Divine character should be vindicated among the children of men; content, if need be, to lie dying in the ditch, so long as we can hear the shouts of triumph amid which our King rides over us to victory.

III. THE ELEMENTS IN ABRAHAM'S INTERCESSION. *It was lonely prayer.* He waited till on all that wide plateau, and beneath those arching skies, there was no living man to overhear this marvelous outpouring of a soul overcharged, as are the pools, when, after the rains of spring, they overflow their banks. "He stood before the Lord." It is fatal to all the intensest, strongest devotion to pray always in the presence of another, even the dearest. Every saint must have a closet, of which he can shut the door, and in which he can pray to the Father which is in secret. The oratory may be the mountains, or the woods, or the sounding shore, but it must be somewhere. Pitiable is the man who cannot—miserable the man who dare not—meet God face to face, and talk with Him of His ways, and plead for his fellows.

> For what are men better than sheep or goats,
> That nourish a blind life within the brain,
> If, knowing God, they lift not hands of prayer
> Both for themselves and those who call them friends.

It was prolonged prayer. "Abraham stood yet before the Lord." The story takes but a few moments to read, but the scene may have lasted for the space of hours. We cannot climb the more elevated pinnacles of prayer in a hasty rush. They demand patience, toil, prolonged endeavor, ere the lower slopes can be left, and the brooding cloud line passed, and the aspiring soul can reach that cleft in the mountainside, where Moses stood beneath the shadow of God's hand. Of course, our God is ever on the alert to hear and answer those prayers which, like minute guns, we fire through the livelong day, but we cannot maintain his posture of ejaculatory prayer unless we cultivate the prolonged occasions. How much we miss because we do not wait before God! We do not give the sun a chance to thaw us. We do not linger long enough upon the quay to see the vessels return freighted with the answers we had been praying for. If only we had remained longer at the palace door, we might have seen the King come out with a benediction in His fact and a largess in His hands.

It was a very humble prayer. "Behold, now, I have taken upon me to speak unto the Lord, which am but dust and ashes." "Oh let not the Lord be angry, and I will speak." "Behold, I have taken upon me to speak unto the Lord." "Oh let not the Lord be angry, and I will speak yet but this once." The nearer we get to God, the more conscious are we of our own unworthiness; just as the higher a bird flies in mid-heaven, the deeper will be the reflection of its snowy pinions in the placid mere beneath. Let the glowworm vie with the meridian sun; let the dewdrop boast itself against the fullness of the ocean bed; let the babe vaunt its knowledge with the intelligence of a seraph—before the man who lives in touch with God shall think of taking any other position than that of lowliest humiliation and prostration in His presence. Before Him angels veil their faces, and the heavens are not clean in His sight. And is it not remarkable that our sense of weakness is one of our strongest claims and arguments with God? "He forgetteth not the cry of the humble." "To that man will I look who trembleth."

This prayer was based on a belief that God possessed the same moral intuitions as himself. "Wilt Thou destroy the righteous with the wicked? That be far from Thee that the righteous should be as the wicked!" "Shall not the Judge of all the earth do right?" There is an infinite interest in this. It is as if the patriarch looked up from the clear depths of his own integrity into the azure heights of the Divine Being, and saw there enthroned a moral nature, at least as upright, fair and true as his own; and to that he made his appeal, sure of a favorable response.

It was as if he had said: "Almighty God, I could not think it right to destroy the righteous with the wicked; and I am sure that any number of righteous men would shrink from doing so. And if this is binding on man, of course it must be much more binding on Thee, because Thou art the Judge of all the earth." And God was not angry; indeed He assented to Abraham's plea. And may we not go further, and say?—that though God may act in ways above our reason, yet He will not contradict those instincts of the moral sense which He has placed within our hearts. And if at times He seem to do so, it is because we have falsely conceived of His dealings, and put an erroneous interpretation upon them.

It was a cherished motto of bygone days that "the king could do no wrong." Alas! it was a vain dream. But what was untrue of the Stuarts is literally true of the Eternal God. He cannot outrage the moral nature in man, which is made in the likeness of His own. Let us possess our souls in patience, sure that any appearances to the contrary are the mists generated by our own evil natures or limited intelligence, and will be swept away from obscuring that everlasting righteousness which is steadfast and changeless as the great mountains.

This prayer was persevering. SIX TIMES Abraham returned to the charge, and as each petition was granted, his faith and courage grew; and, finding he had struck a right vein, he worked it again, and yet again. It looks at first sight as if he forced God back from point to point, and wrung his petitions from an unwilling hand. But this is a mistake. In point of fact, *God was drawing him on;* and if he had dared to ask at first what he asked at the last, he would have got more than all that he asked or thought at the very commencement of his intercession. This was the time of his education. He did not learn the vast extent of God's righteousness and mercy all at once; he climbed the dizzy heights step by step; and, as he gained each step, he was inspired to dare another. What a pity that he stopped at ten! There is no knowing what he might have reached, had he gone on. As it was, the Almighty was obliged by the demands of His own nature, to exceed the limits placed by Abraham, in bringing out of Sodom the only persons that could, by any possibility, be accounted "righteous."

It is so that God educates us still. In ever widening circles, He tempts his new fledged eaglets to try the sustaining elasticity of the air. He forces us to ask one thing; and then another, and yet another.

And when we have asked our utmost, there are always unexplored re-mainders behind; and He does exceeding abundantly above all. There were not ten righteous men in Sodom, but Lot and his wife, and his two daughters, were saved, though three of them were deeply infected with the moral contagion of the place. And God's righteousness was clearly established and vindicated in the eyes of the surrounding peoples.

In closing, we remark *one of the great principles in the Divine government of the world.* A whole city had been spared, if ten righteous men had been found within its walls. Ungodly men little realize how much they owe to the presence of the children of God in their midst. Long ere now had the floods of deserved wrath swept them all away, but judgment has been restrained, because God could not do anything while the righteous were found among them. The impatient servants have often asked if they should not gather out the tares. But the answer of the righteous Lord has ever been: "Nay, lest while ye gather up the tares, ye root up the wheat also with them." Ah, how little the world realizes the debt it owes to its saints, the salt to stay its corruption, the light to arrest the reinstitution of the reign of chaos and night! We cannot but yearn over the world, as it rolls on its way towards its sad dark doom. Let us plead for it from the heights above Mamre. And may we and our beloved ones be led out from it into safety, ere the last plagues break full upon it in inevitable destruction!

17

Angel Work
in a Bad Town

Genesis 19.

The waters of the Dead Sea ripple over a part of the site where once stood the cities of the plain, with their busy stir of life, and thought, and trade. But all the sounds of human joy, sorrow, or industry, the tread of the soldier, the call of the herdsman, the murmur of the market, the voices of little children playing in the open spaces—*all* are hushed in that awful solitude, the aspect of which is a striking testimony to the truth of the inspired Word.

Embosomed in gaunt mountains, the Dead Sea lies thirteen hundred feet below the level of the Mediterranean Sea. So weird and desolate is the scene, that it was long believed that no birds would fly across the sullen waters; no shells line the strand; no trace of living verdure is found along the shores: but, strewn along the desolate margin lie trunks and branches of trees, torn from the thickets of the river jungle by the violence of the Jordan, borne rapidly into the Sea of Sodom, and cast up again from its depths, encrusted with the slat which makes those waters utterly unfit to drink. And as the traveler wanders around the spot, he is irresistibly reminded of the time, when "the Lord rained upon Sodom and upon Gomorrah brimstone and fire from the

Lord out of heaven; and He overthrew those cities, and all the plain, and all the inhabitants of the cities, and that which grew upon the ground."

THE REASONS WHICH JUSTIFIED THIS SUPREME ACT OF DE-STRUCTION:

(1) *It was a merciful warning to the rest of mankind.* The lesson of the Flood had well nigh faded from the memory of man; and, heedless of all restraint, the human family had made terrible advances in the course of open and shameless vice—so much so that there seemed an imminent danger of men repeating the abominable crimes that had opened the sluices of the Deluge. It was surely, therefore, wise and merciful to set up a warning, which told its own terrible story, and reminded transgressors that there were limits beyond which the Judge of all the earth would not permit them to go.

It is true that the visitation, if it temporarily alarmed the nations of the immediate neighborhood, did not prevent them from reaching a similar excess of immorality some centuries later, or from incurring at the edge of Joshua's word the doom which heaven's fire had executed on their neighbors in the Jordan plain. Still, God's warnings have a merciful intention, even where they are unheeded; and this Sodom catastrophe has been well said to belong to that class of terrors in which a wise man will trace "the lovingkindness of the Lord."

(2) *Moreover, in this terrible act the Almighty simply hastened the result of their own actions.* Nations are not destroyed until they are rotten at the core; as the northeast wind which snaps the forest trees only hastens the result for which the borer worm had already prepared. It would have been clear to any thoughtful observer who had ventured out after dark in Sodom that it must inevitably fall. Unnatural crime had already eaten out the national heart, and, in the ordinary course of events, utter collapse could not be long delayed.

Go into the tents of Abraham, and you find simplicity; hospitality; the graces of a truly noble character, which guarantee the perpetuity of his name, and the glorious future of his children. Now go to Sodom: and in that sultry climate you find a population enervated with luxury; debased by cowardly submission to a foreign tyrant; cankered to the core with vice; not ten righteous men among them all; while the purity and sanctity of home are idle words. All these symptoms prognosticate, with prophetic voice, that their "sentence lingereth not, and their destruction slumbereth not."

This suggests a solemn lesson for ourselves. The tide of empire has ever set westwards. India, Babylon, Egypt, Greece, and Rome, have successively wielded supreme power, and sunk into oblivion. Shall it depart from Britain, as it has departed from the rest? It need not do so. Yet, as we remark the increase of extravagance and luxury; the reckless expenditure on pleasure; the shameless vice that flaunts itself in our streets; the adulation of wealth; the devotion to gambling which so largely supports the weekly and daily Press; the growing laxness of the marriage tie—we may well entertain the darkest fears about the future of our fatherland. The only hope for us is based on the important part which we are called to play in facilitating the evangelization of the world. Should we once fail in this—or should we send out more opium chests than Bible, more spirit sellers than missionaries—nothing can avert our fall.

(3) *Besides, this overthrow only happened after careful investigation.* "I will go down now and see." Beneath these simple words we catch a glimpse of one of the most sacred principles of Divine action. God does not act hastily, nor upon hearsay evidence; He must see for Himself if there may not be some mitigating or extenuating circumstances. It was only after He had come to the fig tree for many years, seeking fruit in vain, that He said, "Cut it down: why cumbereth it the ground?" And this deliberation is characteristic of God. He is unwilling that any should perish. He is slow to anger. Judgment is His strange work. He tells us that some day, when we come to look into His doings, we shall be comforted, concerning many of the evils which He has brought on the world, because we shall know that he has not done *without cause* all that He has done (Ezek. 14:23).

(4) *There is this consideration also—that, during the delay, many a warning was sent.* First, there was the conquest by Chedorlaomer, some twenty years before the time of which we write. Then there was the presence of Lot, which, indeed, was enfeebled by his inconsistencies, but was yet a protest on the behalf of righteousness (2 Pet. 2:7, 8). Finally, there was the deliverance and restoration by the energetic

interposition of Abraham. Again and again had God warned the men of these cities of their inevitable doom, if they did not repent. To use His own expressive words, He "rose up early" to send His messengers, but the people would not hear.

Nor is His usage different in the case of individuals. The course of every sin is against a succession of menacing red lights and exploding fog signals, warning of danger if that course be pursued. Just as the quivering of the nerves tells when the system is overstrained, and demands immediate rest at the risk of certain paralysis, if that warning be disregarded; so has God arranged that no downward step can be taken, without setting going vast numbers of shrill bells that tell of danger ahead. Transgressor, the signals are all against thee!

To regard these alarm tokens is to be saved. To disregard them, persevering in spite of all, is to deaden the soul and harden the heart, and run the risk of blasphemy against the Holy Ghost. For that unpardonable sin is not an act, but a state—the condition of the soul that does not, and cannot, feel; that is utterly insensible and careless of its state; that drifts heedless to its doom; and is not forgiven, simply because it does not admit or feel its need of forgiveness, and, therefore, does not ask for it.

(5) *It is worthy of notice that God saved all whom He could.* Lot was a sorry wreck of a noble beginning. When he started forth, as Abraham's companion, from Ur, he gave promise of a life of quite unusual power and fruit. But he was one of those characters which cannot stand success. There is no temptation more insidious or perilous than that. The Enchanted Ground is more to be dreaded than the open assaults of Apollyon. More are ruined by the deceitfulness of riches than by the cares of life.

When first Lot went down to Sodom, attracted by the sole consideration of its pastures, it was no doubt his intention to keep aloof from its people, and to live without its walls. But the moth cannot with impunity flutter about the flame. By and by he abandoned the tent life altogether, and took a house inside the city. At last he betrothed his daughters to native Sodomites, and sat in its gateway as one of its aldermen. He was given to hospitality, but in the proposals by which he endeavored to vindicate its exercise, he proved how the air of Sodom had taken the bloom off his purity. He was with difficulty dragged out of Sodom, as a brand plucked from the burning; and over the closing scenes of his life it is decent to draw a veil. And yet such a wreck was saved!

Nor was he saved alone, but his wife also, who did not take many steps outside the city, before, by looking back, with a mixture of disobedience and regret, she showed herself utterly hopeless; and her two daughters, whose names are branded with eternal infamy. If God was so careful to secure their safety, how bad must those have been whom He left to their fate! Is it not clear that He saved all who at all came within the range of mercy's possibilities? There will not be one soul among the lost who had the faintest claim to be among the saved; and there will be a great many among the saved whose presence there will be a very great surprise to us. "They shall come from the east and west . . . but the children of the kingdom shall be cast out."

THE MOTIVES OF THE ANGELS' VISIT. These were three:

(1) *The proximate, or nearest cause was their own love to man.* The angels love us. Though they know that we are destined to a dignity before which that of the loftiest seraphs must pale, no envy eats out the pure benevolence which throbs within their holy spirits. It is enough that God has willed it so, and that we are dear to their sweet Master, Christ. It is then no hardship for them to leave "their golden bowers," or "cleave the flitting skies," that they may come and hasten lingerers to repentance. If there were any hardship, it would be in their mission to destroy.

(2) *The efficient cause was Abraham's prayer.* "And it came to pass, when God destroyed the cities of the plain, that God remembered Abraham, and sent Lot out of the midst of the overthrow" (Gen. 19:29). Pray on, beloved reader, pray on for that dear one far away in the midst of a very Sodom of iniquity. It may seem impossible for you to go down into it for his rescue, or to help him in any other way, but, in answer to your prayer, God will send His angels to that ship laboring in midocean; into that log house in the Canadian clearing, or that shanty by an African diamond mine; or away to that abode dedicated to vice or drink. God's angels go everywhere. A Sodom cannot hold its victims back from their touch, any more than their bright presences can be soiled by the polluting atmosphere through which they pass. While you

are praying, God's angels are on their way to perform your desire, albeit that their progress may be hindered by causes hidden from our ken (see Dan. 10:12).

(3) *But the ultimate cause was God's mercy.* "The Lord being merciful to him." Mercy: that is the last link in the chain. Is it not the staple in the wall? There is nothing beyond it. The Apostle himself cannot allege a more comprehensive or satisfactory reason for his position in the sunlit circle of salvation than this: "I obtained mercy." "By the grace of God, I am what I am." And this shall be our theme also through that eternity whose day star has already arisen in our hearts.

It seems marvelous that God should employ sons of men to win men to Himself. Surely angels could to it better! Nay, did they not save Lot with a pertinacity, and a holy ingenuity, which are full of teaching and stimulus to ourselves, as workers for the Lord? The world is full of Sodoms still; and Lots, whom we have known and loved, or who have a claim on us, are sitting at their gates. Oh, why are we behind the angels in eagerness to pluck them as brands from the burning? Bright spirits, ye shall read us some holy lessons as to methods of Christian work; and we will try and emulate you—lest the time should come when we shall be dismissed from our posts; and heaven's doors flung wide open each dawn to let out your rejoicing crowds, to take our place in class, or pulpit, or squalid court!

THE ANGELS WENT TO WHERE LOT WAS. "There came two angels to Sodom at even." What! Did angels go to Sodom! Yes, to Sodom—and yet angels. And as a ray of light may pass through the fetid atmosphere of some squalid court, and emerge without a stain on its pure texture, so may angels spend a night in Sodom, surrounded by crowds of sinners, and yet be untainted angels still. If you go to Sodom for your gains, as Lot did, you will soon show signs of moral pollution. But if you go to save men, as these angels did, you may go into a very hell of evil, where the air is laden with impurity and blasphemy, but you will not be befouled. No grain of mud shall stick. "No weapon that is formed against thee shall prosper; and every tongue that shall rise against thee in judgment thou shalt condemn" (Is. 54:17).

This is the spirit of Christ's Gospel. "He goeth after that which is lost, till He find it." "He put forth His hand and touched him" (Matt.

8:3; Luke 15:4). We must not wait for sinners to come to us; we must go to them—to the banks of the stream, where the fish hide in the dark, cool depths; to the highways of the town, where men congregate; to public houses, music halls, stews of crime, and homes of poverty; yea, and to the most distant parts of the world—wherever men are found we must go to them, to preach the Gospel. The most unlikely places will yield Lots, who would have died in their sins, if they had not been sought out.

THEY WERE CONTENT TO WORK FOR VERY FEW. Special value attaches to hand-picked fruit. Too often we, in our ignorance, prefer to go into the orchard and shake down from the trees the abundant crop, until the ground far and near is littered with fruit. But we forget how much waste there is in the process; and how much of the crop becomes bruised: while some is torn prematurely from the parent bough.

So far as we can gather, all our Lord's choicest followers were the result of His personal ministry. To one and another He said, "Follow Me!" His life was full of personal interviews. He sought out individual souls (Matt. 4:19, 21; 9:9; Luke 19:5). He would spend much time and thought to win one solitary woman, her character none too good (John 4). He believed in going after one sheep that was lost. And the steadfastness of their characters vindicated His methods. And it is most beautiful to trace the same characteristic in the Apostle Paul, who says that he "warned every man, and taught every man, that he might present every man perfect in Christ Jesus" (Col. 1:28).

It is a question whether more men are not saved by individual appeal than by all our preaching. It is not the sermon which wins them, but the quiet talk with a worker at an after-meeting, or the letter of a parent, or the words of a friend. When Christ said, "Preach the Gospel to every creature," did He not suggest that we were to set ourselves to the work of leaving the proclamation of heaven's love at every door, and to every child of Adam, throughout the world?

We never know what we do when we win one soul for God. Is not the following instance, culled from the biography of James Brainerd Taylor—called home to God too early, and yet not before he had won hundreds of souls by his personal appeals—a fair specimen of myriads more?

On one occasion he reined up his horse to drink at a roadside well. The servant of God, as the horses were eagerly quenching their thirst, turned to the stranger, and spoke some burning words concerning the duty and honor of Christian discipleship. In a moment more they had parted, and were riding in different directions. But the word of God remained as incorruptible seed, and led to the conversion of that wayside hearer. He became a Christian and a missionary. Often he wondered who had been the instrument of his conversion, and sought for him in vain. But he did not succeed in identifying him till years after, when, in a packet of books, sent him from his native land, he opened the story of that devoted life, and in the frontispiece beheld the face which had haunted him, in sleeping and waking hours, ever since that slight but memorable interview.

It has been said that the true method of soul winning is to set the heart on some one soul; and to pursue it, until it has either definitely accepted, or finally rejected, the Gospel of the grace of God. We should not hear so many cries for larger spheres, if Christians only realized the possibilities of the humblest life. Christ found work enough in a village to keep Him there for thirty years. Philip was torn from the great revival in Samaria to go into the desert to win one seeker after God.

Have you ever spoken to your servant, your shoeblack, your postman, your companion, your neighbor? Ah, it would not take long to evangelize the world, if every man would teach his neighbor, and every man his brother, saying, "Know the Lord."

THEY TOLD LOT PLAINLY OF HIS DANGER. "Hast thou here any besides? . . . bring them out of this place: for we will destroy this place, because the cry of them is waxen great before the face of the Lord; and the Lord hath sent us to destroy it" (Gen. 19:12, 13). We are rather squeamish nowadays of talking to men thus. We have lined our lips with velvet. We aim to be gentler than Christ. He did not hesitate to speak of an undying worm and a quenchless flame. The gnashing of teeth; the wail of despair; the knock to which no door would open— were arguments which came more than once from His lips. (See. Matt. 8:12; 13:42, 50; 22:13; 24:51; 25:10–12, 30; Mark 9:43–48; Luke 13:25–28). He evidently taught as if men might make a mistake which they could not possibly repair. If certain elements are wanting in food, the children will grow up boneless and unhealthy; and if we do not take care, the deficiency of our modern teaching will have disastrous results. Whether we talk about it or not, it is yet as true as the nature of God, that those who obey not the Gospel of our Lord Jesus Christ "shall be punished with everlasting destruction from the presence of the Lord, and from the glory of His power" (2 Thess. 1:9). And "if we sin willfully after that we have received the knowledge of the truth, there remaineth no more sacrifice for sins, but a certain fearful looking for of judgment and fiery indignation, which shall devour the adversaries (Heb. 10:26, 27).

It may be that the day of grace is nearer to its close than we think. The clock of destiny may have struck; the avalanche may have commenced to roll forward its overwhelming mass; while the storm clouds may brood heavily over a godless age, for which, in the Day of Judgment, it shall be worse than for Sodom and Gomorrah. There may be nothing to portend this momentous fact. "The sun was risen upon the earth when Lot entered into Zoar." Nature keeps God's secrets well. No portent in heaven, no driving up of the cloud wrack in the clouds, no tremor on the earth, but the axe suddenly driven home to the heart of the doomed tree. Escape, my reader, for thy life; look not behind thee, neither stay thou anywhere short of the cleft side of Jesus, where only we may hide from the just judgment of sin. Rest not till thou hast put the Lord Jesus between thyself and the footsteps of pursing justice.

THEY HASTENED HIM. "When the morning arose, then the angels hastened Lot" (19:15). They had been reluctant to stay in his house, unlike the alacrity with which they accepted Abraham's hospitality; and they spent the short sultry night in urging on Lot the certainty and terror of the approaching destruction. So much so that they actually got him to go to arouse his sons-in-law. But an inconsistent life cannot arrest the wanderer, or startle the sleeper into wide awakeness about his soul. People say that we must conform a little to the manners of our time, if we would exert a saving influence over men. It is a fatal mistake. If we live in Sodom, we shall have no power to save the people of Sodom. You must stand outside of them, if you would save them from the gurgling rapids. Yes, dwellers in Sodom, you cannot level

Sodom up, but it will certainly level you down, and laugh at you, when you try to speak. "He seemed as one that mocked unto his sons-in-law."

But when he came back from his ineffectual mission, Lot seemed infected by the skepticism which had ridiculed his warnings. "He lingered." How could he leave his children, and household goods, and property, on what seemed to be a fool's errand? Surely all things would continue as they had been from the beginning of the world. "And while he lingered, the men laid hold upon his hand."

It was hand-help. It was the urgency of a love that would take no denial. The two angels had but four hands, but each hand was full, and each clasped the hand of a procrastinating sinner. Would that we knew more fully this divine enthusiasm, which pulls men out of the fire! (Jude 1:23).

Nor were they satisfied, till their *proteges* were safe without the city; and were speeding towards the rampart of the distant hills. So Lot was saved from the overthrow. But though he was sent out of Sodom, he took Sodom with him; and over the remainder of his history we must draw a veil. Still, it is a marvelous testimony to the power of intercessory prayer, to learn that a man so low in the moral scale, together with his daughters, was saved for Abraham's sake; and if he had finally settled at the little city of Zoar, that too would have been spared for his sake.

Let us hasten sinner. Let us say to each one: "Escape for thy life; better lose all than lose your soul. Look not behind to past attainments or failures. Linger nowhere outside the City of Refuge, which is Jesus Christ Himself. Haste ye! Habits of indecision strengthen; opportunities are closing in; the arrow of destruction has already left the bow of justice": "behold, now is the accepted time: behold, now is the day of salvation."

18

A Bit of the Old Nature

Then Abimelech called Abraham, and said
unto him, What hast thou done unto us?
and what have I offended thee, that
thou hast brought on me and on
my kingdom a great sin?
—Genesis 20:9

For long years an evil may lurk in our hearts, permitted and unjudged, breeding failure and sorrow in our lives, and some unnoticed and forgotten sewer may secretly undermine the health of an entire household. In the twilight we overlook many a thing which we should not allow for a single moment if we saw it in its true character; and which, amid the all-revealing light of the perfect day, we should be the first to fling away in horror. But that which escapes our ken is patent in all its naked deformity to the eye of God. "The darkness and the light are both alike to Him." And He will do direct the discipline of our lives as to set in clear prominence the deadly evil which He hates; so that, when He has laid bare the cancerous growth, He may bring us to long for and invite the knife which shall set us free from it forever.

These words have been suggested by the thirteenth verse of this chapter, which indicates an evil compact, into which Abraham had entered with Sarah some thirty years before the time of which we write. Addressing the king of the Philistines, the patriarch let fall a hint which sheds a startling light upon his failure, when first he entered the

Land of Promise, and, under stress of famine, went down into Egypt; and upon that repetition of his failure which we must now consider. Here is what he said: "And it came to pass, when God caused me to wander from my father's house, that I said unto my wife, This is thy kindness which thou shalt show unto me; at every place whither we shall come, say of me, He is my brother."

In a certain sense, no doubt, Sarah was his sister. She was the daughter of his father, though not the daughter of his mother. But she was much more his wife than his sister; and to withhold that fact was to withhold the one fact that was essential to the maintenance of his honor, and the protection of her virtue. We are not bound to tell the whole truth to gratify an idle curiosity, but we are bound not to withhold the one item, which another should know before completing a bargain, if the knowledge of it would materially alter the result. A lie consists in the motive quite as much as in the actual words. We may unwittingly say that which is actually false, meaning above all things to speak the truth, and, though a lie in form, there is no lie in fact. On the other hand, like Abraham, we may utter true words, meaning them to convey a false impression, and, in the sight of Heaven we are guilty of a deliberate and shameful falsehood.

This secret compact between Abraham and his wife, in the earliest days of his exodus, was due to his slender faith in God's power to take care of them, which again sprang from his limited experience of his Almighty Friend. In this we may find its sole excuse. But it ought long before this to have been canceled by mutual consent. The faithless treaty should have been torn into shreds, and scattered to the winds of heaven. It was not enough that they did not act on it for many years; for it was evidently still in existence, tacitly admitted by each of them, and only waiting for an emergency to arise from the dusty obscurity into which it had receded, and to come again into light and use.

But the existence of this hidden understanding, though perhaps Abraham did not realize it, was inconsistent with the relation into which he had now entered with God. It was altogether a source of weakness and failure. And, above all, it was a secret flaw in his faith, which would inevitably affect its tone, and destroy its effectiveness in the dark trials which were approaching. God could afford to pass it over in those early days, when faith itself was yet in germ, but it could not be permitted, when that faith was reaching to a maturity in which any flaw would be instantly detected; and it would be an unsuitable example in one who was to become the model of faith to the world.

The judgment and eradication of this lurking evil were therefore necessary, and were brought about in this wise.

The day before Sodom's fall, the Almighty told Abraham that, at a set time in the following year, he should have a son and heir. And we should have expected that he would have spent the slow-moving months beneath the oak of Mamre, already hallowed by so many associations. But such was not the case. It has been suggested that he was too horrified at the overthrow of the cities of the plain, to be able to remain any longer in the vicinity. All further association with the spot was distasteful to him. Or it may have been that another famine was threatening. But in any case "he journeyed from hence toward the south country, and dwelled between Kadesh and Shur, and sojourned in Gerar" (Gen. 20:1).

Gerar was the capital of a race of men who had dispossessed the original inhabitants of the land, and were gradually passing from the condition of wandering shepherd life into that of a settled and warlike nation; afterwards to be known to the Hebrews by the dreaded name, Philistines: a title which, in fact, gave to the whole land its name of Palestine. Their chieftain bore the official title of Abimelech, "My Father the King."

Here, the almost forgotten agreement between Sarah and himself offered itself as a ready expedient, behind which Abraham's unbelief took shelter. He knew the ungoverned license of his time, unbridled by the fear of God (v. 11). He dreaded, lest the heathen monarch, enamored with Sarah's beauty, or ambitious to get her into his power for purposes of State policy, might slay him for his wife's sake. And so he again resorted to the paltry policy of calling her his sister. As if God could not have defended him and her, screening them from all evil; as He had done so often in days gone by.

HIS CONDUCT WAS VERY COWARDLY. He risked Sarah's virtue, and the purity of the promised seed. And, even if we accept the justification of his conduct proposed by some, who argue that he was so sure of the seed promised him by God that he could dare to risk what otherwise he would have more carefully guarded, his faith leading him into the license of presumption, yet, it was surely very mean on his part to permit Sarah to pass through any ordeal of the sort. If he had such superabundant faith, he might have risked his own safety at the hand of Abimelech rather than Sarah's virtue.

IT WAS ALSO VERY DISHONORING TO GOD. Among those untutored tribes Abraham was well known as the servant of Jehovah. And they could not but judge of the character of Him whom they could not see, by the traits they discerned in His servant, whom they knew in familiar intercourse. Alas that Abraham's standard was lower than their own! So much so that Abimelech was able to rebuke him, saying: "Thou hast brought on me and on my kingdom a great sin: thou hast done deeds unto me that ought not to be done." Such an opinion, elicited in such a way, must have been an unpropitious preparation for any attempt to proselytize Abimelech to the Hebrew faith. "Not so," we can imagine him saying: "I have had some experience of one of its foremost representatives, and I prefer to remain as I am."

It is heartbreaking when the heathen rebukes a professor of superior godliness for speaking lies. Yet it is lamentable to confess that such men often enough have higher standards of morality than those who profess godliness. Even if they did not fulfill their own conceptions, yet the beauty of their ideal is undeniable, and is a remarkable vindication of the universal vitality of conscience. The temperate Hindu is scandalized by the drunkenness of the Englishman whose religion he is invited to embrace. The Chinaman cannot understand why he should exchange the hoary religion of Confucius for that of a people which by superior armaments forces upon his country a drug which is sapping its vitals. The employee abhors a creed which is professed by his master for one day of the week, but is disowned on the other six. Let us walk circumspectly towards them that are without; adorning in all things the Gospel of Jesus Christ; and giving no occasion to the enemy to blaspheme, save as it concerns the law of our God.

IT ALSO STOOD OUT IN POOR RELIEF AGAINST THE BEHAVIOR OF ABIMELECH. As to his original character, Abimelech commends himself to us as the nobler of the two. He rises early in the morning, prompt to set the great wrong right. He warns his people. He restores Sarah with munificent presents. His reproach and rebuke are spoken in the gentlest, kindest tones. He simply tells Sarah that her position as the wife of a prophet would, not in Philistia only, but wherever they might come, be a sufficient security and veil (v. 16). There is the air of high-minded nobility in his behavior throughout this crisis which is exceedingly winsome.

It would almost appear as if the Spirit of God took delight in showing that the original texture of God's saints was not higher than that of other men, nor indeed so high. What they became, they became in spite of their natural selves. So marvelous is the wonder-working power of the grace of God that He can graft His rarest fruits on the wildest stocks. He seems to delight to secure His choicest results in natures which men of the world might reject as hopelessly bad. He demands no assistance from us, so sure is He that when once faith is admitted as the root principle of character, all other things will be added to it.

Oh, critics of God's handiwork, we do not deny the inconsistencies of a David, a Peter, or an Abraham, but we insist that those inconsistencies were not the result of God's work, but in spite of it. They indicate the hopelessness of the original nature—the moorland waste to which He has set His cultivating hand. And shall we blame the Gardener's skill, when, in the paradise which it has created, we encounter a bit of original soil, which, by force of contrast, indicates the marvel of His genius; and which, before long, if only we exercise patience, will yield to the selfsame spell, and blossom as the rest?

And you, on the other hand, who aspire for the crown of saintliness, to which ye are truly called, take heart! There is nothing which God has done for any soul that He will not do for you. And there is no soil so unpromising that He will not compel it to yield His fairest results. "What is impossible to man is possible to God." The same power in all its matchless energy, which raised the body of our Lord from its sleep in the grave of Joseph, to sit at the Father's side in the heights of glory, in spite of opposing battalions of evil spirits—is ready to do as much for each of us, if only we will daily, hourly, yield to it without reserve. Only cease from your own works, and keep always on

God's "lift," refusing each solicitation to step off its ascending energy, or to do for yourself what he will do for you so much better than you can ask or think.

Let us ponder, as we close, these practical lessons:

I. WE ARE NEVER SAFE SO LONG AS WE ARE IN THIS WORLD. Abraham was an old man. Thirty years had passed since that sin had shown itself last. During that time he had been growing and learning much. But, alas! the snake was scotched, not killed. The weeds were cut down, not eradicated. The dry rot had been checked, but the rotten timbers had not been cut away. Never boast yourself against once-cherished sins: only by God's grace are they kept in check; and if you cease to abide in Christ, they will revive and revisit you, as the seven sleepers of Ephesus reappeared to the panic-stricken town.

II. WE HAVE NO RIGHT TO THROW OURSELVES INTO THE WAY OF THE TEMPTATION WHICH HAS OFTEN MASTERED US. Those who daily cry, "Lead us not into temptation," should see to it that they do not court the temptation against which they pray. We must not expect angels to catch us every time we choose to cast ourselves from the mountain brow. A godly fear will avoid the perilous pass marked by crosses to indicate the failures of the past, and will choose a safer route. Abraham had been wiser had he never gone into the Philistines' territory at all.

III. WE MAY BE ENCOURAGED BY GOD'S TREATMENT OF ABRAHAM'S SIN. Although God had a secret controversy with His child, He did not put him away. And when his wife and he were in extreme danger, as the result of his sin, their Almighty Friend stepped in to deliver them from the peril which menaced them. Again, "He reproved kings for their sakes, saying, Touch not My anointed, and do My prophets no harm." He told Abimelech that he was a dead man; put an arrest upon him by the ministry of an ominous disease; and bade him apply to the intercession of the very man by whom he had been so grievously misled, and who, in spite of all his failures, was a prophet still, having power with God.

Have you sinned, bringing disrepute on the name of God? Do not despair. Go alone, as Abraham must have done, and confess your sin with tears and childlike trust. Do not abandon prayer. Your prayers are still sweet to Him; and He waits to answer them. It is only through them that His purposes can be fulfilled toward men. Trust then in the patience and forgiveness of God, and let His love, as consuming fire, rid you of concealed and hidden sin.

19
Hagar and Ishmael Cast Out

*Cast out this bondwoman and her son: for
the son of this bondwoman shall
not be heir . . . with Isaac.*
—Genesis 21:10

Even though we were hearing this story for the first time, and did not know of the grave crisis to which we were approaching in the next chapter, we might be sure that something of the sort was imminent; and we should rest our conclusion on the fact of the stern discipline through which the great patriarch was called to pass. Faith is the expression of our inner moral life; and it cannot be exercised in its loftiest form so long as there is any obliquity of the heart, any hidden or unholy affection. These things must be cut away, or passed through the fiery discipline of sorrow; that, being freed from them, the heart may exercise that supreme faith in God which is the fairest crown of human existence.

The Almighty Lover of souls knew the trial which awaited His child in the near future; and set Himself to prepare him for it, by ridding him of certain clinging inconsistencies, which would have paralyzed the action of his faith in the hour of trial. We have already seen how one of these—the secret compact between himself and Sarah—was exposed to the light and judged. We have now to see how another matter, the patriarch's connection with Hagar and her child, was also dealt with by

139

Him, who acts on us either as fuller's soap, or if that be not strong enough, as a refiner's fire.

In what way the presence of Hagar and Ishmael hindered the development of Abraham's noblest life of faith, we cannot entirely understand. Did his heart still cling to the girl who had given him his firstborn son? Was there any secret satisfaction in the arrangement, which had at least achieved one cherished purpose, though it had been unblessed by God? Was there any fear that if he were summoned to surrender Isaac, he would find it easier to do so, because, at any moment, he could fall back on Ishmael, as both son and heir? We cannot read all that was in Abraham's mind, but surely some such thoughts are suggested by the expressions which to this hour record the history of the anguish of this torn and lonely heart, as one darling idol after another was rent away, that he himself might be cast naked and helpless on the omnipotence of the Eternal God. "The thing was very grievous in Abraham's sight" (v. 11).

It may be that not a few who read these lines sigh to possess a faith like that which Abraham had: a faith which staggers not through unbelief; a faith to which God cannot give a denial; a faith which can open and shut heaven, and to which all things are possible. But are you willing to pay the cost—the cost of suffering; the cost of rending from your heart all that would frustrate the operation of so glorious a principle; the cost of seeing one cherished idol after another cast out; the cost of being tripped even to nakedness of all the dear delights in which the flesh may have found pleasure? "Are ye able to drink of the cup that I shall drink of, and to be baptized with the baptism that I am baptized with? They say unto Him, We are able" (Matt. 20:22; Mark 10:38, 39). You hardly realize all that is meant when you say so much, but it shall be revealed to you step by step; and nothing shall be too difficult, all being measured out according to your strength by Him who knows our frame and remembers that we are dust. Let us not dread the pruning knife; for it is wielded by the hand of One who loves us infinitely, and who is seeking results that are to fill our hearts with eternal gratitude, and heaven with praise.

The final separation from Abraham of ingredients which would have been prejudicial to the exercise of a supreme faith was brought about by the birth of the long-promised child, which is alluded to at the commencement of this chapter (Gen. 21), and which led up to the crisis with which we are now dealing.

"The Lord visited Sarah as He had said, and the Lord did unto Sarah as He had spoken" (Gen. 21:1). It is impossible to trust God too absolutely. God's least word is a spar of imperishable wood driven into the Rock of Ages, which will never give, and on which you may hang your entire weight forevermore. "The counsel of the Lord standeth forever; the thoughts of His heart to all generations" (Ps. 33:11).

BUT WE MUST BE PREPARED TO WAIT GOD'S TIME. "Sarah bare Abraham a son in his old age, *at the set time* of which God had spoken unto him." God has His set times. It is not for us to know them; indeed, we cannot know them; we must wait for them. If God had told Abraham in Haran that he must wait for thirty years until he pressed the promised child to his bosom, his heart would have failed him. So, in gracious love, the length of the weary years was hidden, and only as they were nearly spent, and there were only a few more months to wait, God told him that "according to the time of life, Sarah shall have a son" (18:14). The set time came at last; and then the laughter that filled the patriarch's home made the aged pair forget the long and weary vigil. "And Abraham called the name of his son that was born unto him, whom Sarah bare unto him, ISAAC" (*that is* LAUGHTER). Take heart, waiting one, thou waits for One who cannot disappoint thee; and who will not be five minutes behind the appointed moment: ere long "your sorrow shall be turned into joy."

"A woman, when she is in travail, hath sorrow, because her hour is come: but as soon as she is delivered of the child, she remembers no more the anguish, for joy that a man is born into the world" (John 16:21). That joy may give the clue to the unwonted outburst of song on the part of the happy and aged mother. The laughter of incredulity, with which she received the first intimation of her approaching motherhood (18:12), was now exchanged for the laughter of fulfilled hope. And she gave utterance to words that approached the elevation of a rhythmic chant, and which served as the model of that other son with which the virgin mother announced the advent of her Lord. So Sarah said,

> God hath made me to laugh:
> Every one that heareth will laugh with me.

And long after, one of her daughters said,

> My soul doth magnify the Lord;
> And my spirit hath rejoiced
>   In God my Savior.
> For He that is mighty
> Hath done to me great things;
>   And holy is His name.
>
>   Luke 1:46–49

Ah, happy soul, when God makes thee laugh! Then sorrow and crying shall flee away forever, as darkness before the dawn.

The peace of Abraham's house remained at first unbroken, though there may have been some slight symptoms of the rupture which was at hand. The dislike which Sarah had manifested to Hagar, long years before, had never been extinguished: it had only smoldered in her bosom, waiting for some slight incident to stir it again into a blaze. Nor had the warm passionate nature of Hagar ever forgotten those hard dealings which had driven her forth, to fare as best she might in the inhospitable desert. Abraham must have been often sorely put to it to keep the peace between them. At last the women's quarters could conceal the quarrel no longer, and the scandal broke out into the open day.

THE IMMEDIATE OCCASION OF THIS OPEN RUPTURE was the weaning of the young Isaac. "The child grew, and was weaned: and Abraham made a great feast the day that Isaac was weaned." But amid all the bright joy of that happy occasion, one shadow suddenly stole over the scene, and brooded on the mother's soul. Sarah's jealous eye saw Ishmael mocking. It was hardly to be wondered at. The lad had recently suffered a severe disappointment. He had grown up as the undisputed heir of all that camp, accustomed to receive its undivided loyalty; and it must have been very difficult to view with equanimity the preparations made in honor of the child who was destined to supersede him: and so, under the appearance of sportive jesting, he jeered at Isaac in a way which betrayed the bitterness of his soul; and which indeed he was at no pains to conceal. This awoke all Sarah's slumbering jealousy; which may have often been severely tested during the last few years by Ishmael's assumption and independent bearing. She would stand it no longer. Why should she, the chieftain's wife, and mother of his heir, brook the insolence of a slave? And so she said unto Abraham with a sneer and the sting of the old jealousy, "Cast out this bondwoman and her son; for the son of this bondwoman shall not be heir with my son, even with Isaac."

WE CANNOT BUT RECALL THE USE WHICH THE GREAT APOSTLE MAKES OF THIS INCIDENT. In his days the Jews, priding themselves on being the lineal descendants of Abraham, refused to consider it possible that any but themselves could be children of God, and the heirs of promises. They arrogated to themselves exclusive privileges and position. And when large numbers of Gentiles were born into the Christian Church under the first preaching of the Gospel, and claimed to be the spiritual seed, with all the rights pertaining thereunto; they who, like Ishmael, were simply born after the flesh, persecuted them which, like Isaac, were born after the Spirit. Everywhere the Jews set themselves to resist the preaching of the gospel, which denied to them their exclusive privileges; and to harry those who would not enter the Church through the rites of Judaism. And ere long the Jewish nation was rejected; put aside; cast out. Succeeding ages have seen the building up of the Church from among the once-persecuted ones, while the children of Abraham have wandered in the wilderness fainting for the true water of life (Gal. 4:29).

BUT THERE IS A STILL DEEPER REFERENCE. Hagar, the slave, who may even have been born in the Sinaitic Desert, with which she seems to have been so familiar, is a fit representative of the spirit of legalism and bondage, seeking to win life by the observance of the law, which was given from those hoary cliffs. Hagar is the covenant of Mount Sinai in Arabia, "which gendereth to bondage," and "is in bondage with her children" (Gal. 4:24, 25). Sarah, the free woman, on the other hand, represents the covenant of free grace. Her children are love, and faith, and hope; they are not bound by the spirit of "must," but by the promptings of spontaneous gratitude; their home is not in the frowning clefts of Sinai, but in Jerusalem above, which is free, and is the mother of us all. Now, argues the Apostle, there was no room for Hagar and Sarah, with their respective children, in Abraham's tent. If Ishmael was there, it was because Isaac was not born. But as soon as Isaac came in, Ishmael must go out. So the two principles—of legalism, which insists on the performance of the outward rite of circumcision; and of faith, which accepts the finished work of the Savior—cannot coexist in one heart. It is a moral impossibility. As well could darkness coexist with light, and slavery with freedom. So, addressing the Galatian converts, who were being tempted by Judaizing teachers to mingle legalism and faith, the Apostle bade them follow the example of Abraham, and cast out the spirit of bondage which keeps the soul in one perpetual agony of unrest.

You, my readers, are trusting Christ, but, perhaps, you are living in perpetual bondage to your scruples; or, perhaps you are always endeavoring to add some acts of obedience, by way of completing and assuring your salvation. Ah! It is a great mistake. Cease to worry about these legal matters. Beware of morbid scrupulosity of conscience, one of the most terrible diseases by which the human spirit can be plagued. Do not always imagine that God's love to you depends on the performance of many minute acts, concerning which there are no definite instructions given. Trust Christ. Realize His wonderful and complete salvation. Work not towards sonship, but from it. "Cast out the bondwoman and her son." Live the free, happy life of Isaac, whose position is assured; and not that of Ishmael, whose position is dependent on his good behavior. "The servant abideth not in the house forever, but the son abideth ever."

The remaining history is briefly told. With many a pang—as the vine which bleeds copiously when the pruning knife is doing its work—Abraham sent Hagar and her child forth from his home, bidding them a last sad farewell. In the dim twilight they fared forth, before the camp was astir. The strong man must have suffered keenly as he put the bread into her hand, and with his own fingers bound the bottle of water on her shoulder, and kissed Ishmael once more. And yet he must not let Sarah guess how much he felt it. How many passages in our lives are only known to God!

Yet it was better so. And God provided for them both. When the mother's hopes were on the point of expiring, and the lad lay dying of thirst in the scorching noon, under the slender shade of a desert shrub, the Angel of God stayed her sobs, pointed out the well of water to which her tears had made her blind, and promised that her child should become a great nation. Ishmael would never have developed to his full stature if he had perpetually lived in the enervating luxury of Abraham's camp. There was no room enough there for him to grow. For him, as for us all, there was need of the free air of the desert, in which he should match himself with his peers, becoming strong by privation and want. That which seems like to break our hearts at the moment, turns out in after years to have been of God. "And God said unto Abraham, Let it not be grievous in thy sight; in all that Sarah hath said unto thee, hearken unto her voice" (21:12).

One more weight was laid aside, and one more step taken in the preparation of God's "friend" for the supreme victory of his faith; for which his whole life had been a preparation, and which was now at hand.

Some flowers are the result of a century of growth; and the Divine Husbandman will consider Himself repaid for years of loving, patient care, if the life He has tended will bloom out into but one act, like that which we are soon to record. Such acts scatter the seeds of noble and heroic deeds for all future time.

20
A Quiet Resting Place

And Abraham planted a grove in Beersheba,
and called there on the name of the Lord, the
everlasting God: and Abraham sojourned in
the Philistines' land many days.
—Genesis 21:33, 34

When a river is approaching its plunge down some mighty chasm, its waters flow with placid stillness; every ripple is smoothed out of the peaceful surface, and the great volume of water is hushed and quieted. There could hardly be a greater contrast than that which exists between the restfulness of the river before it is torn by the ragged rocks in its downward rush, and its excitement and foam at the foot of the falls. In the one case you can discern, through the translucent waters, the stones and rocks that line its bed; in the other you are blinded by the spray and deafened by the noise.

Is not this an emblem of our lives?—Our Father often inserts in them a parenthesis of rest and peace, to prepare us for some coming trial. It is not invariably so. We need not always temper our enjoyment of some precious gift with a foreboding dread of its afterwards. But this, at least, is largely true: that if every season of clear shining is not followed by a time of cloud, yet seasons of sorrow and trial are almost always preceded by hours or days or years of sunny experience, which lie in the retrospect of life, as a bright and comforting memory, where the soul was able to gather the strength it was to expend, and to prepare itself for its supreme effort.

Thus it happened to Abraham. We have already seen how wisely and tenderly his Almighty friend had been preparing him for his approaching trial; first, in searching out his hidden compact with Sarah; and then in ridding him of the presence of Hagar and her son. And now some further preparation was to be wrought in his spirit, through this period of peaceful rest beside the well of the oath. Leaving Gerar, the patriarch traveled with his slow moving flocks along the fertile valley, which extends from the sea into the country. The whole district was admirably suited for the maintenance of a vast pastoral clan. In the winter the valley contains a running stream, and at any time water may be obtained by digging at a greater or less depth. Having reached a suitable camping ground, Abraham dug a well, which is probably one of those which remain to this day; and of which the water, lying some forty feet below the surface, is pure and sweet. Drinking troughs for the use of cattle are scattered around in close proximity to the mouth, the curbstones of which are deeply worn by the friction of the ropes used in drawing up the water by hand. It is not improbable that these very stones were originally hewn under the patriarch's direction, even though their position may have been somewhat altered by the Arab workmen of a later date.

Shortly after Abraham had settled there, Abimelech, the king, accompanied by Phichol, the chief captain of his host, came to his encampment, intent on entering into a treaty which should be binding, not only on themselves, but on their children: "Swear unto me here by God, that thou wilt not deal falsely with me, nor with my son, nor with my son's son" (v. 23). Before formally binding himself under these solemn sanctions, Abraham brought up a matter which is still a fruitful subject of dispute in Eastern lands. The herdsman of Abimelech had violently taken away the well of water which the servants of Abraham had dug. But the king immediately repudiated all knowledge of their action. It had been done without his cognizance and sanction. And in the treaty into which the two chieftains entered, there was, so to speak, a special clause inserted with reference to this well, destined in after years to be so famous. Writing materials were not then in use, but the seven ewe lambs, which Abraham gave Abimelech, were the visible and lasting memorial that the well was his recognized property. Thus it happened that as the solemnly-sworn covenant was made beside the well, so its name became forever associated with it, and it was called "Beersheba," the well of the oath, or "the well of the seven" with reference to the seven gifts, or victims, on which the oath was taken.

In further commemoration of this treaty, Abraham planted a tamarisk tree, which, as a hardy evergreen, would long perpetuate the memory of the transaction in those lands, where the mind of man eagerly catches at anything that will break the monotony of the landscape. There also he erected an altar, or shrine, and called on the name of the Lord, the Everlasting God. "And Abraham sojourned in the land of the Philistines many days." Ah, those long, happy days! Their course was only marked by the growing years of Isaac, who passed on through the natural stages of human growth—from boyhood to youth, and from youth to opening manhood—the object of Abraham's tender, clinging love. No words can tell the joy of Abraham over this beloved child of his old age. "Thine only son Isaac, whom thou lovest." It seemed as if perpetual laughter had come to take up its abode in that home, to brighten the declining years of that aged pair. Who could have foretold that the greatest trial of all his life had yet to come, and that from a clear sky a thunderbolt was about to fall, threatening to destroy all his happiness at a single stroke?

None of us knows what awaits us. This at least is clear, that our life is being portioned out by the tender love of God; who spared not His own Son, and has pledged Himself, with Him, also freely to give us all things. Here is one of the unanswerable questions of Scripture: What will not God do for them that love Him? No love, no care, no wisdom, which they need, shall be spared. And yet, with all this, there may be keen suffering to bear. We sometimes seem to forget that what God takes He takes in fire: that nothing less than the discipline of pain can ever disintegrate the clinging dross of our natures; and that the only way to the resurrection life and the ascension mount is the way of the garden, the cross, and the grave. Nothing will dare to inflict so much pain—as the love which desires the richest and sweetest life of the object of its affection. "Whom the Lord loveth He chasteneth; and scourgeth every son whom He receiveth." Let us prepare them for coming hours of trial by doing as Abraham did.

I. LET US LIVE BY THE WELL. There is a great tendency among Christians today to magnify special places and scenes which have been associated with times of blessing; and to obtain from them a supply which they store up for their maintenance in after days. But so many of these, and of others, are in danger of forgetting that instead of making an annual pilgrimage to the well, they might take up their abode beside it, and live there.

The water of that well speaks of the life of God, which is in Jesus Christ our Lord, and is stored up for us in the fathomless depths of the Word of God. The well is deep; yet can faith's bucket reach its precious contents, and bring them to the thirsty lip and yearning heart.

One of the greatest blessings that can come to the soul is to acquire the habit of sinking wells into the depth that lieth under, and to draw water for itself. We are too much in the habit of drinking water which others have drawn; and too little initiated into the sacred science of drawing for ourselves.

It is my growing conviction that if Christians would not attempt to read so many chapters of the Bible daily, but would study what they do read more carefully, turning to the marginal references, reading the context, comparing Scripture with Scripture, endeavoring to get one or more complete thoughts of the mind of God, there would be a greater richness in their experience; more freshness in their interest in Scripture; more independence of men and means; and more real enjoyment of the Word of the living God. Oh for a practical realization of what Jesus meant when He said—"The water that I shall give him shall be in him a well of water, springing up into everlasting life."

Oh, my readers, open your hearts to the teaching of the Holy Ghost. Rest content with nothing short of a deep and loving knowledge of the Bible. Ask that within you there may be a repetition of the old miracle, "when Israel sang this song: Spring up, O well; sing ye unto it" (Num. 21:17). Then "in the wilderness shall waters break out, and streams in the desert: and the parched ground shall become a pool, and the thirsty land springs of water" (Is. 35:6, 7).

II. LET US SHELTER BENEATH THE COVENANT. Abraham was quiet from the fear of evil, because of Abimelech's oath. How much more sure and restful should be the believing soul, which shelters beneath that everlasting covenant which is "ordered in all things and sure." There are some Christians doubtful of their eternal salvation, and fearful lest they should ultimately fall away from grace and be lost, to whom this advice is peculiarly appropriate: "Live by the well of the oath."

In the eternity of the past, the Eternal Father entered into covenant with His Son, the terms of which covenant seem to have been on this wise. On the one hand our Lord pledged His complete obedience and His atoning death on behalf of all who should believe. And, on the other hand, the Father promised that all who should believe in Him should be delivered from the penalty of a broken law; should be forgiven; adopted into His family; and saved with an eternal salvation. This is but a crude and inadequate statement of mysteries so fathomless that the loftiest seraphs peer into them in vain. And yet it sets forth, in the babbling of human language, a truth of the utmost importance, behind which the weakest believer may securely shelter.

The one question is, Do you believe in Jesus Christ? Or, to put it still more simply, Are you willing that the Holy Ghost should create in you a living faith in the Savior of men? *Would you believe if you could?* Is your will on God's side in this matter of faith? Are you prepared to surrender anything and everything that would hinder your simple-hearted faith in Jesus? If so, you may appropriate to yourself the blessings of the Covenant confirmed by the counsel and oath of God. Your faith may be weak, but it is faith in the embryo and germ. And as the Ark saved the squirrel as well as the elephant, so does the Covenant shelter the weakest and feeblest believer equally with the giant in faith.

This, then, becomes true of us, if we believe. We are forgiven; our name is inscribed on the roll of the saved; we are adopted into the family of God; we have within us the beginning of a life which is eternal as the life of God. "The mountains shall depart and the hills be removed, but My kindness shall not depart from thee, neither shall the covenant of My peace be removed, saith the Lord that hath mercy on thee" (Is. 54:10). And shall not this comfort us amid many a heartbreaking sorrow? Nothing can break the bonds by which our souls are knit with the eternal God. "Although my house be not so with God; yet He hath made with me an everlasting covenant, ordered in all things and sure; for this is all my salvation, and all my desire, although He make it not to grow" (2 Sam. 23:5).

Rejoice in all the good things which the Lord thy God giveth thee. Plant thy trees; be comforted by their shade, and fed by their fruit. Listen to the ringing laughter of thine Isaac. Dread not the future, but trust the great love of God. Live by the well, and shelter beneath the covenant. So, if trial is approaching, thou shalt be the better able to meet it with a calm and strong heart.

21

The Greatest
Trial of All

Take now thy son, thine only son Isaac, whom
thou lovest; and offer him for a burnt offering.
—Genesis 22:2

S o long as men live in the world, they will turn to this story
with unwaning interest. There is only one scene in history by
which it is surpassed; that where the Great Father gave His
Isaac to a death from which there was no deliverance. God and Abraham were friends in a common sorrow up to a certain point; though
the infinite love of God stepped in to stay the hand of Abraham at the
critical moment, sparing His friend what He would not spare Himself.

"GOD DID TEMPT ABRAHAM."—A better rendering might be, "God
did put Abraham to the test." Satan tempts us that he may bring out
the evil that is in our hearts; God tries or tests us that He may bring out
all the good. In the fiery trial through which the believer is called to pass,
ingredients of evil which had counteracted his true development drop
away, shriveled and consumed; while latent qualities—produced by
grace, but not yet brought into exercise—are called to the front; receive
due recognition; and acquire a fixity of position and influence which
nothing else could possibly have given them. In the agony of sorrow we
say words and assume positions, which otherwise we should never
have dreamed of, but from which we never again recede. Looking

back, we wonder how we dared to do as we did: and yet we are not sorry—because the memory of what we were in that supreme hour is a precious legacy; and a platform from which we take a wider view, and climb to the further heights which beckon us.

The common incidents of daily life, as well as the rare and exceptional crises, are so contrived as to give us incessant opportunities of exercising, and so strengthening, the graces of Christian living. Happy are they who are ever on the alert to manifest each grace, according to the successive demands of the varied experiences of daily life. If we were always on the outlook for opportunities of manifesting the special qualities about Christ's character, which are called for by the trials, and worries, and vexations of common experience, we should find that they were the twenty thousand chariots of God, waiting to carry us up to heights which could never otherwise be trodden by our feet.

BUT GOD SENDS US NO TRIAL, WHETHER GREAT OR SMALL, WITHOUT FIRST PREPARING US. He "will with the temptation also make a way to escape, that ye may be able to bear it" (1 Cor. 10:13). Trials are, therefore, God's vote of confidence in us. Many a trifling event is sent to test us, ere a greater trial is permitted to break on our heads. We are set to climb the lower peaks before urged to the loftiest summits with their virgin snows; are made to run with footmen before contending with horses; are taught to wade in the shallows, before venturing into the swell of the ocean waves. So it is written: "It came to pass *after these things,* that God did tempt Abraham."

Moreover, GOD OFTEN PREPARES US FOR COMING TRIAL BY GIVING US SOME NEW AND BLISSFUL REVELATION OF HIMSELF. I notice that, at the close of the preceding chapter, we are told that Abraham called on the name of the everlasting God." Now, we do not learn that he had ever looked on God in this light before. He had known Him as God, the Almighty (17:1), but not as God, the Everlasting. The unchangeableness, the eternity, the independence of change, and time, and tense, which mark the Being of Jehovah—all these broke suddenly on his soul about that time in a fresh and more vivid manner. Who that can remember seeing the sea for the first time can ever forget the first impression of its grandeur and far-spread mirror-like expanse? And the soul of the patriarch was thrilled with the lofty train of high and holy thought, as he used that name in prayer beside the well, and beneath the spreading shade of the tree he had planted. And with him, as so often with us, the new name was to enable him the better to withstand the shock of coming sorrow.

THE TRIAL CAME VERY SUDDENLY. As we have seen, life was flowing smoothly with the patriarch—courted by Abimelech; secure of his wells; gladdened with the presence of Isaac; the everlasting God his friend. "Ah, happy man," we might well have exclaimed, "thou hast entered upon thy land of Beulah; thy sun shall no more go down, nor thy moon withdraw itself; before thee lie the sunlit years, in an unbroken chain of blessing." But this was not to be. And just at that moment, like a bolt out of a clear sky, there burst upon him the severest trial of his life. It is not often that the express trains of heaven are announced by a warning bell, or falling signal; they dash suddenly into the station of the soul. It becomes us to be ever on the alert; for at such an hour and in such a guise as we think not, the Son of Man comes.

THE TRIAL TOUCHED ABRAHAM IN HIS TENDEREST POINT. It concerned his Isaac. Nothing else in the circumference of his life could have been such a test as anything connected with the heir of promise, the child of his old age, the laughter of his life. *His love was tested*. For love of God, he had done much. But at whatever cost, he had ever put God first, glad to sacrifice all, for very love of Him. For this he had torn himself from Charran. For this he had been willing to become a homeless wanderer; content if at the last he became an inmate of God's home. For this he had renounced the hopes he had built on Ishmael; driving him, as a scapegoat, into the wilderness to return no more. But, perhaps, if he had been asked if he felt that he loved God most of all, he would not have dared to say that he did. We can never gauge our love by feeling. The only true test of love is in how much we are prepared to do for the one to whom we profess it. "He that hath My commandments, and keepeth them, he it is that loveth Me." But God knew how true and strong His child's love was, and that he loved Him best. So He put him to a supreme test, that all men might henceforth know that a mortal man could love God so much as to put Him first, though his dearest lay in the opposite scale of the balance of the heart. Would not you like to love God like this? Then tell Him you are willing to pay the cost, if only He will create that love within you. And, remember: though at first He may ask you to give up your Isaac to Him, it is only that you may take up your true position, and evince to the world your choice; for He will give your beloved back again from the altar on which you have laid him. "Take now thy son, thine only son Isaac, whom thou lovest, and offer him for a burnt offering" (Gen. 22:2).

IT WAS ALSO A GREAT TEST OF HIS FAITH. Isaac was the child of promise. "In Isaac shall thy seed be called." With reiterated emphasis this lad had been indicated as the one essential link between the aged pair and the vast posterity which was promised them. And now the father was asked to sacrifice his life. It was a tremendous test to his faith. How could God keep His word, and let Isaac die? It was utterly inexplicable to human thought. If Isaac had been old enough to have a son who could perpetuate the seed to future generations, the difficulty would have been removed. But how could the childless Isaac die; and still the promise stand of a posterity through him, innumerable as stars and sand? One thought, however, as the Epistle to the Hebrews tells us, filled the old man's mind, "GOD IS ABLE." He "accounted that God was able to raise him up, even from the dead" (Heb. 11:19). He felt sure that somehow God would keep His word. It was not for him to reason how, but simply to obey. He had already seen Divine power giving life where all was as good as dead; why should it not do it again? In any case he must go straight on, doing as he was told, and calculating on the unexhausted stores in the secret hand of God. Oh for faith like this! Simply to believe what God says; assured that God will do just what He has promised; looking without alarm, from circumstances that threaten to make the fulfillment impossible, to the bare word of God's unswerving truthfulness. Surely this habit is not so impossible of attainment. Why then should we not begin to practice it, stepping from stone to stone, until we are far out from the shore of human expediency leaning on the unseen but felt arm of Omnipotence?

IT WAS A TEST OF ABRAHAM'S OBEDIENCE. It was in the visions of the night that the word of the Lord must have come to him: and early the next morning the patriarch was on his way. The night before, as he lay down, he had not the least idea of the mission on which he would be started when the early beams of dawn had broken up the short Eastern night. But he acted immediately. We might have excused him if he had dallied with his duty; postponing it, procrastinating, lingering as long as possible. That, however, was not the habit of this heroic soul, which had well acquired the habit of instantaneity, one of the most priceless acquisitions for any soul ambitious of saintliness. "And Abraham rose up early in the morning" (Gen. 22:3). No other hand was permitted to saddle the ass, or cleave the wood, or interfere with the promptness of his action. He "saddled his ass, and clave the wood for the burnt offering, and rose up, and went unto the place of which God had told him." This promptness was his safeguard. While the herdsmen were beginning to stir, and the long lines of cattle were being driven forth to their several grazing grounds, the old man was on his way. I do not think he confided his secret to a single soul, not even to Sarah. Why should he? The lad and he would enter that camp again, when the short but awful journey was over. "I and the lad will go yonder and worship, and come again to you."

THIS TEST DID NOT OUTRAGE ANY OF THE NATURAL INSTINCTS OF HIS SOUL. First of all, he was too familiar with God's voice to mistake it. Too often had he listened to it to make a mistake in this solemn crisis. And he was sure that God had some way of deliverance which, though he might not be able to forecast it, would secure the sparing of Isaac's life. Besides, he lived at a time when such sacrifices as that to which he was called were very common; and he had never been taught decisively that they were abhorrent to the mind of his Almighty Friend. We must, in reading Scripture, remember that at first all God's servants were more or less affected by the religious notions that were current in their age; and we must not imagine that resulted from the twilight revelation in which they lived, but have since become dissipated before the meridian light of the Gospel. One of the first principles of that old Canaanitish religion demanded that men should give their firstborn for their transgression, the fruit of their body for the sin of their soul. On the altars of Moab, and Phoenicia, and Carthage; nay, even in the history of Israel itself—this almost irrepressible expression of human horror at sin, and desire to propitiate God, found terrible expression. Not that fathers were less tender than now, but because they had a keener sense of the terror of unforgiven sin; they cowered before gods whom they knew not, and to whom they imputed a thirst for blood and suffering; they counted no cost too great to appease the awful demands which ignorance, and superstition, and a consciousness of sin, made upon them.

Perhaps Abraham had lately witnessed these rites; and as he did so, he had thought of Isaac, and wondered if he could do the same with him; and marveled why such a sacrifice had never been demanded at his hands. And it did not, therefore, startle him when God said, "Take now thy son, and offer him up." He was to learn that while God demanded as much love as ever the heathen gave their cruel and imaginary deities, yet Heaven would not permit of human sacrifices or of offered sons. A Greater Sacrifice was to be made to put away sin. Abraham's obedience was, therefore, allowed to go up to a certain point, and then peremptorily stayed—that in all future time men might know that God would not demand, or permit, or accept human blood at their hands, much less the blood of a bright and noble lad; and that in such things He could have no delight.

Here let us ask ourselves whether we are of this same mind; holding our treasures with a loose hand; loving God most of all; prepared to obey Him at all costs; slaying our brightest hopes if God bid it—because so sure that he will not fail or deceive us. If so, may God give us this mind, and keep us in it, for His glory, and for the maturing of our own faith.

What those three days of quiet traveling must have been to Abraham, we can never know. It is always so much easier to act immediately and precipitately, than to wait through long days, and even years, but it is in this process of waiting upon God that souls are drawn out to a strength of purpose and nobility of daring, which become their sacred inheritance for all after-time. And yet, despite the patriarch's preoccupation with his own special sorrow, the necessity was laid upon him to hide it under an appearance of resignation, and even gladsomeness; so that neither his son nor his servants might guess the agony which was gnawing at his heart.

At last, on the third day, he saw from afar the goal of his journey. God had informed him that He would tell him which of the mountains was the appointed spot of the sacrifice: and now probably some sudden conviction seized upon his soul, that an especial summit which reared itself in the blue distance, was to be the scene of that supreme act in which he should prove that to his soul God was chiefest and best. Tradition, which seems well authenticated, has always associated that "mountain in the land of Moriah" with the place on which, in after days, stood the threshing floor of Araunah the Jebusite and the site of Solomon's Temple; and there is a wonderful appropriateness in the fact that this great act of obedience took place on the very spot where hecatombs of victims and rivers of blood were to point to that supreme Sacrifice which this prefigured.

As soon as the mountain had loomed into view, Abraham said unto his young men: "Abide ye here with the ass; and I and the lad will go yonder and worship, and come again to you." What a significant expression, in this connection, is that word WORSHIP! It reflects the mood of the patriarch's mind. He was preoccupied with that being, at whose command he had gone forth on this sorrowful errand. He looked upon his God, at the moment when He was asking so great a gift, as only deserving adoration and worship. The loftiest sentiment that can fill the heart of man swayed his whole nature; and it seemed to him as if his costliest and dearest treasure was not too great to give to that great and glorious God who was the one object of his life.

It is of the utmost importance that we should emphasize the words of *assured confidence*, which Abraham addressed to his young men before he left them. "I and the lad will go yonder and worship, and come again to you." This was something more than unconscious prophecy: it was the assurance of an unwavering faith, that somehow or other God would interpose to spare his son; or at least, if necessary, to raise him from the dead. In any case Abraham was sure that Isaac and he would before long come again. It is this which so largely removes the difficulties that might otherwise obscure this act; and it remains to all time a most striking proof of the tenacity with which faith can cling to the promises of God. When once you have received a promise, cling to it as a sailor to a spar in the midst of the boiling waters. God is bound to be as good as His word. And even though He may ask you to do the one thing that might seem to make deliverance impossible;

yet if you dare to do it, you will find not only that you shall obtain the promise, but that you shall also receive some crowning and unexpected mark of His love.

THE INFLUENCE OF ABRAHAM'S BEHAVIOR WAS FELT BY HIS SON. He caught his father's spirit. We do not know how old he was; he was at least old enough to sustain the toil of a long march on foot, and strong enough to carry up hill the faggots, laid upon his shoulders by his father. But he gladly bent his youthful strength under the weight of the wood, just as through the *Via Dolorosa* a greater than he carried His cross. Probably this was not the first time that Abraham and Isaac had gone on such an errand, but it is beautiful to see the evident interest the lad took in the proceedings as they went, "both of them together."

At all previous sacrifices, Abraham had taken with him a lamb, but on this occasion Isaac's wondering attention was drawn to the omission of that constant appendage to their acts of sacrifice; and with a simplicity which must have touched Abraham to the quick, he said, "My father, behold the fire and the wood! But where is the lamb for a burnt offering?" What a stab was this to that sorely-tried heart, which dared not even then reveal the secret beneath which it bowed; and which eagerly caught at a subterfuge to enable it to postpone the answer. Thus with a gleam of prophetic insight, mingled with unwavering faith in Him for whose sake he was suffering, the father answered, "My son, God will Himself provide a lamb for a burnt offering." So they went both of them together.

CAN WE WONDER THAT ABRAHAM SHRANK FROM DISCLOSING ALL THE FACTS? We all have our treasures whom we fondly love. We shudder at the remotest thought of losing them. With breaking hearts we watch the color fade from the cheek of a darling child, or mark the slow progress of disease in some twin soul, but Abraham must submit to a keener test than these. Our dear ones depart in spite of all we do to keep them, but in Abraham's case there was this added anguish, that he was to inflict the blow. The last thought that Isaac would have of him would be holding the uplifted knife; and even though the lad might be restored to him—yet would it not be a revelation to the young heart to discover that it was possible for his father to do to him an act of violence like that?

BUT AT LAST THE DISCOVERY COULD NO LONGER BE WITHHELD. "They came to the place which God had told him of, and Abraham built an altar there, and laid the wood in order." Can you not see the old man slowly gathering the stones; bringing them from the furthest distance possible; placing them with a reverent and judicious precision; and binding the wood with as much deliberation as possible? But at last everything is complete; and he turns to break the fatal secret to the young lad who had stood wondering by. Inspiration draws a veil over that last tender scene—the father's announcement of his mission; the broken sobs; the kisses, wet with tears; the instant submission of the son, who was old enough and strong enough to rebel if he had had the mind. Then the binding of that tender frame; which, indeed, needed no compulsion, because the young heart had learned the secret of obedience and resignation. Finally, the lifting him to lie upon the altar, on the wood. Here was a spectacle which must have arrested the attention of heaven. Here was a proof of how much mortal man will do for the love of God. Here was an evidence of childlike faith which must have thrilled the heart of the Eternal God, and moved Him in the very depths of His being. Do you and I love God like this? Is He more to us than our nearest and dearest? Suppose they stood on this side, and He on that side: would we go with Him, though it cost us the loss of all? You think you would. Aye, it is a great thing to say. The air upon this height is too rare to breathe with comfort. The one explanation of it is to be found in the words of our Lord: "He that loveth father or mother, son or daughter, more than Me, is not worthy of Me" (Matt. 10:37).

The blade was raised high, flashing in the rays of the morning sun, but it was not permitted to fall. With the temptation God also made a way of escape. "And the angel of the Lord called unto him out of heaven, and said, 'Abraham!' " With that avidity would that much-tried soul seize at anything that offered the chance of respite or of pause! And he said, his uplifted hand returning gladly to his side, "Here am I!" Would that we could more constantly live in the spirit of that response, so that God might always know where to find us; and so that we might be always ready to fulfill His will. Then followed words that spoke release and deliverance: "Lay not thine hand upon the lad, neither do thou anything unto him: for now I know that thou fearest God, seeing thou hast not withheld thy son, thine only son, from Me" (v. 12).

When we have given our best and costliest to God, passing our gifts through the fire, surrendering them to His will, He will give them back to us as gold refined—multiplied, as Job's belongings were. But it is also quite likely that He will not do so until we have almost lost all heart and hope. "Abraham called the name of that place Jehovah-Jireh," "The Lord will provide." And so it passed into a proverb, and men said one to another, "In the mount of the Lord deliverance shall be seen." It is a true word. Deliverance is not seen till we come to the mount of sacrifice. God does not provide deliverance until we have reached the point of our extremest need. It is when our Isaac is on the altar, and the knife is about to descend upon him, that God's angel interposes to deliver.

Nearby the altar there was a thicket; and, as Abraham lifted up his eyes and looked around, he beheld a ram caught there by its horns. Nothing could be more opportune. He had wanted to show his gratitude, and the fullness of his heart's devotion; and he gladly went and took the ram, and offered him up for a burnt offering instead of his son. Here, surely, is the great doctrine of substitution; and we are taught how life can only be preserved at the cost of life given. According to one of the early Church writers, there is a yet deeper mystery latent here; viz., that while Isaac represents the Deity of Christ, the ram represents His human nature, which became a sacrifice for the sins of the world. I am not sure that I would altogether accept this interpretation, because it is the Deity of Christ working through His humanity which gives value to His sacrifice, but all through this marvelous story there is an evident setting forth of the mysteries of Calvary.

Abraham's act enables us to better understand the sacrifice which God made to save us. The gentle submission of Isaac, laid upon the altar with throat bare to the knife, gives us a better insight into Christ's obedience to death. Isaac's restoration to life, as from the dead, and after having been three days dead in his father's purpose, suggests the resurrection from Joseph's tomb. Yet the reality surpasses the shadow Isaac suffers with a clear apprehension of his father's presence. Christ, bereft of the consciousness of His Father's love, complains of His forsakenness. All was done that love could do to alleviate Isaac's anguish, but Christ suffered the rudeness of coarse soldiery, and the upbraidings of Pharisee and Scribe. Isaac was spared death, but Christ drank the bitter cup to its dregs.

Before they left the mountain brow, the angel of Jehovah once more addressed the patriarch. God had often promised: now for the first time He sware; and since He could swear by no greater He sware by Himself, and said: "By Myself have I sworn, because thou hast done this thing, and hast not withheld thy son, thine only son; that in blessing I will bless thee; and in multiplying I will multiply thy seed as the stars of heaven, and as the sand which is upon the seashore; and thy seed shall possess the gate of his enemies; and in thy seed shall all nations of the earth be blessed, because thou hast obeyed My voice" (v. 16, 17). Think not, O soul of man, that this is a unique and solitary experience. It is simply a specimen and pattern of God's dealing with all souls who are prepared to obey Him at whatever cost. After thou has patiently endured, thou shalt receive the promise. The moment of supreme sacrifice shall be the moment of supreme and rapturous blessing. God's river, which is full of water, shall burst its banks, and pour upon thee a tide of wealth and grace. There is nothing, indeed, which God will not do for a man who dares to step out upon what seems to be the mist; though as he puts down his foot he finds it rock beneath him.

ALL WHO BELIEVE ARE THE CHILDREN OF FAITHFUL ABRAHAM. We then, Gentiles though we are, divided from him by the lapse of centuries, may inherit the blessing that he won; and the more so as we follow closely in his steps. That blessing is for us if we will claim it. That multiplication of seed may be realized in our fruitfulness of service. That victory over all enemies may give us victory in all time of our temptation, and that blessing for all the nations of the earth may be verified again as we go forth into all the world telling the story of a Savior's death.

From that eminence Abraham looked across the vale of centuries, and saw the day of Christ. He "saw it, and was glad" (John 8:56). With a new light in his heart, with a new composure on his face, talking much with Isaac of the vision which had broken upon his noble soul, Abraham returned to his young men. "And they rose up and went together to Beer-sheba, and Abraham dwelt at Beersheba", but the halo of the vision lit up the common places of his life, as it shall do for us, when from the mounts of sacrifice we turn back to the lowlands of daily duty.

22
Machpelah, and Its First Tenant

Give me a possession of a burying place with you;
that I may bury my dead out of my sight.
—Genesis 23:4

And Abraham buried Sarah, his wife, in the cave
of the field of Machpelah, before Mamre.
—Genesis 23:19

W hen Abraham came down the slopes of Mount Moriah, hand in hand with Isaac, fifty years of his long life still lay before him. Of those fifty years, twenty-five passed away before the event recorded in this chapter. What happened in those serene and untroubled years which lie between these two chapters, as a valley between two ridges of hills, we do not know. In all likelihood one year was as much as possible like another. Few events broke their monotony. The river of Abraham's life had passed the rapids and narrows of its earlier course, and now broadened into reaches of still water, over which its current blinded with an almost imperceptible movement.

The changes that mark the progress of our year are unknown beneath those glorious skies which rain perpetual summer on the earth; and the equableness of the climate is symbolical of the equableness of the simple patriarchal life. The tending of vast flocks and herds; the perpetual recurrence of birth, marriage, and death, among the vast household of slaves; the occasional interchange of hospitality with neighboring clans; special days for sacrifice and worship—these would be the most exciting episodes of that serene and calm existence, which is separated

165

as far as possible from our feverish, broken lives. And yet, is there so very much that we can vaunt ourselves in, when we compare our days with those? True, there was not the railway; the telegraph wire; the journal; the constant interchange of news. But perhaps life may more fully attain its ideal and fulfill its purpose, when its moments and hours are not dissipated by the constant intrusion of petty details, like those which for most of us make up the fabric of existence.

Perhaps we can never realize how much the members of such a household as Abraham's would be to one another. Through long, un-broken periods they lived together, finding all their society in one another. The course of pastoral life left ample leisure for close personal intercourse; and it was inevitable that human lives spent under such circumstances should grow together; even as trees in a dense wood, wherein they sometimes became so entangled and entwined that no human ingenuity can disentangle one from another. Thus it must have happened that the loss through death of one loved and familiar face would leave a blank never to be filled, and scarcely ever to be for-gotten. We need not wonder, therefore, that so much stress is laid upon the death of Sarah, the chief event of those fifty years of Abraham's life; nor need we regret that such ample details are given of her death and burial; since they enable us to get a glimpse of the patriarch, and see if he has altered at all during the quarter of a century which has passed over him.

I. WE ARE FIRST ARRESTED BY ABRAHAM'S TEARS. "And Sarah died in Kirjath-Arba; the same is Hebron in the land of Canaan." Abraham seems to have been away from home, perhaps at Beersheba, when she breathed her last, but he came at once "to mourn for Sarah, and to weep for her." This is the first time we read of Abraham weeping. We do not read that he wept when he crossed the Euphrates, and left forever home and kindred. There is no record of his tears when tidings came to him that his nephew Lot was carried into captivity. He does not seem to have bedewed his pathway to Mount Moriah with the tears of his heart. But now that Sarah is lying dead before him, the fountains of his grief are broken up.

What made the difference? Ah! there is all the difference between *doing* God's will and *suffering* it. So long as we have something to do for God—whether it be a toilsome march; or a battle; or a sacrifice— we can keep back our tears, and bear up with fortitude. The multiplicity of our engagement turns away our attention from our griefs. But when all is over; when there is nothing more to do; when we are left with the silent dead, requiring nothing more at our hands; when the last office is performed, the last flower arranged, the last touch given— then the tears come.

It is not wonderful that Abraham wept. Sarah had been the partner of his life for seventy or eighty years. She was the only link to the home of his childhood. She alone could sympathize with him when he talked of Terah and Nahor, or of Haran and Ur of the Chaldees. She alone was left of all who thirty years before had shared the hardships of his pilgrimage. As he knelt by her side, what a tide of memories must have rushed over him of their common plans, and hopes, and fears, and joys! He remembered her as the bright young wife; and the fellow pilgrim; as the childless persecutor of Hagar; as the prisoner of Pharaoh and Abimelech; as the loving mother of Isaac; and every memory would bring a fresh rush of tears.

There are some who chide tears as unmanly, unsubmissive, unchristian. They would comfort us with chill and pious stoicism, bidding us meet the most agitating passages of our history with rigid and tearless countenance. With such the spirit of the Gospel, and of the Bible, has little sympathy. We have no sympathy with a morbid sentimentality, but we may well question whether the man who cannot weep can really love; for sorrow is love, widowed and bereaved—and where that is present, its most natural expression is in tears. Religion does not come to make us unnatural and inhuman, but to purify and ennoble all those natural emotions with which our manifold nature is endowed. Jesus wept. Peter wept. The Ephesian converts wept on the neck of the Apostle whose face they thought they were never to see again. Christ stands by each mourner, saying, "Weep, my child; weep, for I have wept."

Tears relieve the burning brain, as a shower the electric clouds. Tears discharge the insupportable agony of the hearer, as an overflow lessens the pressure of the flood against the dam. Tears are the material out of which heaven weaves its brightest rainbows. Tears are transmuted into the jewels of better life, as the wounds in the oyster turn to pearls. Happy, however, is that man who, when he weeps for his departed, has not to reproach himself with unkindnesses and bitter words. We cannot always understand what makes people weep, when we stand with them on the loose earth beside the open grave. In many cases their sorrow is due to pure affection; in some cases, however, there is an additional saltness in their tears, because of unspoken regret. "I wish that I had not acted so: that I could recall those words: that I had had another opportunity of expressing the love I really felt, but hid: that I had taken more pains to curb myself; to be gentle, loving, endearing, and endeared. Oh for one hour of explanation and confession and forgiveness!" Let us see to it that we may never have to drink such bitter ingredients in the cup of our bereavement; and that we may not, let us not fail to give expression to those nobler feelings which often strive within our breasts, but which we too often repress.

And if some should read these words whose tears are the more bitter because they themselves are unsubmissive, let such remember that where they cannot feel resigned, they must will to be resigned, putting their will on God's side in this matter; asking him to take it and fashion it according to His own; and remembering that our only province is with the will. This is all God asks, and if this is right with Him, He will subdue every other thought, and bring the whole being into a state of glad acquiescence. "I delight to do Thy will, O my God." "Though He slay me, yet will I trust in Him!"

II. NOTICE ABRAHAM'S CONFESSION. "Abraham stood up from before his dead, and spake unto the sons of Heth, saying, I am a stranger and a sojourner with you; give me a possession of a burying place with you" (23:3, 4). See how sorrow reveals the heart. When all is going well, we wrap up our secrets, but when sorrow rends the veil, the *arcana* of the inner temple are laid bare! To look at Abraham as the great and wealthy patriarch, the emir, the chieftain of a mighty clan, we cannot guess his secret thoughts. He has been in the land for sixty-two years; and surely by this time he must have lost his first feelings of loneliness.

He is probably as settled and naturalized as any of the princes around. So you might think, until he is widowed of his beloved Sarah! Then, amid his grief, you hear the real man speaking his most secret thought: "I am a stranger and a sojourner with you."

There are very remarkable words; and they were never forgotten by his children. Speaking of the land of promise, God said, through Moses, to the people, "The land shall not be sold for ever; for ye are strangers and sojourners with Me." When David and his people made splendid preparations to build the Temple, as their spokesman he said, "Who am I, and what is my people, that we should be able to offer so willingly? for all things come of Thee; for we are strangers before Thee and sojourners, as were all our fathers. Our days on the earth are as a shadow, and there is none abiding." And, further, in one of his matchless Psalms, he pleads, "Hear my prayer, O Lord! Hold not Thy peace at my tears; for I am a stranger with Thee, and a sojourner, as all my fathers were." So deeply had those words of Abraham sunk in the national mind, that the Apostle inscribes them over the cemetery where the great and the good of the Jewish nation lie entombed: "These all died in faith, not having received the promises, but having seen them afar off, and were persuaded of them, and embraced them; and confessed that they were strangers and pilgrims on the earth" (Heb. 11:13).

We may ask what it was that maintained this spirit in Abraham for so many years. There is but one answer: "They that say such things declare plainly that they seek a country" (Heb. 11:14). That country is never looked upon by the sun, or watered by the rivers of the earth, or refreshed by the generous dews. It is the better country, even the heavenly; the city which hath foundations, whose builder and maker is God; the land that needs neither sun nor moon, because the Lord God and the Lamb are the light thereof. Uprooted from the land of his birth, the patriarch could never take root again in any earthly country; and his spirit was always on the alert, eagerly reaching out towards the city of God, the home where only such royal souls as his can meet their peers, and find their rest. He refused to be contented with anything short of this; and, therefore, God was not ashamed to be called his God, because He had prepared for him a city. How this elevation of soul shames some of us! In our better moments we say that we are "the burgesses of the skies", but our conversation is not in heaven, in our practical ordinary daily life. We profess to look for a city, but we take good care to make for ourselves an assured position among the citizens of this world. We affect to count all things dross, but the eagerness with which, muck rake in hand, we strive to heap together the treasures of earth is a startling commentary upon our words.

III. NOTICE ABRAHAM'S FAITH. Men are wont to bury their dead beside their ancestors. The graves of past generations are the heritage of their posterity. By them rather than by the habitations of the living do tribes and races of men find their resting place. The American loves to visit the quiet English churchyard where his fathers lie. The Jew elects in old age to journey to Palestine, that dying he may be buried in soil consecrated by the remains of his race. And it may be that Abraham first thought of that far distant grave in Charran, where Terah and Haran lay buried. Should he take Sarah thither? "No," thought he, "that country has no claim upon me now. The only land, indeed, on which I have a claim is this wherein I have been a stranger. Here in after-days shall my children live. Here the generations that bear my name shall spread themselves out as the sands on the seashore, and as the stars in the midnight sky. It is meet, therefore, that I should place our grave, in which Sarah their mother, and I their father, shall lie, in the heart of the land—to be a nucleus around which our descendants shall gather in all coming time. What though, as God has told me, four hundred years of suffering and furnace fire must pass, yet my children shall ultimately come hither again: and I will hold the land in pledge against their coming, sure that it shall be as God has said!"

It is very beautiful to remark the action of Abraham's faith in this matter; and to see its outcome in his utter refusal to receive the land as a gift from any hand but that of God. When the chieftains to whom he made his appeal heard it, they instantly offered him the choice of their sepulcher affirming that none of them would withhold his sepulcher from so mighty a prince. And afterwards, when he sought their intercession with Ephron the son of Zohar, for the obtaining of the cave of Machpelah, which was at the end of his field, and

Ephron proposed to give it him in the presence of the sons of his people, Abraham steadfastly refused. It was all his as the gift of God; it would be all his some day in fact; and in the meanwhile he would purchase the temporary use of that which he could never accept as a gift from any but his Almighty Friend.

And so after many courteous speeches, in the dignified manner which still prevails among Orientals, "the field, and the cave, and all the trees, were made sure unto Abraham for a possession in the presence of the children of Heth, before all that enter in at the gate of his city" (Gen. 23:17, 18). Their witness had the same binding effect in those rude days as legal documents have in our own.

There Abraham buried Sarah; there Isaac and Ishmael buried Abraham; there they buried Isaac, and Rebecca his wife; there Jacob buried Leah; and there Joseph buried Jacob his father; and there in all likelihood, guarded by the jealous Moslem, untouched by the changes and storms that have swept around their quiet resting place, those remains are sleeping still, holding that land in fee, and anticipating the time when on a larger and more prominent scale the promise of God to Abraham shall be accomplished.

Not yet has the Divine promise been fully realized. The children of Abraham have possessed the Land of Promise for "but a little while" (Is. 53:18). For long ages their adversaries have held sway there. But the days are hastening on when once more God will set His hand to gather His chosen people from all lands; and the infidel shall no longer desecrate those sacred spots, but once again shall the hills and valleys, and pasture lands of Palestine come into the possession of the seed of Abraham, the friend of God.

23

The Soul's Answer
to the Divine Summons

I WILL GO!
—Genesis 24:58

Carry back your mind for thirty-seven centuries. The soft light of an Oriental sunset falls gently on the fertile grazing grounds watered by the broad Euphrates; and as its gloom lights up all the landscapes dotted by flocks, and huts, and villages, it irradiates with an especial wealth of color the little town of Haran, founded one hundred years before by Terah, who, traveling northwards from Ur, resolved to go no further. The old man was smarting keenly at the recent loss of his youngest son, and after him the infant settlement was named. And so in time houses were built, and girdled by a wall in Oriental style. There Terah died, and thence the caravan had started at the command of God across the terrible desert, for the unknown Land of Promise. One branch of the family, however—that of Nahor—lived there still. His son, Bethuel, was the head; and in that family, at the time of which I speak, there was at least a mother; a brother named Laban; and a daughter in the first flush of girlish beauty, Rebecca.

It is Rebecca who occupies the central place in the pastoral scene before us. All her young life had been spent in that old town. Daughter of the Sheikh though she was, yet she was not kept in that listless

indolence which dares not soil the fingers with honest work: an indolence which is the curse of so many well-born girls today. She could
make savory meat, and tend the flocks, as her niece Rachel did in after
years on that same spot, and carry her pitcher gracefully poised upon
her shoulder. She knew by name all the people who dwelt in that little town; and she had heard of those of her kindred who before her birth
had gone beyond the great desert, and of whom hardly a word had traveled back for so many years. She little guessed the great news of the
world, and of her place in it; and in her wildest dreams she never
thought of doing more than living and dying within the narrow limits of her native place. Elastic in step, modest in manner, pure in heart,
amiable and generous, with a very fair face, as the sacred story tells us—
how little did she imagine that the wheel of God's providence was
soon to catch her out of her quiet home, and whirl her into the mighty
outer world that lay beyond the horizon of desert sand.

On a special evening a stranger halted at the well, without the little town. He had with him a stately caravan of ten camels, each richly
laden, and all bearing traces of long travel. There the little band
waited, as if not knowing what next to do. Its leader was probably the
good Eliezer, the steward of Abraham's house, who had come there on
a solemn commission from his master. Abraham was now advanced in
years. Isaac his son was forty years of age, and the old man longed to
see him suitably married; and though his faith never doubted that God
would fulfill His promise of the seed, yet he was desirous of clasping
in his aged arms the second link between him and his posterity. He had
therefore bound his trusty servant by a double oath: first, that he
would not take a wife for Isaac from the daughters of the Canaanites
around them, but from his own kith and kin at Haran; and secondly,
that he would never be an accomplice to Isaac's return to the land which
he had left. This solemn oath was lit up by the assurance of the old
man, that the Lord God of heaven, who took him from his father's
house and the land of his kindred, would send His angel before him,
and would crown his mission with success.

Having arrived at the city well towards nightfall, "even, the time
that women go out to draw water"—the devout leader asked that
God would send him "good speed," addressing the Almighty as the

Lord God of his master Abraham, and pleading that in prospering his way He would show kindness to his master. The simplicity and trustfulness of his prayer are very beautiful; and are surely the reflection of the piety which reigned in that vast encampment gathered around the wells of Beersheba, and which was the result of Abraham's own close walk with God. There would be less fault to find with servants in the present day, if they were treated as servants were once treated—as souls rather than hands; and if they were encouraged to imitate, because they had learned to admire, the character of those with whom they live in such close contact. Alas that servants in Christian homes often find so little to attract them to the godliness which is professed, but scantily practiced!

It is our privilege to talk with God about everything in life. The minutest things are not too small for Him who numbers the hairs of our heads. No day can we afford to spend, without asking that He would send us good speed. Well would it be for us, as we stand by the well at morning, or at eventide, to commit our way unto the Lord, trusting that He should bring it to pass. And if this be true of ordinary days, how much more of those days which decide destiny, which are the watershed of life, and in which plans are concluded which may affect all after years! Nor is it wrong for us to ask a sign from God, if by this we mean that He would permit the circumstances of our daily lot to indicate His will: to confirm by inner inspiration from Himself, and to embody, in fact, that which has already been impressed upon our own conscience. We have no right to ask for signs for the gratification of a morbid curiosity, but we are justified in asking for the concurrence of outward providence indicating the will of God. It was a holy and a happy inspiration that led the godly servant to ask that the damsel, who responded with courteous alacrity to his request for water, should be she whom God had appointed as a bride for his master's son; and it happened to him as it will always happen to those who have learned to trust like little children, that "before he had done speaking," his answer was waiting by his side.

We need not tell in detail all that followed: the gifts of heavy jewelry; the reverent recognition of God's goodness in answering prayer, as the man bowed down his head and worshiped the Lord; the swift run home; the admiration of mother and brother at the splendid gifts; the breathless telling of the unexpected meeting; the proffered hospitality of Laban, whose notions of hospitality were quickened by his keen eye for gain, and who spoke the words of welcome with extra heat because he saw the rich lading of the camels; the provision of straw and provender for the camels, of water for the feet of the weary drivers, and of food for their leader, and the refusal to eat until his errand was unraveled and its purpose accomplished; the story, told in glowing words, of Abraham's greatness; the narrative of the wonderful way in which the speaker had been led, and Rebecca indicated; the final request that her relatives would deal kindly and truly in the matter; and their unhesitating and swift consent in words that drew the old servant prostrate to the ground in holy ecstasy as he worshiped the Lord. "Behold," they said, "Rebecca is before thee; take her and go: and let her be thy master's son's wife, as the Lord hath spoken."

Then from his treasures he brought forth jewels of silver and jewels of gold, and raiment with which to deck Rebecca's fair form; her mother and Laban also received precious things to their hearts' desire. "Then they did eat and drink, he and the men that were with him, and tarried all night." In the early dawn, refusing all invitation to further waiting, Abraham's steward started back again, carrying with him Rebecca and her nurse; and through the fragrant morning air the blessings of that little cluster of friendly hearts were wafted to her ear, as seated on her camel; and wrapped in a dream of girlish hope and wonder, she caught the last voice from her home. "They addressed Rebecca and said unto her, Thou art our sister: be thou the mother of thousands of millions; and let thy seed possess the gate of those which hate them."

We must thus pass over the details of this story, which carries on its forefront the stamp of inspiration and of truth; suffice it to say that it has no superior in this book for its rich, soft, placid style. It is full of those touches of nature which make all men kin, and which move them everywhere alike. Let us now elicit two or three further lessons to illustrate by it the Divine summons, and the answer of the soul.

I. A LESSON TO THOSE WHO CARRY THE SUMMONS OF GOD. *Let us saturate our work with prayer.* Like his master, the servant would not take a single step without prayer. Not that he always spoke aloud. No one would have known that the old man prayed as he stood there by the well. Nor did he arbitrarily dictate to God, but he threw the whole responsibility of the matter upon Him who had ever shown Himself so true a Friend to his beloved master. He had a most difficult thing to do, in which strong chances were running against him. Was it likely that a young girl would care to leave her home to cross the vast expanse of sand in company with himself, a complete stranger, and to become the wife of one whom she had never seen? "Peradventure the woman will not follow me!" And if she were willing, her relatives might not be, but he prayed, and prayed again, and God's good speed crowned his errand with complete success.

We too are sometimes sent on very unlikely errands. Humanly speaking, our mission seems likely to prove a failure: but those who trust in God have not the word "failure" in their vocabulary. Their hearts are centers from which the fragrance of silent prayer is ever exhaling into the presence of God. They succeed where they seem menaced with certain disappointment. Christian worker! Never start on any mission for God, whether to an individual soul or to a congregation, without the prayer, "Send me good speed on this day."

We must also wait upon God for direction. Abraham's steward asked that the chosen bride should be willing to draw water for his camels. A trifle this must seem to some; and yet it was a true test for a girl's nature. It showed a ready kindliness of heart, which was prepared to outrun the requirements of conventional politeness. It indicated a nature in which haughty pride had no place. Is it not a fact that in such trivial, unstudied acts there is a sure index of character? Very often God's servants make great mistakes, because they force themselves on souls, not living in the will of God, not seeking the indication of His bidding, not waiting until He should open the door of circumstance into some new life. We do not always realize the solemn mystery that surrounds each human soul; or the depths into which all spiritual consciousness may have receded; or the thick cake of worldliness and carelessness which may have trusted over the sensibilities of the being. God only understands all this; and we should do very wisely to wait expectantly and trustfully for Him to open up the way of access into the citadel of the heart. We may be sure that in this God will not fail us, but that while we are speaking He will hear and answer.

Let us say much in praise of our Master. It is beautiful to notice how eloquent the old man is about his master. He does not say one word about himself, or extol himself in any way, so absorbed was he in the story of his absent, distant lord. Was not this also characteristic of the Apostles, who preached not themselves, but Christ Jesus the Lord; and whose narratives are like colorless glass, only letting His glory though? Alas! that we so obtrude ourselves, that men go away talking of us. Let us lose ourselves in our theme. And while we show the jewels of Christian character in our own deportment, let the theme of our message be: "The Lord Jehovah hath greatly blessed our Master, Christ, and has given Him a name which is above every name; and has raised Him to His own right hand in the heavenly places, far above all principality and power, and every name that is named: and He is worthy to receive power, and riches, and strength, and honor, and glory, and blessing." And when success attends your words, be sure to give all the glory to Him from whom it has come.

II. THE SUMMONS ITSELF was a call to a simple, penniless girl to ally herself in marriage to one of the wealthiest and noblest of earth's aristocracy. It was not sent because of her worth, or wealth, or beauty, but because it was so willed in the heart and counsel of Abraham. Such a call is sent to very soul that hears the Gospel. In yonder azure depths lives the great Father God. He has one Son, His only-begotten and well-beloved. He has resolved to choose from among men those who as one Church shall constitute His bride forever. He sends this call to you, not because you are worthy, or wealthy, or beautiful, but because He has so willed it in the counsels of His own heart: and He longs that you shall be willing to detach yourself from all that you hold dear. This is His message: "Hearken, O daughter, and consider, and incline thine ear! forget also thine own people and thy father's house: so shall the King greatly desire thy beauty: for He is thy Lord; and worship thou Him" (Ps. 45:10, 11).

And if that call is obeyed, thou shalt lose thine own name, sinner, in His name; thou shalt be arrayed in His fair jewels; thou shalt share

His wealth; thou shalt sit down with Him on His throne; all things shall be thine. Wilt thou go with this Man? Wilt thou leave all to be Christ's? Wilt thou give thine unseen Lover thine heart, to be His forever? Come and put yourselves under the convoy of the blessed Holy Spirit, who pleads the cause of Jesus, as did Abraham's servant that of Isaac; and let Him conduct you where Jesus is.

III. How to deal with this summons. *We must find room for it.* "Come in, thou blessed of the Lord; wherefore standest thou without? for I have prepared a house and room." The Master saith, "Where is the guest chamber?" There was no room for Christ in the inn: but we must make room for Him in the heart; or, at least, we must be willing that He should make room for Himself.

We must bear witness. "The damsel ran, and told them of her mother's house." As soon as you have heard the call, and received the jewels of promise, which are the earnest of your inheritance, you must go home to your friends and tell them what great things the Lord hath done for you.

We must not procrastinate, or confer with flesh and blood. Men, and circumstances, would fain defer our starting on pilgrimage. This is Satan's method of breaking off the union forever. There must be no dallying or delay: but when the inquiry is put to us, "Wilt thou go with this man?" we must promptly and swiftly answer, "I will go."

The journey was long and toilsome, but all the way the heart of the young girl was sustained by the tidings told her by the faithful servant, who beguiled the weary miles with stories of the home to which she was journeying, and the man with whom her life was to be united— "Whom having not seen, she loved; and in whom, though she saw him not, she rejoiced." She already loved him, and ardently longed to see him.

One evening the meeting came. Isaac had gone forth to meditate at eventide, sadly lamenting the loss of his mother, eagerly anticipating the coming of his bride, and interweaving all with holy thought. And when he lifted up his eyes across the pastures, lo, the camels were coming, and the two young souls leapt to each other. Happy meeting, which made Rebecca oblivious to all the trials and hardships of her journey and the loss of her friends! Was it not also an emblem of the moment when the work of the Holy Spirit, our gracious Conductor, will conclude in the presence of our Lord, the true Bridegroom of saintly hearts, and we shall see his face, to be forever with Him, going no more out forever?

And after awhile in that silent home, there was again the prattle of childish voices; and for several years the patriarch rejoiced in the presence of his grandchildren, to whom he would tell the history of the past, on which his aged soul loved to dwell. And of one narrative those lands would never tire; that which told how their father had once climbed the summit of Moriah, to be, as it were, raised from the dead.

24
Gathered to His People

*These are the days of the years of Abraham's
life which he lived; a hundred, threescore,
and fifteen years. Then Abraham gave up the
ghost, and died in a good old age,
an old man, and full of years; and
was gathered to his people.*
—Genesis 25:8

No human name can vie with Abraham's for the widespread reverence which it has evoked among all races and throughout all time. The pious Jew looked forward to reposing, after death, in the bosom of Father Abraham. The fact of descent from him was counted by thousands sufficient to secure them a pass3port into heaven. Apostles so opposite as Paul and James united in commending his example to the imitation of primitive Christians, in an age which had seen the Lord Jesus Himself. The medieval Church canonized Abraham alone among Old Testament worthies, by no decree, but by popular consent. Devout Mohammedans reverence his name as second only to that of their prophet. What was the secret of this widespread renown? It is not because he headed one of the greatest movements of the human family; nor yet because he evinced manly and intellectual vigor; nor because he possessed vast wealth. It was rather the remarkable nobility and grandeur of his religious life that has made him the object of veneration to all generations of mankind.

At the basis of his character was a mighty Faith. "Abraham believed God." In that faith he left his native land, and traveled to one which was promised, but not clearly indicated. In that faith he felt able to let Lot choose the best he could for himself, because he was sure that none could do better for himself than God was prepared to do for the one who trusted Him. In that faith he waited through long years, sure that God would give him the promised child. In that faith he lived a nomad life, dwelling in tents, and making no attempt to return to the settled country from which he had come out. Indeed, his soul was consumed with the passionate expectancy of the city of God. In that faith he was prepared to offer Isaac, and buried Sarah.

Do not suppose that his faith dwelt alone. One the contrary, it bore much fruit; for if we test him by those catalogues of the fruits of faith which are provided in the New Testament, we shall find that he manifested them each and all. Take, for instance, that chain of linked graces enumerated in the Second Epistle by the Apostle Peter; a kind of golden ladder, stretched across the chasm between heaven and earth, and uniting them.

To Faith he added Virtue, or Manly Courage. What could have been more manly than the speed with which he armed his trained servants; or than the heroism with which he, with a train of undisciplined shepherds, broke on the disciplined bands of Assyria, driving them before him as the chaff before the whirlwind, and returning victorious down the long valley of the Jordan?

And to Manly Courage he added Knowledge. All his life he was a student in God's college of divinity. Year by year fresh revelations of the character and attributes of God broke upon his soul. He grew in the knowledge of God and the Divine nature, which at the first had been to him a *terra incognita*. An unknown country grew beneath his gaze; as he climbed through the years into closer fellowship with God, and from the summit looked down upon its lengths and breadths, its depths and heights, its oceans, mountain ranges, and plains.

And to Knowledge he added Temperance, or Self-Control. That he was master of himself is evident from the way in which he repelled the offer of the King of Sodom; and curbed his spirit amid the irritations caused by Lot's herdsmen. The strongest spirits are those which have the strongest hand upon themselves, and are able, therefore, to do things which weaker men would fail in. There is no type of character more splendid than that of the man who is a master of himself, because he is the servant of God; and who can rule others rightly because he can rule himself well.

And to Temperance, Patience. Speaking of him, the voice of New Testament inspiration affirms that he "patiently endured" (Heb. 6:15). No ordinary patience was that which waited through the long years, not murmuring or complaining, but prepared to abide God's time; weaned from the breasts of earthly consolation, and help, and quieted after the manner of the Psalmist, who said, "I have quieted myself as a child that is weaned of his mother: my soul is even as a weaned child. Let Israel hope in the Lord from henceforth and forever" (Ps. 131:2, 3).

And to his Patience he added Godliness. One of his chief characteristics was his piety—a constant sense of the presence of God in his life, and a love and devotion to Him. Wherever he pitched his tent, there his first care was to rear an altar. Shechem, Hebron, Beersheba—alike saw these tokens of his reverence and love. In every time of trouble he turned as naturally to God as a child to its father; and there was such holy intercourse between his spirit and that of God, that the name by which he is now best known throughout the East is "THE FRIEND"— a name which he holds *par excellence,* and which has almost overshadowed the use of that name by which we know him best.

And to Godliness he added Brotherly Kindness. Some men who are devoted towards God are lacking in the tenderer qualities towards those most closely knit with them in family bonds. Not so was it with Abraham. He was full of affection. Beneath the calm exterior and the erect bearing of the mighty chieftain there beat a warm and affectionate heart. Listen to that passionate cry, "Oh that Ishmael might live before Thee!" Remember God's own testimony to the affection he bore towards Isaac—"Thy son, thine only son, whom thou lovest." Abraham's nature therefore may be compared to those ranges of mighty hills, whose summits rear themselves above the region of storms, and hold converse with the skies; while their lower slopes are clothed with woods and meadows, where homesteads nestle and bright children string their necklaces of flowers with merry laughter.

And to Brotherly Kindness he added Charity, or Love. In his dealings with men he could afford to be generous, open-hearted, open-handed;

willing to pay down the large price demanded for Machpelah's cave without haggling or complaint; destitute of petty pride; affable, courteous, able to break out into sunny laughter; right with God, and therefore able to shed upon men the rays of a genial, restful noble heart.

All these things were in him and abounded, and they made him neither barren nor unfruitful; they made his calling and election sure; they prepared for him an abundant entrance into the everlasting kingdom of God our Savior. The thought that underlies the expression in the Greek (πλουσίως ἡ εἴσοδος) [*plousīos he eísodos*] is richly significant. The words denote the welcome given by choral songs and joyous greetings to the conqueror who, laden with spoils, returned to his native city; and they indicate that for some favored souls, at least, there is waiting on the threshold of the other world a welcome so exuberant, so boisterous in its unutterable joy, so royally demonstrative, as to resemble that given in all times to those who have conferred great benefits, or who have learned the art of stirring the loyal devotion of their fellows. If such an entrance could be accorded to anyone, certainly it would be Abraham, when, stooping beneath the weight of one hundred threescore and fifteen years, "he gave up the ghost, and died at a good old age, an old man, full of years, and was gathered to his people."

"Abraham gave up the ghost." There was no reluctance in his death; he did not cling to life—he was glad to be gone; and when the angel-messenger summoned him, without a struggle, nay, with the readiness of glad consent, his spirit returned to God who gave it.

He was gathered to his people. This cannot refer to his body; for that did not sleep beside his ancestors, but side by side with Sarah's. Surely then it must refer to his spirit. The world's grey fathers knew little of the future, but they felt that there was somewhere a mustering place of their clan, whither devout and holy souls were being gathered, one by one, so that each spirit, as it passed from this world, went to rejoin its people; the people from which it had sprung; the people whose name it bore; the people to which by its tastes and sympathies it was akin.

What a lovely synonym for death! TO DIE is to rejoin our people; to pass into a world where the great clan is gathering, welcoming with shouts each newcomer through the shadows. Where are your people? I trust they are God's people; and if so, those that bear your name, standing on the other shore, are more numerous than the handful gathered around you here; many whom you have never known, but who know you; many whom you have loved and lost awhile; many who without you cannot be made perfect in their happiness. There they are, rank on rank, company on company, regiment on regiment, watching for your coming. Be sure you do not disappoint them! But remember, if your people are God's people, you cannot be gathered to them unless first in faith and love you are gathered to Him.

Little doubt had this noble man of the recognition of saintly spirits in the other world; and indeed, it is an untrue conception which has filled the future with strange spirits, unknowing and unknown. Heaven is not a prison with tier on tier of cells, but a HOME. And what is home without the recognition and love of fond hearts? So long as we read of David going to his child; of Paul anticipating the pleasure of meeting again his converts; of the women and disciples being able to recognize the appearance and the love of the Savior amid the glory of the resurrection body—we may be prepared to believe, with the patriarch, that dying is reunion with those to whom in the deepest sense we are related. Spiritual affinities are for all time and for eternity, and will discover themselves through all worlds.

"And his sons, Isaac and Ishmael, buried him in the cave of Machpelah." There were great differences between these two. Ishmael, the child of his slave: Isaac, of the wedded wife. Ishmael, the offspring of expediency: Isaac, of promise. Ishmael, wild and masterful, "the wild ass"; strongly marked in his individuality; proud, independent, swift to take an insult, swift to avenge it: Isaac, quiet and retiring, submissive and meek, willing to carry wood, to be kept in the dark, to be bound, to yield up his wells and to let his wife govern his home. And yet all differences were wiped out in that moment of supreme sorrow; and coming from his desert fastnesses, surrounded by his wild and ruffian freebooters, Ishmael united with the other son of their common father, who had displaced him in his inheritance, and who was so great a contrast to himself, but all differences were smoothed out in that hour.

Many ancient chieftains may have been gathered by that ancient cave, to join in one last act of respect to the mighty prince who had dwelt among them for so long. Amid the wail of the women, and the dirge which even to this day tells of sorrow for departed worth in Eastern lands—borne by a band of his trusted retainers, while a vast concourse of the camp stood wrapped in reverent silence around—the remains of the man who had dared to trust God at all costs, and who with pilgrim steps had traversed so many weary miles, were solemnly laid beside the dust of Sarah, his faithful wife. There, in all probability, they rest even to this day, and thence they will be raised at the coming of the King.

Out of materials which were by no means extraordinary, God built up a character with which He could hold fellowship as friend with friend; and a life which has exerted a profound influence on all after-time. It would seem as if He can raise any crop He chooses, when the soil of the heart and life are entirely surrendered to Him. Why should not we henceforth yield ourselves utterly to His divine husbandry, asking Him to fulfill in us the good pleasure of His goodness, and the work of faith with power? Only let us trust Him fully, and obey Him instantly and utterly; and as the years pass by, they shall witness results which shall bring glory to God in the highest, while they fill us with ceaseless praise.

II
Israel: A Prince with God

✠

Preface

It was the custom with some of the older commentators to write as though their loyalty to God's Spirit required that they should show that the acts of the Old Testament saints were all of them consistent with the highest morality. This was especially evident in their remarks on the career of the patriarch whose name stands on our title page. Ingenious attempts have been made to palliate episodes and transactions in his life, which at first sight certainly conflict with our conceptions of righteousness.

It was this that led me in the first instance to prepare this book. I wrote it with the avowed purpose of telling the story of Jacob's life, extenuating nothing; portraying his failures as well as his victories; and endeavoring to show that the Word of God does not hesitate to describe the imperfections and native deformities of its most conspicuous characters, because of the incalculable benefit which may accrue in the two following directions.

First, mankind is taught that the love of God is not determined by what it finds in man. God loves, not because we are good, but to make us so. He is not surprised by the evil He discovers in us, and His lovingkindness is not turned away by our sin.

Secondly, it is a great comfort to find that the saints of Bible story were men of like passions with ourselves; and if God was able to shape materials so rough into vessels so fair, there is hope that He will not fail nor be discouraged until He has done the like for us.

It will also be a great pleasure if these pages will serve to show some of my fellow workers, weary with the incessant demands of their congregations, how they may find a constant wellspring of freshness, variety, and interest, in the glorious biographies of Scripture. To recruit a dwindling congregation; to sustain interest in a crowded one; to awaken new devotion to the Bible; and to touch the many chords of human life—there is nothing to be compared with a reverent re-telling of the stories of Bible Heroes and Saints.

F. B. Meyer.

1
First Impressions

One adequate support
For the calamities of mortal life
Exists—one only: an assured belief
That the procession of our fate, however
Sad or disturbed, is ordered by a Being
Of Infinite benevolence and power;
Whose everlasting purposes embrace
All accidents, converting them to good

Genesis 25   Wordsworth

An old-world story this! In its strange Eastern dress, it appears to be as remote from us as the garb of an Arab, or the barter of an Oriental bazaar. And yet human life is much the same, whether lived eighteen hundred years on this side or eighteen hundred years on that side of the Cross; whether hidden beneath our broadcloth, or the flowing robes of an Arab Sheikh; whether spent in modern towns, or on the free, open pasture lands of Southern Palestine.

Our critics complain of our poring over these time-worn pages of ancient biography, but, with all deference to them, we feel bound to say that we learn better how to live, we inhale more spiritual ozone, we see further into the reasons of God's dealings with men, when doing so, than when scanning the pages of yesterday's newspaper, or of a society journal.

With human life and discipline, one day is as a thousand years, and a thousand years as one day. Souls grasp hands across the intervening centuries. Thousands of miles cannot part us from our kin across the seas; and thousands of years cannot part us from our kin across the ages, or sever the readers of these words—who daily weep over an often dropped ideal—from that son of Isaac, who, nearly drowned in the seas

of his own craft and cunning, at length emerged a new man, and a
prince with God.

There are many reasons which invest this story with absorbing interest:

I. JACOB WAS THE FATHER OF THE JEWISH RACE, AND A TYPICAL
JEW. The Jews called themselves by the name of Jacob; and surnamed
themselves by the name of Israel (Is. 44:5). God calls them children of
Israel. We call them Israelites. We speak of Jacob, rather than Abraham,
as the founder of the people to which he gave his name, because,
though Abraham was their ancestor, yet he was no so exclusively. He
is the founder of a yet richer, mightier line. The wild son of the desert
claims him as father equally with the bargain-loving Jew. Nor is that
all. We Gentiles have reason to be proud to trace back our lineage to
the first great Hebrew, the man who *crossed over*,[*] and whom God designated
as His friend. He is the father of all who believe: not of the circumcision
only, but of those who walk in the steps of the faith which
he had, even before he was circumcised (Rom. 4:12). *We* go to make
up the sands on the shore and the stars of the heavens, which he saw
in the vision of God (Gen. 22:17).

But Jacob is the typical Jew. His life is the epitome of that wonderful
people, who are found in every country and belong to none; who
supply us with our loftiest religious literature, and are yet a byword for
their craft, their scheming, and their love of money; who have supplied
us with our highest ideals of nobility, and our lowest types of villainy;
who have played so great a part in the history of the past, and are
only waiting now for the final catastrophe which is to replace them in
the van of the world's progress.

No thoughtful man can ignore this wonderful people. Their history
is, without doubt, the key to the complications of modern politics;
and it may be that their redemption is to be the fruit of that mighty
travail, which is beginning to convulse all peoples, announced as it is,
by throes of earthquake and the rumors of war.

---

[*] The word "Hebrew," according to the generally-accepted interpretation, signifies *the
man who had crossed the river-flood*—the man who came from beyond the Euphrates.
(See Stanley's *Jewish Church*, i, p. 10.)

If we can understand the life of Jacob, we can understand the history of his people. The extremes which startle us in them are all in him. Like them, he is the most successful schemer of his times; and, like them, he has that deep spirituality and that far-seeing faith which are the grandest of all qualities, and make a man capable of the highest culture that a human spirit can receive. Like them, he spends the greatest part of his life in exile, and amid trying conditions of toil and sorrow; and, like them, he is inalienably attached to that dear land, his only hold on which was by the promise of God and the graves of the heroic dead.

But Jacob's character was purified by tremendous discipline. The furnace into which he was cast was heated one seven times more than it is wont to be heated for ordinary men. He stands among the peers in the kingdom of sorrow; and through it all he passed into a peerage of moral and spiritual power, which made the mightiest monarch of his times bend eagerly for a blessing from his trembling hand. Through such discipline his people have been passing for centuries; and surely, before its searching fires, the baser elements of their natures will be expelled, until they recognize the true Joseph of their seed—who has sent them many generous gifts; whom yet they have not known, but towards whom they are certainly being brought. Then shall they share His glory (Gen. 45:13, 18); and they shall be among many people, "as a dew from the Lord" (Mic. 5:7); yea, in them shall be fulfilled the ancient promise, "I will bless thee; and thou shalt be a blessing" (Gen. 12:2).

II. JACOB ALSO HAS SO MANY POINTS OF CONTACT WITH OURSELVES. Newman has said truly, "Abraham was a hero; Jacob was a plain man dwelling in tents. Abraham we feel to be above ourselves; Jacob like ourselves. We no longer stand in the unclouded golden dawn of the patriarchal age; it is overcast with clouds, and is more like our own checkered life."

His *failings* speak to us. He takes advantage of his brother when hard pressed with hunger. He deceives his father. He meets Laban's guile with guile. He thinks to buy himself out of his trouble with Esau. He mixes, in a terrible mingle-mangle, religion and worldly policy. His children grow up to hatred, violence, and murder. He cringes before the

distant Egyptian governor, and sends him a present. Mean, crafty
and weak, are the least terms we can apply to him. But, alas! who is
there that does not feel the germs of this harvest to be within his
own breast, hidden there as seed germs in a mummy case, and only
waiting for favorable conditions to ripen them to the same disastrous
groth. "There goes myself, but for the grace of God."

His *aspirations* speak to us. We, too, have our angel-haunted
dreams, and make our vows when we leave home. We, too, count hard
work a trifle, when inspired by all-mastering love. We, too, cling in a
paroxysm of yearning to the departing angels, that they should bless us
ere they go. We, too, get back to our Bethels, and bury our idols.
We, too, confess ourselves pilgrims and strangers on the earth. We, too,
recognize the shepherd care of God (Gen. 48:15). We, too, wait for
God's salvation (Gen. 49:18).

His *sorrows* speak to us. In every life there is a leaving home to go
forth alone; and a weary struggle for existence; and a limp which reminds us of some awful crisis; and an Allon-bachuth (an oak of weeping, Gen. 35:8); and a lonely grave on the way to Ephrath, which holds
some priceless jewel case; and a lost Joseph; and the grey hairs of sorrow. And we have mourned over hopes, which have mocked us with
their non-fulfillment; "I have not attained" (Gen. 47:9).

What a comfort it is to find that the Bible saints, who now shine
as stars in the firmament of heaven, were men of like passions with ourselves! They were not always saints; they sinned, and murmured, and
rebelled—as we do. Heaven's rarest blades were not wrought of finer
metal than that which is within our constitution. God's choicest vessels were not turned from superior earth to that of which we are
made. The jewels which now lie at the foundation of the new Jerusalem
were once obscure, unnamed men of no finer texture than ourselves.
Look to the quarry whence they were hewn, and the hold of the pit
whence they were digged; and say if there was much to choose between
their origin and your own. And then, take heart; for if God were able
to take up such men as Jacob, and Simon Bar-Jona, and make of
them princes and kings, surely He can do as much for you. The discipline may be keen as fire, but the result shall be glorious: and all eternity shall ring with the praises of Him who raises up the poor out of

the dust, and lifts up the beggar from the dunghill, and makes them kings and priests unto God.

III. In Jacob we can trace the Workings of Divine Love. "Jacob have I loved" (Mal. 1:2). It was *pre-natal* love. Before the child was born, it was the object of God's love (Rom. 9:11). In God's heart all his members were written, when as yet there was none of them. Though God forecasted his disposition and habits, yet He loved him. It is ever sweet to rest on a love which is dated not in time but eternity, because one feels that as God's love did not originate in any unforeseen flash of excellence in us, so it will not be turned away by any unexpected outbreak of depravity. It did not begin because of what we were; and it will continue in spite of what we are.

It was *fervent* love. So strong that, in comparison, the love which shone around Esau might be almost termed hatred (Rom. 9:13). For God loved Esau as he loves all men. He hates nothing that He has made. But there were as many degrees of temperature between His love to Jacob and that to Esau, as there are in human hearts between love and hate. Sometimes in an early morning the moon shines in the same sky as the sun—her beams still fall on all things, but one might almost assert that she did not shine, by reason of the brilliance of his beams. So was it with these two men. And who shall find faith? There must be degrees in the love of God. Was there not one disciple "whom Jesus loved?" (See also Matt. 10:37 and Luke 14:26).

It was a *disciplinary* love. We have low thoughts of love. *We* can only count that as love which caresses, and soothes, and says sweet things, and makes of itself a shield so that no rough wind may breathe on us. We have no notion of a love that can say, "No"; that can use the rod, and scourge, and fire; that can sustain the long discipline by which the mean and false and evil elements are driven out of the beloved soul. But such is the love of God. "The grace of God hath appeared, bringing salvation to all men, instructing us" (disciplining us, Titus 2:12, R.V.). So it came to Jacob.

If we had been asked to tell which of these two men was Heaven's favorite, we should, in all likelihood, have selected the wrong one.

Here stands Esau, the shaggy, broad-shouldered, red-haired hunts-man, equipped with bow and arrows, full of generous impulse, affec-tionate to his aged father, forgiving to the brother who had done him such grievous wrong. He became a chieftain of renown, and the an-cestor of a princely line (Gen. 36). He was happy in his wives and chil-dren; we read of no such outbreaks as embittered Jacob's lot. He was so rich that he could make light of Jacob's presents; and so powerful that Jacob's company was helpless in his hand. His people were happily set-tled in their rich territories; while the children of Jacob were groaning in Egyptian bondage. And, as we consider him, we are inclined to im-itate the words of Samuel, when Jesse's eldest son entered his presence, and say: "Surely, the Lord's anointed is before Him!"

There, on the other hand, is Jacob. In his young manhood, an exile from his father's house. In his mature manhood, a hireling, in the employ of a kinsman. In his declining years, worn by anxiety and trouble. In his old age, a stranger in a strange land. Few and evil were the days of the years of his pilgrimage. Yet *he* was the beloved of God; and it was because of that especial love that he was exposed to such searching discipline. "Whom the Lord loveth He chasteneth, and scourgeth every son whom He receiveth" (Heb. 12:6).

Earthly prosperity is no sign of the special love of Heaven; nor are sorrow and care any mark of God's disfavor, but the reverse. "Jesus loved Martha, and her sister, and Lazarus. When He had heard, therefore, that he was sick, He abode where He was," and let Lazarus die. God's love is robust, and true, and eager—not for our comfort, but for our lasting blessedness; it is bent on achieving this, and it is strong enough to bear misrepresentation and rebuke in its attempts to attune our spir-its to higher music. It therefore comes instructing us.

Let us enter ourselves as pupils in the school of God's love. Let us lay aside our own notions of the course of study; let us submit ourselves to be led and taught; let us be prepared for any lessons that may be given from the blackboard of sorrow; let us be so assured of the inexhaustible tenacity of His love, as to dare to trust Him, though He slay us. And let us look forward to that august moment when He will give us a rea-son for all life's discipline, with a smile that shall thrill our souls with ecstasy, and constrain sorrow and sighing to flee away forever.

IV. Jacob's Life gives a Clue to the Doctrine of Election.
There was election here. The Apostle Paul uses it to illustrate that mysterious truth (Rom. 9:11). And it is obviously so. Jacob was the younger son; and his life is as much a Gospel for younger sons as is that matchless parable of the prodigal. The children were not born when God foretold and fixed their destiny.

It is impossible to ignore election; it has been truly said to be the the key to the order of all nature and history. "There are elect angels; elect stars; elect races of animals; elect flowers and fruits; elect human souls. Nowhere do we meet with equality, uniformity, the monotony of a dull level. Everywhere things and beings, with superior endowment to other things and beings, seem made to head them, and sweep them along in the orbit of their motion by the attraction of the superior on the inferior spheres. One star differs from another star in glory; some flash forth resplendent, regal gems in the diadem of night, while others are scattered faint and dim like seed pearls on her dusky robe."

So is it with souls. Some men are evidently born to be the leaders, teachers, masters of mankind. Thus it was with Jeremiah the prophet (Jer. 1:5); with Cyrus the conqueror (Is. 45:1, 4); and John the Baptist (Luke 1:17)—and these are types of myriads more.

But to what are these elect? To comfort, ease, success? Nay, for these things fall to the lot rather of the Esaus than the Jacobs. The elect of God seem chosen to stand in the front rank, and bear the brunt of the storms of sorrow, pain, and care.

Are they, then, elect to personal salvation? Many of the cases in which the words occur do not demand this as their exclusive meaning. Indeed, Scripture does not certainly exclude Esau himself from a share in Abraham's bosom. He lost his birthright, truly, and he could not recover it by strong cryings and tears, but the loss of his birthright did not necessarily entail the loss of his soul.

But may we not hold that election refers largely, if not primarily, to the *service* which the elect are qualified to render to their fellows throughout all coming time? They are elect, not for themselves, or for the sake of their own future, but rather for the sake of the work which their position of privilege may enable them to do for mankind.

This, certainly, has been one result of the election of Jacob and his people. They were elect to be the spiritual leaders and teachers of mankind; to furnish us with a matchless religious literature; to provide a suitable platform on which the Savior of the world should appear, and from which He might influence the world. Not for the sake of their own comfort, but for the sake of the dark and dying world, God gave them light and life, and sustained them in existence against overwhelming odds, and stored in them streams of electric force, as in some mighty battery.

This, then, will explain also the terrific discipline through which they passed. It was needed, not for their sakes alone, but also for the race they were destined to serve; that they might be set free from deteriorating influences, and stand forth as God's chosen vessels, brimming with blessing for the world.

Seeking souls need not then concern themselves with this mysterious subject. Outside the house of salvation, there is no word but this—"whosoever." When once we have crossed the threshold and looked around, we may find some such text as that with which Peter begins his first epistle; and we may find that God had some purpose of mercy to others, when He first drew us to Himself.

But his and many other similar questions will receive new and beautiful illustrations, as we pursue our studies of Jacob's life.

The Sale of the Birthright

We shape ourselves the joy or fear
Of which the coming life is made;
And fill our future's atmosphere
With sunshine or with shade.
The tissue of the life to be
We weave with colors all our own;
And in the fields of Destiny
We reap as we have sown.

Genesis 25   Whittier

Brothers were these two men, yes, twin brothers, but brothers could not differ more widely. Before their birth their difference was foretold. At their birth it was evident. From their birth it began to broaden and increase. The linked hands of the brothers, reaching across the tiny rill of their earliest infancy, were soon parted, as the stream of life widened between them, and they passed to their destiny along the opposite banks.

They differed in appearance. Esau was rough, ruddy, and hairy. He would give the impression of great bodily strength; capacity for vast physical fatigue; and a temperament which would incline him to exciting and hazardous pursuits. Jacob was the reverse: smooth in skin; dark in feature; slight in build; no match for his burly brother in physical force, but more than his match in guile.

They differed in pursuits. Esau was a cunning hunter, a man of the field and chase. Had he been living now, he would have been foremost in all manly, daring, outdoor sports. Nor would it be difficult to find his duplicate today among our high-born youth: with handsome face, generous disposition, and open hand; quick to resent, and quick to forgive; perfect in dress; polished in manner; a rare shot, a splendid rider, an expert in all manly exercise; and certain to marry well—as Esau did—and found a strong and noble house. Jacob, on the other hand, loved the home life. The violent exercise and hazards for which Esau pined, as an imprisoned eagle for its rocky, storm-beaten crags, had no fascination for him. And while Esau was away, he was content to dwell among the flocks and herds of the camp; content with the peaceful occupations of an uneventful pastoral life. Each man to his taste!

They differed most in character. There is much in Esau which makes us like him; and we should have been certainly more quickly attracted to him than to his brother. If he was impetuous, he was generous. If he was rash, he was frank. If he was singularly wanting in religious fervor, he was a good son. If his heart doted on the pleasures of the chase, he was splendid company, and every inch a man. But, for all this, he was decidedly sensual—Scripture calls him *profane*—i.e., he was a slave to his senses; he hailed anything that would thrill him with pleasant though transient excitement; he was willing to purchase pleasure at any price, though he had to pawn the most priceless jewels of his spirit; he was, indeed, too enamored with the claims of the passing hour to care for unseen realities; or to seek the eternal harvest which lies beyond the bitter sowing times of patience, and waiting, and pain. Alas, that he should have had such a host of imitators!

Jacob was a "plain" man (a 'quiet' man, R.V. *marg.*), but under that calm exterior there were depths and depths. Amid all the craft and duplicity of his nature, there was immense capacity for religious fervor and religious faith. He could understand, as Esau never could, the meaning of the birthright, with all its spiritual glow and glory. He could draw aside the veil of the unseen, and weigh its promises, and compare its treasures with the shows of earth. He could dream angel-haunted dreams, that threw a mystic ladder over the abyss of space, linking all worlds. And while Esau was occupied with pleasure, Jacob would feel within him the strange stirrings of a nature which could not be satisfied with anything within the narrow limits of his tents, but which yearned for that spiritual heritage which was summed up in the word "birthright."

Let us consider—the Birthright; the Barter; and the Bitter Cry.

I. THE BIRTHRIGHT. What was it? It was not worldly prosperity; for though Esau lost it, he had an abundant fortune: four hundred armed retainers followed at his heel; the great country of Edom owned his sway; till, after a life of splendid and unbroken prosperity, he went down to the grave in peace and a good old age. There is nothing in the brief record which we have of him to make us think that he lived a broken or disappointed life. All that this world could give was his. The sunshine of worldly prosperity touched with golden light all the wavelets that broke upon the beach of his life. The exceeding bitter wail of momentary disappointment was soon forgotten in his satisfaction at having lost nothing which he really cared for, while so much was still left to him that his soul loved. Whatever the birthright was, it evidently was not worldly prosperity; for of this, Esau, who lost it, probably had more than Jacob, who won it.

It was not immunity from sorrow. When Jacob had secured it, it seemed as if the mystic box of Pandora had been opened in his home; for every human ill was let free into his life. Staff in hand, he tears himself from home, and seeks a distant country. A hireling in a kinsman's house, he spends the best years of manhood's prime. Halting on his thigh, he bows before Esau; buries his favorite Rachel; chafes over the open sores of his home life; is bereaved of his children; and moans that the days of the years of his pilgrimage have been evil and few. Few have trodden a more rugged path, or bound about their brows a crown more set with thorns. It was a sad and weary life that breathed itself out in that hieroglyphed chamber in the land of the Pharaohs, when for the last time he gathered his feet into his bed, and was gathered unto his people. Whatever the birthright was, it evidently was not freedom from pain and grief; for of these, Jacob, who won it, had infinitely more than Esau, who lost it.

The birthright was a spiritual heritage. It gave the right—which ever belonged to its possessor—of being the priest of the family or clan. It carried the privilege of being the depository and communicator of the Divine secrets. It constituted a link in the line of descent by which the Messiah was to be born into the world. The right of wielding power with God and men; the right of catching up and handing on—as in the old Greek race—the torch of Messianic hope; the right of heirship to the promises of the covenant made to Abraham; the right of standing among the spiritual aristocracy of mankind; the right of being a pilgrim of eternity, owning no foot of earth, because all heaven was held in fee—this, and more than this, was summed up in the possession of the birthright.

It was a fair heritage, but a fairer one is the birthright of every reader of these lines. You have been born into a world which has been trodden by the feet and wet by the tears of the Son of God. You have been born of a race whose redemption has been purchased at the exceeding great price of His precious blood. You have been born of a nature which has been taken up by Him, who passed by that of angels. And such a birth carries with it rights, given by the matchless grace of God, which as much outshine the birthrights of the old world, as the regalia of England does the crown of Alfred.

Your birth gives you the right to be translated from the kingdom of darkness into the kingdom of God's dear Son; the right to claim of the Holy Ghost the second birth; the right to be forgiven and saved; the right to become the sons and daughters of the Lord God Almighty; the right to stand side by side with the Son in His glory, joint heirs with Him of all that is His; the right to be more than conquerors over all the power of our foes; the right to be delivered from sin, and to join the jubilant throng that stands on the shores of the sea of glass mingled with fire.

This may be your glorious heritage. It cannot be purchased, or won by might of arm. It is reserved for those only who, having been born of woman, have also been born of the Holy Ghost. It may be amid tears and storm that the heart will first realize its right to participate in this inheritance; yet, even then, the thought and hope of its future heritage will cheer the spirit when passing through the stern discipline of life, on its way to the promised rest. That hope shall not be shamed. And surely it will be the standing marvel of eternity that a destiny so bright was ever put within the reach of the fallen children of this sin-cursed earth.

II. THE BARTER. One day Jacob was standing over a caldron of savory pottage, made of those red lentils which to the present day form a dish highly relished in Syria and in Egypt. The appetizing odor soon filled the air, enticing enough for a full, to say nothing of a hungry man. At that moment, who should come in but Esau, faint with hunger. He did not know the name: his active life left him little time for such trifles as domestic cookery, but the sight and smell were quite enough to convince him that Jacob's preparations would be marvelously suitable to stay the cravings of his hunter's hunger. "Give me some of that red—that red," he cried impatiently.

Now Jacob was not wholly a selfish man, but it suddenly occurred to him that this would be a good opportunity of winning the right to be the spiritual leader of the clan. So, knowing well how little his brother counted on his rights, he made the extraordinary proposal to exchange the mess of pottage for the birthright.

Esau closed with the proposal. "Behold," said the bluff hunter, "I am on the point to die; and what profit shall this birthright do to me?" On the one hand was the birthright—a myth, so far as he could see, a vision of the far future, wholly unseen and spiritual. On the other hand was this pottage, right before him, and very tempting to his hunger. So he made over his birthright to Jacob. And Jacob gave him bread and pottage of lentils; and he did eat and drink, and went his way—not, I think, without some qualms of conscience: and thus Esau despised his birthright.

We cannot exonerate either of these men from blame. Jacob was not only a traitor to his brother, but he was faithless towards his God. Had it not been distinctly whispered in his mother's ear that the elder of the brothers should serve the younger? Had not the realization of his loftiest ambition been pledged by One whose faithfulness had been the theme of repeated talks with Abraham, who had survived during the first eighteen years of his young life? He might have been well assured that what the God of Abraham had promised He was able also to perform; and would perform, without the aid of his own miserable schemes. But how hard is it for us to quietly wait for God! We are too apt to outrun Him; to forestall the quiet unfolding of His purposes; and to snatch at promised blessings before they are ripe.

And as for Esau, we can never forget the beacon words of Scripture: "Look diligently, lest there be any profane person, as Esau, who for one morsel of meat sold his birthright" (Heb. 12:6). Yet let us, in condemning him across the ages, look close at home. How many are there among ourselves, born into the world with splendid talents; dowried with unusual powers; inheritors of noble names; heirs to vast estates; gifted with keys to unlock any of the many doors to name, and fame, and usefulness—who yet fling away all these possibilities of blessing and blessedness, for one brief plunge into the Stygian pool of selfish and sensual indulgence!

The strongest and bravest men in build and muscle are often the weakest in resisting the appeals of momentary passion. Esau is mastered by the fragrance of a mess of pottage; Samson by the charms of a Philistine girl; Peter by the question of a servant. There is no strength apart from the strong Son of God.

And the appeals to sense come most often when we are least expecting them. When we say, Peace and safety, then sudden destruction comes. The foe creeps through the postern gate. The arrow penetrates the joints of the harness. The moment of crisis is the moment when we come in from the dangers of the chase to the home which promised us immunity from the attack. "Watch ye, therefore, and pray always; that ye may be accounted worthy to escape all these things."

These appeals, moreover, come in the most trivial things. One mess of pottage; one glass of drink; one moment's unbridled passion; one afternoon's saunter; a question and an answer; a movement or a look. It is in such small things—small as the angle at which railway lines diverge from each other to east and west—that great alternatives are offered and great decisions made. When we fail in some such thing, we often comfort ourselves with the reflection that we could and would do right in some all-important crisis. We cannot pray in a bedroom, but we could burn at a stake. We cannot speak to an individual, but we could preach at a Pentecost. We little understand ourselves. We do not see that trifles are the truest test of character; and that if we cannot run with footmen, we certainly could not contend with horses; and if we have been wearied in the land of peace, we certainly shall stand no chance when we are called to battle with the swellings of Jordan. There are no trifles in Christian living. Everything is great, because the mightiest events revolve on the smallest pivots; and the greatest harvests for good and ill spring from the tiniest seeds.

Had we been at Esau's side, how eagerly should we have laid our hand upon his shoulder, entreating him to pause and consider, before he bartered the spiritual for the physical; the eternal for the temporal; the unseen for the seen. "Will it pay?" "Is it wise?" "Will you get an equivalent for that which you forfeit now forever?" And such questions are asked still of all Esaus who are tempted to barter their peace, their manhood, their heaven, for one mess of the devil's pottage. It steams. It smells savory. It promises to do more good to you than all the Bible put together. The tempter whispers, "Thou shalt not surely die. Bow down and worship me, and all shall be thine. Give me that which thou hast; and I will give thee this and much more." Then it is that a still small voice asks, "What shall it profit a man if he gain the world and lose himself? How much less will it profit him to lose his all for one small mess of pottage, which will only secure a brief respite from the cravings of appetite." Learn to master appetite in Christ's strength; this will serve thee better far than warding off its urgency for a time, leaving it to return with whetted hunger, like a pack of wolves which have tasted blood. "Hold that fast which thou hast, that no man take thy crown."

III. THE BITTER CRY. When Esau saw that God had taken him at his word, and had taken away from him the birthright of spiritual primacy, "he cried with an exceeding great and bitter cry" (Gen. 28:34, R.V.). But that cry came too late to alter the consequences of his rash act. "He found no place of repentance" (no way to change his father's decision), "though he sought it carefully with tears."

"No place of repentance!" On many hearts those words have rung the knell of hope. As the heartbroken sinner has reviewed a blighted past with bitter tears and cries, the adversary of souls has whispered that he has sinned too deeply for repentance, and wandered too far to return; and he has backed the insinuation with these terrible words—*"no place of repentance."*

And is it so? Is it possible for a soul, on this side of death, to reach a position where tears and prayers will strike against the brazen heavens, and rebound, only an echo? It cannot be. It is possible that a man should become too callous and hard to desire salvation: *this* is the sin unto death; *this* is the sin that hath never forgiveness; and it has no forgiveness because the sinner does not desire or seek it. But it is impossible for a man to desire to repent and not find a ready help in the grace of the Holy Ghost. It is impossible for a man to seek forgiveness with bitter tears, and not obtain it. It is impossible for a man to knock at the door of mercy, and not find it open at last, though after long delay: "All manner of sin and blasphemy shall be forgiven unto me." In point of fact, these desires and tears and prayers are blessed symptoms that the work of grace and forgiveness has begun within the soul. They are not of man; or of the will of the flesh: but of God. And when God puts His hand to the plow in a human spirit, He never looks back.

But the "repentance" mentioned here is not repentance to salvation, but the power of reversing the past. Esau could not undo what he had done. He had long despised his birthright. That act of surrender was not a solitary one, but the outcome of a state of heart. It simply revealed thoughts that had been long admitted guests in the inner chamber of his being. But when once this temper had taken effect in a definite promise, asseverated by an oath, God held him to it—yea, nature and righteousness and conscience held him to it too; and he could not alter it by his tears or bitter cries.

The sinful past is irrevocable. Eve might bitterly regret her choice, but as she stood with Adam outside the cherub-guarded gate, with the faded rose in her hand—of which Rabbis tell us—her bitter regrets could not replace the apple on the tree, or reinstate her within the golden bowers of Paradise. Peter went out and wept bitterly, but those tears of uncontrollable anguish could not recall the words of denial, or blot from his memory that look of pain. The Virgins might beat their breasts in bitter self-reproach, but no complaints, however pitiable, could reverse the decision of the Bridegroom's lips.

We all know this. We remember bursts of passion which have broken hearts; sundered ties of love; clouded sunny skies; withered hopes; and shattered promising prospects. We would give worlds to blot out the record, and to make them as if they had never been. But it is impossible. We cannot bring back the shadow on the dial. We cannot reverse the writing of the faithful chronicler. We cannot find a chance for altering the decisions, which had been long floating in solution in our minds, but which have had one fatal and irrevocable crystallization in word or act. There is no place of repentance, though we seek it carefully and with tears. You cannot undo.

But though the past is irrevocable, it is not irreparable. In the garden of Gethsemane our Lord said mournfully to the chosen three, "Sleep on now, and take your rest," but He instantly added, "Arise: let us be going." In the first sentence, He taught the irrevocableness of the past; they might as well sleep, for any good that watching could now do. But in the second sentence, he taught that there was still a future before them, with new chances, and opportunities, and hopes.

So shall it ever be. God Himself cannot undo the past. But He can and will forgive. He will not mention the past, but give us a fair, fresh start. He will even "restore the years that the cankerworm has eaten." He will give us new opportunities of showing how truly we repent the decisions of the past; and how loyally we desire to serve Him in the decisions of the future. He will not even mention the thrice denial, but He will give us three opportunities of saying how much we love Him, as He thrice bids us tend His flock. "The King is dead!"—that is the proclamation of the irrevocable past. "Long live the King!"—that is the announcement of an available future.

3

The Stolen Blessing

No action, whether foul or fair,
Is ever done, but it leaves somewhere
A record, written by fingers ghostly
As a blessing, or a curse; and mostly
In the greater weakness or greater strength
Of the acts which follow it: till at length
The wrongs of ages are redressed
And the justice of God made manifest.

Genesis 25   Anonymous

In many a picturesque English village there lies a pond of stagnant water, which has been there as long as the oldest inhabitant can remember. It looks innocent enough when the winds of March sweep it, or the leaves of October bestrew it, but when it is exposed to the scorching rays of a summer sun, it pours forth volumes of poisonous gases, which had lurked unnoticed in its depths, and typhoid fever is sown in the homes that cluster round. Such is the heart of man. We do not think, we do not care to know, how much evil lies within. We read with listless interest the terrible photograph given by One who could not exaggerate (Mark 7:21); and attach a vague meaning to other words which characterize the human heart as "desperately wicked." And yet we do not feel so bad; nor shall we truly verify those words; nor realize how evil our nature is; or what a dying need we have for God—until we have been exposed to some searching test, which shall reveal us to ourselves.

Temptation is such a test. There is no sin in being tempted. Our great High Priest was "tempted in all points like as we are, yet without sin." And temptation need not necessarily lead to sin; so long as the steadfast will, inspired by the Holy Spirit, keeps the door of the nature shut and locked. Nay, temptation is even a blessing: "Blessed is the man that endureth temptation," when it leads a man to discover tendencies, movement, appetites within him—unknown before, but against which he must henceforth be on his guard.

God our Father permits us to be tempted, to lead us to see the hidden evils of our heart—to hold up a looking glass before us, in which we may behold what manner of people we are; and to make us so sensible of our own worthlessness and deformity as to drive us to hand ourselves over to Him, to do anything He may please, if only we may be delivered out of this body of death. To know oneself, and to despair of oneself, is to come within the sweep of that gracious power, which can fashion a temple column out of a bruised reed; and a noble vessel out of a lump of clay; and an Israel out of a Jacob.

We need not be at all astonished, then, to learn that temptation was allowed to come to Jacob from an unexpected source, taking him unawares. And if you are truly desirous of ascending the higher reaches of Christian thought and life, you must not be astonished if, in answer to your prayer for more grace and life, your heavenly Lover should take some unexpected means of showing you what you are. So Newton found—

> I asked the Lord that I might grow
> In faith, and love, and every grace;
> Might more of His salvation know,
> And see the glory of His face.
>
> Instead of this, He made me feel
> The hidden evils of my heart;
> And let the angry powers of hell
> Assault my soul in every part.

I. The Temptation originated in a sensuous request of Isaac. We sometimes find it hard to think that the Isaac of this chapter is the same person as the submissive boy who carried the altar wood on his stalwart young shoulders, and wondered about the lamb, and meekly submitted to be bound as a sacrifice. That was a radiant dawn for a human life, which for some reason became quickly overcast.

What was that reason? Was it the prosperity of which we read in the previous chapter? "The man waxed great, and went forward, and grew until he became very great." It would not be the last time that prosperity has choked off spiritual growth. Was it a too-easy disposition, of which we catch a glimpse in his readiness to abandon well after well, if only he might be left in peace? It would not be the only time that a molluscous lack of backbone has barred the path of a noble career. Was it an inordinate love for the pleasures of the table? There seems to have been too much of this in his constitution. He said to Esau, "Make me savory meat, such as I love." Rebekah was keenly aware of her husband's weakness in this respect: "I will make for thy father savory meat such as he loveth." There is a sad suggestiveness in all this, and enough to account for all. The man who, on the supposed point of death, thinks most of all of a good dish of delicious venison, is not likely to shine as a specially brilliant star in the heavenly firmament.

We need to take warning against the twin sins of gluttony and drunkenness. Intemperance in eating may not result in the same outward degradation as in drinking, but it is as harmful to the spirit. The question is, whether average Christian people do not eat much more than is good for the health of either body or spirit. Certainly the world and the Church are filled with numberless cases of men, the brilliance of whose minds has been obscured, and the edge of their spiritual life blunted, by their habitual and greedy indulgence in superfluous and luxurious food. With every grace we say at our meals, we need to ask that we may eat and drink, not merely at our own caprice, but to the glory of God. "Take heed to yourselves, lest at any time your hearts be overcharged with *surfeiting*, and drunkenness, and cares."

Many years had passed since that memorable day on Mount Moriah; and many signs told Isaac that his sun was setting. Chief among these was dimming sight. God has mercifully arranged that such reminders, like warning bells, should ring out to show us how far we have traveled, and how near we are to the terminus of life. Many a man, who otherwise had dropped carelessly into the grave, has been awakened by such things to say to himself, "Behold, now I am old; I know not the day of my death. I must begin to prepare for the final act."

There are glimpses of the better things in Isaac's character in the threefold preparation he made for his end.

He made his last testamentary disposition. If you have not done this, do it at once—no time is so good as this. Leave nothing uncertain; nothing to chance; no loophole for heart burning or heartbreak among your heirs. *He laid aside his earthly cares.* He lived for several years after this, but he was a man set apart. It was the gloaming of his life; not quite dark, yet not light enough to work—the fittest time for meditation and prayer. It was ever the ambition of Dr. Chalmers to have such a time of Sabbath calm after the busy rush of his life of working days, and before the final act. *He handed on the blessing.* Even though he proposed to counterwork the purposes of God, yet there is a significant beauty in the desire of the old man to bless before he died. Aged people, we younger ones have surely a right to expect some blessing, ere you leave us, of ripe counsel; of matured wisdom; of prophetic experience.

II. This Temptation was presented to Jacob through the Unscrupulous Love of Rebekah. Jacob was her favorite son. There was a closer relationship between them than there could be between her and the more random Esau. As soon as she overheard Isaac's request to Esau, she resolved at once to win his blessing for her younger boy. And if a momentary qualm suggested itself, she, doubtless, quieted it by the reflection that she was simply trying to ratify the bargain which he had made for himself.

We cannot but admire her love. She threw herself away on this lad, whom she was never to see again. She was reckless of personal consequences. She cared not what might come to herself, so that he might win. "Upon me be thy curse, my son." For him she sacrificed husband, elder son, principle—*all*. It is with such prodigality of affection that women constantly give themselves for their beloved. Their love is often worthy of a better object; and yet it is beautiful. Oh that all such knew of Him on whom the saint of the home at Bethany, and the sinner in the house of Simon, broke their alabaster boxes in a very prodigality of love, and yet there was no waste!

But Rebekah's love was not based on principle. And such love is as terrible as the fire which has burst from the restraints of iron bars, and leaves behind it a scorched and blackened trail. Love is either the bliss or bane of life: it is bliss, if rooted and grounded in an all-mastering and all-penetrating devotion to purity, truth, principle—or in a word, to God, but it is curse, if, like some pirate crew, it steers the ship of life according to its own wild whim. Let us keep our hearts above all that we guard, since out of them are the issues of life. And if we are ever prompted to act according to the strong solicitation of mere natural affection, let us remember the havoc which such a course produced in that far-off Eastern home, under the black tents of the patriarch Isaac: how it deceived the husband; wronged the elder son; drove the younger to an enforced exile; and blasted the reputation of this woman, who otherwise had been honored and beloved.

But Rebekah is not the only mother who has acted thus. As we review her life, we find its counterpart in many: who will scheme, maneuver, palter with truth and righteousness, and cast even conjugal love into the scale, if only, at all hazards, they can advance the interests of their child. How little do they realize the harvest of which these are the seeds—a harvest of misery for the home; of heart burning and hatred; of sorrow for those whom they would benefit; and of heartbreaking anguish for themselves.

In another sense than our Savior meant, a man's foes may be they of his own household. We exert a vast influence—not only by what we say, but by the spirit of our lives—on those who dwell under the same roof, and address us by the tenderest names. And, alas! this influence is often sadly averse to their nobler life, withering it, as gas does flowers. They see us in our most careless moments, when we have ungirded ourselves, and lie at ease on the grass. They catch up our least guarded words. They take us at a disadvantage, when, biased by love, we try to solve their problems and answer their questions so as to make life's pathway as easy as possible for their feet. And one drop of poison instilled into the heart by a loved and trusted friend is enough to spoil a life. We drink more unquestioningly of the poisoned chalice, when put to our lips by one we love. We enter more unsuspectingly the pathway to ruin, when the hand of parent or friend points the way. The course of deceit is less forbidding, when urged on us by those who, like Rebekah, can gain nothing if we succeed; who are willing to assume all responsibility if we fail; and who profess that they are inspired by no other motive than the most unselfish devotion to our interests.

How careful should we be, then, of all suggestions and advice we give to those accustomed to look up to us; lest, wittingly or not, we should place a stumblingblock and occasion to fall in another's way. In such matters affection is no true guide, unless regulated, as God's is, by the dictates of righteousness and truth; if these be absent, there is terrible danger lest we should make again the mistake of Rebekah, and follow again in the footsteps of her sin, against her sons, herself, and her God.

III. This Temptation was greedily responded to by the Weak and Crafty Nature of Jacob. Jacob was not a thoroughly vicious man, but he was deplorably weak: and weakness is close akin to the sin to which it inevitably leads. He would not have concocted this plot or laid the train himself. He would have preferred not to act the liar. He was really afraid of the result. But he had not the courage to say "No" to the strong will and wish of his mother, especially when she was ready to take all risks. He tried to quiet his conscience by the consideration that he was only trying to get his own; and that Esau had no right to think of getting back from their father the birthright which he had certainly sold. And so, when his mother put strong pressure on him, summoning him by the obedience he owed her as her son (v. 8), he weakly did not refuse on the ground that it was unlawful, but suggested it was inexpedient, lest they should be found out. "Behold, Esau my brother is a hairy man, and I am a smooth man; my father peradventure will feel me, and I shall seem to him as a deceiver, and I shall bring a curse upon me, and not a blessing." When a man retreats from the position of what is right, to the urging of what is likely to be expedient and to pay—that man is near a fall, swift as the archangel's from heaven to hell.

Such a fall was Jacob's. It is impossible to emphasize this point too earnestly, especially for the young. So long as we take our stand on what is lawful—as John the Baptist did, when he strode into the royal presence and told Herod that he had *no right* to take his brother's wife—we are impregnable. But when once we retreat from this, and argue with the tempter on the lower grounds of possible discovery and failure, we shall find ourselves outmatched by his arithmetic, and led as garlanded oxen to the slaughterhouse. Into this fault, to which all weak men are so liable, Jacob fell; and so, when, a second time, his mother commanded him to obey her voice (v. 13), and go to the flock for two good kids of the goats, "he went, and fetched, and brought them to his mother."

When once the first step had been taken, it was quickly followed by others which it seemed to render needful. Sin never comes alone. The first act of sin is like the boy put through a narrow window into a burglar-beset house, who creeps round to pen the door for the entire gang; or it is like the first link of the rusty chain, which draws all the rest into the hold of the ship. If the graces come with linked hands, so do the vices. They are sporadic. That first sin of Jacob led to many others.

He simulated his brother's dress and skin. While the meat was cooking, Rebekah was engaged in turning over Esau's wardrobe, to find some suitable garments, highly perfumed, as is the custom with the Easterns to this day. This done, she prepared the delicate skins of the kids for his hands and neck. All was done with haste; lest Esau might come in. And when all was ready, Jacob arrayed himself to play his part.

He deceived his father with a direct falsehood. "I am Esau, thy firstborn; I have done according as thou badest me; eat of my venison, that thy soul may bless me."

He made an impious use of the name of God. In answer to Isaac's question as to how he had found it so quickly, he dared to say, "The Lord thy God brought it to me."

Yet what horror must have thrilled him as he found himself forced to take step after step, aware that he was being carried out by a rushing stream towards an ocean of ink; yet not daring to stop—nay, compelled to press still further out to sea. How his heart must have stood still when the old man became suspicious, and doubted his voice, and insisted on feeling, smelling, and having him near! What if God should strike him dead! What a relief when he came out again in the fresh air, though the words of the coveted blessing hardly repaid him for the agony he had passed through! How he must have loathed himself, and longed to change places with the lizards that crept about the tents, or the little naked slave children that laughed so merrily at play! The sun itself seemed shorn of half its light.

Yet this is the man who became the Prince of God. And if he became so, is there not hope for us, who can trace in him many resemblances to ourselves? "Though we have lien among the pots, yet may we be as the wings of a dove, covered with yellow gold." If the Almighty Workman could fashion such clay into so fair a vessel, what may He not do for us? Our only hope is to hand ourselves over to Him, in an act of entire self-surrender; conscious that we are useless and worthless, deserving rather to be trampled under foot than fashioned by his hand; conscious, too, that if He do not work for us, we are undone; willing to be and do anything He may direct; careful to work *out* all that He may work *in*. If only we will to do this, and yield ourselves to God, and be willing to be made willing to have his will done in us, by us, and about us, then God will be able to work in us also some fair design of beauty and use. Oh, do not mar His work; or lead Him to make of thee some inferior vessel to that which thou mayest become! (Jer. 18:4).

But, remember, God must implant the nature which He educates into Israel the Prince. When we speak of God's education, we must be very careful what we mean, and how we express it; lest we should countenance error. Amidst all his sin, there must have been in Jacob a better self, which was capable of receiving the education of God, and of being developed into Israel. You may call this *faith*, or what you will, but it was there. And it was the possession of this better nature that made Jacob stand in a different relation towards God than Esau did; and made him capable of rising to a spiritual level, for which Esau had neither the aptitude nor the taste.

No doubt the God of love had thoughts of love towards Esau, but there was not, in his worldly nature, the faith, or the elements of nobility, which, through faith, had been implanted in his brother's heart. Put a stone into a flowerpot; cover it with mold; give it water and sunshine, and light and air—it will always be a stone: so if Esau had passed through the discipline of Jacob, he would always have been an

Esau—he never could have been an Israel; unless there had been also in him the better nature which is associated with faith. You may develop intelligence, by education and mind culture, but the faculty must be already present, otherwise your best methods will be abortive. You can develop the rudimentary germ, but when it is absent, you cannot create it. So the discipline of God's grace in a human life can do nothing, unless there be the germ of that new and divine nature of which our Lord spoke to Nicodemus: "That which is born of the flesh is flesh; that which is born of the Spirit is spirit. Ye must be born again."

If, then, you are conscious of a depraved nature, capable of the faults which disfigure the character of Jacob, be anxious to inquire if, besides this, there is the new nature, born of God, and capable of being educated into His image. If it be there, be thankful; and ask the Holy Spirit to lust against and repress the Jacob-nature, so that you may not do the things that you would (Gal. 5:17, R.V.), and to hasten your Israel-beauty. If it be not there, your duty is to look at once to the Lamb of God, who was delivered for your sins, and was raised again for your justification; and the imparting, by the Holy Ghost, of the germ of the new and better nature will be simultaneous with the first real longing, transforming look of faith to the Lord Jesus.

4

The Angel Ladder

Though like the wanderer,
Daylight all gone,
Darkness be over me,
My rest a stone:
Yet, in my dreams, I'd be
Nearer, my God, to Thee,
Nearer to Thee

Genesis 28   S. F. Adams

When Esau found that Jacob had stolen his blessing, he hated him, and vowed to kill him. This was nothing less than might have been expected from his headstrong and impetuous nature. These threats came to Rebekah's ears, and filled her with fear, lest she should be deprived of them both in one day— Jacob, the jewel of her eye, by the hand of his brother; and Esau, by being compelled, like a second Cain, to become an outlaw for his brother's murder.

But there was one source of relief which presented itself to her mother's love and woman's wit. She understood Esau's temperament perfectly. She knew that a passionate, hasty man is less to be feared than a man who gives no sign of the tumult raging within. Rage like Esau's would soon expend itself in words and threats and burn itself out, like a quick and furious fire, for want of fuel. If only Jacob absented himself for a short time, all would be forgotten. So Rebekah made up her mind that he should go across the desert to Haran; to abide for a time with her brother Laban, from whom she had been parted since that memorable day, when, with many a girlish dream floating before her dark eyes, she had started with Abraham's servant for her new home. She did not tell her husband all her reasons—it would have done more harm than good, but she adduced very good and obvious ones, in the necessity of preserving from defilement the holy seed, and of procuring for Jacob a suitable wife.

Isaac fell in with the proposal; and "called Jacob, and blessed him, and charged him, and said unto him, Thou shalt not take a wife of the daughters of Canaan. Arise, go to Padan-aram; and take thee a wife of the daughters of Laban, thy mother's brother. And God Almighty bless thee!" And Jacob, not without many a tear, went out from Beer-sheba, and went toward Haran. And it was on his way that this revelation of the Angel-Ladder was made to him.

I. THE CIRCUMCISION IN WHICH THIS REVELATION WAS MADE TO HIM. Jacob was lonely. He was not what we should call a young man; he had reached mature years: but it is almost certain that this was the first time of his leaving the shelter of his home. Led far from home in pursuit of the fleet deer, his hunter brother may often have passed the night amid the wilds, comfortable and content. But Jacob had no taste for such experiences. For him solitude had no charms; he loved to hear the sounds of human voices, and the stir of the camp. In the early morning light, as he started forth there may have been an exhilarating sense of independence, freshness, and novelty, but as night drew its curtains over the world, and the stars glimmered out of the depths, and the solemn boulders lay so still on the moorland around him—with no tent for shelter, no fire form warmth, no pillow for rest, there stole over his mind a sense of loneliness and melancholy. This was God's chosen time, when He drew near to his spirit, and said, "Behold, I am with thee; and will keep thee in all places whither thou goest; and will bring thee again into this land: for I will not leave thee, until I have done that which I have spoken to thee of." And so it has often been with men. We must be withdrawn from the rush and hum of the busy marketplace, if in the old minister we would see the calm angel faces carved in stone, or hear the thrilling notes of the chorister boys. Recall, for a moment, your first night away from home—as a schoolboy; or apprentice; or servant; or student: and answer, if that were not a sacred epoch in your history, when God took up the trailing tendrils of your love, and twined them around Himself, and you realized His presence, and clung to Him as never before.

Jacob was also standing on the threshold of independence. It is a solemn moment when a man enters on independence—fairly afloat like a swimmer without forks; adrift like a boat's crew who have seen the waves close over their ship. Childhood sleeps peacefully, because it has no responsibilities; the flower is sheathed in its green case; the nestling is fed and shielded by the untiring care of the parent bird. But this does not last long; and none need wish prematurely to exchange such dependence for the independence that must needs care for itself. The child must go forth at last to earn his own living; to win his spurs; to stand alone; to choose and act for himself. It is a solemn crisis.

But it is at such a moment that the Almighty, as a wayfaring man, offers His company for the untrodden path. Happy is he who accepts the proffered help; and transfers the feeling of dependence from the earthly to the heavenly Friend. It is almost worthwhile being cast off by father and mother, if one may be taken up by the Lord. And when one is willing to be taken up by Him, there need be no further anxiety or care; for directly a human spirit yields itself to its Almighty Lover, that moment He takes it, and assumes all responsibility, and makes Himself answerable for all its needs. There is but one condition: "Seek ye first the Kingdom of God, and His righteousness; and all these things shall be added unto you." As Queen Elizabeth said once to one of her Court: "Sir, if you will look after my business, I will make yours my care." Would that all the children of God might know what it is to hand over, moment by moment, as they occur, all worries, anxieties, and cares, to the compassionate Lord, sure that He takes them straight from their hands! We need never feel, then, as if all depended on our tired brain or failing strength, because the Lord Himself would supply all our need, according to his riches in glory. There is, indeed, no real independence for the believer. To be independent of Christ is to be cast forth as a branch to wither. The secret of rest, and fruit, and power, is an abiding union with Him—which time cannot impair, and death cannot dissolve.

Jacob was also in fear. What should hinder Esau, when he heard of his flight, from pursuing him? He was well acquainted with those parts; was fleet of foot; or might use dogs, so as to track him and run him down. Besides, the country was full of robbers and wild beasts. And it was then that God calmed his fears, by showing him that that lone spot was teeming with angel-hosts, willing and eager to encamp about him, with celestial watch and ward. The most lonely spot is as safe for us as the most crowded, since God is there. It is His presence that keeps us safe amid the crowded city; and it is not in the smallest degree withdrawn when, benighted on some desolate moorland, we lay ourselves down to sleep. Into the low dungeon, where the true-hearted prophet lies (Lam. 3:55); into the prison cell, where the heroic apostle awaits his doom (Acts 23:11); into the cabin of the creaking, laboring vessel, threatened each moment with destruction (Acts 27:24)—there comes this assurance of One who cannot lie: "Fear not!" so that we may boldly say, "The Lord is my helper: and I will not fear what man shall do unto me" (Heb. 13:6).

II. THE ELEMENTS OF WHICH THIS REVELATION CONSISTED. The Spirit of God always conveyed His teachings to His servants in language borrowed from their surroundings. John's records of heaven are full of reminiscences of the Aegean; which sometimes murmured around the cliffs of his prison isle as a sea of glass bathed in fire, and at other times broke on them in yeasty foam. David's Psalms make constant reference to the wild hill country of Judea, in which so many of them were composed; Daniel's visions commemorate the giant forms familiar to him in Babylon; and Amos casts his prophecies in molds borrowed from a herdsman's life. So was it here.

Bethel was a bleak moorland that lay in the heart of Palestine. There was nothing remarkable about it; it was "a certain place." The hillsides and upland slopes were strewn with large sheets of bare rock: most of which lay flat upon their faces, like huge fallen gravestones; whilst some few were standing erect, like the cromlechs of our Druid circles.

Fleeing northwards, the wanderer suddenly found himself overtaken by the swift Eastern night, whilst on this desolate and unpeopled waste. There was no help for it but to lie down on the hard ground, taking the stones thereof as a pillow for his head. And thus he slept; and as he slept he dreamed: and in his dream his mind wove together many of his waking thoughts in fantastic medley. The striking appearance of those huge boulders; the memory that Abraham had built one of his earliest altars there, remnants of which may have been still standing; his last look upwards at that wondrous heaven, studded with the brilliant constellations of an Eastern night—all these wove themselves into his dreams. It seemed as if the huge slabs of limestone came near together, and built themselves up into a gigantic staircase, reaching from the spot where he lay to the starry depths above him; and on that staircase angels came and went, peopling by their multitudes that most desolate region, and evidently deeply concerned with the sleeper that lay beneath. Nor was this all; for, from the summit, the voice of God fell like music,

There are here three points of interest.

(1) *The Ladder*. Jacob may have been oppressed by a sense of his insignificance, and sin, and distance from home. And it was very pleasant to know that there was a link between him and God. Earth is not a wandering star: it is bound to heaven, not by the golden chains of which our Laureate sings; not by the iron fetters of necessity, as a slave ship to its captor; not by the silken ties of gravitation which thread the worlds—but by a ladder, denoting communion, fellowship, passage to and fro.

That ladder is Jesus Christ Himself (John 1:51). He took upon Himself our nature, built up from the dust; and in that nature passed upwards from the brow of Olivet, beyond principalities and powers, thrones and dominions, to the very throne of God: and in doing so, He has left a trail of light behind; and become "the way" by which we may approach the High and Lofty One that inhabits eternity, whose name is Holy. There is no other way; "no man cometh unto the Father but by Him." To neglect Him is to drift past the only medium by which a sinner may come into the Light and Love and Life of God. And yet the weakest and most sinful may climb through Jesus from the verge of the pit of hell to the foot of the eternal throne.

> The sons of Ignorance and Night
> May dwell in the Eternal Light
> Through the Eternal Love.

Milton, in his sublime poem, tells how Sin and Death followed the track of Satan, and paved after him a broad and beaten way over the dark abyss, whose boiling gulf tamely endured a bridge of wondrous length from hell, continued to the utmost orb of this frail world; so that the wicked spirits of his court might easily pass to and fro to tempt us mortals. *That* is imagination: *this* is fact, that there is a "Mediator between God and men, the Man Christ Jesus" (1 Tim. 2:5).

Sometimes, when the sky is beclouded, we do not see that across the garden path there sways a ladder of gossamer, linking tree with tree, but when the sun shines, it is revealed by its silver sheen. So, as the infidel looks upwards, he can see no bond of union between this atom of stardust and the metropolis of the universe, until his eyes are opened, and he sees the ladder left by the trail of the departing Savior. Thank God, we are not cut adrift to the mercy of every current; this dark coal ship is moored alongside the bright ship of heavenly grace; yes, and there is a plank from the one to the other.

(2) *The Angels.* The angels ascended: there is the ascent of our prayers. The angels descended: there is the descent of God's answers. We are reminded of the afferent and efferent nerves of the body—up which flash the sharp stings of pain from the extremities to the head; and down which come the directions how to act. It would be well to ponder more frequently the ministering care of the angels. They keep pace with every railway train, at whatever speed it travels, which bears some child of God to his appointed destination. They convoy every ship plowing its way through the troubled sea, which carries an heir of salvation to the haven where he would be. They encamp with horses and chariots of fire about every city, however beleaguered, in which God's servants are found. They minister to our needs. They prepare for us strengthening meals when we sink exhausted on the desert sands and wish to die. They whisper comfort into our troubled hearts. They carry our departing spirits upwards in the hour of death. "And all for love, and nothing for reward." God gives His angels charge concerning us, to keep us in *all* our ways; they bear us up in their hands. "The angel of the Lord encampeth round about them that fear Him, and delivereth them." They are "sent forth to minister to the heirs of salvation."

What comfort Jacob must have realized! He found, to his great surprise, that that lone spot was as thickly populated as *the gate* of some Eastern town, which is the place of concourse and barter. But it was *the gate of heaven;* for it seemed as if the populations of heaven were teeming around him, thronging to and fro; and all engaged in the beneficent work of bringing in the needs of men, and carrying out the blessings of God heaped up, after the overflowing measure with which He is wont to give. We need never yield to feelings of loneliness again, if we remember that, in our most retired hours, we are living in the very heart of a vast throng of angels; and we should hear their songs, and see their forms, if only our sense were not clogged with sin.

(3) *The Voice of God.* God answered his thoughts. He felt lonesome, but God said, "I will be with thee." He feared Esau, but God said, "I will keep thee." He knew not what hardships he might meet with; and God promised to bring him, safely back again. He seemed forsaken of friends, but God gave him the assurance, "I will not leave thee." Appearances seemed to contradict the Divine promise, but God said, "I will do that which I have spoken to thee of." These are precious words, but they only belong to those who lie at the foot of that wondrous Cross which unites earth with heaven. If your place is there, you may freely claim all the comfort that they contain.

Is it not remarkable that Jacob did not see these glorious realities until he slept? God was as much brooding in the wilderness before he slept as afterwards; *only he knew it not.* It was only when he slept that he came to know it. "Gradually slumber stole upon him, and folded him in her arms; gradually the fever cooled, the excitement subsided, the anxiety ceased. He grew tranquil and still; he lost himself—the flurried, heated, uneasy self that he had brought with him from Beersheba: and, *while he slept,* the hitherto unperceived Eternal Presence came out softly, largely, above and around him. He saw His glory, and heard His voice; the solitary waste trembled, flushed, and overflowed with God."[*]

It is impossible to walk with God, unless we have these seasons of quiet vision. Some are ever dwarfed, and driven to and fro by every wind, because they do not make times of respite from the whirl of occupation,

---

[*] Rev. S. A. Tipple.

and the fret of daily work and care. We need to escape from our-selves, our cares and gains, our personal individualities, in order that we may be at leisure to receive the revelations of God. And if we are to have this blessed sleep, it must be the gift of God in answer to our child-like trust.

In our next paper, we shall detail the effect which this marvelous vision produced on the awe-struck fugitive, but ere we close, we ask you to think of that mystic ladder, which descends from the throne of God to the spot, however lowly, where you may be, as you read these lines. It may be a moorland waste; a humble cottage; a ship's cabin; a settler's hut; a bed of pain: but Jesus Christ finds you out, and comes just where you are. The one pole of this ladder is the gold of His Deity; the other is the silver of His Manhood; the rungs are the series of events from the cradle of Bethlehem to the right hand of power, where He sits. That ladder sways beneath a weight of blessing for you. Oh that you would send away your burdens of sin and care and fear, by the hands of the ascending angels of prayer and faith, so as to be able to receive into your heart the trooping angels of peace, and joy, and love, and glory.

5

The Noble Resolve

I slept and dreamt that life was beauty;
I waked and found that life was duty
Was thy dream, then, a shadowy lie?
Toil on, sad heart, courageously,
And thou shalt find thy dream to be
A noon-day light and truth to thee.
Dreams grow holy put in action,
Work grows fair through starry dreaming:
But where each flows on unmingling,
Both are fruitless and in vain.

Genesis 28

A. A. Procter

We are studying the education of a human spirit in the story of Jacob, who became Israel the Prince. But before you can benefit by it, you must be quite sure that there is something in you capable of being educated. Education means *drawing out*; as culture will draw fragrance, color, and graceful beauty, out of the bulb which looks uninteresting and dead. No amount of education could draw such products from a stone. Education only avails when there is some latent germ containing the promise and potency of life. So the discipline of God will be a failure, so far as you are concerned, unless you have got within you, as Jacob certainly had, the principle of a nobler life than that which comes by nature. In a word—Have you been born again? Has there been placed within you, by the Spirit of God, the principle of a new and better life? Is there within you a something which is not of self, or of man, or of the will of the flesh, but of God? If so, you are welcome to acquire any help that may be afforded by a study of God's dealings with Jacob, in whose original constitution there was little to admire. There were *three steps* in God's dealings with this mean and crafty spirit; and, in one form or another, they have a universal application.

227

To begin with, God revealed Jacob to himself. He might have gone on for years in dreamy self-content, ignorant of the evils that lurked within his breast. So a strong temptation was permitted to cross his pathway. There was no necessity for him to yield, but he did yield. And in yielding, he stood face to face with the unutterable baseness of his own heart. A rock, jutting up in the midst of a stream, often reveals the set of the languid current. Fling a strong light into a cave: and the wretched tenants will hurry out screaming, as they behold the loathsome creatures that had crept around them. This is the first step towards soul health. A Nathan must be sent to unveil the evils that fester within, and to accost us with the terrible apostrophe. "Thou art the man!" If, of late, you have begun to see the hidden evils of your heart; and to discover the workings of things of which you could not have supposed yourself capable; and to loathe yourself, as Job did: then take heart. God is dealing with you; and is commencing a work which He will never abandon, till you are presented faultless in His presence, with exceeding joy. The first and indispensable work of the Holy Ghost, in the human spirit, is to convict of sin.

In the next place, God permitted Jacob to suffer the loss of all earthly friends and goods. The prodigal, in the far country, was reduced to heart rending straits. "When he had spent all, there arose a mighty famine in that land: and he began to be in want. And he was sent into the fields to feed swine; and no man gave unto him." And yet he was not much worse off than Jacob was at this moment. We saw in our last chapter that he was lonely, destitute, and in fear. He had little or no property, but a cruse of oil (v. 18) and his staff (32:10). He dreaded his brother's wrath. He was compelled to content himself with a stone for his pillow on the moorland waste. But he was not the last man who has had reason to bless God, to all eternity, for having swept his life clear of much which he had accounted absolutely needful to his existence. The "still small voice" can only be heard when all other voices are hushed. The silver stars can only be seen in the dark. It is when the weary fishers have toiled all the night, without taking a solitary fish, that they are prepared to see, in the morning haze, the form of One who loves them standing on the shore. Do not be surprised if to soul-trial there have been added other bitter trials beside.

Finally, God thrust in Jacob's life a revelation of His love. "Behold, a ladder set up on the earth, and the top of it reached to heaven." That ladder symbolized the love of God. All through his life, that love had surrounded Jacob with its balmy atmosphere, but he had never realized, or returned, or yielded to it. But now it was gathered up and crystallized into one definite appeal, and thrust upon him; so that he could do no other than behold it. And in that hour of conviction and need, it was as welcome as a ladder put down into a dark and noisome pit, where a man is sinking fast into despair; he quickly hails its seasonable aid, and begins to climb back to daylight.

Can you not remember the moment when the love of God in Jesus Christ first broke on you? You were deeply convinced of sin; you dreaded lest at any moment the sword of the Avenger should smite you down; you would have gladly exchanged places with the dumb animals around you; you were broken by trouble, anxiety, and care. And just then you were arrested by the cross of Jesus. At first you only looked on it with the casual gaze of curiosity, but as you looked, your attention became so fixed that you were spellbound. You saw it transfigured beneath the light of heaven; you felt that Divine love shone in those dying eyes; and streamed in tides of blessing from every open wound; and spoke in every accent of that faltering voice. And as you lingered still, there stole into your heart the conviction that it was all for you— a conviction which forced tears to your eyes, and these words from your lips: "He loved *me*, and gave Himself for *me*. *My* sins nailed Him there; *my* curse poured its vials upon that drooping head; *my* stripes broke that royal heart."

"So I saw in my dream, that just as Christian came up with the cross, his burden loosed from off his shoulders, and fell from off his back, and began to tremble; and so continued to do till it came to the mouth of the sepulcher, where it fell in, and I saw it no more. Then was Christian glad and lightsome; and said, with a merry heart,

He hath given me rest by His sorrow,
And life by His death.

Then he stood still awhile to look and wonder; even till the springs that were in his head sent the waters down his cheeks."

Has this been your experience? If not, seek it; ask that your eyes may be opened to see the love of God to you, revealed in the cross of Jesus, and let down into your life. Then will you also give three leaps for joy, and go on your way singing.

The revelation of God's love will have five results on the receptive spirit.

I. IT WILL MAKE US QUICK TO DISCOVER GOD. Jacob had been inclined to localize God in his father's tents: as many localize Him now in chapel, church, or minster; supposing that prayer and worship are more acceptable there than anywhere beside. *Now* he learned that God was equally in every place—on the moorland waste as well as by Isaac's altar, though his eye had been too blind to perceive Him. In point of fact, the difference lay not in God, but in *himself;* the human spirit carries with it everywhere its own atmosphere, through which it may see, or not see, the presence of the Omnipresent. If your spirit is reverent, it will discern God on a moorland waste. If your spirit is thoughtless and careless, it will fail to find Him even in the face of Jesus Christ. There are many men, who might have kept as close to the Apostle Paul as his shadow, who would not have seen one angel vision or heard one heavenly word. On the other hand, if the Apostle were to spend a day with us, he would see traces of the glorious presence of God in our busy streets and wrangling marts. The difference is not in the place, or in the degrees of God's presence, but in the keenness of the spiritual eye, since all places are equally hallowed, and God is everywhere.

When we have been touched and solemnized by some stately service or stirring discourse, we are disposed to say, "This is none other but the house of God; and this is the gate of heaven." But we are not disposed to say as much of the shop or counting house in which we spend the greater part of our time. The reason for this is to be found in the materialism of our spirit. If only we were full of God, we should find that every spot was sacred, every moment hallowed, every act a sacrament; from every incident we should see a ladder stretching up to heaven: and our happy spirits would be constantly availing themselves of the opportunity to run up the shining way and embrace their dearest Lord.

Similarly, when we have met with a great deliverance—as Abraham on Mount Moriah—we are led to exclaim, "This is the finger of God." But we are not apt to say as much of every trivial incident in daily life. The reason, again, is in ourselves. We need the quick insight which only love can give. It was the disciple to whom Jesus had revealed His special love that discerned Him on the lakeshore, and cried, "It is the Lord." And if we were as willing as he was to drink in the love of Jesus, we should be as quick as he was in discerning the presence of the Lord.

Up to this moment, the Lord has been in many of the moorland wastes of your lives, but *you have not known it.* He has been beside you in that lonely chamber of pain; in that irksome situation; on that rugged pathway; by that bitter cross; amid those godless companions; during those hours which you have counted secular and profane—but your eyes have been holden. What wonder that your path has been so drear! But if you will only take home to yourself the message of the cross of Jesus, "God loves me"; and if you will let it shed its perfume through your secret heart—then you will never feel lonely or outcast again. You will be able to see Him where no other eye can discern Him. You will feel the ruddy glow of His love when others carry chilled and torpid hearts. You will discover that a desolate moor is one of the mansions of your Father's house. You will detect your Father's handwriting in every letter; your Father's seal on every parcel; your Father's will in every event. You will be able to commune with Him equally on the hillside as amid the congregation. And you will be often compelled to exclaim, as you meet with fresh revelations of Himself, in the most unlikely places, "*This* is none other but the house of God; and *this* is the gate of heaven."

II. IT WILL INSPIRE US WITH GODLY FEAR. "He was afraid, and said, How dreadful is this place!" "Perfect love casteth out fear"—the fear that hath torment, but it begets us in another fear, which is the beginning of wisdom and the foundation of all noble lives; the fear that reveres God, and shudders to grieve Him; and dreads to lose the tiniest chance of doing His holy will. True love is always fearless and fearful. It is fearless with the freedom of undoubting trust, but it is fearful lest it should miss a single grain of tender affection, or should bring a moment's shadow over the face of the beloved. Those who look from without sometimes rebuke us for dwelling so constantly on the infinite love of God, surrounding us, as the warm Southern seas lap around shores enameled with shells. Some say, "You will lead people to live loosely, if you tell them that there is no sin which may not be instantly forgiven." Ah! they do not know that there are none who fear sin so much as those who know that they are greatly loved. For them every spot is full of the presence of the Beloved. Heaven itself does not more evidently glow with it than each spot of earth. And thus, though all other fear has fled before all-mastering love, there will have come into the spirit another fear, which distrusts self and clings to Christ, and works out its salvation with fear and trembling.

III. IT WILL CONSTRAIN US TO GIVE OURSELVES TO GOD. The ordinary reading might lead us to suppose that, true to his worse self, Jacob tried to make a bargain with God; and promised to take Him as his, on certain conditions. "*If* God will be with me, and keep me in my way, and give me bread to eat and raiment to put on: *then*—" But a better reading relieves him of this sad imputation; and tones the words down to mean that if the Lord would be his God, then the stone should be God's house. But, however the words may run, this was evidently the moment of his consecration. He was constrained by love of God, "no longer to live to himself, but to Him."

Have you done thus, dear reader? It is the sole condition of soul health, and peace, and power. You are Christ's by right, but you have been living as if you were your own, and had never been bought by His precious blood. Is it then to be wondered at, that your life has been such a miserable failure? You are robbing Jesus of His own purchased possession; and you cannot expect to enjoy the fullness of His salvation. Give yourself to Him now. And, as soon as you will to do so, He takes that which you give. Or, if you cannot give yourself, then lie low at His feet, and ask Him to take all you are and have. And so soon as the words have passed your lips, He will answer your prayer, and make you His forever.

IV. IT WILL PROMPT US TO DEVOTE OUR PROPERTY TO HIM. "Of all that Thou shalt give me, I will surely give the tenth unto Thee." There is no reason to doubt that this became the principle of Jacob's life: and if so, he shames the majority of Christian people—most of whom do not give on principle; and give a very uncertain and meager percentage of their income. The Church would have no lack if every one of its members acted upon this principle. Let the proportion be diminished, if you will; though *that* were surely unworthy of us, who sing,

> Were the whole realm of nature mine,
>   That were an offering far too small;
> Love so amazing, so divine,
>   Demands my life, my soul, my all.

But whether the proportion be diminished or not, let each Christian person resolve to give systematically to the Lord's cause; and to put aside, as firstfruits from all profits and receipts, a certain part, which shall be considered as distinctly and exclusively the Lord's, to be applied as He may direct.

There is something better than this—viz., to consider oneself, one's earnings, one's strength, one's all, as belonging to the dear Master; as the rages, and earnings, and jewels, of slaves belonged absolutely to their owners, who had bought them off the block. But many, admitting this theoretically, do nothing practically; and, therefore, it is better to give a regular proportion certainly, and as much more as you choose, as a perpetual reminder that all you have and are is not your own, but Jesus Christ's.

It is failure in this which so often brings barrenness and joylessness into Christian lives. This is the reason that so many of the ascending angels never come down again, or return with empty hands. This is why we sow much, and bring in little; eat, and have not enough; drink, and are not satisfied; and put our wages into a bag with holes. We have robbed God in tithes and offerings. But if we would resolve to give Him tithes of all, and to bring them into His storehouse, we should find that He would open the windows of heaven, and pour us out such a blessing that there would not be room to receive it.

V. IT WILL FILL US WITH JOY. "Then Jacob lifted up his feet" (29:1, *marg.*). Does not that denote the lighthearted alacrity with which he sped upon his way? His feet were winged with joy, and seemed scarcely to tread the earth. All sorrow had gone from his heart; for he had handed his burdens over to those ascending angels. And this will be our happy lot, if only we will believe the love that God hath to us. We, too, shall lose our burdens at the foot of the cross; and we shall learn the blessed secret of handing over, as soon as they arise, all worries and fears to our pitiful High Priest. Then shall our mouth be "filled with laughter, and our tongue with singing." Our heart shall "bubble over with good matter." "Our soul shall make her boast in the Lord; the humble shall hear thereof, and be glad."

6

The Education of Home

Life is only bright when it proceedeth
Towards a truer, deeper Life above;
Human Love is sweetest when it leadeth
To a more Divine and perfect Love.
A. A. Procter

Genesis 29

Next to the love of God comes the love of man or woman, as a factor in the education of a human spirit. Each one of us is capable of giving out a vast wealth of love; we must love and be loved: and almost everything depends on the twin spirit whom we choose as the object of our affection; and as the hearth at whose fires we may warm ourselves, when chilled and repelled by an unfriendly world. That love may make or mar us; may transfigure or degrade us—and which it shall be is settled by the objects whom we choose, and the way in which we treat them.

Jacob's encounter with Rachel at the first well he came to reminds us that though there is nothing more important than the union of heart with heart, there is nothing into which people drift more heedlessly. A fancy, a look, a smile, a touch, a moment's talk in a crowded room, amid the excitement of an evening's gaiety—any of these is deemed sufficient to justify a choice which may affect the destiny of the spirit forever.

Of course we do not deny that Jacob may find his other self in the beautiful girl at the well, under the Eastern noon; and that she may prove to be the one without whom his life would be incomplete. It may so happen, through the kind providence of God, which shields us

235

from dangers we do not perceive, and loads us with benefits we do not deserve. Nevertheless, it is the highest folly to leave so momentous a matter to be decided by a transient passion, or by the charms of a fascinating manner and pretty face. Do not carry your heart on your sleeve. Do not let your affections trail loosely on the ground, to catch in every thorn-brake. Gird up the loins of your mind; test the spirits whether they be of God. Do not take an irrevocable step without earnest prayer that He will still the voices of self-choice; keep you from making a mistake; and reveal to you His will.

It is not enough to think and pray thus when a new affection has already flung its spell over you. At such a time, the soul is thrilling beneath its new-found rapture; and it is much harder for the judgment to discover the voice of God, because the heart deflects it—as the mass of iron in a modern steamboat deflects the needle from the pole. And therefore, it is of the highest importance that these subjects be made a matter of prayer and thought in the earlier stages of life, when a supreme affection is, as yet, an ideal and a dream. Let mothers speak of them to their daughters; and fathers to their sons—as Isaac did to Jacob (28:1, 2). Let young men, whenever they think of these matters, turn their thoughts into prayers that God would guide them—as He did Abraham's servant—to the woman whom He has chosen to be their helpmeet. And let Christian women lay aside all ideas of attracting men to themselves. Let them quiet their hearts as weaned babes. Let them constitute themselves the wards of God: leaving Him to choose for them the one who shall give them strength for sweetness; defense for weakness; protection for helplessness; and love for love.

There is no training of such value to man or woman as the training of the home—to which the deep instincts of our nature, and the most solemn sanctions of the Bible, point us. Jacob found it so. Rachel and Leah had a very powerful influence upon his character and life; and we need to take warning by his mistakes, and reap his rewards.

I. THE FOUR CONDITIONS OF A TRUE HOME. (1) *There must be a supreme affection.* This was clearly a love match. "Jacob loved Rachel" (v. 18), is a sufficient explanation. And no marriage is heaven made, heaven sent, or heaven sanctioned, which does not spring from a supreme love. Alas, how many marry from some less worthy motive! Some for a home; others to escape from uncongenial surroundings; others for position; others for baser reasons still. All these sin against God's purpose; they sin against one another; and, not least, they sin against themselves. No two should marry unless each feels that life without the other would be incomplete. Less than this will never suffice. If one loves, and not the other, there cannot be true happiness for there is no reciprocity; no mutual satisfaction. To give without receiving is to run to waste; to take without giving is to harden the heart, till it becomes ice. If neither loves, what is it less than the crime which cries myriad-tongued to heaven on every night breeze? But if there be true love, then, though one has been taken from the other by death before they stand together at the marriage altar, yet in the sight of God's high angels those twain are one forever.

It is needless to show how the necessity of the presence of a supreme love is the ground and justification of monogamy, the union of two. This has been the pride and glory of the German peoples, as even Tacitus discerned; and this has been the cradle of all those higher ministries which distinguish our people, and assign us the leading position among the nations of the earth. "Therefore take heed to your spirit, and let none deal treacherously against the wife of his youth."

You have no right to excite that love, or play with it, unless you are prepared to satisfy it, as far as you may. You have no right to give that love away, till you discover that all other conditions are assured. You have no right to marry if this love be absent. You would have no right to treat either man or woman as you would not like your brother or sister to be treated, or as you would not like to be treated yourself.

(2) *Marriage must be "only in the Lord."* Jacob's was so. He might have taken a wife of the daughters of Heth, as Esau did, steeped in the idolatries and impurities which cursed the land. But, guided by his parents' counsels, he crossed the desert to obtain a wife who had been reared in a home in which there lingered still the memory of the worship of the God of Abraham, of Nahor, and of their father Terah (31:53).

The Bible rings from end to end with warnings against mixed marriages. "Thou shalt not give thy daughter unto his son; nor take his daughter unto thy son; for they will turn away thy son from following Me, to serve other gods" (Deut. 7:3). "Be ye not unequally yoked together with unbelievers; for what fellowship hath righteousness with unrighteousness; light with darkness; Christ with Belial?" (2 Cor. 7:14, 15). "She is at liberty to be married to whom she will; only in the Lord?" (2 Cor. 7:39).

We need not be surprised at these strong and repeated prohibitions. A mixed marriage is a prolific source of misery. In the course of a considerable pastoral experience, I have never known one to result in perfect happiness. Believers, in such unions, do not level their unbelieving partners up to Christ, but are themselves dragged down to infinite misery and self-reproach. "Did not Solomon, king of Israel, sin by these things? Yet among many nations was there no king like unto him, who was beloved of his God: and God made him king over all Israel. Nevertheless, even him did outlandish women cause to sin" (Neh. 13:26). How can there be sympathy in the deepest matters? Each feels that there is one subject on which they are not agreed; and this is a fatal barrier to perfect union. The ungodly partner despises the Christian for marrying in the teeth of principle. The Christian is disappointed because the apparent influence gained before marriage is dissipated soon after the knot is irrevocably tied. Well might Rebekah be weary of her life through those daughters of Heth! Many a Christian girl has married an unbeliever, in the hope of saving him, and has bitterly rued her choice: she has seen her influence wane; and has learned, though too late, that the Holy Spirit will not cooperate with our efforts, if they are based on distinct disobedience to one of the clearest commands of the Bible. If a man threatens that if you deny yourself to him, he will take violent or fatal steps, *let him!* He has no right to put you in that position; he simply wants to get you into his power: and he will be much too great a coward to carry out his threats. Do right in the sight of God; and leave *him* to settle the matter with his Maker.

(3) *A true home should be based on the goodwill of parents and friends.* This is not necessary where sanction is withheld from caprice. But where it can possibly be obtained, there is the halo of a brighter promise encircling the union of two young hearts, when it is ratified amid the congratulations of rejoicing friends. So it was with Jacob:

"Isaac called Jacob, and blessed him, and sent him away" (Gen. 28:1–5). It is wise and right, where practicable, for children to consult, in such matters, those whose love has made them the eager guardians of their opening life; and to do so by courtesy, even when mature years have given them the right to choose and act for themselves. But if parents would have such confidences when their children are old, they must make themselves their confidants while they are young; they must give as well as receive; they must exercise their authority by love and reasoning, rather than by constraint; and they have no right to let their decision be warped, through any personal whim, from the straight line of what would best serve the highest interest of a beloved child.

(4) *There should be some prospect of suitable livelihood.* In the broad wealthy land where Jacob found himself, there was not much difficult about that. It is a much more complicated matter amid the conditions of our crowded modern life. Yet there ought to be some security of a competence. Young people have no need to begin where their parents are leaving off; to do so would avoid much wholesome difficulty and the opportunities for mutual help: but it is equally absurd to run the risk of a late repentance for a rash marriage. Young man, select as your partner one who, with refinement and culture, is not above turning her hands to the practical details of household management, and who knows what to do and how to do it. Young women, give your hearts to men who love you well enough to earn you through years of faithful and steadfast courtship, if so it must be. Anyone could do one deed of gallantry; it took a true man to serve for seven long years.

If these four conditions are fulfilled, there will be the strongest reasons for anticipating a union which shall be a miniature picture of that sublime event for which the whole creation groans: when the midnight air shall be startled by the tidings of the Bridegroom's advent; and the Church shall pass as the Bride into the wedding feast.

II. THE EXPULSIVE POWER OF SUPREME AFFECTION. "Jacob served seven years for Rachel; and they seemed unto him but a few days, for the love he had to her" (v. 20). That sentence always charms us for its beauty and its truth. Love has the power of making a rough road easy, and a weary waiting time short. It makes us oblivious to many things, which, for lack of it, would be insupportable. The three mighty men break through the armed host of the Philistines, to get one draft of water from the well for their beloved chieftain, oblivious of personal risk—*the love they bare to him*. The trembling women, on the resurrection morning, ventured out into the perils of the crowded city, while it was yet dark, that they might embalm the body of their Lord; nor do they appear to have considered the perils amid which they threaded their way to His grave—*for the love they bare to Him*. The martyrs died amid bitter torture, with a smile on their faces and a song on their lips, not counting their lives dear, but reckoning it an honor to spill their heart's blood—*for the love they bare to Him*. Many a woman has nursed her children through loathsome disorders, doing for them what no money would hire a servant to do, but she has not considered the cost—*for the love she bare to them*. Yea, Jesus Christ Himself endured the cross, and despised the shame; stooped to a felon's death; bore the base treatment of coarse and brutal soldiery; and rejoiced to lay down His life—*for the love He bare to us*.

Do you find it hard to deny yourself, to make the required sacrifices for doing His will, and to confess Him? There is one cure, a short and easy one. Go to the Holy Ghost, and ask Him to shed the love of Christ abroad in your heart, and so teach you to love Him who first loved you. Then, as the tides of that love rise within your heart, they will constrain you to live, not for yourself, but for Him; then burdens will be light that once crushed; roads will be pleasant that once strained and tired; hours will fly that were once leaden-footed; years will seem as a day. Love's labor is always light.

III. SOME CLOSING WORDS. Are you unmarried? Do not bewail yourself, as if your life must be incomplete. Yours is not a higher state, as the priest has falsely taught, but it is neither a failure nor a shame. It will attain to finished beauty, if only you walk in the path which your Heavenly Father has prepared for you. Cease to measure yourself by human standards. Find rest in being just what your Heavenly Father wills you to be. Break the alabaster box of your affection on Him, and His, for His sake. It may be that you have been kept free from the limited circle of a home, in order to pour your love on those who have no one else to love them. But remember, it is possible for all such to live in perfect self-restraint and purity, through the power of the Holy Ghost, "which is in us."

Are you disappointed? Jacob was disappointed in poor Leah; and she spent many a bitter hour of anguish. Her father had forced her on a man who did not love her, and who wanted to be rid of her. She had a woman's heart, and pined for love that never came. There are few stories more touching than the secret history of Leah, as revealed in the names she gave her boys, and her reasons in giving them. Yet remember, she had her compensations in the love of those strong, healthy lads, who greeted her with the title, "Mother," so dear to a woman's heart. And there are, doubtless, compensations in your lot, if you are not too bitter to see them. And this is the best of all: "The Lord will look upon your affliction" (v. 32). Meanwhile, do not flinch from doing your duty as in His sight.

Are you happily married? Then beware lest you make an idol of your happiness; or suppose that there is no further need to watch. Is it not remarkable that Jacob's dearest wife was the source of his defeat and disgrace, in after years, because he hid in her baggage the household idols of her father? That was a remarkable command that Moses gave to Israel: "If the wife of thy bosom entice thee secretly, saying, Let us go and serve other gods, thou shalt not consent unto her; neither shalt thou spare, but thine hand shalt be first upon her to put her to death." Does it not teach us that we are not to receive, without question, the suggestions of even our dearest? We must ever put God first. "If any come to Me, and hate not his father, and mother, and wife, and children, and brethren, and sisters, yea, and his own life also, he cannot be My disciple."

Have you become a Christian since you were married to an unbeliever? Then do not seek, in any wise, to alter your relations (1 Cor. 7:13, 14), but expect, in all assurance, that you will be the happy means of winning that beloved one to Christ. And seek this, not so much by frequent speech—there is a time to speak, but also a time to be silent—but rather seek it by the admirable beauty and consistency of your life: "That if any obey not the word, they may without the word be gained by your manner of life beholding your behavior" (1 Pet. 3:1).

Above all, withhold not your love from the dear Master, Christ. Hold all human love in Him. You may love to the uttermost of your power, if only you make Him first; and take your love as His gift; and enjoy it in Him; and thank Him for it. So human love will teach you to understand Divine love; and from your thoughts you may understand His thoughts: "Every one that loveth . . . knoweth God." "That being rooted and grounded in love, we may be able to comprehend . . . the love of Christ."

7

The Mid-Passage of Life

Genesis 30

In our last chapter, we saw how Jacob built for himself a home. But ah—what a home! The presence of the two sisters there was fatal to its peace. They who had been happy enough as sisters before he came, could not now live in such close quarters, as wives of the same husband, without incessant jealousy and heart-burning. Each had her own grievance. Poor Leah knew that Jacob had never loved her; and that she was not the wife of his choice: and though God compensated her by giving her that pride of Oriental women, a family of sons, yet even this was a new source of anguish to her; for Rachel envied her. Frightfully desolate was she in that home; and the names or her sons are like so many landmarks of her misery. But Rachel must have been equally miserable: true, she had her husband's love, but she could not be sure of keeping it; and she had the mortification of seeing her sister's children growing up as her husband's heirs. How eagerly she prayed, and fretted, proudly chafed!

What wonder, then, that the children grew up wild and bad? Reuben, unstable as water, excitable and passionate; Simeon, quick to obey, but quick to desperate cruelty; and Levi, a willing accomplice in his crime. When children turn out badly, and the beautiful fate of childhood does not lead to the fair temple of mature life, it is generally the fault of the home training; and it is more often the result of what they see than of what they are taught. Whatever Jacob may have been—and I fear that his example was none of the best—yet the impressions received in the women's tents, of high words and evil passion, would be enough to ruin any child. Beware how you act at home. Remember what keen little eyes are watching you; and with what absolute mimicry they will repeat what they see.

But it is not so much Jacob's home life, as his business dealings, that we have now to consider.

He served fourteen years, as a dowry for his two wives; and at the time when Rachel gave birth to her firstborn Joseph, that period had elapsed. So soon as mother and child were able to undertake so long and fatiguing a journey, Jacob declared his intention of returning to Canaan; and this resolve was perhaps precipitated by a message from Rebekah, to say that there was now no further reason for his absence.

This proposal alarmed Laban, who had learned to value his services; and was much too astute to let him go, without making an effort to retain so valuable a servant. "Tarry," said he, "I pray thee, if I have found favor in thine eyes; for I have learned by experience that the Lord hath blessed me for thy sake." Jacob at once caught at the opportunity of making an independent provision for his large and increasing family; and the bargain was struck.

Eastern sheep are almost wholly white; the goats black; the particolored rare. Jacob proposed, therefore, that all the brown and speckled should be at once removed; and that all of that color, which the flock produced afterwards should be his wage. There was no harm in this; unless he had already made up his mind to take the unfair advantage of Laban, which is a dark blot on his name. Supposing that this were the case, we have here a humiliating picture of two unprincipled men, each trying to outwit the other: Laban chuckling over his bargain, and taking care to remove, not only the young, but the old, and sending them off under the care of his sons; Jacob, laughing in his sleeve, because he knew, or thought he knew, a plan of winning to himself a great advantage. But whether this were premeditated in the first instance or not, it is certain that Jacob acted as a cheat and a rogue. Laban entrusted his flocks to his care without supposing for a moment that he would tamper with the usual course of nature. Jacob, on the other hand, did not scruple to use every art to secure his own advantage at Laban's cost; taking means to procure for himself the produce of the strongest of the flock, and to leave to Laban the enfeebled and the weak.

It is very surprising to find how eagerly some of the older commentators try to vindicate Jacob in this. They might almost as soon sprinkle rosewater on a sewer. And it certainly lowers the standard of morality to attempt to prove that there was not very much harm after all in what Jacob did. I feel no temptation to do this.

The Bible does not hesitate to tell us the very worst about its heroes; that we may better magnify the grace of God, which, out of such materials, could create trophies of mercy. Let Jacob be painted in colors borrowed from Rembrandt's brush; and there is all the more wonder that the grace of God could overcome his duplicity and cunning, and make of him a diamond of the very first water.

Let us draw near, and remonstrate with Jacob, as he sits beside his flocks, in the scorching Eastern sun; and let us carefully notice his excuses and pleas.

He might urge, first, the necessity of self-protection. "My uncle is bent on defrauding me, and keeping me down; and, if I did not do this, he would succeed. You must meet a man on his own ground; and, as he has chosen to play the rogue with me, I cannot see the harm of turning his own weapons on himself." This reasoning did not die with Jacob: it is still passed round the world in act and word; and good men are sometimes sorely tempted to make use of it. It is undoubtedly hard to find that another man is taking an unfair advantage of you by maneuvers which, from your soul, you loathe. But is that a justification for you to resort to them? This has come into your life as a test; to prove whether you believe the world is ordered by God or the devil. If you believe it is the devil's world, it is quite likely that you will try to hold your ground, or gain an advantage by arts, which he alone would approve. But if you really believe in the Almighty God, you will be sure that falsehood must ultimately fail, and righteousness finally win: and you will meet fraud by faith; cunning by conscience;

and violence by a Divine virtue. Goliath may wear armor, but that is no reason why David should. Remember how the Lord hath said: "I will keep thee." Your competitors may do mean and dirty tricks, but you will live to see them trapped in their own pits, and pierced by their own swords: while if you continue to do right, you will go steadily forward to success; as the sun at noon rids himself of the clouds that obscured his early rays. "Trust in the Lord, and do good; so shalt thou dwell in the land, verily thou shalt be fed. Fret not thyself in any wise to do evil; for evildoers shall be cut off." "The Lord shall be thy confidence, and shall keep thy foot from being taken."

He might urge, as a second plea, the familiar formula. Business is business. "It is quite right to speak of Bethel when that scared anniversary comes round, but it is out of the question to suppose that I can act and speak in my daily business, as I did when that angel ladder glistened before my view. Business must be regulated on its own distinct laws; and they are quite different to those which obtain at Bethel." It is strange to hear professing Christians speak thus. They have one standard of morality for the Lord's day; and another for the other six. They permit things in business which are contrary to the spirit and letter of the Word of God; and which they would not sanction for a moment in the ordinary dealings of daily life; and they quiet their conscience by the easy motto, Business is business. I never can understand what difference there is in the morality of an act, because it has to do with buying and selling; or why we should not apply to such an act the same principles by which we judge other actions. According to the practice of some, we should read the golden rule thus: "Do as you would be done by—except in business." "Do not steal" applies everywhere—except in shops and factories. "Lying lips are always an abomination to the Lord"—except when a salesman wants to dispose of some soiled goods. If this were the case, the larger part of the life of most men would be outside the circumference of God's commands. But it cannot be. The moralities of the Gospel resemble the law of gravitation: to which nothing is secular; nothing common, but which determines the pathway of a grain of dust on the autumn breeze, as well as the march of worlds.

But Jacob might urge, as his third plea, that this was the general practice. "Other shepherds practice it. Laban must know all about it;

or he might know. When you are with Chaldeans, you must do as Chaldeans do. I am not worse than others." But a universal practice does not condone sin; this is the difference between God's laws and man's. Let all men break a human law: it stands abrogated on the statute book; it cannot be enforced. But though all men break a Divine law, it will exact its penalty from all. Multitudes may have sinned together, but they will not be able to screen each other, or to escape. And if you do a mean thing, it will come back to roost in you heart; and will find you out with its curse, though you may be one of a crowd.

But he might urge, as his fourth plea, that chicanery was necessary to obtain bread. "A man must live, you know." But the plea cannot stand. There is no *must* about it. Where should we have been today if all the martyrs had argued that it was more important to live than to do right? Every man has to choose between these two. Many men deem life more important than righteousness; and, like the nautilus, they drop out of sight when storms sweep the sea: they are fair weather Christians, and are of too soft a stuff to make martyrs. Others reckoned that it is not necessary for them to live, but it is necessary for them to do right. They say what Pompey said when his friends besought him not to risk his life upon a tempestuous sea—"It is necessary for me to go; it is not necessary for me to live." This surely is the logic of faith. A man may be well content to suffer the loss of all things, and to die, if he may keep inviolate the priceless jewels which God has entrusted to his care.

Jacob's double-dealing appeared to be a success. "The man increased exceedingly; and had much cattle, and maidservants, and menservants, and camels, and asses." But that which men call success, and which is sometimes a very superficial and temporary thing, proves nothing as to the rightness or wrongness of a life. It is not by the glitter of gold that God rewards His faithful servants. Many a noble life in the sight of God has been a sad failure, when judged by human standards. And many a failure in the judgment of man has been a royal success in the estimation of the angels. When a tide of gold has been setting in towards some men, it has been allowed to come as a judgment and a curse, that they might be blinded to destruction. And in many cases, the tide has been restrained, that it might be more possible for the soul to attain to perfect health.

I demur to the common use of the phrase, "Honesty is the best policy"; no doubt, it is so in reality and at the end, though not always in appearance and at the beginning. But if we are simply going to be honest because it pays, we are basing the fabric of our lives on too low a level; and our foundation may give way in days of storm. We must be honest—not because of good policy, but because of good principle, because it is right, and noble, and God-like; yea, because it pleases God. Let us do right; and we shall be happier with scanty means and a good conscience, than those who have all that a heart could wish, but are haunted by memories of the means by which their fortunes were acquired—memories which, like the ghost of the murdered king, in the immortal drama, arise to mar the merriment of the splendid feast. "A little that a righteous man hath is better than the riches of many wicked."

Do not draw a line of separation between the house of God and the house of business. The counting house and the shop may be as much the house of God as the holiest shrine, where generations have knelt in prayer. A devout soul will find God everywhere; and will abide with God in every calling in which it is called. If you cannot have the companionship of Jesus in the paths of daily business, by all means abandon them. But if they are at all legitimate, you will find Him at your side, though His presence is veiled from all other eyes.

Do what you have to do in the name of the Lord Jesus. In that name you are wont to pray. In that name learn to do your work. Speak that name over the most menial tasks; and they will glisten with heavenly beauty. Speak it over doubtful things; and their true character will be revealed—as the tempter sprang from the toad, when touched by the spear of Ithuriel. Speak it over difficulties; and the iron gates will own the spell, and open to you of their own accord.

Take the Lord Jesus into your partnership. Consult Him before branching out into new directions; or consigning goods to fresh customers; or making large purchases. Let every transaction and every entry be freely open to His eye. Let every transaction be laid before Him, for Him to close or open as He will. And be sure to divide with Him the profits, which are His due. A business life, with such sanctions, could never strand on the shoals of bankruptcy.

Above all, realize that you are the *slaves* of Jesus Christ. In the olden days of slavery, a master would sometimes put a trusted slave into a position of great responsibility, where he was permitted even to trade for his owner. But his brains, his muscles, and his gains were all another's. Everything had to be used and accounted for on that one condition. And what are we but the purchased possession of the Son of God? What is our business, but a branch of our stewardship for Him, as it is also a training school for us? What is there we can call our own? It is He that gives us power to get wealth; and His image and superscription are evident on every coin. "Ye are not your own; ye are bought with a price: wherefore glorify God in your body and in your spirit, which are God's."

8
The Stirring Up
of the Nest

O Father! the untrodden path how shall we dare to tread?
We see not what is in the clouds now hanging o'er our head.
Thou hid'st the future from our ken. Oh, be Thy children's light!
Guide Thou our halting footsteps in the day or in the night.

Genesis 31

Marianne Farningham

In that sublime song with which the great Lawgiver closed his words to Israel, we are carried through the steeps of air, to stand beside an eagle's eyrie, perched amid the inaccessible cliffs. Here we may find a clue to explain the ways of God to man. The young eaglets are old and strong enough to fly, but they cling to the familiar nest, with its scant shelter. They dare not venture forth upon the untried air, or trust their fluttering wings. But they *must* learn to fly. There are joys awaiting them in the wide oceans of space, which far outvie those of the rude nest in which they have been nurtured. And so the eagle stirs up the nest, and drives them forth. What anguish the young birds feel, as they see that nest destroyed; and themselves thrust forth, as it might seem, to certain destruction! But when once they are launched upon the upbearing air, and learn by glad experience the freedom, the ecstasy of flight—how grateful should they be to the parent bird, who flinched not from the unwelcome task; and who still swoops and flies beneath them, ready to catch them up if their powers should flag, and to bear them sunwards. There, in mid-heaven, she lets them fall again; and again she catches them: and thus, each moment they increase in confidence and strength; and develop powers of sustained flight, of which they were unconscious when they lingered by the nest.

It is a beautiful parable of human life. We all cling to the old nest —the old home where we were born; the dear protection of strong, true hearts, that screen us from every breath; the place where we are known; the faces with which we are familiar; the competence which we have won. We say, with eager petulance, "Let us stay here forever. Do not speak to us of that great outer world; or of the opportunities which lie hidden there; and which, you say, might bring out powers of muscle, and brain, and heart, of which we now know nothing. We would rather that they should remain hidden, than that we should have to suffer the anguish of their development amid the strain and trial of that rude, strange world of which we now catch but distant rumors. We are content; let us stay." But the great love of God has provided some better thing for us. He knows that there are heights and depths of life hidden from us till we go forth. Keen may be the agony of the moment in which we see the nest stirred up, and find ourselves flung forth into a strange element. But it is not worthy to be compared with the glory instantly revealed; for that light affliction, which is but for a moment, works out for us a far more exceeding and eternal weight of glory: the glory of a faith that poises itself on the unseen; the glory of a hope that breasts the thundercloud; the glory of a love that soars ever upward to the sun. "They change their strength, and mount up with wings as eagles."

These thoughts give the key to the next experience in Jacob's troubled life. There is reason for every step in our education, whether we see it or not: and, though Jacob could not have guessed it at the time, yet, as we look back, we can easily understand why his residence at Haran was suddenly closed; and his home broken up; and he driven across the desert, as a fugitive, hotly pursued—much as he had been years before, only in the reverse direction.

In point of fact, Jacob was becoming too contented in that strange land. Like Ulysses and his crews, he was in danger of forgetting the land of his birth; the tents of his father; and the promises of which he was the heir. He was fast losing the pilgrim spirit, and settled into a citizen of that far country. His mean and crafty arts to increase his wealth were honeycombing his spirit, and eating out his nobler nature, prostituting it to the meanest ends. His wives, infected with the idolatry of their father's house, were in danger of corrupting the minds of his children; and how then would fare the holy seed, destined to give the world the messages of God? It was evident that his nest must be broken up in Haran; that he must be driven back into the pilgrim life—to become a stranger and a sojourner, as his fathers were. And this was another step nearer the moment when he became an Israel, a prince with God. This may be your destiny, my reader; and, if it be, accept meekly the discipline which forces you towards it. It is the hand that was pierced with nails that breaks up the nest of the past, and beckons you to the untried but blessed realities in front.

I. THE SUMMONS TO DEPART. "And the Lord said unto Jacob, Return unto the land of thy fathers, and to thy kindred; and I will be with thee." Whether there was voice audible to the outward ear I cannot tell, but there was certainly the uprising of a strong impulse within his heart. Sometimes on a sultry summer day we suddenly feel the breeze fanning our faces, and we say that the wind is rising, but we know not whence it comes, or whither it goes: so does the Spirit of God frequently visit us with strong and holy impulses. There is a divine restlessness; a noble discontent; a hunger created in the heart, which will not be satisfied with the husks on which the swine feed. We cannot always understand ourselves, but it is the Lord saying to us, Arise and depart; for this is not your rest.

There are many kinds of voices in the world, and none of them is without signification; and sometimes it is difficult to know the voice of the Lord. But the more truly we partake of the nature of "His own sheep," the more unerringly shall we detect the voice of the Good Shepherd. If you are not quite sure, wait till you are. It is the Shepherd's business to make His presence and wish understood by the timid and perplexed in His flock. The only necessity is to be willing to do His will so soon as it is clearly seen. If you are in doubt, wait in faith till every other door is shut, and one path only lies open before you, and you are able to say: "He leadeth me in the paths of righteousness for His name's sake."

God's voice to the heart is generally corroborated by the drift of outward circumstances. "Jacob beheld the countenance of Laban, and, behold, it was not towards him as before." For some time their relations had been strained. Ten times in six years had Laban altered the method of computing his wages; and now there were symptoms of open rupture. It is always wise to be on the outlook for any evident symptoms of God's will; and here was one.

It is very bitter to behold a change passing over men and women in their behavior towards us; a change which we cannot avert. We dread it as the timid passenger by the night mail dreads the roar of the waves, as they seethe, white with rage, outside the harbor bar. And yet God is undoubtedly in all this. It is the way which He is taking through the deep. Listen to the Divine assurance, "I am with thee." The Good Shepherd Himself is putting you forth from the warm fold, now almost bare, that He may conduct you to green pastures and living waters. The Master Himself is emptying you from vessel to vessel; lest you should settle on your lees. The Husbandman Himself is exposing you to that painful process of transplanting, which is said to be one of the surest methods of luxuriant growth. Take heart: it is only part of the process of making you a prince; you need it badly enough—in no other way can your mean Jacob-nature be replaced by something better.

II. The Tenacity of Circumstances. When the pilgrim spirit essays to obey the voice of God, the house is always filled with neighbors to dissuade from the rash resolve. "As Christian ran, some mocked; others threatened; and some cried after him to return." There was something of this in Jacob's case. The bird-lime clung closely to him, as he began to plume his wings for his homeward flight.

He was evidently afraid that his wives would hinder his return. It would have been natural if they had. Was it likely that they would at once consent to his proposal to tear them from their kindred and land? This fear may have greatly hindered Jacob. He at least thought it necessary to fortify himself with a quiver full of arguments, in order to carry his point. In those arguments we catch another glimpse of his cowardly and crafty nature. They are a strange medley of lies, and cant, and truth. He might have saved himself from all this, if he had only trusted God to roll away the stones from the path of obedience. For God had been at work before him; and had prepared their hearts, so that they at once assented to his plan, saying: "We have no further ties to home; now then, whatsoever God hath said unto thee, do." If we would only go forward in simple obedience, we should find that there would be no need for our diplomacy; He would go before us, making the crooked straight, and the rough smooth.

In the endeavors of Laban to retain Jacob, we have a vivid picture of the eager energy with which the world would retain us, when we are about to turn away from it forever. It pursues us, with all its allies, for seven days and more (v. 23). It asks us why we are not content to abide with it (v. 27). It professes its willingness to make our religion palatable, by mingling with it its own tabret and dance (v. 27). It appeals to our feelings, and asks us not to be too cruel (v. 28). It threatens us (v. 29). It jeers us with our sudden compunction, after so many years of contentment with its company (v. 30). It reproaches us with our inconsistency in making so much of our God, and yet harboring some cunning sin. "Wherefore hast thou stolen my gods?" (v. 30). Ah, friends, how sad it is, when we, who profess so much, give occasion to our foes to sneer, because of the secret idols which they know we carry with us! Sometimes it is not we who are to blame, so much as our Rachels—our wives, or children, or friends. But we should never rest till, as far as we know, our camp is clear of the accursed thing.

At last, our Labans, who would hold us fast, having tried every expedient, content themselves with groaning, "What can I do this day?" Blustering often ends in bewailing over an unalterable destiny.

Thus the heap of witness is raised at length. Oh that you might break away from that life of worldliness in which you have tarried too long! Make a clean break with it! Only do not do it secretly, as Jacob did. Better so, than not at all: but it is mean-spirited and cowardly; it always arouses intenser opposition; and it is not worthy of one whose escort is God Himself. The straightforward and outspoken course—which nails its colors to the mast—is always the easiest, and safest, and best.

A midshipman, who was about to leave the sailor's home, where he had been converted, came to the superintendent on the day of going on board, and asked him to write on a card, in plain bold characters, the words, "I am a Christian." When he was asked his object, he said, "As soon as I get on board, I shall go to my hammock, and put this card where everybody can see it: it will save a lot of trouble; for everyone will know at once which side I am on, and will expect me to keep true to it." This is raising the heap of witness.

Let us raise that heap: let me help you rear it; gather stones, and pile them into the form of that cross by which the world was crucified to St. Paul, and he to the world. Eat there the feast that speaks of life through death. Call your friends to witness your solemn act; above all, call God to witness your resolve—that never again shall the world, the flesh, or the devil, come over to you, or you pass over to them. This is the true Mizpah, of the Lord's watch.

III. THE DIVINE CARE. Well might Jacob have thrilled with joy, as he said to his wives, "The God of my father has been with me." When God is for us, and with us, who can be against us? Blessed is he who is environed by God, and for whom God fights. He must be more than a conqueror. So Jacob found it; and, at the end of his encounter with Laban, he was able to repeat his assurance, that the God of his father had been with him (v. 42).

At the head of his flocks and herds, with wives and children and slaves, he struck across the Euphrates and the desert, at the utmost speed possible to his encumbered march, but God's angels accompanied him. He met their radiant hosts afterwards (32:1). His flight remained unsuspected for three days; then Laban set off with swift camels in pursuit, and overtook them, when still threading their way among the richly wooded and watered hills of Gilead. It was a moment of real danger; and it was then that God interposed. "God came to Laban the Syrian by night." That dream laid an irresistible spell on Laban, which prevented him from carrying out his design to do Jacob hurt.

Jacob was an erring and unworthy child, but God did not leave or forsake him. He does not love us (as we so often falsely tell little children) because we are good, but to make us so. As He does not set His love on us because of our deserts, so He does not turn it away from us because of our sins. He hates our sins, but He loves ourselves with a love that sin can neither wear out, nor turn away. Thus He was able to throw His protection round His erring child; and this was part of the loving discipline which was leading Jacob to a goal of which he never dreamed.

Jacob conceived that he was a model shepherd (v. 38), but he little realized how lovingly he was being protected by the shepherd care of Him who keeps Israel, and who neither slumbers nor sleeps. That protection may be ours.

O Thou, who art the Good Shepherd; who does guard Thy flock, in drought and frost, with untried and unabated tenderness; who does go after that which is gone astray, until Thou does find it, bringing it back upon Thy shoulders—we, too, have gone astray like lost sheep. Seek Thy servants; at whatever cost, disentangle us from the meshes of the world; and take care of us until Thine own ideal is realized in our lives.

9

The Midnight Wrestle

The Sun of Righteousness on me
Hath rose, with healing in His wings.
Withered my nature's strength; from Thee
My soul its life and succor brings;
My help is all laid up above;
Thy nature and Thy name is Love!
Contented now, upon my thigh
I halt, till life's short journey end;
All helplessness, all weakness, I
On Thee alone for strength depend;
Nor have I power from Thee to move:
Thy nature and Thy name is Love!

Genesis 32

Wesley

In the morning after his interview with Laban, Jacob broke up his camp on the heights of Gilead, and slowly took his journey southwards. He little knew that that day was to be the crisis of his life. "Thou knowest not what a day may bring forth," not of evil only, but of blessing. It may be that this day has been predestined from all eternity to be that of thy transformation from the craft and cunning of years, to a life of subjection to the will of God, and of power over men.

This wondrous scene does not, in my opinion, correspond to that change which we call conversion. That was determined, surely, by the angel vision at Bethel. But it may rather be compared with that further blessing, which sometimes comes to a Christian after some years of religious experience and profession. There is no reason, in the nature of things, why it should be so. There is no reason why, at the moment of conversion, we should not at once step into the realization and enjoyment of all the possibilities of Christian living. But still, as a matter of fact, it very often happens that some years of wilderness wandering do intervene between the deliverance of the Passover and the passage across the Jordan into the land of promise, and rest, and victory. Many a child of God who has no doubt of acceptance and forgiveness, is conscious of a broken and fitful experience: often foiled and overthrown; wishing to do good, but unable to do it; full of self-reproach and bitterness of soul. Then there comes a time when he is almost forced into a new experience. He passes into a climate that brings into glorious fruitage the seed germs which were lying in his nature undeveloped. He receives an abounding freshet of grace, that lifts him sheer above all the former levels of his existence, and launches him on the flood tide of blessedness. If you have never known this in happy experience, you can hardly understand what an extraordinary change comes over all things; or how great a contrast severs the new from the old. Such an experience fell to Jacob's lot after that memorable night.

Three events are narrated in this chapter, corresponding to morning, afternoon, and night of that memorable day.

(1) IN THE MORNING, we are told that the angels of God met him. Those words tremble with mystic and indescribable beauty. How did it befall? Did they come in twos or threes? Or, as he turned some corner in the mountain pass, did he see a long procession of bright harnessed angels, marching four abreast, with golden bands girding about them their lustrous robes, while the music of heaven beat time? Would it not remind him of Bethel, that lay across the chasm of five-and-twenty years? Would it not nerve and prepare him for coming danger?

Doubtless these angel bands are always passing by us; only our eyes are holden so that we do not see them. But whether we see them or not, we may always reckon on their being at hand—especially when some heavy trial is near. "The angel of the Lord encampeth round about them that fear Him, and delivereth them." This is Mahanaim. Here two hosts are meeting; the mountain is full of horses and chariots of fire around us; more are they that are with us than all they which are against us.

(2) As the day wore on to AFTERNOON, Jacob's spirit was shaken to the center by ominous tidings. He had sent messengers, as Arab chiefs would do still, to announce to Esau his return, and to ascertain his mind. They now returned in breathless haste to say that Esau was coming to meet him, with four hundred men at his back. Jacob was panic-

stricken; and well he might be. His all was at stake—wives and children; herds and cattle; the careful gains of six laborious years. The Mizpah tower barred the way back; his bridge was, so to speak, burned behind him. Around him were robber tribes, eager to seize on the rich booty, if he showed the least sign of vacillation or fear. But to go on seemed to involve a risk of inevitable ruin. There was just one alternative—which most men will only turn to when all other expedients have failed: he could at least pray; and to prayer he betook himself. It may have been a long time since he prayed like this.

For years his nobler self had been overgrown by a noxious growth of weeds, and drugged to unconsciousness by the cares of this life; the deceitfulness of riches; and the lusts of many things. The evil conscience cannot pray. Prayer cannot live in the heart with deceit, and craft, and villainy, but passes out unnoticed and unmissed. But now, under the shock of this terrible danger, the olden spirit revived in him; and the hair of consecration began to grow again. (See Num. 6). Is not this the key to God's dealings with us all? He brings us into sore straits; He shuts us up in a corner; He causes the walls and ceiling and floor of our room to draw together, as if to crush us. At such moments there is only one resource left. It is Himself. We must fly to God, to escape from God. We are driven to our knees, with no language but a cry. And though that cry consists mostly of a confession of unworthiness, yet it is enough: the silence is broken; the avenues are cleared of their choking undergrowth; the child has already left the far country, and is on his way home. Was not this the experience of the Syro-Phoenician woman? Her utter misery made her seek Christ; she found Him out in a retirement which would have concealed Him from all save one in her dire need; and His apparent denial drove her to climb an altitude of faith, and to utter words of desperate boldness, from which she would have shrunk except under the pressure of that terrible agony of soul. The love of God is great enough to cause us pain—if only it can force us to positions from which we had heretofore shrunk, but from which we shall never again recede.

There are many healthy symptoms in that prayer. In some respects it may serve as a mold into which our own spirits may pour themselves, when melted in the fiery furnace of sorrow.

He began by quoting God's promise: "Thou saidst." He did so twice (9, 12). Ah, he had got God in his power then! God puts Himself within our reach in His promises; and when we can say to Him, "Thou saidst," He cannot say nay—He must do as He has said. If Herod was so particular for his oath's sake, what will not our God be? Be sure, in prayer, to get your feet well on a promise; it will give you purchase enough to force open the gates of heaven, and to take it by force.

He next went to confession: "I am not worthy." There passed before his mind his deceit to his aged father; his behavior to Esau; his years of trickery to Laban. All the meanness of his heart and life stood revealed, as a landscape is revealed when the midnight sky is riven by the lightning flash. Conscience came forth from its retreat in the dungeons of his nature, and climbed the stairs, and stood in the throne room of his spirit: as Nathan before David; or John the Baptist before Herod; or Paul before Felix, the Roman governor, who trembled as he spake of righteousness, temperance, and judgment to come. And as the sea of memory gave up the dead past to a terrible resurrection, and as it all stood in vivid minuteness before him, was there not plenty to justify his penitent confession?—"I am not worthy." Great soul anguish will generally wring some such cry from our startled and stricken hearts. If there is one position that better becomes us than another, it is that of the publican with downcast eyes; nor can we improve on his prayer, "God be merciful to me, *the* sinner."

Then he passed on to plead for deliverance: "Deliver me, I pray thee, from the hand of my brother, from the hand of Esau." It was, of course, quite right to pray thus, but I cannot feel that it was a wholehearted prayer: for he had hardly finished it, when he reverted to the plan on which he had been busy before he turned aside to pray. Jacob's first thought was always a plan. He had a plan for Isaac's blessing; and another for his property; and now another to appease Esau. Of course, I have no word to say against planning, when that is evidently God's method of delivering us, but I am desperately afraid lest our planning should take the place of simple waiting on God, till the cloud rises, and moves forward, and shows us our path across the trackless sands. We are all so apt to pray, and then to try and concoct a plan for our own deliverance. Surely the nobler attitude is, after prayer, to stand still for God to develop His plan, leading us in ways that we had never guessed. The blessed life of our Lord was absolutely planless.

There was too much selfhood in Jacob; as there is also in us. This must be broken down, and put in the place of death. The I-life must be crucified before the Christ-life can take its place. The sinews of the old nature must be utterly shriveled; that the new nature, whose only strength is to cling, may be manifested in power. This was the object of that mysterious conflict, which left so deep an impression on Jacob's life.

(3) IT WAS MIDNIGHT. Jacob had already sent across the Jabbok his property, his children, even the beloved Rachel. It seemed as if, amid the awful pressure of that anxiety, he could not bear the noise of the camp; the prattlings of the children; or even the presence of the only woman he ever really loved. "He caused them to pass over the brook; and sent over that he had. And Jacob was left alone." When the soul enters its Gethsemane, it withdraws a stone's cast from its most trusted friends. Around him was the profound stillness of those most desolate regions; beside him the murmur of the rapid brook over the stones; above him the infinite depths of heaven, bejeweled with stars. There, alone, he considered the past; and anticipated the future; and felt the meanness of the aims for which he had sold his soul; and saw the wretched failure of his life: and so, suddenly, he became aware that a mysterious combatant was at his side, drawing him into a conflict, half literal and half spiritual, which lasted till break of day.

Was this a literal contest? There is no reason to deny it. We know that the Son of God sometimes anticipated His incarnation by assuming literal physical shapes. "His delights were of old amongst the sons of men." And it would have been as possible for Him to wrestle literally with Jacob, as for Him to offer His hands to the touch of Thomas after His resurrection. The physical must have been largely present, because, when he resumed his journey, Jacob halted upon his thigh: It was a physical fact; physically commemorated by the Israelites to this day, who abstain from eating of that part in animals which corresponds to the sinew that shrank in Jacob's thigh. Men do not become lame in imaginary conflicts. But, in any case, the outward

wrestling was only a poor symbol of the spiritual struggle which con-
vulsed the patriarch's soul; and is as real in the experience of earnest men
today as when the world was young.

Remember that the conflict originated not with Jacob, but with the
angel: "There wrestled a Man with him." This passage is often quoted
as an instance of Jacob's earnestness in prayer. It is nothing of the
sort. It is an instance of God's earnestness to take from us all that
hinders our truest life; while we resist Him with all our might and main.
It was not that Jacob wished to obtain aught from God, but it was that
He—the angel Jehovah—had a controversy with this double-dealing
and crafty child of His; desirous to break up his self-sufficiency forever;
and to give scope for the development of the Israel that lay cramped
and coffined within.

There is an illustration of this in the life of Moses. For forty years
he lived in the retirement of the desert. At last he set out for Egypt, accompanied by his wife and children. Concerning those children, in deference to their mother's wish, he seems to have neglected a rite,
binding, by Divine command, on every son of Abraham. And it came
to pass in the way, that the Lord barred his journey, and even threatened him with death, until he had obeyed the injunction he had ig-
nored; then He let him go. So it was with Jacob. There was much in
him that needed to be laid aside; much self-sufficiency requiring to be
broken down; much dross that had to be burned out by a consuming
fire; and so the Love of God drew near to him on that solemn night,
to wrest these things from him at whatever cost.

Has not "this Man" that wrestled with Jacob found you out? Have
you not felt a holy discontent with yourself? Have you not felt that certain things, long cherished and loved, should be given up, though it
should cost you blood? Have you not felt that you should yield your
whole being to God, but there has been a rebellious uprising of self-will
within you, as if it were impossible for you to make the surrender? Have
you not felt in an agony, between the stirrings of God's good Spirit on
the one hand, and the preferences of your own choice on the other?
Have you not felt as if some mighty power were wrestling with you,
against you, and for your good? Surely these convulsive throes; these
heaven-born strivings; these mysterious workings—are not of man, or

of the will of the flesh, but of God. It is God that works in you, and wrestles with you. Glory be to Him for His tender patience, interest, and love!

At first Jacob held his own. "He saw that he prevailed not against him." The strength that, years before, had rolled the stone from the well for Rachel's sheep, was vigorous yet; and he was in no humor to submit. And thus we do all resist the love of God. We carry out our own plans; we follow our own will; we are strong in our own self-sufficiency. "When thou wast young, thou girdedst thyself, and walkedst whither thou wouldest." Each one of us is dowered with that wonderful power of holding our own against God; and He knows, sorrowfully, that He cannot prevail against us, without taking some severe measures which will give us no alternative but to yield.

Then the angel touched the hollow of his thigh. Whatever it is that enables a soul, whom God designs to bless, to stand out against Him, God will touch. It may be the pride of wealth; or of influence; or of affection, but it will not be spared—God will touch it. It may be something as natural as a sinew, but if it robs a man of spiritual blessing, God will touch it. It may be as small a thing as a sinew, but its influence in making a man strong in his resistance of blessing will be enough to condemn it—and God will touch it. And beneath that touch it will shrink and shrivel; and you will limp to the end of life. Remember that the sinew never shrinks save beneath the touch of the Angel hand— the touch of tender love. This is why your schemes have miscarried; and your children have faded in untimely decay; and your life has been haunted by disappointment. God has touched the sinew of your strength; and it has dried up. Oh, you who are still holding out against Him, make haste to yield, lest some worse thing come upon you!

Then Jacob went from resisting to clinging. As the day broke, the Angel would be gone, but He could not, because Jacob clung to Him with a death grip. The request to be let go indicates how tenaciously the limping patriarch clung to Him for support. He had abandoned the posture of defense and resistance; and had fastened himself on to the Angel—as a terrified child clasps its arms tightly around its father's neck. That is a glad moment in the history of the human spirit, when it throws both arms around the risen Savior; and hangs on

Him, and will not let Him go. It is the attitude of blessing. It is the posture of power. It is the sublime condition in which Christ will whisper His own new name, which no man knows saving he that receives it. Have you ever come to this? Have you abandoned the art of self-defense for the artlessness of clinging trust? Have you felt able to rejoice in your inability to stand alone, because it has made the Lord Jesus so real? Have you reached the point of self-surrender? If not, ask God to show you what sinew it is that makes you too strong for Him to bless you; ask Him to touch it, so that you shall be able to hold out no more. And then you will discover the threefold blessing which is yours.

(1) *The changed name.* In olden days, names were given not for euphony, or by caprice, but for character. A man's character was in his name. Now, when Jacob came into the attitude of blessing—an attitude which has two parts: viz.; absolute abandonment of self, and a trust which clings to Christ—then immediately the Angel said, "What is thy name?" And he said, "Jacob. By nature I am a supplanter, a rogue, and a cheat." Never shrink from declaring your true character: "My name is Sinner." "And he said, thy name shall be no more Jacob, but Israel: a prince with God." The changed name indicated a changed character. Jacob was swallowed up of light. He was clothed upon with the name and nature of a prince. There is only one way to princeliness— it is the thorn-set path of self-surrender and of faith. Why should you not now yield yourself entirely to God, and give Him your whole being? It is only a reasonable service: and out if it will spring a tenacity of faith; and a power for service; and a royalty of character— enough to make you willing to bear the limp, which proves that your own strength has passed away forever.

(2) *Power.* The better rendering of these words would be: "As a prince hast thou power with God; and with man thou shalt prevail." We sigh for power—power over ourselves; power for service; power over the principalities of wicked spirits. But before we can receive power with the creature, we must obtain it from the Creator. The man who would have power with men must first have it with God; and we can only get power with God when our own strength has failed, and we limp. "I glory in infirmity, that the power of Christ may rest upon me; for when

I am weak, then am I strong." Oh for the withered sinew of our own strength, that we may lay hold on the strength of God!

(3) *The beatific vision.* "I have seen God face to face." Our moments of vision come at daybreak: but they are ushered in by the agony of dread; the long midnight vigil; the extreme agony of conflict; the shrinking of the sinew. Yet, when they come, they are so glorious, that the frame is almost overpowered with the brightness of that light, and the exceeding weight of glory. The price is dear, but the vision is more than worth it all. The sufferings are not worthy to be compared with the glory revealed.

This is life; a long wrestle against the love of God, which longs to make us royal. As the years go on, we begin to cling where once we struggled; and as the morn of heaven breaks, we catch glimpses of the Angel face of love, and hear His whispered name: and as He blesses us, we awake to find ourselves living, and face to face with God—and that is heaven itself.

10
Failure

Or sometimes strangely I forget;
And, learning o'er and o'er
A lesson all with teardrops wet,
Which I had learnt before.
He chides me not, but waits awhile;
Then wipes my heavy eyes;
Oh, what a Teacher is our God—
So patient and so wise!

Genesis 33, 34   F. R. Havergal

That midnight wrestle, which last engaged our thoughts, made an epoch in Jacob's life. It was the moment in which he stepped up to a new level in his experience—the level of Israel the prince. But, let us remember, it is one thing to step up to a level like that; it is quite another to keep it. Some, when they touch a new attainment, keep to it, and are blessed forevermore; others, when they have stood there for a moment, recede from it. Yet it is well for them to have stood for even a moment on the shining tablelands, where God Himself is sun: for, when once they have caught sight of a new ideal, they will never be satisfied to live as they have lived; and, even if they do not win it at once as an abiding experience, they will come to it afterwards. Jacob, alas! soon stepped down from that glorious level to which the Angel had lifted him.

This descent is indicated by the retention, in the sacred record, of the name Jacob. We should have expected that it would have been replaced by the new title, Israel—as Abram was by Abraham, but it is not so. How could he be called Israel, when he had so soon reverted to the life of Jacob; and had gone back from the life of clinging, to the

269

cringing, crafty, scheming life which he had been leading all too long? The time will come when Israel shall become his habitual designation, but not yet—not yet. Our Heavenly Father is very tender with us; and if we do not learn His lessons at once, He will present them to us again and again—now in one form, then in another—until at last His ideal is accomplished in our characters and lives.

We have to consider now the three evidences of failure; which are recounted in these chapters.

I. THE FIRST FAILURE WAS IN HIS MANNER OF MEETING ESAU. As the morning broke, "Jacob lifted up his eyes, and looked; and, behold, Esau came, and with him four hundred men." Such is life. It is filled with sharply varied experiences. Now the Angel; then the coming of Esau. Now forty days on the brow of Sinai with God; then the golden calf. Now the Mountain of Transfiguration; then the bitter cross. Now Patmos, with its visions; then the cold grey rock, and the commonplaces of captivity and loneliness.

Yet, how grateful should we be that it is so! Life might have been full of Esaus, and no Jacobs; full of Gethsemanes, and no glimpses into heaven; full of grey commonplaces, and no rapturous visions. The bright days of our lives outnumber the dark ones. There are more sweets than bitters; more smiles than tears; more mercies than miseries.

How often do we find that a great blessing—like that which came to Jacob by the fords of the Jabbok—is sent to prepare us for a great trial. God prevents us, and prepares us, with the blessings of His goodness. He takes us up the Hill Difficulty; into the House Beautiful: where we sleep in the Chamber of Peace, which looks toward the sunrise. Not that we should stay there: but that we should be rested, and accoutered, and prepared to meet Apollyon in the Valley; and to pass unscathed through the Shadow of Death and Vanity Fair. Do not be surprised or discouraged if a time of fiery trial should follow a season of unusual blessing; indeed, you may be rather surprised if it does not. But when it comes, be sure to do as Jacob did not do, and draw heavily upon all those resources of strength and comfort which have been stored up during the previous days of clear shining and peace.

There are two ways of meeting troubles: the one is the way of the flesh; the other, of the Spirit. The flesh anticipates them with terror; prepares against them with trembling hands; prays in a panic, and then cringes before them—as Jacob, who bowed himself to the ground seven times, until he came near his brother. The way of faith is far better. She clings to God; she hears God say, "I am with thee, and will keep thee"; she believes that He will keep His word; she reviews the past, when the hands of Laban were tied, and argues that God can do as much again; she goes to meet trouble, not cringing but erect, sure that God has already been at work in the heart of difficulty: and that, however grim they may seem in the distance, yet the lions are chained, the wolf claws are extracted; and the arrows have been deprived of their barbed tips.

I have always admired the refusal of the members of Lord Elgin's suite to crawl on the ground into the presence of the Emperor of China. When they learned that that was the posture which all foreigners were expected to assume, they indignantly replied that they certainly would not give to the Emperor of China a homage which their own Most Gracious Sovereign did not require; and, in the end, they were permitted to enter his presence erect. This is the natural posture of an Englishman, but it is more surely the native posture of faith.

Some who read this may be dreading a meeting with their Esaus tomorrow: some creditor; some demand for payment; some awkward problem; some difficulty. And you are today worrying, planning, scheming, and contriving, as Jacob did, in arranging his wives, and children, and servants, while tomorrow you will go cringing and creeping towards it.

Listen to a more excellent way. Do not lift up your eyes and look for Esaus. Those who look for troubles will not be long without finding trouble to look at. But lift them higher—to Him from whom our help comes. Then you will be able to meet your troubles with an unperturbed spirit. Those who have seen the face of God need not fear the face of a man that shall die. To have power with God is to have power over all the evils that threaten us.

Besides all this, when prayer has preceded trial, the trial turns out to be much less than we anticipated. The women found, when they reached the sepulcher, that the dreaded stone had been rolled away. When Peter reached the outer gate, that threatened to be an insurmountable obstacle to liberty, it opened to him of its own accord. So Jacob dreaded that meeting with Esau, but when Esau came up with

him, he ran to meet him, and embraced him, and fell on his neck, and
kissed him: and they wept. The heroic Gordon used to say that, in his
lonely camel rides, he often in prayer encountered and disarmed hostile chiefs, before he rode, unaccompanied, into their presence. None
can guess, if they have not tried it for themselves, what a solvent
prayer is for the difficulties and agonies of life.

It is very beautiful to see that, in this, God was better to Jacob than
his fears, or his faith. While he was foreboding the worst, his heavenly
Friend was preparing deliverance; as, years after the Lord stretched out
His hand and saved from the yeasty waves the faithless Apostle, who
had looked away from Himself to the terrors of the storm.

II. THE SECOND FAILURE WAS IN THE SUBTERFUGE TO WHICH
JACOB RESORTED, TO FREE HIMSELF FROM ESAU'S COMPANY. When Esau
offered him the protection of his armed men, he was at once in a
panic; for he dreaded them even more than the Bedouins of the wilds.
He tried to evade the proposal by many excuses; especially explaining
that his flocks and his children could not keep up with their more rapid
pace. And finally, still further to reconcile Esau to the separation, he
promised to come at last to Seir, where Esau had fixed his abode.

Now I do not, for a single moment, believe that Jacob really meant
to go to Seir; for as soon as he had seen the rear of Esau's retiring forces,
he journeyed in the contrary direction to Succoth. All such subterfuge
and lying were utterly unworthy of the man who had seen God's angels
face to face.

What wretched failure was here! The bright dawn was all too
speedily overcast and clouded; and if it had not been for the marvelous
tenderness of God, there is no telling how much further Jacob would
have drifted, or how indefinitely distant the day would have been in
which he should be worthy to bear the name of Israel.

III. THE THIRD FAILURE WAS IN SETTLING AT SHECHEM. God
had not said, Go to Shechem, but, "I am the God of Bethel." Bethel,
rather than Shechem, was his appointed goal. But alas! we are all too
ready to fall short of God's schemes for our elevation and blessedness.
And so Jacob came to Shalem, a city of Shechem.

But he did worse; he pitched his tent before the city—as Lot did when he pitched his tent before Sodom. What took him there? Was it that Rachel persuaded him that a little society would be a pleasant relief to the monotony and seclusion of the camp life? Was it that his children urged him to it against his better mind? Was it some idea of obtaining eligible alliances for his children among the children of the land? Whatever may have been his reason, there stands the sad and solemn fact that Jacob pitched his tent *before the city*.

Are not many Christians doing so still? They live on the edge of the world, just on the borderland; far enough away to justify a religious profession, yet near enough to run into it for sweets. They send their children to fashionable schools, that they may acquire the false veneer of the world, and pass muster in its drawing rooms. They remove into the fashionable quarters of a town; and adopt a certain style; and throw themselves into the swim of all manner of worldly engagements—that they may get in with "society." They choose their Church, their pastimes, their friendships, on the sole principle of doing as others do; and of forming good alliances for their children. What is all this but pitching the tent towards Shechem?

"But what are we to do?" say they; "our children must have society; they cannot be recluses, or be forever shut up in our homes." But why need we cater for them by rushing into the world? Are there not plenty of innocent pastimes, on which worldliness has never breathed its withering breath? Are there not enough elements in the bright social intercourse of the family circle; in the play of imagination and wholesome merriment; in games of skill; in the charms of books; in the recital of travel and adventure; in the witchery of wholesome songs and music; and even in the revelations of modern popular science—to beguile the hours of long winter evenings, without calling in the aid of worldly society, whose brightest hours leave a sense of vacuity and thirst, to say nothing of a positive sting? The most earnest religion does not debar us from manly sports: the swift movement of the skater over the frozen lake; the evening row; the exhilarating climb: or from the culture of the faculties of art; and music; and imagination; of science and poesy. Surely, in all these there is enough to brighten Christian homes, without grieving the Holy Spirit, or lowering their tone. But if parents and guardians will insist on something more exciting and stimulating than these, they must reckon on being called upon to pay the price. They may have the dicebox, the theater, the dance, if they will, but they must learn, by sad experience, the bitter cost. He needs a long spoon who sups with the devil. The fact is, it is much easier to give these things than to arouse oneself to provide something better. The something better needs time and thought; and staying at home from religious meetings, to give it effect: but the ultimate benefit will more than repay the self-denial.

We cannot put old heads on young shoulders; or our experience into young hearts. We must let our children see a brightness in our behavior which shall not repel them from us, but win them to our Savior. But in doing this, it is quite unnecessary to go to those empty cisterns which the children of the world have hewn for themselves, and which yield no water. We may find, with a little trouble, other wells, through which the living water rises with a sparkle and a beauty that cannot fail to attract young hearts not yet spoiled by the world's glamour and show.

But Jacob did still worse. Not content with pitching his tent before the city, he bought the parcel of ground "where he had pitched his tent." Abraham bought a parcel of ground in which to bury his dead; and this was no declension from the pilgrim spirit—it rather placed it in clearer relief. But as Jacob paid down his hundred pieces of money, each of which bore the rude imprint of a lamb, he was abandoning the pilgrim spirit and the pilgrim attitude, and was *buying* that which God had promised to *give* to him and to his seed. The true spirit of faith would have waited quietly, until God had made good His repeated promise.

It may be that Jacob sought to conciliate his conscience by building the altar, and dedicating it to the God of Israel. Or perhaps he thought to counteract the effect of the idolatrous city, by this means. In some such way professing Christians sometimes try to find an antidote for a week of worldliness in the religious observance of the Lord's day. They allow their children to go into the world, but they insist on their attending family worship before they retire to rest. Where the altar and the world are put into rivalry, there is no doubt as to which will win the day: the Shechem gate will appeal too strongly to our natural tendencies; and we shall find ourselves and our children drifting into Shechem—while the grass of neglect grows up around the altar, or it becomes broken down and disused.

"And Dinah, the daughter of Leah, which she bare unto Jacob, went out to see the daughters of the land." It is a startling announcement, but it contains nothing more than might have been expected. Poor girl! A moth fluttering about a flame! A foolish fish nibbling at the bait! Was she lonely, being the only girl? Did she want to show off some piece of jewelry or dress? Did she long for more admiration, or fascinating society, than she could find at home? Was there a secret drawing to the young men of the place? She went along a path, that seemed to her girlish fancy ever so much more attractive than the dull routine of home. She took no heed to the warnings that may have been addressed to her. And it all ended—as it has ended in thousands of cases since—in misery, ruin, and unutterable disgrace.

She was kindly received. The world will always give a hearty welcome to those who bear a Christian name. Perhaps there is a sense of relief in feeling that it cannot be so bad after all, since Christians do not hesitate to take part with it. The welcome and "well-done" of worldly men should always put us on our guard. "What evil thing have I done," said a shrewd observer, "that yonder worldling speaks so well of me?"

She fascinated the young prince, and fell. It is the old, old story, which is ever new. On the one hand—rank, and wealth, and unbridled appetite; on the other—beauty, weakness, and dallying with temptation. But to whom was her fall due? To Shechem? Yes. To herself? Yes. But, also to Jacob. He must forever reproach himself for his daughter's murdered innocence. But of what use were his reproaches when the deed was done; and the honor of his house was gone; and his name stank among the inhabitants of the land? Would that some Christian parents, reading these words, might take warning as to the end of a pathway on which they are encouraging their children to tread! To stay now may save them tears of blood, and years of fruitless agony. In the strongest terms, let me entreat them not to play on the rim of the whirlpool: lest its hurrying waters catch the too-hazardous craft before they are aware; and whirl them round in an ever giddier dance; and finally engulf them in its eddying vortex.

And all this came because Jacob stepped down from the Israel level back to his old unlovely self. Not improbably you, my reader, have done the same. You have attended meetings which had stirred you to the very depths; and beneath their spell you have thought that life could never be the same again, but that the common round of daily duty would be radiant with the lingering glory of the Transfiguration Mount. You have even gone further: at the Jabbok ford you have met with the Angel Jehovah, the sinew of your strength has shrunk beneath His touch, and you have bent beneath the blessing of His hand. But, notwithstanding all, you have stepped back and down into the old low-level life. You wonder how you were ever so mightily affected, and why the whole experience has faded from you, as some radiant glory which for a moment shone in the western sky, but has died away into dusky twilight.

Let us understand the causes of this relapse, and see how we may guard against its recurrence.

It arises, first, from trusting in the impulse received at a given moment, as though that were sufficient to carry the soul forward through all coming days; and there is, therefore, a relaxation of watchfulness, and prayer, and Bible study. We are all so apt to substitute an experience for abiding fellowship with the Son of God; to dwell in the past, instead of in the living present; to take out the dry and moldy manna we gathered yesterday, instead of being on the alert in the early dawn to get new manna fresh from its baptism of dew. This mistake in Christian experience can only be obviated by careful cultivation of the daily, hourly, friendship of the living Savior. And even this cannot be attained by any effort or resolution of our own, but by the grace of the Holy Spirit, who alone can teach us the art of daily abiding.

Secondly, it may arise from the energy of the self life, which the Apostle Paul calls *the flesh*. Before regeneration we attempt to justify ourselves; being regenerate, we attempt to sanctify ourselves. At meetings of consecration, well-meaning persons endeavor to consecrate themselves. In each case, the element of self makes every effort abortive. We can no more consecrate, in the deepest meaning of that word, than we can justify ourselves. God must be all in all. Let us ask Him to take, keep, and seal us, by the Holy Ghost. There must be more of God in our lives. We must speak less of God helping us, and more of His performing all things for us, as He did for the Psalmist.

Thirdly, these failures arise because we are conscious of the subsidence of the keen emotions which once filled our hearts, and suppose that in losing these we have really lost that spiritual attitude which we then assumed. It can never be too often repeated that all the deepest experiences in Christian life consist in acts of the will, which may or may not be accompanied by emotion, and which remain when the glow of feeling has passed. It would not do for us to live in perpetual sunshine, nor in unbroken rapture; we should be exhausted by an over-expenditure of the vital forces of our souls. God, therefore, withdraws the life of emotion that He may train us to live by faith, and in our wills. We must dare to believe that the blessed experience has not gone, if we can look up to heaven and say, "I *will* to be as I was in the glad hours that bore me to a higher level than any before attained."

Whatever failure comes may also be associated with our reluctance to confess to others the blessing which has irradiated our inner life. It is not necessary to unbare the deepest exercises of our souls to every passerby, but we should not hesitate to confess with our mouth that Jesus Christ is Lord, and tell those with whom we are most intimate what great things the Lord has done for us. To withhold confession, is often to staunch the flow of blessing.

If you are conscious of having failed in any of these respects, ask to be forgiven and restored; put back just where you were; and trust Him, who is the keeper of the faithful soul, to hold you as a star in His right hand, and to trim you as the light of the sacred temple lamps.

11
Back to Bethel

O God, man's heart is darkened,
He will not understand!
Show him Thy cloud and fire;
And, with Thine own right hand
Then lead him through his desert,
Back to Thy Holy Land!

Genesis 35   E. A. Procter

In itself, Bethel was not much. Imagine a long range of broken hills running north and south. The eastern slopes, bleak and tempest riven, descend to the Jordan. The western slopes lie towards the more thickly-peopled parts of Palestine. In the valley at their foot runs the main thoroughfare of Palestine, which has been trodden by centuries of travelers—a rough, broken mountain roadway, following the uneven course of the valley, and intersected by innumerable watercourses. From this track and upwards the mountain slopes are strewn with large sheets of bare rocks—most prone as gravestones, some erect as Druid cromlechs. No house is within sight; no cultivated lands break the stretch of mountain pasture; no domestic animals share the rule of the eagle, the wild goat, and the rabbit.

But to Jacob, Bethel was the most memorable and sacred spot in all the earth. It was there, on the first night of his flight from home, that the mystic ladder had seemed to link earth to heaven, thronged by angels engaged in holy ministry.

Many years had passed since then—years of searching discipline, which had revealed the meanness, the craft, the weakness of his nature.

He had fallen far below the promise of his early vows; his better nature had held but a spasmodic supremacy over his worse; even the angel wrestle had only momentarily lifted him to the level of Israel, the Prince. And of late it would seem that even worse symptoms had begun to show themselves. His life at the gate of Shechem had done much to lower his standard and aims; and to assimilate them to those of the people with whom he had been associated. He seems even to have winked at the idols which were in common request among his people, and of the presence of which he was perfectly well aware. There had been a time when, if his dearest wife wished for graven images, she must have them surreptitiously, but now he had become so lax himself, that there was no need for concealment on the part of any (v. 2). Alas! what a fall was this for the man who had built so many altars to Jehovah; and was the chosen depository of those truths for which the world was waiting! For the world's sake, and for his own, it was essential that he should be compelled to regain the ground which he had so grievously lost. It was then that he said to his household, "Let us arise, and go up to Bethel."

This impulse was natural. The emigrant who lives in the soft Bermudas, or in a Canadian log house, as he reaches mature life, will find a strange yearning rising within him for the Highland glen in which he was born. He sends many a longing look towards the Northern stars; and at last starts on pilgrimage. He may find the scene desolate and deserted; yet he is not wholly disappointed: he needed the glut of reality to satisfy the long fever of his soul. It was something like this that came to Jacob. A voice (shall I not call it an instinct, within him?) cried: Go and dwell for a season at Bethel; gaze once more on the familiar scene; put your head down again upon that stone which you set up for a pillar; and review the way in which the Lord thy God hath led thee.

But his untoward circumstances gave a yet further reason. He was in terrible trouble. He had settled himself down, and sunk a well for his supply, which became so famous as to be known through all succeeding time as Jacob's Well; he was intimately identified for several uneventful years with the life of the locality; and then his sons had made his name stink among the inhabitants of the land, by the frenzied passion with which they had revenged their sister's dishonor. He was in imminent danger of destruction from the infuriated tribes around him. He must go somewhere; and it was at this moment that the impulse came to him to go up to Bethel. He might not have heeded it, if the waters of earthly comfort had sufficed for his urgent need. But now that they threatened to fail, and even to turn to poison, he was the more ready to try what Bethel might afford of comfort and safety, of satisfaction and restoration. A drying well will often lead the spirit to the river that flows from the throne of the Lamb.

But, above all, that impulse originated in God Himself, "God said unto Jacob, Arise, go up to Bethel, and dwell there." No human ear now catches the tones of that majestic voice. Yet, God often speaks to us also—through our own consciousness, and within our own souls. Yes, and He speaks more often than most of us are aware. We do not always distinguish the voice within us to be the voice of God. We act on an impulse, we know not why. But as we review our path from the sweet summit of religious revival to which we have been led, we recognize, with thankful awe, that the voice to which we listened was none other than that voice which Jacob first heard speaking to him in his angel-haunted sleep. Has it not been so with you? You have followed an inward impulse, not knowing whence it came, or whither it led; you have wandered blindly on, reaching positions of which you had never dreamed, but which are evidently your special sphere: and it is only on looking backwards that you realize how every step of your way has been ordered by a wisdom not your own; how the impulse originated in Him who prompts the swallows to follow the sun to warmer climes; and how the voice that called you was the voice of God.

But there is something better than this blind obedience, and it would be a happy thing if every child of God had reached it. God is always speaking to us in the incidents of daily life; He has a meaning, and transmits to us a message, in everything which He permits to happen. We are wise, therefore, when we set ourselves to decipher the hieroglyphics in which His meaning is enwrapped; and to question each event as to the tidings which He has entrusted it to bring. We are wiser still, when we lovingly, yea joyfully, accept, and unquestioningly obey.

And why did God wish Jacob to go back to Bethel? Because Bethel was associated with one of the most blessed spiritual experiences of his life. And the summons to go back to Bethel was equivalent to an invitation to return to that fervor, that devotion, and those holy vows, which had made that bare mountain pass the very house of God and the gate of heaven. "Come back; and be as near to Me as you were when you first set up that stone, and annointed it with oil."

There are some words which cannot be spoken in our ears without arousing in us an immediate and touching response. They come on us as a strain of music; or a whiff of perfume on the summer breeze—awakening far-off memories, and exciting emotions long gone by. So must the word *Bethel* have sounded in the ear of Jacob: stirring all his better nature—bidding it arise, and come forth from its long death sleep; and lighting up the nobler spirit of his life. It met with an instant response: "Then Jacob said unto his household, and to all that were with him, Put away the strange gods that are among you; and be clean, and change your garments. And let us arise, and go up to Bethel."

And so he came to Bethel, protected by God's watchful care; and he built there an altar, and God appeared unto him again.

I. MANY CHRISTIANS ARE SUFFERING FROM SPIRITUAL DECLENSION. They hardly realize it, it has crept on them so quietly, but they have drifted far away from their Bethel and Peniel. Grey hairs are on a man before he knows. Summer fruit is beginning to rot within, long before its surface is pitted with specks. The leaf's connection with the branch is severed, even when it looks green. The devil is too shrewd to make Judases at a stroke; he wins us from the side of Christ by hair breadths. We would never think of letting in the lion, but we spare the little foxes, which break down the hedge—through which the lion comes presently. We would never think of letting Delilah cut off our seven locks of hair, but we do no so much object to her binding it with her green withes, though she will creep on to the other. So insensible have you been slipping back; until you are infinitely farther from God than you were in the sacred, happy days that are past.

II. IDOLS ARE THE INEVITABLE SYMPTOM OF INCIPIENT DECAY. Go at autumn into the woods, and see how the members of the fungus tribes are scattered plentifully throughout the unfrequented glades. All through the long scorching summer days their germs were present in the soil, but they were kept from germinating by the dryness of the air, and the heat of the sun. However, there is now nothing to prevent it; nay, the dank damp of decay is the very food of their life. Where the shade is deepest, and the soil most impregnated with the products of corruption, they love to pitch their tents. Wherever, therefore, you find these fungus growths, you may be sure that there is corruption and decay. Similarly, whenever there has set in upon the spiritual life the autumn of decay, you will be sure to find a fungus growth of idols—the sorrowful symptoms that the bright summer time has passed, or is passing away from the soul.

You may hide your idols, like Rachel, but they will not remain hidden: they will work their way forward, until what was hidden as a sin becomes paraded as a boast. It may be that some backslider shall read these lines, conscious that things are not now what they were between him and God. Such a one will bear witness from his own bitter experience, that in proportion to the decay of the inner life there has been the growth of some idol love. You have set your heart on making a reputation, or a fortune; you have loved some worthless friend with an inordinate affection; you have lavished yourself on something or someone outside of God—and as your energies have waxed in this direction, they have waned in the other. "No man can serve two masters: either he will love the one, and hate the other; or else he will hold to the one, and despise the other."

III. THESE IDOLS MUST BE SURRENDERED BEFORE THERE CAN BE VICTORY OR PEACE.

The reason for Jacob's flight before those alien tribes was, of course, the censurable and merciless action of his sons, but above and beyond this, lay the fact that Jacob had been giving some measure of countenance to the existence of idolatry in the camp. I always find, in Christian experience, that failure and defeat indicate the presence of some idol somewhere, and the need of more complete consecration to God. It may be a hidden idol; and it may be hidden by the Rachel of your heart, lovely and beloved: but if it be there, it will be the certain cause of disappointment. You say that you do not find yourself able to overcome besetting sin; that you are tripped up before you look to Christ; that you are sometimes hot as juniper coals, and then cold as ice; you talk about your experience as if Christ had failed—no such thing! Get down on your knees; search out the idols; ransack all the camel baggage, in spite of all that Rachel may say bring out the accursed things, and bury them. Put away the garments spotted with the flesh; only thus will you enter upon the life of victory, or will God appear unto you again.

How wise it was for Jacob to bury those idols right away! If he had kept or carried them with him, he might have been tempted to bring them out again. It was so much better to leave them right there, under the oak in Shechem, before he started for Bethel. I do not think he could have counted on God's delivering care, if he had not acted with such promptness and decision. God would not have been the escort of a pack of idols! Burn the books that have polluted your mind. Cut off the hand that has made you offend. Renounce the drink that has obtained such a power over you; and pour the contents of your cellars down the gutter, lest you be tempted to return to them again. Burn your bridge behind you. Hide the idols under the oak. "Mother," said a betting man, "I have taken the first step to Christianity; I have burned my betting books." We cannot be surprised at the mighty work of God in Ephesus after the splendid *auto-da-fé* that took place in the marketplace (Acts 19:19).

What a man is, that in most cases his family will also be. When Jacob's camp saw that he was himself in earnest, they gave him all the strange gods that were in their hand, and all the earrings that were in their ears. What a solemn responsibility rests on us all in our family life, that we should not, by our silence, connive at either follies or sins. If those around us see that we are consistent and determined, they will not let us go to heaven alone. Christiana and her children will sooner or later follow Christian. "Jacob came to Luz that is, Bethel, he and *all the people that were with him.*"

This, then, is our closing message: put away your idols, and get back to Bethel. Repent, and do the first works. Pray as you used to pray. Study the Bible as you used to study it. Spend the Lord's day as you used to spend it. Build an altar now on the same site on which you built it years ago. Give yourself again to God. True, a sad life of wasted opportunities lies behind you, but do not waste more time in fruitless regrets. Forget the things that are behind; stretch forward to those that are before. And God will appear to you again; and will renew the Princely Name and the Princely Blessing to which you might have thought that you had forfeited all right; moreover, He will promise you marvelous fruitfulness in service, and far-reaching possessions in the Land of promise (vv. 11, 12). All these things are in store for you—if only you will bury your idols, and go up to Bethel, and dwell there. "Goodness and mercy shall follow you all the days of your life; and you shall dwell in the house of the Lord forever." "Return, ye backsliding children; and I will heal your backslidings. Behold, we come unto Thee; for Thou art the Lord our God."

12

The School of Sorrow

The ills we see—
The mysteries of sorrow deep and long,
The dark enigmas of permitted wrong—
Have all one key:
This strange, sad world is but our Father's school;
All chance and change His love shall grandly overrule.

Genesis 35—42   F. R. Havergal

I n manufactories of chinaware there are processes which illustrate our lives with startling force and beauty. Among others which read us deep and helpful lessons, is the burning in of the colors, which had been previously painted on the ware. It is only the skilled hand that can delineate those designs which delight our fancy, but no skill of the painter could make them other than evanescent, unless there were some other method of rendering them permanent. This is accomplished by placing the newly-painted ware in a kiln or furnace, where it is exposed to very intense heat; and the colors are burned in and fixed.

It is very often thus that God makes permanent some great blessing which we have received. He burns it in by placing us amid the fires of keen suffering and sorrow. So often have I noticed this, that I am never surprised to hear men date an unusual amount of trial from the moment in which heaven seemed nearer, and Christ dearer, than ever before. It must be so: or the blessing which they had obtained would fade from their soul—as the tints of sunset fade off earth and sky; or as the photograph fades from the plate, unless it has been "fixed" in the dark chamber. In this respect, there is a precise analogy between the experience of Jacob and ourselves: teaching us again that spiritual life is one, though severed by the centuries; and that the Bible is evidently the Word of God, because it is so certainly the book of man.

When, having left his idols behind, Jacob had got back to Bethel, and had built again the altar of renewed consecration, we are told significantly that "God appeared unto him again, and blessed him." Are all the readers of these lines conscious that the blessing of the Almighty is resting upon them—as the light of the transfigured body of our Lord fell upon the virgin snows of Hermon, and made the darkness light? Has God revealed Himself to you again, after the long, sad lapse of fellowship and communion? Is the backslider back again in the house of God, and at the gate of heaven? If not, would it not be wise to do as Jacob did? Ask God to show you what your idols are. Tell Him that you want to be only, always, all for Him. Put away not only your sins, but your weights—i.e., aught that hinders you in the Christian race. If you cannot do this yourself, tell Him that you are willing for Him to take them from you. If you cannot say that you are willing, tell Him that you are willing to be made willing. And when you have thus surrendered your will, give yourself again to Him; entreat Him to take full possession of your entire being; ally yourself as an Isaac upon the altar of self-dedication; and remember that He takes all we give, and at the moment of our giving it. It may be that He will appear to us at once, flooding our spirits with the old unspeakable joy; or He may keep us waiting for a little. But it matters comparatively little, if only we can say, with the assurance of an unwavering faith, "We are His; nothing shall henceforth separate us from the love of God."

It was a great blessing, indeed, that God vouchsafed to Jacob. "God said unto him, Thy name is Jacob: thy name shall not be called any more Jacob, but Israel shall be thy name." The angel had said as much as this at Peniel; and, for a brief moment, he had shone in the transfiguring gleam of royalty. But the gleam was transient enough; like that which sometimes breaks for a moment far out upon a stormy sea, and is instantly veiled again. But there had been wrought on him a deep spiritual change since then; and his experience had been brought into more constant conformity with the level of Israel, the Prince—which was not reaffirmed as his perpetual designation. And forthwith he was plunged into a fiery furnace of trial, which made both name and character permanent.

But this was not all: God constituted him father of nations and kings; and promised to give to him the land in which he was a wanderer, as his fathers before him. Now these two items of fruitfulness and possession are only possible to those who have passed through the school of suffering. It is in soul travail that our children are born; and it is through much tribulation that we enter into the Kingdom. Let no man think that he can win the highest spiritual attainments without paying the price for them. Our Lord could only be perfected as our Captain and High Priest by the things that He suffered; through His sufferings He became the Author of eternal salvation to all who believe.

We need not dwell further, then, on the probable reasons why, from this moment, Jacob's path was draped in the gathering shadows of outward sorrow. But we may notice what those shadows were. And we may interest ourselves in remarking how, as the sorrows gathered, there was a fuller life, and fruitfulness, and royalty. Jacob is increasingly replaced by Israel, the Prince. Does it not remind us forcibly of another, who said, "Though our outward man perish, the inward man is renewed day by day?" (2 Cor. 4:16). Our affliction is light, and for a moment, compared with the weight of glory which it is working out.

There are four burials in one chapter (Gen. 35), including that of the idols in Shechem. These were the beginning of sorrows.

First, Deborah died; the old favorite nurse, who had accompanied her young mistress, when, long years before, she had left her home across the Euphrates to become Isaac's bride. What a link she must have been with that sacred past! What stories she could tell of the glory of that camp presided over by Abraham, the friend of God! And often she would live again in the past, and tell how bitterly Rebekah rued the fatal advice she gave to her favorite son—whom she was never to see again; and for lack of whom she pined, until she drooped in death, while he still tarried across the distant Euphrates' flood. Rebekah's death may have made the camp of Isaac distasteful to the faithful old servant; and she took the first opportunity of coming to spend her remaining days with him whom, in memory of the long past, she too loved with the tenacious affection of her race. It must have been a sad wrench to Jacob to lay the remains of his mother's closest friend beneath that oak in Bethel. The grief occasioned by her death was evidently quite unusual; since even the oak became known, in after years, as "the oak of tears."

But a worse sorrow was in store. They journeyed from Bethel, and there was but a little way to come to Ephrath. The foremost ranks of the march were already in sight of the hostelry, and were eagerly pressing on for the camping ground. But suddenly a summons from the rear bade them halt. The beloved Rachel cannot go another step. The tidings of her extreme agony and peril silence the motley groups of drovers and slaves, and servants and sons. Gathered in confusion upon the road, they await the issue with the dread suspense which breathlessly marks each flicker of life's taper. That scene would never be forgotten by any of them, least of all by Jacob. When he, too, lay upon his dying bed, in that hieroglyphed Egyptian chamber, it came back to him, with touching force and pathos, such as told the freshness of the wound, and the anguish of the grief, which thirty years could not dull. Ah, sorrow! nature may cast its mantle of greenery over her scars, and golden grain may stand in serried ranks upon the field of Waterloo, but thou can inflict wounds which never seam together, but gape, and gape.

But all the agony of those devoted hearts could not stay that departing spirit: the mother only lived long enough to see her second babe, and to enshrine her sorrow in its name; and then she died, and was buried there in the way to Ephrath, which is Bethlehem. It was a matter of evident regret to Jacob, in after years, that she did not lie, with the rest of her kin, in Machpelah's ancient cave, but he could never forget that lone spot on the way to Ephrath (48:7). And when the wheel of time had brought many changes, and that spot had become famous as the birthplace of the great son of Jesse, still it seemed to the anointed ear of the prophet as if Rachel's spirit haunted the spot, wailing for her children. And even to this day travelers turn aside to visit Rachel's tomb.

Yet another heart pang was measured out to that much-tried man. We suffer keenly through the sins of those we love; and when the father saw his Reuben and his Judah stained with the soil of nameless impurity, he drank perhaps the bitterest cup of his life.

Nor was this all. He lived to see dissension and hatred rend his home. The elder brethren envied and hated their younger brother, Joseph; the son of the beloved Rachel, and the child of his old age. His partiality most certainly added fuel to the flame. It was a great mistake to confer the costly coat that indicated the heir and prince of an Eastern clan. But we can easily understand how naturally the old man would turn to the promising lad, whose dreams bespoke his regal future, and reminded him of his own. "His brethren envied him, but his father observed the saying."

But there was worse to follow. One day the sons brought home the coat he knew so well, but it was daubed with blood, and stained. "This have we found; know now whether it be thy sons' coat or not." It may be that a suspicion even then crossed his mind that there had been foul play. But if it did, he kept it to himself, and only let it slip afterwards in the bitterness of his grief (42:36). He at least professed to believe that an evil beast had devoured the beloved body, and that Joseph had been rent in pieces. How he mourned only those know who have passed through similar anguish. The father's grief touched unwonted chords in the hearts of his children. They rose up to comfort him. "But he refused to be comforted; and said, I will go down to the grave unto my son mourning. Thus his father wept for him."

But another sorrow was in store. Jacob was next called upon to see his aged father breathe his last; and perhaps once more to hear those trembling lips pronounce the blessing which had cost so much. "Isaac gave up the ghost and died, and was gathered unto his people." He joined the great gathering of his clan, in the ranks of which are numbered all meek and true-hearted souls. Who are *our* people, to whom *we* shall be one day gathered? And the two sons buried him. Esau came from Edom—the successful man of the world, who had anticipated this moment years before, as likely to suit his purpose for slaying Jacob, but who was sweetened and softened by the mellowing influence of time. And Jacob, limping in his step; broken by hard toils; stricken by his recent losses—came to help him. There they stood for a moment: the twins whose lives had been such a struggle and such a contrast, reconciled in the presence of the great silence of the grave; and soon to take their several ways, never again to meet, but to tread ever diverging paths, both they and their children, and their children's children. We link hands with the playmates and companions of early life across the tiny stream, and for some distance we can keep them linked, albeit that the streamlet widens between us; then loosing hands, we walk side by side, keeping each other well in view, and talking merrily: but, at last, the mighty river spreads its volume between us; and we can neither see nor hear anything, save the break of the sea upon the shore. It is all important that those who love should be on the same right side of the stream, if they would escape an eternal separation.

On the heels of bereavement came one of those terrific famines to which Eastern countries are subject, and which sweep them bare of people. The family of Jacob was not exempt. The sons seem to have sat down in the stolid indifference born of long privation; and were only aroused by their father's appeal, "Why do ye look one upon another?' They went down into Egypt—in all ages the granary of the world; and after an agonizing interval of suspense returned. But Simeon was not with them; and to get him, and more corn, Jacob must risk the son of his right hand—the lad who had cost him so much in Rachel's death. Who does not sympathize with the cry of agony wrung from that quivering heart, a cry that revealed that depth of love of which it was capable? "Me have ye bereaved of my children: Joseph is not, and Simeon is not; and ye will take Benjamin away: all these things are against me. Ye shall bring down my grey hairs with sorrow to the grave."

In addition to all this, there was growing upon him a sense that his life was closing; that his strength was failing; and that he must prepare to follow his father into the unseen. His years had been few in comparison with those of his forefathers; and he had the weary sense of failure, in that he had "not attained" (47:9). It is a pitiful thing, when an old man finds life ebbing fast away from him; while all his regrets cannot recall one single mistake, or give him the consciousness of having done all he could. Such sorrows fell to Jacob's lot: they fall to our lot still; and when they do, let us learn how to behave ourselves.

I. DO NOT JUDGE BY APPEARANCE. Jacob said, "*All* these things are against me." It was a great mistake. Joseph was alive—the governor of

Egypt; sent there to preserve their lives, and to be the stay of his closing years. Simeon was also alive—the blessed link which was drawing and compelling his brothers to return into the presence of the strange Egyptian governor. Benjamin would come safely back again. All things, so far from being against him, were working together for good to him; and if only he would trust God, he would live to see it so. All things are yours, if you are Christ's. All things serve you. Even those that seem most awry and trying are really promoting your best interests. If you knew as much about them as God does, you would go down on your bended knees and thank Him, with streaming eyes, for the most untoward of your circumstances. The seed buried in the ground may rejoice in the frost as much as in the genial sunshine. And even though some events cut us to the quick, if we believe that the infinite love of God is working in and through them, we may sing as Paul and Silas did, albeit that our feet are fast in the stocks. Let us cultivate the habit of looking at the bright side of things. If there are only a few clouds floating in your sky, do not say that the whole is overcast; and if all the heaven is covered, save one small chink of blue, make much of that; and by all means do not exaggerate the darkness.

II. BE SURE THAT GOD HAS A PURPOSE IN ALL YOUR SORROW. The apparent aimlessness of some kinds of pain is sometimes their sorest ingredient. We can suffer more cheerfully if we can clearly see the end which is being slowly reached. But if we cannot, it is hard to lie still and be at rest. But the believer knows that nothing can come to him, save by the permission of God's love. Every trial must reach him through the mystic barriers that engird him; and must show a permit signed by the hand of God Himself. Nothing comes by chance, or by the will of friend or foe, but all is under law. And each several calamity has a specific purpose. "Fitches are not threshed with a sharp threshing instrument, neither is a cartwheel turned about upon the cummin, but the fitches are beaten out with a staff, and the cummin with a rod."

And as the farmer carefully adjusts his method to various kinds of grain, and to accomplish the object he has at heart, so the Almighty varies his method of dealing with us: He ever selects the precise trial that will soonest and best accomplish His purposes; and He only continues it long enough to do all that needs to be done. "Bread corn is bruised: but He will not ever be threshing it; nor break it with the wheel of his cart; nor bruise it with his horsemen." I commend that precious promise to those who think their sorrows past endurance. They will not last forever; they will be suited to our peculiar needs and strength. They will accomplish that on which the great Husbandman has set His heart.

III. REMEMBER THAT NOTHING CAN SEPARATE YOU FROM THE LOVE OF GOD. When Jacob reviewed these dark passages of his life from the serene heights of his dying bed, he saw—as he had never seen it before—that God had shepherded him all his life long; and His Angel had redeemed him from all evil (48:15, 16). We do not realize this at the time: but there is never an experience in life without the watch of that unsleeping Shepherd-eye; never a peril without the interposition of that untiring Shepherd hand. The hand of the Good Physician is ever on the pulse, as we pass through the operation. "Who shall separate us from the love of Christ? Shall tribulation, or distress, or persecution, or famine, or nakedness, or peril, or sword? Nay." These things may sever God from our eyes, and shut away the realization of His love, but they cannot make Him cease to love us; or hide us from Him; or separate us from Him. Take heart, you who are descending into the dark valley of shadow; the Good Shepherd is going at your side, though you see Him not. His rod and staff shall comfort you: yea, His own voice shall speak comfortably to you. Fear not!

IV. ANTICIPATE THE "AFTERWARD." Look not at the things which are seen, but at those which are not seen. Cast into the one scale your sorrows, if you will, but put into the other the glory which shall presently be the outcome of the pain. Consider how splendid it will be, when the discipline is over; and the lovely shape is acquired; and the lesson learned; and the pattern fixed forever. Anticipate the time when every vestige of Jacob shall have been laid aside, and Israel is become the befitting title for your soul. Will not that repay you—because you will have been brought into a oneness with Christ which shall be heaven in miniature?

Take heart, thou bit of heaven's porcelain: thou must be shaped and fashioned on the rapid wheel; thy fairest hues must be burnt in amid the most fiery trials—but thou shalt yet grace the table of thy King; and shalt be used of Him for His choicest purposes.

"Wherefore, let them that suffer according to the will of God, commit the keeping of their souls to Him, as unto a faithful Creator" (1 Pet. 4:19).

13
Glimpses
of the Israel-Nature

I held it truth with him who sings
To one clear harp in diverse tones,
That men may rise on stepping stones
Of their dead selves to higher things.

Genesis 47   Tennyson

A s a brook runs, it clears itself. It was so with Jacob's life. The discipline of life, like a refining fire, did not fail in its purpose. The dross of his nature was at last well nigh worked out; and the nobler Israel nature became more and more apparent. This change is marked by the change in the name by which he is designated on the inspired page. The old term, Jacob, is used but sparingly; and for the most part Israel is the title of his nobility.

Before we can study the traces of his increasing princeliness of character, we should do well to notice that the name Jacob, though used sparingly, is not wholly dropped. We can never forget what we were. We can never forget what we might be, were it not for the restraining grace of God. I cannot agree with those who think that the Jacob nature may be expunged, wiped out from our being. In my judgment, both Scripture and experience are dead against them. "The flesh lusteth against the Spirit"; and will lust, though with ever decreasing force, unto the end. But it is my joyful belief, also, that "the Spirit lusteth against the flesh"; and represses it with such growing power that it is reduced to the last extremity: and we are kept from doing the things that we otherwise would. Indeed, the self-life can scarcely be said to live, since it makes but the faintest response to temptation. If only we walk in the Spirit, and live in the Spirit, and are led by the Spirit, we shall not fulfill the lusts of the flesh: we shall hardly be aware of their presence in our being; we shall be as good as dead to them. But, in the moment that we cease to abide in living union with the Blessed Spirit, we shall find that the old nature will revive again, in horrid resurrection; and will sweep us down to a sin like that which blackened and saddened all David's later years.

Germs of disease may be constantly breeding in an infected house, but, so long as the disinfecting fluid is well sprinkled on the floors and pendant sheets, they are killed off as soon as they are formed. So sin, though present in the heart, may be choked off, so as to be almost unperceived, because the Holy Ghost is ever at work acting as a disinfectant: but, so soon as His grace is withdrawn, sin regains its old deadly sway, and breathes forth its pestilential poison. It is of the utmost importance, then, to keep in with the Holy Ghost.

One more illustration, though some may deem it far-fetched, will clench and illustrate my meaning. A mesmerist may weave a spell, by passing hands over a man of weaker mind, so as to cast him into all the appearances of death. But he is not dead; and when the charm is broken, the processes of life resume their course. So, beneath the spell of the grace of God's Holy Spirit, our evil self life may lie as dead, only giving faint signs of life; and yet, if that spell be spoken, it will spring up with robust and deadly vigor. It becomes us then to watch and pray, lest we enter into temptation.

There is a beautiful experiment, which the readers of these lines may try for themselves; and which will give them a vivid idea of how the law of the Spirit of life in Christ Jesus can make them free from the law of sin and death. If you take a heavy book and hold it at arm's length, the pull of the law of gravitation will soon draw it downwards, but if some friend will pour down that arm a constant stream of electricity, the flow of the electric current will set you free from the effect of the downward pull. It will still be there, though you will have become almost unconscious of it. Thus it will be when we are filled by the Spirit of God: the downward tendency may be in us yet, but it will be more than counteracted by the habit of that new life, in which the power of the living Savior is ever at work, through the grace of the Holy Ghost.

In the earlier stages of the Christian life, the habit of abiding ever in communion with the Spirit of God is difficult to form and maintain. Some seem to acquire it more habitually and unbrokenly than others. Where this is the case, the Jacob-nature begins to disappear with a suddenness that reminds us of a rapid thaw, which, in a single night, may rid the streets of tons of snow. In the case of those who learn the sweet lesson of unbroken fellowship more slowly, the Jacob-nature keeps breaking in upon the Israel-life as the underlying rock strata will break up through the green sward of a highland valley. Yet, as the years pass on, and the habit of fellowship becomes a permanent possession, these eruptions become less and less frequent; so that at last the Israel-nature has the almost undisputed sway in the life.

We have to notice some manifestations of this Israel-nature in Jacob, like the outshinings of the sun; which, in the early morning, has fought with heavy mists for his supremacy, but at last shines out in a cloudless sky, and sets in radiant glory.

For more than twenty years Jacob mourned for Joseph as dead. The monotony of those years was only broken by new misfortunes, which came upon each other's heels, as the messengers of calamity to Job. We only catch some few sobs from that stricken heart; like the cries of the Crucified from amid the dense gloom of the cross. On first seeing the bloodstained coat, "I will go down into the grave mourning"; on learning the first tidings about the rough governor, the lord of the land, "Me have ye bereaved of my children"; on the appeal of his sons to spare Benjamin, "My son shall not go down with you, lest ye bring down my grey hairs with sorrow to the grave"; on their renewed appeal. "Wherefore dealt ye so ill with me as to tell the man ye had a brother?" On giving his final consent, in addition to the direction that they should take some few delicacies from their almost emptied stores, he said sadly and almost despairingly, "God Almighty give you mercy before the man, that he may send away your other brother, and Benjamin. If I be bereaved of my children, I am bereaved."

But the night of weeping was followed by the morning of joy. Joy looked in at the old man's window; and sorrow and sighing fled away.

What a confusion of emotion must have filled his heart when the completed band of his sons stood once again before him with such amazing tidings! Benjamin was there, and Simeon. Love had welded them together in the furnace of sorrow, like a twelve-linked chain, no link of which would ever again be missing. The God of their fathers had met with them; and henceforward would supply their needs so fully, that they could have no further lack, though the famine should last thrice seven years. And, above all, Joseph was yet alive; and he was governor over all the land of Egypt. What wonder that the aged heart stood still, and its machinery almost threatened to break down, beneath the pressure of sudden rapture. At first he could not believe it all. But the sight of the wagons convinced him. Then there came forth a gleam of the royal spirit of faith—the spirit of Jacob revived, and *Israel* said, "It is enough: Joseph my son is yet alive; I will go and see him before I die."

Before he left Canaan, he had one final interview with his Almighty Friend. It happened at Beersheba—the last halting place amid the green pasture lands of the Land of Promise, and before they struck into the sand waste that lay between them and Egypt. Everything there reminded him of his own early life which was spent there. He could find the ruins of his father's altar; and the well which his father had sunk; and "he offered sacrifices unto the God of his father Isaac." At that time his mind was engaged in eager debate as to the path of duty. On the one hand, love to Joseph and his necessities drew him to Egypt; on the other, the memory of how much evil had befallen his ancestors whenever they went down to Egypt, made him eagerly question whether he was justified in going. It was at that time that God made his path clear, by saying, "Fear not to go down into Egypt; for I will there make of thee a great nation: I will go down with thee into Egypt; and Joseph shall put his hand upon thine eyes." How comfortably our God speaks to us when we are sore perplexed. If we will only wait, we shall hear a voice behind us saying, "This is the way, walk ye in it." But, since the voice speaks from behind, we must not run on too far or fast in front.

(1) There is a glimpse of the Israel-nature in his meeting with Joseph. How feverishly the old man anticipated it! And when, on the confines of Egypt, he learned that the second chariot in the land was

bringing his long lost son to his embrace, he roused himself to meet him; not as the Jacob of olden days, but as Israel the Prince. "And Israel said unto Joseph, Now let me die, since I have seen thy face, because thou art yet alive."

(2) There is yet another glimpse of the Israel-nature in his blessing of Pharaoh. Joseph might almost have been ashamed of his aged father, and left him in the background. He was old, and decrepit, and lame. He had spent all his life in tents and sheep farms, and was totally ignorant of the manners of a court. He was an exile, an emigrant, a man who had failed. His very presence there was due to his ruinous losses. What a contrast between him and the glorious Pharaoh, whose court teemed with science and wit; with soldiers and priests; with wealth and splendor! And yet, when he stood before Pharaoh, there was so much moral grandeur about him that the greatest monarch in the world bent eagerly beneath his blessing. "How old art thou?" was the kind inquiry of the mighty monarch, to commemorate whom a massive pyramid, destined to outlast his race, was in course of erection. The question was perhaps suggested by his bent form and withered look. The reply was sad enough; and it was the Jacob-nature that uttered it. It seemed like an anticipation of the cry of Ecclesiastes, "Vanity of vanities, all is vanity." It was lit up by no single ray of thankfulness, or faith, or hope: "My life has been a pilgrimage; its days have been few and evil." *Few,* in comparison with those of Terah, Abraham, and Isaac. *Evil,* in comparison with that of Esau, who stood at the head of a great kingdom, the progenitor of a line of kings. And yet, with this confession ringing in his ears, Pharaoh was blessed by those outstretched trembling hands, and by that quavering voice. Esau never could have done that.

"Without all contradiction the less is blessed of the better." Jacob must have had something about him that rendered him superior to the greatest monarch of his time. There were two kings in that royal chamber decorated by weird hieroglyphs and long lines of fantastic figures: the one, royal with the adventitious distinction of birth and rank; the other, a wayworn pilgrim, royal with the divine patent of royalty—a noble character. And, as they stood together, it was shown to all the world that the spiritual is greater than the material; and that God can endow a human spirit with such moral splendor as to compel the world's conquerors to confess themselves conquered before its power. You may be crafty, mean, and bargain-loving; yet if you will but yield yourself to God, and submit to his loving discipline, He will make you truly royal, and give you the moral power, which masters all other power beside.

(3) There is yet another glimpse of the Israel-nature in his solemn injunctions to Joseph about his burial. "The time drew nigh that *Israel* must die; and he called his son Joseph, and said unto him. . . . And *Israel* bowed himself upon the bed's head" (47:29, 30). It is the death scene which shows the true nature of a man; and its darkness set Jacob's better nature in full relief.

He was evidently a man of faith. He knew the ancient promise made by God, of which Abraham may have often spoken to him in his early life—that their seed should inherit Canaan. He was sure, therefore, that his people would not always abide in Egypt—however fertile its Goshens, or friendly its peoples. The trumpet would sound the summons for their departure. If then he were buried in Egypt, he would be left behind, a stranger among strangers; and this could not be. He must be where his people were. To him, therefore, burial in the most splendid mausoleum that was ever constructed to that land of silent tombs was not for one moment to be compared with burial in Machpelah's solitary and humble cave; which at that time was a mere outpost in a distant and hostile land. And he desired it, not only because the mortal remains of Abraham and Sarah, of Isaac and Rebekah, and of Leah lay there, but because he foresaw the time when it would be surrounded by the teeming myriads of his children.

He could only see this by faith. He "had not received the promises, but, by faith, he had seen them afar off, and was persuaded of them, and embraced them." It was by faith that he was able to say, "Behold I die: but God shall be with you, and bring you again unto the land of your father. Bury me not in Egypt, but I will lie with my fathers, and thou shalt carry me out of Egypt, and bury me in their burying place." Was it not *Israel* that spoke thus? Faith made him royal; as it will ennoble the coarsest and commonest nature, lifting the beggar from the dunghill, and making him sit among princes. And these noble utterances prove how truly God had done his work of ennoblement; and how royal was the spirit of the dying patriarch.

(4) There is yet another glimpse of the Israel-nature in his dealings with Joseph's sons. In the chapter that records that solemn scene, it is almost entirely on Israel that our attention is fixed. "Israel strengthened himself on his bed." "Israel beheld Joseph's sons." "Israel stretched out his right hand." "Israel said unto Joseph."

The sands of time had nearly run out in that aged and battered body; and when Joseph arrived at his dwelling, the gift of his own munificence, the dying man seems to have been lying in the extreme of physical exhaustion. But the sound of the beloved name of "Joseph" rallied him; and, propped by pillows, he sat up upon his bed.

Then, with that wonderful accuracy of memory which is so remarkable in the dying, he reviewed the past. The vision of the wondrous ladder, with its troops of angels; the precious words of promise, which one hundred years could not obliterate from the tablets of memory; the scene on the hilly road to Bethlehem, where he buried Rachel; the successive instance of the guardian care of the Angel who had tended him, as a shepherd does his flock, all his life long until that day—all passed before his eye, dim with age, but bright with memory and hope.

Amid this reverie, the old man became aware of the presence of Joseph's two sons, and inquired who they were; and when he knew, he asked that they might be brought near enough for him to give them an old man's blessing. He did this with great affection and solemnity. He kissed and embraced them; and asked that his good angel might bless the lads. He ranked them among his own sons: and was led by prophetic insight to distinguish between them, crossing his hands, and laying his right on the head of the younger, whom Joseph had placed before his left; and his left on the head of the elder, whom the father had placed before his right. When Joseph remonstrated with him, thinking it was a mistake due to his age and blindness, the old man still held to his choice, as one conscious of a prerogative in which not even Joseph must interfere.

This touching interview ended by the gift to Joseph of the parcel of ground which he had wrested from the Amorites in Shechem. It had long ago returned to its original owners, but he saw, down the vista of the future, that there would be a reversion of the whole to him and his—and it was of that future that he spoke in faith.

The whole of this scene is replete with a dignity, born of moral greatness, and worthy of Israel, the Prince.

Time fails to bring out the traits of royalty in the closing scene of all, which must yield us material for our next chapter. It is enough to remind you of them, ere we close. They are evident enough. Twelve strong, bearded men stand around him. He is in the last extreme of physical decrepitude, but he does not cower or shrink before them, as in other days. His face may be shadowed with death, but his eye gleams with the light of prophecy. He calls out their names one by one. He arraigns them at the bar of judgment. He reviews their past. He apportions them their praise or blame. He allots their future. "These are the twelve tribes of Israel; and this is it that their father spake unto them."

We need not go into further particulars, because enough has been said to convince the most careless reader of the royalty that shone forth from this aged man, as the gleaming torch lights flashed from the breaking pitchers of Gideon's host. And there is enkindled in our hearts the hope that God will do as much for us, through Him who loveth us, and by His death hath made us kings unto God, with whom we shall one day reign on the earth.

14
Rest,
and the Rest Giver

Oh, the little birds sang east, The little birds sang west!
And I said in underbreath, All our life is mixed with death:
And who knoweth which is best?
Oh, the little birds sang east, The little birds sang west!
And I smiled to think God's good flowsAround our incompleteness;
Round our restlessness He's rest!

Genesis 44   Mrs. E. B. Browning

There is much of interest in these dying words of Jacob, through which Israel the Prince shines so conspicuously. We can but touch them as we pass, as the sea bird touches the wave; for higher themes allure us.

It would, for instance, be interesting to mark their accuracy. Reuben, though the firstborn, never excelled; no judge, prophet, or ruler, sprang from his tribe. Simeon was almost absorbed in the nomad tribes, of Southern Palestine. The cities in which the sons of Levi dwelt were scattered throughout all the tribes. Vestiges of terraced vineyards still attest how well the hilly province assigned to Judah suited the culture of the vine. Zebulun embosomed the lake of Galilee, and stretched away toward the coast of the blue Mediterranean. Esdraelon, the battlefield of Palestine, where Assyria from the north and Egypt from the South often met in deadly feud, lay within the limits of Issachar. Dan was small as an adder, but like it, could inflict dangerous wounds on any invader who had to pass by it towards the heart of the country. Gad, much pressed by border war; Asher, notable for fertility; Naphtali, famous for eloquence; Benjamin, cruel as a wolf. All these justified the prophecy of their dying ancestor; while the mighty tribes of Ephraim and Manasseh, sprung from the sons of Joseph, inherited to the full "the blessings of heaven above; blessings of the deep that lieth under; blessings of the breasts and of the womb; blessings to the utmost bound of the everlasting hills."

It would be interesting, also, to mark the beauty of these dying words. They abound in observation and description of animal nature; indicating the habits of the shepherd's life, with which, from his earliest days Jacob must have been familiar. The lion's whelp, couching in his lair, refusing to be roused up, because satisfied with a sufficient meal. The ass, and her colt browsing on the young grapes of the vine. The serpent lurking in the sand; and springing out as the horse passes him, with venomous sting. The wolf, with stealthy tread, seeking his prey at night. The slender, gentle hind. Then, too, the vineyards, rich with grapes, that stain the garments of the peasants with blood-red juice, as they stamp them in the vats. The boughs running over the vineyard walls, in rich bounty, and giving refreshment to weary passers by. The bubbling waters of the spring. The beach of the distant sea. The blue outline of the everlasting hills in the far distance. All these bespeak a mind that loved natural beauty.

It would be interesting, also, to mark the close connection between the awards and the character of the bearded sons who stood around the withered, propped-up body of that dying man; while his spirit was flaming out in one last splendid outburst of prophetic and princelike glory, too much for the frail tenement to endure. Take, for example, the case of Reuben: he had committed a nameless sin years before; he might have hoped that it was all long since forgotten, but no, here it reappears, dragged into inevitable light—as ours must be, unless hidden beneath the Blood of Jesus. That sin deprived him of the primacy—*that one sin*. Was not this arbitrary? Not so: since it was the index of his character, and was the unerring evidence of an unstable nature; for sensuality and instability are one. As sensual indulgence palsies the nerves of the body, so it paralyzes the strength and decision of the spirit. And there was this further dread effect of Reuben's sin: he not only entailed a loss of position and prestige on his descendants, but he transmitted to them his own character. On the threshold of Canaan they asked for land east of Jordan; they could not wait: they showed all the characteristics of the man of appetite, who places the present above the future, and seen above the unseen. And Deborah, in her war song, changed the requiem of the martial valor of the tribe.

But amid all this change of character, condition, and estate, there comes, in these dying words, the announcement of a personality, mysterious, ineffable, sublime, which dwarfs all others—as Mont Blanc the lesser elevations of his mountain realm; and before which that aged spirit bows in worship, illumining the withered face with a light not born of earth. What does he mean by those mystic words, describing the Shiloh; and His coming; and the gathering of the peoples to Him? There is a power in them that strangely stirs our spirits. We feel instinctively that we are face to face with Him before whom angels bow, veiling their faces with their wings. Again the words ring in our hearts: "The scepter shall not depart from Judah, nor a lawgiver from between his feet, until Shiloh come; and unto Him shall the gathering of the peoples be."

I. LET US TRY TO UNDERSTAND THEM. The primacy of Israel, forfeited by Reuben, was transferred to Judah. The scepter, or staff, surely indicates legislative authority; the lawgiver, some kind of legislator: and the drift of meaning in the verse is that Judah should retain the primacy of the tribes; and should not fail to have some kind of government, and some kind of governor, until One came, of whom Jacob spoke as Shiloh.

And who is this Shiloh? The greatest modern Hebrew critics tell us that it is like the German *Frederick*—Rich in Peace; the Rest Giver; the Man of Rest. And of whom can this be true, but of One? Amid the vice and crimes of their times, an aged pair gave to their newborn son the name of Noah—*Rest;* and hoped that he would live to comfort them. It was, alas! a vain hope; the waters of the deluge were destined to sweep over their home and world. No *man* can give us rest. He who shall give rest to the toiling populations of earth, must be more than man; and must be superior to those changes that toss us on their tumultuous billows. The true Shiloh can be none other than the Son of God; who, standing among earth's toiling millions, said, "Come unto Me, all ye that labor and are heavy laden, and I will give you rest."

I have sometimes wondered where Jacob learned this most sweet and true name of our Lord Jesus. Was it flashed into his heart, at that moment, for the first time? It may have been. But there is another supposition which has often pleased me. You will remember that at Peniel, Jacob asked the mysterious combatant His name. What answer did he receive? When Manoah asked a similar question, the angel of the Lord told him it was secret. But no such negative was spoken to Jacob. The angel simply said: "Wherefore is it that thou dost ask after My name? And he blessed him there." I have sometimes thought that, as He blessed him, He whispered in his ear this lovely title; which lingered in the old man's mind, as the years went on, and became invested with ever fuller and richer meaning, as he felt to need more urgently the balm and strength which it contained. To him that overcomes Christ promises to give a white stone; and in that stone a new name written, which is only known to him that receives it. Why should He not have done as much for that old world patriarch, who had overcome in his defeat; and had gone from wrestling in full strength to halting on shrunken thigh? And it would be only natural that, at the moment of full surrender, He should teach him the secret of rest. This is the universal order of Christian living: first the resistance; then the shrunken sinew; then the yielding and clinging; and finally rest.

Jacob, then, believed that the Rest Giver would come at length; and that, when He came, people would be gathered to Him—not driven, as he had seen long strings of Nubian slaves driven through the streets of Egyptian towns: but gathered as a hen gathers her chickens beneath her wing; or as the magnet attracts steel filings to itself.

II. LET US NOTE, ALSO, THEIR LITERAL FULFILLMENT. For long centuries, Judah held the proud position assigned by the dying chieftain. The lion of the tribe of Judah brooked no rival. Jerusalem lay in his territory. David sprang from his sons. Throughout the long captivity, princes still claimed and held their right; for we are told, when Cyrus issued the proclamation that gave them liberty, "there arose up the chief of the fathers of Judah, and numbered unto them Sheshbazzar, the prince of Judah." It was Judah that returned from the captivity and gave the title *Jew* to every member of the race; and even up to the times of our Lord, there were vestiges of the ancient government in the council before which He was arraigned.

But the system had become decrepit, and showed signs of passing away. We are told, for instance, when the Idumean Herod was placed upon the throne, all Jewish patriots were in deep consternation. Men with wild and haggard looks, their garments rent, and ashes on their heads, went about the streets crying, "Woe unto us! Woe unto us! For the scepter is departed from Judah; and a lawgiver from between his feet." Still the complex machinery of inferior and superior courts lingered on, until that mighty explosion burst beneath the Jewish State— leaving not a single Jew within fifty miles of Bethlehem; and making it utterly impossible for Shiloh to come out of Judah.

Before this entire breakup of the Jewish system, the Shiloh came. When they were expecting Him at the front door, He stole in the back. While they were expecting Him with outward show, He came as the spring comes, and as day breaks. He had rest in Himself. What else could have kept Him so calm—amid the tumult at Nazareth; and the raging of the storm on the Lake of Galilee; and the mob in Gethsemane? And He gave rest: rest from weary years of pain; rest from tears and heartache; rest from sin.

And as He has spoken through the centuries, His still small voice has been heard above the fevered throb and pulse of human life, saying, "Come unto Me, come unto Me!" and spirits have arisen and gone forth to Him: drawn to Him as the publicans and sinners were of old; gathering to Him as the oppressed in the old kingdom of Saul gathered to David in Adullam's cave, furnishing material for a host which was to carry everything before its victorious arms. "Thy people shall be free will offerings in the day of thy power."

III. LET US REALIZE THEIR TRUTH. What a variety of weary eyes will read these words—weary eyes, aching heads, tired bodies, breaking hearts! Tired of sitting at the task which barely suffices to get bread for hungry little ones; tired of waiting for one who never comes; tired of hearing the slow torture of never-ceasing pain: tired of the strain of competition, ever waxing keener and more merciless; tired of the conflict against the evil around; tired of the war with self and sin within; tired of life—

> Lord, oftentimes I am a weary quite
> Of my own self, my sin, my vanity;
> Yet be not Thou (or I am lost outright)
>   Weary of me.

Would to God that each of these could understand that Jesus Christ, the true Shiloh, is able to give them, now and forevermore—rest! "Come unto Me, *all* ye that are heavy laden, and I will give you REST."

It is a royal word. If this were the only scrap of His words, we should feel Him to have been the most royal man that ever trod our world. He knows exactly what men want; and He feels that He has the secret, and is Himself the universal and unfailing reservoir of rest. What must not be the ocean fullness of His heart—which can fill up every void and vacancy in all human spirits: as the tides of the Pacific, the stormless, restful ocean, fill up all the myriad indentations of every continent, and coral reef, and emerald isle, washed by their waves! What certainty is here! No doubt, or question, or fear of failure; no faltering in that clear voice; no hesitancy in that decisive accent. We may trust Him, brothers and sisters. He at least has learned the law of equilibrium. He speaks that which He knows. He has Himself the rest He promises. Put yourselves into His hand. It will not take Him longer to give you rest, than it took Him to still the waves; they did not even need to rock themselves to rest: "*Immediately* there was a great calm."

The Shiloh-rest is not for heaven. We need not ask for the wings of a dove to fly away to it. We should not find it hereafter, if we did not first find it here. "We which believe DO enter into rest." The rest remains, only in the sense of being unexhausted by all who have gone before. It awaits us in unstinted abundance.

The Shiloh-rest is not in Circumstances. That thought lies at the root of the teaching of the Epicurean, the Stoic, the worldly philosopher. But circumstances will never bring it; any more than change of posture will bring permanent relief to the pain-racked body. Here is a truer science: rest within—rest within the heart, while storms, and per-plexities, and trials are swirling through the world; as the ocean depths are still enough to permit of perpetual deposits while hurricanes sweep the surface; and as there is a point of calm in the midst of the fiercest whirlwind that ever marched across the desert sands.

The Shiloh-rest is not in Inaction. He invites us to no bank of roses; to no Elysian plain; to no parade ground. In heaven, though they rest, yet they rest not. They rest in their blessed service. They serve with-out breaking their rest. There is the strenuous putting forth of energy, but no strain, no effort, no sense of fatigue. And such is the rest He gives. Does He not speak of a "burden" and a "yoke" in the same breath as He speaks of Rest?

And it is not hard to get it. See! He *gives* it; and it does not need much effort to take a gift. He shows just where to look for it; and it is easy enough to *find* a thing if we know just where it lies. There seems to be but three conditions to be fulfilled by us.

(1) *Surrender all to Him.* As long as you try to wield that scepter, or permit your will to be the lawgiver of your life, the Shiloh cannot come to you. You must give up your own efforts to save yourself—your own ideas of getting right with God; your own choice; your own way; your own will. You must as absolutely cease from your own works as God did from His on the Sabbath of His rest. You must hand over your sinful spirit to be saved by Him; you must surrender the keys of every room in your heart; you must be willing for Him to be supreme monarch of every province of your being; you must lie naked and open to Him as the victim before the priest. So only can you ex-pect rest. And if you cannot bring your nature into this posture, ask Him to do it for you. Let your will crown Him—as our own Alfred was crowned, when most of England was still ravaged by the Danes. He will not fail nor be discouraged, till He hath put down all rule and authority and power, and made Himself supreme throughout heart and life.

(2) *Trust Him, by handing over all to Him.* Hand over to Him all your sins and all your sorrows. He takes away the sin of the world. Do not wait till sins have accumulated into a cloud or a mountain. Do not tarry till the time has come for evening prayer. Do not delay till you are alone. But as swiftly as you are conscious of any burden, pass it on

to Jesus; cast all your care upon Him, for he cares for you. His eye is quick to see each effort to believe; and His heart is large enough to hold the troubles of the world. So soon as you give, He takes; and what He takes He also undertakes; and will see it made right for you, to your rejoicing and to His glory. This is the Blessed Rest of Faith; the Land of Promise into which our Joshua waits to lead all who trust Him.

(3) *Take His yoke, and learn of Him*—i.e., do as He did. What did He do? What was His yoke? A yoke means submission. To whom did He submit? Not to man; not even to His mother, not the suggestions of Satan: but to the Father's will. Whenever He saw the handwriting of that will, He meekly yielded submission. This was the secret of His rest. To live in the will of God—this is rest. Be ever on the outlook for it: in every event; in every kindness or insult; in every letter; in every new friendship; in every discipline of Providence; and in every test of Scripture. And whenever you see it, *take it*. Do not wait for it to be forced on you; as a yoke on a heifer unaccustomed to it, which struggles till a deep wound is cut in its flesh. But *take* the yoke; be meek and lowly; imitate Him who said, "The cup which my Father hath given me, shall I not drink it?" The language which best befits such a one is that wonderful sentence, in which simplicity and sublimity struggle for mastery: "Even so, Father; for so it seemed good in Thy sight."

A gentleman once visited a school of deaf and dumb children, and was asked to write them a question on the blackboard; and he wrote: "Why did God make you deaf and dumb, while I can hear and speak?" Tears filled their eyes; and after a slight pause, a little boy stepped forward, and took the chalk and wrote beneath, "Even so, Father; for so it seemed good in Thy sight." If you can say that, you have learned the secret of rest; and Shiloh has already come to you; and you are one of those that are being gathered to Him through the long weary ages to share His ultimate triumph and reign.

15
Home: At Last!

What is death? Oh, what is death?
'Tis slumber to the weary;
'Tis rest to the forlorn;
'Tis shelter to the dreary;
'Tis peace amid the storm;
'Tis the entrance to our home;
'Tis the passage to that God
Who bids His children come,
When their weary course is trod.

Genesis 50   Anonymous

The end is come at last! And we stand with those stalwart men in that heiroglyph-covered chamber, silent with the hush of death, to see the wayworn pilgrim breathe his last. His life has been a stern fight; his pathway not strewn with roses, but set with flints; few and evil the days of the years of his pilgrimage. Compared with the brilliant career of Esau, his life might be almost considered a failure—estimating it by all human standards of failure and success. But as the scaffold is taken down piece by piece, we catch glimpses of the real manhood which God has been so carefully building up, through long years of pain and sorrow; and as it comes into view, we feel that it is more than enough to justify all. Better a hundredfold to be Israel the Prince, though an exile; than Esau, the founder of a line of dukes. The glory of moral and spiritual rank will glisten when the crowns of earthly splendor shall have moldered into dust; and the name of Israel will be an unfailing inspiration to those who, conscious of untold weakness and unloveableness, shall yet strive to apprehend that for which they were originally apprehended by Christ Jesus.

We, too, if the Lord tarry, shall lie someday in a chamber of death, surrounded by our dear ones. Our spirits must poise themselves for their final flight, and stand waiting at the Beautiful Gate of the temple of life. And as Jacob has taught us how to live, so let him teach us how to die. "Come," said the dying Havelock to his son, "and see how a Christian can die." Some such summons calls us now: for even we, living in the noontide of the Gospel, may obtain salutary hints for our own death hour from one who once seemed to mean to teach us anything, but who now, through the stern discipline of the Angel of Love, stands forth to lead faithful souls through the dark gorge of death into the land of the eternal morning.

Before the mind of the dying patriarch three visions seemed to float in that solemn hour. He was thinking of the City of God; and of the gathering of his clan; and of that lone and distant cave in Canaan where his fathers lay, and which he had so often visited.

I. THE CITY OF GOD. We are expressly told in the Epistle to the Hebrews that Jacob was one of those "who died in faith." He was the heir of Promise. The land promised to Abraham and Isaac had not as yet passed into his possession; it was still held by the wandering and settled tribes, who had eyed his journeyings with such evident suspicion. All he had was the assured promise that in the coming days it should be his through his seed. Perhaps, in the dawn of early vigor, he may have hoped to live until those fair pasture lands and terraced hills had literally passed into his possession. The yearning comes out in the deep drawn ejaculation, flashing through his dying charge to his sons, "I have waited for Thy salvation, O Lord!"

But as the years passed on, and clouds closed over this azure aperture of earthly hope, he was compelled to realize that he would never live to be lord of Canaan. Nevertheless, he clung tenaciously to the blessed promise, so often reiterated to Abraham, that the land should become his people's; and his assurance that God would keep His word flung a radiance, which neither sorrow nor adversity could dim, over his dying moments. Oh, glorious faith! It carries a torch through the long catacombs of sorrow, keeping the heart from fainting, until the welcome dawn of accomplishment grows upon the sight. What cannot faith do for those whom God has taught to trust! "My soul, wait thou only upon God; for my expectation is from Him."

As it became clear to Jacob that *he* was not to inherit Canaan, he seems to have fixed his mind with increasing eagerness on heaven. He felt that if God had not destined for him an earthly resting place, yet He had prepared for him a City. Its foundations had not been laid by man; its walls bore no mark of human workmanship; its atmosphere could not be stained with the smoke or dust of earth. And it was for that glorious city, the city of the saints, that his pilgrim spirit now yearned. It was the vision of that city which had enabled him to confess to the mighty Pharaoh that he was a pilgrim and a stranger on the earth. And now it was his close proximity to it that stirred his aged spirit, and drew it on with breathless eagerness and rapid steps.

The sacred writer employs a beautiful similitude when he says of Jacob and the rest of the patriarchs, that they greeted the promises from afar (Heb. 11:13). When the traveler returns from distant lands, and from the summit of some neighboring hill catches the first glimpse of his still distant home, with its spiral column of blue smoke curling up amid the trees, he is disposed to fall upon the greensward, and with outstretched hands thank God and greet his home. "Hail! Happy scenes of childhood; and blest abode of manhood's prime." So Jacob, as he neared the City of God, so dear to faithful hearts, approved his kinsmanship with the elect spirits of all ages, by reaching forth towards it his aged, trembling hands. And as God looked down upon that eager attitude of faith, and hope, and desire, He was not ashamed to be called his God.

Modern commentators have wrangled fiercely as to how much or how little of the future life was realized by these ancient saints. Into that controversy I have no desire to enter. But I find a large answer to their questions in the assurance of Scripture, that Jacob and the men of his type desired "the better country, that is, a heavenly." The future was less indistinct to them than we sometimes suppose. They, too, stood on Pisgah heights and beheld a Land of Promise: not that on which the veteran lawgiver gazed, bounded by the blue waters of the Mediterranean, but that which is never shadowed by night, or swept by wild tempests of wind and rain—the true Home of the saints. On such a Pisgah height Jacob was standing; and as all earthly objects, even the face of Joseph, grew indistinct to his dimming eyes, those rapturous and celestial scenes grew upon his spiritual vision, and beckoned to him.

In what relation do you, my readers, stand to that City of God? Do not imagine that it will gladden your dying gaze, unless it has often been the object of your loving thought in the days of health and vigor. Your citizenship must be in heaven now, if you would feel attracted to it as your true home at last. Is it so? Do you feel content to live in tents, having no fixed hold upon this fleeting scene; and confessing yourselves pilgrims and strangers on the earth—because you are looking for the City? Do you feel the *pull* of that city, as the sailor does of the anchor, which keeps him from drifting with the tide? Do you anticipate it, like the children in the Children's Crusade, who asked of every city they entered, "Is this Jerusalem?" If so, it shall gladden your dying moments. You shall see the holy city descending out of heaven from God, as a bank seems to approach the nearing vessel. And you shall have the blessedness, assured by the living Savior to those who wash their robes, of the right to enter in, through the gates, into the City (Rev. 22:14, R.V.).

II. THE GATHERING OF THE CLAN. "I am to be gathered unto my people." When the dying patriarch spoke thus, he meant something more than that his dust should mingle with all that was mortal of his forefathers. He expresses that thought in the following sentence: "Bury me with my fathers." No; he meant something more than this. He surely looked upon the City as the gathering place of his clan; the metropolis of true and godly hearts; the *rendezvous* of all who were *his* people, because they were people of God.

How much truer is this thought of heaven than that which is entertained by many Christian people! "What do you think of the intermediate state?" "Shall we be consciously happy from the very moment of death?" "Shall we know one another on the other side?" These are the doleful questions asked on many sides; and they present a melancholy contrast to the words of the dying Jacob, "I am to be gathered unto my people."

What as to the intermediate state? At the best "we know not what we shall be." We cannot penetrate the veil that only opens wide enough to admit the entering spirit. It is clear that our spirits will not reach their full consummation and bliss till the morning of the resurrection, when body and spirit will be reunited, but it is equally clear that they will not be unconscious, but will enter into the blessed presence of our Lord.

This was taught by Christ Himself, when He quoted the words, "I am the God of Abraham, Isaac, and Jacob"; and added the comment, "He is not the God of the dead, but of the living." That grand formula was spoken years after Jacob had fallen asleep; and yet God speaks of Himself as his God: and since He could not be the God of dead mummies only, or of unconscious spirits, Jacob and all the rest must have been living. Yes, they were living then, and are living now, possessed of all the vivid life that made them what they were.

There is no accent of uncertainty in the New Testament. As soon as the tent is taken down, the mansion is entered (2 Cor. 5:2). Absent from the body, the believer is present with the Lord. "To die is gain"; which were an impossibility if the spirit did not have more of Christ than is possible on this side of the Golden City (Phil. 1:21). The dying Stephen went direct into the hands of his Lord (Acts 7:59). Do not puzzle over useless questionings: be content to know that death is not a state, but an act; not a resting place, but a transition; a passage, a birth, a crossing the Bridge of Sighs from the prison to the palace.

> Death is another life. We bow our heads
> At going out, we think; and enter straight
> Another golden chamber of the King's,
> Larger than this we leave, and lovelier.

What as to the recognition of the departed? It would not have been an object of anticipation to Jacob to be gathered to his people, if he would not know them when he reached their blessed society. When the Jew thought of the unseen world, he expected to meet the saints, of whom he had been wont to hear from childhood, and especially Abraham. Was not the Jew wiser than most Christians? What! has the body powers of recognition, and the spirit none? Shall love, which has molded the life, range through eternity unable to find the twin spirit with which it had become entwined? Can that be a Father's home, where the brothers and sisters do not know each other?

But these questions have always been solved, to me at least, by a careful study of the facts of our Lord's resurrection body—the model to the likeness of which we are to be conformed (Phil. 3:21). Those who knew Him before His death, recognized Him after. His very voice had in it intonations familiar to those who loved Him (John 20:16). His mannerisms were identical; and sufficient to identify Him to the two disciples with whom He sat (Luke 24:31). And as it was with Him, so shall it be with us and our beloved.

We shall be gathered to our people. Death will not usher us into a chill, unfriendly circle, but into a great gathering of loving and sympathizing friends, who shall give us a choral welcome as we enter into the eternal kingdom of our Lord (2 Pet. 1:11; see the Greek).

Throughout the ages the elect souls of our race have been gathering there. Are they our people? Can we claim kinship with them. There is but one bond, as we are taught in Hebrews 11. That bond is not of dispensation; or of knowledge; or of exploits, but of faith—such faith as may exist in a beggar or a king, in a child or a philosopher. It is independent of age, or sect, or knowledge, or work. But, wherever it is found, it designates the owner to be one of those who can claim kinship with the saintly inhabitants of the City of God. The test question of qualification for the franchise of the New Jerusalem is: "Dost thou believe in the name of the only begotten Son of God?"

III. THE CAVE OF MACHPELAH. "Bury me with my fathers in the cave that is in the field of Ephron the Hittite." For seventeen years he had lived in Egypt, surrounded by all the comforts that Joseph's filial love could devise, and his munificence execute. He must have become familiar with Egypt's splendid temples and obelisks and pyramids, with which that cave could not for one moment be compared. But he would not rest in any of them. He must be laid where Abraham and Sarah, Isaac and Rebekah, and the faithful Leah awaited resurrection.

This was something more than the natural sentiment which impels us to request burial in some quiet spot in God's acre, where our family name is inscribed on many of the gravestones around. He felt that Machpelah's cave was the first outpost in the land which was one day to belong to his people; and he wanted, so far as he might, to be there with them, and to share in the land of promise.

The last word was spoken, the last commission given, and he knew the end was come. "He gathered up his feet into the bed"; *i.e.,* he met death quietly, calmly, manfully. He was not dragged away as a criminal; he went to meet it with complacency and with joy. The servant might have a grim face and a sable suit, but he had come to take him home. He quietly breathed out his spirit, and was gathered unto his people. And at that moment sorrow and sighing which had been his close companions in life, fled away forever.

How calm and noble that face looked, fixed in the marble of death! The Jacob-look had vanished from it; and it was stamped with the smile with which the royal Israel-spirit had molded it in its outward passage.

> So, pilgrim, now thy brows are cold,
>   We see thee what thou art; and know
>   Thy likeness to the wise below,
> Thy kindred to the great of old.

What wonder, then, that Joseph fell upon his father's face, and wept upon him, and kissed him! He had borne the strain as long as he could; and now nature must vent herself in manly, filial grief.

The body was carefully embalmed. No time, or pains, or cost, were spared. Egypt herself mourned for him for seventy days. And then one of the most splendid funeral processions that ever gathered to lay saint, or sage, or hero to his rest, carried that precious casket in solemn pomp from Egypt up to Canaan. The chivalry of Egypt, its statesmen and counselors, its princes and priests, joined with the shepherds of Goshen in accompanying the *cortége*. And the signs of mourning were so great as to impress the inhabitants of the land, the Canaanites.

The stone was rolled away, and the remains laid on their appointed niche; and in all probability they are there, in a state of perfect preservation, unto this day. Many a storm has swept over them—Assyrian, Egyptian, Babylonian, Grecian, Roman, Saracenic, and Mohammedan. But nought has disturbed their quiet rest; and they hold the land in fee, till God shall fulfill, in all its magnificence, the promise which He made and has never recalled—that He would give the land to Jacob's seed for an everlasting inheritance. So rest thee, ISRAEL, THE PRINCE!

16
The God of Jacob

With all thy heart, with all thy soul and mind,
Thou must Him love, and His behests embrace;
All other loves—with which the world doth blind
Weak fancies, and stir up affections base—
Thou must renounce, and utterly displace;
And give thyself unto Him full and free,
That full and freely Gave Himself to thee.

Psalm 46   Spenser

I t is very comforting to discover in how many parts of Scripture
God calls Himself the God of Jacob. He seems to take special
delight in the title which links His holy nature with one who, so
far from giving promise of saintship, was naturally one of the meanest of men. We should not have been surprised to find Him speaking
of Himself as the God of Israel, the Prince, but it is as startling as it is
reassuring to find Him speaking of Himself still more often as the God
of Jacob.

But as we notice the careful reiteration of the designation—especially in the Psalms of David and the prophecies of Isaiah—we learn this
priceless lesson: that He has not changed since He took Jacob in hand;
that He feels towards such characters now as He did when He began his
gracious work of renewal in that poor cramped heart; and that He is
ready to do as much for all who are conscious of being equally worthless by nature, and who are willing to put themselves into His gracious
hands—which reach down from heaven to earth, "molding men."

There is little doubt that God would do as much for all the readers of these lines, if only they were willing. And it is the object of this

321

closing appeal to urge my readers to let Him have His gracious way with
them. As we have studied together Jacob's life and character, have
you not been keenly conscious of similarities between him and yourself? *You* too may be cunning, crafty, and deceitful; or you may be prone
to outbursts of ungovernable temper; or you may be cursed by unholy
desires that honeycomb your better nature; or you may be constantly
brought into captivity to some tyrannous sin. Now there is no need for
this to be your hapless lot for one moment longer, if only you will hand
yourself over to the mighty God of Jacob.

At the door of a mission hall in a low and degraded neighborhood,
a Christian man, one evening, was inviting the passersby to go in to the
service, which was about to commence. "But my coat is in rags,"
replied a wretched looking man. "That is no matter," was the answer; "there's a man inside *without a coat at all.*" It was quite enough
to remove all further hesitation; and he entered. Forgive the simple illustration by which I wish to press home my meaning on those who
may question if their nature is not too ignoble, and their evil habits too
confirmed, for them to entertain the hope of saintliness. Your case is
not hopeless. If God could make a prince of Jacob, He can do as
much for anyone. It is hardly possible for one of us to be more hopeless than Jacob was to begin with; and the same Lord who was so
rich in mercy to him, will be as rich to all them that call upon Him in
truth.

I. Cultivate a Holy Ambition. There is no tendency of the un-
renewed heart more subtle or dangerous than ambition. "By this sin fell
the angels." And yet, if it is properly curbed and kept, ambition plays
a useful part among the motive forces of human life. It is a bad sign
when a lad, or a man, has no desire to improve his position and get on.
In all likelihood he will always lie with the rest of the rabble at the bottom of the hill, without the desire or power to stir. And it is well to cultivate a holy ambition to be all that God can make us; to grasp all the
possibilities that lie within the reach of faith; and to apprehend that for
which we have been apprehended of Christ Jesus.

Such an ambition fired the heart of the Apostle when he said:
"Not as though I had already attained, either were already perfect, but

I follow after: . . . forgetting those things which are behind, and reaching forth unto those things which are before, I press toward the mark for the prize of the high calling of God in Christ Jesus" (Phil. 3:12–14). Does not this stir you? Do not be content to be always a Jacob. Do not settle down to lifelong slavery beneath your merciless oppressors. Do not suppose that you must always be what you have been. "The arrows are beyond thee"; make for them!

This holy ambition may be aroused by the study of Christian biography. Every time you read or hear of God's grace being magnified in some beautiful and noble life, thank Him; let your own ideal be raised, and ask Him to do as much for you. But there is nothing which will quicken this sacred spark into a flame so soon as the devout study of the Bible. There are such wonderful openings up of the possibilities of Christian living and being in almost every paragraph. Constant familiarity may have rubbed them bright and smooth, like some well worn coin, but if only we will let the Holy Ghost recut them for us, we shall be perfectly astonished. And as, one after another, these ideals of God's own heart open to our gaze, let us entreat Him "to fulfill in us the good pleasure of His goodness, and the work of faith with power."

Let this be deeply engraven on your heart, as the sacred page is turned—that every promise is for you; and that God is able to do exceeding abundantly above all you can ask or think; and then look up to Him, and claim that He should do as He has said.

II. MAKE A COMPLETE SURRENDER TO GOD. Before God will commence His gracious work on a human spirit, it must be entirely surrendered to Him. The key of every room, and closet, and cupboard, in the being must be put into His hands. Every province of the life must be placed under His government. There must be no keeping back, no reserve: to withhold one thing, even the least, will vitiate the whole transaction; and leave a foothold for the self life from which it will speedily spread back throughout the whole nature.

Who would take a house recently infected by smallpox unless the whole of it were thrown freely open to the officers of health? Who would pretend to advise a friend involved in financial difficulties, unless the whole of his liabilities were freely disclosed? Who would pre-scribe for a disease, unless the patient told all the symptoms and entirely gave up all other means of cure? And so God will not undertake the case of any poor child of His unless there be first a complete and entire sur-render of the whole being to His gentle healing work.

Some time ago, as I was passing down one of the poorer streets in Leicester, I remarked a notice in the window of a most dilapidated shop, the trade of which had for some time past been ebbing away. The no-tice was to the following effect: "This shop will shortly be opened under entirely new management." And as I stood for a moment there, it seemed as if the whole building put on a kind of hopeful smile, as much as to say, "I am so glad that I am to be put under an entirely fresh man-agement." Several days afterwards, as I passed that way again, I found a small army of whitewashers and paperhangers at work; and on the next occasion, the change in management was evident to the most ca-sual eye, for the whole place had a clean, sweet look about it which was quite attractive.

Now this is just what you require—you with the Jacob nature. You have been trying to manage yourself all too long. A change is evi-dently needed, but it must be complete. There must be nothing left of yourself at all. Everything must be absolutely surrendered to that mighty God of Jacob whom the Psalmist made his refuge; and who is able to take bankrupt souls, and make them heirs of God, and joint heirs with Christ. Why should you not make that surrender now?

Instances crowd upon my pen, eagerly asking mention, of those who have entered into experiences of undreamt of blessing through the strait gate of entire surrender. But I forbear to give them here. It is enough to point the way; and leave all to enter the golden land who will.

When you come to the point of self-surrender, it is highly proba-ble that some one thing will suggest itself to your mind which it is very difficult to transfer from your control to that of the Lord Jesus. You would so much prefer to retain it under your own management. You are not quite sure whether He may not introduce some sweeping, and painful changes. You stand in dread, as the lad before he throws himself into the buoyant waves. But such fears are most unworthy of our loving Master. He will take away nothing which it will do us no harm to keep. He never amputates a limb without using some anodyne to lessen the pain without injuring the health. He will never give us one thrill of anguish from which it would be possible to save us.

Do not be afraid of giving all up to the lovely will of Him who is love; and who will not break the bruised reed or quench the smoking flax. If your child were to say, "I am going to give my life over to your ordering; do all you will," would you begin to make him miserable? Would you not rejoice in the opportunity of arresting him in courses which were harming him? Would you not gladly embrace the opportunity of filling him with joys that he could never have realized for himself? And your heavenly Father will not do less for you; only trust Him with all.

And should there be things in your life which you find it hard to abandon—dear as right eye, or hand, or foot; involving the happiness of others as well as your own—tell God that you give them over to Him; and that you are willing to have His will done, if He only will bring it to pass in His own good time and way. And if you cannot say as much as that, tell Him *that you are willing to be made willing*: hand over your will to Him, though it seem to be as a piece of cold, hard iron; sure that He can soften and weld it into the pattern on which He has set His heart.

> Renew my will from day to day;
> Blend it with Thine, and take away
> All that now makes it hard to say,
>   Thy will be done.

There is even a more excellent way than any, which is within the reach of the feeblest hand; and that is to ask the Lord to come into your life *to take* that which you do not feel able to give. The only matter of which you need be careful, is your willingness that He should have all; if that is assured, the rest may be safely left to His gracious arrangement. Directly you are willing, the door is opened to Him, and He instantly takes full possession.

III. Be careful not to thwart God's good workmanship. Of course, there is a sense in which we cannot resist or impede the execution of His sovereign will. "He doeth as He will amongst the armies of heaven and the inhabitants of earth." And yet, on the other hand, we may hinder and counterwork His loving purposes, "How often would I . . . but ye would not!" Let us be on the guard against this disastrous resistance; and be ever on the alert to work out that which God is working in us, "both to will and to do."

Once, the prophet Jeremiah was led to go down into the valley where the potter was at work, molding clay on a wheel (Jer. 18). And as he stood by to watch the skillful manipulation of the clay, the prophet had, of course, no idea what pattern was in the designer's mind; though, probably, it was one of the noblest conception, and destined for some royal or special purpose. And so, beneath those rapid revolutions of the wheel, the ideal began to take shape. Then suddenly the clay was taken from the wheel with an exclamation of disappointment, and the design was foiled and spoiled. Why? Because the potter was wanting in skill? No, but because the clay refused to take on the shape which he had designed. His work was, therefore, marred on the wheel; and he was compelled to make of that clay some inferior vessel from that which he had intended. It might have served a noble purpose in the royal household, or even in the Temple service, but it was now fashioned into a coarser form, for some mean purpose in a peasant's home. The lesson was meant for Israel, but it will serve for us.

Speaking after the manner of men, may we not say that when God created us anew in Christ Jesus He conceived a noble ideal, after the pattern of which we might have been conformed? And if we had only yielded to Him more completely, that ideal would long ago have revealed itself in our experience. But alas! We have not always been plastic in His hands; we have not obeyed the promptings of His Spirit; we have quenched and grieved Him; and we are far different today from what we might have been, and from what God intended us to become. Shall we not confess this with tears and shame? Shall we not take unto us words, and turn to Him, saying, "Now, O Lord, we are the clay, and Thou our potter; we are all the work of Thy hands. Be not wroth very sore." And if a man purify himself from the sins which have hindered the Divine Workman, he shall yet become "a vessel unto honor, sanctified, and meet for the Master's use, and prepared unto every good work."

I do not deny that God will fulfill His purpose in us, even though we hinder Him, but it will be carried through, as it was in the case of Jacob, at a terrible expenditure of agony, and the shriveling of the sinew of our strength. The yoke will have to be borne, and the long furrows cut; and if the unaccustomed heifer prove restive, its struggles will only chafe sores about its neck—but it will ultimately be broken in. On the whole, therefore, it is always better to *take* the yoke of Divine purpose, offered by our Lord as His: "Take *My* yoke." And remember, a yoke is for two. Our Lord yokes Himself at our side; and paces by us, step by step, doing for us what Simon the Cyrenian once did for Him, on the way to Golgotha.

IV. SEEK THE FULLNESS OF THE SPIRIT. That Spirit dwelt in Israel; as the sun flushes the topmost summits of the Alps with a roseate glow, long before it bathes the valleys in its meridian light. But in this blessed dispensation, He is given—not to saints and prophets only, but to all: to sons and daughters; to old men and children; to servants and handmaidens. "The promise is to you and to your children; and to all that are afar off, even as many as the Lord our God shall call" (Acts 2:39). And it is only as we receive this sacred gift, in all its fullness, that we can hope to attain to the royal standard of the Israel-life. That blessed Spirit is the Spirit of the Son—the Spirit of the one royal Man that ever walked the world; and if we would have His nature, we must have His Spirit: not in drops, but in rivers; not as a zephyr breath, but as "a rushing mighty wind."

This is the dying need of the Christian Church in this country. We have learning, rhetoric, fashion, wealth, splendid buildings, and superb machinery, but we are powerless, for lack of the power which can only be obtained through the fullness of the Spirit. Of what use is a train of sumptuous Pullman cars without an engine throbbing with the power of steam? We have too largely forgotten the exhortation; "Be filled with the Spirit." We have thought that the fullness of the Spirit was a specialty for the apostolic age, instead of being for all time. And thus the majority of Christians are living on the other side of Pentecost. We can never be what we might be until we have got back to apostolic theory and practice in respect to this all-essential matter.

Oh that God, in these last days, would raise up some fire-touched tongue to do for this neglected doctrine what Luther did for justification by faith!

In the meanwhile seek this blessed filling. It is only possible to emptied hearts, but just so soon as a vacuum has been created by the act of entire surrender, there will be an instantaneous filling by the Holy Ghost in answer to expectant desire and eager faith. For the Holy Ghost longs to enter the human heart; resembling in this the air, which is ever seeking to enter our homes by every keyhole, crack, and aperture. Do not wait to *feel* that you have Him. Be sure that you do possess His fullness, if only you have made room for Him; and go on acting in the strength of His mighty power. So shall you be an Israel, and have power with God and man.

The words, of course, apply only to those who by faith have become the justified children of God. If any who are not assured of this should have read thus far, let them now make a complete abandonment of themselves to the Son of God, to be saved by His death and life, just as He will. This is the first essential step towards royalty. To as many as receive Him, to them He gives the right to become children of God, even to as many as believe on His name (John 1:12).

Life is not child's play to those who enter into God's purposes, and in whom He is fulfilling His sublime ideals. But, with the dying Kingsley, we are sure that all is right and well since "all is under law." When the discipline is over, we shall be more than satisfied with the result; and, taking our stand among the princes of the royal blood, we shall ascribe eternal glory to Him who loved us in spite of all, and washed us from our sins in His own blood, and out of Jacobs made us KINGS UNTO GOD.

III
Joseph: Beloved, Hated, Exalted

Preface

My first essay at Scripture biography was made on the life of Joseph. And ever since, Joseph's life has had a special charm for me, not only for its intrinsic beauty, but because of its vivid anticipations of the Life that lights all lives.

I remember seeing the huge Matterhorn reflected, in its minutest details, in a small mountain lakelet, many miles distant; and similarly, the life of Jesus is remarkably mirrored in this touching story.

In fact, there are scenes in the life of Joseph which probably fore-shadow events that are timed to happen in the near future, and which depict them with a vividness and minuteness not to be found elsewhere on the pages of Scripture. It is here only that we can fully realize what will take place when the Lord Jesus makes Himself known to his brethren according to the flesh, and they exclaim, "It is Jesus our brother!"

The substance of this Biography was published some years ago, but it has been re-written, and much new matter has been added; so that in fact this is a new book: and it is offered to the Christian public in the hope that it may find favor, and be of special interest and use to the young, and, indeed, to all who love to hear again the stories that fascinated their earliest years, as they were, perhaps, first told by sainted lips, now forever silent.

F. B. Meyer.

1

Early Days

*Behind our life the Weaver stands
And works his wondrous will;
We leave it all in his wise hands,
And trust his perfect skill.
Should mystery enshroud his plan,
And our short sight be dim,
We will not try the whole to scan,
But leave each thread to Him.*

Genesis 37   C. Murray

It was said by Coleridge that our greatest mission is to rescue admitted truths from the neglect caused by their universal admission. There is much force in this. When a truth is fighting for existence, it compels men, whether they love it or not, to consider it. But when its position is secured, it becomes like a well-used coin, or the familiar text which hangs unnoticed on the wall. It is a great mission to rescue such truths from neglect; to flash upon them the strong light which arrests attention; to play the part of Old Mortality, who, chisel in hand, was wont to clear the mold of neglect from the gravestones of the Covenanters, so that the legend might stand out clear cut. It is something like this that I attempt for this exquisite story. We think we know all about it; and yet there may be depths of meaning and beauty which, by their very familiarity, escape us. Let us ponder together the story of Joseph; and as we do so, we shall get many a foreshadowing of Him who was cast into the pit of death, but who now sits at the right hand of Power, a Prince and a Savior.

I. THE FORMATIVE INFLUENCES OF HIS EARLY LIFE. Seventeen years before our story opens, a little child was borne by Rachel, the favorite wife of Jacob. The latter was then living as manager for his uncle Laban, on the ancient pasture-land of Charran, situated in the valley of the Euphrates and the Tigris, from which his grandfather Abraham had been called by God. The child received an eager welcome from its parents, and from the first gave unusual promise. He was like one of those children, whom we sometimes meet in large families, who bears a marked contrast to the rest; and who grow up like some fair Saxon child amid the swarthy natives of a tent of gypsies who have made it their prize.

But what a history has passed in that interval! When yet a child he was hastily caught up by his mother, and sustained in her arms on the back of a swift camel, urged to its highest speed, in the flight across the desert that lay, with only one oasis, between the bank of the Euphrates and the green prairies of Gilead. He could just remember the panic that spread through the camp when tidings came that Esau, the dread uncle, was on his march, with four hundred followers. Nor could he ever forget the evening full of preparation, the night of solemn expectancy, and the morning when his father limped into the camp, maimed in body, but with the look of a prince upon his face.

More recently still, he could recall the hurried flight from the enraged idolaters of Schechem; and those solemn hours at Bethel where his father had probably showed him the very spot on which the foot of the mystic ladder had rested, and where the whole family formally entered into a new covenant with God. It may be that this was the turning point of his life. Such events make deep impressions on young hearts. As they stood together on that hallowed spot, and heard again the oft-told story, and clasped each other's hands in solemn covenant, the other sons of Jacob may have been unmoved spectators, but there was a deep response in the susceptible heart of the lad, who may have felt, "This God shall be my God forever and ever; He shall be my Guide, even unto death."

If this were so, these impressions were soon deepened by three deaths. When they reached the family settlement, they found the old nurse Deborah dying. She was the last link to those bright days when her young mistress Rebekah came across the desert to be Isaac's bride; and they buried her with many tears under an ancient but splendid oak. And he could never forget the next. The long caravan was moving slowly up to the narrow ridge along which lay the ancient village of Bethlehem: suddenly a halt was called; the beloved Rachel could go not another step; there as the sun was westering, amid scenes where in after years Ruth met Boaz, and David watched his sheep, and the good Joseph walked beside the patient ass with its precious burden—there Rachel, Joseph's mother, died. This was the greatest loss that he had ever known. A little while after, the lad stood with his father and brethren before Machpelah's venerable grave, to lay Isaac where Abraham and Sarah and Rebekah awaited him, each on a narrow shelf; and where, after a space of seven-and-twenty years, he was to place the remains of his father Jacob.

These things made Joseph what he was. And the little sympathy that he received from his family only drove him more apart, and compelled him to live "by the well" (Gen. 49:22), and to strike his roots deeper into the life of God.

It may be that these words will be read by youths of seventeen who have passed through experiences not unlike Joseph's. They have lost sainted friends. They have been emptied from vessel to vessel. They feel lonely in the midst of their home. Let me solemnly ask them if they have entered into covenant with God. Have you avouched God to be your God? Have you put your hand into the hand of "the mighty God of Jacob"? It is an urgent question, for the answer to it may mark the crisis of your lives. Choose Christ; and, in choosing Him, choose life, and blessedness, and heaven. And when you have chosen Him, cleave close to Him, and send the rootlets of your existence deep down into the hidden wells of communion and fellowship.

II. THE EXPERIENCES OF HIS HOME LIFE. *Joseph was endowed with very remarkable intelligence.* It would almost seem as if he were chief shepherd (Gen. 37:2), the sons of Bilhah and Zilpah acting as his subordinates and assistants. The Rabbis describe him as a wise son, endowed with knowledge beyond his years. It was this, combined with the sweetness of his disposition, and the memory of his mother, that won for him his father's peculiar love. "Israel loved Joseph more than all his children."

And this love provided the coat of many colors. We have been accustomed to think of this coat as a kind of patchwork quilt, and we have wondered that grown men should have been moved to so much passion at the sight of the peacock plumes of their younger brother. But further knowledge will correct these thoughts. The Hebrew word means simply a tunic reaching to the extremities, and describes a garment commonly worn in Egypt and the adjacent lands. Imagine a long white linen robe extending to the ankles and wrists, and embroidered with a narrow stripe of color round the edge of the skirt and sleeves, and you will have a very fair conception of this famous coat.

Now we can understand the envy of his brothers. This sort of robe was worn only by the opulent and noble, by kings' sons, and by those who had no need to toil for their living. All who had to win their bread by labor wore short, colored garments that did not show stain, or cramp the free movement of the limbs. Such was the lot of Jacob's sons, and such the garments they wore. They had to wade through morasses, to clamber up hills, to carry wandering sheep home on their shoulders, to fight with robbers and beasts of prey; and for such toils the flowing robe would have been quite unfit. But when Jacob gave such a robe to Joseph, he declared in effect that from such hardships and toils his favorite son should be exempt. Now in those times the father's will was law. When, therefore, they saw Joseph tricked out in his robe of state, the brethren felt that in all likelihood *he* would have the rich inheritance, while *they* must follow a life of toil. "And when his brethren saw that their father loved him more than all his brethren, they hated him, and could not speak peaceably unto him."

The case was aggravated by his plain speaking. "He brought unto his father their evil report." At first sight this does not seem a noble trait in his character. Love covereth the multitude of sins, as the two elder sons of Noah covered their father's shame. At the same time there may have been circumstances that justified, and even demanded, the exposure. It is sometimes the truest kindness, after due and repeated warning, to expose the evil deeds of those with whom we live and work. If they are permitted to go on in sin, apparently undetected, they will become hardened and emboldened, and eager to go to greater lengths. Moreover, Joseph was probably placed over them, and was responsible to his father for their behavior. He was jealous for the family name which they had already "made to stink among the inhabitants of the land." He was eager for the glory of God, whose name was continually blasphemed through their means. And, therefore, without attempting to conceal the evil, he told their father just how matters stood.

But this was enough to make them hate him. "Every one that doeth evil hateth the light." "I hate him," said the infuriated Ahab when speaking of Micaiah, "because he doth not prophesy good of me, but evil." "The world cannot hate you," our Lord said sadly; "but Me it hateth, because I testify of it, that its works are evil." So will it be always: if the world loves us and speaks well of us, we may gravely question if we are salt, pure and stinging, amid its corruption, or lights in its midnight gloom. As soon as our lives become a strong contrast and reproof, we shall arouse its undying hate. "What evil have I done," said the ancient Cynic, "to make all men speak well of me?"

But still further, *Joseph dreamed that he should become the center of the family life.* All young people dream. Unless our lot has been peculiarly hard and untoward, we all in the sunny days of youth, don Joseph's tunic, and dream—how great and successful we shall be! How noble and heroic! How much good we are to get and give! The heavens shall rain soft showers of benediction! The earth shall yield flowers for our feet and fruits to our taste! We shall surpass all who have preceded us; sitting on the throne of supremacy, while our detractors and foes do us obeisance! Alas, our raiment soon drips with blood, and we find ourselves down in the pit, or sold into captivity. But there was this in Joseph's dreams, they foretold not only his exaltation, but his brothers' humiliation. If he were the central sheaf, their sheaves must do obeisance, by falling to the earth around it. If he were on the throne, sun, moon, and stars must do him homage. This was more than the proud spirits of his brethren could brook, and "they hated him yet the more."

But the root of their enmity lay even deeper. In Eden, when addressing the serpent, God said: "I will put enmity between thee and the woman, and between thy seed and her seed." That is one of the profoundest sayings in the Bible. It is the key to Scripture. All that comes after only proves the virulence and the universality of the conflict between the children of God and the children of the devil. It broke out between Cain and Abel. It has embittered every family. It has rent every home. It shall yet convulse the universe. This was the secret of the conflict that raged around Joseph. I grant that the home was ill-organized; that all the evils incident to polygamy were there; that Jacob was incompetent to rule. But still I see there an instance of that conflict of which Christ spake: "I am come to set a man at variance against his father, and the daughter against her mother; . . . and a man's foes shall be they of his own household."

Do you know by sad experience what Joseph felt beneath those Syrian skies? Do the archers shoot at you? Are you lonesome and depressed, and ready to give up? Take heart! See the trampled grass and the snapped twigs; others have gone this way before you. Christ your Lord suffered the same treatment from His own. Go on doing right, in nothing terrified by your adversaries. Be pitiful and gentle, forgiving and forbearing. Be specially careful not to take your case into your own hands; demanding redress in imperious and vindictive tones. If you are servants, forbear to answer back. Give your backs to the smiters, and your cheeks to them that pluck off the hair. Avenge not yourselves, but rather give place unto wrath. Put down your feet into the footprints of your Savior, who left an example that we should follow Him. He did no sin, neither was guile found in His mouth: and yet, when He was unjustly reviled, He reviled not again; when He suffered beneath undeserved contumely and reproach, He did not even remind the perpetrators of the righteous judgment of God, but was dumb as a lamb, and threatened not, and committed Himself to Him that judgeth righteously.

And what was the result? Joseph was carried through the hatred and opposition of his foes; and his dreams were literally fulfilled in the golden days of prosperity, which came at length. Just as Jesus was eventually seated at the right hand of God, as Prince and Savior. And your time, sufferer, shall come at length, when God shall vindicate your character, and avenge your sorrows. "Trust in the Lord, and do good; fret not thyself in any wise to do evil; for evil-doers shall be cut off: but those that wait upon the Lord, they shall inherit the earth. He shall bring forth thy righteousness as the light, and thy judgment as the noonday" (from Ps. 37).

2
The Pit

Genesis 37

All is of God that is, and is to be;
And God is good! Let this suffice us still;
Resting in childlike trust upon his will,
Who moves to his great ends, unthwarted by the ill.

J. G. Whittier

The cross of our Lord Jesus Christ is the center of human history. It is the sun around which the firmament circles; the key to all Scripture history and type; the fact which gives meaning and beauty to all other facts. To ignore the cross is to repeat the error of the old philosophers; who thought that the earth, and not the sun, was the center of our system, and to whom therefore the very heavens were in confusion. To know and love the cross—to stand beside it as the faithful women did when Jesus died—is to obtain a deep insight into the harmonies of all things in heaven and earth.

It is remarkable to learn that, on the day of our Savior's passion, it being equinox, the whole habitable world was lit up between the hours of 9 A.M. and 6 P.M. Could an angel have poised himself in mid-air during those memorable hours, he would have seen each continent bathed in successive sunshine. At 9 A.M. it was noon in India, and all Asia was in light to its far eastern fringes; at noon all Europe and all Africa was in light; at 6 P.M. the whole continent of America had passed into the golden glory. This may serve as a parable. Poise yourself above the cross; look back to the morning of earth's history, and onward to its evening—and all will be light. The radiance that streams from the cross illumines all events, and banishes all darkness.

When an artist in music, color, or stone, conceives a beautiful idea, he seems reluctant to let it drop: he hints at it before he expresses it in complete beauty; nor is he satisfied until he has exhausted his art by the variety of ways in which he has embodied his thought. The practiced sense may detect it now in the symphony, and then in the chorus; now in the general scheme, and again in the minute detail. It recurs again and again. There is the hint, the outline, the slight symptom, anticipating the fuller, richer revelation. Is not this true also of the death of our beloved Lord? The Great Artist of all things, enamored with the wondrous cross, filled the world with foreshadowings and anticipations of it long before it stood with outstretched arms on the little hill of Calvary. You may find them in heathen myths, or in ancient sayings and songs. You may find them in touching incidents of human history. You may, above all, find them upon the pages of the Bible. The ages that lie on this side of the cross are full of references to it—it shapes them as it shapes each cathedral church, but I suppose that the ages on the other side were quite as full, though the observers may not have been so keen to see them.

The sun which now shines, so to speak, from the other side of the cross, so as to fling its shadow forward clear and sharp on the canvas of the present, once shone from where we now stand, and flung its shadow backward upon the canvas of the past. One of these shadows is caught and photographed for us in this sweet story of Joseph.

To the casual reader the story of Joseph's wrongs, and of his rise from the pit to vice-regal power, is simply interesting, as an old world story must ever be, for its archaic simplicity and the insight into the past which it affords. But to the man on whose heart the cross is carved in loving memory there is a far deeper interest. It is Calvary in miniature. It is the outline sketch of the Artist's finished work. It is a rehearsal of the greatest drama ever enacted among men.

We can do no better than take it line by line, and mark the fulfillment of the shadow in the glorious reality.

I. JOSEPH'S MISSION. *"Jacob dwelt in the land* of his father's so-journings." When he had buried his old father he continued to reside in the Vale of Hebron, where Isaac had dwelt for nearly two hundred years, and where Abraham abode before him. This was the head-quarters of his vast encampment. But rich as were the pasture lands of Hebron, they were not sufficient to support the whole of the flocks and herds. The sons were compelled to drive these by slow stages to distant parts of the land; and were even forced, by stern necessity, to brave the anger of the people of Shechem, whom they had grievously wronged, and who had vowed vengeance on them for their foul behavior.

It was this that gave point to Jacob's question, "Do not thy brethren feed the flock at Shechem?" He had heard them speak of going there in search of pasture; long weeks had passed since he received tidings of their welfare, and the memory of the past made him very anxious about them. And this solicitude became so overpowering that it forced him to do what otherwise would never have entered his thoughts.

He was alone in Hebron with Joseph and Benjamin: they were his darlings; his heart loved them with something of the intense devotion which he had felt towards their mother. Benjamin was young, but Joseph was seventeen years old. The old man kept them with him, reluctant to lose them from his sight. Hebron means fellowship,[*] and was a fitting residence for hearts so closely knit as theirs. But still, on the other hand, the old man yearned with anxious love over his absent sons; and at last, after many battlings and hesitations, he suddenly said to the dearly loved Joseph, "Come, I will send thee: go, I pray thee, and see whether it be well with thy brethren, and bring me word again."

On Joseph's part there was not a moment's hesitation. In the flash of a thought he realized the perils of the mission—perils of waters, perils of robbers, perils of wild beasts, perils in the lonely nights, perils among false brethren, who bitterly hated him. But "none of these things moved him, neither counted he his life dear unto himself." As soon as he knew his father's will, he said, "Here am I." "So Jacob sent him; and he came."

---

[*] *Khevrōn:* Associating, joining together.

But Joseph did not go in search of his brethren simply because his father sent him. Had this been the case, he would have returned home when he found that they had safely left the dreaded Shechem. But instead of that he sought them, because he loved them, and went after them until he found them.

Is not all this full to overflowing of a yet loftier theme? Our Lord never wearied of calling Himself the Sent of the Father. There is hardly a page in the Gospel of John in which He does not say more than once, "I came not of Myself, but My Father sent Me." He loved to find an analogy to His mission in the name of the brooklet that flowed "hard by the oracle of God," and which was called Siloam (which is by interpretation, "Sent"). Thus it became a constant expression with the New Testament writers, "God sent forth his Son"; "The Father sent the Son to be the Savior of the world."

It must have cost Jacob something to part with the beloved Joseph: and this can be gauged by those who have lost their beloved. But who can estimate how much it cost the Infinite God to send his only-begotten Son, who had dwelt in his bosom, and who was his Fellow from everlasting? Let us not think that God is passionless as the sphinx, which, with expressionless face and with stony eyes, stares unmoved, unfeeling, over the desert waste. If his love be like ours (and we know it must be), He must suffer from the same causes that work havoc in our hearts, only He must suffer proportionately to the strength and infiniteness of his nature. How much, then, must God have loved us, that He should be willing to send his Son! Truly God *so* loved the world! But who shall fathom the depths of that one small word?

But our Savior did not come solely because He was sent. He came because He loved his mission. He came to seek and to save that which was lost. And He especially came in search of his brethren, his own, the children of the Hebrew race. Could you have asked Him, as you met Him traversing those same fields, "What seekest Thou?" He would have replied in the self-same words of Joseph, "I seek my brethren." Nor was He content with only *seeking* the lost; He went after them *until* He found them. "Joseph went after his brethren until he found them in Dothan."

Beautiful as is the parable of the Prodigal Son, to me there is no less priceless beauty in the parables of the Lost Sheep and the Lost Silverling, because in each of these two there was seeking on the part of one who could not bear to lose, and the seeking was never abandoned until the lost was found. It may be that the Lord Jesus is seeking *you:* for many weary days He has been seeking for you, with bleeding feet or with a lighted candle. You of yourself might never have the desire or the courage to seek *Him;* yet take heart, since He will never rest till He has found *you.*

II. JOSEPH'S RECEPTION. "They saw him afar off, even before he came near unto them, and they conspired against him to slay him." And he would doubtless have been ruthlessly slain, and his body flung into some pit, away from the haunts of men, if it had not been for the merciful pleadings of Reuben, the eldest brother. "And it came to pass, when Joseph was come unto his brethren, that they stripped him of his coat, his coat of many colors, and they took him, and cast him into a pit." Our mother earth has seen many dark crimes committed on her surface by her children, but she has never seen a darker one than this. It was a mean, cowardly, dastardly deed for nine grown men to set upon one timid, unresisting lad.

The calm prose of the historian does not dwell on the passion of the brothers, or on the anguish of that young heart, which found it so hard to die, so hard to say goodbye to the fair earth, so hard to descend into that dark cistern, whose steep sides forbade the hope that he could ever scramble back into the upper air. But the confession of those cruel men, made to one another after the lapse of twenty-five years, enables us to supply the missing coloring for the deed of horror.

Years after they said one to another, "We are verily guilty concerning our brother, in that we saw the anguish of his soul, when he besought us and we would not hear." What a revelation there is in these words! We seem to see Joseph, in those rude hands, like a fleecy lamb in the jaws of a tiger. He struggles to get free. He entreats them with bitter tears to let him go. He implores them for the sake of his old father, and by the tie of brotherhood. The anguish of his soul is clearly evident in his bitter cries, and tears, and prayers. Alas, poor young sufferer! Would that we could believe that thine were the only anguished cries which brutal passion has extorted from gentle innocence!

What a genesis of crime is here! There was a time when the germ of
this sin alighted on their hearts in the form of a ruffled feeling of
jealousy against the young dreamer. If only they had quenched it
then, its further progress would have been stayed. Alas! they did not
quench it; they permitted it to work within them as leaven works in
meal. And "lust, when it had conceived, brought forth sin; and sin,
when it was finished, brought forth death." Take care how you permit
a single germ of sin to alight and remain upon your heart. To permit
it to do so, is almost certain ruin. Sooner or later it will acquire overwhelming force. Treat that germ as you would the first germ of fever
that entered your home. At the first consciousness of sin, seek instant cleansing in the precious blood of Christ.

Unforgiven sin is a fearful scourge. Year passed after year, but the years
could not obliterate from their memories that look, those cries, that
scene in the green glen of Dothan, surrounded by the tall cliffs, over-
arched by the blue sky, whose expanse was lit up by a meridian sun.
They tried to lock up the skeleton in their most secret cupboard, but
it contrived to come forth to confront them even in their guarded
hours. Sometimes they thought they saw that agonized young face in
their dreams, and heard that piteous voice wailing in the night wind.
The old father, who mourned for his son as dead, was happier than
were they, who knew him to be alive. One crime may thus darken a
whole life. There are some who teach that God is too merciful to
punish men; yet He has so made the world that sin is its own Neme-
sis—sin carries with it the seed of its own punishment. And the men
who carry with them the sense of unforgiven sin, will be the first to believe in a vulture forever tearing out the vitals, a worm that never
dies, a fire that is never quenched.

But Joseph's grief was a true anticipation of Christ's. "He came to his
own, but his own received Him not." They said, "This is the heir, come
let us kill Him, and the inheritance shall be ours." "They caught
Him, and cast Him out, and slew Him." "They parted his raiment
among them." They sold Him to the Gentiles. They sat down to
watch Him die. The anguish of Joseph's soul reminds us of the strong
cryings and tears wrung from the human nature of Christ by the near
approach of His unknown sufferings as the scapegoat of the race.

The comparative innocence of Joseph reminds us of the spotlessness of the Lamb who was without blemish, and whose blamelessness was again and again attested before He died. No victim destined for the altar was ever more searchingly inspected for one black hair or defect thanwas Jesus, by those who were compelled to confess, "The Man hath done nothing amiss."

Here, however, the parallel stays. Joseph's sufferings stopped before they reached the point of death; Jesus tasted death. Joseph's sufferings were personal; the sufferings of Jesus were substitutionary and mediatorial; "He died for us"; "He gave Himself for me." Joseph's sufferings had no efficacy in atoning for the sin that caused them, but the sufferings of Jesus atone not only for the guilt of his murderers, but for the guilt of all; "He is the propitiation for our sins; and not for ours only, but also for the whole world."

III. Joseph's Fate. "They sat down to eat bread." With hardened unconcern they took their midday meal. Just at that moment a new and welcome sight struck their gaze. They were sitting on the plain at Dothan, a spot which still retains its ancient name; and anyone stationed there, and looking eastward towards the valley of Jordan, would be able to trace the main road that led from the fords of the Jordan towards the coast of the Mediterranean. This road was one of the main thoroughfares of Palestine; it connected Gilead and the other territories beyond the Jordan with the seacoast; and when once the coast was struck, the way was easy southwards through Philistia to the Delta of the Nile. Along this road at that moment a caravan was traveling. The brothers could readily descry the long string of patient camels moving slowly up the valley towards them. They guessed at once who the parties were and whence they came. Without doubt they were of the Arab race, the sailors of the desert in all ages, descendants of Ishmael; and they were coming from Gilead, bearing spicery and balm and myrrh, natural aromatic products which abound in the woods and pasture lands of Eastern Palestine, and which were in great request in Egypt for purposes of embalment.

The sight of these traveling merchants gave a sudden turn to the thoughts of the conspirators. They knew that there was in Egypt a great demand for slaves, and that these merchantmen were in the habit of buying slaves in their passage and selling them in that land, which has always been the great slave-mart of the world. Why not sell their brother? It would be an easy way of disposing of him. It would save them from fratricide. So, acting upon the suggestion of Judah, they lifted Joseph out of the pit, and as money was no object to them, they sold him for twenty rings of silver—about three pounds.

It was the work of a few minutes; and then Joseph found himself one of a long line of fettered slaves, bound for a foreign land. Was not this almost worse than death? What anguish still rent his young heart! How eager his desire to send just one last message to his father! And with all these thoughts, there would mingle a wondering thought of the great God whom he had learned to worship. What would He say to this? Little did he think then that hereafter he should look back on that day as one of the most gracious links in a chain of loving providence; or that he should ever say, "Be not grieved, nor angry with your-selves: God did send me here before you." It is very sweet, as life passes by, to be able to look back on dark and mysterious events, and to trace the hand of God where we once saw only the malice and cruelty of man. And no doubt the day is coming when we shall be able to speak thus of *all* the dark passages of our life.

Joseph was betrayed by his brothers; Jesus by His friend. Joseph was sold for money; so was our Lord. Joseph followed in the train of cap-tives to slavery; Jesus was numbered with transgressors. The crime of Joseph's brothers fulfilled the Divine plan; and the wicked hands of the crucifiers of Jesus fulfilled the determinate counsel and foreknowl-edge of God.

God will "make the wrath of man to praise Him; and the re-mainder of wrath will He restrain." "Oh, the depth of the riches both of the wisdom and of the knowledge of God! How unsearchable His judgments, and His ways past finding out!"

3

In the House of Potiphar

Many, if God should make them kings,
Might not disgrace the throne He gave;
How few who could as well fulfill
The holier office of a slave!

Great may he be who can command,
And rule with just and tender sway;
Yet diviner wisdom taught
Better by him who can obey.

Genesis 39   A. A. Proctor

The Midianite merchantmen, into whose hands his brethren sold Joseph, brought him down to Egypt—with its riband of green pasture-land amid the waste of sand. In some great slave market he was exposed for sale, together with hundreds more, who had been captured by force or stealth from the surrounding countries. No doubt the regions of the Upper Nile and of Central Africa were drained then as now, to meet the insatiable demand for slaves. And the delicately complexioned lad may have found himself close to the swarthy children of the lands that lie beneath the tropic sun; lands which have been trodden in recent times by English soldiers, and which will forever be sacred to our countrymen because of the soldiers' graves that seam the wastes of sand. He was bought by Potiphar, "the captain of the guard." The margin tells us he was the chief of the slaughtermen or executioners. He was, in all likelihood, the chief of the military force employed as the royal bodyguard, in the precincts of the court. The Egyptian monarchs had the absolute power of life and death; and they did not scruple to order the infliction of a variety of summary or sanguinary punishments, the execution of which was entrusted to the

military guard, which was always at hand, and afforded the readiest and
most efficient instrument for torture or death.

Potiphar was an Egyptian grandee; a member of a proud aristocracy; high in office and in court favor. He would no doubt live in a
splendid palace, covered with hieroglyphs and filled with slaves. The
young captive, accustomed to the tendernesses of his simple and
beloved home, must have trembled as he passed up the pillared avenue,
through sphinx-guarded gates, into the recesses of that strange, vast
Egyptian palace, where they spoke a language of which he could not
understand a word, and where all was so new and strange. But "God
was with him"; the sense of the presence and guardianship of his father's God pervaded and stilled his soul, and kept him in perfect
peace; and, though severed from all whom he knew, it was rest and
strength to feel that the mysterious wings, engraved on the porticoes
of so many Egyptian buildings, were emblems to him of the outstretched wings of his great Father's care—an unsleeping care beneath which his soul might nestle evermore. Who would not rather,
after all, choose to be Joseph in Egypt with God, than the brothers with
a blood-stained garment in their hands and the sense of guilt on
their soul?

Let us consider how Joseph fared in Potiphar's house.

I. JOSEPH'S PROMOTION. "The Lord was with Joseph; and he was
a prosperous man." The older versions of the Bible give a curious
rendering here: "The Lord was with Joseph; and he was a lucky fellow."
I suppose the meaning is that everything he handled went well. Success followed him as closely as his shadow, and touched all his plans
with her magic wand. Potiphar and his household got into the way of
expecting that this strange Hebrew captive could untie every knot, disentangle every skein, and bring to successful issues the most intricate
arrangements. This arose from two causes.

In the first place, *though stripped of his coat, he had not been stripped
of his character.* See to it, young people, that no one rob you of that:
everything else may be replaced but that! He was industrious, prompt,
diligent, obedient, reliable. When sent to find his brothers, he had carried out, not the letter only, but the spirit of his father's instructions,

and did not rest till he had traced them from Shechem to Dothan. And this was the spirit of his life. He did his work, not because he was obliged to do it, but because God had given it to him to do, and had called him to do it. He read the will of God in "the daily round, the common task." He said to himself, as he said in afterlife, "God did send me hither" (45:5). He felt that he was the servant, not so much of Potiphar as of the God of Abraham and Isaac. There, in the household of Potiphar, he might live a devout and earnest life as truly as when he spent the long, happy days in Jacob's tent: and he did. And it was this which made him so conscientious and careful, qualities which in business must ensure success.

When his fellow servants were squandering the golden moments, Joseph was filling them with activities. When they were content with a good surface appearance, he toiled upward to success from carefully laid foundations. When they worked simply to avoid the frown or the lash, he worked to win the smile of the great Taskmaster, whose eye was ever upon him. They often pointed at him with envy, and perhaps said, "He is a lucky fellow." They did not think that his luck was his character; and that his character meant God. Men often speak thus of each other, "He was always a lucky fellow"; "He was born beneath a lucky star"; "He is sure to have good luck." But there is no such thing as luck, except that luck means character. And if you wish to possess such a character as will insure your success in this life, there is no true basis for it but Jesus Christ. You must build on Him, or your structure will be swept away in the first hurricane. But when once you have touched Him, the living stone, with the first courses of faith—then rear the building after the plan given in His own lovely life. Tier on tier let it rise: and you will find that "Godliness is profitable unto all things, and has the promise of the life that now is, and of that which is to come."

In the second place: "*The Lord made all that he did to prosper. The Lord blessed the Egyptian's house for Joseph's sake; and the blessing of the Lord was upon all that he had in the house, and in the field.*" This blessing was not the exclusive privilege of Joseph: it is promised to overtake all those "who hearken diligently unto the voice of God, and who observe to do all His commandments" (Deut. 28:1, 2). Such blessing would oft be ours if we walked as near to God as Joseph did. It is of little use to cry with Jabez, "Oh that Thou wouldest bless me indeed!" unless, like him we add, "Keep me from evil." But when the blessing comes, "it maketh rich, and addeth no sorrow." Let us see to it that we live so that God may be with us. "The Lord is with you, while ye be with Him: and if ye seek Him, He will be found of you, but if ye forsake Him, He will forsake you."

These words may be read by servants of various kinds—the household domestic, the office boy, the apprentice, the clerk. And if so, they will surely be helped by the example of this noble youth. He did not give himself to useless regrets and unavailing tears. He girded himself manfully to do with his might whatsoever his hand found to do. He was "faithful in that which was least," in the most menial and trivial duties of his office. He believed that God had put him where he was; and in serving his earthly master's will he felt that he was really pleasing his great heavenly Friend, who was as near him in those hieroglyphed palaces as in Jacob's tents. This is the spirit in which all service should be done. "Stay where you are," said the apostles to the vast slave populations of their time, who gladly embraced the Gospel that made them free with a freedom which no thongs or chains could limit. But "let every man, wherein he is called, therein abide with God. Art thou called, being a servant? Care not for it; for he that is called in the Lord, being a servant, is the Lord's freeman." "Ye serve the Lord Christ. Whatsoever ye do, do it heartily, as to the Lord, and not unto men." "Be obedient to them that are your masters, in singleness of heart, as unto Christ." "Adorn the doctrine of God our Savior in all things." "Christ"—the great Servant—"suffered for us, leaving us an example that ye should follow His steps."

These voices from the page of inspiration still speak to servants. If only they were acted upon, all such would as much ask the will of Christ before leaving a situation as a minister before leaving his charge. The most trifling things would be done on the loftiest principles, just as the shape of a dewdrop upon a rose leaf is determined by the same laws as controlled the molding of our earth into its present form. Yes: and every kitchen, dwelling room, and office, would be trodden with the same reverence and love as the floors of a temple or the golden pavement of heaven. Our lots in life are much more even than we think. It is not so important what we do as how we do it. The motive that inspires us is the true gauge and measure of the worth or importance of our life. A mean man may belittle the most momentous affairs by the paltriness of his spirit. A noble man may so greaten trifles by his nobility, that they shall become subjects for the conservation of burning seraphim, or of cherubim with folded wing.

These words may be read by masters. We cannot estimate the worth of a true Christian servant. Happy the household which is thus equipped! The Egyptian Potiphar must have been agreeably surprised at the sudden tide of prosperity which set in towards him. All things went well with him—his cattle throve in the field; his affairs prospered in the house. He may often have questioned the cause, but little guessed at first that it was owing to the Hebrew slave. "The Lord blessed the Egyptian's house for Joseph's sake"; He paid him handsomely for His servant's keep. So is it still. Ungodly masters owe many a blessing to the presence of some Christian servant or *employee* beneath their roof. No angel would ever alight there; no living spring would bubble there; no music would ever sweeten the daily din of work; no ladder would link that building to the skies—if it were not for some Eliezer, or Joseph, or Rhoda, that was living there. When we reach heaven, and are able to trace the origin of things, we shall find that many of the choicest blessings of our lives were procured by the prayers or presence of very obscure and unrecognized people who were dear to God.

II. JOSEPH'S TEMPTATION. Years passed on, and Joseph became a prosperous man, the steward and bailiff in his master's house. "He left all that he had in Joseph's hand; and he knew not aught he had, save the bread which he did eat." And it was just here that Joseph encountered the most terrible temptation of his life.

We may expect temptation in days of prosperity and ease rather than in those of privation and toil. Not on the glacier slopes of the Alps, but in the sunny plains of the Campagna; not when the youth is climbing arduously the steep ladder of fame, but when he has entered the golden portals; not where men frown, but where they smile sweet exquisite smiles of flattery—it is *there*, it is *there*, that the temptress lies in wait! Beware! If thou goest armed anywhere, thou must, above all, go armed here. Yet this is so hard. It is easy to keep the armor on when we ascend the desolate mountain pass, struggling against the pitiless blast, and afraid that any boulder may hide an assassin. It is hard to keep it buckled close when we have reached the happy valley, with its sultry air. But unless we keep armed there, we are lost. "Watch and pray, that ye enter not into temptation. The flesh is weak."

Temptation is hardest to resist when it arises from the least expected quarter. Egyptian women in those days enjoyed as much liberty as English women do now: this is conclusively proved by the Egyptian monuments, which also testify to the extreme laxity of their morals. It may be that Potiphar's wife was not worse than many of her sex, though we blush to read of her infamous proposals. They must have startled Joseph like a shock of earthquake, and filled him with a sudden tumult of thoughts. The sudden appeal to his passions invested the temptation with tenfold force. God has so arranged it that, for the most part, the sailor is warned against the coming storm; he is able to reef his sails, and close his portholes: but, alas for him if he is caught by a sudden squall! Christian, beware of sudden squalls! Men are suddenly overtaken by faults.

Policy and conscience are often at variance in respect to temptation. It seemed essential to Joseph to stand well with his master's wife. To please her would secure his advancement. To cross her would make her his foe, and ruin his hopes. How many would have reasoned that, by yielding for only a moment, they might win influence which they could afterwards use for the very best results! One act of homage to the devil would invest them with power which they might then use for his overthrow. This is the reasoning of policy, one of the most accursed traitors in man's heart. It is this policy which leads many to say, when tempted to do wrong, by master, or mistress, or foreman, or chief customer, "I did not care for it, or wish it. I yielded because my bread depended on it; I did not dare offend them." The only armor against policy is FAITH that looks to the long future, and believes that in the end it will be found better to have done right, and to have waited the vindication and blessing of God. Well was it for Joseph that he did not heed the suggestions of policy: had he done so, he might have acquired a little more influence in the home of Potiphar, but it could never have lasted—and he would never have become prime minister of Egypt, or had a home of his own, or have brought his boys to receive the blessing of his dying father.

The strength of a temptation lies in the response of our nature to its suggestions. It is said that the germs of the potato and vine disease are always floating in the air, but they can find no place of operation—no bed—in healthy plants. But directly plants become degenerate and unable to resist their attacks, then they sweep away the farmer's hopes in dreadful ruin. So it is with us; if only we were like our Lord, we should pass unscathed through a whirlwind of temptations; they would find nothing in us. It is because our hearts are so desperately wicked that we need to stand in constant watchfulness. "Keep thy heart with all diligence; for out of it are the issues of life." There is no sin in having certain tendencies, appetites, and desires; else there would be sin in hunger, and in drowsiness leading to soft sleep. But the danger lies in the fear that they should be gratified to an immoderate excess, or from wrong and improper sources. Human nature is very liable to this. It is biased thus; and stolen waters are sweet. Therefore Joseph must have suffered the more.

We should always carefully distinguish between the appetites and desires which are natural to us; and those which we have acquired by evil habit. About the latter we need have no hesitation. We can give them no quarter. They must be cut up root and branch; as weeds from garden soil are thrown upon the bank, that the sun may scorch out their life. But the former need careful watching, because though in themselves they are natural and beautiful, yet they are always liable to demand excessive gratification in respect to right objects, or gratification in directions which are unnatural and forbidden. We must never expect the time to arrive, on this side of death, when these natural tendencies will be rooted out; and so long as they remain in us, they will constitute a *nidus* in which the germs of temptation may sow themselves, and fruit. No thoughtful man, who knows his own weakness, can ever dare affirm his immunity from temptation, or the impossibility of his yielding. If he stand it is only by the grace of God.

There were peculiar elements of trial in Joseph's case. The temptation was accompanied by opportunity: "there were none of the men there within." It was well timed, and if he had yielded, there was not much fear of detection and punishment; the temptress would never publish her own shame. The temptation was also repeated day by day. How terrible must have been that awful persistence! Water, by constant dropping, will wear away rocks; and the temptation that tries at last to win its way by its very importunity is to be feared most of all.

Yet Joseph stood firm. He reasoned with her. He urged his master's kindness and trust. He held up the confidence which he dared not betray. He tried to recall her to a sense of what became her as his master's wife. But he did more. He brought the case from the court of reason to that of conscience, and asked in words forever memorable, and which have given the secret of victory to tempted souls in all ages: "How shall I do this great wickedness, and sin against God!"

There are few subjects which require more notice both from speakers and writers than this great subject of chastity. Society is merciless on the occasional consequences of unchastity and on the wretched victims, but it hears of the sin itself with an averted smile, or calls it by some other name. But there is no one sin which sooner corrupts the heart, weakens the intellect, and destroys the body. The poet Robert Burns wrote out of a bitter experience in his "Letter to a Young Friend":

> The hallowed lowe o' weel-placed love,
>   Luxuriantly indulge it;
> But never tempt the illicit rove,
>   Though naething should divulge it.
> I waive the quantum o' the sin,
>   The hazard o' concealin';
> But oh, it hardens a' within,
>   And petrifies the feelin'.

And Lord Byron, ending his brief and unchaste life at the age of thirty-six, closed his last poem with these mournful words:

> My days are in the yellow leaf,
>   The flower and fruit of love are gone;

> The worm, the canker, and the grief,
> Are mine alone!

There is no one sin which will sooner bring about a nation's fall. If history teaches anything, it teaches that sensual indulgence is the surest way to national ruin. In not condemning this sin, society condemns herself.

It is said that the temptation of our great cities are too many and strong for the young to resist. Men sometimes speak as if sin were a necessity. Refuse to entertain such thoughtlessness and dangerous talk. While the case of Joseph remains on record, it is a standing contradiction to the whole. A young man *can* resist; he *can* overcome; he *can* be pure, and chaste, and sweet. We must, however, obey the dictates of Scripture and common sense. Avoid all places, books and people which minister to evil thoughts. Resist the first tiny rill of temptation, lest it widen a breach big enough to admit the ocean. Remember that no temptation can master you unless you admit it *within* your nature; and since you are too weak to keep the door shut against it, look to the mighty Savior to place Himself against it. All hell cannot break the door open which you entrust to the safe keeping of Jesus.

What a motto this is for us all! "How can *I* do this great wickedness?" *I*, for whom Christ died. "How can I do this great *wickedness?*" Others call it "gaiety"; "being a little fast"; "sowing wild oats." I call it SIN. "How can I do this *great* wickedness?" Many wink at it; to me it is a *great* sin. "How can I sin *against God?*" It seems only to concern men, but in effect it is a personal sin against the holy God.

It might have been better if Joseph had not gone into the house to do his business, but probably he had no choice except to go. He took care not to be with her (v. 10) more than he could help. We have no right to expect God to keep us if we voluntarily put ourselves into temptation. But if we are compelled to go there by the circumstances of our life, we may count upon His faithfulness. If the Spirit driveth us into the wilderness to be tempted, we may expect to enjoy also the ministry of the angels.

Joseph did a wise thing when he fled. Discretion is often the wisest part of valor. Better lose a coat and many a more valuable possession than lose a good conscience. "Flee youthful lusts." Do not parley with temptation. Do not linger in its vicinity. Do not stay to look at it. It will master you if you do. "Escape for thy life; look not behind thee, neither stay in all the plain."

There is no sin in being tempted. The Sinless One Himself was tempted of the devil. The mob may batter at the palace gates, but the national life is safe so long as sin does not penetrate into the throne room, and thrust itself into the royal seat. The will is the citadel of our manhood; and so long as there is no yielding there, there is none anywhere. I cannot be accused of receiving stolen goods, if I am simply asked to take them in—a request which I indignantly repudiate. The sin comes in when I assent, and acquiesce, and yield. At the same time, it is in the highest degree unwise to relinquish the battle until it comes into the inner shrine of our being. Much better fight it in the first circle of defense—in the first suggestion, or insinuation, or desire. Resist the devil there, and he will flee from you; and you will be saved a struggle within, which will leave its scar on your soul for years to come.

May we have grace and faith to imitate the example of Joseph, and, above all, of our stainless Lord. We may be quite sure that no temptation will be permitted to assail us—but such as is common to man, or that we are able to resist. The onset of temptation indicates that God knows that we are strong enough to resist, and that sufficient grace is surely within our reach. And the Almighty Father would lead us to put forth that strength, and to avail ourselves of His resources. "He that abideth in Him sinneth not. He that sinneth hath not seen Him, neither known Him." Never forget that we who believe in Jesus are seated with Him at the right hand of power; nor that Satan is already, in the purpose of God, a defeated foe beneath our feet. Let the Overcomer into your heart, for Him to overcome in you, as He overcame in His own mortal life (1 John 4:4; John 16:33). Open your whole being to the subduing grace of the Holy Spirit. And thus we shall be more than conquerers through Him who loves us.

4

The Secret of Purity

Genesis 39.
See also Prov.
4:23; 2 Pet. 1:5;
2 Tim. 1:12

Against the threats of malice, or of sorcery, or of that power
Which erring men call Chance, this I hold firm:
Virtue may be assailed, but never hurt;
Surprised by unjust force, but not enthralled;
Yea, even that which mischief meant most harm,
Shall, in the happy trial, prove most glory.

Milton

Joseph learned, hundreds of years before our Savior taught it from the Mount of the Beatitudes, the blessedness of the pure in heart. He could not have anticipated the exquisite symmetry of the form in which the law of that blessedness was expressed. That could only be coined and minted by the lips which spake as never man spake. But he most certainly drank a deep draft of divine sweetness and light from the crystal vase of his manly purity.

There is nothing which we more earnestly admire than purity, like that which Milton, our great Puritan bard, so exquisitely paints in his "Comus"; and which, like the sunbeam striking through the atmosphere of some fetid court, can pass through the murkiest conditions, without surrendering a ray of its celestial glory. Men familiar with the secret of self-control—or who, not having been exposed to the gusts of temptation which sweep over and master other lives, have never sullied their robes—always attract to themselves the admiration and reverence of their fellows. The snow capped summits of purity, in their lofty, heaven-reaching majesty, appear so inaccessible to ordinary men, that they wonder greatly at any who are able to scale their rugged sides and breathe the rare atmosphere of the heavenly world.

We must always bear in mind that there is not part of our nature, no function of our human life, which is in itself common or unclean. As Adam came from his Maker's hand, and stood before Him in his native innocence, he did not even need the fig leaf drapery. All was sweet, and pure, and right, and very good. There was no desire or appetite of his nature which in itself was less sacred than any other. And if only he had ever willed God's will—if only the will, and law, and purpose of God had been kept supreme in his inner economy—there had been no lust, no inordinate desire, no passion, in the world. Like Moses, the great lawgiver, on the wilderness march, who received the commands of God and handed them to the officers and elders for the obedience of the host, so could conscience have received from God, and transmitted to the entire economy of our human nature, those enactments, the legitimate outworking of which had been towards the glory of God on the one hand, and man's well being on the other.

But when man sinned in the glades of Paradise, he changed the pivot of his being from God to self; he loved and served the creature more than the Creator; he took the sun out of the center of the inner sphere, which immediately fell into confusion, each part working for its own selfish and immediate gratification. And from that time man's highest law has consisted in the indulgence of appetite, flinging the reins on the neck of inordinate desire, whether of gross physical indulgence, or of imagination and thought; the only restraint being imposed by the fear of disastrous consequences in name or position; in mind, body, or estate.

This fact must be borne in mind then, in considering ourselves or others; and we must take into account the operation of the great law of heredity, by which we have become possessed of appetites and tendencies, which, however pure in their original intention, have been vitiated through the abuse of the many generations from which we have sprung. And there is, therefore, a strong tendency in us all by nature towards the forbidden fruit. Who among us has not been often conscious of a bias towards selfish indulgence in two distinct ways; first, to gratify the senses in directions which are wholly forbidden; and next, to gratify them to an excessive extent in directions which are in themselves legitimate?

It is inevitable, therefore, that we should begin life under serious disadvantages, since by our very origin we are closely related to a race which, through ages of previous history, has been tainted by the poison of self-will, and swept by the storms of passion. We cannot but start under serious disadvantages as compared with Adam. Not that we are condemned for his sin, for we are told that the second Adam has met for us all those penal consequences which must otherwise have accrued to us on that account, but that we are terribly handicapped by the disadvantage of being the children of a fallen race. And is not this what is meant by the theological term, *original sin*; and by St. Paul's phrase, "the law in the members"? And if it should be alleged that some mysterious change has passed over our physical nature, by which the inherited morbid operation of natural appetite has been reversed, we ask for proof and Scriptural warrant. Certainly, the presence of disease in the bodies of some of the holiest people is a strong presumptive proof against any such change having been effected. We must either hold that we have already received the resurrection body, or that there are perverted natural tendencies towards unholy and selfish gratification.

To guard against all possible misconstruction, we reiterate that we do not hold sin to consist in a merely physical state or act, but that we are predisposed to sin by the very nature which we have inherited, and which is so susceptive of Satanic temptation on the one side, and so subtle, swift, and disastrous in its influence on the will upon the other: and no philosophy of the inner life can be satisfactory that does not recognize the presence of this body of flesh, which is not in itself sin, but which so readily lends itself to evil suggestion, that, falling on it as sparks on gunpowder, tends to inflame the imagination, heart, and will.

So long, therefore, as we are in the body, we cannot say that we stand where Adam stood when he first came from the molding hand of God. There is a great difference between us and him, in that at that moment his nature had never yet yielded to evil; while ours has done so thousands of times, both in those from whom we have received it, and in our own repeated acts of self-indulgence. The glad time is coming when we shall exchange this body of humiliation for one in the likeness of our Savior's Resurrection. Then one great source of temptation and failure will be removed, and we shall no longer have to complain that the law in our members wars against the law of our mind, with the design of bringing us into its fatal captivity.

Is there then no deliverance in this life from that bondage? Surely there is. The law in the members may war against the law of the mind, and yet not succeed in bringing it into captivity, because it shall be garrisoned and held by the law of the Spirit of Life, which is in Christ Jesus, and which makes free from the law of sin and death.

The one-sufficient power by which the promptings of our evil nature can be held in check is by the indwelling and infilling of the Holy Spirit. "Walk in the Spirit, and ye shall not fulfill the lust of the flesh. The flesh lusteth against the Spirit, and the Spirit against the flesh, that ye may not do the things that ye would."

Never in this life will the tempter cease to assail. Even in the heavenly places—the upper regions of spiritual experience—we shall still be exposed to the attacks of the hosts of wicked spirits; and so long as we tabernacle in this body, we shall carry with us that susceptibility to evil which is the bitter result of Adam's fall. Like a thrill of electricity which pervades in a single moment the entire range of a telegraphic system, so some flash of unholy suggestion may rush through our nature, causing it for a moment to vibrate and thrill.

But when the Holy Spirit fills us, the tempter may do his worst, and his suggestions will fall fruitless and ineffectual at our feet; our nature will not respond to the solicitations which are made to it from without. We all know what happens when matches are struck on damp surfaces; and it will be thus with our temptations. The old nature, which was once as inflammable as gunpowder, will be deprived, so to speak, so long as the Spirit is in possession of its terrible facility of response. And even more, when the Spirit is in mighty power within, He will take away the very desire to yield to sin, and change the old love into hate, so that we shall loathe and shudder at things which we formerly chose and reveled in.

And in many cases, where He is trusted to the uttermost, He does his work so quietly and effectually in keeping the sinful tendencies in the place of death, that the happy subject of His grace supposes that they have been extracted from the nature. They are as if they were not. The self-life seems to hibernate; and this blessed experience continues, just so long as the soul lives in the full enjoyment of the Blessed Spirit's work.

Would that it might be the happy portion of each reader of these lines!

5

Misunderstood
and Imprisoned*

*Choose for us, Lord, nor let our weak preferring
Cheat us of good Thou hast for us designed;
Choose for us, Lord; Thy wisdom is unerring,
And we are fools and blind.*

*Let us press on, in patient self-denial,
Accept the hardship, shrink not from the loss:
Our portion lies beyond the hour of trial,
Our crown beyond the cross.*

Genesis 39, 40.

See also Ps. 105:17–19

W. H. Burleigh

Between the pit and the prison there was only a transient gleam of sunlight and prosperity. The sky of Joseph's life was again soon overcast. For when Potiphar heard the false but plausible statement of his wife, and saw the garment in her hand, which he recognized as Joseph's, his wrath flamed up; he would hear no words of explanation, but thrust him at once into the state prison, of which he had the oversight and charge.

I. THE SEVERITY OF HIS SUFFERINGS. It was not a prison like those with which we are familiar—airy, well lit, and conducted by humane men. To use Joseph's own words, in the Hebrew, it was a miserable "hole."** "I have done nothing that they should put me into the 'hole'." We are reminded of the words, describing old Bedford prison, with which Bunyan commences his matchless allegory: "As I walked through the wilderness of this world, I lighted on a certain place

---

* Some thoughts in this chapter were suggested by an article in the "Expositor's Notebook" by Rev. S. Cox.   ** Bōr.

where was a den, and I laid me down in that place to sleep; and, as I slept, I dreamed a dream." Two or three little rooms, crowded with prisoners, stifling in air, fetid with ill odors, perhaps half-buried from the blessed sunshine—this was the sort of accommodation in which Joseph spent those two miserable years.

Those who have seen the dreary prison at Tangier will be able to form a better conception of what that "hole" must have been like. Imagine a large gloomy hall, with no windows, paved with flags black with filth, no light or air, save what may struggle through the narrow grated aperture, by which the friends of the wretched inmates, or some pitying strangers, pass in the food and water which are the sole staff of life: no arrangements of any kind being made for cleanliness, or for the separation of the prisoners. All day long there is the weary clank of fetters around manacled feet, as the victims slowly drag themselves over the floor, or revolve again and again around the huge stone columns which support the roof, and to which their chains are riveted. In more ways than one does the Gospel of Christ preach deliverance to the captives. In some such sunless "hole" must Joseph have been confined.

And this was hard enough for one who was wont to wander freely on the broad Syrian plains. Confinement is intolerable to us all, but especially to youth, and of all youth most so to those in whose veins flows something of that Arab blood which dreads death less than bondage. I do not wonder at the pathetic story which tells how, on London Bridge, a sunburned sailor, fresh from the docks, bought cage after cage of imprisoned wild birds, and let them fly rejoicing to their native woods, assigning as his reason to the wondering onlookers that he had languished too long in a foreign prison not to know how sweet freedom was. We do not realize how priceless freedom is, because we have never lost it. And Joseph never valued it as he did when he found himself shut up in that stifling "hole."

But in addition to the confinement of the prison, *there was the constant clank of the fetter.* He was bound, and his feet were hurt by fetters. True, he enjoyed the favor of the keeper of the prison, and had exceptional liberty within the gloomy precincts so as to reach the inmates, but still, wherever he moved, the rattle of the iron reminded him that he was a prisoner still. You remember a touching allusion of another of the Lord's prisoners to this selfsame thing. So Paul took from the hand of his amanuensis the pen with which to write his autograph, "the token in every epistle" of genuineness and authenticity; and as he did so, he felt the pull of the chain that fastened him to the soldier of the imperial guard; and we can almost hear the clanking of the iron in the words, "Remember my bonds" (Col. 4:18).

But besides all this, *his religious notions added greatly to his distress.* He had been taught by Jacob the theory which comes out so prominently in the speeches of Job's three friends, and which was so generally held by all their teachers and associates in that olden, Eastern, philosophic, deeply-pondering world: that good would come to the good, and evil to the bad; that prosperity was the sign of the Divine favor, and adversity of the Divine anger. And Joseph had tried to be good. Had he not always kept his father's commandments and acted righteously, though his brethren were men of evil report, and tried to make him as bad as themselves? But what had he gained by his integrity? Simply the murderous jealousy and hatred of his own flesh and blood. Had he not, in the full flush of youthful passion, resisted the blandishments of the beautiful Egyptian, because he would not sin against God? And what had he gained by that? Simply the stigma which threatened to cling to him of having committed the very wickedness it was so hard not to commit; and, in addition, an undeserved punishment. Had he not always been kind and gentle to his fellow prisoners, listening to their stories, speaking comfort to their hearts? And what had he gained by that? To judge by what he saw, simply nothing; and he might as well have kept his kindness to himself.

Was it of any use, then, being good? Could there be any truth in what his father had taught him of good coming to the good, and evil to the bad? Was there a God who judgeth righteously in the earth? You who have been misunderstood, who have sown seeds of holiness and love to reap nothing but disappointment, loss, suffering, and hate—*you* know something of what Joseph felt in that wretched dungeon hole.

Then, too, disappointment poured her bitter drops into the bitter cup. What had become of those early dreams, those dreams of coming greatness, which had filled his young brain with splendid phantasmagoria?

Were these not from God? He had thought so—yes, and his venerable father had thought so too; and *he* should have known, for he had talked with God many a time. Were those imaginings the delusions of a fevered brain, or mocking lies? Was there no truth, no fidelity, in heaven or earth? Had God forsaken him? Had his father forgotten him? Did his brothers ever think of him? Would they ever try and find him? Was he to spend all his days in that dungeon, dragging on a weary life, never again enjoying the bliss of freedom: and all because he had dared to do right? Do you wonder at the young heart being weighed almost to breaking?

And yet Joseph's experience is not alone. You may have never been confined in a dungeon; and yet you may have often sat in darkness, and felt around you the limitation which forbade your doing as you wished. You may have been doing right, and doing right may have brought you into some unforeseen difficulty; and you are disposed to say, "I have been too honest." Or you may have been doing a noble act to someone, as Joseph did to Potiphar, and it has been taken in quite a wrong light. Who does not know what it is to be misunderstood, misrepresented, accused falsely, and punished wrongfully?

Each begins life so buoyantly and hopefully. Youth, attempting the solution of the strange problem of existence, fears nothing, forbodes no ill. The minstrel, Hope, keys her chords to the loftiest strains of exultation. The sun shines; the blue wavelets break in music around the boat; the sails swell gently; Love and Beauty hold the rudder bands; and though stories of the wreckage of the treacherous sea are freely told, there is no kind of fear that such experiences should ever overtake that craft. But presently disappointment, sorrow, and disaster overcloud the sky and blot out the sunny prospect; and the young mariner wakes as from a dream, "Can this be I, who imagined that I should never see it?" Then come several tremendous struggles of the soul to wrench itself free. The muscles are strained as whipcord; the beads of perspiration stand on the brow: but every effort only entangles the limbs more helplessly. And at last, exhausted and helpless, the young life ceases to struggle, and lies still, cowed and beaten, as the wild denizen of the plains, when it has lain for hours in the hunter's snare.

Surely there was something of this sort in Joseph's condition, as he lay in that wretched dungeon.

II. THESE SUFFERINGS WROUGHT VERY BENEFICIALLY. Taken on the lowest ground, *this imprisonment served Joseph's temporal interests.* That prison was the place where state prisoners were bound. Thither court magnates who had fallen under suspicion were sent. Chief butler and chief baker do not seem much to us, but they were titles for very august people. Such men would talk freely with Joseph; and in doing so would give him a great insight into political parties, and a knowledge of men and things generally, which in after-days must have been of great service to him.

But there is more than this. Psalm 105:18, referring to Joseph's imprisonment, has a striking alternative rendering, "His soul entered into iron." Turn that about, and render it in our language, and it reads thus, *Iron entered into his soul.* Is there not a truth in this? It may not be the truth intended in that verse, but it is a very profound truth, that sorrow and privation, the yoke borne in the youth, the souls' enforced restraint, are all conducive to an iron tenacity and strength of purpose, an endurance, a fortitude, which are the indispensable foundation and framework of a noble character. Do not flinch from suffering. Bear it silently, patiently, resignedly; and be assured that it is God's way of infusing iron into your spiritual make.

As a boy, Joseph's character tended to softness. He was a little spoiled by his father. He was too proud of his coat. He was rather given to tell tales. He was too full of his dreams and foreshadowed greatness. None of these were great faults, but he lacked strength, grip, power to rule. But what a difference his imprisonment made in him! From that moment he carries himself with a wisdom, modesty, courage, and manly resolution, that never fail him. He acts as a born ruler of men. He carries an alien country through the stress of a great famine, without a symptom of revolt. He holds his own with the proudest aristocracy of the time. He promotes the most radical changes. He has learned to hold his peace and wait. Surely the iron had entered his soul!

It is just this that suffering will do for you. The world wants iron dukes, iron battalions, iron sinews, and thews of steel. God wants iron saints; and since there is no way of imparting iron to the moral nature than by letting his people suffer, He lets them suffer. "No chastening for the present seemeth to be joyous, but grievous; nevertheless afterward it yieldeth the peaceable fruit of righteousness unto them which are exercised thereby." Are you in prison for doing right? Are the best years of your life slipping away in enforced monotony? Are you beset by opposition, misunderstanding, obloquy, and scorn, as the thick undergrowth besets the passage of the woodsman pioneer? Then take heart; the time is not wasted; God is only putting you through the iron regimen. The iron crown of suffering precedes the golden crown of glory. And iron is entering into your soul to make it strong and brave.

Is some aged eye perusing these words? If so, the question may be asked, Why does God sometimes fill a whole life with discipline, and give few opportunities for showing the iron quality of the soul? Why give iron to the soul, and then keep it from active service? Ah, that is a question which goes far to prove our glorious destiny. There must be another world somewhere, a world of glorious ministry, for which we are training. "There is service in the sky." And it may be that God counts a human life of seventy years of suffering not too long an education for a soul which may serve Him through the eternities. It is in the prison that Joseph is fitted for the unknown life of Pharaoh's palace; and if he could have foreseen the future, he would not have wondered at the severe discipline. If only we could see all that awaits us in the palace of the Great King, we should not be so surprised at certain experiences which befall us in earth's darker cells. You are being trained for service in God's Home, and in the upper spaces of his universe.

III. Joseph's Comfort in the Midst of these Sufferings. "He was there in the prison, but *the Lord was with him.*" The Lord was with him in the palace of Potiphar, but when Joseph went to prison, the Lord went there too. The only thing which severs us from God is sin: so long as we walk with God, God will walk with us; and if our path dips down from the sunny upland lawns into the valley with its clinging mists, He will go at our side. The godly man is much more independent of men and things than others. It is God who makes him blessed. Like the golden city, he has no need of sun or moon, for the Lord God is his everlasting light. If he is in a palace he is glad, not so much because of its delights as because God is there. And if he is in a prison, he can sing and give praises, because the God of his love bears him company. To the soul which is absorbed with God, all places and experiences are much the same. "If I say, Surely the darkness shall cover me; even the night—(of sorrow and of confinement)—shall be light about me: yea, the night shineth as the day."

Moreover, *the Lord showed him mercy*. Oh, wondrous revelation! He did not stand in a niche on the mountainside, as Moses did, while the solemn pomp swept past; and yet the Lord showed him a great sight—He showed him his mercy. That prison cell was the mount of vision, from the height of which he saw, as he had never seen before, the panorama of Divine loving kindness. It were well worth his while to go to prison to learn that. When children gather to see the magic lantern, the figures may be flung upon the sheet, and yet be invisible, because the room is full of light. Darken the room, and instantly the round circle of light is filled with brilliant color. God our Father has often to turn down the lights of our life because He wants to show us mercy. Whenever you get into a prison of circumstances, be on the watch. Prisons are rare places for seeing things. It was in prison that Bunyan saw his wondrous allegory, and Paul met the Lord, and John looked through heaven's open door, and Joseph saw God's mercy. God has no chance to show his mercy to some of us except when we are in some sore sorrow. The night is the time to see the stars.

God can also raise up friends for his servants in most unlikely places, and of most unlikely people. "The Lord gave him favor in the sight of the keeper of the prison." He was probably a rough, unkindly man, quite prepared to copy the dislikes of his master, the great Potiphar, and to embitter the daily existence of this Hebrew slave. But there was another Power at work, of which he knew nothing, inclining him towards his ward, and leading him to put him in a position of trust. All hearts are open to our King: at his girdle swing the keys by which the most unlikely door can be unlocked. "When a man's ways please the Lord,

He maketh even his enemies to be at peace with him." It is as easy for God to turn a man's heart, as it is for the husbandman to turn the course of a brook to carry fertility to an arid plot.

There is always alleviation for our troubles in ministry to others. Joseph found it so. It must have been a welcome relief to the monotony of his grief when he found himself entrusted with the care of the royal prisoners. A new interest came into his life, and he almost forgot the heavy pressure of his own troubles amid the interest of listening to the tales of those who were more unfortunate than himself. It is very interesting to notice what a deep human interest he took in the separate cases of his charges, noticing the expression of their faces, inquiring kindly after their welfare, sitting down to listen to their tale. Joseph is the patron of all prison philanthropists, but he took to this holy work not primarily because he had an enthusiasm for it, but because it gave a welcome opiate to his own griefs.

There is no anodyne for heart sorrow like ministry to others. If your life is woven with the dark shades of sorrow, do not sit down to deplore in solitude your hapless lot, but arise to seek out those who are more miserable than you are, bearing them balm for their wounds and love for their heartbreaks. And if you are unable to give much practical help, you need not abandon yourself to the gratification of lonely sorrow, for you may largely help the children of bitterness by imitating Joseph in listening to their tales of woe or to their dreams of foreboding. It is a great art to be a good listener. The burdened heart longs to pour out its tale in a sympathetic ear. There is immense relief in the telling out of pain. But it cannot be hurried; it needs plenty of time; it cannot clear itself of its silt and deposits unless it is allowed leisure to stand. And so the sorrowful turn away from men engaged in the full rush of active life as too busy, and seek out those who, like themselves, have been "winged," and are obliged to go softly, as Joseph was, when the servants of Pharaoh found him in the Egyptian dungeon. If you can do nothing else, listen well, and comfort others with the comfort wherewith you yourself have been comforted by God.

And as you listen, and comfort, and wipe the falling tears, you will discover that your own load is lighter, and that a branch or twig of the true tree—the tree of the Cross—has fallen into the bitter waters of your own life, making the Marah, Naomi, and the marshes of salt tears will have been healed. Out of such intercourse you will get what Joseph got—the key which will unlock the heavy doors by which you have been shut in.

And now some closing words to those who are suffering wrongfully. Do not be surprised. You are the followers of One who was misunderstood from the age of twelve to the day of his ascension; who did not sin, and yet was counted as a sinner; concerning whom the unanimous testimony was, "I find in Him no fault at all"; and yet they called Him Beelzebub! If they spoke thus of the Master of the house, how much more concerning the household! "Think it not strange concerning the fiery trial that is to try you, as though some strange thing happened unto you"; only be sure that you suffer wrongfully, and as a Christian.

Do not get weary in well-doing. Joseph might have said, "I give all up; of what profit is my godliness? I may as well live as others do." How much nobler was his course of patient continuance in well-doing! Do right, because it is right to do right, because God sees you, because it puts gladness into the heart. And then, when you are misunderstood and ill-treated, you will not swerve, or sit down to whine and despair.

Above all, do not avenge yourselves. When Joseph recounted his troubles, he did not recriminate harshly on his brethren, or Potiphar, or Potiphar's wife. He simply said: "I was stolen away out of the land of the Hebrews, and here also have I done nothing that they should put me into the hole." He might have read the words of the apostle, "Avenge not yourselves, but rather give place unto wrath." "If when ye do well, and suffer for it, ye take it patiently, this is acceptable with God." We make a great mistake in trying always to clear ourselves; we should be much wiser to go straight on, humbly doing the next thing, and leaving God to vindicate us. "He will bring forth our righteousness as the light, and our judgment as the noonday." In Psalm 105:19 there follow words which, rightly rendered, read thus: "The word of the Lord cleared him." What a triumphant clearing did God give His faithful servant!

There will come hours in all our lives, when we shall be misconstrued, misunderstood, slandered, falsely accused, wrongfully persecuted. At such times it is very difficult not to act on the policy of the men around us in the world. They at once appeal to law and force and public opinion. But the believer takes his case into a higher court, and lays it before his God. He is prepared to use any means that may appear divinely suggested. But he relies much more on the divine clearing than he does on his own most perfect arrangements. He is content to wait for months and years, till God arise to avenge his cause. It is a very little thing for him to be judged adversely at the bar of man: he cares only for the judgment of God, and awaits the moment when the righteous shall shine forth in the kingdom of their Father, as the sun when it breaks from all obscuring mists. "When Christ, who is our life, shall be manifested, then shall ye also with Him be manifested in glory." Ah! What a clearing up of mysteries, what dissipating of misunderstandings, what vindication of character shall be there! Oh, slandered ones, you can afford to await the verdict of eternity; of God, who will bring out your righteousness as the light, and your judgment as the noonday.

In all the discipline of life it is of the utmost importance to see but one ordaining overruling will. If we view our imprisonments and misfortunes as the result of human malevolence, our lives will be filled with fret and unrest. It is hard to suffer wrong at the hands of man, and to think that perhaps it might have never been. But there is a truer and more restful view, to consider all things as being under the law and rule of God; so that though they may originate in and come to us through the spite and malice of our fellows, yet, since before they reach us they have had to pass through the environing atmosphere of the Divine Presence, they have been transformed into his own sweet will for us.

It was Judas who plotted our Savior's death, and filled the garden with the capturing bands and flashing lights; and yet the Lord Jesus said that the Father was putting the cup to his lips. And though He was murdered by the chief priests and scribes, yet He so thoroughly acquiesced in the Father's appointment, that He spoke of *laying down* His life, as if His death were entirely His own act. There is no evil to them that love God; and the believer loses sight of second causes, so absorbed is he in the contemplation of the unfolding of the mystery of his Father's will. As the dying Kingsley said, "All is under law."

We must not be surprised when dark passages come in our outward life, or our inner experience. Unbroken sunshine would madden our brains, and unsullied prosperity of soul or circumstance would induce a spiritual excitement, which would be in the last degree deleterious. We must be sometime deprived of feeling, that we may acquire the art of walking by faith. We must lose the supporting cork belts that we may be compelled to trust ourselves to the buoyant wave. We must descend into the darksome glen, that we may test for ourselves the reliability of the staff and the rod, which before we may have considered as superfluities or as ornaments.

6

The Steps of the Throne

The heights by great men reached and kept
Were not obtained by sudden flight;
But they, while their companions slept,
Were toiling upward in the night.

Standing on what too long we bore,
With shoulders bent and downcast eyes,
We may discern—unseen before—
A path to higher destinies!

Genesis 41   Longfellow

The facts of Joseph's exaltation from the prison cell in which we left him, to the steps of Pharaoh's throne, are so well known that we need not describe them in detail. We will dwell briefly on the more salient points.

I. HOPE DEFERRED. "Remember me when it shall be well with thee." It was a modest and pathetic prayer that Joseph made to the great officer of state, to whose dream he had given so favorable an interpretation. Some, however, have said he had no right to make it. They have said that he had no right to ask this man to plead with Pharaoh, when he himself had access to the King of kings, and could at all times plead his case at His court. The Moslem thought embodies itself in a characteristic legend. It says that God had changed his cell into a pleasant cheerful place by causing a fountain to spring up in the midst, and a tree to grow at the door with shadowing branches and luscious fruit: but that, when he made this request to the chief butler, the fountain fell down and the tree withered; and this because, instead of trusting in God, he had relied on the help of a feeble man.

Well, there may be some truth at the foundation of all this; and yet it ill becomes us to bear hardly on the captive in the hour of his soul's deepest anguish. The strongest faith has wavered at times. Elijah sank down on the desert sand, and asked that he might die. John the Baptist, daunted and despondent, sent from his gloomy cell in Herod's castle to know if Jesus were indeed the Christ. Savonarola, Luther, Edward Irving, passed through darkness so thick that it almost put out the torch of their heroic faith; and if at this moment Joseph eagerly snatched at human help, as being nearer and more real than the help of God, who of us can condemn him? Who of us can help sympathizing with him? Who of us would not have behaved in like manner? Many a time when we have professed that our soul waited only upon God, we have either eagerly hinted at or openly shown our needs to those whom we thought likely to assist.

This cry, "Remember me," reminds us of the prayer of the dying thief to our Lord, as he was entering into the thick darkness. But how different the reply! The promise was quickly made and swiftly kept. And as the sun was setting over the western hills, the believing penitent had entered the city which is never bathed in sunset glory, and had learned what it is to be in Paradise with Christ. Far otherwise it was with Joseph.

The great man no doubt readily acceded to his request, and promised all he asked. "Remember you," he said; "of course I will." And, doubtless, in the fullness of his heart, he resolved to give Joseph a place among the under-butlers, or perhaps in the vineries. And as he passed out, we can imagine him saying, "Goodbye: you will hear from me soon." But he "forgot." Oh that word "Forgot"! How many of us know what it means! Day after day, as Joseph went about his duties, he expected to receive some token of his friend's remembrance and intercession. Week after week he watched for the message of deliverance, and often started because of some sudden knock which made him think that the warrant for his release had come. Then he invented ingenious excuses for the delay. No doubt the butler had had to receive the congratulations of his friends; arrears of business had perhaps accumulated in his absence, and now engrossed his attention; many things had probably gone wrong which required time and pains to set right; or perhaps he was waiting for a good opportunity to urge the claims of his prison friend on the king. How many hours of anxious thought were spent thus, hoping against hope, combating a sickly fear, which he hardly dared to entertain! But at last it was useless to hide from himself the unpalatable truth, which slowly forced itself upon his mind, that he was forgotten.

Hope deferred must have made his heart sick. But he kept steadfast. If he was disappointed in man, he clung the more tenaciously to God. "My soul," said he, in effect, "wait thou only upon God; for my expectation is from Him. He only is my rock and my salvation." Nor did he trust in vain; for, by a chain of wonderful providences, God brought him out of prison, and did better for him than could have been done by the chief butler of Pharaoh's court.

It may be that some who read these lines are in perplexity or distress which may be compared to that of Joseph when in the dungeon. And they have again and again schemed to effect their own deliverance. They helped a friend to emigrate, on the understanding that, if he got on well, he should send money to help them over too. They have applied to people who were befriended by them when they lived in the same poor street, but who have subsequently risen greatly in the world. They have got certain manufacturers and men of influence to make a note of their name and address in their pocketbook. But nothing has come of it all. They were at first very hopeful. They thought each post would bring the expected letter. There was a woman in America who went every morning for ten years to the village postmaster to ask for a letter from her son, which he promised to send, but which had never come. But the members have grown colder and colder still. Hope has flickered out. It is sad enough to be disappointed, but the sting of disappointment is when we are forgotten.

II. THREE BRIEF PIECES OF ADVICE TO THOSE IN SIMILAR CIRCUMSTANCES. 1. *Cease ye from man, whose breath is in his nostrils!* We cannot live without human sympathy and friendship. We long for the touch of the human hand and the sound of the human voice. We eagerly catch at any encouragement which some frail man holds out, as a drowning man catches at twigs floating by on the stream. But men fail us; even the best prove to be less able or less willing than we thought: the stream turns out to be a very turbid one when we reach it, in spite of all reports of its sufficiency. "Cursed be the man that trusteth in man, and maketh flesh his arm, and whose heart departeth from the Lord: for he shall be like the heath in the desert, and shall not see when good cometh, but shall inhabit the parched places in the wilderness, a salt land and not inhabited."

2. *Turn from the failure and forgetfulness of man to the constancy and faithfulness of God!* "He abideth faithful." He cannot promise and fail to perform. He says Himself: "Thou shalt not be forgotten by Me." A woman may forget her sucking child, and be unmindful of the son of her womb, "yet will I not forget thee." He may leave you long without succor. He may allow you to toil against a tempestuous sea until the fourth watch of the night. He may seem silent and austere, tarrying two days still in the same place, as if careless of the dying Lazarus. He may allow your prayers to accumulate like unopened letters on the table of an absent friend. But at last He will say, "O man, O woman, great is thy faith: be it unto thee even as thou wilt."

3. *Wait for God!* We are too feverish, too hasty, too impatient. It is a great mistake. Everything comes only to those who can wait. "They that wait on the Lord shall inherit the earth." You may have had what Joseph had when still a lad—a vision of power and usefulness and blessedness. But you cannot realize it in fact. All your plans miscarry. Every door seems shut. The years are passing over you with the depressing sense that you have not wrought any deliverance in the earth. Now turn your heart to God; accept his will; tell Him that you leave to Him the realization of your dream. "Wait on the Lord, and keep his way, and he shall exalt thee to inherit the land: when the wicked are cut off thou shalt see it." He may keep you waiting a little longer, but you shall find Him verify the words of one who knew by experience his trustworthiness: "The salvation of the righteous is of the Lord; He is their strength in the time of trouble. And the Lord shall help them, and deliver them; He shall deliver them from the wicked and save them, because they trust in Him."

III. THE LINKS IN THE CHAIN OF DIVINE PROVIDENCE. First, the wife of Potiphar makes a baseless charge, which leads to Joseph's imprisonment; then, the young prisoner ingratiates himself with the keeper of the prison, and is allowed to have free access to the prisoners; then it happens at the very time that two state officials are thrown into jail on suspicion of attempting to poison their royal master; then the verification of Joseph's interpretation of their dreams shows that he is possessed of no common power; then that department of memory in which Joseph's face and case are hidden becomes sealed, lest anything premature should be attempted on his behalf; then, after two full years, the king of Egypt dreams. To the casual observer there might seem a great deal of chance in all this, but the historian, directed by the Holy Spirit, lifts the veil, and shows that God was working out, step by step, His own infinite plans.

The dream was twice repeated, so similarly as to make it evident to the dullest mind that something was intended of unusual importance. The scene in each case was the river bank; first the green margin of grass, next the rich alluvial soil. To say the least, it was a bad omen to see the lean kine devour the fat, and the withered ears devour the full: nor can we wonder that the monarch of a people who attached special importance to omens and portents should send in hot haste for the army of priests who were always in close attendance upon him; and who on this occasion were reinforced by all the wise men, adept in this branch of science. But there was none that could interpret the dream of Pharaoh. "God made foolish the wisdom of this world."

Then, amid the panic of the palace, the butler suddenly remembered his prison experiences, and told the king of the young captive Hebrew. Pharaoh eagerly caught at the suggestion: he sent and called Joseph; and they brought him hastily out of the dungeon—the margin says, "they made him run." Still the king's impetuous speed was compelled to wait till he had shaved himself and changed his prison garb. Perfect cleanliness and propriety of dress were so important in the eyes of Egyptians that the most urgent matters were postponed until they were properly attended to. Alas, that men should be so careful of their appearance before one another, and so careless of their appearance before God! Many a man who would not think of entering a drawing room if his linen were not snowy white is quite content to carry within his breast a heart as black as ink.

It is beautiful to notice Joseph's reverent references to God in his first interview with Pharaoh. "It is not in me: God shall give Pharaoh an answer of peace." "God hath showed Pharaoh what He is about to do." "The thing is established by God; and God will shortly bring it to pass." The hypocrite is quick enough to interlard his conversation with the name of God: no doubt this is owing to his belief that a true child of God will often do so; and there is some truth in the belief. When the heart is full of God, the tongue will be almost obliged to speak of Him; and all such references will be easy and natural as flowers in May. Oh that our inner life were more full of the power and love and presence of Jesus! If our hearts were indicting a good matter they would boil over, and we should speak more frequently of the things that touch our King. Joseph was not ashamed to speak of his God amid the throng of idolaters in the court of Egypt: let us not flinch from bearing our humble witness in the teeth of violent opposition and supercilious scorn.

This position of recognizing Jehovah being assumed and granted, there was no difficulty in interpreting the consumption of the seven good kine by the seven lean kine, and of the seven full ears by the seven empty ears, blasted by the east wind; or of indicating that the seven years of great plenty should be followed by seven years of famine, so sore that all the plenty should be forgotten in the land of Egypt, and that plenty should consume the land.

Now that the interpretation is before us, it seems wonderful, not that Joseph gave it, but that the wise men of Pharaoh's court failed to discover it. But perhaps God ordered it that the diviners should be rendered stupid and "mad," so that an opportunity should be made for the advancement, to which, from his childhood, Joseph had been destined. In this, as so often befalls, there was an illustration of the Divine words, "Thou hast hid these things from the wise and prudent, and hast revealed them unto babes: even so, Father, for so it seemed good in thy sight."

Then, in the presence of the thronged and breathless court, surrounded by the evil eyes of the magicians, who could ill afford to surrender their prestige and place, or the rich emoluments of their office, the young Hebrew interpreted the royal dream. That dream was framed in a thoroughly Egyptian setting, and was connected with the Nile, whose waters were regarded by the natives with an enthusiastic regard, whether for their peculiarly luscious, refreshing, and nutritive qualities, or for the annual inundation which bore far afield the rich, fertilizing soil. Indeed, for these and similar considerations the river was the object of idolatrous worship. The buffalo, a species of ox, well known anciently in Egypt, delights to stand in the water in hot countries, remaining for hours in that cooling bath, with all the body, except the head, immersed. The sight of horned cattle coming up out of a river would, therefore, not be a rare occurrence; and Joseph had no difficulty in carrying his audience with him, when he said that these seven kine—as also the seven ears of corn on one stalk, after the nature of that species of bearded wheat still known as Egyptian wheat—were emblems of seven years of great plenty throughout all the land of Egypt.

But perhaps the thing which gave Joseph most influence in that court was not his interpretation, but the wise and statesmanlike policy on which he insisted. As he detailed his successive recommendations: the appointment of a man discreet and wise with this exclusive business as his life work; of the creation of a new department of public business for the purpose of gathering up the resources of Egypt in anticipation of the coming need; of the vast system of storage in the cities of the land—it was evident that he was speaking beneath the glow of a spirit not his own; and with a power which commanded the instant assent of the monarch and his chief advisers. "The thing was good in the eyes of Pharaoh, and in the eyes of all his servants. And Pharaoh said unto his servants, "Can we find such a one as this is, a man in whom the Spirit of God is?" Oh that we might carry with us, even into business relationships, the evident stamp of the Spirit of God! It were worth languishing, even in a dungeon, if only we might have time to seek it. But it is to be had on easier terms: "Ask and have; seek and find; open your heart and receive."

There is an interesting illustration given to us here of the words, "Them that honor Me, I will honor." When Joseph had interpreted the dream and given his advice—little thinking as he did so that he was sketching his own future—Pharaoh said unto his servants, "Can we find such a one as this is, a man in whom is the Spirit of God?" Then he turned to Joseph and said, "Forasmuch as God hath showed thee this, there is none so discreet and wise as thou art: thou shalt be over my house, and according to thy word shall all my people be ruled: only in the throne will I be greater than thou. See, I have set thee over the whole land of Egypt."

It was a wonderful ascent, sheer in a single bound from the dungeon to the steps of the throne. His father had rebuked him; now Pharaoh, the greatest monarch of his time, welcomes him. His brethren despised him; now the proudest priesthood of the world opens its ranks to receive him by marriage into their midst, considering it wiser to conciliate a man who was from that moment to be the greatest force in Egyptian politics and life. The hands that were hard with the toils of a slave are adorned with a signet ring. The feet are no longer tormented by fetters; a chain of gold is linked around his neck. The coat of many colors torn from him by violence and defiled by blood, and the garment left in the hand of the adulteress, are exchanged for vestures of fine linen drawn from the royal wardrobe. He was once trampled upon as the offscouring of all things; now all Egypt is commanded to bow before him, as he rides forth in the second chariot, prime minister of Egypt, and second only to the king. What a comment is this on that rapturous outburst, on the model of which the Virgin Mother composed her happy ode!

> The Lord killeth, and maketh alive;
> He bringeth down to the grave,
> And bringeth up.
> The Lord maketh poor, and maketh rich;
> He bringeth low, and lifteth up.
> He raiseth up the poor out of the dust,
> And lifteth up the beggar
> From the dunghill,
> To set them among princes,
> And to make them inherit
> The throne of glory.

All this happened because one day, for the sake of God, Joseph resisted a temptation to one act of sin. If he had yielded, we should probably never have heard of him again; he would have been slain by the siren who has slain so many more strong men, and would have gone down to the dark chambers of death. No happy marriage, no wife, no child, would have fallen to his lot. No honor or usefulness, or vision of the dear faces of his kin, would ever have enriched his life with their abundant blessing. What a good thing it was that he did not yield!

Let us stand firm; let us seek first the kingdom of God and his righteousness; let us deny ourselves immediate pleasure for the sake of the far-off harvest of content; let us honor God by obedience to his least command; let us dare say, No; let us be willing to decrease. And then the tide will turn: God will not be unfaithful to forget; He will turn again and have mercy upon us, and will exalt us to inherit the earth.

And when that day comes, let us ascribe all to God. I admire the names which Joseph gave to his sons. They show the temper of his heart when in the zenith of his prosperity. Manasseh means "forgetting"— God had made him forget his toils. Ephraim means "fruitfulness"— God had caused him to be fruitful. Be true! *You* shall forget your sorrow and long waiting; *you* shall be fruitful. Then be sure and give God the praise.

IV. THE PARALLEL BETWEEN JOSEPH AND THE LORD JESUS. It is surely more than a coincidence. "Coming events cast their shadows before." The Holy Spirit, enamored with the mystery of love which was coming, anticipated its most striking features in the life of Joseph. Joseph was rejected by his brethren; Jesus by the Jews, his brethren according to the flesh. Joseph was sold for twenty pieces of silver to the Ishmaelites; Jesus was sold by the treachery of Judas for thirty pieces, and then handed over to the Gentiles. Joseph was cast into prison: Jesus abode in the grave. Joseph in prison was able to preach the gospel of deliverance to the butler; Jesus went and preached the gospel to the spirits in the prison. The two malefactors of the cross find their counterpart in Joseph's two fellow prisoners. Joseph, though a Jew by birth and rejected by his own brethren, nevertheless was raised to supreme power in a Gentile state, and saved myriads of them from death; Jesus, of Jewish birth and yet disowned by Jews, has nevertheless been exalted to the supreme seat of power, and is now enthroned in the hearts of myriads of Gentiles, to whom He has brought salvation from death, and spiritual bread for their hunger. The very name that Pharaoh gave to Joseph meant "Savior of the world"—our Savior's title. Yes, and we must carry the parallel still farther. After Joseph had been for some time ruling and blessing Egypt, his very brethren came to him for forgiveness and help; so in days not far away we shall see the Jews retracing their steps and exclaiming—as thousands are now doing in Eastern Russia—"Jesus is our Brother." So all Israel shall be saved!

We have now, therefore, to think of Jesus as seated on his throne. Prime Minister of the Universe, the Interpreter of his Father's will, the Organ and Executor of the Divine decrees. On his head are many crowns; on his finger is the ring of sovereignty; on his loins the girdle of power. Glistening robes of light envelop Him. And this is the cry which precedes Him, "Bow the knee!" Have *you* ever bowed the knee at his feet? It is of no avail to oppose Him. The tongue of malice and envy may traduce Him, and refuse to let Him reign. But nothing can upset the Father's decrees and plan. "Yet have I set my Son upon my holy hill." "In his name every knee shall bow, and every tongue shall confess that He is Lord." Agree with Him quickly. Ground your arms at his feet. "Kiss the Son, lest He be angry."

V. THE WORLD'S NEED FOR CHRIST. You remember Pharaoh's dream. Seven buffaloes, which had escaped from the torturing heat into the comparative coolness of the water, came up on to the banks and began feeding on the sedge. Shortly after, seven lean kine came up, and, finding nothing left for them to eat, by one of those strange transformations common to dreams, swallowed up their predecessors. So the seven shriveled ears devoured those which were rank and good. This is a symbol of a fact that is always happening, and is happening now.

Our rulers, like Pharaoh, are having troublesome visions just now. In Europe and in England weak things are destroying the strong; hungry creatures are devouring the flourishing and the fat; the sterile is swallowing up the fruitful: and there is no visible improvement.

Those who know how much we spend each year for drink and for our army; for extravagance and show—will understand what I mean. Oh, it is grievous to see how much is being squandered to no purpose on all these things, when our toiling masses are sinking deeper and deeper into misery and need! And where is the cure? It seems beyond our reach. Our wisdom, with its parliaments, its learned articles, its congresses, seems at its wits' end and non-plussed. At this very hour, for want of something better, millions of men are under arms to keep the hungry and weak from further devouring the flourishing and fat. For God Himself is bringing Egypt to despair, that it may learn the need of that Jesus who—like Joseph once—is now hidden from its view. Then these Bibles shall be searched for guidance, and places of Christian worship shall be crowded; and the Rejected One shall reign, and his bride shall be given Him. Then shall earth rejoice; for He cometh to rule in equity, and his reign is goodwill to men!

It may be that seven years of famine have been passing over you, devouring all that you had accumulated in happy bygone times, and leaving you bare. Do you not guess the reason? There is a rejected Savior transferred to some obscure dungeon in your heart. There never can be prosperity or peace so long as He is there. Seek Him forthwith. Cause thyself to run to Him. Ask Him to forgive years of shameful neglect. Reinstate Him on the throne. Give the reins of power into his hand. And He shall restore to thee the years that the cankerworm has eaten.

Joseph's First Interview
with His Brethren

Oh hateful spell of sin! When friends are nigh
To make stern memory tell her tale unsought,
And raise accusing shades of hours gone by,
To come between us and all kindly thought!

Genesis 42   Keble

The life of Joseph, as the Prime Minister of Egypt, was a very splendid one. Everything that could please the sense or minister to the taste was his. The walls of Egyptian palaces still exist in the rainless air to attest the magnificent provision that was made for all necessaries and luxuries. In point of fact, the civilization of our nineteenth century in many points has nothing of which to boast over that of the age in which he lived, and of which the record still remains. His palaces would consist of numberless rooms opening into spacious courts, where palms, sycamores, and acacia trees grew in rare luxuriance. The furniture, consisting of tables, couches, and consoles, would be elegantly carved from various woods, encrusted with ebony and adorned with gilding. Rare perfumes rose from vases of gold and bronze and alabaster; and the foot sank deep in carpets covering the floors, or trod upon the skins of lions and other ferocious beasts. Troops of slaves and officials ministered to every want. Choirs of musicians filled the air with sweet melody. Such is said to be a true description of the outward circumstances of Joseph's lot.

But though one of rare splendor, *his life must have been one of considerable anxiety.* He had to deal with a proud hereditary nobility, jealous of his power, and with a populace made with hunger. During the first seven years of his premiership he went throughout all the land of Egypt superintending the dikes and ditches which should utilize as much as possible the unusual rise of the Nile; building vast granaries, and buying up a fifth of the vast profusion of grain. "The earth brought forth by handfuls; and Joseph gathered corn as the sand of the sea, very much, until he left numbering, for it was without number." All this must have involved a great deal of anxiety; it must have been difficult for this young foreigner to carry out his wide-reaching plans in face of the stoic apathy or the active opposition of great officials and vested interests.

He was, however, *eminently qualified for this work;* for there was something in him that could not be accounted for by any analysis of his brain. As Pharaoh had said most truly, "He was a man in whom was the spirit of God." Oh, when will men learn that the Spirit of God may be in them when they are buying and selling, and arranging all the details of business or home? When will they believe that those will do their part best in the marketplace, and in the house, who are most sensible of the gracious and forceful indwelling of the Holy Ghost? May God send us all the simple reverent spirit of this man, who amidst the splendor and business of his proud position set God always before his face! Such a temper of mind will make us a blessing to our times; for, at last, when the days of famine came, Joseph was able, as he afterwards said, to be a "father" unto Pharaoh, and to save the land.

All these events took time. Joseph was a lad of seventeen summers when he was torn away from his home; and he was a young man of thirty when he stood for the first time before Pharaoh. Seven years for the golden time of plenty must be added; and perhaps two more while the stores of the granaries were being slowly exhausted: so that probably twenty-five years had passed between the tragedy at the pit's mouth and the time of which we are thinking now. During those years the life in Jacob's camp had flowed uneventfully and quietly through the same unchanging scenes, like the course of some river in a flat, unbroken country, where a quick eye is required to discover the direction of the stream. The chief sign of the number of the slow passing years was the growing weakness in the old father's step and the increasing infirmity of his form. He pathetically speaks much of his "grey hairs." The sons of Israel had need to "carry Jacob their father." This was not simply the result of age, but of sorrow; he bore in his heart the scars of many wounds, the chief of which was grief for his beloved Joseph. It was grief that he was compelled very largely to nurse alone; and it was, perhaps, the keener because of the suspicions of foul play that seem to have suggested themselves to his mind. He went step by step down towards the grave "mourning for his son." He never could forget the sight of the blood-bedabbled coat, the dear relic of one whose face he never thought to see.

Meanwhile, the sons had become middle-aged men, with families of their own. They probably never mentioned that deed of violence to each other. *They did their best to banish the thought from their minds.* Sometimes in their dreams they may have caught a glimpse of that young face in its agony, or heard the beseechings of his anguished soul, but they sought to drown such painful memories by deep drafts of the Lethe-stream of forgetfulness. Conscience slept. Yet the time had come when God meant to use these men to found a nation. And in order to fit them for their high destiny it was necessary to bring them into a right condition of soul. Yet how could their soul be in health, so long as they had not repented of the sin which cast its lurid light over their history? The great Physician never heals over a wound from above, but from below, and after careful probing and searching. The foundations of noble character must touch the rock of genuine repentance. But it seemed almost impossible to secure repentance in those obtuse and darkened hearts. However, the Eternal brought it about by a number of wonderful providences; and as we study them, let us notice how God will subordinate all the events of our outward lives to try us and prove us, and see what there is in our hearts, and to bring us to Himself.

This, then, is our theme: God's gracious methods of awakening the consciences of these men from their long and apparently endless sleep. And it is a theme well worth our study; for if there is one thing more than another that is needed in Christian congregations and in the world, it is the deep conviction of sin. Well would it be if some resurrection trumpet could sound and awaken the sleeping consciences of men, causing long-forgotten but unforgiven sins to arise and come forth from their graves. Of what use is it to present the Savior to those who do not feel to need Him? And who can scatter seed with hope of harvest, unless the plowshare has first driven its iron into the soil?

I. THE FIRST STEP TOWARDS THEIR CONVICTION WAS THE PRESSURE OF WANT. There was dearth in all lands, and the famine reached even to the land of Canaan. Often before, in the lives of the patriarchs, had they been driven by famine down to Egypt; and Jacob aroused his sons from the hopeless lethargy into which they were sinking by saying, "Why look ye on one another? Behold, I have heard that there is corn in Egypt; get you down there and buy for us, that we may live and not die. And Joseph's ten brethren went down to buy corn in Egypt."

So long as the hills were green and the pastures clothed with flocks; so long as the valleys were covered over with corn and rang with the songs of reapers—just so long Jacob might have mourned alone, but Reuben, Simeon, and the rest of them would have been unconcerned and content. But when the mighty famine came, the hearts of these men were opened to conviction; their carnal security was shattered; and they were prepared for certain spiritual experiences of which they would never have dreamed. Yes; and they were being prepared for the meeting with Joseph.

It is so that God deals with us. He breaks up our nest. He looses our roots. He sends a mighty famine which cuts away the whole staff of bread. And at such times, weary, worn, and sad, we are prepared to confess our sins, and to receive the words of Christ, when He says, "Come unto Me, all ye that labor and are heavy laden, and I will give you rest." Is your life just now passing through a time of famine? Do your supplies threaten to fail? Does your heart fail you, as you look forward to the disasters that menace you? Yet take courage; this is simply the motion of the current which is drifting you to Christ and to a better life. In afterdays those men looked back upon that time of sore straitness as the best thing that could have happened to them: nothing less would have brought them to Joseph. Yes, and the time is coming when you will bless God for your times of sorrow and misfortune. You will say, "Before I was afflicted I went astray, but now have I kept thy Word."

II. THE SECOND STEP WAS THE ROUGH USAGE THEY RECEIVED AT THE HANDS OF JOSEPH. It would seem that in some of the larger markets he superintended the sale of the corn himself. He may even have gone there on purpose, prompted by a sort of hope that he might catch sight of one of the Ishmaelites, whose faces he never could forget; or in some other way hear tidings of his home. He may have even cherished, and prayed over, the fancy that his brethren might come themselves. At last the looked-for day arrived. He was standing as usual at his post, surrounded by all the confusion and noise of an Eastern bazaar, when all of a sudden his attention was attracted by the entrance of those ten men. He looked with a fixed, eager look for a moment, his heart throbbing quickly all the while; and he needed no further assurance: "he knew them."

Evidently, however, they did not know him. How should they? He had grown from a lad of seventeen to a man of forty. He was clothed in pure white linen, with ornaments of gold to indicate his rank, a garb not altogether unlike that famous coat, which had wrought such havoc. He was governor of the land, and if they had thought of Joseph at all when entering that land (and no doubt they did), they expected to see him in the gangs of slaves manacled at work in the fields, or sweltering in the scorching brickyards, preparing material for the pyramids. So, in unconscious fulfillment of his own boyish dream, they bowed down themselves before him with their faces to the earth.

Joseph instantly saw that they failed to recognize him; and partly to ascertain if his brethren were repentant, partly in order to know why Benjamin was not with them, he made himself strange unto them. He spake roughly to them. He accused them of being spies. He refused to believe their statements, and put them in prison until they could be verified. He kept Simeon bound.

In all this, I believe *he repeated exactly the scene at the pit's mouth*; and indeed we may perhaps see what really happened there, reflected in the mirror of this scene. It is not unlikely that when they saw him coming towards them, in his prince-like dress, they had rushed at him, accusing him of having come to spy out their corrupt behavior, and take back an evil report to their father, as he had done before: if so, this will explain why he now suddenly accused them of being spies. No doubt the lad protested that he was no spy—that he had only come to inquire after their welfare, but they had met his protestations with rude violence in much the same was as the rough-speaking governor now treated them. It may be that they had even thrust him into the pit with the threat to keep him there until his statements could be verified, in much the same way as Joseph now dealt with them; and Simeon may have been the ringleader. If this were the case—and it seems most credible—it is obvious that it was a powerful appeal to their conscience and memory, and one that could not fail to awaken both.

You remember the story of Hamlet. Hamlet's uncle murdered his brother, the father of Hamlet, and King of Denmark. The deed was done secretly, but the young prince knew of it, and instructed the players to repeat the murder, in dumb show, before the royal but guilty pair, and their guests. They did so. At last the king could bear it no more. He rose hastily from his seat and went from the hall, saying:

> Oh, my offense is rank, it smells to Heaven;
> It hath the primal eldest curse upon it,
> A brother's murder.

And as those men, each in his dungeon, considered the usage which they had experienced, it must have vividly brought to their minds their treatment of that guileless lad, years on years before.

There is another story in the Old Testament of which we are reminded now—that scene at Zarephath when the child died, and the mother burst into the presence of the prophet saying, "Hast thou come to call my sin to remembrance?" She had tried to forget her sin. She had buried it deep in a far down dungeon, like that in the old castle of Chillon beneath the blue waters of Geneva's lake. But there was something in that dead child which brought it all back to her mind; she lived it over again: but not its pleasure, that had long since passed away; only its pain was left.

Memory is one of the most wonderful processes of our nature. It is the faculty that enables us to record and recall the past. If it were not for this power the mind would remain forever in the blank condition of childhood, and all that had ever passed before it would leave no more impression than images do upon the plain surface of a reflecting mirror. But important as it is, it conducts its operations in perfect mystery. The room is shuttered from all human gaze; the camera is covered by a black veil. This, however, is the one fact of interest to us—that it has a universal retentiveness. Nothing has ever passed athwart it that has not left a record on its plastic slabs.

It is important, however, to distinguish between memory and recollection. We remember all things: there is a record of everything that ever we saw or did somewhere in the archives of memory, but we cannot always recollect an incident, or recall it at the required moment. Supposing you were never to burn your letters, but kept them all in one huge box—that would resemble memory, but supposing you were never to index or classify them, so as to be unable readily to lay your hands on the one required—that would be like a failure of recollection; while a ready recollection would find its analogy in the ease with which you could produce a required letter at a given time. The failure to find a letter would not argue that the letter was not in the box, but simply that the classification was bad; so the failure to recall the past does not argue that it is lost to memory, but simply that the power of recollection is feeble. In other words, our memory really retains everything; and though sometimes our recollection is bad, yet a very trivial thing may excite it and enable it to fetch up things long past from the deep compartments of memory into which they have been cast, and in which they have been unceasingly held.

The reader may have been brought up in a house surrounded by an old-fashioned country garden, but you have not thought of it for years, till the other day you happened to see a plant or smell a scent peculiarly associated with it, which brought the whole back to your recollection. So it is with sin. Long years ago, you may have committed some sin; you have tried to forget it. It has not been forgiven and put away; you have almost succeeded in dropping it from your thoughts: but believe me, it is still there; and the most trivial incident may at any moment bring it all back upon your conscience, as vividly as if committed only yesterday. If sin is forgiven, it is indeed forgotten: God says, "I will remember it no more." But if only forgotten, and not forgiven, it may have a most unexpected and terrible awakening.

This was the case with Joseph's brethren. They said one to another, as they heard the reiterated demand of the strange governor for evidence that they were not spies, "We are verily guilty concerning our brother; in that we saw the anguish of his soul, when he besought us, and we would not hear: therefore is this distress come upon us."

III. THE THIRD STEP TOWARDS CONVICTION WAS THE GIVING OF TIME FOR THEM TO LISTEN TO GOD'S SPIRIT, SPEAKING TO THEM IN THE SILENCE OF THE PRISON CELL—Without the work of the Holy Ghost they might have felt remorse, but not guilt. It is not enough to feel that sin is a blunder and a mistake, but not guilt. This sense of sin, however, is the prerogative of the Spirit of God. He alone can convict of sin. When He is at work, the soul cries out, "Woe is me, I am a sinful man!" "We are verily *guilty* concerning our brother."

Will not these words befit some lips that read these pages? Are *you* not verily guilty? In early life you may have wronged some man or some woman. You may have taught some young lad to swear. You may have laughed away the early impressions from some anxious seeker, until they fled to return no more. You may not have done your best to save those committed to your care. And now others seem to be treating you as you treated the associates of earlier days. You now are eager for salvation; and you learn the bitterness of being ridiculed, thwarted, tempted, and opposed. You recall the past; it flashes before you with terrible intensity. You cry, "God forgive me! I am verily guilty concerning that soul whom I betrayed or wronged." And this is the work of the Holy Spirit. Let Him have his blessed way with you till you are led by Him to the foot of that tree which buds like Aaron's rod, though for eighteen hundred years it has ceased to grow, and the leaves of which are for the nations!

There is at least one Brother whom you have wronged. Need I mention his name? He is not ashamed to call you brother, but you have been shamed of Him. He did not withhold Himself from the cross, but you have never thanked Him. He has never ceased to knock at the door of your heart for admittance to bless you, but you have kept Him waiting amid the dropping dews of night. He has freely offered you the greatest gifts, but you have trampled them beneath your feet, and done despite to Him, and crucified Him afresh. There is, no doubt, a time coming when the Jews shall say of Him, whom they once rejected and put into the pit of death, but who has since been giving corn to the Gentiles, "We are verily guilty concerning our Brother." But these words may also be humbly and sorrowfully appropriated by many of us. We must plead, "Guilty! Guilty! Guilty! Guilty concerning our Brother!"

Whilst these men spoke thus, Joseph stood by them. There was no emotion on those compressed features, no response in those quiet eyes. "They knew not that he understood them." Ah, how often do anguished souls go to priests, ministers, and friends, with the bitter tale of anguish! They knew not that One is standing by who hears and understands all, and longs to throw aside every barrier in order to bring them aid. True, He speaks to them by an interpreter, but if they would only speak straight to Him, He would speak directly to their waiting hearts.

There is a curious contrast in the twenty-fourth verse. First, we learn that "he turned himself about from them and wept"; and next we are told that he "took Simeon and bound him before their eyes." The brethren saw only the latter of these two actions, and must have thought him rough and unkind. How they must have trembled in his presence! But they knew not the heart of tender love that was beating beneath all this seeming hardness. Nor could they guess that the retention of Simeon was intended to act as a silken cord to bring the brothers back to him, and as part of the process of awakening the memory of another brother, whom they had lost years before.

It is thus continually in life's discipline. We suffer, and suffer keenly. Imprisoned, bereaved, rebuked, we count God harsh and hard. We little realize how much pain He is suffering as He causes us pain; or how the tender heart of our Brother is filled with grief, welling up within Him as He makes Himself strange, and deals so roughly with us. If we could but see the tender face behind the vizor, and know how noble a heart beats beneath the mailed armor, we should feel that we were as safe amid his rebukes as ever we were amid his tenderest caresses.

There were alleviations also in their hardships. The sacks were filled with corn; provision was given for the journey home, so that they needed not to come on the stores they were carrying back for their households; and every man's money was returned in his sack's mouth (v. 25). All this was meant in tender love, but their hearts failed them with fear, as they emptied their sacks and saw the bundles of money fall out among the corn. A guilty conscience misinterprets the kindest gifts and mercies which God sends to us, and with evil ingenuity distills poison out of the sweetest flowers. How often, like these men, we cry, "What hath God done to us?" And we are filled with fear, when, in point of fact, God's dealings with us brim with blessing, and we are working out a purpose of mercy which shall make us rejoice all our days.

There is no lot, however hard, without its compensations. Be sure to look out for these. Prize the little touches of tender love which reveal the heart of Jesus, as a girl will dwell upon the slightest symptoms of an affection which, for some reason, must be concealed beneath a strange and unconcerned exterior. Amidst his chastenings, the Master inserts some delicate souvenirs of his love to keep the heart from entire despair. Make much of them until the discipline is over, and the sun of his regard bursts from all restraining clouds.

> Judge not the Lord by feeble sense,
> But trust Him for his grace;
> Beneath a frowning Providence
> He hides a smiling face.

8

Joseph's Second Interview with His Brethren

Kind hearts are here; yet would the tenderest one
Have limits to its mercy: God has none.
And man's forgiveness may be true and sweet,
But yet he stoops to give it. More complete
Is Love that lays forgiveness at thy feet.
And pleads with thee to raise it. Only heaven
Means crowned, not vanquished, when it says "Forgiven!"

Genesis 43   A. A. Proctor

Where is there such another story as this of Joseph? It seems sometimes impossible to believe that the events happened thirty-five centuries ago, in the solemn, rainless land of the Nile and the Pyramids. They might have occurred within our own memory, the experience is so natural, so lifelike, so like our own. At yet orientalists assure us that, in its minutest details, it is verified by the painting which, to this day, exist on the walls of palaces and temples, unimpaired and fresh.

I feel it impossible to dwell on it line by line; I must content myself with taking only the broad outlines of the story.

Our next chapter will deal with that affecting scene, when Joseph caused every man to go out from him, while he cast aside his dignity, stepped down from his throne, and fell upon the necks of his brethren and wept. We have a lesser task just now, yet full of interest; we have to consider the successive steps by which that wayward family was brought into a position in which its members could be forgiven and blessed. May the Holy Spirit help us to understand this, because Joseph, who was exalted from the pit to the palace, is an evident picture of Him who lay in the grave, but is now exalted to the right hand of the Father to give repentance unto Israel and the remission of sins! And as we review the successive steps by which Joseph led his brethren, we shall probably catch a glimpse of those various processes by which the Savior humbles us and leads us to Himself. Should these words be read by the members of some family which is living in this famine-stricken world, minding only the things of sense and sin, ignorant of the great Brother who lives yonder on the throne of God and loves us—let them read, mark, learn, and inwardly digest them, for they may shed a light on some dark landings of their life, and explain things hard as the riddle of the Sphinx.

I. THERE WAS THE PRESSURE OF POVERTY AND SORROW (43:1). Jacob had never turned his thoughts to Egypt if there had been plenty in Canaan. The famine drove the sons of Israel into Egypt to buy corn. And even though poor Simeon was bound in Egypt, the brothers had not gone a second time if it had not been for the rigor of that necessity, which sometimes drives the most timid birds and deer to the homes and haunts of men. At first the old father strongly opposed the thought of their taking Benjamin, even if they went themselves; and his children lingered.

There is a touching picture given of the conversation between the old man and his sons, a kind of council of war. Reuben seems already to have lost the priority which his birthright would have secured, and Judah held the place of spokesman and leader among the brethren. He undertook to deal with the old man for the rest. At the outset, Jacob's request that they should go down to buy food was met with the most distinct refusal, unless Benjamin was permitted to accompany them. And when he complained of their having betrayed the existence of another brother, the whole of them vindicated their action, and declared that they could not have done otherwise. At last Judah made himself personally responsible for the lad's safety, a pledge which, as we shall see, he nobly redeemed. And so, at last, the old man yielded, proposing only that they should take a present to mollify the ruler's heart, a double money to replace what had been returned in their sacks, and uttering a fervent prayer to the Almighty on their behalf.

Thus God in his mercy shut up every other door but the one through which they might find their way to plenty and blessedness. There was no alternative but to go down to Egypt.

So is your life. You have had all that this world could give. Beauty, money, youth, health, success, have come up and poured their horns of plenty into your lap. You have had all that man could wish. But what has been your state of heart meanwhile? Have you bethought yourself of your ill-treatment of your great Elder Brother? Have you set your affections upon things above? Have you lived for that world which lies beyond the narrow horizon of the visible? You know you have not. So God has called for a famine on your land, and broken the whole staff of your bread. You have lost situation and friends. Your business is broken. Beauty, youth, health—all have vanished. Joseph is not; Simeon is not; and Benjamin is on the point of being taken away. Everything has been against you.

It is a severe measure: how will you bear it? In the first burst of the tempest, you say stubbornly, "I will not go down; I will not yield; I will stand out to the last." But, beware! It is a fatal mistake to wrestle against the love of God. Jacob tried it by the Jabbok ford, and he limped on a halting thigh until he gathered his feet up into his deathbed. God will have his way at last if not at first. The famine must continue until the wanderer arises to return to the Father, with words of penitent contrition on his lips. It is in vain to row to bring the ship to land: the sea will not cease her raging until the runaway prophet is on his way back to his home. "I will be," saith the Lord, "unto Ephraim as a lion, and as a young lion to the house of Judah. I, even I, will tear and go away; and none shall rescue. I will go and return to my place, till they acknowledge their offense, and seek my face; in their affliction they will seek Me early." Oh that your reply might be, "Come, let us return unto the Lord; for He hath torn, and He will heal us; He hath smitten, and He will bind us up."

II. There was the Awakening of Conscience. For twenty years conscience had slept. And as long as this was the case there could be no real peace between Joseph and his brethren. *They* could never feel sure that he had forgiven them. *He* would always feel that there was a padlock on the treasure store of his love. You never can feel at perfect rest with your friend, so long as there is some unexplained wrong between you. Conscience must awake and slowly tread the aisles of the temple of penitence, telling the beads of confession. This is the clue to the understanding of Joseph's behavior.

Joseph, to arouse their dormant consciences, repeated as nearly as possible to them, their treatment of himself. This has already engaged our thought. "Ye are spies," was the echo of their own rough words to himself. The prison, in which they lay for three days, was the counterpart of the pit in which they placed *him.* Men will best learn what is the true nature of their own iniquities when they experience the treatment which they meted out to others. And Joseph's device was a success. Listen to their moan, "We are verily guilty because of our brother."

Here again is a clue to the mysteries of our own lives. God sometimes allows us to be treated as we have treated Him, that we may see our offense in its true character, and may be obliged to turn to Him with words of genuine contrition. Your child has turned out badly enough: you did everything for him; now he refuses to do what you wish, and even taunts you. Do you feel it? Perhaps this will reveal to you what God feels, in that, though He has nourished and brought you up, yet you have rebelled against Him. Your neighbor, when in trouble, came to you for help, and promises to repay you with interest, with many protestations: now he prospers, and you ask him to repay you, but he either laughs at you, or tells you to wait. Do you feel it? Ah, now you know how God feels, He who helped you in distress, to whom you made many vows, but who reminds you in vain of all the past. You know what it is to stand day after day a suppliant, waiting at a gate which never opens, listening for a footstep that never comes. Do you feel it? Ah, now you know what *He* feels who twenty years ago stood at the door of your heart and knocked, and is there now waiting, full-handed, to enrich you. That conscience must indeed be fast in slumber that awakens not at such appeals.

III. There was the Display of much Tender Love towards Them. As soon as Joseph espied them he invited them to his own table to feast with him. The brothers were brought into his house, where every kindness was shown to them; as if, instead of being poor shepherds, they were the magnates of the land. Their fears as to the return of the money were allayed by the pious, though prevaricating, assurance of the steward that if they had discovered it in their sacks it must have been put there by God, as there was no doubt about the price of their corn having come into his hands. And when Joseph came they prostrated themselves before him in striking fulfillment of his own boyish dream. He asked them tenderly about the well-being of their father; and there must have been a pathos in his words to Benjamin which would have revealed the whole secret if they had not been so utterly unprepared to find Joseph beneath the grange guise of the great Egyptian governor.

What an inimitable touch is that, which tells us how Joseph's heart welled up into his eyes, so that he needed to make haste to conceal the bursting emotion, which threatened to overmaster him. "He sought where to weep, and he entered into his chamber, and wept there. And he washed his face, and went out, and refrained himself, and said, Set on bread."

There may be prophetic touches here. And we may yet see the counterpart of this scene literally fulfilled, when the Lord comes forward to recognize and receive his ancient people. *But in the meanwhile what shall we say of his love to ourselves?* Ah, we need the fervid heart and the burning words of a Rutherford to deal with such a theme. The rejected Brother may seem strange and rough. He may cause sorrow. He may bind Simeon before our eyes. But, beneath all, He loves us with a love in which is concentrated the love of all parents to their children, and of all friends for their beloved. And that love is constantly devising means of expressing itself. It puts money into our sacks; it invites us to its home, and spreads banquets before us; it inclines stewards to meet us peacefully; it washes our feet; it takes a tender interest in those we love; it wishes us grace from God; it adjusts itself to our temperaments and puts us at our ease, so that gleams of light as to the love of Jesus strike into our hearts! He feels yearnings over us which He restrains, and dares not betray till the work of conviction is complete, and He can pour the full tides of affection on us, without injury to others or harm to ourselves.

IV. THERE WAS THE DESTRUCTION OF THEIR SELF-CONFIDENCE.
They thought their *word* was good, but when they told their family history, Joseph refused to believe it, and said it must be proved. They were
confident in their *money*; and as they paid down the shining pieces, they
congratulated themselves that in this respect at least they were even with
this rough governor—now at least he cannot touch them or count them
as defaulters. But when they reached their first halting place on their
way home, "as one of them opened his sack to give his ass provender,
he espied his money; for, behold, it was in the sack's mouth: and he said
unto his brethren, My money is restored; and lo, it is even in my
sack: and their heart failed them, and they were afraid, saying one to
another, What is this that God hath done unto us?"

How often this happens in the experience of sinful men! They want to
stand right with God, but they like to do so in their own way. Like
Cain, they bring the fruit which their own hands have raised. Like these
men, they bring prayers and tithes and gifts. But when these gifts
have been laid upon the altar, their donors are amazed to find that they
count for nothing, *and are even given back*. No! The mercy of God,
which is the true bread of the spirit, is not to be bought by anything
we can bring; it must be received as a gift without money and without
price. Jacob said, "Peradventure it was an oversight," but it was not; it
was part of a deeply laid plan, designed and executed for a special purpose. There is no oversight, and no peradventure, in the life of man.

> All nature is but art unknown to thee;
> All chance, direction which thou canst not see;
> All discord, harmony not understood;
> All partial evil, universal good.

They were confident also in their *integrity*. Little knowing what was
in the sack of one of them, when the morning was light they started
on their return journey for the second time. They were in high spirits. Simeon was with them; so was Benjamin, notwithstanding the ner-
vous forebodings of the old father. They were evidently in high favor
with the governor, else they had not been treated to so grand a feast on
the previous day. Their sacks were as full as they could possibly hold.
But they had hardly got clear of the city gate, when they were ar-

rested by the steward's voice. "Stop! Stop! Why have ye rewarded evil for good?" And they said, "Wherefore saith my lord these words? Behold, the money which we found in our sacks' mouths we brought again unto thee: how then should we steal silver of gold out of thy lord's house?" And, so sure were they of their integrity, that they went further and said: "With whomsoever thy master's cup is found, let him die, and we also will be my lord's bondmen." Then they speedily took down every man his sack to the ground, and opened every man his sack." And the steward searched them there on the bar road, beginning with the eldest to the youngest, "*and the cup was found in Benjamin's sack.*" Well might Judah and his brethren come to Joseph's house and fall before him on the ground, and say, "What shall we say unto my lord? What shall we speak? Or how shall we clear ourselves? God hath found out the iniquity of thy servants." They were stripped of every rag of self-confidence, and were shut up to his uncovenanted mercy.

Some men resemble Benjamin. They are naturally guileless and beautiful. Some faint races of original innocence linger about them. Their type is shown forth in the young man whom Jesus loved, as he stood before Him breathless with haste, protesting that he had kept all the commandments blameless from his youth. We do not reckon sin to such; and they do not reckon it to themselves. The publican and the sinner may stand in urgent need of the blood of Christ, but surely nitre and soap will suffice for them. But this reasoning is full of flaws. Such people seem good, only because they are compared with sinners of a blacker dye. Compare them with the only standard of infinite purity; and they are infinitely condemned. "If I wash myself with snow water, and make my hands never so clean, yet shalt Thou plunge me in the ditch, and mine own clothes shall abhor me." The servants think the linen clean as it hangs upon the line, contrasted with the dingy buildings around, but when the snowflakes fall, they wonder that they never before discerned its lack of whiteness. The schoolboy thinks his writing good, only so long as he contrasts it with that of a worse penman than himself, but he soon alters his opinion when he catches sight of the copy. So estimable characters pride themselves on their morality, only until they behold the seamless robes of Christ, whiter than any fuller on earth could whiten them. But *these* must be taught their utter sinfulness; *they* must learn their secret unworthiness; *they* must be made to take their stand with the rest of men. Benjamin must be reduced to the level of Simeon and Judah. The cup must be found in *Benjamin's* sack.

A preacher of the Gospel was once speaking to an old Scotch-woman, who was commonly regarded as only of the most devout and respectable people in that part of the country. He was impressing on her her need of Christ. At last, with tears in her eyes, she said, "Oh, sir, I have never missed a Sabbath at the kirk; and I have read my Bible every day; and I have prayed and done good deeds to my neighbors; and I have done all I knew I ought to do: and now do you mean to tell me that it must all go for nothing?" He answered, "Well, you have to choose between trusting in these and trusting in the redemption which God offers you in Christ. You cannot have both. If you are content to part company with your own righteousness, the Lord will give you his, but if you cling to your Bible-reading and Sabbath-keeping and good deeds, the Lord's righteousness cannot be yours." It was quite a spectacle, he said afterwards, to see that old woman's face. *The cup was found in Benjamin's sack.* For some time she sat in silence, her elbows on the table, her face buried in her hands: a great struggle was going on within. At length the tears began to stream from her eyes, and lifting up her clasped hands to heaven, she cried out, "Oh, my God, they shall all gang for naething!" In a moment more she cast herself on her knees and accepted the Lord Jesus as her Savior. It is when the cup is found in Benjamin's sack that he, too, is brought to the feet of Jesus.

There is a stolen cup in your sack, my respectable, reputable, moral friend. You are probably unconscious of it. You pride yourself upon your blameless life. You suppose that Christ Himself has no controversy with you. But if you only knew, you would see that you are robbing Him of his own. You use for yourself time and money and talents which He bought with his own precious blood, and which He meant to be a chosen vessel unto Himself. It is remarkable that you, who are so scrupulous in paying every man his dues, should be so careless of the daily treachery of which you are guilty in defrauding the Lord of his own purchase. But if you hide the unwelcome truth from yourself, you cannot hide it from your Lord. "Know ye not that such a one as He can certainly divine?" "He searcheth the hearts and trieth the reins of the children of men." And "he that is first in his own cause seemeth just, but his neighbor cometh and searcheth him."

How then shall we act? First, *Do not linger.* "Except we had lingered, surely now ere this we should have returned twice." Except you had lingered, ere this you would have become an earnest, happy Christian. "The angels hastened Lot as he lingered." Make haste! The door is shutting; and when it shuts it will lock itself. The entrance is nearly bricked up. The hourglass is nearly run out, and when its last grain has gone the court of mercy will close.

Secondly, *Make full confession or restitution.* "They came near to the steward of Joseph's house and communed with him," and told him all about the finding of the money, and offered it back in full weight. Commune with Christ as you close this story. Tell Him all that is in your heart. Restore what you have taken wrongfully from Him or from others. Make full and thorough restitution. "When I kept silence, my bones waxed old through my roaring all the day long; for day and night thy hand was heavy upon me: my moisture was turned into the drought of summer. I acknowledged my sin unto Thee, and mine iniquity have I not hid. And thou forgavest the iniquity of my sin." "He that covereth his sins shall not prosper, but whoso confesseth and forsaketh them shall have mercy."

Thirdly, *Throw yourself on the mercy of Christ.* Judah did not excuse himself or his brethren; he had been non-suited if he had. He adopted a wiser course—he pleaded for mercy. Mercy for their own sakes! Mercy for the lad's sake! Mercy for the sake of the old father with his grey hairs at home! Try that plea with your Lord. You will find that it will not fail you. Say, as you beat upon your breast, "Be merciful unto me, *the* sinner!" He will not be able to refrain. He will say, in broken accents, "Come near unto Me; I am Jesus your Brother: your sins nailed Me to the cross, but speak of it no more; grieve not for it. God has overruled it for good, that I might save your lives by a great deliverance."

9

Joseph Making Himself Known

Thou know'st our bitterness—our joys are Thine—
No stranger Thou to all our wanderings wild:
Nor could we bear to think, how every line
Of us, thy darkened likeness, and defiled,
Stand in full sunshine of thy piercing eye,
But that Thou call'st us Brethren: sweet repose
Is in that word—the Lord who dwells on high
Knows all, yet loves us better than He knows.

Genesis 45

Keble

The cup was found in Benjamin's sack. What a discovery was that! There in the open road, in the early morning light, as the villagers were passing into the city with melons and leeks and onions, and as the city was beginning to bestir itself, the cup of the great Premier, in whose hands was the power of life and death, was found lying in the corn, half hidden, as by stealth. But how did it come there? The brothers could not tell. They neither could nor would believe that Benjamin had known anything of it. Yet how to explain the mystery was a problem they could not solve. It seemed as if some evil genius were making them its sport, first in putting the money in their sacks, and then in concealing the cup there.

And yet, in a moment, each brother must have wished that the cup could have been found in any sack rather than in Benjamin's. They all remembered their father's strange unwillingness to let him come. The old man had seemed to have a presentiment of coming disaster. When first they returned from Egypt he said decisively, "My son shall not go down with you; for his brother is dead, and he is left alone: if mischief befall him by the way in the which ye go, then shall ye bring down my grey hairs with sorrow to the grave." And when the pressure of famine compelled them, the last words of the timid and stricken parent were, "God Almighty give you mercy before the man, that he may send away your other brother, and Benjamin. If I be bereaved of my children, I am bereaved." All the time his heart was filled with the presages of coming sorrow; and now those forebodings seemed about to be fulfilled. Each of those men must have thought to himself, as he followed in the sad procession back, "How dare I face my father? When first we reach home, he will be sure to look first for Benjamin; and if he does not see him with us, he will receive a stab of grief in his heart from which he will never rally, and his grey hairs will go down with sorrow to the grave." But there was nothing for it except to reload their asses and return. Oh, how different the road seemed to what it had been a little before! The same sun was shining; the same busy scene surrounded them—but a dark veil was spread over sky and earth.

Let us study the scene that followed. It demands our care; for it throws light on our Lord's dealings with contrite souls, and it is an anticipation of the time when Israel shall seek with tears unto Him who once was nailed by them to the cross, but who is "exalted a Prince and a Savior, to give repentance unto Israel, and forgiveness of sins."

I. NOTICE THE CIRCUMSTANCES IN WHICH THEY FOUND THEMSELVES. *Their conscience was now awakened, and it was ill at ease.* There was no need for them to mention that crime of twenty years before; and yet it seemed impossible for them to refrain from mentioning that which was uppermost in their minds. They were evidently thinking deeply of that dark deed by the pit's mouth; their own sorrows had brought the sorrows of that frail young lad to their minds; they could not but feel that there was some connection between the two; and thus the first words uttered by Judah their spokesman, as they entered the audience chamber of Joseph, betrayed the dark forebodings of their thoughts: "What shall we say unto my Lord? What shall we speak? Or how shall we clear ourselves? God hath found out the iniquity of thy servants."

God will always find out our iniquity. The sleuth-hound is on your track: it may take years to run you down, but it will never leave the trail until it has discovered your hiding place and found you out. "Be sure your sin will find you out." Tens of years may pass over your life; and like these brethren you may be congratulating yourself that the sin is forgotten, and you are safe; and then a train of circumstances, little suspected, but manipulated by a Divine hand, will suddenly bring the truth to light, and write God's sentence in flaming characters upon the walls of the house in which you riot in careless ease. The unforgiven sinner is never safe. A terrible incident in point is recorded by Dr. Donne, once Prebendary of St. Paul's. On one occasion some excavations were being made in the precincts of the cathedral, and among other relics thrown up to the surface, there was a skull with a nail in it. He happened to be standing by; and having taken up the skull, and examined it, he asked the old sexton if he knew whose it was, and how the owner died. "Ah," said he, carelessly, "it is the skull of an aged man, who died very suddenly some years ago: his wife is living yet; she married again soon after his death." Dr. Donne found her out, and confronted her with the skull. The woman turned at once deadly pale; and confessed that she had taken her husband's life, and that she had had no rest since by day or by night. This is a terrible example of a frequent law of God's world. And if all sin is not raced home to its authors in *this* world, at least there is enough to show how terrible that moment will be, when, at the "great white throne," the secrets of all hearts will be disclosed, and God will bring to light the hidden things of darkness. There is absolutely no chance of escape for a man, save in the wounds of Jesus; these are the city of refuge into which the pursuer cannot enter, and in which the fugitive is safe.

But, in addition, they felt that they were absolutely in Joseph's power. There he stood, second to none but Pharaoh in all the land of Egypt. Legions of warriors, like those depicted on the pyramids, were at his beck and call. If he had said that these men were all to be taken and imprisoned for life, or that Benjamin should be retained while the others were set free, there was absolutely no appeal: none could hinder him for a single moment. And the counterpart of this must surely be an alarming thought to the awakened sinner—that he is entirely at the mercy of the Judge of the quick and dead. There is none that can deliver out of his hand, or say, "What doest Thou?" The lamb in the power of the lion, the moth in the grasp of the hand, are not more entirely helpless than are sinners in the hand of God. "Agree with thine adversary quickly, while thou art in the way with him; lest haply the adversary deliver thee to the judge, and the judge deliver thee to the officer, and thou be cast into prison."

Moreover, they saw that appearances were strongly against them. There was no doubt that the cup had been found in Benjamin's sack; and though they were certainly innocent of the theft, yet they could not but feel that they were unable to clear or excuse themselves. As far as the evidence went, it pointed clearly and decisively to their guilt.

The divining cup is familiar enough to all students of ancient literature. It was sometimes made of crystal and of precious stones; and it was supposed that all secrets would be reflected by the liquid it contained. Homer sings of the cup of Nestor. And our own Spenser tells us how the royal maiden, Britomart, found Merlin's cup in her father's closet, and used it to discover a secret which closely concerned her. We, of course, do not believe that Joseph used such a cup for such a purpose, but it was his desire to maintain the character of an Egyptian of high rank. All Egyptian noblemen used such a cup. To appeal to it was most natural; and in their conscience-stricken condition, the brothers were too depressed to contest its decisions, or to ask for one more decisive test of their innocence or guilt.

II. NOTICE THEIR BEHAVIOR. "*They fell before him on the ground.*" As they did so, they unconsciously fulfilled his own prediction, uttered when a boy. How vividly that memorable dream of the harvest field must have occurred to Joseph's mind! Here were their sheaves making obeisance to his sheaf, standing erect in the midst.

But who was to be their spokesman? Reuben had always had something to say in self-justification, and had been so sure that all would be right that he had pledged the lives of his children to his father for the safety of Benjamin, but *he* is dumb. Simeon was probably the cruel one, the instigator of the crime against Joseph, but *he* dares not utter a word. Benjamin, the blameless one, the prototype of the young man whom Jesus loved, is convicted of sin, and has nought to say. Who then is to speak? There is only one, Judah, who at the pit's mouth had diverted the brothers from their first thought of murder. And notice how he speaks. He does not attempt to hold up any extenuating circumstances, or to explain the past, or to excuse Benjamin or themselves. He throws himself helplessly on Joseph's mercy: "What shall we say unto my lord? What shall we speak? Or how shall we clear ourselves?"

This is a good example for us to follow still. There is no doubt about our guilt. We are verily guilty concerning our treatment of that great Brother-man, who once lay in the pit, but who is now seated at the right hand of power. If we try to extenuate our faults, to excuse ourselves, to explain away the past, we shall only make bad worse: we shall be brought face to face with the damning evidence of our guilt; every mouth will be stopped; and we shall be obliged to cry, "God hath found out the iniquity of his servants." But if we throw ourselves on his mercy, we cannot fail.

We stand on surer ground than ever they did. They had no idea of the gentleness of Joseph's heart; they had not seen him turn aside to weep; they had not understood why on one occasion he had hastened from their presence; they could not guess how near the surface lay the fountains of his tears. They only knew him as rough, and stern, and hard. "The man, who is lord of the land, spake roughly to us." But we know the gentleness of the Lord Jesus. We have seen his tears over Jerusalem; we have listened to his tender invitations to come to Him; we have stood beneath his cross and heard his last prayers for his murderers, and his words of invitation to the dying thief; we know that He will not break the bruised reed, nor quench the smoking flax. We then need not fear for the issue when we cast ourselves upon his mercy. We then need not stand trembling in the ante-chamber, saying, "If I perish, I perish." We need not look nervously towards his throne to see if the golden scepter of his grace is extended towards us. Failure and rejection are alike impossible to the soul that pleads guilty, and that casts itself on the mercy of God which is in Jesus Christ our Lord.

In all literature, there is nothing more pathetic than this appeal of Judah. The eagerness that made him draw near; the humility that confessed Joseph's anger might righteously burn, since he was as Pharaoh; the picture of the old man, their father, bereft of one son, and clinging to this little one, the only relic of his mother; the recital of the strain which the governor had imposed on them, by demanding that they should bring their youngest brother down; the story of their father's dread, only overmastered by the imperious demand of a hunger that knew no law, and brooked no check; the vivid picture of the father's eagerness again to see the lad, in whose life his own was bound up; the heart-breaking grief at not seeing him among them; the heroic offer to stay there a slave, as Benjamin's substitute, if only the lad might go home; the preference of a life of slavery rather than to behold the old man sinking with sorrow into his grave—all this is touched with master hand. Oh, how much of poetry and pathos lie behind some of the roughest men, only waiting for some great sorrow to smite open the upper crust, and bore the Artesian well! But if a rough man could plead like this, think, ah think, what must not those pleadings be which Jesus offers before the throne! What moonbeams are to sunshine; what the affection of a dog is to the passionate love of a noble man— such is the pleading of Judah compared to the intercession of our great High Priest! We have an Advocate in the Court of King's Bench who never lost a case: let us put ourselves into his hands, and trust Him when He says, "I have prayed for thee." "Such a High Priest became us."

Thus Joseph's object was attained. He had wished to restore them to perfect rest and peace, but he knew that these were impossible so long as their sin was unconfessed and unforgiven. But it had not been abundantly confessed. Then, too, he had been anxious to see how they felt toward Benjamin. With this object in view he had given him five times as much as he had given them. Some think that he did this to show his special love. It may have been so, but probably there was something deeper. It was his dream of superiority that aroused their hatred against himself: how would they feel toward Benjamin, if he, the younger, were treated better than them all? But notwithstanding the marked favor shown him, they were as eager as before for his return with them. Besides, he wanted to see if they could forgive. It was Benjamin who had brought them into all this trouble: had they treated him in the spirit of former days, they would have abandoned him to his fate, but if so, they could not have been forgiven. "If ye forgive not men their trespasses, neither will your Heavenly Father forgive you." But they had no malice against this young lad. So far from showing malice, they tenderly loved and clung to him for the old father's sake and his own. Evidently then all Joseph's purposes were accomplished; all the conditions were fulfilled; and nothing remained to hinder the great unveiling that was so near.

III. NOTICE THE REVELATION AND RECONCILIATION. "*Then Joseph could not refrain himself.*" There was no effort needed to bring himself to the point: the effort consisted in having restrained himself so long. If he had yielded to his natural feelings, he would have broken out long before. It was only because he studied their lasting welfare, that he refrained himself so long. But when Judah's voice ceased its pathetic pleading, he could restrain himself no more. It may be that someone will read this who has been disposed to think that our Savior is hard to please; needing so much ere He unbends; distant and reticent. Ah, it is the other way! He is gentle and easy to be entreated; He is brimming over with yearning love: and if He seem indifferent, it is not for want of love—it is indeed a positive effort to Him even to seem so, but He will go through with it in order to prove, and test, and teach us. He loved the dear inmates of the home in Bethany, but He refrained Himself, and abode two days still in the same place where He was, so that Lazarus died; and then He went that He might work his greatest miracle at the grave in which hope itself lay buried. While we are being tried, He will invite us to his table, and speak some words of love; yet there will be a veil between us: but when the trial is over, He will refrain Himself no more, but will manifest Himself to us as He does not unto the world. "His going forth is prepared as the morning."

And Joseph cried, "Cause every man to go out from me." There was great delicacy here. He did not want to expose his brethren; and yet he wanted to say words which could not be understood by the curious ears of mere courtiers and place seekers. His brethren, too, must have a chance to be themselves. "And so there stood no man with him, while Joseph made himself known unto his brethren." We must stand alone before Christ, if we would know Him. The priest, the minister, or the Christian friend, must alike go out. There are joys, as there are sorrows, in which no stranger can intermeddle. As Peter met our Lord alone on the resurrection morning, for "He was seen of Cephas"—so alone must each man meet Christ. Why not at once?

And he wept aloud. He gave forth his voice in weeping, so that the Egyptians heard the unusual sounds and wondered. Was this joy or grief? I am disposed to think it was neither. It was pent up emotion. For many days he had been in suspense; so anxious not to lose them, so afraid that they might not stand the test. When from some secret coin of vantage he had watched them leave the city in the grey light, he may have chided himself for letting them go at all. His mind had been on the stretch; and now that the tension was removed, and that there was no further necessity for it, he wept aloud. Ah, sinner, the heart of Christ is on the stretch for thee!

And he said, "I am Joseph." He spoke in deep emotion; yet the words must have fallen on them like a thunderbolt. "Joseph!" Had they been dealing all the while with their long lost brother? "Joseph!" Then they had fallen into a lion's den indeed. "Joseph!" Could it be? Yes, it must be so; and it would explain a great many things which had sorely puzzled them. Well might they be troubled and terrified. Astonishment as at one risen from the dead, terror for the consequences, fear lest he would repay them the long-standing debt—all these emotions made them dumb. They could not answer him. So he said again, "I am Joseph, *your brother*, whom ye sold into Egypt"; and he added very lovingly, "Be not grieved, nor angry, for God did send me." How much this reminds us of another scene, not far from the gates of Damascus, when Jesus arrested the young persecutor with the words, "Saul, why persecutest thou Me?" And he said, "Who art Thou, Lord?" And the answer came back, "I am Jesus, whom thou persecutest." Penitent sinner! it is thus that thy Savior speaks to thee. "I am Jesus, your brother, whom thou hast sold and crucified; yet grieve not for that. I was delivered by the determinate counsel and foreknowledge of God; though the hands have been none the less wicked by whom I have been crucified and slain. But if you repent, your sins shall be blotted out. All manner of sin shall be forgiven unto the sons of men, and the blasphemies wherewith soever they may have blasphemed."

"And Joseph said unto his brethren, Come near unto me." They had gone farther and farther back from him, but now he bids them approach. This is a beautiful illustration of the way in which a sinner may

be reinstated in the loving favor of God. We are not set to serve a time of probation. We need not stand afar off. We may step right into the deepest and closest intimacy with the Son of God. Once "far off," but now "made nigh" by the blood of Jesus. One moment the rugged road of repentance; the next the Father's kiss and the banquet in the Father's home.

A moment more saw him and Benjamin locked in each other's arms, their tears freely flowing. And he kissed *all* his brethren. Simeon? Yes. Reuben? Yes. Those who had tied his hands and mocked his cries? Yes. He kissed them *all*. And after that they talked with him. So shall it be one day. The Jews are slowly filtering back to Palestine in unbelief. Sore troubles await them there, to prepare them to recognize their rejected Messiah. But the time is not far distant when they shall be prepared to hear Him say, "I am Jesus, your brother, whom ye crucified, but be not grieved with yourselves, for God has brought good out of evil, both for Gentile and for Jew, by saving life with a great deliverance." "And they shall look upon Him whom they pierced, and mourn because of Him." "And so all Israel shall be saved."

10

Joseph's
Administration of Egypt

We see him as he moved,
How modest, kindly, all-accomplished, wise,
With what sublime repression of himself,
And in what limits, and how tenderly.

Genesis 47   Tennyson

While all the domestic details on which we have been med-
itating were transpiring, Joseph was carrying his adopted
country through a great crisis—I might almost call it a revolution. When he became Prime Minister, the Egyptian monarchy was
comparatively weak, but after he had administered affairs for some thirteen years, Pharaoh was absolute owner of all the land of Egypt. As it
was in England in the old feudal times, so it was in Egypt: all the land
became held in fief from the crown. The history of this change deserves
more attention than we can give it now, but from first to last it was due
to the statesmanship of the young Hebrew. Nor is this the only instance
of a Hebrew conducting his adopted country through extraordinary
perils by the exercise of extraordinary genius.

During the seven years of plenty, Joseph caused one-fifth of all the
produce of every district to be hoarded up in its town; so that each town
would contain, within immense granaries, the redundant produce of
its own district. At last the years of famine came. And recent sad experiences in India will help us to realize something of the meaning of
the words: "There was no bread in all the land, for the famine was very

sore; so that the land of Egypt, and all the land of Canaan, fainted by
reason of the famine." No doubt, had there been no provision made
by Joseph, the streets would have been filled by emaciated skeletons
picking their way feebly amid the heaps of the dying and the dead; men,
women, and children would have fallen before the scythe of famine-
fever; and it would have taken years for the country to be repopulated
to its former extent.

The slender stores of the Egyptians were soon exhausted; and
when all the land of Egypt was famished, the people cried unto Pharaoh,
saying: "Bread! Bread! Give us bread!" Did they invade the palace
precincts, flow into the corridors, and force their way into the royal presence, as the Parisian mob has done more than once in the awful days
of revolution? We do not know. But Pharaoh had a ready answer: "Go
unto Joseph; and what *he* saith unto you, do." "Then Joseph opened all
the storehouse and *sold* unto the Egyptians." This was right and wise.
It would have been a great mistake to *give*. In the Irish famine the Government set the people to earn their bread by making the roads, since
it would have done them lasting injury to have allowed them to receive
help without rendering some kind of equivalent. And it is not too
much to say that it would have taken the Egyptians one or two generations to recover their moral tone if, instead of selling, Joseph had
given the corn. Joseph's policy was in exact accord with the maxims of
modern political economy.

But the money was soon exhausted: it lasted just one year. What
was to be done now? There was nothing left but persons and lands; the
people were naturally loath to pledge these, but there was no alternative; and so they came to Joseph, and said, "Why should we die? Buy
us and our land for bread." In other words, they became Pharaoh's tenant farmers, and paid him twenty per cent, or one-fifth of their returns,
as rent. This may seem a heavy tax, but it is not heavier than the
rentage in almost every European country in the present day.

I. LET US STUDY THE SPIRIT OF JOSEPH'S ADMINISTRATION. It is
summed up in three brief sentences: He was "diligent in business, fervent in spirit, serving the Lord."

Of his *diligence in business* there is ample proof. When first raised to the proud position of Premier, "he went out through all the land of Egypt." The granaries were built and the corn stored under his personal supervision. And when the famine came, the corn was sold under his own eye. The whole pressure of arrangements seems to have rested entirely upon his shoulders. Pharaoh wiped his hands of it, and said, Go to Joseph. Joseph gathered up all the money that was found in all the land of Egypt. Joseph bought the whole land for Pharaoh; and Joseph superintended the removal of the people into the cities from one end of the country to the other for the easier distribution of food. Joseph made the laws. "Seest thou a man diligent in his business, he shall stand before kings, he shall not stand before mean men." Young men, make Joseph your model in this. Some men do their lifework as if every joint were stiff with rheumatism, or as if they were exuding some adhesive viscus, making their snail progress as painful as it is slow. Others are somnambulists, looking for something and forgetting what they seek; not able to find their work, or, having found it, not able to find their tools: always late, taking their passage when the ship has sailed; insuring their furniture when the house is in flames; locking the door when the horse is gone. Beware of imitating any of these. First choose a pursuit, however humble, into which you can rightly throw your energy, and then put into it all your forces without stint.

These are simple rules, but most important. *Make the most of your time.* The biggest fortunes that the world has seen were made by saving what other men fling away; so be miserly over the moments, and redeem the gold dust of time, and they will make a golden fortune of leisure. *Be punctual.* Some men are always out of step with old Father Time. They do not miss their appointments, but they always arrive five minutes late. It would seem as if they were born late, and have never been able to catch up their lost moments. *Be methodical.* Arrange, so far as you can, your daily work, as postmen do their letters, in streets and districts; subject always, of course, to those special calls which the Almighty may put in your way. *Be prompt.* If your work must be done, do it at once: well-earned rest is sweet. *Be energetic.* An admirer of Thomas Carlyle met him once in Hyde Park, and broke in upon his reverie with an earnest request for a motto. The old man stood still for a moment, and then said, "There is no better motto for a young man than the words of the old book: 'Whatsoever thy hand findeth to do, do it with thy might.'"

But Joseph was also *fervent in spirit*. "He was a fruitful bough by a well, whose branches ran over the wall." It is almost impossible to exaggerate the beauty of this similitude. Yonder is the scorched land. You dare not expect verdure, much less fruit. Suddenly you descry greenery, and far-reaching boughs laden with luscious grapes. Why? Ah! down there lies a deep, deep well, and the rootlets of the vine go down into those cool depths, and draw up a moisture which the torrid heat cannot exhaust. Joseph's life was spent in a dry and thirsty land; there was not much in Egypt to nourish his spiritual life, yet to its close he bore fruit, which refreshed man and pleased God. Love, joy, peace, long-suffering, meekness, goodness, self-control, all those were in him even to abounding. And it was, no doubt, owing to his fervor of heart. It is related of a Grand Vizier, who in early life had been a shepherd, that he set apart one room in his palace for his exclusive use. No one was permitted to enter it. It was filled with the simple furniture of his early home, and the implements of his humble calling. And he entered it each day for quiet meditation on what he had been, that he might not be proud. So surely, in Joseph's palace there was a retired room, where he spent many hours each week in communion with the God of his fathers, to whom he owed everything he had.

Would that more of our businessmen were "fervent in spirit"! There is too little of this. Time for the ledger, but none for the Bible. Time for the club or society, but none for the prayer meeting. Time for converse with friends, but none for God. And, as the result, the bloom soon passes off the spirit, and the light dies away from the eyes, and the elasticity from the step. Men get to look wearied, tired, restless, and dissatisfied. Life bears a somber aspect. And men in this condition are not able to refresh weary souls that pass hard by, searching in vain for the rich clusters of refreshing fruit. We cannot produce fruit by any efforts of our own. We can only be fruitful by sending our rootlets down to the well. We must make time for private prayer and for the loving study of the Bible. Then the glow of fervor would never die down in the heart; and the leaf would never look sere; and seasonable fruit would never be wanting. Think not that fervor of spirit is impossible to those who live amid the stir of business. It was not impossible to Joseph: it need not be impossible to any who will adopt the simple rules of the Bible and of common sense. It is not enough to light a fire—we must feed it. And yet how many of my readers may have gradually sunk into habits of carelessness in private devotion, such as are bound to reduce and extinguish fervor of soul! There is the well of God's own Word! Get near it; strike deep into it; draw up from it by loving habitual study. Thus shall you be able to resist the insidious agencies that would drain away your enthusiasm and your power.

But Joseph was also a *servant of God*. God was in all his thoughts. "I fear God," was his motto. "It was not you that sent me hither, but God; and *He* hath made me . . . ruler throughout all the land of Egypt": this was the inspiration of his life. In saying that, he showed that he felt accountable to God for all he was and did. Now we surely need a principle to bind together our daily life and our religious exercises. So many live in business on one set of principles—and put on another set with their Sunday clothes. Where is the principle that will bring all our life beneath one blessed rule? I know of no other principle than that laid down by the good centurion, when he said, "A man under authority." We must feel hour by hour that we are men and women under the authority of the Lord Jesus Christ. The law of gravitation rules the sweep of the planets round the sun, and the course of a grain of dust in the autumn breeze. So obedience in everything to our Savior will simplify and regulate all things, and reduce the chaos of our life to one symmetrical and beautiful whole. If there is anything in your life, any habit, any dress, any pursuit, which Christ cannot approve, it must be laid aside. His name must be written upon all the bells of life, or they must cease to ring. The Apostle invested with new dignity the existence of the poor slaves of his time, by saying, "Ye are servants of Christ: do service with a will, not as unto men, but as unto Christ." And it is of no consequence how menial your position is, you may do it for your dear Lord, whispering again and again, "This is for Thee, gracious Master, all for Thee." What a check this would put on hurried and superficial work!

There are a good many unfaithful servants about in the world; and if you rebuke them, you receive as answer, "My wages are so poor"; "My mistress takes no interest in me"; "I am treated as a slave"; "I shall leave as soon as I can." Stop! Who put you where you are? Had Christ anything to do with it? If not, how came you there without asking his leave? If He had, how dare you leave unless you are sure He calls you away? And as for service—why do you serve? For money, or thanks, or habit? No, *for Christ*. Then do your best for Him. Every room you enter is a room in his temple. Every vessel you touch is as holy as the vessels of the Last Supper. Every act is as closely noticed by Him as the breaking of the alabaster box. On every fragment of your life you may write, Sacred to the memory of Jesus Christ." This would give a new dignity to toil, and a new meaning to life. Let us never forget how the thought of our dear Lord will equalize all life, and act as the complement of its needs. Those who are called as free, are slaves to Him; and those who are slaves to men are free in Him. And all life reaches its true unity and ideal just insofar as He is its Head, and Lord (1 Cor. 7:22).

II. NOTICE THE CONFESSION OF THE EGYPTIANS. "Thou hast saved our lives" (Gen. 47:25). What a splendid endowment is coolness, foresight, presence of mind! They are the gifts of God; and they have enabled many men to be the saviors of their fellows. That engineer had it who, some time ago, turned off the steam from the broken cylinder on the ocean steamer that seemed doomed. Livingstone and Stanley have had it among travelers; and it often saved them and their followers from infuriated mobs of savages. Cromwell and Wellington had it among soldiers, and it enabled them to extricate their men from positions in which death seemed certain. Cavour, Pitt, and Bright have had it preeminently among statesmen. Any of these might have been addressed in the words of the Egyptians: "Thou hast saved our lives."

But there is something higher than this. As I see these Egyptians crowding round Joseph with these words upon their lips, it makes me think of Him of whom Joseph was but a type. Joseph lay in the pit; and from the pit was raised to give bread to the brethren who had rejected him, and to a nation of Gentiles. Jesus lay in the grave; and from its dark abyss He was raised to give salvation to his brethren the Jews, and to the millions of Gentile people. Already I hear the sound of countless myriads, as they fall before the sapphire throne, and cry, "Thou hast saved us!" The Egyptian name of Joseph meant, "the Savior of the world," but the salvation wrought by him is hardly to be named in the same breath with that which Jesus has achieved. Joseph saved Egypt by sagacity; Jesus saved us by laying down his life. Joseph's bread cost him nothing, but the bread which Jesus gives cost Him Calvary. Joseph was well repaid by money, cattle, and land, but Jesus takes his wares to the market of the poor, and sells them to those who have no money or price. He can supply all our need. His only condition is that He should do it freely. To offer Him anything in exchange is to close all dealings with Him. But if you are willing to go without gold in your hand, and with an empty sack, He will give without stint, with both hands, pressed down, and running over. "He will feed the hungry with good things, but the rich He will send empty away." "Blessed are ye poor, for yours is the kingdom of heaven."

III. REMARK, THE RESOLVE OF THESE EGYPTIANS. "Let us find grace; and we will be Pharaoh's servants." "Thou hast saved our lives; and we will be thy servants." How could we state better the great argument for our consecration to our Savior? "He has saved us: ought we not to be his servants?"

There are many arguments by which we might urge acceptance of the yoke of Christ. There is such *dignity* in it: the old butler is proud to wear the livery of a ducal house, but what livery is so worthy as that which Christ's servants wear? "I bear the marks of the Lord Jesus." There is such *happiness* in it; it is perfect freedom. To be free of Christ is to grind in slavery. To obey Christ—is to go forth into the glorious liberty of the sons of God.

But I pass by these arguments now to present one more cogent, more pathetic, more moving. It is this: Jesus has saved you—will you not serve Him? These are the successive steps: mark them well! Recognize that Jesus bought you to be his by shedding his own blood as your ransom price, and by giving his flesh for you and for the life of the world. Then give yourself entirely to Him, saying, humbly, lovingly, trustfully, "I do now, and here, offer a present unto Thee, O Lord, myself, my soul and body, to be a reasonable, holy, and lively sacrifice to Thee." From that moment you are no more your own, but his; He takes what we yield, at the moment of yielding; reckon on Him to keep you, and to supply all your need. Take Jesus to be moment by moment your Savior, Friend, and Lord; and yield to Him an obedience which shall cover the entire area of our being, and shall comprehend every second of your time. When solicited to leave Him, appropriate the words of the ancient Hebrew slave, and say, "I love my Master; I will not go out free."

He deserves this. For you He lay in Bethlehem's manger. For you He was homeless and poor. For you He sweat the drops of blood and poured out his soul unto death. For you He pleads in heaven. "I beseech you then, by the mercies of God, that ye present yourselves to Him, living sacrifices, which is your reasonable service.

11
Joseph's Father

We live in deeds, not years; in thoughts, not breaths;
In feelings, not in figures on a dial;
We should count time by heart's throbs. He most lives
Who thinks most, feels the noblest, acts the best.

Genesis 47:1–11   P. J. Bailey

We always turn with interest from an illustrious man to ask about his father and his mother. The father of Martin Luther and the mother of the Wesleys hang as familiar portraits in the picture gallery of our fancy. It is not, therefore, to be wondered at that we find in the Bible something to gratify this innocent curiosity; and especially in the story of Joseph we are permitted glance behind the scenes, and to consider the relations between him and his old father, Jacob.

I. JOSEPH'S UNDIMINISHED FILIAL LOVE. From the first moment that Joseph saw his brethren among the crowd of all nationalities that gathered in the corn-mart, it was evident that his love to his father burnt with undiminished fervor. Those brethren little guessed how eager he was to learn if the old man was yet alive, nor what a thrill of comfort shot through his heart when they happened to say, "Behold, our youngest brother is this day with his father." Evidently, then, though twenty-five years had passed since he beheld that shrunken, limping, yet beloved form, his father was living still.

And when his brethren came the second time, they must have been surprised to notice the delicate tenderness with which he asked them of their welfare, and said, "Is your father well, the old man of whom ye spake? Is he yet alive?" Yes; and Judah little realized what a tender chord he struck, and how it vibrated, almost beyond endurance, to his touch, when he spoke again and again of the father at home, an old man, who so tenderly loved the young lad, the only memorial of his mother: that father who had been so anxious lest mischief should befall him; and whose grey hair would go down with sorrow to the grave, unless he came back safe. It was this repeated allusion to his father that wrought on Joseph's feelings so greatly as to break him down. "He could not refrain himself." and so the very next thing he said, after the astounding announcement, "I am Joseph," was, "Doth my father yet live?" And in the tumultuous words which followed, words throbbing with passion and pathos, sentences about the absent father came rolling out along with utterances of reconciliation and forgiveness to his brethren: just as the swollen mountain flood hurries along in its eddies, boulders, timber, and everything that barred the way. "Haste ye, and go up to my father, and say unto him: Thus saith thy son Joseph, 'God hath made me lord of all Egypt: come down unto me; tarry not'. . . . And ye shall tell my father of all my glory in Egypt, and of all that ye have seen; and ye shall haste, and bring down my father hither."

The weeks and months that intervened must have been full of feverish anxiety to Joseph; and when at last he heard that the old man had reached the frontier of Egypt, in one of the wagons which, with thoughtful consideration, he had sent to fetch him, he "made ready his chariot, and went up to meet Israel his father." Oh, that meeting! If the old man was sitting in some recess of the lumbering wain, weary with the long journey, how he would revive when they said, "Joseph is coming!" I think he would surely dismount, and wait, straining his aged eyes at the approaching company, from out the midst of which there came the bejeweled ruler to fall on his neck and weep there a good while. "Let me die," said he, as he looked at him, from head to foot, with glad, proud, satisfied eyes: "let me die, since I have seen thy face, because thou art yet alive." I wonder how he felt, as he recalled his sad lament, "All these things are against me."

But this was not all. Joseph loved his father too well to be ashamed of him. When Pharaoh heard of the arrival of his father and brethren, he seemed mightily pleased, and he directed Joseph to see to their welfare. "The land of Egypt is before thee; in the best of the land make thy father and brethren to dwell; in the land of Goshen let them dwell: and if thou knowest any men of activity among them, then let them be rulers over my cattle." After this Joseph brought in Jacob his father, and set him before Pharaoh.

We cannot but admire the noble frankness with which Joseph introduced his father to the splendid monarch, habituated to the manners of the foremost court of the world. There was a great social gulf fixed between Egypt and Canaan, the court and the tent, the monarch and the shepherd. And if Joseph had been any less noble or simple than he was, he might have shrunk from bringing the two extremes together; might have feared to recall the comparative lowliness of his origin; might have been shamed of his relations, who needed to become pensioners on the land of his adoption. But all these thoughts were forgotten in presence of another: this withered, halting, famine-pursued man was *his father.*

There is a great laxity in these respects in all classes of our community, but especially among the children of working men in large industrial towns. The young people are able to earn such good wages as to be largely independent of their parents. And when they have paid some small amount for their keep, they are apt to imagine that their parents have further claim. They forget the long arrears of obligation. They do not care to remember the cost of those long years of helpless childhood, when they were only a burden and a care. They are unmindful of the tender kindness that nursed them through long and dangerous illnesses; that freely sacrificed sleep and rest; that thought them angels, saints, and heroes; that bore with their petulance and fretfulness; or that sat far into the night, contriving dresses, playthings, and other pleasant surprises.

In some cases the behavior of grown-up children to their parents is still more dishonorable. It is a common thing to see men rise in a few years from obscurity to considerable wealth. With increasing money there comes a vast change in a man's social position. He puts the magic letters

"Esq." after his name. He lives in a fine house, and gives large parties. He keeps his carriage, and sends his children to expensive schools. But what of his aged parents? He allows them a meager annuity, but takes care to keep them out of his family and his home—for, to tell the truth, he is rather shamed of them. It is a false shame indeed! And the man who does so is almost certain, unconsciously, to say or do something which will reveal to his new associates his lowly origin far more readily than the mere presence of his parents at his board could do. I prefer the noble magnanimity of Joseph, who seemed proud to introduce the withered, crippled patriarch to his mighty friend and liege lord.

Young people, honor your parents! Do not treat them the worse, just because you know they love you enough to bear with your impertinences. The politeness is mere veneer which is not gentle to near kin. Do not call them by slang or unmeaning names: glory in the noble titles, "Father," "Mother." They may have their peculiarities and faults, but it is ungenerous and unkind to dwell on them. It is possible so to fix your attention on these minor points as to become oblivious to many noble qualities, which are more than a compensation. Imitate the sons of Noah in the filial respect which flung a mantle even over their father's sin.

II. PHARAOH'S QUESTION. "How old art thou?" This was Pharaoh's first inquiry, as Jacob entered his presence. It was, perhaps, suggested by the patriarch's withered look and bent form. It is a question that often rises to our lips, but it is suggested by a very false standard of estimating the length of a man's life.

The length of a life is not measured by the number of its days; no, but by the way in which its days have been used.

> We live in thoughts, not breaths;
> In feelings, not in figures on a dial.

Some live for many years, and at the end have little or nothing to show for them. Take out the wasted hours, hours of drowsy lethargy, hours of luxurious sloth, and hours of self-indulgence; and only a few hours of real life are left. There are men who will be seventy next birthday, but who have only lived six months out of the whole time.

It is surprising in Liverpool to see the great bales of cotton compressed under the vast pressure of the hydraulic press; and so lives shrink into a very insignificant space, beneath the mighty pressure of reality. Our real life dates, not from our first birth, but from our second. All before that counts for nothing.

Others live for few years, but they have crowded them with strenuous, noble life: they have been punctual, industrious, methodical: they have redeemed the time; they have treasured the moments with frugal and miserly care; they have made the most of odd bits which others would have flung away as useless—and, as the result, they have much to show. What books they have read! What deeds they have done! What ministries they have set afoot! What friends they have made! What characters they have built up! They have lived long. They will be thirty next birthday, but in those few years they have lived the life which most men live in sixty years.

Permit a stranger to ask of each reader, standing in the palace of life, "How old art thou?"

How old art thou? *Seventeen?* That is indeed a critical time. It is the formative time: what thou art now, thou wilt be. Thou art leaving the sheltered bay of early life to launch out into the great ocean. Beware! It is winsome-looking, but it is treacherous. Be sure and take on board the great Master, Christ: none but He can pilot thee through the shoals and quicksands which lie hidden on thy course. Take on board none but those whom He chooses as the crew.

How old art thou? *Twenty-one?* It was at that age that our Lord emerged from obscurity: and think how many men have lived a great life and died before they reached this age. Alexander among generals; Rosetti among singers; McCheyne and Spencer among ministers. What art thou doing in the world? Come, make haste! Thy life will soon slip away. Take care, lest at the close thou be constrained to say, "I have spent my life in laboriously doing trifles."

> 'Tis a mournful story,
> Thus in the ear of pensive eve to tell
> Of morning's firm resolves the vanished glory,
> Hope's honey left within the with'ring bell,

And plants of mercy dead, that might have
bloomed so well.

But this need not be your sad retrospect, if only you will yield your
whole being to the Lord Jesus, asking Him to keep down your self-life,
and to think in your brain, to live in your heart, to work through your
life, and to fulfill in you the good pleasure of his will, "and the work
of faith with power."

How old art thou? *Forty*? Take care! Very few are ever converted
who have reached the downward slopes of forty. If thou art not Christ's
yet, the chances of thy becoming his lessen at a tremendous ratio
every week.

How old art thou? *Fifty*? *Sixty*? *Seventy*? The snows are beginning
to silver thy head. Familiar pursuits must be abandoned. Familiar
places must be visited no more. Affairs once thy pride must be given
over to the stronger nerve of others. The dip in yonder path shows how
near is the valley of the shadow of death, with its dark, dark river. How
art thou going to meet it? Shivering, cringing, cowering, the victim of
an irresistible fate? Or with brave welcome, such as animated the
worn prisoner of the Mamertime dungeon? "I have fought a good fight,
I have finished my course, I have kept the faith; henceforth there is laid
up for me a crown of righteousness." Old friends, we look on you to
teach us how to await our end, and how to die.

It is a solemn question, How old art thou? It is well to face the
frown fewness of our years; to see how envious Time is eating away the
narrow shoal on which we stand. My favorite piece in all Milton's
works is his address to Time; and often have I loved to read the passage
in Charles Kingsley's Life, which tells how on his dying bed he read it
again and again—

Fly, envious Time, till thou run out of race.

Oh, to be able to say that without tremor or misgiving!

III. JACOB'S ANSWER. "And Jacob said unto Pharaoh, The days of
the years of my pilgrimage are a hundred and thirty years; few and evil
have the days of the years of my life been, and have not attained unto

the days of the years of the life of my fathers in the days of their pilgrimage." They had been *few* in comparison with those of his ancestors. Terah reached the age of 205; Abraham of 175; Isaac of 180. But "the whole age of Jacob was a hundred forty and seven years." They had been *evil*. As a young man he was wrenched from his dearest associations of home and friends, and went forth alone to spend the best years of his life as a stranger in a strange land. Arduous and difficult was his service to Laban, consumed in the day by drought, and in the sleepless night vigils by frost. He escaped from Laban with difficulty; and no sooner had he done so than he had to encounter his incensed and impetuous brother. In the agony of that dread crisis he met with the Angel Wrestler who touched the sinew of his thigh, so that he halted to the end of his life. These calamities had hardly passed when he was involved in extreme danger with the Canaanites of Shechem, and passed through scenes which have blanched his hair, furrowed his cheeks, and scarred his heart. Thus he came to Luz, and Deborah, Rebekah's nurse, died, and was buried beneath an oak, which was thenceforth called the Oak of Weeping. "And they journeyed from Bethel, and there was but a little way to come to Ephrath, and Rachel (his favorite wife) bare a son; and it came to pass, as her soul was departing, for she died, that she called his name Ben-oni, the son of my sorrow." A little further on he came to Mamre, arriving just in time to bear the remains of his own father to the grave. And what sorrows befell him after that, have already touched our hearts, as we have studied the wondrous history of his son, Joseph. Reuben involved his name in shameful disgrace. Judah trailed the family honor in the mire of sensual appetite. To all appearance Joseph had been torn to pieces by wild beasts. The dissensions of his sons must have rent his heart. And even after his meeting with his long-lost son he was to linger for seventeen years a pensioner on the bounty of the king of Egypt: far from the glorious heritage which had been promised to his race.

Such was the exterior of Jacob's life. Few have trod a path more paved with jagged flints, or bound around their brows a crown more full of thorns. You would have called his life a failure. Compare it with the lot of Esau; and what a contrast it presents! Jacob obtained the birthright, but what a life of suffering and disaster was his! Esau lost the birthright, but he had all that heart could wish. Wealth, royalty, a line of illustrious sons—these were the portion of his cup. The thirty-sixth chapter of Genesis contains a list of the royal dukes of his line. How often must Esau have pitied his brother! "My poor brother, he was always visionary, counting on the future, building castles in the air; as for myself, I say, make the best of this world while it lasts. Let us eat and drink, for tomorrow we may die."

And yet when this same Jacob stands before Pharaoh, the greatest monarch of the world bends eagerly to catch his blessing. "Jacob blessed Pharaoh." I know that Jacob in his earlier life was crafty, a mere bargain maker, a trickster, but all seems to have been eliminated in the fierce crucible of suffering through which he had passed; and he had reached a grandeur or moral greatness which impressed even the haughty Pharaoh. Esau would never have been able to bless Pharaoh. But this way-worn pilgrim can now do that which his wealthy and successful brother never could have done. "Without contradiction, the less is blessed of the greater." Evidently, then, Jacob was a greater man than the greatest monarch of his time. There is, therefore, a greatness which is wholly independent of those adventitious circumstances which we sometimes associate with it. The ermine does not make a judge; a crown does not make a king; nor does wealth, or rank, or birth make a great man. Jacob was one of the truly great. He was a royal man with a Divine patent of royalty. God Himself said, 'Thy name shall be no more called Jacob, but Israel (a prince of God), for as a prince hast thou power with God, and with men."

Three things made Jacob royal; and will do as much for us. (1) *Prayer*. On the moorland, strewn with boulders, he saw in his dreams the mighty rocks pile themselves into a heaven-touching ladder. This struck the keynote of his life. He ever after lived at the foot of the ladder of prayer, up which the angels sped to carry his petitions, and down which they came, with beautiful feet, to bring the golden handfuls of blessing. Learn to pray without ceasing. It is the secret of greatness. He who is oft in the audience chamber of the great King becomes knife-like.

(2) *Suffering*. His nature was marred by selfish, base, and carnal elements. He took unlawful advantage of his famished brother; de-

ceived his aged father; increased his property at the expense of his uncle; worked his ends by mean and crafty means. But sorrow ate away all these things, and gave him a new dignity. So does it work still on those who have received the new nature, and who meekly learn the lesson which God's love designs to teach them. Do not shrink from pain and sorrow; they come to crown you. The Lamb sits on the throne today because He was slain; and the throne is reserved for those who have learned to suffer with Him, and with Him to die.

(3) *Contact with Christ.* "There wrestled a man with him until the breaking of the day." Who was He? Surely none less than the Angel Jehovah, whose face may not be seen, or his name known. It was the Lord Himself, anticipating his incarnations, and intent on ridding his servant of the evil and weakness which had clung so long and so closely to him, sapping his spiritual life. And from that hour Jacob was "Israel." Ah, my readers, be sure of this, that Jesus, the immortal lover of souls, is wrestling with you, longing to rid you of littleness and selfishness, and to lift you also to a royal life. Yield to Him, lest He be compelled to touch the sinew of your strength. If you let Him have his way, He will make you truly Princes with God; and even those above you in this world's rank will gladly gather round you for the sake of the spiritual blessings you shall bestow.

12

Joseph at the Deathbed of Jacob

This hath He done; and shall we not adore Him?
This shall He do; and can we still despair?
Come, let us quickly fling ourselves before Him,
Cast at His feet the burden of our care.
Yea, thro' life, death, thro' sorrow, and thro' sinning,
He shall suffice me, for He hath suffered:
Christ is the end—for Christ was the beginning;
Christ the beginning—for the end is Christ.

Genesis 47:27–31

F. W. H. Myers

J acob dwelt in the land of Goshen; there his sons led their flocks over the rich pasture lands, and laid the foundation of the great wealth which has ever been a distinguishing mark of this highly-favored nation. "They grew and multiplied exceedingly." So seventeen uneventful years went by. And as the old man became more and more infirm, his spirit was cheered and sustained by the love of Joseph, and by the satisfied joy of his heart in the honor and splendor of his son. Evidently Joseph was the stay of that waning life; and it is not re-markable therefore that the patriarch summoned him not once, or even twice, but thrice, to his deathbed. It is on those visits that we may dwell for a little now.

Evidently there is something to repay us. The Bible is a book of life. Its pages are devoted to the deeds rather than the deaths of its heroes. Their biographies fill whole books, while single verses are enough for their dying words. Whenever, therefore, a death scene is described with some minuteness, we may be sure that there is something which demands our attentive heed. So it is here.

I. JOSEPH'S FIRST VISIT—"The time drew nigh that Israel must die."
How inexorable is the "must" of death! There is no possibility of
evading its summons. When it lays its long, cold hand on the shoulder of the Ancient Mariner, however eager the guests to hear his story,
he must arise and follow. By many years had Jacob exceeded the ordinary span of modern life; and, in spite of much hardship and privation, like the apple at the extremity of the bough, which eludes the
hand of the gatherer, he had evaded the reach of death, but this could
not be forever. The failing powers of his life gave warning that the silver cord was strained to breaking, and that the machinery of nature was
on the point of giving way. He must die.

But his death was a rift in the dark clouds that veiled the future
world from his sons and their children, giving them a glimpse of its reality and beauty. And we can gather some of the conceptions which
must have flashed across the mind of Joseph, as he obeyed the summons
of his father, and stood beside that dying bed.

One of the most sublime verses in the New Testament declares that
"Christ has abolished death, and brought life and immortality to light
through the Gospel." There is a most inspiring rhythm in the words,
but we must not suppose that the Gospel has revealed that concerning
which nothing was previously known. Long before our Lord walked in
this world, carrying at his girdle the keys of Resurrection and Life, men
cherished the hope of eternal life: the Gospel simply threw fuller light
on that which had been before partially hidden, as the rising sun reveals
the clear outlines of the landscape which had lain indistinct and hazy
in the grey dawn. Christ drew from the window the curtain, through
which the morning light had been feebly struggling to the sleeper's eyes.

The evidence of this is not far to seek. Daniel teaches in plainest
language the truth of a general resurrection to endless life or endless
shame. Ecclesiastes closes with an explicit statement of the spirit's return to its giver, and of final judgment. The book of Job, whatever date
may be assigned to it, has been called a very hymn of immortality: he
knew at least that his "Redeemer lived, and that he should stand up at
the last upon the earth, and after his skin had been destroyed, yet from
his flesh he should see God" (Job 19:25, 26, R.V.). In the Book of
Psalms we have no uncertain evidence of the tenacity with which

pious Jews clung to these hopes. "Thou wilt not leave my soul in Sheol; neither wilt thou suffer thine Holy One to see corruption. Thou wilt show me the path of life" (Ps. 16:10, 11, R.V.). And it is just this faith in and yearning after a life beyond the grave which is the true keynote of the lives of the three great patriarchs who lie together in Machpelah's ancient cave.

Why did they wander to and fro in the land of promise as sojourners in a strange land? Why were they content to have no inheritance—no, not so much as a place to put their feet on? Why did Abraham dwell with Isaac and Jacob in frail, shifting tents, rather than in towns like Sodom and Gomorrah? What did Abraham mean when he said to the sons of Heth, "I am a stranger and a sojourner with you"? And what was the thought in Jacob's mind, when, in the presence of the haughty Pharaoh, he described his life as a "pilgrimage?" The answer is clearly given in the roll call of God's heroes contained in Hebrews 11: "They sought a country, a fatherland." And they were so absorbed with this one thought, that they could not settle to any inheritance in Canaan. Their refusal to have anything more than a grave in the soil of the promised land shows how eagerly they looked for the land that was very far off.

At first, no doubt, they thought that Canaan was to be the land of promise. But when they waited for it year after year, and still it was withheld, they looked into the deed of gift again, and learned that there were depths in it of which they had never dreamed; and as they still watched and waited, the gauzy mists of time parted, and in the dim haze there loomed upon their vision a land of which the land of milk and honey was a poor type; and instead of a city built by human hands, there arose before them the fair vision of the crystal walls and the pearly gates of the city which hath foundations, whose builder and maker is God, and which He had prepared for them that love Him. Yonder was their fatherland. Yonder their true city. Yonder their home. And their pilgrim life bore evidence to the reality and certainty of their faith.

This belief in "in the city of God," of which in afterdays Augustine wrote on the coast of Africa, and which has sustained so many saintly souls, animated their lives, cheered them in death, and cast a bright ray across the gloom of the grave. "These all died in faith, not having received the promises, but having seen them afar off (as the minarets and parapets of some distant city), and were persuaded of them and embraced them." The Revised Version says, "They greeted them from afar," as the wanderer greets his longed-for home, when he sees it from afar. With what eagerness, with what earnest yearnings, with what fond anticipation, must these weary wanderers have looked for heaven! Well might Jacob, on this his deathbed, stay the progress of his parting exhortations to say, "I have waited for thy salvation, O Lord." This took the bitterness out of his death.

And notice, *Jacob did not regard the future life as a mere state of existence* stripped of all those associations which make life worth the having. Indeed, in this he seems to have had truer thoughts than many who are found in Christian churches. He said, "I am to be gathered unto my people." He surely did not mean simply that he was to be buried in their tomb, for he expresses that thought afterwards in the words, "Bury me with my fathers in the cave of Machpelah." Nay, he meant to say that for him the city to which he went was the gathering place of his clan, the rendezvous of elect souls, the home of all who were *his* people because they were *God's*.

Year after year the people have been gathering there, as highland clans in olden days were gathered to a central trysting-place by the bearers of the Fiery Cross. All noble, saintly souls are assembled yonder, and await us. And when we leave this world, it will not be to go into a cold, unsympathizing, grave-like realm, where no voice shall greet, no smile welcome us. But we shall go to our people; those whom we have loved and lost; those who are awaiting our coming with fond affection, and who will administer a choral entrance to us into that world of everlasting reunion.

But it was not simply to express these hopes that the dying patriarch summoned the beloved Joseph to his side. The father wanted to bind the son by a solemn promise not to have him buried in the land of his exile, but to carry him back to that lone cave, which seemed an outpost in the hostile and distant land of Canaan. For seventeen years Jacob had been familiar with Egypt's splendid temples, obelisks, and pyramids; he had been surrounded with all the comforts that Joseph's filial love could devise or his munificence execute, but nothing could make him forget that distant cave, which was before Mamre, in the land of Canaan. To him interment in the most splendid pyramid in Egypt was not for a moment to be compared with burial in that solitary and humble sepulcher, where the mortal remains of Abraham and Sarah, of Isaac and Rebekah, and of the faithful Leah, lay waiting the day of resurrection.

Human nature was not different then from what it is today. Our truest home is still by the graves of the beloved dead. Wherever we wander, our hearts return thither, as the eye of the sailor to the Pole star. And for this cause, many a warrior, dying in some distant land, has asked that his remains might be placed, not in the splendid Minster or the nation Walhalla, but in the quiet country graveyard, where the moss-covered tombstones repeat in successive generations, the family name. It was natural, then, for Jacob to wish to be buried in Machpelah.

But there was something more than natural sentiment. He was a man of faith. He knew and cherished the ancient promise made by God to His friend, the patriarch Abraham, that Canaan should become the possession of his seed. That promise was the old man's stay. He knew that Canaan and not Egypt was the destined abiding place of his people. They would not always live in Egypt, however fertile its Goshens or friendly its peoples. The trumpet would sound the summons of their departure. If, then, he were buried in Egypt, he would be left behind, a stranger among strangers. No, this could not be. If they are to leave, he must leave before them. If they are to settle in the land of promise, he will go first as their forerunner. And though he could not share the perils and pains and glories of the exodus, he will be there to meet them when in after years their bands enter upon their inheritance.

"If now I have found grace in thy sight, put, I pray thee, thy hand under my thigh, and deal kindly and truly with me. Bury me not, I pray thee, in Egypt: but I will lie with my fathers; and thou shalt carry me out of Egypt and bury me in their burying place." What son could resist that appeal? Can any of us resist the last appeals of our beloved? Joseph was too good and tender to hesitate for a single moment. "And he said, I will do as thou hast said." But the old man was not content with a mere promise. "And he said, Swear unto me. And he swore unto him. And Israel bowed himself upon the bed's head." So ended Joseph's first visit to his dying father.

II. JOSEPH'S SECOND VISIT. Tidings came to the Prime Minister of Egypt that his father was sick and wished to see him. And he went to him without delay, taking with him his two sons, Manasseh and Ephraim. He, no doubt, guessed that his father's sickness was the last stage of his decay; and the form of the message may have been agreed on by them in previous conversations as the significant sign from one to the other that the sands of time had nearly run out in that aged, battered, and time-worn body.

When Joseph arrived at his father's dwelling, the gift of his own munificence, the aged patriarch seems to have been lying still, with closed eyes, in the extreme of physical exhaustion. He was too weak to notice any of those familiar forms that stood around him. But when one told him and said, "Behold, thy son Joseph is come," the sound of that loved name revived him, and he made a great effort, and, propped by pillows, sat up upon the bed.

There was clearly no decay in his power of recollection, as the old man reviewed the past. Again he seemed to be lying at the foot of the mystic ladder, with its angels trooping up and down, while God Almighty stood above, and pledged Himself to make him fruitful, and to give to him and his seed the land in which is forefathers had been strangers, for an everlasting possession. No lapse of time could erase the impression which those words had made. Even though he had lived to out-measure the years of a Methuselah, they would still ring in musical cadence within his heart. And had not God fulfilled them a thousand times over, so that no one good thing had failed? And his seed was sure of the land, though as yet far removed from its actual possession. And as his recollection embraced the past, it was also vividly alive to more recent incidents in the family history. He did not forget that Joseph, who leaned over his dying form, had two sons; and he announced his intention of adopting them as his own. "Thy two sons, which were born unto thee in the land of Egypt, before I came unto thee into Egypt, are mine: as Reuben and Simeon, they shall be mine."

By that act, while Joseph's name was expunged from the map of Canaan, yet he himself became possessed of a double portion of his area, because Ephraim and Manasseh would henceforth stand there as his representatives.

And when he had said so much, his mind wandered away. He saw again that scene on the hilly road to Bethlehem, just outside the little village, where his onward progress was suddenly halted, and all his camp was hushed into the stillness of a dread suspense, as the life of the beloved Rachel trembled in the balance. He could never forget that moment. His dying eyes could see again the spot where he buried her, "there in the way of Ephrath."

> Be near me when all else is from me drifting,
> Stars, sky, home pictures, days of shade and shine,
> And kindly faces to my own uplifting,
> The love that answers mine.
>
> Suffice it, if my good and ill unreckoned,
> And both forgiven by Thine abounding grace,
> I find myself by hands familiar beckoned,
> Unto my fitting place.
>
> WHITTIER

When the old man came back from his pathetic reverie, the first sight which arrested him was the presence of the awestruck boys, who were drinking in every look and word, with fixed and almost breathless heed.

"Who are these?" said Israel.

"They are my sons," was the proud and immediate reply, "whom God hath given me in this place."

And Israel said, "Bring them, I pray thee, unto me, and I will bless them."

And so they were brought near, and the aged lips were pressed on the young foreheads, and the aged arms were put feebly around the young and slender forms. And then again the dying man wandered back to a grief which had left as deep a scar as his sorrow for the beloved Rachel, and turning to Joseph, he reminded him of the long years

during which he thought he would never look again upon his face. But
now, God, who may keep men waiting, but loves to fill their lives ultimately with blessing, had shown him also his seed.

With prophetic insight he crossed his hands, as the two lads waited
before him for his blessing, so that his right found its way to the head
of the younger, while his left alighted on that of the elder. By that act
he reversed the verdict of their birth, and gave the younger prece-
dence over the elder. It was useless for Joseph to remonstrate, and to
urge the claims of his firstborn. The old man knew quite well what he
was doing, and that he was on the line of the divine purpose. "I know
it, my son, I know it; he also shall become a people, and he also shall
be great: but truly his younger brother shall be greater than he, and his
seed shall become a multitude of nations."

There was nothing arbitrary in this; for in all likelihood there
were qualities in Ephraim, as afterwards in his descendants, which naturally put him in the foremost place. The Old Testament is full of hope
for younger sons: Jacob was a younger son; so was Moses; so was
Gideon; so was David. It is not an unmitigated blessing to be born into
the world with a great name and estate and traditions; it is better to
trust in one's own right arm and in the blessing of the Almighty. God
is no respecter of persons, and He will lift the youngest into the front
rank if only he sees the qualities which warrant it; while He will put
back the foremost into the lower ranks if they are deficient in noble attributes. Thus the first become last, and the last first.

With hands crossed over the young heads the patriarch spoke
sweet and grateful words of the Angel who had redeemed him from all
evil; and his words are so chosen, and that name is so placed in a
parallelism with the name of God who had shepherded him all his life
long, that we are convinced that he is speaking of the Angel-Jehovah,
who is so often referred to on the pages of the Old Testament; and who
can be no other than the Second Person of the ever-blessed Trinity,
whose delights have always been with the sons of men, and who, before He took on Himself the form of a man, was often found in that
of an angel.

We, too, have an Angel guardian, yea, *the* Angel, who is Jesus
Christ the Lord. If you want to be redeemed from all evil, especially

from the evil of sin, make much of Him. And if He began his redemptive work long years before He suffered, died, and rose, how
much more will He do for us now that He sits on the right hand of
God! Take heart, you who are anxious about your daily food. Listen to
the testimony of this dying man, that God had fed him all his life long
unto that day. And if God did so for a hundred and forty-seven years,
surely He will not forget you during the briefer span of your few
days.

There was one thing only more to say, before this memorable interview ended. Years before, Jacob had become embroiled through
the dastardly treachery of his sons, in conflict with the original inhabitants of Canaan, and had been compelled, in self-defense, to acquire by force a parcel of land, with his sword and with his bow. *This*
he gave as an additional portion to his favorite son.

Would that all young persons who read these lines may so act towards their parents that they may never give them an anxious moment:
that they may be their pride in life; their stay in death: so that in
after years they may have the memory of deathbed blessings, and
may have nothing to regret! A parent's dying blessing is a richer legacy
than gold or lands.

III. JOSEPH'S THIRD AND LAST VISIT. Once more Joseph visited that
death chamber. This was the third time and the last. But this time he
stood only as one of twelve strong, bearded men, who gathered around
the aged form of their father, his face shadowed by death, his spirit
aglow with the light of prophecy. How intense the awe with which they
heard their names called, one by one, by the old man's trembling
voice, now pausing for breath, now speaking with great difficulty!
The character of each is criticized with prophetic insight; the salient
points of their past history are vividly brought to mind; and some foreshadowing is given them of their future.

This scene is an anticipation of the Judgment seat: where men shall
hear the story of their lives passed under review; and a sentence passed,
against which there shall be no appeal.

But the dying patriarch speaks with peculiar sweetness and grace,
when he comes to touch on the destiny of his favorite son. His words

brim with tenderness, and move with a stateliness and eloquence, which indicate how his heart was stirred to its depths. This was his swan song, the final outburst of the music of his soul, the last flash of that Spirit of Inspiration, which dwelt also in him. What a glimpse is given to us into the depths of his soul; the secret thoughts of fruitfulness, patience, and strength, and the far-reaching conceptions of blessedness, which had been wrought out within him by the slow process of years of sorrow and training!

A few more sentences to Benjamin, and the venerable patriarch drew up his feet into his bed, and quietly breathed his last, and was gathered unto his people. But that eager, much-tried spirit passed up and away into other scenes of more exalted fellowship and ministry, with no pause in his life, for in afteryears God attested his continued existence and energy when He called Himself "the God of Jacob," for God is not God of the dead, but of the living. And Joseph fell upon his father's face, and wept upon him, and pressed his warm lips on the death-cold clay; and he commanded the physicians to embalm his body, so cheating death of its immediate victory.

13

The Secret of Fruitfulness

*Do I need here
To draw the lesson of this life: or say
More than these few words, following up the text:
The vine from every living limb bleeds wine,
Is it the poorer for that spirit shed?
Measure thy life by loss instead of gain;*

*Not by the wine drunk, but the wine poured forth;
For love's strength standeth in love's sacrifice;
And whoso suffers most hath most to give.*

Genesis 49:22   Mrs. Hamilton King

A fruitful bough by a well." Often had the eyes of the dying man been refreshed by such a spectacle greeting him amid wastes of sand—an oasis in the desert. For hours the weary caravan has been pressing on, parched tongues cleaving to the mouths, eyes scorching in the head, the strength of the patient beasts and of the women and children almost giving out. When, lo, the monotony of desert is broken by a welcome sight! Over some grey crumbling stones a vine reaches out its verdant and fruitful arms; and all press forward with redoubled haste, knowing most surely that down beneath, the rootlets must be spreading themselves in dark, cool depths, where the longed-for water is stored.

It will well repay us to go into the vinery, and talk with some experienced vinedresser of the growth of the vine, which had been a familiar object with our blessed Lord from early boyhood, and led Him to select the vine as the emblem of the union between Himself and those who believe. "I am the true Vine," said He, the Vine of which all others are parables and types. He might have chosen the summer corn, or the olive, or the forest tree, but He chose the vine, which clings, stretching out innumerable tendrils by which to hold and climb.

443

> And as it grows it is not free to heaven,
> But tied unto a stake; and if its arms stretch out
> It is but crosswise, also forced and bound;
> And so it draws out of the hard hillside
> Fixed in its own place, its own food of life.

Visit the vine in the late autumn, when its treasures have been torn from it. While the land is full of joy it stands stripped and desolate. Its sap sinks down to the root; its branches are cut back to the stem; its very bark is peeled off; and it is left to the nipping of the merciless frost. Nothing more desolate and dismal can be conceived in plant life than the death which reigns supreme over the vine through the long, lone winter. And as we contrast the glory of the spring with such desolation, we remember the words of Him who said, "Except a corn of wheat fall into the ground and die, it abideth alone, but if it die, it bringeth forth much fruit"; and how, outcast and forsaken, He hung upon the Cross, in what may well be said to have been the darkest, saddest, hour of winter through which earth ever passed.

But when the sun leads back the spring, the sap begins to flow again; and beneath its impulse the branches start right and left from the long bare stems, and presently, when there is sun, flowers and the promise of fruit appear.

> The flower of the vine is but a little thing,
> The least part of its life. You scarce could tell
> It ever had a flower; the fruit begins
> Almost before the flower has had its day.

Sunshine is essential. Without it the vine bears "nothing but leaves"—leaves in profusion, but leaves only. It is not enough for us to be connected by a living faith to Jesus: we must hold fellowship with Him, sunning ourselves in his smile, communing with Him, and surrendered to his companionship; so only can we hope to bear something more than the leaves of a mere profession.

But though the vine needs sunshine, *it must also have the darkness.* During the night it is said to rest: it does not grow, but it recuperates itself and prepares for the putting forth of fresh energy. During the day it consumes more sap than it can draw up from the root; and during the dark hours of night it is accumulating stores on which to feed. And this may suggest why sometimes after periods of much activity the great Husbandman draws down the blinds and he plunges us into the black night of sorrow, or solitude, or depression. We have been too prodigal of our resources, and need time in order to recuperate our exhausted vigor, and to gather up stores for days to come.

The fruitfulness, however, of the vine largely depends on the care with which it is pruned. There is no tree pruned so mercilessly and incessantly, first with the sharp knife, and then with scissors. The Lord has many such implements. There is the *golden* pruning knife of his Word, by which He would prune us if we would let Him (John 15:3), so escaping the rougher and more terrible discipline of the *iron* pruning knife of affliction. Our Lord uses the knife, with its sharp clean strokes, which cut deep into our nature, and leave scars which it will take years to heal, or even to conceal. And there are the scissors also in his hand—cross events, daily circumstances which appear contrary to each other, but which nevertheless work together in the end for good.

So great are the spring prunings that more branches are taken out than left in; and the cuttings which litter the ground are said to be utterly worthless and fit only for the fire. Apple and pear prunings are used in many ways, such as supports for young and frail plants, but not so these. And so there are many professors among us, who have neither part nor lot with us, who must be taken away; just as there are many things in us all which need pruning out. What a comfort it is that the Vinedresser leaves the pruning to no 'prentice hand! The novice does anything but that. No hand but the most skilled may handle the knife. "My Father is the husbandman."

It is a recognized rule that no shoot should have more than one bunch of grapes. All but that one are nipped off. And I am told that the vinedresser will obtain a greater weight of better grapes in that one bunch, than he would by permitting two or three clusters to form. And so with merciless hand he picks off bunch after bunch of unformed fruit and berry after berry from the reddening swelling cluster. It is thus that we are sometimes shut away from one after another of our chosen directions of Christian activity: not that our father would diminish our fruitbearing, but that the strength of our life may be saved from dissipation, and conducted by one channel to a better and richer fruitage.

How many pruned ones may read these words! They are inclined to say that the Lord hath dealt very bitterly with them. Husband and sons buried in a distant land; poverty and want supreme in a deserted and darkened home; only one left of all the merry circle of bygone years: and yet out of all this shall come a golden harvest of blessing; and the one little grandson pressed to the heart, and his line to David, the sweet Psalmist and mighty king, shall be better than seven sons, and shall make the aged heart young again. "No chastisement for the present seemeth to be joyous, but grievous: nevertheless afterward it yieldeth the peaceable fruit of righteousness unto them which are exercised thereby" (Ruth 4:15; Heb. 12:11).

It is very needful that the pruned branch should abide constantly in the vine. "Abide in Him!" (1 John 2:28) This command was given first to *little children.* It was thus the beloved Apostle, whose head was silvered with many winters, wrote to young men and fathers, in the tender relationship of their father in the Gospel of Jesus. But there is a sense in which we too must become as little children, ere we can learn this sweet lesson of abiding in Him.

The little child is not self-confident: it fears the untried and unknown; it seeks the companionship of mother or friend; and it is willing to be led. Oh for the child heart, with its simplicity and trust; its unbounded faith and lovely guilelessness! Many strong men may read these words who glory in their strength, but they must be converted, and become as little children, if they would learn the secret of abiding in Him. When we are emptied of our own strength and self-confidence, and are utterly beaten and broken, we shall be ready to obey this saintly counsel, which is the echo of the master's own command—"Abide in Me!"

It is said of the great soldier Naaman that "his flesh came to him as the flesh of a little child." It was a splendid combination! The stalwart form of the man of war combined with the soft, sweet flesh of childhood. And these qualities should blend in each of us—strong and simple, manly and childlike; like David, the champion of Israel, whose heart was not haughty, or exercised in matters too great, but was like a child weaned from its mother. Such are counted by the father as his babes; fed with the sincere milk of the Word; taught secrets which are hidden from the wise and prudent; and instructed in the art of abiding in Him.

It is not easy to abide in Christ all at once. It is the growth of years; the result of perpetual watching and self-discipline; the outcome of the blessed Spirit's tender influence on the inner life. It is not at first easy to get the creeper to entwine itself in some chosen direction. The string, and hammer, and knife, must be used, but in time it is satisfied to adopt the new and forced attitude. And the clinging of the soul to Christ comes as the result of prolonged habit and self-discipline beneath the culture of the Spirit of God.

The Holy Spirit will teach us to abide in Him. "The anointing which ye have received of Him abideth in you"; and *anointing* is always used as a symbol of the Spirit's grace. *"And even as it hath taught you, ye shall abide in Him."* This blessed art is taught by the Holy Spirit to those who are willing—eager—to learn. Never leave your room in the morning without lifting up your heart to Him and saying, "Teach me, O blessed, to abide in Christ for today: keep me in abiding fellowship with Him; even when I am not directly thinking of Him, may I be still abiding." Expect that He will do this. And when drifting from these moorings lift up your heart and say, "O my Lord, who art the Life and Light of men, give me more of thy Spirit, that I may better abide in Thee."

Abiding in Christ does not mean that you must always be thinking about Christ. You are in a house, abiding in its enclosure or beneath its shelter, though you are not always thinking about the house itself. *But you always know when you leave it.* A man may not be always thinking of his sweet home circle, but he and they may nevertheless be abiding in each other's love. And he knows instantly when any of them is in danger of passing out of the warm tropic of love into the arctic region of separation. So we may not always be sensible of the revealed presence of Jesus; we may be occupied with many things of necessary duty—but as soon as the heart is disengaged it will become aware that He has been standing near all the while; and there will be a bright flash of recognition, and a repetition of the Psalmist's cry, "Thou art near,

O Lord!" Ah, life of bliss, lived under the thought of his presence, as dwellers in Alpine valleys live beneath the solemn splendor of some grand snowcapped range of mountains!

Abiding in Christ means a life of converse with Him. To tell Him all; to talk over all anxieties and occurrences with Him; to speak with Him aloud as to a familiar and interested friend; to ask his counsel or advice; to stop to praise, to adore, and utter words of love; to draw heavily upon his resources, as the branch on the sap and life of the vine; to be content to be only a channel, so long as his power and grace are ever flowing through; to be only the bed of a stream hidden from view beneath the hurrying waters, speeding without pausing towards the sea. This is abiding in Christ; this is what David must have meant when he said, "One thing have I desired of the Lord, that will I seek after, that I may dwell in the house of the Lord all the days of my life: to behold the beauty of the Lord, and to inquire in his temple."

When this abiding is secured, the root will supply all needed power in fruit-bearing. Methinks I have overheard the branches complaining that it is quite impossible to expect from them the ruddy clusters of the autumn. "Alas!" they sigh, "if you look for fruit from us, you are expecting impossibilities: we can never produce it." But they are not expected to produce it; they have only to be still, and let the root pour its tides of sap through their open ducts. And it will be discovered in blessed experience that there need be no striving, no effort, no "must" in the matter, but that spontaneously and naturally and easily the juices of the plant will break forth into manifestation, and will swell into the luscious cluster of purple grapes. The difficulty will not be in bearing, but in not bearing. There is a whole heaven of difference between *fruit* and *works*—the fruits of the Spirit, and the works of the flesh.

Oh that Christian people would learn that there is a great danger in their putting forth their own self-directed energies in Christian living; and that their true power consists in being still, while Jesus from his hidden life in heaven pours out through them his grace and power and blessing on the world.

This is the true cure for depression on the one hand, and for pride on the other. For depression: because however weak we are, our weakness cannot be a barrier to the forth-putting of his might. Indeed, it will be the chosen condition of its greatest manifestation; for surely more glory will accrue to Him, if He produces much fruit through those from whom no such results could otherwise have been anticipated. For pride: because clearly the branch cannot exalt itself as the creator of the fruit, when it has been simply the channel through which the fruit has been produced.

The whole life of the vine with its fruitful boughs is a parable of self-sacrifice. The one aim of its existence is to bear fruit, "to cheer God and man." Not even rule over the trees is to be compared with this (Judg. 9:13). And the passion which fills the heart of Jesus, and of us also, if we have drunk into his spirit, is to bear fruit for the glory of the Father, in the blessing and salvation of men. Our Lord is set on revealing to men those hidden beauties of the nature of God, with which He has been familiar from before the birth of time; and He communicates this desire to his true disciples (John 15:8).

It is clear, therefore, that our pleasure and plans and personal gains must all be laid aside in order that this purpose may be secured. It was said by James Hinton, who had seen deeply into the heart of Christ, "If God could give us the best and greatest gift, that which above all others we might long for and aspire after, even though in despair, it is this—that He must give us the privilege He gave his Son, to be used and sacrificed for the best and greatest end." But how few of us have really entered into the spirit of this thought! We seek our life; we hedge ourselves about; we are ambitious to get a brief power; we give to others what we can easily spare. And so we lose from our lives their joy and power. But if we could but learn to efface ourselves in daily, hourly self-sacrifice, always considering what Jesus desires to do by us, and what will best promote the highest welfare of earth's weary and toiling myriads, then our joy would be full; we should live at the well-head of life; we should climb with elastic steps those higher levels of experience, where men may see the pavement of sapphire stones and the clearness of the light of heaven.

14
The Secret of Strength

My faith looks up to claim that touch divine
Which robs me of this fatal strength of mine,
And leaves me wholly resting, Lord, on thine.

Yea, make me such a one as Thou canst bless;
Meet for thy use, through very helplessness—
Thine, only thine, the glory of success.

Genesis 49:24   Lucy A. Bennett

s the battle swept over the fatal field of Mount Gilboa, on
which David wished that no dew might ever fall again, as if
to make his horror as the tragedy enacted there; we are told
that "the battle went sore against Saul, and the archers hit him; and he
was sore wounded of the archers." A side light is thus cast on the
dying words of Jacob, in which he referred to the cruelty and malignity
which had followed his beloved Joseph from childhood. "The archers,"
said the old man, "have sorely grieved him, and shot at him, and
hated him." One can almost see the faces of those bitter foes, stern with
cruel hate, the bowstrings drawn tight back against their ears, as they
hotly follow on the steps of their prey, and sorely grieve him.

Is it not marvelous then that he should be able to add, "but his bow
abode in strength"? It is one of those strange paradoxes, of which
there are so many instances in Scripture. Here are some of them: "The
lame take the prey"; "When I am weak, then am I strong"; "God hath
chosen the weak things of the world to confound the things which are
mighty." These are specimens of many more, in which the natural
weakness and impotence of the mortal is nevertheless made sufficient

451

to withstand the onsets of the foe, and hurl them back, becoming more than victorious.

Has not this been also proved true in our own experience? We are too weak enough, sorely pressed by our foes, and sometimes almost driven to despair. And yet we have continued until now; nay, we have been enabled to abide in some measure of strength. The foe has not prevailed. At the moment when he seemed on the point of victory, he has suddenly been compelled to give way; his legions have been scattered as by the invisible, but irresistible breath of God. The fire has burned under water. One has chased a thousand; and two have put ten thousand to flight.

The secret is not a hidden one. It is clearly revealed in the following words, which tell us that

> The arms of his hands were made strong
> By the hands of the mighty God of Jacob.

It is a beautiful picture. There stands the weak child in whose slender arms there are no muscles strong enough to draw the string or bend the bow, which he vainly tries to use. They resist his utmost endeavors. Evidently he has neither might nor strength.

But now see, on his weak hands there are laid other hands, mighty hands, hands that wove the tapestry of the heavens, and that hold in their hollows the depths of the seas: one of these is placed where the left hand holds the bow; the other where the right hand plucks the string. And now with what ease those thin hands wield the bow; it is a plaything in their grasp; and without apparent strain the arrow flies to its mark. Is not this what David meant in after days, when he sang,

> He teacheth my hands to war,
> So that a bow of steel is broken
> By mine arms?

There is another Old Testament incident, which gives a vivid illustration and enforcement of these striking words. Elisha was near his end. His had been a mighty life. Like a war chariot with its fiery steeds he had brought deliverance to his fatherland. What wonder then, in that sad time when disasters were falling thick and fast on Israel and the royal house, that the king came down for a final word of cheer and help. The answer of the dying seer was remarkable. It seemed as if the heart of a soldier had beaten under his prophet's robe, and that the ruling passion had flamed up strong in death.

"Take bow and arrows," said he. "And the king took unto him bow and arrows." Then as the king put his strong muscular sun-browned hands on the bow, the old man put his above them, and the two shot the arrow of the Lord's deliverance through the window opened toward the sunrise, where beyond the Jordan valley the land of the Syrians lay.

Perhaps this touching incident would have better illustrated the words of Jacob, if the chill hands of the dying prophet had been under the warm powerful palms of the king. But still the main point is to notice the combination; and to see how weakness becomes able for deeds of strength, when it permits itself to be molded, guided, wielded, used, by the hands of a mighty man of valor.

The Apostle, who was the most like Christ, and the best loved, tells us a secret when he says, "Our fellowship is with the Father, and with his Son, Jesus Christ." And the word rendered *fellowship* might be translated *partnership;* the common interests into which the saintly heart may enter with the mighty God. Ah, what a combination is here! We cannot, but He can! Our weakness supplemented by his Strength! Our impotence married in immortal union with his Omnipotence. Here, indeed, is a compensating balance. The less there is of us, and the feebler our condition, the greater scope is there for the putting forth of a Might before which cables snap as stalks of straw; and by which opposition is swept away as the cobweb swung across the garden path is caught on the dress of the impetuous child rushing along in an ecstasy of exuberant life.

The old legend tells us that Ulysses, returning home after long years, proved his identity by bending a bow which had defied the efforts of these toutest heroes who had tried it in his absence. There are a good many of these defiant bows lying all around us. Tasks that deride our puny efforts; empty churches that will not fill; wicked neighborhoods that will not yield; hardened soils that will not admit the plowshare to cut into their crust. The one thing of which we need to assure ourselves is—whether it be God's will for us to take them in hand: if not, it is useless to attempt the task; we may as well husband and reserve our strength. But if it is made clear to us that we are to take up armor, methods, instrumentalities, once wielded by giant hands, but now as unbefitting these poorer times as the armor of the age of chivalry mocks at the smaller make of modern warriors—let us not hesitate for a single moment, let us assume the armor of defense and the weapons of attack; and, as we do so, we shall become aware of a strength being infused into us—not ours, but his: "the arms of our hands will be made strong by the hands of the mighty God of Jacob."

The condition of this strength is our consciousness of utter weakness. We are too strong for God. Our self-confidence shuts Him out of our lives. We require to be taken down to Gideon's brook, that we may be reduced to the minimum of our own energy, and be filled to the maximum of his. It was this that made Paul glory in his infirmities, where other men would have thought their infirmities debarred them from Christian usefulness. He accounted that they were the greater reason for anticipating success. Tell him that his words lacked eloquence, or that his appearance was unprepossessing, or that his thorn in the flesh made him a cripple in Christ's army—he would have answered, "I rejoice in them all—nay, I glory in them. All hail, ye blessed arguments for self-abasement, and for reckoning more completely on the mighty power of Christ!"

Do not longer assume that you cannot bend the bow of difficulty lying at your feet. You cannot do it alone, but God and you can do it together. Only do not try to feel able to do it before you take it up. You will never feel strong enough, but when you take it in hand and try to bend it, you will discover that as your day so is your strength. In the act of getting up, the paralyzed man received strength to stand. Act as if you had omnipotent power; and you will discover that you have it allied with you, and working through you, to the accomplishment of purposes of which you had not dared to dream in the wildest flights of fancy.

"All power," said our Lord, "is given to Me in heaven and on earth: go ye therefore, and teach." And it is added, with blessed emphasis, by another evangelist, and in beautiful corroboration of the spirit of these words, "They went forth and preached everywhere; the Lord working with them, and confirming the Word with signs following." This was no extraordinary circumstance; it is simply the normal state of those who have yielded themselves up as channels for the mighty God to work through their lives.

A telegraph wire may as easily carry the power generated by a Niagara as by a waterwheel, to light some distant city, or drive some vast machinery. And we can be vehicles through whom Divine power can reach a dying world. Till now our own energy and might have passed through us as a slow goods train over the metals, but they will as easily sustain the rush of the express. There is no reason why, from this moment, each earnest reader of these lines may not become a medium through whom the mighty God of Jacob shall work some marvelous exhibition of power: and when it is achieved there shall be no envy or pride, because it will be obvious that He has a perfect right to use what vessel He pleases, and the glory of the issue must be given to Him whose mind planned, and whose power executed, the fair and blessed result.

15

The Secret of Blessedness

Genesis 49:25, 26

He always wins who sides with God—to him no chance is lost;
God's will is sweetest to him, when it triumphs at his cost.
Ill that He blesses is our good, and unblest good our ill;
And all is right that seems most wrong, if it be His sweet will.

F. W. Faber

Unto what a rapture did the old man rise when describing the blessedness of his favorite son! Indeed his language failed him. His words staggered beneath the weight of meaning with which he charged them. Reverting to the blessings which is progenitors had invoked on their firstborn sons, and recalling the memorable words which in that strange moment of unmingled emotion the patriarch Isaac had uttered years before over his own bowed head, he declared that his blessings prevailed above the blessings of all who had preceded him. And then, as old men will, he traveled away from the flat sand plains of Egypt, unbroken by mound or hill, to the mountainous country of his earliest years, and avowed that his desire for the blessedness of Joseph reared itself above all other, as the everlasting hills tower up above the plains lying outspread at their feet.

But even though he had gone on to heap metaphor on metaphor, hyperbole on hyperbole, he could have given but vague hints of that weight of glory and blessedness which are ours in Him of whom Joseph was an imperfect representative and type. Yea, even the multiplied Beatitudes of Deuteronomy 28 do but furnish the barest outlines

457

for us to fill in with colors borrowed from the palettes of the Gospels and Epistles. The last glimpse that the Apostolic band caught of the ascending Lord was with the outspread hands of blessing. So He left us: so He continues through the ages. He still sits on the Mount, calling his disciples unto Him, and saying "Blessed." And in the Apocalypse there are several additional Beatitudes recorded, a part of a great multitude which no man can number, ever proceeding from his dear lips. "Blessed be the God and Father of our Lord Jesus Christ, who hath blessed us with all spiritual blessings in heavenly places in Christ."

THE BLESSINGS OF DAILY HELP. "The God of thy father shall help thee." The earthly father must die, but the Heavenly Father abides as a very present and unfailing help. In every emergency we may hear His still small voice hushing our fear, and saying—

> Fear thou not; for I am with thee;
> I the Lord thy God will hold thy right hand.
> Saying unto thee,
> Fear not, I will help thee.

Well then may we join with one sacred writer in boldly saying, "The Lord is my helper; and I will not fear what man shall do unto me"; and with the Apostle, who more than most had learned to lean hard on God's helpfulness, "Having, therefore, obtained help of God, I continue unto this day."

God's help does not, for the most part, come miraculously or obviously. It steals as gradually into our life as the grass of spring clothes the hills with fresh and verdant robes. Before men can say, "Lo, here! or lo, there!" it has suddenly entered into our need and met it. A smile, a flower, a letter, a burst of music, the picture of a bit of mountain scenery, a book, the coming of a friend—such are the ways in which God comes to our help. Not helping us far in advance, but just for one moment at a time. Not giving us a store of strength to make us proud, but supplying our need as the occasion comes. Sometimes the Almighty helps us by putting his wisdom and strength and grace into our hearts; sometimes by manipulating circumstances in our behalf; and sometimes by inclining friends or foes to do the very thing we need. But it matters little as to the channel—only let us rest confidently in the certainty of receiving what we need. It may be delayed to the last moment, but it will come. "God shall help when the morning appeareth" (Ps. 46:5, *marg.*). If the last post has come in without bringing the expected assistance, then wait up and expect a special messenger. "There is none like unto the God of Jeshurun, who rideth upon the heaven in thy help, and in his excellency on the sky."

When the godly man ceaseth and the faithful fail, there is no cry that so befits our lips as the brief statement with which the Psalmist commences Psalm 12; and this is the response attested by old experience, and by the spirit of inspiration: "The God of thy father shall help thee."

THE BLESSINGS OF HEAVEN ABOVE. All that God is and has He has deposited in our blessed Lord Jesus, as the Trustee and Representative of his own. "It was the good pleasure of the Father that in Him should all the fullness dwell." And thus it is gloriously true, that "in Him dwelleth all the fullness of the Godhead bodily; and in Him ye are made full" (Col. 1:19; 2:9, 10, R.V.).

This fullness of heavenly blessing is laid up for us in Jesus, as water is stored in Eastern countries for use through the long drought. The only difference being that in the latter case the sun may dry up, or the dam break, or the demand be too great for the supply. But in the case of Christ, the stores of grace have never ceased to brim. In spite of all the demands made on Him by ages of needy saints, He is as full at this hour as ever. The sun may shine less brilliantly; the moon grow withered through the ages; the course of Nature waste more quickly than the reparative processes can renew—but the stores of Jesus are absolutely as they were when, in the first flush of his Ascension glory, He sat down at the right hand of the throne of God. "They shall perish, but Thou continuest: and they all shall wax old as doth a garment; and as a mantle shalt Thou roll them up—as a garment—and they shall be changed: but Thou art the same, and Thy years shall not fail" (Ps. 102: 26, 27, R.V.).

The difference that exists between believers lies, not in any arbitrary distinction in the Divine allotment, for God gives to each one of us all that He has and is; and to each He says, "All that I have is thine." But the difference lies in the use which each makes of his divine portion.

It is as if a wealthy father were to bequeath to each of his five sons the sum £10,000. One of them is unable to believe that so great a sum stands to his name in the bank, and so makes no use of it at all, leads a pauper's life, and dies in an almshouse. Others have faith enough to believe that there may be £10,000 to their credit, and work up to that limit, thankful for so much, but fearing to go beyond. While the fifth, and youngest, believes that the father has not promised what he could not perform, and so goes on claiming more and ever more, till his whole patrimony has been absorbed; and then he discovers that a proviso in his father's will also permits him to use all the unemployed sums which had stood in his brother's names, but which they had forborne to use. "Take the talent from him, and give it unto him which hath ten talents. For unto every one that hath shall be given; and he shall have abundance." The same unsearchable riches are for each and all: but some do not use their rightful portion; others only in part; and the number is comparatively small of those who really dip deeply into the perennial all-sufficiency of Jesus.

It is the work of the Holy Spirit to convey these heavenly blessings into the soul. From his throne our master is ever sending fleets of heavy laden argosies to us beneath the convoy and guidance of the Holy Spirit, who glorifies Christ in revealing what He is, and making us the happy recipients of grace on grace.

What blessedness might be ours if only we opened all the ports of our being to the heavenly merchantmen bearing in to us from all the winds of heaven! It would be in the inner realm, as it is said to have been in Jerusalem in the days when Hiram's navy brought to it the wealth of the Orient: "And the king made silver to be in Jerusalem as stones; and cedars made he to be as the sycamore trees that are in the vale, for abundance."

We are to be in this world as our Master was: we are to have a similar access to the throne of grace, and the same power in prayer; to share his joy, his peace, his power; to be the members of the body through which He works, and on which He expends tender care in nourishing and cherishing it; to be called his friends, to whom He confides those secret things which his Father makes known to Him. We are to be so filled with all the fullness of God; so strong, and healthy, and robust, that there shall not be "one feeble person" in all the host, but that "the feeble shall be as David, and the house of David as God, as the angel of the Lord before them." All this is God's intention for us, and might be ours if only we would arise to claim by faith that which is ours by the gift of our Heavenly Father, and the purchase of the precious blood.

THE BLESSINGS OF THE UNDERLYING DEEP. In all likelihood these words refer to some kind of thought that underneath the surface of the earth there lie vast deeps of water which supply "the brooks of water, of fountains, and depths that spring out of valleys and hills."

There is physical truth in this; and, above all, spiritual truth. For the depths have also blessings for us. The deep things of God, which pass the comprehension of the natural man: which eye hath not seen, nor ear heard, nor the heart conceived, but which God hath prepared for them that wait for Him, and revealed to them that love Him—what deeps are these! The deep of his Eternal prescience and counsel. The deep of his covenant, spanning with rainbow arc the dark mystery of evil, and ordered in all things and sure. The deep of a love which would descend to shame and agony; willing rather to bear our sin than to lose us. The deep of his marvelous patience, which tires not amid our fretful petulance and frequent backslidings. Ah, what deeps are these! Deep calls unto deep, as wave challenges wave; and the Atlantic calls across the Isthmus of Panama to the mighty Pacific, the ocean of the thousand isles. Here is food for thought! How foolish are we so to feed the outer sense, that the spiritual vision becomes darkened through disuse; and we get to know so little of the great abyss which we call God, which engirdles us as a summer sea does the coral islet floating upon its breast. These are things into which angels desire to look, and stoop that they may behold, but we unfortunately refuse to imitate them, and, reversing the Apostle's attitude, look at the things which are seen, rather than at the things which are not seen, and which are eternal. "The deep that lieth under!"

THE BLESSINGS OF CHILDREN. The Eastern glories in the number of his children. "Blessed is the man that hath his quiver full of them," is the glad response to the primal command, "Be fruitful, and multiply, and replenish the earth." Nor was there any need to dread the multiplication of children in a land where shepherds were needed for flocks, and high-born maidens did not shrink from what we should call menial work. And then there were abundant spaces on the rolling pasture lands, or on the lone hillsides, for the vast expansion of the arts of life; and for husbandry and tillage. Under such circumstances children were indeed welcome for the defense and aggrandizement of family life; and such thoughts must have been in the heart of the dying man.

And there is a sense in which we may say that God has no higher blessing to give than to allow us to look on many spiritual children. To be greeted as the instrument of the salvation of many who but for us had never known Christ and his salvation; to anticipate the moment of standing with them before God, saying, "Behold, I and the children whom the Lord hath given me"; to think of the ever-widening circles of influence which must spread from any one soul truly born for our Redeemer: is there under the sun a purer joy than this? But his blessing is within our reach, through the grace of God.

We must never forget, however, *the condition on which all these blessings depend*. "They shall be on the crown of the head of him that was separate from his brethren." We must not expect that we can have these choice blessings from God, unless we devote ourselves exclusively to Him and to his service. He gives his prizes, as the world gives its, to those who devote themselves wholly to their pursuit. Joseph was not only separated from his brethren and father by the distance which lay between Egypt and Canaan, but by the temper of his mind when he lived among them. Their aims were not his; nor his theirs. His heart was absorbed with motives and desires which found no place in theirs, or which would have been treated as unwelcome intruders. And it was this consciousness which embittered them against him, and led to his violent expulsion from their midst. The citizens of Vanity Fair cannot away with pilgrims, whose garb is outlandish, whose faces are set on a goal beyond their city, and who hasten through their streets, crying, "We buy the truth."

We, too, must come out and be separate; not adopting any particular style of dress, but cultivating the inner temple, which confesses that its true home lies beyond the stars; that its aim is to do the will of God; and that its loftiest ambition is to have the smile of the Master's glad "Well done!"

And when once the will has assumed this position, surrendering many things for the one thing—not only is there a great peace in the heart, but there is a growing appreciation of the blessings which we have so inadequately portrayed. They seem to bulk more largely on the vision; to become more real, and precious, and satisfactory; until they engross the soul with their rapturous fascination into an even greater separation from the passing shows of time. These two tempers act and react. On the one side we choose the blessedness of the separated life, because God bids us: and on the other, the more we know of it, the more we are weaned away from the delights with which the world attracts its votaries; and we say with the Psalmist, "Lord, my heart is not haughty, nor mine eyes lofty; neither do I exercise myself in great matters, or in things too high for me. Surely I have behaved and quieted myself, as a child that is weaned of his mother: my soul is even as a weaned child."

16

Joseph's Last Days and Death

Twighlight and evening bell,
And after that the dark;
And may there be no sadness of farewell
When I embark.

For when from out our bourne of time and place,
The flood shall bear me far,
I hope to see my Pilot face to face,
When I have crossed the bar.

Genesis 50:24, 25   Tennyson

God will surely visit you, and ye shall carry up my bones from hence." These were the dying words of Joseph. And it is somewhat remarkable that these are the only words in his while career which are referred to in the subsequent pages of the Scriptures. His life was a noble one, and, with one exception, the most fascinating in the sacred record, but this last dying speech is singled out from all the rest for special notice of the Holy Ghost. Of course, I refer to those words in Hebrews 11, where it is said, "By faith Joseph, when he died, made mention of the exodus of the children of Israel; and gave commandment concerning his bones."

Let us notice—

I. THE CIRCUMSTANCES UNDER WHICH THESE WORDS WERE SPO-KEN. *Jospeh was now an old man.* One hundred and ten years had stolen away his strength, and left deep marks upon his form. It was three and ninety years since he had been lifted from the pit to become a slave. Eighty years had passed since he had first stood before Pharaoh in all the beauty and wisdom of his young manhood. And sixty years had left their papyrus records in the State archives, since, with all the

465

pomp and splendor of Egypt's court, he had carried the remains of his old father to Machpelah's ancient cave. So old was he that he saw the bright young faces of his great-grandchildren: "they were brought up upon Joseph's knees." With long life and many days God had blessed his faithful servant. And now, stooping beneath their weight, he was fast descending to the break-up of natural life.

But the shadows of his own decay were small compared with those which he saw gathering around his beloved people. Sixty years before, when Jacob gathered up his feet upon his bed and died, his favorite son was in the zenith of his glory. The days of mourning for the patriarch, just because he was Joseph's father, were only two less in number than those of a king. There was no difficulty in obtaining from Pharaoh the necessary permission to go three hundred miles to inter the remains beside those of Abraham and Sarah, of Isaac and Rebekah, and of Leah.

And, indeed, the funeral procession must have been of a sort not often seen. There was not only the family of Israel, but the officers of the court, and all the elders of the land of Egypt. In other words, the proud and magnates of Egypt, the most exclusive aristocracy in the world, were willing to follow the remains of a shepherd and a Jew to their last resting place, out of honor for his son. "There also went up chariots and horsemen, so that it was a very great company.

But sixty years had brought great changes of which there is evidence in the text. When Jacob died all was bright; and he was honored with a splendid funeral, because he had given to the land of Egypt so great a benefactor and savior in the person of his son, but when Joseph died, all was getting dark, and the shadow of a great eclipse was gathering over the destinies of his people. No notice seems to have been taken in Egypt of his death. No splendid obsequies were voted to him at public expense. No pyamid was placed at the disposal of his sons. And he addresses his brethren gathered about him as being sorely in need of help. It is as if he had said: "I have done my best for you, but I am dying; nevertheless God will fill my place, and do for you all, and more than all, that I would have done myself." There is a tone of comfort in these words, which indicates how much they needed an advocate at court, and an assurance of Divine visitation.

Three hundred years before, the great founder of the nation had watched all day beside an altar, scaring away the vultures which, attracted by the flesh that lay upon it, hovered around. At length, as the sun went down, the watcher fell asleep—it is hard to watch with God—and in his sleep he dreamt. A dense and awful gloom seemed to enclose him, and to oppress his soul, and on it, as upon a curtain, passed successive glimpses of the future of his race—glimpses which a Divine voice interpreted to his ear. He saw them exiled to a foreign country, enslaved by the foreigner and lingering there whilst three generations of men bloomed as spring flowers, and were cut down before the keen sickle of death. And as he beheld all the terror of that enslavement, the horror of a great darkness fell upon his soul. We know how exactly that horror was justified by the events which were so soon to take place. "The Egyptians made the children of Israel to serve with rigor: and they made their lives bitter with hard bondage, in mortar, and in brick, and in all manner of service in the field; all their service, wherein they made them serve, was with rigor." The first symptoms of that outburst of popular "Jew-hate" were already, like stormy petrels, settling about the closing hour of the great Egyptian premier.

We cannot tell the precise form of those symptoms. Perhaps he had been banished from the councils of Pharaoh; perhaps he was already pining in neglect; perhaps the murmurs of dislike against his people were already rising, just as the roar of the breakers against a harbor-bar tells how the mighty ocean is arousing itself to frenzy; perhaps acts of oppression and cruelty were increasingly rife, and increasingly difficult to bring to justice. In any case, the twilight of the dark night was gathering in; and it was this which made his words more splendid: they shone out as stars of hope.

Moreover, his brethren were around him. His forgiveness and love to them lasted till the testing-hour by the great assayer, Death. Nor did *they* fail. From something narrated in the previous verses of this chapter, it would appear that, for long, his brethren, judging of him by their own dark and implacable hearts, could not believe in the sincerity and genuineness of his forgiveness. They thought that he must be feining more than he felt, in order to secure some ulterior object, such as the blessing and approval of their old father. And so they feared that, as soon as Jacob was removed, Joseph's just resentment, long concealed with masterly art, would break forth against them. It seemed impossible to believe that he felt no grudge, and would take no action at all with reference to the past; and they said, "Joseph will certainly requite us all the evil which we did unto him." And Joseph wept when they spake; wept that they should have so misunderstood him after his repeated assurances; wept to see them kneeling at his feet for a forgiveness which he had freely given them years before. "Fear not," said he in effect; "do not kneel there; I am not God: ye thought evil against me, but God meant it for good, to save much people alive, as it is this day."

This forgiveness might well be wonderful to these men, because it *was not of this world at all.* The Lord Jesus, who lighteth every man coming into the world, was in Joseph's heart, though less clearly in Joseph's creed; and his behavior was a foreshadowing of Incarnate Love. Reader! He waits to forgive thee thus. Though thou hast maligned, and refused, and crucified Him afresh, and put Him to an open shame; yet, for all that, He waits to forgive thee so entirely, that not one of these things shall be ever mentioned against thee again; yea, if they are looked for, they shall never be found, any more than a stone can be found which has been cast into the bosom of the Atlantic waves. Oh, give Christ credit for his free and entire forgiveness! And remember that when once He forgives, it is unnecessary and distrustful to go to Him again about the same sin. He cannot forgive the same sin twice; and when once He has pronounced the Words of Absolution over a kneeling penitent, that penitent need never go to Him, as did the brethren of Joseph, and say, Forgive, I pray thee, my trespass and my sin, concerning which, Thou knowest, I came to thee with tears and sighs so many years ago.

It is said of the love of the Lord Jesus that, having loved his own, which were in the world, He loved them unto the end; or, as the margin of the Revised Version puts it, "to the uttermost." He is able to save to the uttermost, because He loves to the uttermost. So was it with the love of Joseph; it had outlived the frosts of the early spring, and it bore fruit and looked fresh now in the late autumn of his last days. Oh that we might love and forgive like this! It is possible on one condition only: that we open our hearts for the entrance and indwelling of Him who, so long before his incarnation, had already found a home beneath the doublet of this great Egyptian statesman.

Lastly, he was dying. He had warded off death from Egypt, but he could not ward it off from himself. "I die." They were among the last words that he had caught from his father's dying lips (48:21), and now he appropriates them to himself; yes, and in doing so, he touches the zenith of his noble confidence and hope. Oh that each of us may go on shining more and more each day until our last, and that, when heart and flesh are failing most conspicuously, the life of the spirit may flash out with its most brilliant coruscations, like the lights from Gideon's broken pitchers. There is no better proof of immortality than this: that in us must be a something more than flesh and blood, which, when these are most impaired, is most bright and most alive to the realities of the eternal world. And there must be a sphere appropriate to the ethereal tenant, who stands so keen and eager, reaching forth, with unimpaired vitality and with unquenchable vigor.

It was under all these circumstances that Joseph said, "God will surely visit you; and ye shall carry up my bones from hence."

II. LET US INVESTIGATE THE FULL IMPORTANCE OF THESE WORDS. And we may do so best by comparing them with Jacob's dying wish: "Bury me with my fathers in the cave that is in the field of Machpelah." This was most natural: we all love to be buried by the beloved dust of our departed. And Jacob knew that there would be no great difficulty in carrying out his wish. Joseph was then in the plenitude of his power. There was no great faith therefore in asking for that which could so easily be accomplished. But with Joseph it was different. He too wanted to be buried in the land of Canaan, but not at once—not then! There were two things he expected would happen: the one, that the people would go out of Egypt; the other, that they would come into the land of Canaan. He did not know when or how; he was only sure that so it would be: "surely."

To Joseph's natural vison these things were most unlikely. When he spoke, Israel was settled in Goshen, and so increasing in numbers and in wealth that any uprooting was becoming daily more unlikely.

And as to the oppression which was perhaps beginning to threaten them, what chance would they have of ever being able to escape from the detaining squadrons of Egypt's chivalry, supposing they wished to go? But his anticipation of the future was not founded on human insight, but on the distinct announcements of the Almighty. He remembered how God had said to Abraham as he stood upon his mountain oratory, "Look from the place where thou art, northward, and southward, and eastward, and westward; for all the land that thou seest, to thee will I give it, and to thy seed forever." That promise was repeated to Isaac. "Unto thee, and unto thy seed, will I give all these countries; and I will perform the oath which I sware unto Abraham thy father."

Again was that promise reiterated to Jacob as he lay at the foot of the shining ladder, "The land whereon thou liest, to thee will I give it, and to thy seed." These promises had been carefully treasured and handed on, as in the old Greek race they handed on the burning torch. Jacob on his death-bed reassured Joseph that God would certainly bring them to the land of their fathers; and now Joseph re-animated the trembling company that gathered around him with the self-same hope. In the memories of all these men the word spoken two hundred years before rang like a peal of silver bells in a moss-grown tower. "They shall come hither again" (Gen. 15:16). Joseph could not trace the method of Divine workmanship: it was enough for him to know that God had said, "They *shall* come hither again." So he commanded that his bones should be unburied, so that at any moment, however hurried, when the trumpet of exodus sounded, they might be ready to be caught up and borne onward in the glad march for Canaan.

What a lesson must those unburied bones have to Israel! When the taskmasters dealt hardly with the people, so that their hearts fainted, it must have been sweet to go and look at the mummy case which held those moldering remains, waiting there to be carried forward; and, as they did so, this was doubtless their reflection, "Evidently, then, Joseph believed that we were not to stay here always, but that we should sooner or later leave for Canaan: let us brace ourselves up to bear a little longer, it may only be a very little while!" Yes, and when some were tempted to settle down content with prospering circumstances, and to feast upon leeks, garlics, an onions, it was a check on them to think of those bones, and say, "Evidently we are not to remain there always: we should do well not to build all our hopes and comfort of the unstable tenure of our sojourn in this place." And, often-times, when the people were ready to despair amid the difficulties and weariness of their desert march, those bones borne in their midst told them of the confident hope of Joseph—that God would bring them to the land of rest.

We have not unburied bones to animate our faith, or to revive our drooping zeal, but we have something better—we have an empty grave. Oh, what volumes does that mutely tell us! When John the Baptist died, his disciples dispersed; when Jesus died, his disciples not only clung together, but sprang up into an altogether new vigor. And well they might! And the difference was made by that empty grave in the garden of Joseph of Arimathea. And what it did for them it will do for us. It tells us that He is risen. It tells us that not death, but life, is to be the guardian angel of our desert march. It tells us that this world is not our resting place or home, but that we must seek these above, where Christ sitteth at the right hand of God. It tells us that resurrection is not possible only, but certain; and that ere long we shall be where He is. He will go with us along the desert pathway, till we go to be with Him, where the shadow of death is never flung over flower, or child, or friend.

III. LET US REALIZE THE SPIRIT THAT UNDERLAY AND PROMPTED THESE WORDS. It was above all a pilgrim spirit. Joseph bore an Egyptian title. He married an Egyptian wife. He shared in Egyptian court-life, politics, and trade. But he was as much a pilgrim as was Abraham pitching his tent outside the walls of Hebron, or Isaac in the grassy plains of the south country, or Jacob keeping himself aloof from the families of the land. "He filled his place at Pharaoh's court, but his dying words open a window into his soul, and betray how little he had felt that he belonged to the order of things in the midst of which he had been content to live. Though surrounded by an ancient civilization, and dwelling among granite temples and solid pyramids and firm-based sphinxes, the very emblems of eternity, he confessed that he had here no continuing city, but sought one to come."*

* Maclaren's Sermons, second series, p. 139.

We sometimes speak as if the pilgrim-spirit were impossible for us who live in this settled state of civilization. Our houses are too substantial; our lives too unromantic; our movements too closely tethered to one narrow round. But if that thought should ever cross our hearts again, let us turn to the life of Joseph, and remind ourselves how evidently he was animated by the spirit of those "who confessed that they were pilgrims and strangers on the earth." Ah, friends, what are we living for? Are our pursuits bounded by the narrow horizon of earth, and limited to the fleeting moments of time? Are we constantly engaged in lining as warmly as possible the nest in which we hope to spend our old age and die? Are we perpetually seeking to make the best of this world? I fear me, that these are the real aims of many professing Christians; and if so, it is simply useless for them to claim kinship with that mighty stream of pilgrims, which is constantly pouring through the earth, bound to the city which hath foundations, their true home and mother-city. On the other hand, it is quite conceivable that you may be at the head of a large establishment, engaged in many permanent undertakings, closely attached to the present by imperious duties; and yet, like Joseph, your heart may be detached from things seen and temporal, and engaged, in all its secret longings, to the things unseen and eternal.

The pilgrim spirit will not make us unpractical. Joseph was the most practical man in his time. Who are likely to be as prompt, as energetic, as thorough, as those who feel that they are working for eternity, and that they are building up day by day a fabric in which they shall live hereafter? Each day is character-building for better or for worse: each deed, well or ill done, is a stone in the edifice; each moment tells on eternity. We shall receive a reward according to our deeds.

But the pilgrim-spirit will make us simple. There are two sorts of simplicity: that of circumstances; and that of heart. Many a man sits down to bread and milk at a wooden table, with a heart as proud as pride can make it: whilst many another who eats off a golden plate is as simple as Cincinnatus at his plow. The world cannot understand this. But herein Joseph is an illustration. Ah, my friend, it is not the unjewelled finger, nor the plain attire, nor the unfinished room, that constitutes a simple unaffected life: but that vision of the spirit, which looks through the unsubstantial wreath-vapors of the morning to the peaks of the everlasting hills beyond and above.

What a contrast there is between the opening and closing words of Genesis! Listen to the opening words: "In the beginning, God." Listen to the closing words, "A coffin in Egypt." And is this all? Is all God's work to end in one poor mummy case? Stay. This is only the end of Genesis, the Book of Beginnings. Turn the leaf, and there are Exodus, and Joshua, and Kings, and Prophets, and Christ. God is not dependent on any one of us. We do our little work and cease, as the coral-insects which perish by myriads on the rising reef. But God's work goes on. His temple rises age after age. And it is enough for each of us, like Joseph, to have lived a true, pure, strong, and noble life—and to leave Him to see after our bodies; our beloved, whom we leave so reluctantly; and our work. Nor will He fail. "And Moses took the bones of Joseph with him," on the night of the exodus (Ex. 13:19); "and they buried the bones of Joseph in Shechem: . . . and it became the inheritance of the children of Joseph" (Josh. 24:32).

IV
Moses: The Servant of God

✠

Preface

The concept of Moses, which I have elaborated in the following chapters, was suggested years ago by contrast with Michelangelo's statue of him, colossal in proportions, hewn in stone.

Yet one turns away from that mighty head, that pregnant brow, towering height, hopeless of repeating aught of a life, which, if that conception be the true one, must have had so little in common with our own. It is a comfort, therefore, to turn to the record of the New Testament, which tells that he did not spring at a leap to the throne on which he has sat through the ages, but that his character took years to form, and that his mighty deeds were due, not to some rare combination of personal qualities, but to the faith which he had in common with the rank and file of the great army of the saints.

I have tried therefore, to show that Moses was a man like other men; with great qualities that needed to be developed and improved; with flaws that veined the pure marble of his character; with deficiencies that had rendered him powerless but for the all-sufficient grace that he learned to appropriate; and that he wrought his life work by the simplicity of his faith, by communion with God, and by becoming a channel through which the Divine purpose was achieved.

I wish to express my special obligations for geographical and other details to the works of the late Dean Stanley; to the monograph on Moses in the "Men of the Bible" Series; as well as to "Modern Science in Bible Lands," by Sir. J. W. Dawson, F.R.G.S.

F. B. Meyer.

1

Our Standpoint

By faith, Moses. . . .
—Hebrews 11:24

The writer of the Epistle to the Hebrews lays bare the secret of the marvels effected by the heroes of Hebrew story. Obedient to his summons, they range themselves in one general battalion, and with united breath, cry, Why marvel ye at these things? Or why look ye so earnestly on us, as though by our own power or holiness we had effected them? The God of Abraham, of Isaac, and of Jacob, the God of our fathers, made bare his holy arm and wrought by us. And his name, through faith in his name, hath done all these wonderful works.

We make a profound mistake in attributing to these men extraordinary qualities of courage, and strength of body or soul. To do so is to miss the whole point of the reiterated teaching of Scripture. They were not different from ordinary men, except in their faith. In many respects it is most likely that they were inferior to ourselves. We should probably be much surprised if we were to encounter them in the daily walks of modern life, and should find it almost impossible to believe that they wrought such prodigies of valor, endurance, and deliverance. Gideon and Barak, Samson and Jephthah, were rather of the

479

type of the sturdy Borderers of olden days, whose wild doings kept our northern counties in constant agitation, than like our modern clerics or Christian philanthropists. But there was one characteristic common to them all, which lifted them above ordinary men, and secured for them a niche in the Temple of Scripture—that they had a marvelous faculty of faith; which, indeed, is but the capacity of the human heart for God. Four times over this is cited as the secret of all that Moses did for his people.

The same truth is repeatedly corroborated in the teaching of our Lord. He never stops to ask what may be the specific quantity of power, or wisdom, or enthusiasm, which exists in his disciples. In his judgment these things are as the small dust of the balance, not to be taken into serious consideration, and not likely to affect the aggregate results of a man's life. But his incessant demand is for *faith*. If only there be faith, though it be but as a grain of mustard seed, sycamore trees can be uprooted; mountains cast into the midst of the sea; and demons exorcised from their victims. To a father He once said: "There is no *if* in my power; it is in thy faith. If thou canst believe, all things are possible to him that believeth."

And what is this faith? It is not some inherent power or quality in certain men, by virtue of which they are able to accomplish special results unrealized by others. It is rather the power of putting self aside that God may work unhindered through the nature. It is the attitude of heart which, having ascertained the will of God, and being desirous of becoming an organ for it, goes on to expect that God will work out his purposes through its medium. It is, in brief, that capacity for God which appropriates Him to its uttermost limit, and becomes the channel or vehicle through which He passes forth to bless mankind. The believer is the God-filled, the God-moved, the God-possessed man; and the work which he effects in the world is not his, but God's through him.

There are, therefore, these necessary conditions of all true faith:

- The sense of helplessness and nothingness.
- An absolute assurance of being on God's plan.
- Entire consecration, that He may work out his will through heart and life.
- The daily food of promise.
- A daring to act, in utter independence of feeling, on a faith which reckons absolutely on the faithfulness of God.

It will be our contention throughout our study of the remarkable life before us, that, though Moses may have had commanding features of mind and body, and have been versed in all the learning of his time; yet the marvelous outcome of his life work was not due to any of these qualities, but to the faith which knit his soul to God. His faith sufficed to do what all his other qualities, without his faith, must have failed in doing.

We hope to go further, and show that all the blessings which God in his mindfulness of his covenant bestowed on Israel, came to that rebellious and stiff-necked people through the channel of Moses' faith. It is God's method to seek the cooperation of man in the execution of his purposes, and to fulfill his promise through his servants' faith. In this case it was Moses was called into partnership with Jehovah, and it was through his faith that God fulfilled the promise made to Abraham, Isaac, and Jacob.

Each of the above-mentioned conditions of a mighty faith was fulfilled in the history of Moses.

He was allowed to make his first efforts for the emancipation of his people in the energy of his own strength, and to fail egregiously; so that he fled away to Midian, abandoning all hope of delivering them, and spending his years in solitude and exile, until it was with the greatest difficulty that he could be induced to undertake the Divine commission. He was reduced to the last extreme of helpless nothingness when the burning bush flamed in his path, a symbol of utter weakness, possessed and indwelt yet unconsumed by God, who is a consuming fire.

He could have no doubt as to God's plan; for that lay unfolded before him in the promise made to Abraham long years before, fixing four hundred years as the limit of the Egyptian sojourn. And, in addition, God distinctly told him that He had come down to deliver.

He was as thoroughly yielded to the purpose of God, as the staff which he held in his hand was to his own will. Hence his chosen name, "the servant of the Lord"; and the constant recurrence of the phrase, "as the Lord commanded Moses."

He fed daily on the promise of God, pleading them in prayer, and leaning his whole weight upon them. And he often knew what it was to leave behind him the familiar and tried, for the strange and new; at the bidding of God, he stepped out, though there seemed nothing to tread upon, launching himself and three million people absolutely on the care of God, assured that God's faithfulness could not fail.

His faith made Moses all he was. We shall see this more clearly as we proceed. For it is our eager desire to learn exactly how such a faith as his was produced. Why should we not have it? God's methods are never out of date. It is certain that we all have his faith, if we but pay the price of enduring his discipline. And if only we possessed his faith, why should we not see another Exodus? Seas seamed with paths of salvation; foes defied; chains snapped; captives emancipated; and Jehovah worshiped with songs of triumph! Surely there is no limit to the possibilities of a life which has become the aperture or channel through which God can pour Himself forth.

Are you willing to die to your own strength; to forsake your own plans for God's; to seek out and do his will absolutely; to take up the attitude of entire and absolute surrender to his purposes; to feed daily on the promises of God, as a girl on the pledge of her absent lover; to step out in faith, reckoning, without emotion of any kind, on the faithfulness of God, only fully persuaded that He will perform all that He has promised? Then surely through you God will, here or hereafter, work as in the times of old, of which our fathers have told us.

It is certain, as the present age draws to a close, that God has great schemes on hand which must shortly be realized. According to his invariable method He will have to perform them through the instrumentality and faith of men; the one question is, Are we in such a condition, is our faith of such a nature, that He can work by us to the glory of his holy Name? Let us ponder well the lessons taught in the life and character of Moses, that in due time we too may become vessels meet for the Master's use, and prepared to every good work.

2

His Mother's Faith

*By faith Moses, when he was born, was hid
three months of his parents, because they saw
he was a proper child; and they were not
afraid of the king's commandment.*
—Hebrews 11:23

It was on a very unfriendly world that the little babe opened his eyes.
Without, all was as fair as nature and art could make it. Hard by
the mean cottage, which for a brief space was to shelter him, the
mighty Nile rolled between its reedy banks, reflecting on its broad
bosom the deep azure of the arching heavens by day, and the starry con-
stellation of the night. Within the easy distance of a maiden's morning walk stood the great city of Memphis, metropolis of Egypt and seat
of the Court; center of trade, and art, and war, and religion; the focus
to which the national life converged.

Past that cottage home would go royal processions, as in solemn
state the monarch went forth to war, or came down to the Nile brink
to worship. Priests from all parts of the land would pass it on their way
to the mighty Temple of Phthah, whose pillared avenues, and sculptured galleries, and hieroglyphed chambers, were the result of centuries
of industry, and told the story of the generations that had built them,
but how little would they dream that the site of that humble cottage
would attract the interest of generations to the end of time, when
their lordly temple had fallen into an indistinguishable heap! And

the perpetual supply of leeks and melons and garlic, of barley and wheat and rye, of delicate fabrics from the loom, for which the Egyptians became so famous, of spice and balm for the vast City of the Dead, and of all the multitudinous provision for the demands of a large and wealthy population, must have covered the neighboring rods with an unceasing stream of camels and asses and caravans, and the river with an innumerable flotilla of boats, barges, and ships. Not far away, across the level sands, were the Pyramids which even then were becoming venerable with age, and were destined to remain for forty centuries, witnesses alike to man's instinctive belief in his immortality, and to his selfish indifference to the anguish of his fellows. Amid these circumstances of wealth and splendor the little babe was born to an unkindly lot.

He belonged to an alien race. More than three hundred years before, the forefathers of his people had emigrated from the neighboring land of Palestine, at the invitation of the Prime Minister of the time, who was connected with them by the ties of kinship and race. The king had welcomed them as likely to be valuable allies; for he also belonged to a foreign race, and sat on an unstable throne. At his command they had settled in the best of the land, a strip of green, called Goshen, situated amid vast tracks of sand. There they prospered and multiplied till they numbered near upon two million souls. But they remained as distinct a people as they are now in every nation under heaven, and as such were open to suspicious hate.

He belonged to an oppressed race. A different dynasty had succeeded to that which welcomed them, and one to whom the name of Joseph had no charm. At the time of which we write a tiny cloud of impending war trembled on the Eastern sky, and suggested to the reigning monarch the fear that there might be a coalition between his enemies and the Hebrew race, which had grown into such numbers and might, as to be very formidable. He resolved, therefore, to wear them out, and to reduce both their numbers and their spirit by the rigor of their lot.

Suddenly, the shepherds of Goshen found themselves drafted for service in the brickfields, under the eye and whip of cruel taskmasters, who exacted from them daily a certain tale of bricks; or they performed service in the field, drawing water from the river for the irrigation of the land, and toiling in the cultivation of the soil. "And all their service wherein they made them serve was with rigor"; as if every occasion was eagerly taken advantage of for dealing out cruel and merciless punishment.

The father of the little household was, probably, compelled to bear his share in the bondage and blows which made the existence of his people so bitter. From morning to night he would toil, naked, beneath the burning sun, returning often with bleeding wounds torn open by the scourge, and inclined to question the very existence of God and his character for mercy. Very dark was the night which lay heavily on the chosen people in these years of cruel enslavement.

He was born at a time of unusual trouble. The household consisted of father and mother, of an elder sister, some fifteen years of age, marvelously gifted with the power of song, and of a little brother, Aaron, a bright and merry boy of three years of age. When the latter was born, there was apparently no special need of secrecy; for the king was trying to attain his object by the vigorous policy we have above described. But during the interval, he had discovered that it was not stringent enough to attain his end; and he had, therefore, added to it a scheme for the destruction of all the male children, by casting them into the river as they were born.

It is not likely that this decree was in active operation for more than a few months. It was a spasm of cruelty which was inspired by sudden fear, but was too utterly opposed to the better instincts of human nature to secure for itself a permanent position, in the practice of Pharaoh's subordinates. But while it lasted, it was the bitterest element in all that bitter sorrow. Privation, hardship, scorn, and rigor, are easy to bear, if only the beloved circle of the home is left intact, but when that is threatened, and the little fledglings are menaced by the bird of prey, the waters of a full cup are wrung out.

Generally, the birth of a child, and especially of a boy, was heralded with unstinted joy: but now it was the subject of anxiety, and almost of dread. There was no glad anticipation, no welcome, no rapture, to compensate for the mother's anguish, in the thought that a man was born into the world. Yet in spite of all, "the people multiplied and became very mighty." The edict remained in operation for but a short

time, but it was during its enforcement that Moses was born. This is
God's way. In the darkest hours of the night his tread draws near
across the billows. As the day of execution is breaking, the angel
comes to Peter's cell. When the scaffold for Mordecai is complete, the
royal sleeplessness leads to a reaction in favor of the threatened race. Ah,
soul, it may have to come to the worst with thee ere thou art delivered,
but thou wilt be! God may keep thee waiting, but He will ever be
mindful of his covenant, and will appear to fulfill his inviolable word.

But he was the child of believing parents. We know but little of
them. The father is said to have been "a man of the house of Levi," and
we learn afterwards that his name was Amram, and descended from Ko-
hath, the son of Levi, but the tribe of Levi had then no special importance—in fact, it seemed destined to be divided in Jacob, and
scattered in Israel. The mother, Jochebed, belonged to the same tribe,
and, indeed, was related to her husband in a closer consanguinity
than was afterwards permitted. They were humble folk, glad enough
to receive "wages" from the hand of wealth and royalty, but they preserved the best religious traditions of their nation, and in this contrasted
favorably with many of their race.

Dean Stanley has shown that the sojourn in Egypt had produced
a very deleterious result on the children of Israel. "The old freedom, the
old energy, above all, the old religion of the patriarchal age, had faded
away." There are clear evidences in the later Scriptures that the people
participated in the idolatrous rites of the land of their adoption. "Your
fathers," said Joshua, "served other gods in Egypt" (Josh. 24:14). And
through the lips of Ezekiel, Jehovah reminded the nation, at a later date,
of their early unfaithfulness. "In the day that I lifted up mine hand unto
them, to bring them forth of the land of Egypt into a land flowing with
milk and honey, the glory of all lands. Then said I unto them, Cast ye
away every man the abominations of his eyes, and defile not yourselves
with the idols of Egypt; I am the Lord your God. But they rebelled
against Me, and would not hearken unto Me; they did not every man
cast away the abominations of their eyes, neither did they forsake the
idols of Egypt" (Ezek. 20:6–8). The Sabbath was forgotten; the rite of
circumcision, the significant token of the covenant, fell into disuse; the
comparative purity of their forefathers proved unable to resist the li-

centious attractions of heathen festivals, to which in after years they perpetually recurred.

But evidently there were some families who remained faithful
amid the prevalent corruption. Among these was that into which this
child was born. The sacred covenant between God and their race was
reverently remembered, and held by a faith which dared to believe that,
sooner or later, God must interpose. The treasured stories which are preserved to us in the book of Genesis would be carefully taught to the
children as soon as their hearts could appreciate, and their memories
preserve them. The firstborn, Aaron, would be set apart, with some
kind of consecration, to perform the functions of the priest of the
household. And Miriam, the first Mary of Scripture, would be taught
to use her sweet, clear, voice in the praise and worship of the God of
their fathers.

But their religious life was still more manifested by their faith. "By
faith, Moses, when he was born, was hid three months of his parents,
because they saw he was a proper child; and they were not afraid of the
king's commandment." We have often been furnished with a picture
depicting the anxiety with which his parents received their newborn
babe, the distress of Amram, and the fears of Jochebed. Such a picture
may be true of others of the Hebrew parents, but it is not true of them.
"They were not afraid." When it was announced to Jochebed that she
had borne a boy, she was enabled to cast the care of him on God, and
to receive the assurance that he should come to no hurt. And as the couple bent over their child, in that peasant's hut, and saw his exceeding
goodliness, the conviction grew in their hearts that a great destiny
awaited him; and that in some way he would live to see the expiration
of the time of slavery, foretold centuries before in words which had
passed from lip to lip, the one rift of light amid the blackness of their
night. Josephus says that a dream announced to Amram that Moses
would be the deliverer of his people.

Could those downtrodden serfs ever forget what God had told
their great ancestor, when the horror of a great darkness had fallen on
his soul? "Know of a surety that thy seed shall be a stranger in a land
that is not theirs, and shall serve them, and they shall afflict them
four hundred years, but in the fourth generation they shall come

hither again" (Gen. 15:13, 16). The slow moving years had at last accumulated to the prescribed number. Four hundred years had nearly,
if not quite, elapsed. The promise must be on the point of fulfillment. The words, "they shall come out" (Gen. 15:14) rang like a peal
of bells in the mother's heart; and there was a confidence nurtured by
the Spirit of God, and by the loveliness of her child, who was "goodly"
(Ex. 2:2), "proper" (Heb. 11:23), and "exceeding fair" (Acts 7:20), that
in some way he should share in that Exodus.

She was not always on the *qui vive* for the step of officer or mid-
wife. She would take all ordinary precaution, but she would never give
way to excessive fear. Sometimes when her heart grew sick she would
betake herself to her knees, and plead the Divine promise on which she
had been caused to hope. The whole family lived on that woman's faith,
as men live on bread; and God's angels bent over the unconscious babe,
shielding it with their tenderest care, and whispering their love words
into its ear. Finally, the mother was led by the good Spirit of God to
weave the papyrus rushes into a little ark, or boat, coating it with bitumen, to make it impervious to wet. There she put the child with
many a kiss, closed the lid upon its sweet face, with her own hands bore
it to the water's edge, and placed it tenderly among the flags that
grew there. She knew that Pharaoh's daughter came there to bathe, and
it might be that she would notice and befriend the little foundling. Or,
if not, the God whom she trusted would help her in some other way.
But all the while she never lost her simple, steadfast faith. "The Lord
was her light and her salvation: of whom should she be afraid? When
her enemies and foes came upon her to eat up her flesh, they would
stumble and fall. Though a host should encamp against her, yet should
she not fear."

Miriam was set to watch, not with any thought of harm that
would ensue, whether from unfriendly hand, or from beast of prey, but
simply to see "what would be done to him"; and Jochebed went back
to her house, fighting a mother's natural anxiety by a faith which had
enclasped the very arm of the living God, who could not fail her,
though the heavens should fall, or the pyramids be hurled into the broad
bosom of the Nile. That is faith. Can we wonder at the faith of the man
who was born of such a mother, and nurtured in such a home?

3

"Come to Years"

By faith, Moses, when he was come to years,
refused to be called the son
of Pharaoh's daughter.
—Hebrews 11:24

I t all befell according to the mother's faith. The princess, accompanied by a train of maidens, came to the river bank to bathe. She saw the ark among the flags, and sent her maid to fetch it. In the midst of the little group the lid was carefully uplifted; and their eyes were charmed with the sight of the beautiful face, while their hearts were touched with the whimper of the babe, who missed its mother, and frightened by its unwonted surroundings and the many strange faces.

Quickly the woman's heart guessed the secret. The neighborhood of Hebrew huts, the features and complexion of the babe, the unlikelihood of a mother forgetting her sucking child, the sudden recollection of the stern edict which her father had lately promulgated, all pointed to the inevitable conclusion, "This is one of the Hebrews' children." The sudden interposition of Miriam, who had eagerly and breathlessly watched the whole scene, with her naive suggestion of fetching a Hebrew nurse, solved the problem of what should be done with the foundling almost as soon as it could have suggested itself. Quickly the child's mother stood before the princess, and received the precious burden from her hands; and as she did so, was there not something in her almost convulsive movement which revealed to that quick eye the secret of the little plot? Whether it were so or not, the story does not tell. But with what an ecstasy of joy would that mother pour out her heart when the door was closed on the little group? The child's life was secure beneath the powerful protection of Pharaoh's own daughter, who had said, "Nurse it for me." And the wages which she had promised would do more than provide for all their need. God had done "exceedingly abundantly."

How long the boy stayed in that lowly home we do not know—perhaps till he was four or five years old: but long enough, in any case, to know something of the perils and hardships of his people's lot; to learn those sacred traditions of their past, which he was afterwards to weave with such majestic simplicity into the Book of Genesis; and to receive into his heart the love of the only God, which was to become the absorbing passion and polestar of his career. Priests, philosophers, and scholars, might do their best afterwards, but these things had been built into the growing structure of his soul, never again to be disintegrated from its fabric. What an encouragement is suggested by this record to mothers—to make the very most of the early years during which children are confided to their charge. The circumstances must be exceptional indeed under which that charge can be entrusted to others.

At last the time arrived when Thermutis claimed for her own the child whom she had rescued. He had now grown so beautiful that, Josephus tells us, passersby stood still to look at him, and laborers left their work to steal a glance. The mother's heart must have suffered bitterly as she let her boy go into the unknown world within the great palace gate; and very lonely must the little household have felt when the last kisses had been exchanged, the last instruction given, and the last prayer offered. What a crowd of tender thoughts, curious speculations, and eager yearnings must have followed the little nurseling of the Hebrew home, as his mother took him and brought him unto Pharaoh's daughter, and he became her son! But, amid all, faith rose preeminent, and believed that He who had delivered the child from the perils of the Nile, would keep him pure and sweet amid the evils and fascinations of the Court.

What a magnificent land must Egypt have been in those days of which Herodotus and the hieroglyphic records speak! The atmosphere was rainless: the Nile brought from afar the rich alluvial soil, that bore corn enough to feed the world; the banks of the river were covered with cities, villages, stately temples, and all the evidences of an advanced civilization; while mighty pyramids and colossal figures towered to a hundred feet in height. Seven millions of people throve on this green riband of territory; and while the great mass of them were probably poor and ignorant, the upper classes, and especially the priests, were remarkable for their familiarity with much of which we boast ourselves today.

The cream of all this was poured into the cup of Moses. He was brought up in the palace, and treated as the grandson of Pharaoh. If he rode forth into the streets, it would be in a princely equipage, amid the cries of "Bow the knee." If he floated on the Nile, it would be in a golden barge, amid the strains of voluptuous music. If he wished for aught, the almost illimitable wealth of the treasures of Egypt was within his reach.

When old enough he was probably sent to be *educated in the college*, which had grown up around the Temple of the Sun, and has been called "the Oxford of Ancient Egypt." There he would learn to read and write the mysterious hieroglyph; there, too, he would be instructed in mathematics, astronomy, and chemistry, in all of which the Egyptians were adept. There, also, he would acquire a taste for music; so that in after days he could sing glad and triumphant songs of victory, and compose odes which embalmed the history of God's dealing with his people. How wonderfully was God fitting him for his afterlife! Stephen says: "Moses was learned in all the wisdom of the Egyptians" (Acts 7:22). Much of it was undoubtedly the merest folly, but much of it, also, stood him in good stead when he became the founder of a new state.

But Moses was something more than a royal student, spending his years in cultured refinement and lettered ease. *He was a statesman and a soldier.* Stephen tells us that he was "mighty in words and in deeds"; mighty in words—there is the statesman; mighty in deeds—there the soldier. Josephus says that while he was still in his early manhood the Ethiopians invaded Egypt, routed the army sent against them, and threatened Memphis. In the panic the oracles were consulted; and on their recommendation Moses was entrusted with the command of the royal troops. He immediately took the field, surprised and defeated the enemy, captured their principal city, "the swamp-engirded city of Meroë," and returned to Egypt laden with the spoils of victory.

Thus year followed year till he was forty years of age. Already the foremost positions of the State were open to him; and it seemed as if the river of his life would continue in the same bed, undiverted, and only waxing ever broader and deeper in its flow.

But, beneath all, another thought was always present with him, and gradually dwarfed all others as it grew within his soul. He could not forget that his parents were slaves; that the bondmen who were groaning in the brickfields beneath the lash of the taskmasters were his brethren. He never lost the thought of that God to whom his mother had taught him to pray: and in his gayest, most successful moments, when sipping the intoxicating cup of earthly success, he could not rid himself of the impression that his destiny did not lie amid such surroundings as those, but was in some way to be associated with the fulfillment of that promise which he had heard so often from his mother's lips.

Thoughts like these would often cast strange shadows over his face, which baffled those who knew him best. His foster mother might attribute the strange tinge of melancholy to ill health or some unrequited love. His friends and companions would rally him on his absentmindedness. His suite would often discuss the subject of their master's depression, and wonder as to its cause. But the mystery remained locked in his heart till his vague impressions had become settled resolves; and he broke, as gently as he might, the news to his benefactress that he could no longer hold the position to which she had raised him, or be called her son, but must step back to the lowly lot which was his by birth.

The announcement would be, perhaps, met by bitter tears and hot indignation on the part of her to whom he owed so much, but neither the one nor the other made him swerve by a hair's breadth from his purpose. And how great a sensation must have been caused throughout the

Court as the news leaked out! In how many circles it would be discussed, and what different interpretations would be placed on it! Some would attribute it to mortification or jealousy; others to the presence in his veins of base slave blood; others to some scheme of ultimate self-aggrandizement. All would commiserate the princess, whose kindness seemed so rudely requited. But no one guessed the strength or purity of his hidden purpose, born of God, and nurtured by His good Spirit.

I. NOTICE THE NOBLE INGREDIENTS IN THIS GREAT RESOLVE. (1) *It was made in the full maturity of his powers.* The impulsive ardor of youth will sometimes lead a young heart to say, "This people shall be my people, and their God my God." But there was nothing of that kind here. It was the deliberate resolve of a man who had seen much of life, who knew all that could be urged from every side, and who was come to years. With nothing to gain and all to lose, after thoughtful examination, he descended from the footsteps of the loftiest throne in the world.

(2) *It was made when the fortunes of the children of Israel were at their lowest ebb.* They were slaves, were suffering affliction, and were reproached. For a palace there would be a hut; for luxury, hard fare and coarse food; for respect and honor, hatred and contempt: for the treasures of Egypt, poverty and want; for the society of the learned and *élite*, association with the ignorant and depraved. But none of these things moved him. He counted them as the small dust of the balance. With deliberate resolution he bowed his head beneath the yoke, albeit it was right and heavy.

(3) *It was made when the pleasures of sin seemed most fascinating.* There is nothing gained in saying that there are no pleasures in sin. There are. The forbidden fruit is pleasant to the eye and luscious to the taste; the first steps along the broad road are over a carpet of velvet grass, enameled with countless flowers; there are notes of dulcet sweetness in the siren's song, which ravish the heart. Temptation would have no power at all if it were not so. The keen thrill of pleasure is the bait, beneath which the great enemy of souls hides the inevitable hood. And Moses, was not oblivious to all this; yet, in the heyday of his strength,

in the prime of his manhood, in a court where continence and purity must have been unknown, he dared to forego it all.

(4) *It was made decisively.* Many would have tried to retain the proud position and to benefit their enslaved brethren at the same time; to temporize between an outward recognition of Osiris, and a heart-loyalty to Jehovah: to keep on good terms with court and brick kiln. But there was no trace of this in the great renunciation which cut Moses off from the least association with the fond and fascinating associations of early life.

Are there not times in all our lives when a similar step has to be taken by ourselves? We have to die to much that is pleasant and attractive, in order to rise to our true life. Buried, to bear fruit; maimed, to enter life; laying our Isaac on the altar, to become the leader of the faithful; turning aside from the gate of a sunlit garden, to take a darker, stonier, path; renouncing what others hold without rebuke, because of some high purpose which has forced its way into the soul; choosing Gethsemane and Calvary and the grave, in fellowship with the Man of Sorrows; being willing to renounce friends, wealth, reputation, and success, and to be flung like a shipwrecked sailor on some lone shore, because of some vision that beckons us. Those who have done any one of these can understand, as others cannot, the nobility and greatness of Moses' choice.

II. THE THOUGHT WHICH LED TO IT. "By faith Moses refused. . . ." Faith rests on promise; to her the promise is equivalent to fulfillment; and if only she has the one, she dares to count on the other as already hers. It matters comparatively little that the thing promised is not given; it is sure and certain, because God has pledged his word for it, and in anticipation she enters on its enjoyment. She weighs the things that she can touch against those which are only as yet foretold, because in her judgment the latter are as real as the former. Thus it was with Moses.

He believed God's promise to Abraham, that after four hundred years of bondage his people would come out; and he knew that that period had nearly expired. He cherished a fervent belief in that promise made to the chosen people, that from their ranks the true Deliverer would arise—a shadowy belief in the coming Messiah, which, notwithstanding its vagueness, he dared not forfeit. He believed that there was a destiny waiting for the chosen people in the long future, which would throw into shadow all the pomp and splendor of the magnificent Pharaoh. He believed that there was a recompense of reward awaiting them beyond the borne and limit of Egypt, more glorious than the dazzling splendor of its highest rewards and honors. He evidently believed, what he expected his brethren to believe, that God would deliver them by his hand. And it was this that determined him.

Had he simply acted on what he saw, he had never left Pharaoh's palace. But his faith told him of things hidden from his contemporaries; and these altered his course, and led him to act in a way which to them was perfectly incomprehensible.

He did not simply close his eyes to the claims of Egypt, and steel his nerves against the threats of Pharaoh, isolating himself with the exclusiveness of a cynic: that might have been dictated by a strong and wise policy. But he did what he did, because he saw by faith what eye had not seen, or ear heard, or the heart conceived; and these things—that wealth and that reward—being so much better than anything Egypt could offer, he cheerfully took the path of affliction, of self-denial and reproach, which led to them.

See, child of God, what is within thy reach, if only thou wilt dare to deny thyself and take up thy cross! Send the spies into the Land of Promise. Climb the delectable mountains, and put the telescope to thine eyes. And as the far more exceeding and eternal weight of glory breaks on thy vision, thou wilt be prepared to count all things else, which had seemed gain, to be loss and dung, and not worthy to be mentioned in the comparison. Is the renunciation hard? Do not forget that Christ is suffering with you in it all. His steps lie along this road. It is "the reproach of Christ"—a little phase of His long suffering through the sufferings of his people. He knows every step of the way, because He has so often traversed it in the experience of his own. There is no solace to the agonized soul so sweet as the perpetual mention of his dear name, as if it were conscious that in all its afflictions, He is afflicted, and that the angel of his presence is going at its side.

And who can estimate the result? The water streams from the smitten rock; the flower springs from the dead seed; the crystal river flows from the moraine of the glacier; the bright gold emerges from the dark mine and the cleansing fires. An Exodus and the birth of a nation of freemen were the outcome of this great renunciation.

4

Deliverance by Main Force

And seeing one of his brethren suffer wrong, he
defended him, and avenged him that was op-
pressed, and smote the Egyptian. For he sup-
posed his brethren would have understood how
that God by his hand would deliver them: but
they understood not.
—Acts 7:24, 25

There was true heroism in the act, when Moses stepped down from Pharaoh's throne to share the lot of his brethren. He might have contented himself by sending them money from the treasures of Egypt, but it was a greater and nobler thing to give himself. And the true religious instinct of his soul gleamed out as he did so. There was a revelation of the faith which had been kindled within him when he knelt at his mother's side in the slave hut, and had survived all the adverse influences of the Egyptian Court, like a spark of fire living in the heart of black coals.

At the same time there was a great deal for him to learn. In after days he was to know the ways of the Lord—God would make them known to him (Ps. 103:7), but just now he was full of his own ways. In after days he was to be a hand, nerved, and used, and empowered by God Himself (Ps. 77:20), but now he was acting in his own self-energy—rash, impetuous, headstrong, girding himself and walking whither he would. In after days he was to be the meekest and least obtrusive of men, conscious to a fault of his own weakness, and at every step looking up for guidance and help, but now he leaned wholly on his own understanding, and, without taking counsel of God, thought to secure the emancipation of his people by the assertion of his will, and the forth putting of his might.

Ah! there was the making of a saint in him, but it would take many a long year of lonely waiting and trial before this strong and self-reliant nature could be broken down, shaped into a vessel meet for the Master's use, and prepared for every good work. God's work can only be done by his chosen instruments, and they must be specially fitted for the service they are to render. That special adaptation is not natural to any of us, and can only come after years of deep and searching discipline.

I. THE FIRST ATTEMPT AT DELIVERANCE. (1) *It sprang largely from human sympathy.* As soon as he reached Goshen his first act was to go out and see his brethren in the midst of their toils, working amid the conditions of the severest hardship. Brickmaking in stiff clay pits must always be arduous employment, but how much more so when an Egyptian sun shone vertically above them, and a taskmaster stood by with his heavy whip to punish the least attempt to flinch from toil or shirk the collar! Imagine the accomplished courtier, the child of luxury and fashion, the man of letters and of mighty deeds, as he moves amid these long lines of slaves. At first it must have seemed very strange to him to realize that he was bound in bonds of such close kinship to these toiling, suffering, dying, Hebrews. "He went out unto his brethren." But this feeling must soon have given place to an intense commiseration, as he heard the nation sighing by reason of its bondage; and groaning under its accumulated sorrows, his soul would be filled with tender pity. But within a little, that pity for his people turned to indignation against their oppressors. Before he had taken many steps he came on one of the taskmasters cruelly beating a Hebrew; and as he witnessed the horrid spectacle, the heavy blows falling on the unresisting quivering body, he could restrain himself no longer, and felled the caitiff lifeless to the ground, then bore away his body and buried it in the nearest sands, ever waiting to encroach on the more cultivated lands of Egypt.

It was a chivalrous act, well meant, and at least significant of the strength of the emotions pent up within him; but, after all, the mere impulse of pity would never have been strong enough to bear him through the weary years of the desert march. Beneath the repeated provocations of the people it must have given way. He could never have carried them as a nursing-father, or asked that he might be blotted out of the book of life for them, or pleaded with them for God. Nothing short of a reception of the Divine patience, let into his soul as the ocean waves find an inlet into some deeply indented coast, could suffice for the demands which would be made on him in those coming terrible years.

Is there not a lesson here for many of God's workers? They have not learned to distinguish between passion and principle, between impulse and a settled purpose. If some touching tale is told, some piteous appeal made for help, or some crowded gathering swept by a wave of missionary enthusiasm, they are the first to yield to the impulse, to volunteer their service, to give their money and fling themselves into the breach. But, after all, this is not the loftiest motive for Christian service, and it certainly is not the most permanent. After a little while it dies down, and leaves us stranded as by a receding tide. It is better far to sacrifice the mere natural impulse for the strong sense of what is right, and what God requires. If we undertake a definite work because He calls us to it, because it is put before us as a duty for his sake, or because we are channels through which the unebbing torrent of his Divine pity is flowing, we have secured a principle of action which will bear us through disappointment, failure, and ingratitude. The way in which men treat us will make no difference to us, because all is done for Him.

(2) *It was premature.* God's time for the deliverance of his people was not due for forty years. The iniquity of the Amorites had not reached its full, though it was nearing the brim of the cup (Gen. 15:16). His own education was very incomplete; it would take at least forty years to drain him of his self will and self reliance, and make him a vessel meet for the Master's use. The Hebrew people had not as yet come to the pitch of anguish, which is so touchingly referred to, when the death of their principal oppressor seems to have brought matters to a crisis, and they forsook the false gods to which they had given their allegiance in order to return to the God of their fathers (Ex. 2:23).

We all know something of this haste. We find it so hard to sit still, while our great Boaz does his work (Ruth 3:18). We think that the set time of God's salvation must have arrived, long before the clock strikes. As Saul, in presence of the Philistine invasion, we suppose that we cannot last out for another hour, and force ourselves to offer the burnt offering; and are chagrined to see Samuel's figure slowly pacing up the mountain pass as the fire burns down to its last embers, and to hear from his lips the sentence of deposition for our impatience (1 Sam. 13:12–14). Well may our Master say of us, as He did once of his brethren, "My time is not yet come, but your time is always ready" (John 7:6).

Oh for grace to wait and watch with God, though a horror of great darkness fall on us, and sleep steals up into our eyes, and the head becomes thickly sown with the grey hair of age! One blow struck when the time is fulfilled is worth a thousand struck in premature eagerness. It is not for thee, O my soul, to know the times and seasons which the Father hath put in his own power; wait thou only upon God; let thy expectation be from Him; wait at the gates of thy Jericho for yet seven days; utter not a sound till He says, Shout: but when He gives the signal, with the glad cry of victory thou shalt pass over the fallen wall into the city.

(3) *It was executed in the pride of human strength.* It was but natural that Moses should suppose that he could do something for the amelioration of his people's lot. He had always been accustomed to have his way. Crowds of obsequious servants and courtiers had yielded to his slightest whim. By his strong right hand he had hewn out a great career. He was conscious of vast stores of youthful energy and natural force, untapped by sufficient calls, and undiminished by physical excess; surely these would count for something. He would make that nation of oppressors reel before his blows, and of course he would be hailed by his brethren as their God-sent deliverer.

It was a rude surprise, on the second day, he went out to continue his self-imposed task, and essayed to adjust a difference between two Hebrews, to find himself repulsed from them by the challenge, "Who made thee a prince and a judge over us?" He had never expected a rebuff from that quarter. "For he supposed his brethren would have understood how that God, by his hand, would deliver them: but they understood not." Evidently then, God's time had not arrived; nor could it come until the heat of his spirit had slowly evaporated in the desert air, and he had learned the hardest of all lessons, that "by strength shall no man prevail."

We have been disposed to attribute too much of the success of the Exodus to the natural qualities of the great leader, but we must always remember that, like Gideon's host, he was at first too strong for God. God cannot give his glory to another. He dare not entrust his power to men, till they are humbled and emptied, and conscious of their helplessness. Even the Son learned obedience by the things that He suffered, and descended into the dust of death, crying, "I am a worm and no man," ere He could say, "All power is given unto Me in heaven and in earth." The most eminent of his saints must suffer from a thorn in the flesh, to remind him of his weakness; and he confessed himself grateful for it, because only when he was weak could he be strong. When the soul is inflated with a strong reliance on its own sufficiency, the power of God is unable to effect an entrance, or use that soul as a channel for its work. It is when we are willing to be accounted as worms, as broken reeds, as little children, as foolish, weak, base, despised, as "things which are not," that we become aware of being vehicles for the working of the might of his power, which He wrought in Christ when He raised Him from the dead. You must be brought to an end of yourself before God can begin with you. But when once you have come to that point there is no limit to what may be wrought during a single life by the passage through it of his eternal power and Godhead.

(4) *It was too apprehensive of the judgment of other men.* We are told that he looked this way and that way before he smote the Egyptian; and when he found that his deed of revenge was known, he feared and fled (Ex. 2:15). But suppose that he had felt that he had been divinely commissioned to execute judgment upon Egypt; suppose he had realized the Divine Presence with him; suppose he had known that he was on the line of Divine purpose—would he have cared who was looking, and what was being said? It would not have been possible. Fixing his eyes on the movement of the Divine cloud, absorbed in the one passion of doing God's will, sure that he was immortal till his work was done, he

would have been perfectly indifferent to the praise or blame of men. Whenever men look this way and that to see what other men are doing or saying, you may be quite sure that they do not know certainly their Master's plan; they are in front of Him, and are acting from the prompting of their own self-will, though perhaps under the cover of religious zeal.

There has been only one perfect Servant of God who has ever trodden our world. He never looked this way nor that. Away on the mountain height of unbroken fellowship He received the plan of his life, which He wrought out in daily detail, and He alone could say, "He that sent Me is with Me; the Father hath not left Me alone, for I do always those things that please Him." Oh for the single eye, that our whole body also may be full of light!

II. THE FLIGHT TO THE DESERT. The great news of Moses' first attempt came to the ears of Pharaoh, and he sought to slay Moses. But Moses feared, and fled from the face of Pharaoh. In after years, under similar circumstances, it is said, "He forsook Egypt, not fearing the wrath of the king" (Heb. 11:27). And when we ask the reason of his fearlessness, we learn that it was by faith he did so; for "he endured, as seeing Him who is invisible." But if such were the case afterwards, why was it not so at the time with which we are dealing? Why did he not exercise faith in the visible God? Why did not his heart beat with even throb in the one crisis as in the other? The reason is obvious.

Faith is only possible when we are on God's plan, and stand on God's promise. It is useless to pray for increased faith until we have fulfilled the conditions of faith. It is equally useless to spend time in regrets and tears over the failures which are due to our unbelief. "And the Lord said to Joshua, Get thee up; wherefore liest thou thus upon thy face?" Faith is as natural to right conditions of soul, as a flower is to a plant. And among those conditions this is the first—ascertain your place in God's plan, and get on to it; and this is the second—feed on God's promises. And when each of these is realized, faith comes of itself; and there is absolutely nothing which is impossible. The believing soul can "do all things" with God, because it has got on to God's lines; yea, it is itself as the metal track along which God travels to men in love, grace, and truth.

But Moses was out of touch with God. So he fled, and crossed the desert that lay between him and the eastern frontier; threaded the mountain passes of the Sinaitic peninsula, through which in after years he was to lead his people; and at last sat wearily down by a well in the land of Midian. There his chivalrous interference was suddenly elicited on behalf of the daughters of the priest of Midian, who seem to have suffered daily from the insolence of shepherds appropriating the water which the shepherd maidens had drawn for their flocks. That day, however, the churls met their match, and were compelled to leave the water troughs to the women; who hurried home, unexpectedly early, to tell, with girls' enthusiasm, of the Egyptian who had delivered them from the hand of the shepherds. It was a good office that could not pass without requital in that hospitable land, and it opened the door to the chieftain's tent; ultimately to marriage with one of those same shepherdesses; and finally to the quiet life of a shepherd in the calm open spaces of that wonderful land, which, on more than one occasion, has served for a Divine school.

Such experiences come to us all. We rush forward, thinking to carry all before us; we strike a few blows in vain; we are staggered with disappointment, and reel back; we are afraid at the first breath of human disapprobation; we flee from the scenes of our discomfiture to hide ourselves in chagrin. Then we are hidden in the secret of God's presence from the pride of man. And there our vision clears: the silt drops from the current of our life, as from the Rhone in its passage through the deep waters of Geneva's lake; our self-life dies down; our spirit drinks of the river of God, which is full of water; our faith begins to grasp his arm, and to be the channel for the manifestation of his power; and thus at last we emerge to be his hand to lead an Exodus. "This also cometh forth from the Lord of hosts, who is wonderful in counsel, and excellent in working."

5

The Marvelous Colloquy

God called to him out of the midst of the
bush, and said Moses, Moses.
And he said, Here am I.
—Exodus 3:4

A memorable day. There are days in all lives which come unannounced, unheralded; no angel faces look out of heaven; no angel voices put us on our guard: but as we look back on them in after years, we realize that they were the turning points of existence. Perhaps we look longingly back on the uneventful routine of the life that lies beyond them, but the angel, with drawn sword, forbids our return, and compels us forward. It was so with Moses.

Quite ordinary was that morning as it broke. The sun rose as usual in a dull haze over the expanse of sand, or above the gaunt forms of the mountains, seamed and scarred. As the young day opened, it began to shine in a cloudless sky, casting long shadows over the plains; and presently, climbing to the zenith, threw a searching, scorching, light into every aperture of the landscape beneath. The sheep browsed as usual on the scant herbage, or lay panting beneath the shadow of a great rock, but there was nothing in their behavior to excite the thought that God was nigh. The giant forms of the mountains, the spreading heavens, the awful silence unbroken by song of bird or hum of insect life, the acacia bushes drooping in the shadeless glare—

505

these things were as they had been for forty years, and as they threatened to be, after Moses had sunk into an obscure and forgotten grave. Then, suddenly, a common bush began to shine with the emblem of Deity; and from its heart of fire the voice of God broke the silence of the ages in words that fell on the shepherd's ear like a double knock: "Moses, Moses."

And from that moment all his life was altered. The door which had been so long in repairing was suddenly put on its hinges again and opened. The peaceful quiet, the meditative leisure, the hiding from the strife of tongues, the simple piety of the homestead—where the priest of Midian ministered, and Zipporah welcomed him with his boys, as he brought the flock home to its fold—suddenly vanished, as a tract of land submerged beneath the ocean. And he went forth, not clearly knowing whither; knowing only that he dared not be disobedient to the heavenly vision, or refuse the voice of Him that spoke.

That voice still speaks to those whose hearts are hushed to hear. By written letter or printed page, by the beauty of a holy life, the spell of some precious memory, or the voice of some living teacher, the God of past generations still makes known his will to the anointed ear. Nor will our lives ever be what they might until we realize that God has a plan for every hour in them; and that He waits to reveal that plan to the loving and obedient heart, making it known to us by one of the ten thousand ministries that lie around us. Insensibly to ourselves we contract the habit of thinking of Him as the God of the dead, who spoke to the fathers in oracle and prophet; whereas the I AM is the God of the living—passing through our crowded thoroughfares, brooding over our desert spaces, and seeking hearts which are still enough from their own plannings and activities to listen.

The main point for each of us is to be able to answer his summons with the response, "Here am I." It may seem long to wait, and the oft-expected day so slow in coming, that the heart sinks down, oppressed with the crowd of common days, and relinquishes hope, but your opportunity will come at last. Be always ready! Never let the loins be ungirded, or the lamps expire; never throw yourself down at full length by the brook, to drink lazily of the limpid stream. In such an hour as you think not the Lord will come. What rapture to be able to answer his appeal with, "Here am I." If that summons were to come today, too many of us would have to ask for a moment's respite while we went to finish some neglected duty. Oh for the free, untrammeled, unengaged spirit, to be ready to go at any moment whithersoever the Lord may appoint.

I. A REMARKABLE ANNOUNCEMENT. Out of the bush came the voice of God, blending past, present, and future, in one marvelous sentence: *the past,* "I am the God of thy father, the God of Abraham, the God of Isaac, and the God of Jacob"; *the present,* "I have surely seen the affliction of my people which are in Egypt, and have heard their cry by reason of their taskmasters; for I know their sorrows, and I am come down to deliver them"; *the future,* "Come now, therefore, and I will send thee unto Pharaoh" (Ex. 3:6–10).

Deep and searching thoughts arrest us, which should be laid most seriously to heart, especially by the Lord's busiest workers. We are all too apt to run before we are sent as Moses did in his first well-meant, but ill-timed, endeavors. We put our hands, at our own prompting, to a work that needs doing; we ask God to help us, and we go on very well with the momentum of our own energy for at least a day. But on the morrow, when chiding and rebuke and difficulty arise, as they did to Moses, we are disappointed, and throw it all up; betaking ourselves to flight, finding our refuge in the solitudes of the desert.

But what a contrast to all this ineffectual effort and dismal disappointment is presented in those who have learned to wait for God! When the time is full, they hear Him say, *I am come down, and I will send thee;* and from that moment they are no longer promoters, but instruments, agents, and tools, through whom He executes his plans. What, then, are difficulties to them? They anticipate them without anxiety; they pass through them without fear. God must have foreseen all before He put his hand to the work. He must be able to see a pathway threading the apparently trackless waste. He must know a door through what appears to be an impregnable barrier of rock. At any rate, the chosen soul has simply to walk with Him; to be ready to do the errands He requires, whether they consist in accosting monarchs, lifting up a rod, or uttering his words. That is all; and then to stand still to watch the ease with which He cleaves a pathway through the sea, and provides a commissariat in the desert.

II. Divine Longsuffering under provocation. In the first blush of youthful enthusiasm Moses had been impetuous enough to attempt the emancipation of his people by the blows of his right hand. But now that God proposes to send him to lead an Exodus, he starts back in dismay almost petrified at the proposal. But how true this is to nature! The student, as a precocious schoolboy, thinks that he knows all that can be acquired of a certain branch of science, but twenty years after he feels as if he had not mastered its elements, though he has never ceased to study. The believer who began by speaking of himself as "the least of saints" ends by calling himself "the chief of sinners." And Moses, who had run before God in feverish impatience, now lags fainthearted behind Him.

At first he expostulated: "Who am I, that I should go to Pharaoh?" There was something more than humility here; there was a tone of self-depreciation which was inconsistent with a true faith in God's selection and appointment. Surely it is God's business to choose his special instruments; and when we are persuaded that we are in the line of his purpose, we have no right to question the wisdom of his appointment. To do so is to depreciate his wisdom, or to doubt his power and willingness to become the complement of our need.

"And God said, Certain, I will be with thee." "I whose glory shines here, who am as unimpaired by the flight of the ages as this fire is by burning; who am independent of sustenance or fuel from man; who made the fathers what they were; whose nature is incapable of change—I will be with thee." What an assurance was here! And yet something of this kind is said to each of us when we are called to undertake any new charge. We have been called into the fellowship of the Son of God. "He died for us, that whether we wake or sleep, we should live together with Him." He is with us all the days, even unto the end of the age. He will never leave us, neither forsake us. "Fear not," He seems to say; "I am with thee: I who change not, and without whom no sparrow falls to the ground. All power is given unto Me in heaven and in earth. Not an hour without my companionship; not a difficulty without my cooperation; not a Red Sea without my right arm; not a mile of wilderness journeying without the Angel of my Presence." Days break very differently on us. Sometimes we open the door to a flood of sunshine, sometimes to a sky laden with black, dull clouds; now a funeral, and then a marriage; hours in which it is luxury to live, and others which pass with leaden-footed pace, but nothing can part us from our Divine Companion—nothing but needless worry or permitted sin.

In his next excuse Moses professed his inability to answer if he were asked the name of God (13); and this was met by the proclamation of the spirit-stirring name, JEHOVAH: I AM THAT I AM. There we have the unity of God to the exclusion of the many gods of Egypt; the unchangeableness of God, who lives in an eternal present; the self-sufficiency of God, who alone is his own equivalent. No other term can describe Him; when you have said your utmost you must fall back on this—that God is God.

The term JEHOVAH was not wholly unknown to Moses, for it entered into his mother's name, Jochebed—*Jehovah my glory,* but now for the first time it was adopted as the unique title by which God was to be known in Israel. Slowly it made its way into the faith of the people; and whenever employed, it speaks of the self-existent and redeeming qualities of the nature of God, and is forever enshrined in the precious name of our Savior, JESUS. The whole subsequent life of Moses and of Israel was inspired by this name. All through their history the thought of what He was, and what He would be to them, rang out like a chime of bells.

And for us it is full of meaning. "This," said He, "is my name forever, and this is my memorial to all generations" (15). And as its full meaning opens to our vision, it is as if God put into our hands a blank check, leaving us to fill it in as we will. Are we dark? let us add to his I AM the words, *the true Light;* are we hungry? the words, *the Bread of Life.* Are we defenseless? The words, *the Good Shepherd;* are we weary? the words, *Shiloh, the Restgiver.* "In Him dwelleth all the fullness of the Godhead bodily, and in Him ye are made full" (Col. 2:9, 10 R.V.).

Moses' third excuse was that the people would not believe him, nor hearken to his voice (Ex. 4:1). But God graciously met this also by showing him miracles which he might perform in Egypt, and which would read deep lessons to himself. "What is that in thine hand? And he said, A rod." It was probably only a shepherd's crook. What a history, however, awaited it! It was to be stretched out over the Red Sea, pointing a pathway through its depths; to smite the flinty rock; to win victory over the hosts of Amalek; to be known as the Rod of God. When God wants an implement for his service He does not choose the golden scepter, but a shepherd's crook; the weakest and meanest thing He can find—a ram's horn, a cake of barley meal, an ox goad, an earthen pitcher, a shepherd's sling. He employs a worm to thresh the mountains and make the hills as chaff. A rod with God behind it is mightier than the vastest army.

At God's command the rod was cast on the ground, and it became a serpent. In Egyptian worship the serpent played a very conspicuous part. And as it wriggled on the sand, and sought to do him harm, so that he fled from it, it was an emblem of the might of Egypt before which he had become a fugitive. But, when God gave the word, how easily it became once more a rod in his hand, as he fearlessly grasped the venomous animal by the tail. So God would instruct his faith. If only he would dare do as he was bidden, Pharaoh and all his priests, and the whole force of the Egyptian empire would be equally submissive.

The second sign was ever more significant. His hand thrust into his bosom became leprous; and then again pure and white. It was if God met his consciousness of moral pollution, and taught him that it could be put away as easily as his flesh was cleansed through His forgiving grace.

And the third sign, in which it was promised that the water of the Nile should become blood on the dry land, was full of terrible omens to the gods of that mighty country, the people of which depended so entirely on its river, and worshiped it as a god.

We may well ponder these significant signs. Are we only as rods, and rods which were once serpents? Yet God can do great things by us, if only we are willing to be wielded by his hand. Are we polluted with the leprosy of sin? Yet we may be as his hand, thrust into his bosom and made clean and pure. Are our foes many? They are his foes, too, absolutely in his power to cover them with confusion.

The last excuse that Moses alleged was his lack of eloquence. "O Lord, I am not eloquent; I am slow of speech, and of a slow tongue" (v. 10). Probably, like our Cromwell, he had no ready supply of words. But God was willing to meet this also with his patient grace; and if only Moses had been willing to trust Him, it is probable that he would have added the gifts of a persuasive and splendid oratory to the other talents with which he was copiously endowed. "And the Lord said, Who hath made man's mouth? Or who maketh the dumb, or deaf, or the seeing, or the blind? Have not I, the Lord? Now therefore go, and I will be with thy mouth, and teach thee what thou shalt say" (vv. 11, 12).

But Moses would not believe it; so at length the Divine anger burned against him, and the Lord ended the conference by saying that He would send Aaron with him, to be his colleague and spokesman. Ah! Better a thousand times had it been for him to trust God for speech, than be thus deposed from his premiership! Aaron shaped the golden calf, and wrought folly in Israel, and became a thorn in the side of the saint of God. And probably in the eyes of their contemporaries, Aaron engrossed the greater attention, and had most of the honor and credit of the great deliverance.

III. The Final Assent. It was a very grudging one. "And he said, O my Lord, send, I pray Thee, by the hand of him whom Thou wilt send." It was as much as to say, "Since Thou art determined to send me, and I must undertake the mission, then let it be so, but I would that it might have been another, and I go because I am compelled." So often do we shrink back from the sacrifice or obligation to which God calls us, that we think we are going to our doom. We seek every reason for evading the Divine will, little realizing that He is forcing us out from our quiet homes into a career which includes, among other things, the song of victory on the banks of the Red Sea; the two lonely sojourns for forty days in converse with God; the shining face; the vision of glory; the burial by the hand of Michael; and the supreme honor of standing beside the Lord on the Transfiguration Mount.

6

"To Egypt"

And Moses returned to the land of Egypt;
and took the rod of God in his hand.
—Exodus 4:20

The fire faded from the bush; the light above the brightness of the sun died away; the voice was still; and Moses looked around on the browsing sheep and the mighty mountains with the strange wonder of a man awaking from a trance. It had been the supreme hour of his life; for which all previous years had been preparing, and from which all future ones would date.

I. First Steps toward Return. Slowly, thoughtfully, perhaps painfully, he prepared to obey the heavenly summons. Gathering his flock together, he conducted it from the backside of the desert, with its stern grandeur, its unoccupied spaces, its intense silence, to Midian, the seat of his clan, where human voices and interests could reassert themselves. "And Moses went and returned to Jethro, his father-in-law." By intermarriage with the tribe of which Jethro was the chieftain, Moses had placed himself under those olden customs which still obtain, as unchanged as the world of nature around them, among the wild sons of the desert. One of these customs demanded that any member of the tribe should seek and obtain permission before starting on a distant errand involving prolonged absence from the camp. This permission Moses sought. "Let me go, I pray thee, and return unto my brethren which are in Egypt, and see whether they be yet alive."

Probably he said nothing of the vision he had seen, or of the mission with which he had been entrusted; and it was a noble reserve. We conserve spiritual strength when we refrain from speaking of our dealings with the Lord. Of course it is sometimes necessary to speak of them, to explain our reasons for action or to lead other souls into the same experiences, but it takes the freshness and delicacy from our inner fellowship with God if we are always talking about it. It is not the nature of the deepest love to unveil all its endearments to unsympathizing eyes. It is much more important that men should see and feed on the fruits and results of such intercourse, than that they should be admitted to study its inner secrets. Moses only sought leave to depart by the way which he had come some forty years before.

The request must have involved surprise and pain to the entire family. They never suspected that strong heart of yearnings for the distant land where his kinsfolk were slaves. His seemed to have become so entirely one with themselves. And his going would involve that of wife and boys, and of the infant son, who seems to have been but recently born. However, no obstacle was thrown in his way, and the permission he asked was granted in the laconic answer, "Go in peace."

But even then he lingered. So utterly had the forty years done their work, that his impulsive, hasty spirit had died down; and he who previously had run before God now began to lag behind Him. He was in no hurry to be gone. Was it that he dreaded the turmoil and stir of the busy crowds of those teeming hives of population? Was it that he had commenced to feel the pressure of growing years, disinclining him from great exertion? Was it that he loved the hush of those desert solitudes, and the companionship of those mighty mountains, and was reluctant to tear himself away from them? Was it that he had misgivings about the safety of his person when exposed to the hatred of king and court? We cannot tell the reason; our only point is to notice the marvelous transformation which had been wrought in his inner life, the deliberation, the self-possession, the reserve. For these qualities were so in the ascendant that it was needful for God to send a second summons into his life. "And the Lord said unto Moses in Midian: Go, re-turn into Egypt; for all the men are dead which sought thy life."

Stirred up by this second summons, as Abraham by the second summons—which came to him also—when Terah was dead, Moses prepared to start for Egypt. It was a very simple cavalcade, reminding us of another which, in similar lowliness, but centuries after, was destined to travel through a part of that same desert towards the same goal. Moses, however, went as the servant who was faithful in all his house, but the infant whom Mary carried was the Son who had built the house, and was coming to live in it forever.

Imagine, then, that setting forth. Zipporah sitting on the ass, perhaps nursing a little babe, newborn, while the husband and father walked beside. And in his hand was the sacred rod—only a shepherd's crook, but now the rod of God—destined to be employed for deeds of transcendent power, and always reminding him of what weak things could do when wielded by strong hands behind them. Three things happened on that journey.

II. A FURTHER REVELATION. "And the Lord said unto Moses, . . ." (21). And there followed a marvelous epitome of events which were to transpire within the next few months, from the making of the water into blood to the slaying of the firstborn.

This was in harmony with one of the greatest principles in the moral and spiritual realm. We only learn as we endeavor to obey. Light is given to us to know what next step we should take—just light enough and no more; a rim of light, hemmed in by darkness falling as a faint circle on our path. Shall we take that step? We hesitate, because we cannot see the step beyond, and the next beyond; or because we fail to see the reason, and are not satisfied to act on the conviction of known duty; or because we dread the awful pain which threatens to benumb us and turn our hearts sick. But so long as we refuse to act, that light cannot increase, but begins inevitably to decline. Obedience is the one condition for its increase, nay, for its maintenance at all.

It may be that you are in darkness like that which enveloped King Saul towards the end of his troubled reign, when the Lord answered him not, "neither by dreams, nor by Urim, nor by prophets." It is long since you heard his voice, or saw his face. But as with Saul so with you, disobedience is the cause. You have neglected to perform the Divine commandments; you have disobeyed the distinct word of the Lord. And you will never get back into the warm, blessed, circle of his manifested presence, where his face smiles and his voice speaks, till you have gone back to the place where you dropped the thread of obedience, and, taking it up where you left it, do what you know to be the word and will of God. Then, as you start to obey, the voice of God will greet you once more with the old familiar tones.

III. A Preparatory Rite. In the caravanserai Moses seems to have been attacked by sudden and dangerous illness, and was on the point of death. What a strange and awful visitation that the destined deliverer of Israel should die amid the hubbub and unrest of an Eastern Khan; his call canceled; his wife returning to her people, a widow; his children fatherless; his people unenfranchised. But amid the horror of that hour, conscience did its work unmolested, and searched the secrets of his heart with her lighted torch. How often have we experienced a similar dealing at the Lord's hands! We have lain all night in a bath of fire; we have suffered almost to the limits of sanity; we have gone down to the depths of the ocean of grief: and as we have raised our weary eyes to God, and asked the reason of discipline so searching, his answer has come back to us in the memory of some hidden sin or neglected duty.

It would seem that for some reason Moses had neglected the rite of circumcision for one of his children, perhaps the newly-born one. That reason may have been due to Zipporah's dislike. He allowed her to have her way, but, as the head of the house, he was held responsible for its omission. We cannot shirk responsibilities placed on our shoulders by God Himself. The husband cannot put them on the wife, nor the wife take them from the husband. And as he seemed to hang in the quivering balance, between life and death, this was brought to mind, and he was compelled to insist that the rite should be performed.

It was a comparatively trivial thing, insignificant in the eyes of man; and yet there are no trifles in a man's dealings with God. Great principles are involved in very insignificant acts, as ponderous bridges revolve on very small pivots. The self-life is sometimes more strongly entrenched in a small thing than in a bigger one. And so he is kept waiting on the threshold of the great enterprise of his life, because this rite of circumcision had not been administered to a little babe. We may be conscious of having been sent to do a great work for God, and yet be shrinking from small known duty; and disobedience here will impede our progress, as the stone in a traveler's shoe. We can never learn the lesson too deeply, that our action in the commonplaces of life is deciding our destiny. What we are in them will affect all our future, making us either the emancipators of our people, or carcasses that bleach on the desert sand.

There is a very striking passage in the Minor Prophets, in which God says, "You only have I known of all the families of the earth; therefore I will punish you for all your iniquities" (Amos 3:2). The more dear we are to God, the more care will He expend on us. The more fruit-bearing qualities we possess, the more thoroughly shall we be pruned. The finest, rarest, metals are exposed to the whitest heat. And it was because Moses was to be so eminently used, that he came into God's most searching discipline. Take heart, suffering child of God! He chastens because He loves, and is about to use you. Be careful to ascertain the evil thing which grieves Him, and put it away; or if it seems impossible to put it out of thy life, ask the Priest to cut it out, for, though touched with our pain, He holds a sharp two-edged sword to pierce to the very borderland of soul and spirit. Then shall God remove the stroke of his hand. "So He let him go."

The exhibition of incompatibility displayed by Zipporah, when she had performed the rite, seems to have led Moses to feel that it would not be wise to take her with him; and, on the whole, it seemed better that she should abide quietly with her own people, until the act of emancipation was wrought. And this was easier, inasmuch as God had so distinctly told him that he should bring the people through those very districts on their way to Canaan (Ex. 3:12). And it befell according to his faith; for in the after narrative we find this record, "Jethro, Moses' father-in-law, came with his sons and his wife unto Moses into the wilderness, where he encamped at the mount of God" (Ex. 18:5).

We are not always to follow this example in ridding ourselves of family ties in order to do God's work. At the same time, a man must always move steadily forward on the appointed plan of his life, not swayed to, but swaying, the members of his home, and bearing them along with him in one common work. The circumstances must be very exceptional that invade the close ties of the home, but when such circumstances arise, they will be so evidently indicated by God's providence that there will be no reflection cast on the character of his servants.

IV. A BROTHERLY ALLIANCE. Recovered from his illness, but lonely, Moses, having sent back his wife and children, started again in his journey, threading his way through those corridors of red sandstone, by which he had passed some forty years ago. But how different it all seemed! *He* was different. No longer a disappointed man, smarting with the sense of recent failure, but strong in the Lord, and in the power of his might, conscious of a great mission, and of the presence of an angel beside him who would be equal to every emergency.

And he knew that the same power which brought him forward was bringing towards him the brother whom he had not seen for forty years. How the hearts of the two throbbed at the thought of meeting! How eagerly would each press forward! How earnestly would each scan the distant figure of the other in the long vista! And, finally, God so contrived it that they met in the Mount of God, where the bush had burned, and the voice of God had summoned Moses from shepherding a flock to become shepherd of a host. Then what greetings! "He kissed him." What interchange of confidences! "Moses told Aaron all the words of the Lord who had sent him." What questionings, as the exile would ask tidings of those whom he had loved!

So we shall meet. God knows where our Aarons are, our twin souls whom we need to have beside us for the completion of our life work. They may be far away now. But He is bringing them to us, and us to them. The Zipporah goes, but the Aaron comes. And we shall not miss each other, since He is Guide. Let us live on his providence and love; and He will so arrange it finally that we shall meet at the Mount of God, some consecrated spot, some bower of holy converse, some blessed trysting place, selected by Himself. And the embrace, the joy, the kiss of welcome, shall in the ecstasy cause us to forget the forty years of exile, loneliness, and sorrow.

7

Failure and Disappointment

*And Moses said, Lord, wherefore hast Thou so
evil entreated this people? Why is it that Thou
hast sent me? For since I came to Pharaoh to
speak in Thy name, he hath done evil to this
people; neither hast Thou delivered
Thy people at all.*
—Exodus 5:22, 23

In loving interchange of thought, the noble and venerable brothers reached Egypt, and in pursuance of the Divine command proceeded to summon the elders of Israel to a conference, at which they should present their credentials, and give utterance to the Divine message with which they were entrusted.

I. The Interview with the Elders. It must have been a very remarkable meeting, perhaps the first of the sort ever held. Never before had this downtrodden nation produced men daring enough to take such a step, the first, indeed, towards national autonomy. We are not told whether there was any disposition on the part of any of these elders, who were probably the heads of the Hebrew families and tribes, to question the right of the brothers to convene them. In all likelihood, they were but too glad to merge all prior and selfish claims in a united effort on their people's behalf; and there were probably many stories afloat of Moses' life and deeds, before his strange and sudden self-expatriation, which predisposed them to obey his call, and gather at some convenient spot within the territory allotted to them to inhabit.

When all were gathered Aaron recited on the behalf of Moses, who probably stood beside him without a word, the magnificent words spoken at the bush (Ex. 3:16–22). We do not know how they were received. Perhaps Moses' own fear was partly realized when he said to God, "They will not believe me, not hearken unto my voice; for they will say, the Lord hath not appeared unto thee." The long years of bondage may have so quenched their hopes and quelled their spirits that they were unable to realize that the hour of deliverance had come. As the inmates of the house of Mary could not believe that Peter, for whose release they had been praying, really stood outside the door; so it was almost impossible to believe that the days of slavery were nearly ended, and that the hands of the clock of their destiny were at last pointing to the hour of release.

At this juncture the brothers would probably give the signs with which God had provided them; the serpent changed into a rod; the leprous hand made natural and whole; the water of the river becoming blood as it was poured out upon the land (Ex. 4:2–9). These won conviction and from that meeting the tidings spread throughout the nation, whispered from hut to hut, told in underbreaths from slave to slave among the brick kilns. "And the people believed; and when they heard that the Lord had visited the children of Israel, and that He had looked upon their affliction, then they bowed their heads and worshiped."

II. THE AUDIENCE WITH PHARAOH. The next point for the brothers was to go to Pharaoh, with the demand that he should let the people go to hold a feast in the wilderness. This was according to the Divine direction (Ex. 3:18); and was moreover a reasonable request. So fastidious a people as the Egyptians could well understand how Israel would prefer to carry out their rites apart from the inspection of strangers, and the contagion of the predominant religious cult surrounding them. Besides, it was like asking for a brief holiday, after an unbroken spell of centuries of incessant toil. It did not set forth all they wanted, but inasmuch as it was a foregone conclusion that Pharaoh would grant nothing, every care was taken to deprive him of the excuse of saying that their demands were preposterous.

It was probably in an audience room of some splendid palace, where the lordly Pharaoh received deputations and embassies, that they met him. How mixed must Moses' feelings have been, entering as a suppliant the precincts in which he had played no inconspicuous part in those buried years! And then Aaron and he uttered the words, which pealed as a thunder clap through the audience, "Thus saith the Lord God of Israel, Let my people go, that they may hold a feast unto Me in the wilderness."

In order to appreciate the audacity of the demand, we must remember the unbridled power and authority which were claimed by the Egyptian monarchs. Each Pharaoh was the child of the sun. He is depicted as fondled by the greatest gods, and sitting with them in the recesses of their temples to receive worship equal to their own. "By the life of Pharaoh," was the supreme oath. Without Pharaoh could not man lift up his hand or foot in all the land of Egypt. For him great Egypt existed. For him all other men lived, suffered, and died. For him the mighty Nile flowed from its unexplored fountains to fructify the soil. For him vast armies of priests, and magicians, and courtiers, wrought and ministered. From his superb throne he looked down on the wretched crowds of subject people, careless of their miseries. What were their tears and groans, and the wail of their bondage, but a fitting sacrifice to be offered to his exalted majesty! In addition, the present monarch had recently, through his generals, achieved certain great victories; and these successes had greatly enhanced his arrogant pride, so that it was in a paroxysm of supercilious scorn that he answered the Divine demand: "Who is the Lord, that I should obey his voice, to let Israel go? I know not the Lord, neither will I let Israel go."

The point of the reply lies in that word *obey*. He saw that these men did not present him with a request, but with a mandate from One of greater authority than himself. This stung him to the quick. He also was a god. Who was this other God, stronger than himself, who dared to issue such a summons! A God of whose existence till that moment he had been unaware! The God of a parcel of slaves! How dare they speak of their paltry Deity in his presence, and in the midst of priests, courtiers, and high officers of state!

The brothers met this outburst with a reiteration of their message, telling how the God of the Hebrews had met with them; and requesting, in a softer tone, that they might be permitted to do as He had enjoined. But the king refused to believe that their plea was genuine; and insisted on regarding the whole matter as a desire to escape from their labors, and as a plea for idleness. Turning sharply on the two brethren, he accused them of hindering their people's toils, and bade them begone to their own share in the clay pit or the brick kiln: "Wherefore do ye, Moses and Aaron, let the people from their works? Get you unto your burdens." What a bitter taunt there was in that last sentence! How the royal lip curled as it was uttered! Already the heart had begun to harden! And so the audience ended, and the brothers came down the crowded corridors amid the titter of the court. A very different scene was to be enacted a few months later, as the news came there of the overthrow of the monarch in the Red Sea—the last stage of the conflict between himself and the God of the Hebrews, whose name he heard that day for the first time.

III. FAILURE AND DISAPPOINTMENT. That same day a new order was issued from the palace, emanating from Pharaoh himself, to the taskmasters of the people. And probably, ere the evening fell, the ominous word had passed from the taskmasters to the head men who were set over their fellow Hebrews, and were, therefore, responsible for the daily delivery of a certain tale of bricks, that they must expect no more straw, though the daily returns must be maintained. "Thus saith Pharaoh, I will not give you straw; go ye, get your straw where ye can find it. Yet not aught of your work shall be diminished."

Then ensued a time of awful anguish. The Hebrew head men told off some of the people to scatter themselves over the country, collecting straw from every quarter, and to do it with all haste. And in the meantime they urged on the rest of the people to compensate for the absence of the straw gatherers by their added energy. Every nerve was strained to the uttermost. From early morning to the last ray of light the whole nation sought to do the impossible beneath the scorching sun, and with never a moment's pause. And yet as the tale of bricks was counted it fell inevitably short. In vain did the taskmasters haste them, saying, "Fulfill your works, your daily tasks, as when there was straw." In vain were the officers of the children of Israel, whom Pharaoh's taskmasters had set over them, beaten, and such beating as they would get might mean death. It was as when a whole crew, stripped to the waist, works at the pumps, but they cannot pump out the water as quickly as it pours in; the waterline will not fall and at length drowning is preferable to the agonized suspense.

Finally, they could stand it no longer, and resolved to make an appeal direct to Pharaoh. "The officers of the children of Israel came and cried unto Pharaoh" (v. 15). It was a bitter day for the two brothers when the people took the matter into their own hands, and, without using them as intermediaries, went direct to the king to get him to put them back to the point at which they stood before that well-meant, but disastrous interference. But it was evidently better that Moses and Aaron should wait outside the palace to learn the result of the interview (v. 20).

It happened just as it might have been expected, the king would not listen to the appeal made to him. "He said, Ye are idle, ye are idle: therefore ye say, Let us go and do sacrifice to the Lord. Go therefore now, and work; for there shall no straw be given to you, yet shall ye deliver the tale of bricks" (vv. 17, 18). It may be that he referred again sarcastically to the "vain words," on which the brothers had caused them to hope (v. 9). And so they came forth from Pharaoh, at the very extreme of agony, dreading the lingering death from exhaustion and stripes, which apparently awaited their whole nation; and as Moses and Aaron stood there they poured on them the bitterness of their spirit. What must it not have been for them to hear from those lips the bitterest reproaches they could frame, cutting them as knives, although they would have gladly given their lives to alleviate the circumstances out of which they sprang? "The Lord look upon you, and judge; because ye have made our savor to stink in the eyes of Pharaoh, and in the eyes of his servants, to put a sword into their hand to slay us."

As we look back on that scene, we can somewhat understand the reason for it all. God can afford to bring us through passages like this, because of "the afterward" to which they lead. It was necessary that Moses, Aaron, and the Hebrews should come to see that their case was desperate, and that no appeals or reasonings or remonstrances could alter it. It was necessary that the leaders should be weaned from the enthusiastic loyalty of the people, that they might lean only on the arm of the living God, and venture forth depending on Him alone. It was necessary that the people should see that they could not better their position by any efforts of their own. Yes, and their thoughts would henceforth be directed past the leaders, who were discredited in their very first endeavor, to the hand and heart of the Almighty.

IV. THE RESORT OF THE BAFFLED SOUL. "And Moses returned unto the Lord, and said, Lord, wherefore hast thou so evil entreated this people? Why is it that thou hast sent me?" (v. 22). There is no other help for us when passing through such stern discipline; and the man who cannot flee thither in similar straits is pitiable indeed. When we see our hopes blasted, our plans miscarry, our efforts do more harm than good, while we are discredited and blamed, pursued with the taunts and hate of those for whom we were willing to lay down our lives, we may preserve an outward calm, but there will be a heartbreak underneath, and the noblest part in us will wither, as corn blasted by an east wind, unless we are able to pour out our whole complaint before God.

The agony of soul through which Moses passed must have been as death to him. He died to his self-esteem, to his castle building, to pride in his miracles, in the enthusiasm of his people, to everything that a popular leader loves. As he lay there on the ground alone before God, wishing himself back in Midian, and thinking himself hardly used, he was falling as a corn of wheat into the ground to die, no longer to abide alone, but to bear much fruit.

Ah, but dying is not pleasant work! It is not easy nor pleasant to forego one's own plans, to cease from one's own works, to renounce one's own reputation, to be despised and flouted by the very slaves you would save. What corn of wheat enjoys having its waterproof sheath torn from it, its elements disintegrated, its heart eaten into, as it lies helpless, exposed to the earth forces, in the cold, damp, dark soil? And yet this is the necessary condition which must be fulfilled, ere it can put forth the slender stalk, like a hand holding to the sun thirty, sixty, or a hundred grains like itself. "That which thou sowest is not quickened except it die, but if it die it bringeth forth much fruit."

It is a lesson for us all. God must bring us down before He can raise us up. Emptying must precede filling. We must get to an end of ourselves before He can begin in us. But what a beginning He makes! "Then the Lord said unto Moses, Now thou shalt see what I will do to Pharaoh, for with a strong hand shall he let them go, and with a strong hand shall he drive them out of his land" (Ex. 6:1). And as those words of encouragement and promise broke on his ear, he must have forgotten the averted looks and bitter words of the people, and risen into a new world of fretful expectation. Deliverance was sure, though he had learned that it did not depend on anything that he could do, but on that all-sufficient God, who had announced Himself as the I AM.

And out of the whole story there comes to us this lesson: we must never suppose that the difficulties which confront us indicate that we are not on God's path, and doing his work. Indeed the contrary is generally the case. If we are willing to walk with God, He will test the sincerity and temper of our soul; He will cause men to ride over our heads; He will bring us through fire and through water. But out of all He will bring us into a large room, and give us the very thing on which we have been taught to set our hearts. The further banks of the Red Sea with their song of victory will wipe out the memory of those bitter disappointments, those sharp speeches, those hours of lonely anguish.

8

The Love of God in the First Four Plagues

Though the Lord cause grief, yet will
He have compassion according to
the multitudes of His mercies.
—Lamentations 3:32

In despair Moses had thrown himself on God, pouring out the story of his failure and shame. "Wherefore hast Thou so evil entreated this people? why is it that Thou hast sent me?" But there was no chiding, no rebuke on the part of his strong and faithful Friend, who knew his frame, and remembered that he was but dust. "Then the Lord said unto Moses, Now shalt thou see what I will do to Pharaoh."

The emphasis lies on the words, *Then—Now—I. Then*—when he had reached the lowest point of self-confidence. *Now*—since all human effort has been put forth in vain. *I,* the self-existent, ever-glorious Lord. He will not give his glory to another. He is for our sakes jealous of his honor. Therefore it is that He brings us down to the dust of self-humiliation, empties us of human pride, divides with his sharp two-edged sword between the energy of our soul-life and the divine energy of His. Only when this is complete, and we have drunk to the dregs the bitter cup of despair of self, does He step in, saying in effect, "Child of my love, stand aside; quiet thyself as a weaned babe, and thou shalt see what I will do. I need thee not, save as the vehicle and expression of the purpose which I have formed in my heart, and which I am prepared to execute by my strong right arm."

The time of depression with the discouraged servant of God is always a time of promise. Then God takes to Himself a new name (Ex. 6:3); then He gives a glimpse of the meaning of his dealings in the past (4); then He reveals the sympathy of his heart, which can detect inarticulate groans (5); then, since He can swear by no other, He pledges Himself with a sevenfold guarantee (6–8). Does any soul, cursed with the tyranny of a bondage beneath which all its energies are pressed to the dust peruse these lines? Let such a one lay to heart the repeated "I will" of this marvelous necklace of promises, which are Yea and Amen in Christ Jesus, applicable to all circumstances, parallel with all ages, unchangeable and eternal as the nature of Jehovah who gave them. "I will bring you out"; "I will ride you"; "I will redeem you"; "I will take you to Me"; "I will be to you a God"; "I will bring you into the land"; "I will give it you"; and notice that this cluster of *I wills* is contained within two brackets, that pledge the very nature of God itself to their accomplishment, "I am the Lord [6] . . . I am the Lord" (8).

God always links obedience and promise. The doing his will must follow close upon hearing his voice. Promise is intended as a spur to action. We hear, that we may pass on to others the words that have stirred our spirits; and, therefore, it befell that Moses was recommissioned to speak, first to the children of Israel, and then to Pharaoh, king of Egypt. It must have been a very memorable day in which the summons came to him *in the land of Egypt,* as it had come before in the wilderness of Sinai (Ex. 7:28).

Had it ever occurred to him that that vision and voice were inseparable from the solitude of those unfrequented wastes, and the silences of those everlasting hills; and that what was possible there, could have no counterpart amid the stir of Egyptian life, and the presence of the hoary monuments of idolatry? If so, the suggestion was at once answered by that voice finding him in Egypt itself. Ah! Souls of men, God speaks not only in the stillness of the hermit's life, but amid the stir of active engagement, and the press of crowds.

It needed more than usual courage for the two brothers to undertake this further ministry; their people were too broken with anguish of spirit and disappointed hope to care very much what was said, especially when it was said by men who had been the cause of the increase of their burdens: and as for Pharaoh, it was idle to suppose that he would be touched by lips which had no power to charm the ears of Hebrews. "And Moses spake before the Lord, saying, Behold, the children of Israel have not hearkened unto me: how then shall Pharaoh hear me, who am of uncircumcised lips?" (6:12). But it was not the time for parley. There was no doubt as to his duty, there should be no hesitation in his obedience.

At the outset of the interview, Pharaoh, as was expected, asked for their credentials, which they gave as God had instructed them. But the evidence was neutralized by the magicians counterfeiting them, either by the dexterity of their sleight of hand, or by collusion with that evil spirit, who has ever sought to mimic Divine work. It was significant, however, that Aaron's rod swallowed up their rods. But the great question would have to be settled on a wider arena, and by a series of more remarkable signs.

It is necessary that we should for a moment consider the underlying principle of God's dealings with Pharaoh, especially in the earlier plagues. And it will not be difficult to discern the operation of the eternal principles of Divine justice and love in the staggering blows which the Divine Power dealt to Pharaoh and his hand.

I. THE LOVE OF GOD. Always and everywhere, God is Love. Whoso is wise with heavenly wisdom, and has eyes purged from the scales of prejudice and passion, will see as much of the tender mercy of God in the Old Testament as in the New; in the storm as in the zephyr; in the earthquake as in the still small voice; in the plagues as in the cross. The very term JEHOVAH, so constantly employed on these pages, indicates, first the unchangeableness, and then the redemptive side, of God's nature. And surely we must believe that Pharaoh was included in the love that gave Jesus Christ to the world; was embraced within the compass of his propitiation; and might have shone as a star in the firmament of blood-bought saints.

It must be possible, therefore, to find a clue which will reconcile the love of God, which brooded over Pharaoh and his land, with the apparent harshness that inflicted the successive plagues. And it will help us if we remember that there is a marked difference between the first four plagues and the rest. In the commencement of God's dealing with the tyrant it would almost appear as if He set Himself to answer the question, "Who is the Lord that I should obey his voice?" and to remove the ignorance of which he complained when he said, "I know not the Lord."

The case was this. Here was a man who from his earliest childhood had been accustomed to think that the deities of his nation were supreme in heaven and on earth; such as the bountiful goddess, who, from her secret urn, was ever pouring forth the waters of the sacred Nile, inundating the land with fertility and beauty; the prolific source of life, whose favorite emblem was the frog, which in unlimited numbers swarmed on the banks of the Nile! while he would attach reverential importance to the purity of the priesthood, and the supremacy of the sun god, of whom the beetle was the sacred sign. It would have been impossible to expect that in a single week he should turn away from these, to accept the commands of One whose name was, for the first time, uttered in his presence by the representatives of a nation of slaves.

When in Athens the Apostle Paul discovered an altar to THE UNKNOWN GOD. He did not rebuke the people for not having given Him suitable worship, but set himself to declare His nature and attributes. And he went on to show that nature, with all her marvelous processes, was due, not to the deities of the heathen Pantheon—though their effigies, sculptured by heart of Phidia, stood out before the gaze of his audience irradiate with the pure light and unstained in the pure air—but was the creation of Him who had spoken to mankind in Jesus, and whose representative he was. And so God set Himself to show that the gods of the heathen were no gods; that the whole system of Egyptian worship must be subordinate to the empire of a greater God than any known to their magicians or priests and that though He had winked at (to use the old expressive term) the days of past ignorance, the time had come when He commanded all men everywhere—Pharaoh on his throne, the priest in his temple, the ryot in his hut—to repent.

"Who is Jehovah?" He is the God of Nature, at whose bidding the Nile no longer blesses, but curses, her devotees; at whose command the objects of Egyptian worship become a loathing and an abomination, and make the land stink; at the expression of whose will the bodies of the priests are covered with the lice that deride all that razor or water can do for their extermination, and at whose summons the sacred beetle corrupts the land. "Not know Him?" He is the God who speaks through human voices; the God of the aged brethren; the God of those groaning serfs; the God who could not run back from a covenant into which He had entered with that longsuffering people; the God of Redemption and of Eternity.

II. THE FAITH OF MOSES. Though it is quite true that the love of God was at work, seeking to reveal itself to Pharaoh by the ordering of the plagues; yet we must always remember that the faith of Moses played no inconspicuous part in respect to them. This is very apparent in connection with the last of the series, concerning which we are told "by faith he forsook Egypt"; and that "he endured, as seeing Him who is invisible." What was true, therefore, concerning the last, was probably true of the rest; and it becomes us to read into the story of Exodus the spiritual qualities unveiled to us in the Epistle to the Hebrews, where the Spirit of God draws aside the veil of the workings of his inner life and manifests him as he was.

In all probability, therefore, throughout the conflict which issued in the emancipation of Israel, Moses was closely dealing with God. God was vividly present to the eye of his soul. He thought much more of the presence and power of Jehovah than he did of the majesty and might of the greatest king of the time; and as God disclosed to him each successive stage of his providential dealings with Pharaoh, his faith claimed that He should do even as He had said. It was therefore through *his* faith, as the medium and instrument, that God wrought with his mighty hand and outstretched arm.

Are there any marvels recorded in Scripture which took place apart from the operation of the faith of some believing soul or souls? If Enoch was translated as a warning to the antediluvian world, it was because he had faith for it. If Isaac was born to a mother who had renounced all hope of childbearing, it was because her faith received strength. If the Red Sea yielded a path to the ransomed hosts, it was because their leader's faith rolled back the glassy billows. If the walls of Jericho fell down, it was because Joshua had faith to believe they would. Just as electricity must have a wire to conduct it, so the almighty power of God demands the organ of our faith. That faith may be very slender; the believer may be very deficient in what the world accounts most precious: but if only there be a genuine connection between the eternal God and the case that has to be met, it is enough. All the Godhead may pass through the slender faith of a very unworthy man; just as the ocean may pass through a very narrow channel. It is with such thoughts in our mind that we consider the first four plagues, and how God showed his love in them.

III. THE PLAGUES. *The River.* One morning, shortly after the events already described, as the sky would be covered with the roseate hue of dawn's first faint blush, Pharaoh, accompanied by high officials, court functionaries, and priests, came down either to perform his customary ablutions or to worship. Upon the river's brink he found Moses awaiting him, with the rod, with which he was already familiar, in his hand. There was no hesitation now in the peremptory summons, "The Lord God of the Hebrews hath sent me unto thee, saying, Let my people go, that they may serve Me in the wilderness." Then follows words which bear out what has been already said of God's purpose in the plagues, "In this shalt thou know that I am the Lord." The first revelation of God was to be made in the smitten water flowing blood; in the death of its fish, that formed not only objects of worship, but provided a large part of the food staple; and in the stench that filled the land with loathing.

The summons was met by the curled lip of scorn or imperturbable silence; and as there was no alternative, Aaron smote the water with the rod in the presence of the court. Most certainly, as he did so, the two brothers exercised faith that God would do as He had said; and according to their faith it befell. An instantaneous change passed over the appearance and the nature of the water. It became blood. From bank to brae, the tide of crimson gore swept on, hour after hour, day after day, till a week was fulfilled. The fish died, and floated on the surface. The air reeked with corruption. And the effects of the visitation extended throughout all the pools, and reservoirs, and cisterns, in places of public resort, as well as in the homes of the people. There was no water in all the land, save the scanty supplies obtained by digging shallow wells, and collecting the brackish surface water.

The magicians, in some way, counterfeited the marvel; and Pharaoh probably thought that on the part of Moses and Aaron there was only a superior sort of legerdemain. Therefore he did not set his heart to it, though he must have realized that he was at issue with a power greater than that of the goddess of the Nile.

Frogs. It has been supposed that the plagues followed in rapid succession, so that the impression of one had not passed away before another succeeded it. And thus the whole conflict was probably comprehended within nine or ten months. It may have therefore been but a few days after, that Moses and Aaron renewed their demand for emancipation, and told the king the penalty of refusal. But there was no response, no proposal, and the inevitable blow fell.

The land suddenly swarmed with frogs. They came up from the river in myriads, till the very ground seemed alive with them, and it was impossible to walk far without crushing scores. Frogs in the houses, frogs in the beds, frogs baked with the food in the ovens, frogs in the kneading troughs worked up with the flour; frogs with their monotonous croak, frogs with their cold, slimy skins, everywhere—from morning to night, from night to morning—frogs. And the aggravation of the plague consisted in the fact of the frog being the emblem of the goddess of fecundity; so that it was sacrilege to destroy it.

This plague elicited from Pharaoh the first symptom of surrender. He sent for the brethren, and implored their prayers that the scourge might be removed, promising that compliance with his request would secure deliverance, "I will let the people go." To make the supremacy and power of God more manifest, Moses bade the monarch fix his own time for the staying of the plague, and then went to cry to the Lord: "Moses cried unto the Lord; and the Lord did according to the word of Moses."

It is remarkable that though the magicians counterfeited the coming of the frogs, they were evidently unable to remove them; and, indeed, the king does not appear to have appealed to them for help in this

direction. Alleviation of human suffering is no part of the program of
the devil or his agents. That can only come from Jehovah, through the
believing cry of his servants. But what a lesson was taught to Pharaoh—
that Jehovah was above all gods, and that He alone could do according to his will!

Lice. The Egyptians were scrupulously clean in their personal
habits, anticipating the habits of our own time. And the priests were
specially so. They bathed themselves repeatedly, and constantly shaved
their persons, that no uncleanliness might unfit them for their sacred duties. What horror, then, must have taken hold of them when
the very dust of Egypt seemed breeding lice; and they found that
they were not exempted from the plague, which was as painful as it was
abhorrent to their delicate sensibility.

Perhaps there is something more than appears at first sight in the
word, "there was lice in man and *in beast.*" Not only on the bodies of
the priests, but on those of the sacred beasts, was there this odious pest.
Each revered shrine boasted its sacred bull or goat, whose glossy skin
was cleansed with reverent care; and it was an unheard of calamity that
it should become infested with this most disgusting parasite. Thus upon
the gods of Egypt did God execute judgment, in order that Pharaoh
might know that He was God of gods, deserving of the allegiance
which He claimed. The magicians themselves seem to have felt that this
plague was a symptom of the working of a higher Power than they
knew; and even they urged Pharaoh to consider that it was the finger
of God. How often do unexpected voices read for us the lessons that
God designs to teach!

The Beetle. It is not perfectly certain what is meant by the word
translated "flies." And though it is possible that is rightly rendered
"flies," yet it is quite as likely that it stands for a peculiar kind of beetle, which was the emblem of the sun god. Their most powerful entity
seemed now to have turned against them, and to have become their
scourge at the behest of the God of these shepherd slaves. The beetles
covered the ground, swarmed into the houses, and spoiled the produce
of their land.

That it was no mere natural visitation was made clear by a division
being made in this plague between the land of Egypt and that of

Goshen, where the Israelites were found. This God, who could turn the very deities of Egypt against their votaries, could as evidently protect his own. And perhaps this wrought on Pharaoh's heart, as nothing else had done; for he was prepared to allow the Israelites to sacrifice in the land. It was a concession which Moses could not accept; alleging that the Israelites would be obliged to sacrifice as victims animals which the Egyptians considered sacred, and irritated feelings might provoke some terrible outbreak of violence. Pharaoh yielded to this reason; and promised to let them go, if they did not go very far on the condition, that Moses should secure the removal of the plague. "And the Lord did according to the word of Moses."

In all this Moses was but the medium, the ambassador, the instrument through whom God wrought. The suggestion of the plagues lay with the Almighty; their execution was effected through the strong faith of the faithful servant, who did as he was told, and spoke as he was bidden. And it was in answer to his believing prayer that the plagues ceased. Through faith like that God will pass out to do his work of might and love and salvation among men.

9

How the Character of Moses Grew

Moses was faithful in all his house.
—Hebrews 3:2

If we were engaged in telling the story of the Exodus, it would become us to study minutely the account of the succeeding plagues. But the story of Israel is, for our present purpose, incidental to the study of that great personage who gave tone and character to the mighty movement which issued in the passage of the Red Sea. It is on Moses that our attention must be focused; and, indeed, it is marvelous to trace the growth of this man, in perhaps a few months, from the diffidence and hesitancy of Midian to the moral sublimity which made him "very great in the land of Egypt," in the sight of the great officials of the court, no less than of the mass of the common people (Gen. 11:3).

We can trace this development of character through the remaining plagues; and as we do so we shall inevitably discover that the secrets of growth consist in an instant and unquestioning obedience, an utter indifference to human opinion, strength of purpose, unfailing patience, indomitable courage, persevering faith and prayer.

Murrain. In the earlier part of his ministry Moses had repeatedly questioned with God before he set about the performance of the

Divine commissions. "Who am I, that I should go in unto Pharaoh?" "How shall Pharaoh hear me who am of uncircumcised lips?" "Behold, I am of uncircumcised lips; how shall Pharaoh hearken unto me?" And, using the language of men, it needed much persuasion and entreaty before he would fulfill Jehovah's word.

But all that had vanished now. Though he had been at least seven times in the royal presence, and each time the bearer of heavy tidings, increasingly abhorred by Pharaoh and his court, and though so far his appearances there had been unsuccessful in securing the great object which God had set before him, yet there was no hesitancy or questioning, when for the eighth time the Lord bade him present himself in the palace to demand the emancipation of the people on pain of a murrain on the beasts.

It is hardly possible to overestimate the value of simple, unquestioning obedience in the growth of character. The rejection of Saul, the first king of Israel, and the selection of David hinged on the fact that the one did not obey the voice of the Lord in performing his commandments, and that the other was a man after God's heart and fulfilled all his will. The stress of our Lord's farewell discourse is on the reiterated word *obey*. Obedience is the test of love; the condition of divine revelation; the precursor of the most sacred intimacy into which God can enter with the human spirit. In proportion as we obey, we become possessed of noble elements of character; which exist in our hearts as vapor until they are condensed in some act of obedience, and become henceforth a permanent property. Disbelief and disobedience are interchangeable terms (Heb. 4:11, *marg.*); from which we may infer that as our obedience is, so will our faith become. Live up to what you know to be your duty; fill in the outlines of God's commands; never stay to count consequences or to question results; if God says, "Go unto Pharaoh and tell him," and you obey, you will not only be set to greater tasks, but you will acquire a character which no amount of meditation or prayer could afford.

The murrain came at the fixed time, "and the cattle of Egypt died." The cattle that fed on the green meadows of the Nile; the horses of the wealthy, for which Egypt was famous; the asses of the poor; the camels that bore the merchandise of Egypt afar, in exchange for spices and balm and myrrh (Gen. 37:25); the oxen that plowed the fields; the sheep which constituted so large a proportion of their wealth—on all of these the murrain fell. The land was filled with death; the rich landowners were greatly impoverished; the poor suffered severely; thousands of shepherds and teamsters were thrown out of work; the routine of business communication was seriously interrupted; and evidence was given of the increasing severity of the plague while God's care of his own was clearly shown in the cordon of protection that He placed around Goshen, concerning which it is said, "Of the cattle of the children of Israel died not one."

Boils and Blains. In estimating a man's work we must always consider the character of the man himself. Certain kinds of work, congenial to some dispositions, are most distasteful to others; and you might as well look for apples on vines as expect to find the two in conjunction. It is much more startling to find certain attributes in some characters than in others—it is like finding a layer of gneiss in chalk. And, surely, it must have been a much greater effort for Moses to be the medium of such judgments, and the object of so much bitter hatred, than for many. He was naturally gentle, tender, and very meek— always ready to pray for the cessation of a plague, and never for its advent; yearning sympathetically over sister and brother, though they had grievously injured him; willing to be accursed if the people might be spared. A man who had kept sheep for forty years would be likely to acquire a tender shepherd-heart. And it must have been no small effort to the instrument for inflicting pain. Yet this fell plentifully to his lot in his terrible vindication of the supremacy and sovereignty of God.

But he flinched not. It was not for him to aspire to be more pitiful than God; and, therefore, when Aaron and he were bidden to take ashes from some expiring furnace, and fling them broadcast on the air, to become a boil breaking forth with blains upon man and upon beast, he did not hesitate. Taking in his hands handfuls of ashes, he accosted Pharaoh on some public occasion, when he and his court of magicians were assembled in the open air, and sprinkled the light grey dust up towards heaven; with such immediate effect that "the magicians could not stand before him because of the boils, for the boil was upon the magicians and upon all the Egyptians" (v. 11), and perhaps, penetrated also to the sacred precincts of the temples, breaking out in the beasts which were there zealously kept free from taint, as gods of the nation (Num. 33:2).

The Hail. As the plagues advance, Aaron is increasingly dropped out of sight. In the first three plagues the Lord said distinctly unto Moses, "Say unto Aaron" (7:19; 8:5, 16). In the fourth (8:20) and fifth (9:1), the word was to Moses only. In the sixth the command is to them both (9:8). But in this, the seventh, the command is given exclusively to Moses. "The Lord said unto Moses, Stretch forth thine hand toward heaven, that there may be hail" (v. 22). And so with the plagues of locusts (10:12), and of the darkness that might be felt (10:21). Why this was we are not told. It does not appear that Aaron had in any way forfeited his position by misconduct, but he may have lacked that simplicity and directness and purity of motive which were so characteristic of his brother: and the faith of Moses grew with every trial of the faithfulness and reliableness of God, till it alone was able to act as the vehicle of the Divine Will. In any case, Moses came increasingly to the front as the wielder of the miracle-working rod, and as the emancipator of Israel.

In the present instance, also, he seems to have acquired to a surprising extent the power of speech. Those stammering lips became the channels of unwonted eloquence, and were kindled by unexpected fire. It was as if he had suddenly felt able to lay side the mediation of Aaron, and to claim those words which the Almighty had promised to put into his mouth. And is it not full of comfort to find that the Lord did not keep him to the mistaken bargain he had made, that Aaron should be his spokesman (Ex. 9:15–17)? We may have said rash things in the past, which we now deeply and seriously regret, but if we show ourselves worthy of a greater distinction than our weak faith imagined possible, God may not tie us to our words, but will open before us possibilities of which we had not dreamed. Aaron shall not be our mouthpiece; we will stand and speak for ourselves.

The warning given to Pharaoh in that early morning was a very solemn one, but it was in vain. He had deliberately hardened himself so often that now both warning and appeal fell on him like rain and sun on granite slabs, and even tended to harden his heart still more. There is no ice so hard as that which melts by day and freezes by night.

And so the storm broke. As the rod was uplifted, vast thunderclouds drifted up from the sea, and covered the land, and poured out their contents in thunder, hail, and fire. Storms of any kind are very rare in Egypt; and this was "very grievous, such as there was none like it in all the land of Egypt since it became a nation." There are several references in the Psalms to this fearful visitation. We can almost hear the peal of the thunder, and detect the devastation caused by the hail, in the vibrating chords of Hebrew minstrelsy. In the intervals of the thunder peals, in which the Almighty uttered his voice, we can hear the pelt of the hailstone chorus and the explosion of the balls of fire (Ps. 18:12, 13). The vines torn from their trellises and beaten into the soil; the sycamore trees blighted as by frost; the forest trees broken down; the crops of flax and barley utterly spoiled; beasts and herdsmen unsheltered in the open fields in defiance of the warning given, smitten to death by hailstones, which fell as thick as rain, and may have weighed (as in exceptional instances hailstones have been known to weigh) from six to eight ounces—such are some of the indications given of the terror of the scene (Ps. 78:47, 48; cv. 32). But from all these the land of Goshen was free.

Through the pelting storm, Moses and Aaron were summoned into the royal presence to hear for the first time from those proud lips the confession of sin (Ex. 9:27) with an urgent entreaty that the mighty thunderings and hail which were then shaking palace and city might cease. Moses had no doubt as to the answer which would come to his prayer, but he had grave doubts of the reliableness of the royal word. However, he did as Pharaoh required. Passing uninjured through the storm, he went beyond the city gates into the open country. It was as if he consciously lived in the secret place of the Most High, and abode under the shadow of the Almighty. With outspread hands he interceded for the land of the oppressors of his people; and God hearkened to his request: so that the thunders and hail ceased, and the rain was no more poured out upon the earth (v. 33).

The Locusts. The tone of Moses rose with every plague. Hitherto he had been content with repeating his demand, but now the failure of the king to keep his royal word had altered the relations between them. Pharaoh had forfeited all claim to his respect. He had made repeated promises and broken them. His confessions of sin had been followed by no efforts at amendment. He was no longer ignorant of Jehovah, but willfully obstinate and defiant. Weak, vacillating, cringing in trial, imperious and truculent in prosperity, he had become unspeakably despicable. And Moses altered his tone; not now treating him as a sovereign, but as a sinner, and dealing directly with his proud and obstinate heart: "Thus saith the Lord God of the Hebrews, How long wilt thou refuse to humble thyself before Me?" The penalty of further delay was to be an infliction of locusts.

The Egyptians well knew what a plague of locusts might mean; and therefore the servants of Pharaoh pleaded with the king to acquiesce in the demand of the Hebrew leaders. Better lose a nation of slaves, said they, then imperil the land. So that from that moment it became a trial of strength between the king of Egypt and God, in whom for the first time in his history he had found more than his match.

Pharaoh, at his servants' suggestion, proposed a compromise. He was willing to let *the men* go, and threatened them with evil if they did not accept this proposition. But there was no hesitation in its instant refusal by the brothers. It could not be. The young and old must go, sons and daughters, flocks and herds—*all*. None was to be absent in that great convocation, which was to assemble somewhere in the desert to hold a feast to Jehovah. The court had never heard the great Pharaoh so addressed; nor could he endure that dauntless speech; so, at a signal from him, they were driven from his presence.

But the locusts came with an east wind, which, blowing straight from the desert, had set in on the land for a whole day and night. "When it was morning, the east wind brought the locusts." Their numbers filled the air, and literally covered the earth. Its green surface was darkened by their brown forms; and every trace of green in the fields, on the fruit trees, and among the plentiful herbs, of which the Egyptians were so fond, instantly disappeared. There was no bud, nor blossom, nor shoot, nor leaf, left anywhere "through all the land of Egypt" (10:15). The animals had perished, and now the produce of the earth. Surely the next visitation must sweep away all human life.

Panic stricken, the king sent for the men whom a little before he had driven from his presence; confessed that he had not only sinned against Jehovah, who had now become an evident Personality to his conscience, but against them; and entreated that this death might be removed. How gracious and longsuffering is God! In answer to Moses' intercession, "the Lord turned a mighty strong west wind, which took away the locusts, and cast them into the Red Sea; there remained not one locust in all the coasts of Egypt" (v. 19). But again Pharaoh went back from his word.

The Darkness. Unannounced, the darkness fell like a pall upon the land, "even darkness that could be felt." Travelers tell us of darkness caused by sandstorm, so thick that it was impossible to see the hand when placed close against the face. From whatever cause, the darkness of this plague must have been of the same description.

"They saw not one another, neither rose any from his place for three days." All the activities of the land were paralyzed. The stoutest hearts were dismayed. It seemed as if their greatest deity had suddenly deserted them, abandoning their case. Perhaps the light would never visit them again. In that land of radiant sunlight it was an awful experience. The very temples were so draped in gloom that the priests could not see the sacred beasts, nor were they able to perform their usual rites. For the first time in perhaps centuries great Memnon's statue failed to greet the beams of the morning sun with music.

When the plague passed away, for the last time the monarch summoned the brothers, and made a final desperate effort at compromise. The nation might go, said he, but the flocks and herds must remain. But Moses penetrated the craft of the proposal, and tore it to shreds. "Our cattle shall go with us, there shall not a hoof be left behind." Clearly they would be required for sacrifice (v. 25). Then, again, the proud spirit of the king, uncowed by repeated misfortune, untaught by the stern discipline of pain, broke vehemently forth; and he said, as if exasperated beyond endurance, "Get thee from me, take heed to thyself, see my face no more; for in that day thou seest my face thou shalt die" (v. 28).

The spirit of Moses, also, was swept with that anger which at rare intervals asserted itself in him, as a storm on a tranquil lake (Ex. 11:8), but he made answer with calm dignity, as became the ambassador of God. "And Moses said, Thou hast spoken well; I will see thy face again no more" (v. 29). But as he turned to leave the royal presence, he raised himself to his full height, and poured one overwhelming torrent of denunciation and warning on the willful spirit that had deliberately chosen evil for its god, and destruction for its doom. "And Moses said, Thus saith the Lord, About midnight will I go out into the midst of Egypt; and all the firstborn of Egypt shall die. And all these thy servants shall come down unto me, and bow down themselves unto me, saying, Get thee out, and all the people that follow thee; and after that I will go out" (11:4–8).

Thus did the bowing reed of Midian become as a rock on which the tempest expends its force in vain; the man who had left that palace in fear, strode its courts as a king; and the faith which fled before the serpent rod became strong enough to wield the thunderbolts of heaven, and to bring the land of Egypt to the very brink of destruction.

10
Preparing for the Exodus

*And it came to pass at the end of the four
hundred and thirty years, that all the hosts of
the Lord went out from the land of Egypt.*
—Exodus 12:4

We have seen how, during those months of agony, Moses
had been the organ through which God wrought out
his purposes; first of informing Pharaoh's mind, and lat-
terly of breaking his stubborn will. And already we have had indications
that through the faith of this man, which was growing exceedingly,
blessing would accrue to the chosen people.

The first three plagues fell equally on the children of Israel as on
the Egyptians, but when the brothers threatened Pharaoh with the
fourth, they were commissioned in the name of God, to utter this further message: "I will sever in that day the land of Goshen, in which my
people dwell" (Ex. 8:22). And from that hour the children of Israel were
exempted from the terrible inflictions by which Egypt was desolated.
Moses claimed that God should do as He had said. And according to
his faith it befell. No murrain swept off their beasts. No boils broke out
on their persons. No tempest swept their fields. No locusts destroyed
their crops. No darkness obscured to them the sun. Thus, while the
minds of their oppressors were engrossed with their own special sufferings, the Hebrews were at peace; and when the Egyptians were

prevented by the darkness from moving, the oppressed population of
Goshen had ample time to prepare for that Exodus which Moses at least
knew was so near.

As we study that strange and marvelous episode, we must never forget the light thrown on it by the memorable verse which tells us that
"*by faith* Moses kept the Passover, and the sprinkling of blood; lest he
that destroyed the firstborn should touch them" (Heb. 11:28). The importance of this verse lies in the fact that it attributes the keeping of the
Passover, the sprinkling of blood on the lintels of the Hebrew houses,
and the immunity of the Hebrew people, to the effect of the heroic faith
which burned so steadily in the soul of this simple-hearted man; the
entirety of whose obedience was only equaled by the absoluteness of
the unquestioning faith, which dared to take God at his word.

I. HIS FAITH WAS BASED ON PROMISE. All faith must rest there.
There must be some distinct word or undertaking on the part of one
who is perfectly trustworthy, or there is no ground for faith to build on.
Here is the difference between faith and credulity; between faith and
following some vain will-o'-the-wisp, generated amid the miasma of an
unhealthy imagination.

We cannot tell the form in which the Divine Word came to the two
brethren. Was it as when a man speaks to his friend? Should we have
heard it, with our uncircumcised ears, had we been in their company? Or was it an impression photographed on the heart of each, up-
turned towards the source of light? But, howsoever the communication
came, in those accents—which first declared what Israel was to do, and
then, with unhesitating precision, announced the successive acts which
would finally smite the fetters from the captives' hands, and free the nation in a single night—they recognized the voice that had bidden
them go to Pharaoh with repeated summonses to surrender.

The directions were substantially these. On the tenth of the following month, the head of each family, whether slave or elder, was to
select a firstling lamb, free of disease and defect. Only if the family were
too small to need a lamb for itself might it join with some neighboring household. There was no question as to the lamb being too little
for the household. Jesus is "enough for all, enough for each, enough

forevermore." The lamb was to be kept from the tenth to the fourteenth of the month, and killed on the latter day, towards the close of the afternoon. The blood, as it gushed warm from the wound, was to be carefully caught in a basin, and sprinkled on the two side posts and lintel of the houses where the Israelites dwelt; the carcass roasted whole, and eaten with unleavened bread and bitter herbs.

Special instructions were also given as to the attitude in which that feast was to be eaten. The whole family was to be gathered around the table, from the grey-headed sire to the newborn babe. There was to be no symptom of lassitude or indolence. The men were to have their loins girt as for a long journey, and to grasp their staves. The women were to have their dough and kneading troughs bound up in little bundles, with their clothes, for easy carriage on their shoulders. All were to have their feet sandalled. The meal was to be eaten in haste. And thus, with ears intent to catch the first note of the trumpet, the whole nation was to await the signal for its Exodus, sheltered by flood; while strength was stored for the fatigues that must be endured ere the land of bondage was left behind forever.

There was a great contrast, therefore, between the attitude of the Israelites in the destruction of the firstborn and in the former plagues. In those they had been perfectly inactive, only reaping the benefits which accrued from the successive victories won through the faith of their great leader. But now they were called upon to appropriate benefits, which might not accrue if they failed to conform to the conditions laid down. And in those demands on their obedience and faith, there surely must have broken, on the minds of the more intelligent at least, the feeling that there was a deeper meaning in the whole transaction than appeared on the surface; and that eternal issues were being wrought out, the meaning of which they could not as yet adequately apprehend.

Moses at least must have felt that God was in effect saying to his people that they were not less guilty, in some respects, than the Egyptians around them. It was not enough for them to allege that they had not gone to the same lengths of stiff-necked rebellion as Pharaoh and his people. Had they not forgotten his Sabbaths, and turned to serve other gods, and mingled in the evil rites of Egyptian idolatry? For these things, at least, they were held guilty in his sight, and liable to lose the firstborn of their homes, unless they kept the sprinkling of blood.

And when all the provision had been thus solemnly recited, there followed the words of promise, on which thenceforward Moses reposed his faith; "I will pass through the land of Egypt, and will smite all the firstborn in the land of Egypt, both man and beast; and when I see the blood, . . . I will pass over you, and the plague shall not be upon you to destroy you, when I smite the land of Egypt" (v. 12, 13).

II. HIS FAITH LED TO ACTION. He gathered the elders of Israel, and informed them of the instructions he had received; and whether it was that some prognostications of their coming deliverance had entered their souls, or that they had come to believe in their great leader to an extent which had been previously impossible, it is certain that they offered neither opposition or suggestion to his proposals. They bowed the head and worshiped, and went their way to do "as the Lord had commanded Moses and Aaron: so did they" (v. 27, 28).

It is a glorious thing for men and angels to see a faith which, with no outward appearance to warrant it, will yet step out on a path of literal obedience, though there seems nothing but thin air to tread upon. It seemed so utterly extraordinary for such a thing to be, as the deliverance of his people, because blood happened to be sprinkled on the outside of their doors. There was no precedent; no apparent reason to justify such a thing to ordinary common sense; no likelihood of obedience having any connection with deliverance. Many such thoughts may have occurred to him, but he dismissed them from his mind, and simply obeyed, believing that there could be no mistake, no shadow of turning in Him to whom he had given the allegiance of his soul.

Oh that such faith were ours! Not arguing, nor questioning, nor reasoning: but believing that the promises of God are Yea and Amen in Christ; and that what He says about accepting all who believe in Christ, making us sit together with Him on his throne, and loving us with the love He bears his Son, He is willing and able to perform.

And such faith becomes contagious. How did that memorable tenth night of the month Abib close in upon Egypt? Did not the air seem oppressed with the burden of the coming woe? Did no priestess, intoxicated with Mephitic vapor, utter in piercing shrieks some warning of the terrible visitation at hand? Did not the wings of the Angel of Death overshadow the doomed land, before he smote with his sword? Surely the fact of the Israelites obtaining so many gifts of jewelry and raiment from the Egyptians indicated that, on both sides, there was an anticipation of their near release. While, however, on the one hand, there must have been grave foreboding and suspense; on the other there were expectancy and hope. The faith of Moses had kindled faith in three millions of people; who stood ready to plunge the knife into the fleecy victim that awaited it, to sprinkle the blood, to start on the distant march, but with no fear that the firstborn of the house should be left a corpse behind. No father eyed his son with anxiety; no mother trembled to hear the rustle of the angel wing; no boy shuddered at the near approach of death. It was enough that God had said, that, when He saw the blood, He would pass over. But though they could not see it or understand it, or fathom the purposes of God, they knew the blood was there to speak for them; and they believed, therefore, that all must be well. And though no one knew exactly their destination, nor how they would reach it, they had no misgiving as to the issue.

III. His Faith was Vindicated. Who can depict that night, ever memorable in the history of our race—when, indeed, as Bunsen says, history itself was born—the night when God brought Israel out of the house of bondage! It was the early spring, and a time of the full silver moon, which shed her soft light in cascades of beauty on the land that lay beneath her; from where, on the Western frontier, the Nile rolled its majestic volumes, to the waters of the Red Sea on the far Eastern border. All was still with an almost preternatural silence; "broken only by the hoot of the owl, the scream of the bittern, the lunge of the monster in the water, or the cry of the jackal on the plains."

But suddenly the stillness was interrupted by a scream of anguish, as a mother rushed out into the night to tell that the Angel of Death had begun his work, and she was presently answered by the wail of a mother in agony for her firstborn; and this by another, and yet another. It was useless to summon priest or physician, magician or courtier; how could they help others who had not been able to ward off death from their own? The maid grinding at the mill and her lady sleeping under curtains of silk were involved in a common sorrow, which obliterated all social distinctions, and made all one. There was not house where there was not one dead—even Pharaoh's palace was not exempt. The news spread like wildfire that the heir to the throne was dead. "And there was a great cry in Egypt."

Ah, Egypt! Bitter as that night was, it did not counterbalance the wrongs that Israel had suffered at thy hands for centuries! Thy tears were as a rill, compared to the rivers of sorrow which had been extorted from that high-spirited people, who were compelled to turn the soil to brick, with no reward but the taskmaster's scourge! Thy loss in sweet and noble life was insignificant, compared with the thousands flung into the Nile, or done to death in the cruel brick kilns! Thy cry, piercing and heartrending though it were, a whisper, compared with the sobs wrung from mothers as their babes were torn from their breasts, the groans of the oppressed as they saw their dear ones failing under a bondage they could not alleviate, or with the cries of the men driven to despair.

"Then Pharaoh rose up in the night, he and all his servants, and all the Egyptians; and he called for Moses and Aaron by night, and said, 'Rise up, and get you forth from among my people.' " There was no attempt at parley. They, their people, their children, and their property, were to be gone. And the bidding of the palace was repeated by ten thousand tongues. The one eager desire of the Egyptians was to get rid of them at all speed, and at all cost. They were glad to give them anything they asked, and thus bestowed some payment for their long unremunerated labor; and even Pharaoh, the haughty monarch, entreated that they would bless him ere they went.

And so the host stepped forth into freedom. For the first time the Israelites realized that they were a nation, and drank the earliest rich deep draft of liberty. A mere horde of slaves, they suddenly crystallized in a people. The spirit of their leader inspired and thrilled them. There was a fire in their eye, an elasticity in their step, a courage in their heart, which told their own story. Then was their mouth filled with laughter, and their tongue with singing. God hath made bare his holy arm in their deliverance. And sentiments began to assert themselves which were destined ere long to roll in thunderous acclaim along the shores of the Red Sea. What faith did for them it will do for thee and me, O soul enslaved by a worse tyranny than Pharaoh's. If only thou would claim deliverance thou should have it. Listen to the son which heralded the work of Christ; "that we, being delivered out of the hand of our enemies, might serve Him without fear, in holiness and righteousness all our days" (Luke 1:74, 75). This is for us. We, too, may overcome by the blood of the Lamb, and by the word of our testimony. By faith we, too, may obtain promises and stop the mouths of lions, and quench the violence of fire. Only claim thy freedom, and thou shalt tread on the lion and adder; the young lion and dragon shalt thou trample under foot.

11

The Passage
of the Red Sea

*The waters were a wall unto them on their
right hand, and on their left. Thus the Lord
saved Israel out of the hand of the Egyptians.*
—Exodus 14:29, 30

I t was not long after the hour of midnight before the entire Israelite
host was on the move; and as the morning light suffused the
cloudlets with its flush, it beheld them marching, the men five
abreast, while wives and children and baggage and cattle followed. From
different points the vast host—which, judging by the fact that the number of the men amounted to six hundred thousand, could not have been
less than two and a half million—converged towards the central meeting place at Succoth.

Moses probably led the largest of several detachments; and we
can almost imagine the flush of honest pride upon his face, mingling
with a sense of profound humility, that he had been honored, in the
hand of God, to become the instrument of so great a deliverance.

Succoth would be about fifteen miles from their starting place, and
there they made their first prolonged halt; baked unleavened cakes of
the dough which they had brought with them; rested the weary
women and children in leafy tabernacles hastily improvised from the
foliage of that region: so that the whole host, heartened and refreshed,
was able to undertake its second state, which was Etham, on the edge

of the wilderness, where the green vegetation of Egypt fades into wastes of sand. There is one episode in this setting forth that we must not forget to mention, and which shows how largely the whole Exodus was wrought in faith, at least in the case of Moses, and perhaps of more. "And Moses took the bones of Joseph with him" (12:10). This great ancestor of their race had been dead some four hundred years, but on his deathbed he had made his brethren swear that when God visited them, as He most surely would, and brought them out of Egypt, they should bear his bones with them in their march. In his death, and through that weary waiting time, he had been the prophet of the Exodus; and how often must those unburied bones have been the theme of conversation in Hebrew homes! And now that they were accompanying their march, all the people realized that the anticipations of generations were being fulfilled. "God had surely visited them."

I. THE GUIDING PILLAR. In the campaigns of Alexander the Great, we are told that a brazier filled with combustibles and elevated on a high pole indicated his pavilion, and directed the march of his victorious armies. But a still greater spectacle came into view as that Hebrew host broke away from the land of bondage. Who has not seen in a summer sky some majestic cumulus cloud sailing slowly through the heavens, as if it had taken the impression of some mighty Alp, whose cliffs, recesses and snow were being reduplicated in its shape and color? Something of this sort must have gathered in the pure morning atmosphere at the head of the vanguard, never again to desert that pilgrim band till the Jordan was crossed and it had settled down to brood over the house of God, But all through the years, when night fell, it burned with fire at its heart; fire, which was always the symbol and sign of the presence of God.

This served many purposes. It was the guide of their march; it was a shadow from the burning heat of a vertical sun, spreading its folds in fleecy beauty to shelter them in a "weary land"; and at night it provided them with a light as it watched over them like the Eye of God. On one occasion, at least, as we shall see presently, it rendered the utmost service by concealing the movements of Israel, lying between them and the pursuit of their foes.

There is no pillar of cloud and fire now—long since it has faded from the sky, but it was in probable allusion to its blessed help that Jesus said, "I am the Light of the World," indicating by his use of a well-known phrase, that what the cloud had been to Israel, He was prepared to be to every soul of man.

He is our Guide; by his Spirit within us, by the example of his life, by the words of his Gospel, and by the manifold indications of his providence, He conducts us over the wastes of our earthly pilgrimage to the land where we would fain be. Do not anticipate Him by rash haste, or by acting on your own hurriedly-formed conclusion. Do not lag behind Him indolently. Dare to wait for months, or even years, if He give no indication that the time has come to strike your tents and follow.

He is our Shield; beneath his canopy we may shelter from the arrows of the sun of temptation or of prosperity, and from the glare of worldly success.

He is our Light; those who follow Him do not walk in the darkness of ignorance, impurity, or sorrow, but have the light of life. Draw the curtain of your tent, Christian pilgrim! Look out into the night already glowing with the myriad stars of promise; amid them all behold the sign that *He* is with you, who slumbers not, nor sleeps, and to whom the night shines as the day.

In the thought of Moses, that cloud by day and night must have been full of reassurance, because it was the very chariot of God, in which He went before his people. And it is very touching to learn that "He took it not away," as if neither sin, nor murmuring, nor disobedience, could ever drive away Him who loves us, not because we are good, but to make us so; and who cannot leave or forsake those whom He has taught to lisp, "Abba, Father."

II. THE ROUTE. The easiest route to Canaan lay through the Isthmus of Suez and the land of the Philistines. A journey of a little over one hundred miles would have conducted them direct to their destination. But God did not permit them to go that way, lest the sight of embattled hosts should unnerve them. In after years, when the education and revelations of the desert were finished, they might behold those scenes undismayed. But as yet they must not know war till they had been more deeply taught in the might and care of God. So is our journey ever adapted to our strength. God is always considering what we are able to bear; never leading us into dangers before which heart and flesh would succumb. "God led them about." The leading about tries our patience, but it is the best route for timid hearts and inexperienced feet.

It must have been a great disappointment when the cloud altered its course, and led them due south. But there was no alternative; and so they finally found themselves encamped in the last place in all the land that human judgment would have selected. It would appear as if Moses himself would have hesitated encamping there, had he not been distinctly commanded to bid the children of Israel take up that position. On one side of them was Migdol (the modern Muktala) and impassable wastes of sand; on the other was the Red Sea. East of them, or, as it might be, in front, was the impassable range of Baal-Zephon.

It was a perfect *cul-de-sac*. There as no egress from it except the way by which they had entered. The most inexperienced eyes in the whole multitude must have seen the apparent absurdity of the movement; and loud and deep must have been the murmurs and protestations of the people. "Is this the way to Canaan? We know better! How dare you presume to lead us, when your very first tactics prove you to be wholly untrustworthy? Well for you and us that Pharaoh has his son to bury; or if he came after us we should be like a penned flock of sheep, the prey of the first wolf that can leap the hurdles!"

Such reflections and reproaches are not easy to bear. They can only be borne by a man who has learned utterly to trust his God. But they made no impression on Moses. He knew Him whom he believed. He had learned to obey Him implicitly, and to see himself always completely vindicated. "Though a host should encamp against him, his heart should not fear; though war should rise against him, in this would he be confident." Oh for more of his simple trusting God, which rests so distinctly in his guidance and help—that the believer will dare to do what to the eye of others are marks of insanity and wild fanaticism, but which are vindicated by the result.

Often God seems to place his children in positions of profound difficulty—leading them into a wedge from which there is no escape; contriving a situation which no human judgment would have permitted had it been previously consulted. The very cloud conducts them thither. You, reader, may be thus involved at this very hour. It does seem perplexing and mysterious to the last degree. But it is perfectly right. The issue will more than Justify Him who has brought you hither. It is a platform for the display of his almighty grace and power. He will not only deliver you, but in doing so He will give you a lesson that you will never forget; and to which, in many a psalm and song in after days, you will revert. You will never be able to thank God enough for having done just as He has. Had you brought yourself into this position by your caprice, you had perished miserably, but since He has brought you here, you have only to stand still and see his salvation, which is prepared as the morning.

III. THE PURSUIT. No sooner had Israel gone than Pharaoh was sorry. The public works stood still for lack of labor. Vast territories were suddenly unoccupied. The labor of this enslaved people was missed on every side, in city and field. There was a sudden loss of revenue and service which he could ill dispense with. And his pride forbade that he should quietly acquiesce in their unhindered Exodus. Besides, in their mad haste to be rid of this people, the Egyptians had laden them with jewels of silver, and jewels of gold, and raiment; so much so that it is distinctly said, "they spoiled the Egyptians." It is clear from the contributions afterwards made to the building of the Tabernacle, that Israel was carrying off a large amount of treasure and valuables. "And the heart of Pharaoh, and of his servants, was turned against the people; and they said, Why have we done this, that we have let Israel go from serving us" (15:5, 6).

At this juncture, the kind heart of the extraordinary movement southwards, which seemed to have thrown them again into his power. Surely his gods were recovering their olden power, and were rallying to his aid! And he said, "I will pursue; I will overtake; I will divide the spoil; my lust shall be satisfied upon them!" Then there was great haste, and the marshaling of the chivalry and the pride of Egypt, six hundred of the chosen chariots, with cavalry and infantry, horsemen and foot soldiers. "And the Egyptians pursued after them, all the horses and chariots of Pharaoh . . . and overtook them" (15:9).

And so as the afternoon closed in, of perhaps the fifth day of the Exodus, the outposts of the fugitive host beheld the dreaded forms of the Egyptian warriors coming over the ridges of the desert hills; and as the night fell they were aware that the whole Egyptian host was encamped in their near vicinity, only waiting for the morning light to swoop down on them, involving them either in a general massacre, or in what was, perhaps, more dreadful, a return to slavery.

It was an awful plight. Terrible, indeed, was the breaking of that news on those craven hearts. They immediately turned on Moses, and spent their fear and anguish on his heart. "Wherefore hast thou dealt thus with us? Were there no graves in Egypt? Better to have perished there than here! Why did you not leave us alone? Where is your God?" And then that noble spirit rose up in the might of its faith, and in the words he spoke we read his own inner attitude. He was not fearful nor dismayed, his cheeks were unblanched, his heart untroubled; he was standing still to see God's salvation, he was perfectly sure that it would be forthcoming that day; and he knew that Jehovah would fight for them, and redeem them, and vindicate his word. So we shall see in our next chapter.

12

The Song of Victory

Sing ye to the Lord, for he hath triumphed
gloriously; the horse and his rider
hath He thrown into the sea.
—Exodus 15:21

When God's cloud brings any of his children into a position of unparalleled difficulty, they may always count upon Him to deliver them. Our Almighty Parent, like the eagle of which Moses sang afterwards, delights to conduct the tender nestlings of his care to the very edge of the precipice, and even to thrust them off into the steeps of air, that they may learn their possession of unrealized powers of flight, to be forever after a luxury; and if, in the attempt, they be exposed to unwonted peril, He is prepared to swoop beneath them, and to bear them upward on his mighty pinions.

A conspicuous example of this is given here. From his chariot cloud their Almighty Friend looked down upon the cowering crowd of fugitives in their sore fear as they cried to Him. "In all their affliction He was afflicted, and the angel of his presence saved them; in his love and in his pity He redeemed them; and He bare them, and carried them" throughout that memorable night and day. As Moses foretold, "He fought for them, while they held their peace."

It would almost seem, from an expression in the Psalms, that the children of Israel yielded to more rebellion at the Red Sea than appears

559

from the narrative of Moses. We are told distinctly that they "provoked him at the Sea, even at the Red Sea, because they remembered not the multitude of his mercies"; so that God saved them in spite of their rebelliousness, for his Name's sake, and "that He might make his mighty power to be known" (Ps. 106:7, 8). And this suggests the further thought, that our deliverance does not depend on our deserts, but upon the Divine purpose. And even though it might be supposed that our behavior, in seasons of peril, must alienate from us the Divine helpfulness, yet it shall not be so, but notwithstanding all, He will work miracles of power for such as have no claim on Him, save that which his love gives.

The one man who seemed unmoved amid the panic of the people was their heroic leader, whose faith was the organ of their deliverance. And therefore it is that in all after-allusions to this great event his hand is always referred to as the instrument through which the might of Jehovah wrought. "Thou leddest," says the Psalmist, "thy people like a flock, by the hand of Moses and Aaron" (Ps. 77:20). "He caused," says Isaiah, "his glorious arm to go at the right hand of Moses" (Is. 63:12, R.V.). The people, therefore, had good reason to remember the ancient days of Moses; for they were made famous by Moses' mighty faith. By his faith they passed through the Red Sea as by dry land.

THE ROD. There is a limit to prayer. While Moses presented an appearance of unbroken fortitude towards the people, rearing himself among them like a rock, before God he bent like a broken reed, crying to Him. That, however, was not the time for heartrending supplication, but for action: he must give to the people the word of advance. Over the sea, on which the shadows of night were falling rapidly, he must stretch out his rod; and by his faith he must afford the power of God a channel through which it should pass to the cleavage of the mighty waters.

That rod had already played many parts; it grew first in some watered glade of the Sinaitic peninsula, little witting of its destiny, till cut down by the shepherd for the purpose of guiding his flock, or clubbing some beast of prey; it was in his hand when God first met with him, and cast upon the ground it became a serpent, emblem of Egyptian pride. Already it had figured in many of the Egyptian plagues;

stretched over the waters of the river to turn them to blood; lifted towards heaven to summon the storm; extended over the land to turn the very dust to lice; hereafter it was to win victory over Amalek, and to open streams from the heart of the rock; everywhere emphatically as "the rod of God." But never in all its history had it done, nor would it do, such marvels as awaited it that night, when at the bidding of God it was stretched over the waters of the Red Sea.

As the rod was in the hands of Moses, so Moses was in the hand of God; and so may each of us be, if only we yield ourselves implicitly to Him for service. By nature we may be of the coarsest texture, not pine, nor oak, nor cedar; by education, we may be uncultured and unpolished; there may be many notches in us which mar our symmetry and beauty: but what do these things matter? The one essential is to know that we are being wielded and used by the hands that shaped the worlds, and built the arch of heaven. The glassblower has beside him on the bench the rudest iron tools to aid him in the execution of the most exquisite designs, but the dexterity of his touch more than compensates for their apparent inaptitude. Be a piece of iron if you will or a rod cut from the forest tree, but be sure that you are in the right hand of the Master Workman.

THE CLOUD. Up till now the pillar of cloud had swept in majestic glory through the heavens, but at this juncture it settled down upon the ground like a great wall of billowy vapor, standing for a fence between the camp of Egypt and the camp of Israel. To the former it was dark and menacing, forbidding progress, and enshrouding the movements of the fugitives; to the latter it gave light, casting a sheen upon the sand and sea, and indicating, with unerring accuracy, the path that soon appeared. All night through, those heaven-lit beacon fires shone out; and in after days the memory of the effect produced by the mingling of their light with the walls of glassy water, supplied the inspired seer with the imagery with which to depict the triumph of the redeemed, who stand on the shores of the "glassy sea mingled with fire, having the harps of God." It seemed as if inspiration itself could find no worthier emblem of that supreme event than the rapture and triumph of the host of Israel on the night, when the glory of the Shechinah flashed back from the crested billows, marshaled on either hand, as the pillared entrance to a mighty temple.

THE PASSAGE. At this point, following the lead of the Psalmist-historian, it is clear that a terrific storm broke upon the scene. The earth shook and trembled; the massy foundations of the mountains rocked; from out the darkness brooding overhead, the curtains of God's pavilion, came the repeated flash of the lightning, followed by the long reverberation of the thunder. The Most High uttered his voice, which was followed by the pelt of the hailstones and the fall of fireballs. The east wind rose in fury, driving before it the retreating waters, which fled at the blast of the breath of his nostrils; then catching them up in its hands it piled them, wave on wave, until they stood up a wall of foam and tumult, from base to top, fretting, seething, fuming, chafing at the unexpected restraint, and wondering at the unwonted posture, but held steadily and always by the pressure of that mighty blast, that gave them no respite, but held them as in a vice; and all the water behind, backed up, leaned upon that rampart, so strangely built, so marvelously maintained.

And on the other side the tide withdrew back and back towards the fountains of the great deep behind. It was as if every wavelet felt the pull, the suction of an abyss opening somewhere far down in the sea, and hastened to fill it, leaving the foundations of the deep naked in the headlong rush. Then the channels of water appeared, the foundations of the world were laid bare, so that rocks and stones deposited in primeval times, and closely veiled from all prying gaze, awoke to find themselves discovered.

Presently it seemed as if there was a pause in the speed of the retreating waters, and they began slowly to return, but as they did so they met with the restraint of the hand of God, which leaving a pathway of sufficient breadth from the wall already formed, commenced to constitute a second, and "so the flood stood upright as a heap, and the deeps were congealed in the heart of the sea."

Shelving down from the shore between these two walls of water, a broad thoroughfare lay outspread, which the prophet compares to those mountain paths by which cattle descend from the heights on which they graze to the valleys where they rest (Is. 68:14). Was there ever such a strange comparison? And yet for the moment it seemed almost as natural; and at that moment the word which had sprung from the lips of the leader, and had been caught by those who stood closest around him, passed like prairie fire, though in a whisper, from lip to lip, "Speak unto the children of Israel that they go forward"; and immediately, without precipitate haste, but with glad obedience, the ransomed host stepped down, rank after rank, and passed between the walls of glass and fir amid the rattle of the storm, which made the withdrawal of their hosts inaudible to their foes.

Imagine, O child of God, if you can, that triumphal march: the excited children restrained from ejaculations of wonder by the perpetual hush of their parents; the almost uncontrollable excitement of the women as they found themselves suddenly saved from a fate worse than death; while the men followed or accompanied them, ashamed or confounded that they had ever mistrusted God or murmured against Moses: and as you see those mighty walls of water piled by the outstretched hand of the Eternal in response to the faith of a single man, learn what God will do for his own. Dread not any result of implicit obedience to his command; fear not the angry waters which, in their proud insolence, forbid your progress; fear not the turbulent crowds of men who are perpetually compared to waters lifting up their voice and roaring with their waves. Fear none of these things. Above the voice of many waters, the mighty breakers of the sea, the Lord sits as king upon the flood; yea, the Lord sits as king forever. A storm is only as the outskirts of his robe, the symptom of his advent, the environment of his presence. His way lies through, as well as *in* the sea, his path amid mighty waters, and his footsteps are veiled from human reason. Dare to trust Him; dare to follow Him! Step right down into the ooze of the sea, to find it rock; go down into the mighty depths, to discover that the very forces which barred your progress and threatened your life, at his bidding become the materials of which an avenue is made to liberty.

THE PURSUIT. As soon as the Egyptians became aware that Israel was escaping, they followed them, and went on after them into the midst of the sea. There was a good deal of pride and obstinacy in this act, which tempted God and presumptuously dared him to do his worst; and forthwith, when the host was between the walls of water, the whole force of the storm seemed to spend itself on them. The Lord looked upon them through the pillar of fire and of cloud, and troubled them; a sudden panic seized them; their heavy chariots could make but ill progress amid the ooze of the sea bottom, and the wheels themselves became clogged and bound so that they could not move; and they turned to flee, conscious that a greater than Israel was engaged against them.

At this juncture the morning light began to break; and, at the bidding of God, Moses stretched out his hand over the sea from that further shore which he and Israel had by this time gained, and the sea returned to its strength. The Egyptians fled against it in vain; they were overwhelmed in the sudden rush of water toppling down on them from either side. They sank as lead in the mighty waters; they went down like a stone into its depths; and in less than it takes to tell the story, not a trace of their proud array remained.

THE SONG OF MOSES. "Then sang Moses." The morning dawn revealed one of the most memorable spectacles of history. A nation of slaves, fleeing from their masters, had suddenly become a nation of freemen, and stood emancipated upon the shores of a new continent. The proud people, which for generations had inflicted such untold griefs upon them, had suffered a humiliation from which it would take them generations to recover. The chivalry of Egypt was overwhelmed in the midst of the sea, there remained not so much as one of them left; and all along the shore lay the bodies of the dead, cast up from the depths of the tide. At this day a significant blank in the hieroglyphed memorials of Egypt tells the story of that overwhelming disaster. And there was given to Israel for all subsequent time an evidence of the trustworthiness of God, which compelled belief, not only in their great Deliverer, but in his servant Moses. It is thus, if only we are still, and commit to Him our cause, that He will vindicate us from the aspersions of our detractors, and bring out our judgment to the light. And we shall look back on the forms which once filled us with dread, dead upon the seashore, unable to pursue or hurt us more.

And from that ransomed host, congregated there in one vast throng, broke forth an anthem, whose sublime conceptions of language rendered it worthy of the occasion, as it has been the model for triumphal songs in all subsequent times.

There is no thought of any but the Lord throughout the entire piece. The song was sung to Him and of Him. It was *He* that had triumphed gloriously, and cast horse and rider into the sea. It was *his* right hand that had dashed in pieces the enemy. It was because *He* blew with *his* wind, that they sank as lead in the mighty waters. It was through the greatness of *his* excellency that they were overthrown who had risen against Him. All the honors of the victory were reverently laid at his feet. Moses is not once referred to.

And the ease of his victory was clearly accentuated. The waters were piled as walls by his breath. He blew with his wind, and a whole army sank as a stone into the depths. He had but to stretch out his right hand, and the sea swallowed the flower of the greatest army of the time.

Note the epithets heaped on God: "My strength and song and salvation"; "glorious in holiness, fearful in praises, doing wonders"; while the men extolled Him as "a man of war," and dwelt on the anguish that must take hold of the inhabitants of Canaan when they heard the story of the overthrow. The women, led by Miriam, replied in a noble refrain, "Sing ye to the Lord, for He hath triumphed gloriously; the horse and his rider hath He thrown into the sea."

Whether or not this ode were composed beforehand in anticipation of this moment we cannot tell. It may have been; else how could it have been sung by those assembled thousands? But this in itself would be a striking token of the faith which dwelt so vigorously in the heart of Moses. It was *his* song preeminently; and in its closing notes we catch a glimpse of his forecast of the future, and the certainty of his convictions: "Thou shalt bring them in and plant them in the mountain of thine inheritance."

So does God turn our anxieties into occasions of singing—weeping endures for a night, but joy comes in the morning. The redeemed obtain gladness and joy; God puts gladness into their hearts, and new songs into their mouths. Long years of waiting and preparation and obedience shall be rewarded at last, as certainly as God is God. If not before, yet surely when the eternal morning is breaking on the shores of time, we shall join in shouts of victory; which shall awaken eternal echoes, as with myriads beside we sing the song of Moses, the servant of God, and the song of the Lamb.

13

Marah and Elim

All these things
happened unto them by way of figure.
—1 Corinthians 10:11, R.V., *marg.*

The peninsula of Sinai, on the shores of which the ransomed people stood, and which for forty years was to be their schoolhouse, is one of the wildest, grandest, barest countries in the world. It has been described as a tangle maze of mountains, piled in inextricable confusion, and gradually rising in height towards the lofty summit of Um-Shomer, to the south of Sinai. Between the Red Sea and the lowest outworks of these mighty citadels of rock there is a plain of gravel; and thence the way climbs slowly upward through long avenues and passes composed of purple granite or brilliant sandstone, which give a richness to the landscape unknown to our bleaker and greyer hills.

We have not now to do with those majestic approaches to the inner sanctuary, but with the sandy plain over which, during the first weeks of wandering, the host was led, skirting the shores of the Red Sea, along which they probably beheld the dead bodies of their foes—a ghastly spectacle!

Though not expressly stated, there must have been a division of the Israelite host, from the point where their first encampments were pitched in the strange new land of freedom. The flocks and herds, as is the custom with modern Arabs, were dispersed far and wide over the country, to crop the scanty "pastures of the wilderness," of which the Psalmist speaks. "Nearly everywhere," Dean Stanley tells us, "there is a thin, it might almost be said a transparent, coating of vegetation. And in some few places there are more marked spots of verdure, the accompaniments, not of the empty beds of winter torrents, but of the few living, perhaps perennial springs; which by the mere fact of their rarity assume an importance difficult to be understood, in the moist scenery of these northern lands." It was there that their flocks and herds were preserved, while the main body of the people marched with Moses.

How marvelous the change! No longer the ceaseless pulse of movement of Egypt, with festival and pageant, song and feast, the court and the army; no longer the green valley of the beneficent Nile, where water never failed, and luscious vegetables, melons, leeks, and garlic, charmed away thirst; no longer the majestic glory of sphinx, and pyramid, and temple: but instead, a silence so intense that the Arabs say they can make their voices heard across the Gulf of Akaba, a waste so waterless, that they might count themselves fortunate if they met a spring in a day's march; while they were literally enclosed within a temple, whose walls were stupendous rocks, such as human hands had never piled. But amid all these checkered and strange experiences, the cloud slowly led them forward; and as the successive scenes crowd on our view, we cannot but see in them an allegory or parable of human life, and we acknowledge the truth of the Apostle's statement, "Now these things happened unto them by way of figure" (1 Cor. 10:11, R.V., *marg.*).

I. THE COURAGEOUS FAITH OF MOSES. He knew that desert well—its wild and desolate character, its dried torrent beds, its lack of all that would support human life; he knew, too, that if they were to follow the northern route it would not take them very long to reach the land of the Philistines, "which was near," and where they would be easily able to procure all necessary supplies either by force or purchase, but we are told, nevertheless, that he deliberately led them southwards and entered the wilderness. "So Moses brought Israel from the Red Sea, and they went out into the wilderness of Shur." He could not do otherwise, because the cloud went that way, but even with that indication of God's will before his eyes, it must have required a heroic faith to lead two millions of people direct into the wilderness (Ex. 13:17; 15:22).

We all of us need the leading about by the way of the wilderness. In its majestic scenery, our minds, dwarfed and stunted by too great familiarity with the works of men, are turned to a higher keynote, and learn to wonder at the littleness of the vanities which engross so many. There we learn to deal with God not at second hand, as is too frequent in human civilization, but directly, as scattering with his own hand the manna for our food, and deriving from "the flinty rock" the living streams to quench our thirst. We lose the luxuries which were sapping and enervating our moral nature, to find ourselves becoming braced and strengthened in every sinew by privation and hardship. Patience, freedom, faith, the pilgrim spirit—all these are children of the wilderness wanderings, that thrive in its rare and peculiar air.

There was good reason, then, why the great leader should follow the lead of the cloud, but it was not the less a sublime evidence of a faith that could trust God to the uttermost, as he turned his back on Philistia, and steadfastly took his course towards the heart of the desert, veiled as yet in those mighty ramparts and walls of rock.

II. THE TESTING OF HIS FAITH. "They went three days in the wilderness, and found no water" (Ex. 15:22). The first day's journey was, doubtless, very distressing—the blinding sandstorms; the glare of the sun reflected from the white limestone plains; the absence of shade, of tree, of water. And the water which they carried in their waterskins must have become hot and unrefreshing.

The second day was not less trying. The sea was now far in their rear, and there was nothing to break the monotony of the treeless, lifeless, waterless horizon. And surely as they pitched their black tents for the night, it was difficult to repress some discontent, or at least anxiety, as to what the morrow might bring to their blistered feet and fevered lips. Their supplies of water were also getting low, if they were not quite exhausted.

The third day broke. Perhaps Moses, knowing that pools of water were not far away, encouraged them to persevere; and every eye was eagerly strained to catch the first sight of palm trees and living verdure. Not more eagerly does the mother look for the symptoms of returning life on the cheek of her child, or the beleaguered garrison scan the horizon for the first signal of the relieving squadron, than did those wistful eyes seek for the promised signs.

And when at last, towards the close of the day, they descried them in the far distance, how glad their shouts, how buoyant their hearts, how ready their expressions of confidence in Moses! Their fatigues and complaints and privations were all forgotten, as with quickened pace they made for the margin of the wells. But ah, how great was their disappointment and chagrin when the first long draft filled their mouths with bitterness, and they discovered that the water was too nauseous to drink!

So long as there was none to be got, they had managed to endure, but this sorrow was harder than they could bear, and they turned on Moses and murmured, "What shall we drink?" "They soon forgot His works." From minstrels they become mutineers.

Do we not all know something of the wilderness march? It may follow on some great deliverance. But how great a contrast there is between the rapturous hallelujahs of the one, and the wearying commonplace of the other! The start is both interesting and delightful, but it is so hard to plod on day after day, amid the dust of the shop, the glare of temptation, the pressure of grinding poverty, the routine of irksome toil. The wilderness is no child's play; it is meant to be our school, our training ground, our arena, where we are being sternly and carefully educated for our great future. And then Marahs will come—bitter disappointments, heart-rending sorrow, as our ideals are shattered and our cherished plans torn to shreds. Ah me! It were better to plod on day by day without the vision of coming bliss, than to awake to discover that it has been an unsubstantial mirage. The Marahs are permitted to prove us, or, in other words, to show what is in us. What pilgrim to the New Jerusalem is there that has not visited those springs, and mingled bitter tears with the bitter waters?

III. MOSES' RESOURCE. "He cried unto the Lord." How much better this than to rebuke the people, or to threaten to throw up his appointment, or to sit down in despondence as utterly out of heart! The disciples of John, when they had buried their beloved leader, went and told Jesus. And in all ages the servants of God have been glad to turn from their discouragements and the ingratitude of those for whom they would have gladly laid down their lives, to Him whose heart is open to every moan, and whose love is over all and through all, and in all.

Beside each bitter Marah pool there grows a tree, which, when cast into the waters, makes them palatable and sweet. It is so ever. Poison and antidote, infection and cure, pain and medicine, are always close together. The word which saves is nigh even in the mouth and in the heart. WE do not always see the "sufficient grace," but it is there. Too occupied with our disappointment, we have no heart to seek for it, but when we cry, it is shown to our weary longing eyes.

And of what is that tree the type, if not of the cross of Jesus—which is the symbol, not only of our redemption, but of a yielded will? It was there that his obedience to the will of his Father reached its supreme manifestation. He became obedient to death, even the death of the cross. Nor is there anything that will so take the bitterness out of disappointment and so make it palatable and even lifegiving, as to look up from it to the cross, and to say, "Not my will, but Thine be done. Thy will is my weal. In Thy will is my bliss."

What a constant lesson Moses was learning from day to day! God must indeed have become a living reality to him. He learned God's ways; we are expressly told "that they were made known to him." And gradually he must have come to feel that the whole responsibility of the pilgrimage was on the great, broad shoulders of his Almighty Friend. Ah, fellow workers, let us not carry the burdens of responsibilities arising out of his work! Our one thought should be to be on his track, and to be in living union with Himself. We may leave all the rest with Him.

IV. ELIM. There are more Elims in the life than Marahs; and we *encamp* by them. WE are not bidden to tarry at the one, but we may spend long blessed days at the other. How refreshing the shadow of those seventy palm trees! How sweet the water of those twelve wells!

How delightful those long restful days! You say that they will never
come to you? Yes, but they will! They come to all tired souls. There is
no desert march without an Elim at last. The Lamb cannot fail to lead
you by living fountains of water, and to wipe away all tears from your
eyes before you pass the gateway of pearl. A lull comes in the storm; an
arbor on the Hill Difficulty; a pause in the march. He makes his
sheep to lie down in pastures of tender grass, and leads them beside waters of rest. "Oh, magnify the Lord with me, and let us exalt his name
together!"

We must read the desert, or we can never come to Elim. But the
desert lends the Elim much of its bliss. The Castle of Doubting makes
the vision from the Delectable Mountains so entrancing. The long illness makes the air so exquisite in the first permitted walk or drive. The
long winter snows paint the fairest colors on the spring flowers. Do not
stay murmuring at Marah; press on! Our Elim is within sight. Hope
thou in God, for thou shalt yet praise Him.

At Marah Moses received from God a glad, fresh revelation, that
God would be the healer of his people in their wilderness march, securing them from the diseases of Egypt. Marvelous that such a message
should be sent at such a time! But the grace of God is not restrained
by human sin from making its glad surprises. And Elim was the vindication of the promise. What a God is ours! He overthrows our foes
in the sea, and disciplines his people in the desert. He leads us over the
burning sand, and rest us in luxuriant glades. He permits disappointment at Marah, and surprises us at Elim. He leads us by a cloud, but
He speaks to us by a human voice. He counts the number of the star,
but He feeds his flock like a shepherd, and gently leads those that give
suck. He chooses a thundercloud as the canvas on which He paints his
promise in rainbow hues. He proves by Marah, and at Elim recruits us.

14

The Gift of Manna

*When the dew that lay was gone up, behold, upon
the face of the wilderness a small round thing,
small as the hoar frost on the ground. And when
the children of Israel saw it, they said one to another, What is it? For they knew not what it was.
And Moses said unto them, It is the bread which
the Lord hath given you to eat.*
—Exodus 16:14–16, R.V.

We may encamp at Elim, and stay for long happy days in its
green bowers, but we may not live there; at least the majority may not. It is so much harder, and needs so much
more grace, to remain devoted and earnest, to retain the girt loin and
the soldier-like bearing, in its soft, enervating climate, than on the bare
and sterile sand of the desert, with its rare and stimulating air. Few characters are able to reach their highest and noblest excellence amid the
genial conditions through which at times each life is permitted to
pass. Therefore it is that, though the cloud of the Divine guidance
broods at Elim long enough to recruit us, it soon gathers up its folds,
and commences its majestic progress over the desert expanse, leaving
us no alternative but to strike our tents and follow. So it is said that
"they took their journey from Elim; and all the congregation of the children of Israel came unto the wilderness of Sin, which is between Elim
and Sinai" (v. 1).

Farewell to the seventy palm trees and the twelve watersprings!
Farewell to the brief, bright hours of respite from the blinding glare of
the desert! But He whose nature was mirrored in that exquisite beauty,

who was able to reproduce any number of Elims if He chose—*He* could never be left behind, but always must accompany his people.

It is immaterial whether He locates us amid verdure or desert, He is responsible to make up from his own resources for that which is lacking in outward circumstance. What if there are no palm trees? The shadow of the Almighty must be our shelter from the sultry heat.

There are things about God and his ability to supply all needs of the soul of man, which could not be learned in any Elim, with all its beauty; and can only be acquired where its bowers are exchanged for those long corridors of rock which lead to the foot of Sinai, as the ancient approaches of obelisks conducted to the pillared halls of Karnak. The eagle wings on which God bears his people are only spread beneath them when the nest is broken up and left. The supremacy of God over all natural laws is only learned when they are seen to stand before Him as the angels who do his bidding, hearkening unto the voice of his word. The patient tenderness of God, the mother side of his nature, is only apparent where a whole host breaks out in to the sobbings of a querulous child. The punctuality of God is more easily discerned in the spread breakfast table of the wilderness than in the procession of the seasons or the march of worlds. It is well, then, to leave Elim; beyond it lie Sinai, Pisgah, and Canaan.

I. THE DESERT MURMURINGS. It was a great aggravation of the responsibilities which already lay heavily on the heart of Moses, to have to encounter the perpetual murmurings of the people whom he loved so well. It only drove him continually back on his Almighty Friend and Helper, to pour into his most tender and sympathizing ear the entire tale of sorrow. But the repeated outbreak of the murmurings all along the wilderness route only sets in more conspicuous prominence the beauty of his gentle meekness, and the glory of his faith, which probably was the one channel through which the power of God wrought for the salvation and blessing of his people.

The race of murmurers is, alas, not extinct. Lips which have joined in singing consecration hymns, sometimes give passage to complaints. And we are none of us so careful as we ought to be to restrain the expression of discontent. How often are murmurings mingled with the food we eat, because we are not exactly pleased with its quality or preparation; with the weather, because it does not quite fit in with our plans; with our daily calling, because it is irksome and distasteful; and with the presence or absence of certain persons in our lives!

Murmurers are short of Memory. It was only one short month since the people had come forth out of Egypt—a month crowded with the wonders which the right hand of the Lord had wrought. The chronicler specially notes that it was the fifteenth day of the second month, and adds, "The whole congregation of the children of Israel murmured against Moses and Aaron in the wilderness; and the children of Israel said unto them, Would to God we had died by the hand of the Lord in the land of Egypt, when we sat by the flesh pots, and when we did eat bread to the full; for ye have brought us forth into this wilderness to kill this whole assembly with hunger" (vv. 2, 3).

They could remember very well the sensual delights of Egypt, but they forgot the lash of the taskmaster, and the anguish of heart with which they wrought at the kneading of the clay. They forgot how graciously God had provided for their needs, ever since they had stood around their tables to eat the flesh of the paschal lamb. They forgot the triumph song, which recorded their undoubting faith that God would bring them in and plant them in the land of their inheritance. None of these things availed to stay the torrent of their murmuring complaining.

Whenever a murmuring fit threatens, let us review the past, and recount the Lord's dealings with us in bygone years. Did He deliver in six troubles, and is He likely to forsake us in the seventh? Has He ransomed our souls from the power of the grave, and will He not regard the body, which is included in the purchase money? When the Psalmist complained, and his spirit was overwhelmed, he tells us that he considered the days of old, the years of ancient times; he called to remembrance his song in the night; he remembered the years of the right hand of the Most High. "I will remember the works of the Lord; surely I will remember thy wonders of old." And as at the summons of memory, the sea of the past gives up its dead, each risen record of God's goodness will condemn the murmur, and rally the wavering faith.

Murmurers are short of Sight. They fail to see that behind all the appearances of things there lie hid the Presence and Providence of God.

Moses called the attention of the people to this fact, which enhanced so gravely the magnitude of their offense. They thought that they were only venting their spleen on a man like themselves. Annoyed and apprehensive, it was some relief to expend their spleen on the one man to whom they owed everything. Ah! How vain it is to trust the populace, which today cries Hosanna; tomorrow, Crucify! But their faithful leader showed them that their insults were directed not against himself, but against Him whose servant he was, and at whose bidding everything was being wrought. "The Lord heareth your murmurings which ye murmur against HIM; and way are we? Your murmurings are not against us, but against the Lord" (v. 8).

It becomes us to ponder well those words. Some of God's children are more willing to admit a general providence than a special particular one. But the former involves the latter. The whole teaching of Jesus compels us to believe in a care which counts the hairs of our heads. The very necessities of our education demand a Divine superintendence of the insignificances and commonplaces of life. God must be in all things, ordaining and permitting them. It is impossible, therefore, to grumble, without the sword of our words cutting through the gauze-like drapery of what we see, and wounding Him whom circumstances scarcely avail to hide. Grumblings, murmurings, complaints, these are directed against the will and arrangement and plan of God. And their cure is to accept all things from his hand, to acquiesce in his wise appointments, and to believe that He is securing the very best results.

Murmurers are Short of Faith. The pressure of want had begun to make itself felt but very slightly, if at all, on the host. It was not so much the hardship that they were at that moment experiencing, but that which they thought to be imminent. Provisions were running short; supplies were becoming exhausted; the slender store refused to be eked out beyond a comparatively short period. It was thus that they came to Moses and murmured.

God often delays his help. He tarries ere He comes, long enough to bring us to the end of ourselves, and to show the futility of looking for creature aid. At such times we too often evade the lesson which He would teach, and bemoan our hard lot, though it is only a suggestion of our fearful hearts. From the marshy swamps of our inner life arises the miasma of unbelief, in the folds of which our imagination affects to descry gaunt and fearful objects; and immediately we think that they have, or will have, a real existence, we fall straightway all along the earth, and are sore afraid, as Saul before the ghost of Samuel.

Too many of God's children despond because of what they dread, and break out into murmurings that they are going to be killed; when if they were to stop to think for a single moment, they would see that God is pledged by the most solemn obligations to provide for them. Why do you murmur? It is because you doubt. Why do you doubt? It is because you will look out on the future, or consider your circumstances, apart from God. But when the eye is single in its steadfast gaze towards Him—his love, his wisdom, his resources—faith grows strong, reads his love in his eyes, reckons on his faithfulness, and realizes that he who spared not his own Son, but delivered Him up for us all, will with Him also freely give us all things.

How different to this murmuring life was that of our blessed Lord, who also was led into the wilderness, and was without food for forty days! But He did not complain; no word of murmuring passed his lips, although He might have remonstrated with the Father for dealing thus with one who had always yielded Him a prompt and glad obedience. And even when He hungered, and the devil suggested that hunger was not becoming to the newly-designated Son of God, He meekly said that it was enough for Him to have his Father's will. He was prepared for all that it might involve. He insisted that if God withheld bread, He would sustain the body He had made in some other way. The Son never for a moment questioned his father's right to follow any line of procedure He chose, and was apparently perfectly satisfied. He had learned the secret of how to be full and to be hungry, how to abound and to suffer need. He did not live by bread alone, but by every word that proceeds out of the mouth of God. And in this Divine patience He has shown how murmuring may find no foothold, and how the soul may be braced to endure hardship.

II. The Wilderness Food. It is not for us to tell here the whole story of the manna, with its wealth of spiritual reference to the true Bread, which is Christ. It is enough to remember:

To look up for our supplies. "He gave them bread from heaven to eat." For the believer there are five sources from which help may come; for in addition to the four quarters of the winds he looks up to the heavens. There came *from heaven* the sound of the rushing of a mighty wind. Look higher, child of God, to the heart and hand of the Father!

To feed on the heavenly bread daily and early. "They gathered it every morning, and when the sun waxed hot it melted." There is no time like the early morning hour for feeding on the flesh of Christ by communion with Him, and pondering his words. Once lose that, and the charm is broken by the intrusion of many things, though it may be they are all useful and necessary. You cannot remake the broken reflections of a lake swept by wind. How different is that day from all others, the early prime of which is surrendered to fellowship with Christ! Nor is it possible to live today on the gathered spoils of yesterday. Each man needs all that a new day can yield him of God's grace and comfort. It must be daily bread.

To feed on Christ is the only secret of strength and blessedness. If only believers in Christ would realize and appropriate the lesson so clearly taught in this narrative, as well as in the wonderful discourse which our Lord founded upon (John 6:22–58), they would find themselves the subjects of a marvelous change. It is almost incredible how great a difference is wrought by the prolonged and living study of what the Scriptures say concerning Him. To sit down to enjoy them; to read two or three chapters, an epistle, or a book, at a sitting; to let the heart and mind steep in it; to do this before other intruders have noisily entered the heart and distracted its attention—ah, how this transforms us!

We close this chapter, however, by calling attention to the remarkable expression used by our Lord, when He said, "Moses gave you not that bread from heaven" (John 6:32); intimating that though Moses did not give that eternal Bread of which He was speaking, yet he did give some sort of bread, *i.e.,* the manna; so that there was a sense in which the faithful servant procured and gave daily the provision on which his people fed.

We are not unfamiliar, in these days, with instances in which the faith of one man avails to procure the daily food of hundreds of orphans and of others. God gives to them that they may give to those with whom they are charged. But all these are dwarfed before the stupendous miracle of a faith that was capable of covering the desert place with food for forty years!

No one who reads these words need ever hesitate to enter into partnership with God for any enterprise to which the Almighty may summon him. The only thing that is at all necessary is to be quick to catch the faintest expression of his will, prompt to obey, and strong to persevere. When these conditions are fulfilled, the soul walks with God in blessed companionship; taking pleasure in difficulty, straitness, famine, and peril, because each of these becomes a foil for the display of the Divine resources, who makes even mountains move. Such a one is perfectly indifferent to murmuring or applause, to censure or praise; since the soul is engrossed with a companionship which is perfect bliss, because perfect satisfaction.

Let us, then, unceasing make our boast in the Lord, as we step out on to the unknown and untried. And who shall lament the beauty of Elim, or the fleshpots of Egypt, or the frugal meals of Jethro's tent, when such lessons are to be learned in the society of our eternal Friend, who can never fail those who dare to trust Him; and who gives to the uttermost capacity of our faith, that we may in turn give as much as they need to those poor friends of ours, who knock us up with entreaties for help and bread (Luke 11:5–9).

15
Rephidim

*And there was no water for the people to drink. And the
Lord said, Thou shalt smite the rock, and there shall come
water out of it. And Moses did so.*

*Then came Amalek and fought with Israel in
Rephidim. . . . And Moses' hands were steady until the going
down of the sun. . . . And Moses built an altar and called the
name of it* JEHOVAH-NISSI—*The Lord my banner.*
—Exodus 17:1–15

If you essay to lead men, you will sooner or later come to a
Rephidim. We are distinctly told that it was according to the
commandment of the Lord that the children of Israel journeyed "by
stages" (v. 1, R.V., *marg.*) from the wilderness of Sin, and pitched in
Rephidim. The character of the worker is as dear to God as the work
he is doing; and no pains must be spared by the Divine Artificer to
complete the design to which He has set his hand. Do not be surprised
then, Christian worker, if you find yourself landed in Rephidim.
There are lessons to be learned there of incalculable worth.

Geographers and historians have found it difficult to fix on its precise locality, but the site is immaterial. It lay, no doubt, somewhere along
that coast in one of the Wadys that lead up into the heart of the
mountains of the central tableland. But the experience of which that
place was the scene are common to all lives, ages, and lands.

I. THERE WE LEARN THE LIMIT OF OUR ABILITY. Few of us can
stand great or long-continued success. It is comparatively easy to walk
in the Valley of Humiliation, when our path is hidden and the faces of

men are averted, but to stand on the height, with none to rival, with nothing left to scale, the wonder and the envy of a host—ah! This is a task in which the brain reels, the step falters, and the heart gets proud. It is easier to know how to be abased than how to abound, how to be empty than how to be full. We are so apt to repeat the folly of Hezekiah in showing his treasures to the ambassadors of Babylon; and to utter the man vaunt of Nebuchadnezzar, "Is not this great Babylon which *I* have built, by the might of my power, and for the glory of my majesty!"

But whenever this happens, directly the heart of man is inflated with pride, and lifts itself up in self-confidence, there is an end to its usefulness. God will not give his glory to another. He will not permit his power to be employed for the inflation of human pride, or to minister to the exaltation of the flesh. It is his solemn decree that no flesh shall glory in his presence. "Shall the axe boast itself, against him that shaketh it? As if the rod should shake itself against them that lift it up" (Is. 10:15).

This is why so many of God's servants, who once did yeoman service, are laid aside. They were marvelously helped till they were strong, but when they were strong, their hearts were lifted up to their destruction. They still preach the old sermons that once pealed like the archangel's trumpet, or thrilled with the wall of Calvary's broken heart, but there is no stir or shaking among the dry bones that strew the valley of vision. They utter the old exorcisms, but the demons laugh at them from behind their ramparts, and refuse to go forth. They know that the Lord has departed from them, and that it is not with them as in the days that are past. If such would only consider and search their hearts, they would find that they had commenced to trust in the momentum of past success; and to think that somehow the draft of fishes was due to their own fisher experience, instead of being the direct gift of One who often traverses all the rules of art by a Divine knowledge and power.

We can easily suppose that Moses was in danger of a similar fall. For the last few months his career had been in uninterrupted line of success. He had brought the proudest monarch of his time to his knees with the cry of a suppliant. He had become very great in the eyes of priesthood and court. He had led the greatest Exodus the world had seen or would see. The parted ocean, the submerged host, the song of victory, the fall of the manna, the evidence of his statesmanship and sagacity as a born leader of men—all combined to place him in an unparalleled position of authority and glory. As the triumphal ode puts it, "He was king in Jeshurun, when the heads of the people were gathered" (Deut. 33:5).

Was there no temptation in all this? Men warn others against temptations on which they have been at the point of sliding to their fall; and may it not have been from his own experience that Moses derived the caution given to the people, "Beware that thou forget not the Lord thy God. . . . lest when all that thou hast is multiplied, thine heart be lifted up, and thou forget the Lord thy God . . . and thou say in thine heart, My power and the might of mine hand hath gotten me this wealth" (Deut. 7:11–17).

Great and good men are not proof against the attacks of pride and vainglory. We are none of us free from the tendency to sacrifice to our net, and burn incense to our drag, because by then our portion is fat, and our meat plenteous. It was for this reason that Paul gloried in his infirmities; finding in them perpetual reminders of his weakness, which kept him low enough for God to choose him as the platform for the putting forth of his might.

It was probable, therefore, that God brought Moses to Rephidim to counteract and check all uprisings of self-sufficiency; to bring him down to the dust of abject helplessness; to teach him the narrow limits of his resources and ability. Lo, all these things does God work, "That He may withdraw man from his purpose, and hide pride from man" (Job 33:17).

Whatever Moses may have begun to think, all self-confidence must have vanished like a wreath of mist among the hills when he found himself face to face with that infuriated mob; who broke through every barrier erected by gratitude, or patriotism, or self-respect, or memory of past deliverances, and violence demanded water. "The people did chide with Moses, and said, Give us water that we may drink. . . . And the people murmured against Moses, and said, Wherefore hast thou brought us up out of Egypt, to kill us and our children

and our cattle with thirst" (Ex. 17:2, 3). And such was their irritation
that they seemed ready to stone him.

Was this the way that they repaid his unstinted service for them? Did
they not care for him more than this? Ah, he was not king of their hearts,
as he had thought and hoped! And as for water, whence could he procure it? No wisdom or power of his could help in such a strait. Nothing that he could suggest would meet the case. He was absolutely at the
end of himself, and "he cried unto the Lord, saying, What shall I do?"

It is a blessed position to which the providence of God reduces us
when we find ourselves face to face with an over-mastering necessity.
Were it a brook, we might ford it, but here is a river! Were it the
thirst of a little child, we might quench it, but there are two millions
of thirsty souls! Were it for the water of earth's wells we might begin to
build aqueducts from the lakes that lie in the bosom of the hills, but
here is thirst for the living water, which issues from the throne of
God and the Lamb! Then we learn the limit of our sufficiency. We cry,
Who is sufficient for these things? And we confess that we are not sufficient of ourselves, to account anything as from ourselves, but our sufficiency is from God. We cannot make a revival; or save a soul; or
convince a heart of sin, or break it down in contrition; we cannot comfort, or counsel, or satisfy the parching thirst. And when we have
reached the end of self, we have got to the beginning of God. It is from
the low threshold of the door that the lifegiving stream gushes on its
heaven-sent way.

II. There We Learn Much About God. This always follows the
other lesson. We are brought to know ourselves that we may be prepared to know God. The Master always says, "Whence are we to buy
bread, that these may eat? How many loaves have ye?" not because He
needs the information, but because He desires to bring his workers face
to face with the utter inadequacy of their supply, and to prepare them
better to appreciate the greatness of his power. But that question,
eliciting the fewness of the loaves, is invariably followed by the demand,
"Bring them hither to Me"; and by the heaps of broken victuals, evidence of the abundance of the supply. So at Rephidim, the need
which abases us and drives us to God, reveals God.

We learn his patience. Not a word of reproach or remonstrance breaks upon the still desert air. If the people had been exemplary in their humble trust, they could not have met with more tender willingness to supply their need. The people, and perhaps Levi especially, proved Him at Masah, and strove with Him at the waters of Meribah, asking whether the Lord were among them or not, though the cloud brooded overhead, and the manna lay each morning around the camp: yet there was no work of rebuke, only directions for the immediate supply of their need. It is only at Rephidim that we learn his patience towards ourselves and towards others, because He will ever be mindful of his covenant. "His mercy endureth forever."

We learn the reality of his spiritual presence. "I will stand before thee upon the rock in Horeb" (v. 6). The people had just threatened to stone Moses, but God, in effect, bade him not to fear. It was as if He said, "Fear not, I am with thee; be not dismayed, I am thy God: none shall set on thee to hurt thee, for I am with thee to deliver thee. Pass on before them, thou shalt take no harm; and this shall be a sign that I am actually there upon the rock, it shall gush with watersprings." Never before had God been more real to his servant than he was that day, when He rose up as a rampart to protect him from the infuriated crowd with their threatening stones. It is when men turn against us most, that the Lord stands beside, as He did to Paul, and says, Fear not!

We learn God's secret storehouses. "Thou shalt smite the rock, and there shall come water out of it." This is strange! A rock would seem the last place to choose for the storage of water. But God's cupboards are in very unlikely places. Ravens bring food. The Prime Minister of Egypt gives corn. Cyrus lets go the people of Israel from Babylon. The Jordan heals the leper. Meal makes poisoned pottage wholesome. Wood makes iron swim. A Samaritan binds up the wounds and saves the life of the pillaged traveler. Joseph of Arimathea buries the sacred body in his own new tomb. It is worth while to go to Rephidim to get an insight into the fertility and inventiveness of God's providence. There can be no lack to them that fear Him, and no fear of lack of those who have become acquainted with his secret storehouses. "Eye hath not seen, nor ear heard . . . the things which God hath prepared for them that love him, but God hath revealed them unto us by his Spirit" (1 Cor. 2:9, 10).

That smitten rock was a type of Christ. A Rock, indeed! Stable amid upheaval, permanent amid change. A smitten Rock! Reproach broke his heart, and the soldier's spear set abroach the blood and water, which they have issued to heal the nations and quench their thirst. "They drank of that spiritual Rock that followed them, and that Rock was Christ." There is no water that will so satisfy thirst as this crystal Rock-water. "Rock of Ages, cleft for me."

III. THERE WE LEARN THE POWER OF PRAYER. The tribe of Amalek was probably descended from Esau; and, like him, was wild and fierce and warlike. Were they likely tamely to submit to the intrusion of a new people into their pasturelands and fastnesses, which they had succeeded in holding against Egypt? It was impossible; and so, according to Josephus, this powerful tribe gathered to this spot all the forces of the desert, from Petra to the Mediterranean; and they "smote the hindmost of the Israelites, even all that were feeble among them, when they were faint and weary."

If Egypt represents the power of darkness. Amalek is a type of the flesh; which, though thoroughly defeated and broken, is always apt to crop up in moments of weakness and unwatchfulness. Far down the history of Israel, Haman, the Amalekite, had nearly compassed the annihilation of the whole people. It is in keeping with this typology that Saul was commissioned utterly to destroy the Amalekites; and that Jehovah solemnly pledged Himself to have war with Amalek from generation to generation.

Moses, now eighty-one years old, shrank from the brunt of the battle. He entrusted the troops to Joshua, here first brought into prominence, while he climbed the hill, with the sacred rod in his hand. Thence he surveyed the battle, and stretched out his hands in prayer— fought with unseen combatants the livelong day, and won the victory by intercession, of which those steady arms were the symbol. It is a most beautiful picture. Three old men in prayer. Two staying up the third!

In Rephidim we learn the lesson that prayer will do what else were impossible. In earlier days Moses would never have thought of winning a battle save by fighting. He now learns that he can win it by praying. Probably Paul, too, learned that lesson in his long and wearisome imprisonments. How they must at first have chafed his eager spirit; accustomed as he was to gird himself, and go whither he would. He may have even been tempted to feel that all his power to affect the destiny of the Church was at an end; when he suddenly discovered a leverage by which he was able to secure greater results than ever; and henceforth each epistle contains a reference to his prayers. Remember his recurring phrase, "I never cease to make mention of you in my prayers."

We cannot compare ourselves with either of these, save as Lilliputians might with a Gulliver; and yet we may, at least, emulate them in their intercessions. According to the prayers of church are the successes of a church. Are they maintained, the banner floats on to victory: are they languid, and depressed, the foe achieves a transient success. Let us, then, learn to pray, filling our Rephidims with strong crying and tears, obtaining by faith for ourselves and others victories which no prowess of our own could win. These shall encourage us like nothing beside, filling our heart with joy, our lips with songs, and our hands with the spoil of the foe. What deliverances might we win for our dear ones, and all others who are strongly molested by the flesh, if only we were more often found on the top of the hill with the uplifted rod of prayer in our steadied hands! Let then the Christ who is in thee, plead through thee for his Peters, that their faith may not fail, but that they may be saved as birds from the snare of the fowler.

16

The God-ward Aspect

*Be thou for the people Godward, that thou
mayest bring the causes unto God.*
—Exodus 18:19

Whsen the Israelite host had left Rephidim, they began to
climb up from the coast of the Red Sea into the heart of
the mountain range of Sinai. Their route has been compared to a stair of rock. Before them, through the pure air, floated the
majestic cloud, leading them they knew not whither. They only knew
that they had no option but to follow, since their supply of manna and
water depended on absolute obedience to its movement. On either side
rose the cliffs of red sandstone, like the walls of some mighty temple,
to the Holy of Holies of which they were ever approaching. It was apparently on the route that the incident reported in this chapter took
place. For the words, "at the mount of God," probably refer to the entire region.

Tidings in the desert fly fast; and the aged priest, in the fastnesses
of Midian, had been kept fully informed of the wonderful series of
events of which his relative had been the center. When, therefore, tidings came of the arrival of the vast host in the vicinity of Sinai, he took
Zipporah, Moses' wife, and her two sons, who had been entrusted to
his care, and brought them unto Moses. After the customary profuse

Oriental salutations, they spoke long and admiringly of the way in which the Lord had led his people. And the day closed with a solemn feast and sacrifice. The morrow seems to have been a rest day. The cloud did not move forward, but remained stationary; as if moored by an invisible cable, and spreading itself out as a refreshing canopy from the burning heat of the sun. And on that day an incident took place which was destined to have important issues on the history of the great leader as well as of the people whom he led. "It came to pass on the morrow that Moses sat to judge the people; and the people stood by Moses from the morning unto the evening" (v. 15).

Moses' Habitual Practice. We get a sudden glimpse here into the kind of life which Moses at this time was leading. When the host encamped, and there was a day at liberty from the weariness of the march, he seems to have sat on a judgment seat, to which all the people came who had any disputes, or grievances, or matters about which they desired to obtain advice and Divine counsel. Despite all their murmurings they looked upon him as the organ for the voice of God, and sought from his lips an authoritative declaration of the Divine will. To use his own words, when the people had a matter, they came unto him to inquire of God; and he made them know the statutes of God and his laws.

It was a Divine work, sufficient to engross his noblest powers, and to tax resources which had been stored up within him through long years of waiting; for what is higher in all this world than to serve as the interpreter of whom Job speaks, "One among a thousand, to show unto man what is right for him" (Job 33:23, R.V.)? To hear the difficulties, perplexities, and hard questions of the anxious and troubled; to inquire for them to God; both bring their causes to his bar for judgment, and to his mercy seat for help: to come back to them to teach them, to show them the way in which they should walk, and the work they should do—this is employment which were worthy of the delicacy and strength of an angel's love, and most nearly approaches the ministry of the Redeemer. This blessed work of mediatorship was not borne by Moses as a Priest, for as yet the Priesthood was not constituted, but as a large-hearted, noble man, who was at leisure from himself, and had the ear of God. He was "for the people to Godward." And it opens up a very interesting vista of service for us all, especially for those who are intimate with the King, and habituated to the royal Court. Why should we not enter more largely into participation with Moses in this delightful service, which is open to those who are low of speech equally as to those who are golden-mouthed; and affords opportunities for the very powers which most shrink from the glare of publicity and the gaze of men?

We can imagine him going to God each day with long lists of questions for one and another of the mighty host. This and the other cause he laid before Him for counsel, quoting names and circumstances, arguments and reasons on either side, and waiting for the message which he was to carry back. What variety! What directness! What reality must have pervaded his prayers! How vividly must he have realized that he was, indeed, in partnership with the Most High, a fellow worker and yoke fellow; and that they had a common interest in the people whom they loved! Why should not we also begin to live such a life? The voice that spake to him speaks to us, "Be thou for the people to Godward, that thou mayest bring the causes unto God" (v. 19). And the gates through which he passed and repassed stand open day and night.

We often wonder at Luther, who spent three hours each day in prayer and meditation; at Bishop Andrews, spending the greater part of five hours every day in fellowship with God; at John Welsh, who thought that day ill spent which did not witness eight or ten hours of closet communion. It seems to us as if such prolonged praying must involve an endless monotony of vain repetitions. We forget that when men are sent to market with a host of commissions from their neighbors and friends, they must needs tarry longer than when they go only for themselves. It would be a very wholesome thing if the causes of others were to detain us more constantly before the Lord.

This "being for the people to Godward" became more and more characteristic of the life of Moses. Whenever the people cried unto him, he prayed unto the Lord. When the spirit of revolt spread through the camp, he fell upon is face. When it seemed likely that the whole nation must perish for their sin, he stood in the breach, and besought the Lord, and turned away the destruction that hung over them like a lurid cloud. Twice for forty days their interests detained him in the holy mount. And in long after years he is classed with Samuel as one who had stood before God for his people.

What a striking type is this of our Lord Jesus, though at the best there is a marvelous gulf between the two. For Moses was faithful over God's household as a servant, but Christ as a Son, whose house we are. All that Moses did He will do, and more. When we have a matter, let us go to Him. He is for us to Godward, and will bring our causes to God. Through Him we may inquire of God; and he will make us know (for the responsibility of *making* us know is on Him, and if one way will not suffice we may trust Him to adopt another) the statutes of God and his laws; and will show us the way in which we should walk, and the work that we must do.

The Tax on Moses' Strength. Work like this cannot be done without severe expenditure of all that is most vital to man. It drains the sympathies, taxes the brain, wearies the heart charged with the anxieties and sorrows, the burdens and needs of a throng of perplexed and troubled souls. You cannot save others and save yourself as well. Virtue cannot go forth to heal without your becoming conscious of the drain. You can only comfort others when you understand them: and you cannot understand them till you have given yourself away to them. But the effort to do this costs you all that you are worth to some other soul. And it therefore became apparent to the keen eye of Jethro's loving solicitude that both Moses and the people were being worn away in his attempt to meet all their demands.

In after years Moses himself seems to have broken down under the burden. "And Moses said unto the Lord, Wherefore hast Thou afflicted thy servant? And wherefore have I not found favor in thy sight, that Thou layest the burden of all this people upon me? Have I conceived all this people? Have I begotten them, that Thou shouldst say unto me, Carry them in thy bosom, as a nursing father beareth the sucking child, unto the land which Thou swarest unto their fathers?" (Num. 11:11, 12). Moses did not feel that strain now when Jethro spoke, for it was as yet fresh on him, but it was, nevertheless, sapping his strength, and Jethro remarked it.

We do not always see the cost at which we are doing our work. We are sustained by the excitement and interest of it. The stir, the rush, the cry of the combatants, the chances and opportunities of the battle, the alluring form of victory, to be won at the price of just one more effort— all these things conceal from us the expenditure of our reserves, which is patent enough to others. Some men get weary of forbearing; they cannot live slowly; they must expend themselves, pouring their lives out as a libation from a bowl. And it is an act of benevolence when some Jethro is prompted to interpose and suggest a mitigation of the fever, a slackening of the eager rush. The Jethros seldom prevail with us. They get scant thanks for their pains. We have to learn by some terrible collapse. But they have at least, deserved well by us.

From man, breaking down under the weight of human care imposed on his heart by his fellows, let us turn to the true Priest and Brother of Man; into whose ear is being poured one incessant stream of complaint and sorrow, of care and need, and sin. It is as if all the letters, deposited in all the receiving boxes of England year by year, were directed to one man, who must open and answer them all himself. But even that illustration gives an utterly inadequate idea of all that devolves on our dear Master, Christ, whose heart is the receptacle of all the anguish, sorrow, and soul-travail of mankind.

Moses' patience lasted for a few months only, but His till the work is done (Deut. 1:31; Is. 63:9; Acts 13:18, R.V.). He faints not, neither is weary, because He combines with a woman's sympathy and delicacy of touch and insight, all the patience and strength of the Divine. But do we sufficiently realize the cost at which, through the ages, He is exercising his ministry on our behalf? Think ye not that the festal processions of the glorified often halt upon their way, like that which stayed on the shoulder of Olivet, because the king is in tears! He is "touched with the feeling of our infirmities."

Moses' Assent to Jethro's Proposal. It cannot be God's will that any of his servants should wear away. He knows our frame too well to overtax its frail machinery. No hard taskmaster is He, driving his slaves beyond the limit of human endurance. The burden of responsibility which He lays upon their shoulders may be heavy, but it is not too heavy. The engagements which He assigns for each day may be many, but not too many for its working hours. The souls committed to their charge may be numbered by thousands, but they are not more than can be overlooked and shepherded. The bell never summons a servant to a duty concerning which God does not say to him, My grace is sufficient for thee; as thy day so shall thy strength be.

Sometimes God's workers make the mistake of burdening themselves with work which others could do as well as themselves, and, indeed, would be the better for doing. This seems to have been the case with Moses. He appeared to think that he alone could judge, manage, and administer the affairs of Israel. And this monopoly of the administration was working adversely. It was overtaxing himself; it was wearing out the people; it was delaying the course of justice; and it was allowing a large amount of talent to lie unused. Jethro's advice was therefore most timely, that he should provide out of all the people able men, with the three important qualifications, that they should fear God, love truth, and hate unjust gain. These were to deal with the small matters, while the greater ones were still brought to himself.

Moses has been blamed for doing this. It has been said that if he had trusted God, the power which was not to be divided among many might have been concentrated on himself; so that he might have continued to bear the responsibility and honor of judgment alone. God could have enabled him to do all the work which these others were not to divide with him.

But, surely, even if that had been the case—and we would not for a moment dispute that it could have been so—yet, it would not have been so well as the division of interest and labor which now took place. It was much better to set all these men to work than to do all their work. It evoked talent; it ennobled them by placing them in positions of responsibility before their fellows; it drove them to personal dealings with God; it inspired them with a fellow feeling with Moses; it turned critics into sympathizers and companions; it educated them for positions for which they might be required in the emergencies of the future. It is a great matter to be a good workman, one not needing to be ashamed, but it is a greater to be able to call out other workmen, and to set them at work.

This policy was that which the apostles adopted when the business of the Church had so grown upon their hands as to engross too much of their time and energy. They could no longer combine the serving of tables with the ministry of the Word; and as they could not hesitate which side of their double office to abandon, they called in the help of Stephen and his colleagues "to serve tables," while they gave themselves to prayer and to the ministry of the Word.

Is there not a thought here for many of the Lord's workers who may read these words? Are we not dissipating our energies over too wide an area? Do we not attempt to embrace in our life many things which others could do as well as ourselves? Ought not those specially, who are gifted with the power of prayer and spiritual insight, to cultivate those special sides of their nature, leaving details of management and direction of finance to others? We should live on the greatest side of our nature, reserving ourselves for that; not careless of minor details, if there is no one else to manage them, but prepared to hand them over to "able men," even though they may have to learn their duties at a cost, in the beginning, of some mistakes and failures. The mountain brow, with its fellowship, affords a leverage from which we may best move earth. We touch men most when we most touch God. The prophet and priest, the man of God, the teacher, these are among the choicest gifts of God to men. And if you are gifted specially in these directions, cultivate such endowments to the uttermost—they are rare enough—leaving other details to be cared for by others who may be cast in a more practical mold.

17

At the Foot of Sinai

And Mount Sinai was altogether on a smoke,
because the Lord descended upon it in fire:
and the smoke thereof ascended as the smoke
of a furnace, and the whole
mount quaked greatly.
—Exodus 19:18

From Rephidim the children of Israel marched slowly and laboriously through the great thoroughfare of the desert now known as the Wady-es-Sheykh, the longest, widest, and most continuous of those vast desert valleys. It must have been an astonishing exchange from the flat alluvial land of Egypt, where the only hills were those raised by the hands of man. On either side of the pilgrim host, lofty and precipitous mountains reared their inaccessible ramparts of red sandstone and variegated granite, without verdure, or gushing rills, or trace of living thing. They must have appeared like the majestic corridors of a vast temple, to the inner shrine of which the pillar of cloud was conducting them by its stately march.

The Red Sea, which must have become like a friend, had been long ago left behind; and there was no chance of retracing their path or returning. There was nothing to allure them or arrest their steps amid the awful desolation and grandeur of those inaccessible precipices. They would be sometimes almost overwhelmed by the bare sterility of the scene, and by the awful silence that was stirred to resent the intrusion of such a multitude upon its ancient reign. But their course was always onwards; and a deepening awe must have grown upon their souls, such as became those who were already treading the precincts of a temple not made with hands, a shrine of incomparable majesty, to which those vast and sublime avenues were the befitting approach.

At last it broke on them. After a march of eighteen miles from the Red Sea, they came out on a perfectly level plain of yellow sand, some two miles long, and half-a-mile wide, nearly flat, and dotted over with tamarisk bushes. The mountains which gather around this plain have for the most part sloping sides, and form a kind of natural amphitheater, but towards the south there is one pile of jagged cliffs which rises sheer upwards in wild precipitousness, while behind lies the granite mass of Gebel Mousa, deeply cleft with fissures, and torn, as though it had fought a hard battle with earthquake, storm, and fire. This pile of rocks is called Ras Sufsafeh, and was probably "the mount that might be touched and burned with fire." It rises from the plain below as a huge altar; and all that transpired on its summit would have been easily visible to the furthest limits of the camp of two million souls pitched beneath.

Such was the chosen scene for the giving of the Law. There the hosts of Israel remained stationary for long weeks; and there, while clouds veiled the heights, and fire played from peak to peak, and mysterious voices, resembling at times a trumpet's notes, awake unwonted echoes in the heart of the hills, God met with his people and gave them his Law; writing his name not on tablets of stone merely, but on the entire course of human history.

I. God's Object at Sinai. We can but briefly touch on this, as we are most of all concerned with the character of the great leader, but in that more exclusive study we may for a moment consider the impressions which the marvelous scenes associated with Sinai were calculated to produce on the people and on himself.

At the time of the Exodus the world was almost wholly given to idolatry. The first objects of idolatrous worship were probably simply the sun and moon and heavenly bodies, or other conspicuous objects of creative wisdom and power. Afterwards the Deity was supposed to reside in men, and even beasts. Of these, images were made and worshiped—at first covered with drapery, but afterwards in a state of nudity, and exerting the most demoralizing effect. "Professing themselves to be wise, they became fools, and changed the glory of the incorruptible God for the likeness of an image of corruptible man, and of birds, and four-footed beasts, and creeping things. Wherefore God gave them up to the lusts of their hearts" (Rom. 1:22–24, R.V.).

In dealing with this deluge of idolatry, God acted as with the deluge of water that drowned the ancient world. He began with a single family, teaching them the sublime lessons concerning Himself; which when they had perfectly acquired, they were to make the common coin of the world.

Let us notice the successive steps.

First Step. God chose from the masses of heathendom one man, "called him alone," and led him to follow Him into a strange land. There, shut away from surrounding peoples, He began to teach him about Himself. As a gardener selects one plant that he may bring it to rare perfection, and make it the means of improving the entire sisterhood, so Jehovah spared no time or pains with the first great Hebrew, that being blessed he might be the means of blessing to the race.

Second Step. God welded the Hebrew people together into one, that they might be able to receive and retain as a part of their national life those great truths with which they were to be entrusted. This welding was accomplished by the tie of common parentage, of which they were justly proud; by the bond of a common occupation, which kept them to themselves as shepherds, apart from the busy traffic of cities and marts of commerce; and, lastly, by the pressure of a common trial, which together with the marvelous deliverance that was ranted them, remained fresh and indelible in all after generations, like those colors in the land of their bondage, which in the dry desert air have lasted in unfading vividness for thirty centuries. So perfectly did God do this work that while other nations have risen, reigned, and fallen, and their disintegration has been utter and final, the children of Abraham endure, like an imperishable rock, undestroyed by the chafe of the waves or the fret of the ages.

Third Step. God revealed his existence. Into the midst of their bondage tidings came that the god of their fathers was a living God;

that He had met one of their number in the desert and had called him by name, and had promised to interfere in their behalf. The news may have excited but a languid interest. They were glad that like other nations of the time they had their tutelary deity, but that was all; and they knew little or nothing beside.

Fourth Step. God showed by the plagues that He was stronger than the gods of Egypt. Can you not imagine the children of Israel saying, "Our God is great, He has turned the water into blood, but perhaps He is not so strong as Isis, or Osiris, or Serapis, or the sacred bull"? But the wonders which were wrought on the gods of Egypt settled that question forever.

Fifth Step. God excited their love and gratitude. You can do anything you like with those you love, but to get, you must give; to excite love, you must declare it. Hence they were touchingly reminded of what He had done: "Ye have seen what I did unto the Egyptians, and how I bare you on eagles' wings, and brought you unto Myself" (Ex. 19:4).

Sixth Step. God set Himself to teach them concerning certain of those great qualities, the knowledge of which lay at the foundation of all right dealings between the people and Himself. And in order to achieve his purpose, He made use of outward significant signs; which did more than the most elaborate discourse to instruct the ignorant and sensual people whom He had taken for his own.

Seventh Step. God clearly designated Moses to be the organ and channel of his communications to man. "Lo, I come unto thee in a thick cloud, that the people may hear when I speak with thee, and believe thee forever" (v. 9). It was impossible to forecast the way in which God was fulfilling his purposes at the time, but as we look back on the story we can detect the development of his plan, just as from the summits of the eternal hills we shall see the way by which He has been leading us all the days of our pilgrimage.

II. THE LESSONS OF SINAI. (1) *The Majesty of God.* The natural scenery was sufficiently majestic, but it became more so as the incidents of the third day were unfolded. Was there not majesty in the thunders and lightnings; in the brooding cloud where clouds were almost unknown; in the flashing lightning dispelling the pitchy gloom; in the trumpet peal echoing through the hills—now soft as a flute rolling through the yielding air, now loud as an organ striking against some outstanding cliff? Meanwhile the clouds dropped water, and there were showers of tropical rain. And it was amid such scenes that God spoke. Could any combination of natural phenomena have given grander conceptions of the Majesty of the Divine Nature?

(1) *The Spirituality of God.* What was their God like? Would He assume the form of anything that is in the heaven above, or in the earth beneath, or in the waters under the earth? Would it be in any, or in a combination of all, of these forms that they should see Him who had brought them out of Egypt? But on that memorable occasion, "when Moses brought forth the people out of the camp to meet God," they saw no likeness. He was there, for He spoke. But there was no outward form for the eye to discern. It was very hard. The extreme difficulty of the human heart accustoming itself to the worship of what the eye cannot perceive, or the imagination realize, has been attested by the repeated relapse into idolatry, from the days of the golden calf to the crucifix which the Roman Catholic devotee presses to her lips. It has not been easy for mankind to learn this lesson so clearly taught on Sinai, that God is a Spirit.

(3) *The Holiness of God.* This primal lesson was also taught in striking fashion by outward signs which impressed the sense. Bounds were erected to keep the beasts from grazing on the thin herbage of the lower slopes; whoever touched the Mount must die; all clothes were to be carefully washed against that third day; absolute purity was to be observed in heart and life; Moses alone was called up to the top of the Mount, where smoke and fire and lightning flash commingled, and the thunder peal viewed with the trumpet blast; and when he had climbed thither, he was sent all the way down again for the express purpose of charging the people, and even the priests, not to break through upon the Lord to gaze, lest God should break forth upon them. All these significant acts converged to give outward and sensible manifestation of the Holiness of God.

(4) *The Royalty of God.* In their triumphal ode of victory by the shores of the Red Sea, the people had confessed the right of Jehovah to reign over them forever, but they were yet to learn that He was indeed

absolute monarch. The Jewish state was a kingdom, and God was
King. And the reality of his government appeared in the way in which
Moses himself obeyed his behest. It was a sign never to be forgotten to
see how their great leader Moses was absolutely subservient to the
command issued from God's pavilion. At the best he was only God's
executor, "the passive instrument of the Divine will." The decalogue
was spoken by God Himself "out of the midst of the fire, of the cloud,
and of the thick darkness, with a great voice" (Deut. 5:22). Every or-
dinance of the Law, every custom and provision for domestic and
civil life, every item in the construction of the sanctuary and in the or-
dering of the priests, was due to the direct will of God, spoken from
his mouth. "God, and not Moses, was the author of each proviso, the
real Legislator, the real Lawgiver, the real King; Moses was but the
mouthpiece, an intermediary to communicate God's decrees to his people." How clear was the testimony to the supremacy of the Most
High! Such were some of the lessons taught at Sinai.

III. MOSES AT SINAI. He seemed at home there. Though as to his
physical system he could not but fear and quake from the unwonted
accompaniments of the Divine Glory, yet there was no slavish dread
such as would make him draw afar off, as the people did. Mark the successive stages in that familiarity between him and God. "Moses went
up unto God" (Ex. 19:3). Having reported God's words to the people,
he returned to tell the people's words to the Lord; for we are told "he
went down from the mount unto the people" (v. 14). When Jehovah
came down in thunder and smoke, for the third time Moses went up
to the top of the mount (v. 20). When the ten words of the Law had
been spoken, Moses drew near to the thick darkness where God was
(Ex. 20:21). After this, he was bidden to ascend the mountain a fifth
time, the elders accompanying him to a certain point, and Joshua
still further, but he alone entering the cloud, which was like devouring fire on the top of the mount: and he remained there forty days and
forty nights to receive the Divine instructions for the erection of the
Tabernacle (Ex. 24:18). A sixth time he returned unto God, offering
to be blotted from his book, if only Israel might be spared, and their
sin atoned (Ex. 32:32). And yet a seventh time he was invited to

come up early in the morning, carrying with him two tablets of stone; and there, as he stood in an alcove of the rocks, the presence of God passed by, and the name of God was proclaimed, and he remained for a second period of forty days and forty nights, descending to the people with shining face, the living evidence of the reality and closeness of the fellowship. "And the Lord spake unto Moses face to face, as a man speaketh unto his friend" (Ex. 33:11).

This fellowship had an ennobling effect on his character. Not only did his face shine, but his life shone also. There was henceforth a supernatural grace and beauty about his aspect and demeanor which clearly marked him out as "the man of God." His meekness, his gentleness under provocation, his jealousy for the name and cause of God, burned with an intenser and more even flame.

The life of fellowship with God cannot be built up in a day. It begins with the habitual reference of all to Him, hour by hour, as Moses did in Egypt. But it moves on to more and longer periods of communion. And it finds its consummation and bliss in days and nights of intercession and waiting and holy discourse. Ah, what patterns are seen on the Mount! What cries are uttered there! What visions are seen there! What revelations are made there! What injunctions are received there! Alas for us that we remove so far away from it! Or at the best are admitted to stand only with the elders, and see paved work of sapphire stone beneath God's feet! Oh for the closer access, the nearer view, the more intimate face to face conversation, such as is open still to the friends of God!

18
The Vision of God
and Its Effect

*It came to pass, when Moses came down
from Mount Sinai, that he knew not that the
skin of his face shone.*
—Exodus 34:29

We are justified by the highest authority in deriving spiritual lessons from this incident in the life of the great lawgiver. The Apostle expressly refers to it when he says that we all may, with unveiled face, behold the glory of the Lord, and be transformed (2 Cor. 3:13–18). That blessed vision which of old was given only to the great leader of Israel, is now within reach of each individual believer. The Gospel has no fences to keep off the crowds from the mount of vision; the lowest and most unworthy of its children may pass upward where the shining glory is to be seen. We are not living in the morning, when the rays of the sun reach only the elect spirits that tower above the rest, but in the noon, when every tiny flower and hidden nook lies in full view of the meridian sun. "We *all* . . . are changed."

I. THE DESIRE TO SEE GOD CARRIES WITH IT THE PLEDGE OF ITS GRATIFICATION. During long years the desire had been growing in the heart of Moses to see the face of God. "Show me now thy way, that I may know Thee"; "I beseech Thee, show me thy glory." Prayers like these were constantly on his lips. And sometimes with him, as with saints of later days, the yearning must have become almost too intense to be borne. No invalid in the dark cold winter days so longs for the summer; no true heart so longs for its mate; no young bride just widowed so longs for the everlasting reunion of heaven, as do some saintly hearts long for God. "Oh that I knew where I might find Him!" "My soul longeth, yea, even fainteth for the courts of the Lord; my heart and my flesh cry out for the living God." "My soul thirsteth for Thee."

But these longings are certain to be fulfilled, because God is faithful. There is no stronger argument for immortality than this; it must be, because all men forecast it. There is no stronger argument for retribution than this; it must be, because men's consciences demand it. There is no stronger argument for the Being of God than to say, It must be, because the heart of man craves infinite love; the mind of man infinite truth; the spirit of man infinite communion with spirit. And in the same way we must infer, that the very presence of these intense yearnings for Himself—for face to face fellowship and intercourse— are the herald symptoms, the premonitory signs, that within our reach there is the possibility of an intercourse with God, which up till now our hearts have not conceived.

And if we garner every opportunity, cultivate every faculty, and keep our faces ever toward the mountain of communion, we shall infallibly find that the heart which yearns for the vision shall not be left without the vision for which it yearns; and that the yearning is the unconscious awakening of the soul to the fact that it is standing on the threshold of the highest privilege possible to man. It is thus that a babe awakens to a mother's tenderness, and a maiden becomes conscious of the great destiny to which an unexpected love, which has stolen so mysteriously upon her, beckons. Oh, these mysterious risings off the water in the river where the barges lie, bearing them upon their arms, rattling their chains, straining their cords, and bringing them an assurance of the swell and fullness and glory of the great ocean, which calls to them to launch forth on its broad expanse and fathomless depths! "And the Lord said unto Moses, I will do this thing also that thou hast spoken; for thou hast found grace in My sight. . . . Be ready in the morning, and come up in the morning unto Mount Sinai."

II. THE GRATIFICATION OF OUR DESIRE DEPENDS ON OUR FUL-
FILLMENT OF CERTAIN CONDITIONS. (1) *We must learn to obey.* This was
the great characteristic of Moses. He was faithful in *all* God's house as
a servant. His proudest title, by which he is known even in heaven, is
"the servant of God." "They sing the song of Moses, the servant of
God" (Rev. 15:3). And the repeated refrain of the books of the Pen-
tateuch is the phrase which sounds deep and often, as the toll of the
Inchcape bell over the waves: "as the Lord commanded Moses, so did
he." God could always depend on him. He was a man after his own
heart, who could fulfill all his will. And it was to him, rather than to
the disobedient hearts of the people, that God revealed Himself.

And this is consistent with the words of our Lord, who said, "He
that hath my commandments and keepeth them, he it is that loveth
Me; and I will manifest Myself unto him" (John 14:21). Clearly, obedience is the stepping stone to vision. We must be servants ere we can
be friends. The path of literal obedience, albeit that it is rough and
steep, is the only path to the mountain summit, with its marvelous revelation. Is it not so always? The discoverer must obey nature, before he
can expect to reach the vantage ground from which to survey the
harmony and helpfulness of her mighty laws, and the mystery of her
secret processes.

Do not be disobedient to heavenly visions; never turn aside to your
own preferences from the narrow path of unswerving loyalty to the
voice of God—speaking in his word, and in your heart, and in circumstance. Dare to do right, though you stand alone among the
recreant hosts; and you will thus fulfill one prime condition of the vision of God.

(2) *We must be willing to pass through the thick cloud.* "God called to
Moses out of the midst of the cloud . . . and Moses went into the midst
of the cloud" (Ex. 24:16–18). Thick banks of dense cloud, dark in
their earthward aspect, though insufferably bright on their inner side, shut
out the light of sun and the spectacles of earth, and shut him in with God.
But he had not seen the vision, had he not been willing to pass through
the cloud and to stand beneath the shadow of the Divine hand.

The traveler who would pass from the wintry slopes of Switzerland
into the summer beauty of the plains of Italy, must be prepared to

tunnel the Alps. The garden, the cross, and the grave, are the only way to the Easter morning. The walls must be toned to a neutral tint on which masterpieces of painting are to be exhibited. And it seems indispensable that we should pass into the shadow of bereavement, temptation, and distress, if we are to emerge into God's marvelous light and estimate its brilliance.

> Not first the light, and after that the dark;
>   But first the dark, and after that the light.
> First, the thick cloud, and then the rainbow are:
>   First, the dark grave, and then the resurrection light.

(3) *We must dare to be alone.* When we read (Ex. 34:2, 3) those solemn words, "Be ready in the morning, and come up in the morning, and present thyself there to Me in the top of the mount: and no man shall come up with thee; neither let any man be seen throughout all the mount, neither let the flocks nor herds feed before the mount"— they seem to echo down to us in other but similar tones, "When thou prayest, enter into thy closet, and when thou hast shut thy door, pray to thy Father which is in secret." Jacob must be left alone if the Angel of God is to whisper in his ear the mystic name of Shiloh; Daniel must be alone if he is to see the celestial vision; John must be banished to Patmos if he is deeply to take and firmly to keep "the print of heaven." The insulated cloud alone contains in its bosom the mighty thunderstorm; that which is stranded on the mountain slope is soon robbed of its electricity.

Valuable as are the prolific opportunities for Christian culture and service which surround us, they will be disastrous indeed in their effect if they rob us of the time that we should otherwise spend with God, or give us a distaste for lonely heart fellowship. Let the first moments of the day, when the heart is fresh, be given to God. Never see the face of man till you have seen the King. Dare to be much alone on the Mount.

III. WHEN THE CONDITIONS ARE FULFILLED, THE VISION IS SURE. Perhaps Moses, as he entered the cloud, expected that the Almighty would pass before him, riding upon a cherub, flying upon the wings of the wind, girded with rainbow and storm, while the thunder rolled as drums in his march. But lo! He seemed to stand in a ravine, upon a ledge of rock, shadowed by a hand, while through that mountain-rent passed the Divine procession; and a voice, still, sweet, penetrating, told that God was Love.

Mark the progress of revelation to the adoring soul. In Horeb, Moses had stood in the outer court, to learn that God is changeless. In the giving of the Law he had stood in the effulgent glory of the Holy Place, to learn that God is righteous. Now he was admitted to the inner shrine, to learn that the Lord God was merciful and gracious, long-suffering and abundant in goodness and truth.

The answers to our prayers for spiritual vision may not always come as we expect. But, however they come, come they will. None of those who wait for Him shall be shamed. He will satisfy desires which He has Himself implanted. The King will be punctual to enter to see the guests who have complied with his conditions. As to Fletcher of Madeley, to Catherine of Siena, to President Edwards, to Dr. Payson, and to hundreds besides, so to you, when least expecting it, will come the beatific vision, perhaps constraining you to cry, as John Tennant did: "Hold, Lord, it is enough! Or the frail vessel will break beneath the weight of glory."

IV. Such Visions Leave Unmistakable Traces. The face of Moses shone: and did not his heart and life shine also? Could it have been otherwise? Linen in which the housewife has laid rosemary and lavender will smell fragrantly; ordinary iron placed near a magnet becomes magnetic; those that are in king's courts catch a refined and courteous mien; the friend of wise men gets wisdom; the members of a closely-knit family contract by association some tiny gesture, a peculiarity which betrays their oneness; it is proverbial how on the faces of an aged couple there is seen a strong resemblance, so that each reflects the other. And it is impossible for us to be much with God without becoming godly, that is, God-like.

The old legends of the saints tell of those who, by long meditation on the crucifixion of the Lord, received in their very flesh the marks of his wounds. There is certainly a spiritual counterpart of this in the long, fixed gaze of the soul on the vision of God, by which the lineaments of the Divine beauty pass into the life, and light it up with a loveliness which is not of earth.

V. SUCH TRACES ARE NOT PERCEIVED BY THOSE WHO PRESENT THEM. "Moses knew not that his face shone." He was glorious in all eyes but his own.

There is a law known to medical men as Holland's law; which affirms that whenever attention is directed specially to any one organ of the body, the action of that organ is more or less disturbed. If, for instance, we begin to think of our heart, counting its beats, and listening to its throbs, we disturb its rhythmic action. There are few who can let the physician feel their pulse with perfect composure; and he is generally obliged to make some allowance for the effects of this self-consciousness. So with the functions of digestion, and respiration, and thought. These great and vital processes of the body go on most healthily and satisfactorily, when they are not made direct subjects of attention. And in these respects we may trace a close analogy between the physical and the spiritual life of man. A counterpart of Holland's law pervades the physiology of the spiritual life. We shall do best, and make quickest progress, when we know it not.

True Christian excellence is as unconscious of its beauty as Moses was; whenever it becomes self-conscious it loses its charm. Beware of the man who talks about his grace. There is such a thing as being proud of humility, and making capital out of our nothingness. The man who boasts of a shining face is a counterfeit and a cheat. The possessor of the genuine article never talks about it, never thinks about it; and would be almost overwhelmed to hear of any such thing being ascribed to him. The charm of a little child is its utter unconsciousness of self; and that is the charm in true God-likeness. It is like the bloom on a peach, the dew-jewels on the morning lawn, or the stillness of the surface of a mountain pool.

19
The Broken Sentence

*Yet now, if Thou wilt forgive their sin—; and
if not, blot me, I pray Thee, out of Thy book
which Thou hast written.*
—Exodus 32:32

This is one of the most pathetic verses of the Bible, which bears on its face the evidence of its genuineness. It could not have emanated from the mind or pen of some later scribe, because it was so entirely unexpected, so strange, and yet so likely. It reminds us of the shaft of a graceful column broken off in the middle; or of a strain of plaintive music hushed to sudden silence by the snapping of a string. It is the fragment of a sentence of which we would have given much to hear the conclusion, but who can presume to finish that, which in this supreme hour was shocked by a paroxysm of grief, a sob of irrepressible emotion?

I. THE PROBLEM WITH WHICH HE HAD TO DEAL. (1) *Their idolatry.* After the utterance of the ten great words of Sinai, the people, frightened by the thunderings and lightnings, and the voice of the trumpet, and the smoke of the mountain, entreated Moses to act as their daysman and mediator. "They said unto him: Speak thou with us, and we will hear, but let not God speak with us, lest we die" (Ex. 20:19). The great lawgiver and leader, acting on their request, thereupon

611

withdrew himself into the divine pavilion, and was absent for about six weeks.

After the return of the seventy elders who had accompanied Moses to some lower ledge of the mountain but had returned without him, the people were doubtless well content. Better to be temporarily deprived of their leader, than be exposed to those terrible thunderings. But, after awhile, they became uneasy and restless. From one to another the word passed, "Where is he? He did not take food enough with him to sustain him for so long. Has he met with some mishap on those lonely steeps? Or perchance he has been destroyed by that burning fire, or absorbed into the unseen." "As for this Moses, the man that brought us up out of the land of Egypt, we know not what is become of him" (Ex. 32:1). And then turning to Aaron, the man of words, sure that neither he nor twenty like him could fill the gap which the loss of Moses had caused, they cried, "Up, make us gods, which shall go before us."

We may notice, as we pass, the essential nature of idolatry. For in this marvelous chapter we have its entire history, from the first cry of the soul, which betrays so marvelous a yearning for an idol, to the draining of the last bitter dregs, with which, when ground to powder, the idolater has to drink its very dust. Men sometimes speak of idolaters bowing down before material forms, whether of gold, stone, or wood, as if they supposed that these were Divine, and possessed Divine attributes—and such may be the case with the more degraded and debased, but in the beginning it was not so. And if we carefully study the question in all its bearings, we shall discover that the idolater does not—in the first instance, at least—look upon his image as God, but as a prepresentation or manifestation of God. It is an attempt on the part of the human spirit, which shrinks from the effort of communion with the unseen and spiritual, to associate God with what it can own and handle; so as to have a constant and evident token of the presence and favor of God.

This was the case of Israel. It was only three months since they had stood by the Red Sea, and seen its waters roll in pride over the hosts of Pharaoh. Every day since then God's love had followed them. For them the heaven had given bread, and the rocks had flowed with water; and his cloud had sailed majestically through the sky, shielding them in the daylight, and burning like a watchfire through the night. And even at the time with which we are dealing the whole summit of the mount was crowned by the pavilion of cloud, which was the emblem of his presence in their midst. But notwithstanding all, they were carried away before that imperious craving of the human heart, which cries out for a sensible image for its worship.

Their idolatry, then, was a violation, not of the first, but of the second commandment. They did not propose to renounce Jehovah—that was left for the days of Ahab, but they desired to worship Jehovah under the form of a calf, and in distinct violation of the emphatic prohibition, which said, "Thou shalt not make unto thee any graven image, or any likeness of any thing that is in heaven above, or that is in the earth beneath; thou shalt not bow down thyself to them, nor serve them." This was the sin also of Jeroboam.

(2) *Their Degradation.* There can be no doubt that the worship of the calf was accompanied with the licentious orgies which were a recognized part of Egyptian idolatry. As much as this is implied in the narrative. "The people sat down to eat and to drink, and rose up to play." In the R.V. a striking emendation is given of the 25th verse. "Moses saw that the people were broken loose; for Aaron had let them loose for a derision among their enemies." And from this we may infer that the bonds of continence, that had restrained them since the Exodus, had been suddenly slackened; with the result of their breaking from all restraint, and giving themselves up to their unholy riot.

(3) *The Claims of God.* There was every reason to believe that God would exact the full amount of penalty; not because He was vindictive, but because the maintenance of his authority seemed to demand it. The righteousness of his character, the inviolability of his oath, the authority of the Ten Commandments, so recently given, combined to make it necessary that He should do as He had said.

And yet, on the other hand, there was the fear lest, if, to use the language of men, God's anger waxed hot and He consumed them, the Egyptians might say, "For evil did He bring them forth to slay them on the mountains, and to consume them from the face of the earth." And thus Jehovah's character might be misunderstood and maligned among the nations around.

How could God maintain his character with his own people without imperiling it with the Egyptians? If he spared the people, they would begin to think that neither his threats nor his promises were worth their heed. And if He destroyed them, his glory would be dimmed; and He might seem to have become unmindful of the oath which He swore by Himself to his servants, Abraham, Isaac, and Israel, that He would multiply their seed, and give the land of Canaan to them as a heritage forever. So greatly did these considerations weigh with Moses, that he refused the Divine offer to make him the only survivor of the host, and the progenitor of a great nation.

It would almost seem as if this proposal resembled the suggestion made to Abraham, that he should offer up his only son, Isaac. In each case God tried—or tested—his servant. But there is this great difference between the temptations of the devil and of God. The former seeks to bring out all the evil, and to make it permanent, as the streams of lava poured from the heart of a volcano: the latter seeks to bring out all the good, and to make it ours; for moral qualities never become ours till we have put them into practice.

II. THE EMOTIONS WITH WHICH HIS SOUL WAS STIRRED. In the mount he acted as intercessor. When God told him all that was transpiring in the plain below, and showed the glittering sword of justice suspended over the guilty nation by a thread, he pleaded for the people whom he loved. "And Moses besought the Lord his God . . . Turn from thy fierce wrath, and repent of this evil against thy people." "And the Lord repented of the evil which He thought to do unto his people."

On his way down from the mount, when he came near enough to see the calf and the dancing, peering over some overhanging ledge of rock, the old impetuous vehemence which had characterized him in earlier life, and had slept for so many years, broke out with all its early intensity. It was not against the people, but against their sin, that his anger flamed out. "Moses' anger waxed hot; and he cast the tables out of his hands, and brake them beneath the mount." Those splintered bits leaping from crag to crag are an apt symbol of the inability of man, even the holiest, to keep intact the holy Law of God.

When he reached the camp, he seems to have strode into the as-tonished throng, broken up their revelry, and overturned their calf, or-dering it to be destroyed, and the fragments mingled with the water they drank. But as this did not avail to stay the inveterate evil, he was compelled to use more drastic measures, and by the sword of Levi to extinguish it with the life blood of three thousand men.

Then when the next day came, when the camp was filled with mourning over those newly-made graves, when the awful reaction had set in on the people and himself, the tide seems to have turned. His indignation was succeeded by bitter sorrow and pity. The thunderstorm was broken into floods of tears. The pitiable state to which their sin had reduced them aroused his deepest compassion; and he said unto the people; "Ye have sinned a great sin: and now I will go up unto the Lord, peradventure I shall make an atonement for your sin" (v. 30), but he did not tell them the purpose which was in his heart, nor the price which he was proposing to pay.

III. THE OFFER THAT HE MADE. He went quietly and thoughtfully back to the presence chamber of God, as the people stood beholding. "Peradventure," he had said—he was not sure. He felt that the sin was very great. He could not see how God could go back from his solemn threatenings. He was convinced that if the merited judgments were averted, it must be in consequence of an atonement. Yet, what atone-ment could there be? Animals could not avail, though they were offered in hecatombs. There was only one thing he could suggest—he could offer himself. He was, of course, by no means clear that even this would be accepted or avail, but he could at least make the offer. This was the secret which he locked in his breast as he climbed the moun-tain. And it was this which made him say, "Peradventure." He could not be sure that the ransom price would be large enough.

It may be asked how he came to think of atonement. But we must remember that probably there had already been much talk be-tween God and himself about the sacrifices which the people were to offer. Again and again had the word *atonement* been employed: he had learned that one by suffering could redeem others; he had seen the deep possibilities in the law of substitution; and it seemed a natural thing, therefore, to propose that he, the chosen servant, the prince and leader of the people, would be weighed in the scale against the nation, and God should accept his blood as a ransom for their life.

And Moses confessed his people's sin to God, and added: "Yet now, if Thou wilt forgive their sin—." He would not finish that sentence. He could not trust himself to depict the blessed consequences that would ensue, if only God would forgive. If Thou wilt forgive, freely, and without a ransom price, *then* thy noblest attributes will appear; *then* my tongue shall sing aloud of thy goodness; *then* I will bind myself to thy service with new enthusiasm; *then* the people surely will become touched with the passion of gratitude and love.

But the dark fear oppressed him that free pardon was too much to expect. Ah, how little did he realize the love of God in Jesus Christ our Lord! And he therefore added, "And if not, blot me, I pray Thee, out of thy book which Thou hast written." That book may be the Book of Life; or it may be the registry of God's people whether in this life or in the next. So that the proposal was whether that he should there and then die, and not see the good land beyond Jordan; or that he should cease to be numbered with God's people, and miss forever the beautiful vision, finding his portion among the reprobate.

This proposal was made deliberately and thoughtfully. He had had ample time to think it over during the long and tedious climb from the mountain foot. He was quite prepared for God to accept it. He would have counted himself highly honored to have been allowed to be a sin offering on those heights. Oh, how the heart of God must have moved towards the faithful servant, whose proposal recalled another scene in the faraway ages of eternity, when the Son of God undertook to redeem man by making an atonement through the shedding of his own blood!

Of course, the offer was not accepted. No one can atone for his own sin, much less for the sins of others. Yet the people were spared. The passing by of their transgression was rendered possible by the propitiation which was to be offered in the course of the ages on the cross (Rom. 3:25). And though they were threatened with the loss of the Divine presence in its richer manifestations, yet the Angel of God was sent before them to lead them into the land of promise.

20

God's Presence
Our Rest

My presence shall go with thee,
and I will give you rest.
—Exodus 33:14

This assurance of rest is as applicable to the present age as to that of the Exodus. Nay, perhaps there is a special message in it to these feverish days, so filled with discord, confusion, and strife. Its very utterance shows a deep acquaintance with the heart of man. For there is a settled conviction with us all that we are not to live ever thus, the victims of merciless disquiet.

Every revolution—the Anarchist's plot and the Socialist's dream, the well-meant effort to bring about the kingdom of heaven by social reconstruction—is a plea on the part of men for rest. But that rest must be sought deeper down than in circumstances. It must begin at the center of our being, and in its accord with the being of God. His presence must be welcome to us, and accompany us, or rest is a vain dream.

I. THE CIRCUMSTANCES BY WHICH THIS ASSURANCE WAS CALLED FORTH. (1) Moses was a very lonely man. Perhaps more lonely in the midst of the two millions of people whom he was leading as a flock, than he had been amid the solitudes of the desert, tending the flock of Jethro. The very contrast between his lofty enjoyment of Divine communion, and the people, always set on sensual pleasure, must have lent intensity to the isolation of his spirit, which reared itself amid their sensual longings, as the peak of Sufsafeh above the lower ranges of Sinai. "And Moses said unto the Lord, See, Thou sayest unto me, bring up this people; and Thou hast not let me know whom Thou wilt send with me." What a sigh there is here for companionship!

It is certain that these words will be read by many whose lives are outwardly solitary. Some are left during long hours to bear the burden of the home, or of suffering, or of foreign service, like a sentry on night duty at a lone post. Others amid crowds are not less solitary; many soldiers, but no brother office; many voices, but the one voice missing; many companions, but no friend. In the physical world we are told that in the most solid bodies the atoms do not touch; and how often though the crowd throngs us we are not conscious that anyone has touched us. It is to that state of mind that the assurance of the text was given.

(2) In addition to this, the hosts were soon to leave the mountain region of Sinai, with which Moses had been familiar during his shepherd life, in order to take the onward road through unknown deserts, infested by daring and experienced foes. What though the pillar and cloud led them slowly along those solemn desert pathways, and at night shed a broad flood of light on the clustered tents of the desert encampment; yet the prospect of that journey through the great and terrible wilderness was sufficient to appall the stoutest heart.

Such a summons to arise and depart is often sounding with its bugle call in our ears. We are not like those who travel by the metal track of the railroad, on which they have been to and fro every day for years, and are able to tell exactly the names and order of the stations, but like an exploring expedition in an absolutely unknown district, when even the leader, as he leaves his hammock in the morning, does not know where it will be slung at night. What seems a monotonous life, always the same, does not revolve around a beaten circle, as the horse or ass winding up buckets from a well, but is ever striking out over new tracts of territory, which we have not traversed before.

(3) Still further difficulties had lately arisen in connection with the people's transgression. From a careful study of the passage it would seem that a change was proposed by their Almighty Friend. Hitherto He had

gone in the midst of them. Now He avowed his intention of substituting an angel for Himself, lest He should suddenly consume the people because of their stiff-neckedness (v. 23). Already the people had been bidden to strip themselves of their ornaments; and the tent, which was recognized as the temporary pavilion for God, must be pitched without the camp, afar off from the camp, so those who sought the Lord were compelled to take a considerable journey to reach his visible shrine. But now it seemed likely that some sensible diminution of the evidence of the Divine presence and favor was about to take place; and the fear of this stirred the soul of the great leader to its depths. Like Jacob at the fords of the Jabbok, he felt that he could not let God go, and he told Him so: "If thy presence go not with us, carry us not up hence." Better abandon thy mighty scheme, slay us at once, and wrap us in a winding sheet of sand, than allow us to take another step without thy presence.

Are there not times with many of us when we have reason to fear that, in consequence of some sad failure or sin on our part, the Lord may be obliged to withdraw the conscious enjoyment of his love? A chill fear lays its icy hand upon the strings of our heart, and almost petrifies it into silence. "Supposing He should be compelled to leave me to myself, to withdraw his tender mercies, to shut up his compassions. Supposing that I should be like a sledge abandoned in Arctic snows, or a ship abandoned by its crew in mid-ocean. Supposing that the fate of Saul should be mine, and that of me God should say, It repenteth me that I have made him king." Such thoughts quicken the pace of the soul as it goes to his footstool.

II. THE PLACE WHERE THIS ASSURANCE WAS GIVEN. The earlier intercourse between the servant, "faithful in all his house," and Him who had appointed him, seems to have been on the mountain summit. But after the outburst of the people's sin, a change was made which did not necessitate such prolonged or distant absences from the camp. Indeed, he was absent for only one other period of forty days (Ex. 34:28) till the time of his death, some thirty-eight years afterwards.

During the prolonged interview which he had been permitted to enjoy, God had spoken to him much of the Tabernacle which was shortly to be reared. He at once saw the blessedness of this proximity of the shrine for worship and fellowship, and his ardent soul seems to have been unable to brook delay. A tent was therefore selected; it may have been his own, or one specially prepared, and was pitched "without the camp, afar off from the camp. And he called it the Tent of Meeting; and it came to pass that everyone which sought the Lord went out into the tent of meeting, which was without the camp" (v. 7, R.V.).

But its special benefit was obvious in the case of Moses himself. It was no longer necessary for him to climb to the mountain summit, entrusted with errands on behalf of the people, or eager for advice in difficult problems. He was able to transact all necessary business by going out to the tent. And when it was rumored through the camp that the was about to do so, "all the people rose up" to see the marvelous spectacle, "and stood, every man at his tent door," looking after him because so soon as he entered into the tent, the pillar of cloud descended from its position in mid-heaven, and stood at the door of the tent, the vehicle and emblem of the Divine presence. Thus "the Lord spake unto Moses face to face, as a man speaketh unto his friend"; and Moses spake to his Father, who is in secret, with the freedom of a child. And as the people beheld that wondrous sight of God stooping to commune with man, they "rose up and worshiped, every man in his tent door" (v. 10).

It was there that this amazing colloquy took place. Moses spoke of his loneliness, and asked who was to be associated with him in his great task; and contrasted this silence on the part of God in a particular which so closely concerned his comfort and efficiency with all his other dealings with him. "Yet Thou hast said, I know thee by name, and thou hast also found grace in my sight" (v. 12). Then it seemed as if that faithful heart suddenly caught sight of a blessing more transcendent in glory than any he had yet dared to ask. His petition was couched in great humility, sandwiched between a double reference to the grace to which he owed everything, but he ventured to suggest that God should Himself show him his ways, that he might know Him. It was as if he said, Wilt Thou Thyself be my comrade and companion—my referee in difficulty; my adviser in perplexity; my friend in solitude?

Thine angels are strong and fair and good: but none of them will suffice me, nothing short of Thyself. Without Thee, it were better for me to relinquish my task and die, but with Thee, no difficulty can baffle, no fear alarm, no obstacle deter.

And God's answer came back on his spirit with music and balm, "My presence shall go with thee, and I will give thee rest" (v. 14). Nothing was said as to the people. The promise of the Divine presence was made apparently to Moses alone.

But faith gets bolder as it mounts. Each answer to its claims makes it claim more. We may seriously question whether our faith is of the right quality if it is unable to compass more in its hand today than it did a year ago. And, therefore, Moses not only took the assurance of the Divine presence for himself, but asked that it would be extended to include the people. "Wherein shall it be known there that I and thy people have found grace in thy sight? Is it not in that Thou goest with us? So shall we be separated, I and thy people, from all the people that are upon the face of the earth" (v. 16).

In this request also he was successful. "And the Lord said unto Moses, I will do this thing also that thou hast spoken; for thou hast found grace in my sight" (v. 17). There are moments of holy intercourse with God, rapturous, golden moments, in the lives of all his servants; when next they visit us, and we would make the most of their brief, bright, rapturous glow, let us plead, not only for ourselves, but for others, asking for them an equal blessedness.

III. THE BLESSEDNESS WHICH THE ASSURANCE GUARANTEED. There was, first, the Divine presence; and there was, secondly, the promised Rest—not the rest of Canaan, for this Moses never saw, but a deeper and more blessed inheritance, which may be the portion of all faithful souls. But at their heart these two are one. The Divine presence is Rest.

Of course, the conscious presence of God with us is only possible on three conditions.

Firstly, we must walk in the light, as He is in the light; for He will have no fellowship with the unfruitful works of darkness, or turn aside to go with us on any crooked path of our own choosing.

Secondly, we must recognize that the blood of Jesus Christ his Son constantly cleanses us from all sin; not only that which we judge and confess, but that also which is only seen by his pure and holy eyes.

Thirdly, we must claim the gracious aid of the Holy Spirit, to make real that presence, which is too subtle for the eye of man, unless it be specially enlightened.

And above all, we must remember that for us, at least, that presence is localized in the man Christ Jesus. For us there is no attenuated mist of presence, though a mist of light, but a Person in whom that presence is made real and touches us. But when these conditions are fulfilled, the blessed soul enters upon an experience of the presence of God which can find no better words to express its bliss than the psalmist's, as he turned from the prosperity of the wicked to consider his own estate: "Nevertheless, I am continually with Thee; Thou hast holden me by my right hand . . . Whom have I in heaven but Thee? And there is none upon earth that I desire beside Thee" (Ps. 73:23, 25).

And the sense of that presence is Rest. I have a vision of a woodland glade. A group of tired, frightened children are cowering around the hole of an old tree, dropping the fragile, withered flowers from their hands and pinafores, as the first great drops of the thunder shower, which had been darkening the sky, begin to fall. They have lost their way; they sob bitterly, and crowd together. Suddenly through the wood there comes a quick step, beneath which the twigs crackle and break—Father has come, and as he carries some in his strong arms through the storm on the nearest trick for home, and the others run at his side, they have learned that there is a presence which is Rest.

21
Tabernacle Building

According to all that I show thee, even so
shall ye make it . . . after the pattern which
was showed thee in the mount.
—Exodus 25:9, 40

The heart of the Jewish people was the Tabernacle, around which their tents circled, and the movements of which determined the journeyings of the host. The Tabernacle also taught them some of the deepest thoughts about God, in a kind of picture language, which was best suited to their immature minds. These we can touch on but incidentally, as our main point is the part borne by Moses in its creation.

We must remember that the children of Israel did not possess a language like our own, with many words, and a rich vocabulary, capable of expressing all kinds of abstract ideas, such as love, wisdom, purity, spirituality, holiness. We hardly realize how great a hindrance to the communication of spiritual truth arises from the lack of suitable words to act as the channels of thought. How could you speak of love to savages, if the only word for it in their language had impure and coarse associations? So that before making his revelation God had to provide language for his thoughts. This He did largely in the construction of the Tabernacle.

I. The Conception of the Tabernacle. The pattern in the mount! Then clearly there must have been some visible phenomenon, some bright apparition, some glorious picture cast on the clouds or built on the old rocks. There may have been stakes and curtains, cherubs and lamps, gold and silver, altar and candlestick, but they would not bear the touch—they existed as a beautiful dream, like some mystery of cloud that stands for a moment in the heavens at sunset, and then is gone.

But it is almost inconceivable that God did not at the same time explain to Moses those wonderful conceptions of his own nature, and his relations to men, which were intended to be set forth in this material structure. In those days of hallowed intercourse, the Almighty Teacher must have impressed on the reverent and receptive mind of his pupil trains of holy thought which engrossed and delighted him. It may be that even to him they were first conveyed under those pictorial forms in which they were afterwards presented to the people, but in any case they were surely communicated by the Spirit which reveals the deep things of God, and makes them known to those who love Him. They were as follows:

God's willingness to share man's life. If the people had only seen the devouring fire on the top of Sinai, the pavilion of God's presence, they would never have dared to think that there was any community of interest between Him and them. To their minds, He would always have seemed distant and unapproachable. So God said, "Let them make Me a sanctuary, that I may dwell among them" (v. 8); and He promised concerning it, "I will dwell among the children of Israel, and will be their God" (Ex. 29:45).

Thus it was ordained that this larger tent should be pitched among them, only differing from their own in its proportions and materials, but standing on the same level sand, struck and pitched at the same hour with theirs, and enduring the same vicissitudes of weather and travel. Did not this say, as plain as words could, that the tabernacle of God was with men, and that He was willing to dwell with them and become their God? Did it not teach that Jehovah had become a pilgrim with the pilgrim host; no longer a God afar off, but a sharer in their national fortunes? And is not this the very lesson of the Incarnation? May we not venture to suppose that the Church, that holy body which was being prepared for the Son of God, was even then revealed to the faithful servant? And that in his wonderful structure he was taught to repeat, in material forms, that mystic union of spirit, soul, and body, in the man Christ Jesus, of which the holy of holies, the holy place, and the outer court were the transient but striking emblem?

It was thus that the mind of man was prepared to learn that God could become flesh, and tabernacle among us. It was thus that the first syllables were coined which were to be built up into the name Emmanuel. It was thus that the Incarnation was prefigured. For the body of Jesus is the true Tabernacle, which the Lord hath pitched, and not man; that body which was born of the pure Virgin, in which He abode with men, and through which He achieved redemption.

The Greatness of God. To this, too, a visible expression was to be given. The Tabernacle was the most superb building of its kind ever reared by man. It must have cost at least a quarter of a million sterling—an immense sum for that fugitive nation of slaves. The silver pedestals placed at intervals along the sand to hold the upright boards; the gorgeous tapestry which composed ceiling and walls; the golden furniture, of which the seven-branched candelabra alone weighed one hundredweight of gold, equal to £5,500 in value; the brass wrought into sixty brazen pillars, with their silver capitals and hooks, from which were suspended curtains of so slight a gauze that people could see all that was transpiring in the outer court. How costly were these!

On that new year's day, the anniversary of the Exodus (Ex. 40:17), as it stood forth completed in the desert sunshine, it must have seemed to all who beheld it as fair as the New Jerusalem did to the eye of the seer, when he beheld it descending out of heaven from God; and must have furnished new and enlarged conceptions of the Divine majesty: though to the eye of Moses there must have been almost a disappointment, because the actual fell so far short of the pattern he had seen.

God's Unity. All around, the nations were under the spell of idolatry. But the Tabernacle, with all its differing parts, and materials, and accessories, was one. One ark; one incense altar; one altar of burnt offering; one sacred purpose in every order and rite for the putting away of uncleanness. It stood, therefore, among men as a perpetual protest against idolatry, and as an emphatic witness to the Unity of God. "Hear, O Israel; the Lord our God is one Lord." Such was the perpetual message that floated on the desert air from that unique structure.

But how sublime, how awe-inspiring must that message have been, as it first broke on the heart of Moses! He knew it before, but he saw it as one who looks into the heart of truth; comparing small things with great, it was as when we look into the eye of our friend, and detect there depths of life and love which we could not put into words, and which had passed our thoughts.

God's Spirituality. On the mountain the lawgiver saw the robes of the King, but not the King; his glory, but not his person; his back part, but not his face; and the conception that God was a spirit was conveyed to the people in that most striking form.

Enter the holy place; your eye is arrested by the heavy but magnificent curtain, wrought with cherubim, that cuts off six feet of the length of the entire structure. Pull that aside, and you pass into a chamber which is a perfect cube, a miniature of the New Jerusalem, whose length, and breadth, and height, are equal, In the Egyptian temple, this apartment would contain the crocodile or ibis, but there was only a box, over which forms of exquisite beauty bent with outspread wings, and between them a light shone which was not borrowed from sun or stars. Could anything more significantly convey the idea that God was a Spirit?

This absence of any visible form in the inner shrine most astonished the rough soldier Pompey, who strode with eager curiosity across the floor, which had never before been pressed by aught but the unsandalled foot of the high priest once a year. He expected to find some visible embodiment of Jehovah, and turned contemptuously away deriding the empty void. But to Moses it must have been an unparalleled conception, overpowering his thoughts.

God's Purity. The impression of this was produced by a series of comparisons. First, the Tabernacle stood within a courtyard fenced from public approach, the outer part could be trodden only by those men who had passed through certain rites of purification; and as to the inner, it could only be trodden once a year by the high priest, carefully cleansed by many rites, and clad in garments of special design, while the blood of slain animals, selected out of the herds of their freedom from any blemish or speck, was sprinkled around. All was done to impress upon the people the care with which they must approach God; and in this way impressions of his holiness were wrought into the national mind, which succeeding centuries have not been able to efface.

And throughout these arrangements, and notably by these repeated references to the blood of sacrifices that was to be shed and sprinkled, Moses became much familiarized with the philosophy of the Atonement. He must have seen across the centuries the cross of Jesus, with its mystery of love and sacrifice and substitution for the sins of men; and there must have arisen a very clear prevision of those various aspects of that marvelous death, which were faintly shadowed forth in the offerings, and which touch God and the believer, the offender in ignorance, and the sinner in presumption, the great world of men, and apparently the universe of God.

Such thoughts as these must have penetrated the soul of Moses as he waited before God, oblivious to the flight of time, the waning love and idolatry of his people, or the demands of the body for food. And as we behold the great spectacle of that rapt and spellbound soul, we get some conception of one part at least of the engagements of eternity, and we are stirred to seek after a more intimate knowledge of God.

Oh to know God! Not to know *about* Him, but to know Him; to "follow on to know the Lord"; to think his thoughts; to give Him time to convey his thoughts into our minds; to acquaint ourselves with Him, who, indeed, invites us to the knowledge, and sets open all the doors of his nature for us to enter. This were better than all beside; no rapturous experience, no deliverance from evil, no flight of emotion, could so repay our soul as this, which must carry in its embrace all of these. It were well, indeed, to suffer the loss of all things to know Him!

II. THE REPRODUCTION OF THE PATTERN. There is a special interest to us all in this. We are not called to build again the Tabernacle, after that old pattern which has served its purpose, and fallen into disuse because superseded by the clearer regulations of the Gospel; yet there is an analogy which is full of instruction and inspiration in the life of every true believer, and deserves our attention for a moment.

As the Tabernacle dwelt in the mind of God before it was reproduced on the desert sands, so does the life of each one exist, as a conception of that same infinite intelligence—which comprehends in its sweep the flight of an angel with the everlasting Gospel, and the fall of a sparrow to the ground.

When a child is born into the world, with all its faculties shut up within it, as a flower in the bud, there is in the mind of God a perfect picture of what that life may become, an ideal to which it may be conformed. There is a clear anticipation of what it will be, but side by side there is a distinct prevision of what it might be. And if only that pattern could be seen and literally reproduced, if only that life could attain to the Divine ideal, there would be no room for regret or disappointment. It would fulfill its complete purpose as a thought of the Divine mind, and attain its perfect consummation and bliss.

So with the believer standing on the threshold of the Christian life, full of hope and purpose. For him also there is a perfect ideal stored in the Divine nature, of a life full of the blessedness of the Beatitudes, and overflowing with the mighty works of the Gospels. If only it were realized from day to day!—of growing glory, from strength to strength, from grace to grace. Alas, that with so many of us, as the years have passed, we have wrought our own evil will and followed our own design!

The main inquiry for us all as we enter on any fresh enterprise, or even pass over the threshold of each new day, should be, *not* How would other men act? *Nor* What will make for my own advantage? *Nor* What would increase my reputation, or add to my gains? But—What is God's ideal, God's thought, God's pattern? And our one aim should be to understand it, sure that to fulfill it is to have lived well.

God's Pattern was Comprehensive. No tassel, nor socket, nor tiny detail, was left to the fancy or ingenuity of the artificers; all was comprehended in the Divine pattern. Of every detail God had a plan, because in each some purpose was hidden, and the symmetry of the whole depended on the perfection of each part. So in life God's thought covers all details. Nothing is too trivial to be made a matter of prayer and supplication. No great life is possible that does not comprehend in its scheme and scope attention to the commonplaces and trifles of character.

God's Plan was unfolded gradually. Probably the account of the revelation of the successive parts of the tabernacle is an exact transcript of the method by which the Divine design was unfolded to Moses' thought. Line upon line, precept upon precept—such is ever the Divine method. If we may so put it, the plan of the life of Jesus was only unfolded to his human intelligence a step at a time. Remember how He said, "the Son can do nothing of Himself, but what He seeth the Father do." "He will show Him greater works than these." The eye of the perfect Servant was always fixed on the development of his Father's scheme for Him; this was shown in the touch of a wasted hand, the cry of an agonized parent, the pressure of the hate of his foes, the demands of the crowds.

We shall not be able to see far in front, nor the whole completed plan of our life, but as we complete one thing, another will be revealed, and then the next, and the next. It may be that we shall have to fulfill the different portions of the Tabernacle of our life, without apparent connection with each other, "by diverse portions and in diverse manners," and we shall not understand the Divine purpose, but at the end of life we shall see that it was one complete and exquisite structure, of which no part was wanting.

God's Plan was commensurate with the people's resources. As the pattern was there on the Mount, there were the materials for its realization in the possession of the people below—the gold and silver and precious stones; the blue and purple and scarlet; the fine linen and goats' hair; the rams' skins and badgers' skins; the genius of the artificers; and the willingness of the people.

God never gives a man a pattern without making Himself responsible for the provision of all materials needed for its execution. Take God's plan, and then trust God utterly for the needful grace; it is there; it only awaits the claim of your faith. All things are added to the man who seeks first and only the kingdom of God. If the materials are not forthcoming, you may seriously question whether you are not working on a plan of your own. God will not provide for a single tassel of your own addition to his scheme.

God's Plan must be resolutely Obeyed. Again and again in the last chapter of Exodus we are told that all was done, "as the Lord commanded Moses." This was his supreme joy and satisfaction, that he had not added to or diminished from the divine command; and so the work was finished. It would be well for us to cultivate the habit of immediate and entire subservience to the prompting of the Divine will repeating it in the tiniest details as well as in the most difficult experiences.

Thus would the human life become harmonious with the Divine, the tabernacles of our lives would become the home of Him that inhabits eternity, and whose name is Holy; and there would be the settling down upon us of the Divine Shekinah, "the cloud by day and fire by night," through all our journeys, till we reach our Father's home.

God's Plan is always Progressive. In pursuing the earlier stages of the Divine tuition, Moses was specially occupied with elaborating the elementary idea of sacrifice, as in the case of the Paschal Lamb. The next stage was the building of the Tabernacle, with which we have now been engaged. But this was not the final form of the Divine revelation to which he was called to give visible shape. In after years, when disease was mowing down thousands of victims throughout the camp, as a judgment on the murmurings of the people, their leader was summoned to make a serpent of brass, and place it on a pole, that all who looked might live.

In that supreme moment, he caught sight of the dying Lord, and discerned, not only the fact, but the method of his death. To no other Old Testament seer, so far as we can learn, was it given to know that Jesus must be lifted up upon a cross. But this was permitted to him who had faithfully wrought out the Divine plan in its earlier stages; and he, too, was privileged to set forth, so graphically and simply, the nature of saving faith. "As Moses lifted up the serpent in the wilderness, so must the Son of Man be lifted up, that whosoever believeth in Him should not perish, but have everlasting life."

Thus is it always. As we climb the hill, the horizon expands; as we do God's will more thoroughly, we know his doctrine more completely; as we follow the Divine plan, we are permitted to look into and proclaim those deeper things, "which God hath prepared for them that love Him."

22
The Start from Sinai

And Moses said unto Hobab, We are jour-
neying unto the place of which the Lord said,
I will give it you. Come thou with us,
and we will do thee good.
—Numbers 10:29

Israel sojourned under the shadow of Sinai for about eleven months—long enough to see the round of the season, but the green verdure of the spring and the fading tints of the autumn would leave no trace on the appearance of those vast sandstone rocks. But what a change had been wrought in their condition! They arrived there a fugitive and unorganized people: they left it a mighty nation in battle array, provided with a sacerdotal system which was to last for centuries, as a type of the Priesthood of Christ and his saints; and furnished with a code of laws and sanitary enactments which have been a model for the most civilized peoples of the world.

The very appearance of the camp indicated this marvelous change. In the midst the sacred tent with its brooding cloud, and around it the goodly tents of the people, "as gardens by the riverside, as lignaloes which the Lord had planted, or as cedars beside the waters." The priests and Levites pitched immediately around it, in the inner circle; and around them again the twelve great tribes, three towards each point of the compass, guarding the Tabernacle as a most sacred charge, and as the center of their national life.

It was a marvelous spectacle, also, when the cloud was taken up, and the priests, through the silver trumpets, gave the signal that the camps on the east side should begin to lead off the march. Then Judah passed on first, followed by Issachar and Zebulun; and the sons of Gershom and Merari, with their six wagons, bearing the heavier portions of the Tabernacle (Num. 7:1–9) came next; and after these Reuben, followed by Simeon and Gad; then the long lines of Kohathites, carrying on their shoulders the vessels of the Holy Service; and, lastly, the remaining six tribes in two great divisions, the one led by Ephraim and the other by Dan.

All was beautifully ordered; and though we may not attribute the mighty revolution which had been thus effected to the unaided genius of Moses, we cannot but feel that, as God for the most part gave his teachings, through minds competent to receive and transmit them, so the mental endowments of Moses must have been of no mean order, that he could so readily take, and keep, and transmit the legislation which made Israel a great people. But side by side with this colossal intellect, there was still a weak, human heart, which betrayed itself in the proposal which he made to Hobab.

I. MOSES' PROPOSAL. During their stay at Sinai, it is probable that deputations from neighboring tribes visited the people, and among them was this chieftain of a tribe closely related to Moses by marriage. Hobab, we are told, was the son of Reuel, the Midianite, Moses' father-in-law. Of course, he knew the country well, every foot of it—where the springs lay, and the pastures, and the safest, shortest routes; and so Moses approached him with the request that he would go with them, to give them the benefit of his practical knowledge. "Leave us not, I pray thee; forasmuch as thou knowest how we are to encamp in the wilderness, and thou mayest be to us instead of eyes" (10:31).

This request was, obviously, most natural. Moses was a very lonely man, as we have seen; and it was pleasant to have one, bound to him by a blood affinity, to unburden himself to, in any special crisis.

At the same time, it was at variance with the general custom, which even then must have commenced strongly to assert itself, or Israelite exclusiveness. This national characteristic was acutely perceived and adverted to by Balaam, when he said: "Lo, the people shall dwell alone, and shall not be reckoned among the nations" (Num. 23:9). The Jews made no intermarriages with neighboring peoples on pain of death; he dressed in a special garb, and differed from all other men to the very dressing of his beard. And all this, to keep the people free from the plague-spots of the earth, which, in the expressive language of Leviticus (18:25), was "vomiting out her inhabitants."

Even though we admit that at the heart of the nation there were more tender emotions towards any who were willing to sympathize with its spirit—to a Rahab and a Ruth; to the strangers within its gates; and to the Gentiles, who might in after days be attracted by the light which shines from Zion's hill—yet it was an unusual thing for the great law-giver to go out of his way to utter this winsome invitation to a Midianite prince. And there must have been a strong reason that prompted it.

And shall we not find it in that instinctive shrinking of the human heart from the strange and unknown way? It was because Moses had never gone that way before that he was so eager to obtain Hobab's company, and offered as a bribe that "what goodness the Lord shall do unto us, the same will we do unto thee" (Num. 10:32). How closely home does this phase of thought come to us all! We do not know what may await us at the next turn of the path, or at the top of the pass; what foes may lurk; what emergencies arise; what unexpected barriers arrest our steps. What if we are going into the midst of the foe; or missing a sweet glen with its luscious herbage; or making for a *cul de sac,* through which we shall find no aperture, and must return! And then how shall we survey the place in time to get suitable camping grounds for the coming hosts! How well to have a Hobab who knows the ground!

We seek our Hobabs in the advice of sage, grey-haired counselors; in the formation of strong, intelligent, and wealthy committees; in a careful observance of precedent. Anything seems better than a simple reliance on an unseen guide. Now, in one sense, there is no harm in this. We have neither right nor need to cut ourselves adrift from others, who have had special experience in some new ground on which we are venturing. It is a mistake to live a hermit life, thinking out all our own problems, and meeting all our own questions as best we may. Those who do so are apt to become self-opinionated and full of crotchets. God often speaks to us through our fellows; they are his ministers to us for good, and we do well to listen to our Samuels, our Isaiahs, our Johns. But there is also a great danger that we should put man before God: that we should think more of the glasses than of that which they are intended to reveal; and that we should so cling to Hobab, as to become unmindful of the true Guide and Leader of souls. When we have given Him his right place, He will probably restore our judges as at the first, and our counselors as at the beginning, but the first necessity is that the eye should be single towards Himself, so that the whole body may be full of light.

II. The Failure of Hobab, and the Divine Substitute. The desert chieftain was by no means enamored of the proposal of his great relative. He had no desire to leave his tribe, his camping ground, his free, careless existence, to link his fortunes to that great but ill-mannered host.

And other considerations may have weighed with him. It was only a month before that Aaron and his sons had been set apart for their sacred work, and the fire of God had fallen on their dedicatory sacrifices. The people had seen and shouted, but before evening their joy had been shrouded in sudden mourning. For some violation of the sacred ritual, or perhaps, as the subsequent prohibition of wine suggests, for personal misconduct while engaged in their ministry, the two young priests had been stricken dead, and Aaron forbidden to weep. This must have struck an awful fear through the camp.

Shortly after this, another incident occurred. The son of an Israelitish woman, whose father was an Egyptian, had blasphemed the holy name of God, and cursed in the midst of conflict with a man of Israel. The blasphemer had been stoned. The sentence must have seemed severe, though, as God was King, the sin had amounted to high treason, but the swift and awful vengeance may have been another deterrent cause in influencing the decision of Hobab.

The result of it all was that in reply to Moses' request, he said bluntly, "I will not go, but I will depart unto mine own land, and to my kindred" (v. 30). Moses still further urged and entreated him, but whether he succeeded or not is doubtful, though there are some reasons for thinking that the second request prevailed, because the descendants of the Kenite are numbered among the chosen people (Judg. 1:16).

But it would seem as if his aid were rendered needless by the provision of guidance immediately promised. Up to this moment the position of the Ark had been in the midst of the host, in front of Ephraim, Benjamin, and Manasseh, but henceforth it went three days' journey in front of the people, "to seek out a resting place for them." We are left to conceive of its lonely journey as it went forward, borne by its attendant band of priests and Levites, and perhaps accompanied by a little group of princes and warriors, and specially by the great lawgiver himself. Far behind, at a distance of miles, followed the camp with its tumult, its murmur of many voices, the cries of little children, the measured tramp of armed bands. But none of these intruded on the silence and solemnity, which, like majestic angels, passed forward with that courier group accompanying the Ark, over which cherubic forms were bending. That Moses was there is indubitable; for the august sentences are recorded with which he announced its starting forth and its setting down. In the one case, looking into the thin air, which seemed to him thronged with opposing forces of men and demons, he cried, "Rise up, O Lord, and let thine enemies be scattered, and let them that hate Thee flee before Thee"; and in the other he cried, "Return, O Lord, unto the many thousands of Israel" (vv. 35, 36). Thus God Himself superseded the proposal of Moses by an expedient which more than met their needs.

What consolation there is to each of us, in realizing the spiritual truth underlying this historical fact! We have to pass into the untried and unknown, and know not the way we should take. Some have to go alone. Some with the memory of companions that once went at their side, but whom they will see no more in this life. Some, though at present dowered with dear fellow pilgrims, are apprehensive and fearful as to the route, and what a day may bring forth. But amid all Jesus is with them, and goes before them, whether for war or rest. He will never forsake nor leave them. And the days as they pass will enable them to say with ever new meaning, "I know whom I have believed."

The Lord Jesus is the true Ark of the Covenant, who has gone before us through the world and death, through the grave and the last rally of the hosts of darkness, to the glory. We have but to follow Him. It is for Him to scatter our enemies, while we stand still and see his salvation. It is for Him to choose our resting place while we lie down and prepare ourselves for new obedience.

Let us not anticipate God's guidance or press on Him unduly. "He that believeth shall not make haste." Let there be an interval between the Ark and your steps, so that you may see, so far as possible, what God would have you do; and then deliberately, thoughtfully, but with fixed determination follow. *He* will "be to us instead of eyes."

And oh, the bliss of knowing that Jesus is not "three days' journey" distant, but near, so that He is ever between us and our foes. Before they can hurt us they must reckon with Him. In Him, too, is rest; so that we may lie under his shadow with great delight, and know that all must be well, since He has chosen our inheritance for us.

23
Noble to the Core

And Moses said, Enviest thou for my sake?
Would God that all the Lord's
people were prophets.
—Numbers 11:29

Uninterrupted success is hard to bear, much more so than perpetual trial. This was the moral of the story of the plains of Capua, where the demoralization, wrought in the troops of Hannibal by the enervating climate, wrought more havoc than the prowess of the legions of Rome. Many who were vigorous and energetic when climbing the steep cliffs of adversity, have succumbed to petty temptations in days of sunny prosperity.

If it should be debated as to whether sunshine or storm, success or trial, were the severer test for character, the shrewdest observers of human nature would probably answer that nothing so clearly shows the real stuff of which we are made as prosperity, because this of all tests is the severest. When the younger son came to possess the portion of goods that fell to him, he went down to feed swine.

For some two years Moses had been borne along on a flowing tide. Through faith in the living Jehovah, he had vanquished the proudest monarch of his time; had conducted nearly three millions of people through the wilderness wastes without a settled commissariat; had disciplined an unorganized multitude into a mighty host, with a

code of legislation and ritual which is the admiration of all thoughtful men. This was success enough to turn the head of any ordinary man
nor could we have wondered if he had shown signs of undue elation
and pride. But the two incidents which we are now to consider show
how absolutely simple and humble he had remained amid a very
summer of success.

ELDAD AND MEDAD. In condescension to his weakness, his
Almighty Friend appointed seventy colleagues to bear with him the burden of the people; and concerning them the somewhat ominous announcement is made that "the Lord came down in a cloud, and took
of the spirit that was upon him and gave it unto them" (Num. 11:25).

I do not agree with those who think that there was any diminution
of the spirit that rested upon Moses. It is very difficult to speak of the
subdivision of spirit. You cannot draw it off from one man to others,
as you draw off water. The whole Spirit of God is in each man, waiting to fill him to the uttermost of his capacity. It seems to me, therefore, that nothing more is intended than to affirm that the seventy were
"clothed upon" with the same kind of spiritual force as that which rested
upon Moses.

In each case of those thus anointed, the accession of spiritual
force was marked by the sudden breaking forth of prophecy; reminding us of that memorable day, of which this was a miniature, when
"they were all filled with the Holy ghost, and began to speak with other
tongues, as the Spirit gave them utterance" (Acts 2:4). May we not say
that the entrance of the Holy Ghost in fullness to the heart of man will
always lead to the utterance of thoughts that strive for expression, as
the ocean wave sweeps along the sea wall seeking for the inlet where it
may expend itself!

For sixty-eight of them the power of utterance was only spasmodic and temporary. "They prophesied, but they did so no more"
(R.V.). Emblems are they of those who, beneath some special influence—like that which cast Saul down among the prophets—suddenly break out into speech and act, and give promises not destined to
be fulfilled. Two, however, of the selected number, who, for some
reason, had remained in the camp, suddenly became conscious of
their reception of that same spirit, and they, too, broke out into

prophecy, and appear to have continued to do so. Instantly a young man, jealous for the honor of Moses, carried to him the startling tidings, "Eldad and Medad do prophesy in the camp"; and as he heard the announcement, Joshua, equally chivalrous, exclaimed, "My lord Moses, forbid them!" eliciting the magnificent answer, "Art thou jealous for my sake? Would God that all the Lord's people were prophets—that the Lord would put his Spirit upon them!"

It was as if he said, "Do you think that I alone am the channel through which the Divine influences can pour? Do you suppose that the supplies in the being of God are so meager that He must stint what He gives through me, when He gives through others? If it should please Him to create new stars, must He rob the sun of its light to give them brilliance? Is the gratification of a mean motive of vanity a matter of any moment to me, who have gazed on the face of God? Besides, what am I, or what is my position, among this people, compared with the benefit which would accrue to them, and the glory which would redound to God, if He did for each of them all that He has done for me?"

This is the spirit of true magnanimity. A spirit of self-aggrandizement is set on retaining its exclusive position as the sole depository of the Divine blessing; though this has the certain effect of forfeiting it, so that fresh supplies cease to pass through. But whenever the eye is single for the glory of God, and position is looked upon only as his gift to be used for his glory, and when the spirit is concentered in one eager and intense desire to see his will done, the glory of that light extinguishes the fires of ambition, and the faithful servant is willing to be anything or nothing, if only the Divine purpose is accomplished.

There is no test more searching than this. Am I as eager for God's kingdom to come through others as through myself? In my private intercessions can I pray as heartily and earnestly for the success of my competitors as for my own? Can I see with equanimity other and younger men coming to the front, and showing themselves possessed of gifts which I always considered to be my special province? Am I conscious of the rising of jealousy or envy when my leadership is subordinated to the claims of rivals? Should I be willing that the will of God should be done through another, if he suited God's purpose better than myself? Few of us could answer these questions without the sense of almost insuperable difficulty in assuming the position taken up by Moses when he heard that Eldad and Medad prophesied in the camp.

And yet, insofar as we fall short of that position, do we not betray the earthly ingredients which have mingled, and mingle still, in our holy service? Yes; it is ourselves that we serve—our schemes, and plans, and selfhood. And if we were to eliminate from Christian service all that has emanated from these sources, what a scanty handful of gold dust would be left! Oh, when shall we be able to say, "Would God that all the Lord's people were prophets," and view with thankful joy the leveling up of all Christians to the tableland of our gifts and grace?

This, however, can never come till we have learned to spend long hours with God; till we have been taken into his secret place; till we have come to care for his honor more than for our own; till we have become absorbed in the one consuming passion to see Him glorified in his saints, and admired in all them that believe. "The zeal of thine house hath eaten me up." Thus does the herald star, which on the fringe of night has told weary eyes that the dawn is near, sink contentedly into a very ocean of light; though not itself less bright because every inch of space is illuminated with a luster like its own.

MIRIAM. We remember her as the little black-eyed, watchful maiden who stood beneath the tall palm trees of the river's brink to watch the bulrush ark; and again as the heroic woman who answered the deep bass of the delivered hosts by leading the women's chorus on the shores of the Red Sea. What did she not owe to Moses? But for him she must have been an unknown slave girl, mated to a toiler in Pharaoh's brickfields, the mother of slaves. But now she was free, and the representative woman of an emancipated race, through the brother whom she had rocked in her arms. Ah, it was sad, indeed, that, at the age of ninety, she should turn against him whom she had tended and loved; and that she should poison the mind of the elder brother who had been his spokesman and right hand.

They spoke against him because of the Ethiopian woman whom he had married. Some have thought that Moses had married a second time, but it seems wiser, since the death of Zipporah is not mentioned, to consider the reproach as applicable to her, especially as she probably bore in her complexion the brand of another race. "Cushite" means black or dark-complexioned. She had comparatively recently come to the camp; and for some time Miriam may have been carefully watching her, with the result, that the whole woman's nature revolted from the thought of having to resign her primacy to such as she was. It is always difficult to see another filling the place which we have looked upon as ours, especially if we are conscious of being able to fulfill its duties better.

How well we can imagine her talking to Aaron and to the women with whom she was intimate, about these "Cushites," until she had raised quite a storm of feeling. This was bad enough in her, but how much worse in Aaron, who held the proudest position in the camp? The function of Moses was temporary, and would pass away with his life; whereas that of Aaron was permanent to himself and his heirs. Yet Aaron could not but feel how vast was the gulf between him and his brother. And out of this there sprang the jealousy which made Zipporah its excuse. "And they said, Hath the Lord indeed spoken only by Moses; hath He not spoken also by us?" How easy it is to disguise jealousy beneath the cloak of zeal for the law of God; and to think ourselves immaculate when rebuking the faults of others.

But how did Moses act—he who, years before, had felled an Egyptian with one blow of his fist? Did he pour out a torrent of indignation, assuring himself that he had just cause to be angry? Did he show them the door of the tent, and bid them mind their own affairs? Did he call on God to strike them down in his anger? Nothing of the sort. He answered not a word; for "the man Moses was very meek, above all the men which were upon the face of the earth" (Num. 12:3). In his bearing he reminds us of Christ in the judgment hall, who, "when He was reviled, reviled not again."

Was this weakness, as some would say? Nay, verily; it was the exhibition of colossal spiritual strength. Only a Samson with unshorn locks could have acted thus. It is the weak man who gives blow for blow; who blurts out his wrath; who cannot control the passion of his spirit. Only the strong man can be perfectly still under provocation, holding himself in, and turning the vehemence of his soul into the heat of an intense love.

It may be well to give some closing rules as to the attainment of this meek and quiet spirit, which in the sight of God is of great price.

First, let us claim the meekness of Christ. This, of course, was not possible for Moses in the direct way in which it is for us. And yet doubtless, in his case also there was a constant appeal for heavenly grace. The humility of Jesus did not forbid his proposing Himself as our model for meekness. "Learn of Me," He said; "for I am meek and lowly in heart." The likeness of the dove that rested on his head, and the lamb to which he was compared, were the sweet emblems of his heart. And in moments of provocation there is nothing better than to turn to Him and claim his calm, sweet silence, his patience and meekness, saying, "I claim all these, my Lord, for the bitter need of my spirit."

Let us cultivate the habit of silence. Express a thought, and you give it strength and permanence; repress it, and it will wither and die. Wisely did the Apostle James lay such stress on the use of the tongue, as the rudder and bit of the whole body; for its use will instantly determine whether the heart is filled with evil or peace. You will often hear it said that the best way of getting rid of an importunate passion is to let it out and have done with it. It is, however, a very mistaken policy. Utterance will give it vigor, and will sow another crop that will soon fruit again. Silence will kill it; as ice kills fish when there are no ventholes by which they can come up to breathe.

Learn to be still; to keep the door of the lips closed; to give, indeed, an answer when it is asked, and an explanation when it is needed to correct a misapprehension. But for the most part imitate the example of David, who was prepared for his victory over Goliath by the previous victory which he won over his elder brother in the soft answer returned to his insulting questions, "Let every man be swift to hear, slow to speak, slow to wrath" (James 1:19).

Next, consider the harm done by the aggressors to themselves. The cloud removed from over the tent, as if it must leave the very spot where the culprits stood; and behold, Miriam was leprous, white as snow. There is a piece of profound instruction here; you cannot say unkind or bitter things about another, without hurting yourself more than you hurt him. Like the boomerang of the savage, curses come back to the spot from which they start. And the wronged one may well forget his own anguish as he pours out his soul in pity and prayer for those, who, in dealing out their bitter words, have contracted the blot of leprosy on themselves.

Let us leave God to vindicate our cause. Moses trusted God to vindicate him; and the Almighty God "rode upon a cherub and did fly; yea, He did fly upon the wings of the wind." The Lord heard all that was said, and spoke suddenly to the three, and told them that while He would speak to others in visions and dreams, it was to Moses only that he would speak face to face, so that he might behold Jehovah's form. "Wherefore then," said He, "were ye not afraid to speak against my servant Moses?" (Num. 12:8). This is the secret of rest—to cultivate the habit of handing all over to God; as Hezekiah did, when he spread out Sennacherib's letter in the house of the Lord.

Commit yourself to Him that judges righteously, in sure certainty that He will vindicate you, and bring out your righteousness as the light, and your judgment as the noonday.

Let us give ourselves to intercessory prayer. Moses cried unto the Lord saying, "Heal her now, O God, I beseech Thee" (v. 13). When we pray for those who have despitefully used and persecuted us, it is marvelous how soon the soul gets calm and tender. We may begin to do it as a duty, in obedience to the command; we soon discover it to be as snow on a fevered forehead, cooling and soothing the soul. Do not wait to feel an inspiration—act on the sense of what your Lord requires; and as you pray, in the calm and holy presence of God, in the secret where your Father is found, you will find that unworthy thoughts will sink, as silt is precipitated to the river bed, leaving the stream pellucid and clear.

And the Lord heard his servant's prayer, and healed Miriam, but the whole host was delayed a week through her sin. We may be forgiven, but these outbreaks of sin always entail disaster and delay. Neither we nor others can be where we might have been had they not occurred.

24

A Bitter Disappointment

Tomorrow turn you, and get you into the
wilderness by the way of the Red Sea.
—Numbers 14:25

It was a weary journey from Kibroth-hataavah to Hazeroth, and
thence to Kadesh, probably the weariest of the entire route. Moses
spoke of it afterwards as "that great and terrible wilderness" (Deut.
1:19). But at last the hosts reached Kadesh-barnea, on the very border
of the Land of Promise; within sight of the low hills, the flying but-
tresses, so to speak, of the verdant tableland, which first arrests the eye
of the traveler coming up from the vast limestone plain of the desert.

How welcome that spectacle, after the four hundred miles of journey which had occupied the people for the past fifteen months! Welcome as the land-haze to Columbus, or as his native village nestling in
the embrace of the hills to the returning traveler. It must have been specially grateful to the eye of Moses.

I. HIS HOPES. As yet God had graciously veiled from him the
weary journeys of the forty years that were to succeed. He had no idea
of them. They had never entered into his calculations. From the way
in which he spoke to the people, he evidently counted on a comparatively brief struggle, sharp, but short, through which they would

pass to their possession. It never occurred to him that anyone but himself would plan that campaign, even if Joshua led it; or that any other hand would settle the people in the land of their eager longings. These are the words he addressed to the people as they camped in sight of the rolling prairies of Canaan: "Ye are come unto the mountain of the Amorites, which the Lord our God doth give unto us. Behold the Lord thy God hath set the land before thee: go up and possess it, as the Lord God of thy fathers hath said unto thee; fear not, neither be discouraged" (Deut. 1:20, 21).

As he said these words, must there not have been, deep in his heart, a sign of relief now that his task was almost done, and he might lay down his weighty responsibilities? God's glory was secured beyond their power to tarnish its luster. The Egyptians and all the neighboring nations must hear and be convinced. And as for himself, surely there were in store some few happy years in which he should repose after the long toils of his life. "Ah, sweet Land, of which God has spoken to me, surely there is within thy precincts some sequestered nook, where I may sit down and rest, and review an accomplished work!"

Who can doubt that some such hopes and thoughts as these filled his soul, and whispered the one deep sweet word, Rest—Rest? No more the daily gathering of manna, because it was a land of wheat and barley, in which they should eat bread without scarceness. No more the quenching of thirst at the water that flowed hot over the desert sand, because there would be vines, and fig trees, and pomegranates: it was a land of brooks of water, of fountains and depths that spring out of valleys and hills. No more the pitching and striking of tent, the setting of the watch, the perpetual movement; for every man would sit under his own vine and fig tree. After a few years spent thus, he might ask to depart in peace, and pass home from the Canaan of earth to the Sabbath-keeping of heaven.

Is it not thus that we all picture to ourselves some blessed landscape, lying warm and sunny under the smile of heaven? Life is pretty hard just now: a march over a great and terrible wilderness; a stern fight; a bearing of burdens, for which we have only just got strength enough. But never mind, it cannot last—there must be respite; the long land must have a turning; the wilderness march must have a Canaan; the lack of sympathy and tenderness must be swallowed up and forgotten in the embrace of a love which shall obliterate the memory of all, so that we shall awake as out of a brief, unpleasant dream. But suppose it be not so! What if He who loves us better than we love ourselves has marked out stations in a desert march, that lead right up to the mount from which we are to ascend to our Father's home! What if we are to fight with Moab, and meet Balaam, and see every one of those with whom we commenced life droop around us! What if we are to lie down to die alone beneath his kiss, away from the prattle of children, and the warm pressure of loving hands, on some Pisgah height! All this may be so, but if it is so, how will we do? Yet this is precisely what came to Moses.

II. THE QUARTER FROM WHICH HIS DISAPPOINTMENT CAME. It came entirely from the people. *Their first mistake was in desiring to spy out the land.* It is certainly said in these chapters that "the Lord spake unto Moses, saying, Send thou men, that they may search the land of Canaan" (Num. 13:1, 2). But the proposal did not emanate from the Lord. It had another origin, which was disclosed by Moses himself forty years afterwards, in words that followed those quoted above, "And ye came near unto me, every one of you, and said, We will send men before us, and they shall search us out the land, and bring us word again" (Deut. 1:22).

As in the case of Saul, the King of Israel, God gave them what they would have. Their self-will was a profound mistake. Had not God promised to give them the land, and could they not trust his choice? Were not his eyes ever upon it, from the beginning to the end of the year? Why need they wish to spy it out? What about his promise to give it them; why, then, need they be so anxious to see whether they could cope with its possessors? They had but, as Moses said, to go up and possess that which He had given.

Their second mistake was in receiving the discouraging report of the majority of the spies. Up to a certain point there was perfect agreement between them. "We came into the land whither thou sentest us, and surely it floweth with milk and honey, and this is the fruit of it." Then the ten said, "The people are strong, the cities are fenced and very great; and, moreover, we saw the children of Anak there. . . . We be not able to go up against the people, for they are stronger than we" (vv. 28, 31, R.V.). But the two, Caleb and Joshua, whose names alone linger on our tongues as household words, replied, "If the Lord delight in us, then He will bring us into the land, and give it us" (Num. 14:8).

The difference between the two lay in this, that the ten looked at God through the difficulties, as when you look at the sun through a reversed telescope, and it seems indefinitely distant and shorn of its glory; while the two looked at difficulties through God. And the people sided with the ten, and turned aside from the thought of God, to dwell long and sadly on the stupendous obstacles that menaced their occupation of the land. Here was a fatal mistake. Unbelief never gets beyond the difficulties—the cities, the walls, the giants. It is always picturing them, dwelling on them, pitting them against its own resources. Faith, on the other hand, though it never minimizes the difficulties, looks them steadily in the face, turns from them, and looks up into the face of God, and counts on Him. This is what the people failed to do; and for this they lost Canaan. "And the Lord said unto Moses, How long will this people not believe in Me" (14:11, R.V.). "We see that they could not enter in, because of unbelief" (Heb. 3:19).

Note, that they lost Canaan, not because of the graves of lust, but because of their unbelief. My brother, do not sit down beside that grave of lust, and suppose that that is going to settle your future. Never! God is not going to tether you forever to a grave. There is a resurrection and a new life before you, even for you; arise in the light of his forgiveness, and walk through the length and breadth of the land to possess it. Know thou this, that the only thing which can exclude thee thence is that thou wilt not believe in a forgiveness and grace, which are like the blue arch of heaven above thee, or like the immensity of eternity itself.

Their next mistake was in their murmuring, which proposed to substitute a captain for their tried friend and God-given leader. "All the congregation lifted up their voice and cried; and the people wept that night. And all the children of Israel murmured against Moses and against Aaron, and said, Would God that we had died in the land of Egypt. . . . And they said one to another, Let us make a captain, and let us return into Egypt" (Num. 14:1–3).

This was perhaps the bitterest hour in Moses' life. They had pro-posed to elect a captain before, but it was when he was away; this pro-posal was made before his face. The people whom he had loved with passionate devotion, whose very existence was due to his intercession on the Mount when they were on the point of being destroyed, had for-gotten all he had done; they actually proposed to supersede his au-thority, and if he would not go with them beneath their new-made captain, to leave him to his own devices there. And he fell on his face before all the assembly of the congregation. What unutterable agony rent his breast! Not only that he would be thus set aside, but that the anger of God should be thus provoked by the people he loved!

And as he lay there, did he not also, in those dark, sad moments, see the crumbling of his fairy vision, the falling of a shadow over the fair prospect of his hopes as when a pelting shower of rain hides a land-scape which a moment before had lain radiant in the summer light? So it has befallen in our own experience, not once, nor twice. We had been on the point of realizing some long-cherished hope. We were within a day's march of it. Our hands had already reached across the frontier line, and plucked the first fruits and pressed the luscious grapes of Es-hcol to our lips. Oh, rapture! Oh, fruition of long expectation! Oh, heaven of bliss! Then suddenly there is someone or more to whom we are tied, and their education is not complete. They cannot yet go over into the good land; and because they cannot, we may not. And as we stand there, the voice says, "Tomorrow turn you, and get you into the wilderness by the way of the Red Sea" (Num. 14:25).

III. HIS REFUSAL TO ESCAPE THE DISAPPOINTMENT. The dream of Moses for a speedy entrance into the land might even yet have been re-alized. If all the people were cut off, and he spared to be a second Abraham, the founder of the nation, it might be possible even yet for him to pass into the good land, and like Abraham settle there. And thus the trial came into his life. Satan tempts us, to reveal the evil in us; God to reveal the good. So God, knowing the hidden nobleness of his faithful servant, and eager that it should be revealed to all the world, suggested to him a proposal, that He should smite the people with

pestilence, and disinherit them, and make of him a nation greater
and mightier than they.

"Accept it," said the spirit of the self-life, "thou hast had trouble
enough with them; it will only hasten the inevitable issue of their
misconduct; besides, think of the rest thou wilt enter and the renown
which will accrue to thee in all after time." "No," said his nobler,
truer self. "It may not be; what would become of Jehovah's fame? and
how can I endure to see my people cut off?"

There are few grander passages in the whole Bible than that in
which Moses puts away the testing suggestion as impossible. "If Thou
shalt kill all this people as one man, then the nations which have heard
the fame of Thee will speak, saying: Because the Lord was not able to
bring this people into the land which He sware unto them, therefore He
hath slain them in the wilderness" (vv. 15 16). Then quoting the words
which God had spoken into his heart on that memorable occasion
when He passed down the mountain gorge, he pleaded that He would
pardon the people according unto the greatness of his mercy, as He had
been doing from the first of leaving Egypt until then. In other words,
Moses would not have the rest he longed for at the sacrifice of a ray of
God's glory, or of the people with whom his life was linked though they
had sadly plagued and disowned him. And so he turned away from the
open gate in Paradise, and again chose rather to suffer with the people
in their afflictions than enjoy the pleasures of Canaan alone. Let us ponder the lesson; and when next a dear delight is within our reach, and it
will be more for the glory of God and the good of others to turn from
it, let us ask grace to take the rugged path of the wilderness though it
mean a lonely life for forty years, and a death on Pisgah.

IV. A CONTRAST TO HIS ENDURANCE OF DISAPPOINTMENT. Little
is said about the leader's bearing. He kept silence, and opened not his
mouth; he hid his face even from good, because God did it. But the
people's behavior throws his into strong relief.

When they heard that they were to wander in the wilderness for
forty years, till their carcasses fill in its wastes, to be interred in the sands
as winding sheets, they rose up early in the morning, and gat them up
to the top of the mountain, saying, "Lo, we be here, and will go up

unto the place which the Lord hath promised. . . . Nevertheless the ark of the covenant of the Lord, and Moses, departed not out of the camp" (vv. 40, 44). By force of will and energy they sought to reverse the sentence just passed on them. Moses meekly bowed his head to it, and accepted the discipline of those long years.

Do not times like this come into our lives? We have come to the brink of some great opportunity, and the prize has seemed within our reach. But by some outburst we have shown ourselves unable or unfit to possess it. God puts us back. He says in effect, You are not yet fit to enjoy the blessing. You must go back to the common round, sit at the daily task, plod around the dull mill wheel. Exercise yourself in toils and frets and trifles, which are not worthy of a place in history; and after awhile come back and stand before these gates again, and you shall be admitted.

But we will not submit to it. "Nay, but we will go up." We will storm the position; we will not be thwarted. It is a hapless and useless resolve. You cannot force the gate. Better a hundred times wait meekly outside, learning the lesson of patience and faith, and you shall stand there again ere long to find it open to the summons of your ennobled and purified spirit.

V. MOSES' SOLACE IN DISAPPOINTMENT. Yet there were springs at which that weary spirit slaked its thirst. The sense that he did the will of God; the blessedness which unselfishness always brings to the elect spirit; the joy of seeing the result of the Divine discipline in the growing earnestness and strength of his people; the reception of daily grace of daily need. All these were his.

But even better than these there was the growing realization that the true rest of which he dreamed was not to be found in any earthly Canaan, however enticing, but in that rest of heart, that Sabbath-keeping of the soul, that repose of the nature in God, which is alone permanent and satisfying, amid the change and transience of all human and earthly conditions. So our God not unseldom breaks up our earthly visions, dear and cherished, in order that our soul, bereaved and solitary, may search for and find those diviner things which the moth of change cannot gnaw into, and the rust of time cannot corrode. "These things God worketh oftentimes with man."

25
Faithful
under Reproach

O God, shall one man sin, and wilt Thou be
wroth with all the congregation?
—Numbers 16:22

Few men have had greater experience of the ingratitude of their fellows than Moses. Here it broke out again, and this time in a formidable conspiracy led by Korah, with whom were associated two hundred and fifty princes, men of renown. The special points were the position he held and the authority he exercised; and the revolt throws some interesting light on the manner in which God's servants should consider the position they occupy in his church.

In the history of all workers for God there will come crises, when wrong motives will be imputed and unkind suggestions passed from mouth to mouth, even by those whose spiritual life has been due to their prayers and tears. Now it is jealousy of growing influence; then it is unwillingness to accept directions and fall in rank at the word of command; again it is the dislike of a carnal soul at the high spiritual demands which are in direct collision with its longings for milk and honey, fields and vineyards. Such disaffection begins with one discontented sensual soul, but it spreads as fire in prairie grass. There are many craven hearts ready enough to follow, who would not dare to lead, in an attempt to subvert some eminent and devoted servant of God.

Sometimes the pretext is no better than in the case of the man who voted for the expulsion of Aristides, for no other reason than that he was tired of hearing him called "the Just."

At such times we do well to turn to this dark chapter in the history of the forty years' wanderings, and learn how men ought to behave themselves in the house of God, which is the church of the living God, the pillar and ground of the truth.

I. LOOK ON YOUR POSITION AS GOD'S APPOINTMENT. Korah and his confederates suggested that Moses and Aaron had taken on themselves the offices which they held, the one as king in Jeshurun, whenever the heads of the people gathered; the other, with his family, as priest. "Why should these offices be exclusively vested in the two brothers? Were there not plenty of men as good as they? Was not all the congregation holy? And might not the presence of Jehovah be had by others as well as by them?" It was a conspiracy of princes against the leader and prince, and of Levites against the priestly family.

Instantly Moses fell on his face before God—his favorite attitude for meeting these outbreaks of popular hatred and discontent—like the bulrush which meekly bows its head as the autumn blast sweeps over the moor. But he made no further attempt to justify his position or Aaron's. He might have alleged his past services, his claims on the gratitude and loyalty of the people; he might have reminded them that their national existence was due, under God, to his faith, his prayers and tears, his intercessions and exertions on their behalf. But on all these points he held his peace, and took the whole matter into the Divine presence, throwing the responsibility on his God.

First, *he reminded the malcontents that their own position had been assigned by the appointment of the Most High.* The God of Israel had separated them from the congregation of Israel, to bring them near unto Himself, to do the service of the tabernacle of the Lord, and to stand before the congregation to minister unto them. It was distinctly *He* who had brought them near, and all the sons of Levi with them. There was, therefore, no cause for jealousy. The places of influence and authority in Israel were not a lottery, where some men might happen to draw prizes and others blanks. Posts were assigned to men, and men to posts, by the distinct interposition of God. And they who had been so distinctly appointed surely should admit that an equally distinct Divine appointment had been made in respect of Aaron and himself.

Next, and as a result of such a conception of the true position of affairs, *the ebullition of anger was shown to be really directed against God Himself.* "Therefore thou and all thy company are gathered together against the Lord; and Aaron, what is he that ye murmur against him?" (v. 11, R.V.). When men turn against us, we are too apt to run away from our position in panic; to make terms with them; or to throw down the reins in a pet. Any of these courses is a profound mistake, and quite incompatible with a right apprehension of our position towards God on the one hand, and man on the other.

There are many passages which show beyond doubt that our positions in the visible church are defined as carefully as of members in the human body. Though you be only a joint or hinge, on which other members articulate and work, you must believe that your position was fixed by the All-wise and Almighty Disposer of all. Is it to be supposed for a moment that He, who appointed the place where each star should shine in the bosom of night, should leave the position of the stars of his church to chance? (Acts 20:28; 1 Cor. 12:28; Eph. 4:11, R.V.).

If, then, disaffection or dissatisfaction arise, they must not in themselves determine your course. It may be that they indicate that the time has come for you to go elsewhere. But this evidence is by no means conclusive. You must go to Him who sent you, whose servant you are, and ask if it is his will for you to vacate your post; and if so, that He should make it clear. If He does not, then let nothing that man can do alarm or trouble you. You must stand to your post, as the lonely sentinel amid the falling lava of the eruption, till the Commander of the Lord's hosts tells you that you may surrender your sacred charge. But if no such orders come, grace and patience will; and you must remain till relieved by death.

Lastly, *Moses left the ultimate decision with God.* They were all to take censers, which were the ordinary prerequisites of the priests alone; and having charged them with fire and incense, were to present themselves before the Lord, at the door of the tent of meeting. It would be then for God to choose who should be holy, and who should be caused to come near unto Him.

What infinite rest would come into the lives of many of God's servants, if only they drank in the spirit of this heroic soul—so resolute to do the Divine will, at all hazards; and to remain at the helm though the fire of popular resentment crept along the bulwarks and blistered the skin from his hands. How often the face is worn with care, and the head streaked with grey, even if the course of the life be not deflected from the straight rule it should follow by thoughts like these—What will my committee, or elders, or supporters say? What will become of my children's bread, if I thwart so influential a contributor? How shall I be able to withstand so strong a popular movement? Must I not yield to the suggestions of friends, or threatenings of foes? Alas! these questions are so often asked, and the course of life decided by the weighing of prudential suggestions, and the consideration of human policy, but with little or no reference to Him, whose slaves we are, selected and appointed for special work.

Let us act as Moses, the faithful servant did, and refer all to the decision of our Master and Lord; and in the meanwhile be at peace. It is such a profound mistake to carry the burdens of the Lord's work. When difficulties come, as they will, they are his quite as much as they are ours. We have no right to carry his anxieties and care for his cares. He asks us to do his work; to obey his behests; to fulfill his commissions; and to transfer all the weary pressure and burden to Himself. If the people do not like us, it is for Him to determine whether He will continue us in our position; and if He choose to do so, He must keep us there, and give us favor with them. If our supplies fall off in doing his work, He must maintain us and our dear ones. A royal court is bound to support its own embassies. If our mission involve the assumption of leadership which is disputed by our fellows, we cannot recede from it, so long as we can say with Moses, "The Lord hath sent me to do all these works, for I have not done them of mine own mind" (v. 28). Thus pride and jealousy are alike impossible. We know we receive nothing except it is given us from heaven; and we refer all disputants to Him who has put us where we are.

II. Cherish Kindly Feelings Towards Those who Oppose. How nobly Moses dealt with this murmuring crowd! When first he heard their contentious voices, he assumed the posture of intercession, and began to plead for those who despitefully used and persecuted him. When it seemed, on the following morning, as if God would destroy not the ringleaders only, but all the congregation who assembled with them at the door of the tent of meeting, he fell on his face and pleaded with the God of the spirits of all flesh not to punish all for the sin of one man. Dathan and Abiram, the sons of Eliab, were specially contumelious; and, when he sent to summon them, returned an insulting message, accusing him of betraying them with false representations, asking why he had not led them into the land of milk and honey. They went so far as to insinuate that they dared not come, lest he should bore out their eyes (v. 14). Moses was naturally very indignant and wounded by these bitter and undeserved reproaches, but he made no attempt to answer them, except in self-vindication before the Lord. And when bidden he did not hesitate to rise up, and go to them, with no trace of vindictiveness in his address.

And on the following day, when the people, unawed by the terrible judgments that had befallen, murmured against Aaron and himself, and accused them of having killed the people of the Lord, he again averted from them the judgment which was threatened—first by his prayers, and then by hastening Aaron to stand, censer in hand, between the plague-stricken and those as yet unreached by the sickle of death. How quick he was to know when wrath had gone out from the Lord! How eager to stay its progress! How generous to make such efforts on the behalf of those who had but an hour before launched at him their bitter reproaches!

This is the true pastor's heart. He partakes of the spirit of the Good Shepherd, who loved those who taunted Him, and pleaded for the forgiveness of his murderers. There is no more resentment in his heart towards those who opposed Him than in a mother's towards the babe who, in its paroxysm of temper, smites her breast with its tiny hands. The grey-headed retainers, who, prepared to die, resist the entrance of the mob at the palace gates, that by their blood they may pur-

chase time for their royal master's escape, do not take the malice of the
bloodthirsty crowd as a mere personal matter, since they know that they
are hated as his representatives, and are proud to suffer for him. Oh for
that chivalrous devotion to Christ, that we may only suffer in fellowship with his sufferings, die only in conformity to his death, identified with Him in all! It is, perhaps, the loftiest summit of devotion
when we crave love only to pass it on to Him; and dread hatred only
because it hurts the hearts that cherish it, and inflicts a wrong on the
dear and glorious Lord.

III. YOU MAY EXPECT GOD TO VINDICATE YOU. "And Moses said,
If these men die the common death of all men . . . then the Lord hath
not sent me. But if the Lord create a creation [*marg.*], and the ground
open her mouth and swallow them up . . . then ye shall understand that
these men have despised the Lord. And it came to pass, as he made an
end of speaking all these words, that the ground clave asunder that was
under them, and the earth opened her mouth and swallowed them up"
(vv. 38–32, R.V.). It was a terrible act of vengeance. It was essential to
the existence of the camp that the mutiny should be stamped out
without mercy. There was no help for it. The cancer must be cut out
of the quivering flesh. The death would be painless for the little ones,
and though cut off from life here they would pass at once into the broad
and blessed spaces of eternity, but for the rest the punishment was merited, and their extermination saved the camp.

Many have essayed to stamp out the church of God, but, like
Haman, have been hanged on the gallows prepared for Mordecai.
Others have spoken against the servants of the Lord, but have suffered
untimely and terrible deaths. The bears out of the wood have devoured. Herod has been eaten by worms. Persecutors have died in
horrible torment. No weapon that has been formed against God's
saints has prospered. Every tongue that has been raised against them
in judgment has been condemned.

Trust Him, O suffering saints, doing his will in the teeth of opposition and hate! Fear not the faces of men; be not dismayed before
their threats—He is with you to deliver you. They may fight against
you, but they shall not prevail; their proudest threats shall fail of their

fulfillment, as the sea billow which flings itself on the boulder is dissolved into a cloud of harmless spray. God loves his saints. They are all in his hand. But especially those are in its covert who are engaged in his sacred work. If only they are faithful to Him and to his behests, and live on his plan, there is nothing He will not do for them. When they call upon Him in their distress, He will deliver them from their strong enemy, and bring them into a large place, because He delights in them, and they put their trust in Him.

25
How It Went Ill
with Him

And Moses lifted up his hand, and with his
rod he smote the rock twice.
—Num. 20:11

It was but one act, one little act, but it blighted the fair flower of a
noble life, and shut the one soul, whose faith had sustained the responsibilities of the Exodus with unflinching fortitude, from the
reward which seemed so nearly within its grasp.

The wanderings of the forty years were almost over. The congregation which had been scattered over the peninsula had converged towards the given meeting place in Kadesh. There the encampment
remained for some months; and there Miriam died—one of the few
with whom that lonely spirit could still hold converse of that life
which lay beyond the desert sands, the valleys of Sinai, and the waters
of the Red Sea, in the distant mighty land of the Pharaohs and the Pyramids. Aaron, Caleb, Joshua (and perhaps the Levites), were the only
relics and survivors of that vast triumphant host, whose voices had rung
out their challenge on the morning of emancipation; and each of the
four thought himself sure, and his comrades also, of going over to "see
the good land that is beyond Jordan, that goodly mountain, and
Lebanon." But this was not to be.

I. How it Befell. The demand of the people on the water supply at Kadesh was so great, that the streams were drained; whereupon there broke out again that spirit of murmuring and complaint which had cursed the former generation, and was now reproduced in their children. Oblivious to the unwavering care of all the preceding years, the people assembled themselves together against Moses, and against Aaron, though it was against Moses that they principally directed their reproach.

They professed to wish that they had died in the plague that Aaron's censer had stayed. They accused the brothers of malicious designs to effect the destruction of the whole assembly by thirst. Although the cloud of God brooded overhead, and the manna fell day by day, they cursed their abiding place as evil. They taunted Moses with the absence of figs, vines, and pomegranates. They demanded water. And this was the new generation of which he had cherished such high hopes, the new growth on the old stock! It could hardly have been otherwise than that he should feel strongly provoked.

However, he resumed his old position, prostrating himself at the door of the tent of meeting until the growing light that welled forth from the secret place indicated that the Divine answer was near. Unlike the injunction on a similar occasion, which now lay back in the haze of years, Moses was bidden, though he took the rod, not to use it, but to speak to the rock with a certainty that the accents of his voice, smiting on its flinty face, would have as much effect as ever the rod had had previously, and would be followed by a rush of crystal water. Yes, when God is with you, words are equivalent to rods; the gentlest whisper spoken in his name will unlock the secrets of rocky chambers, and roll away great stones, and splinter sepulchers where entombed life awaits a summons. Rods are well enough to use at the commencement of faith's nurture, and when its strength is small, but they may be laid aside without hesitance in the later stages of the education of the soul. For as faith grows, the mere machinery and apparatus it employs becomes ever less; and its miracles are wrought with the slightest possible introduction of the material. Years ago you were bidden to use the rod because your faith was untried, but by this time the greater faith should work through a slighter and more fragile means.

Moses might have entered into these thoughts of God in quieter and more tranquil moments, but just now he was irritated, indignant, and hot with disappointment and anger. When, therefore, the assembly was gathered together in their thronging multitudes around him, he accosted them as rebels. He spoke as if the gift of water depended on himself and Aaron, He betrayed his sense of the irksomeness of their demand, and then vehemently smote the rock with his rod twice. And as those blows re-echoed through the still air, they shivered forever the fabric woven by his dreams and hopes.

The vision that had allured him through those long years faded as light off Alpine snows at sunset; and angels were sent to choose the site beneath the cliffs of Pisgah, where his body should keep guard at the gate of the Land, in which he had hoped to lie. What a warning is here, admonishing us that we sometimes fail in our strongest point; and that a noble career may be blasted by one small but significant and forever lamentable failure! "The Lord said unto Moses and Aaron, Because ye believed not in Me, to sanctify Me in the eyes of the children of Israel, therefore ye shall not bring this assembly into the land which I have given them" (v. 12, R.V.).

The people did not suffer through their leader's sin. The waters gushed from out the rock as plentifully as they would have done if the Divine injunctions had been precisely complied with. "The water came forth abundant; and the congregation drank, and their cattle." Man's unbelief does not make the power of God of none effect: though we believe not, yet He remains faithful; He cannot deny Himself, or desert the people of his choice.

II. THE PRINCIPLE THAT UNDERLAY THE DIVINE DECISION.
(1) *There was distinct Disobedience.* No doubt was possible as to the Divine command; and it had been distinctly infringed. He was not to strike, but to speak; and he had twice smitten the rock. In this way he had failed to sanctify God in the eyes of the people. He who ought to have set the example of implicit obedience to every jot and tittle, had inserted his own will and way as a substitute for God's. This could not be tolerated in one who was set to lead and teach the people.

God is sanctified whenever we put an inviolable fence around Himself and his words; treating them as unquestionable and decisive; obeying them with instant and utter loyalty; daring to place them high above all dispute as the supreme rule and guide of conduct. Therefore, when Moses set them aside to follow the behest of his own whim, it was equivalent to a desecration of the holy name of God. "Ye did not sanctify Me in the eyes of the children of Israel."

It is a solemn question for us all whether we are sufficiently accurate in our obedience. It is a repeated burden of those sad chapters of Hebrews, which tell the story of the wilderness wanderings—the cemetery chapters of the New Testament—that "they could not enter in because of unbelief." But throughout the verses the margin suggests the alternative reading of *disobedience,* because disobedience and unbelief are the two sides of the same coin—a coin of the devil's mintage. They who disobey do not believe; and they who do not believe disobey. May the great High Priest, with his sharp, two-edged sword, pierce to our innermost heart, to cut away the least symptom of disobedience; then shall faith be strong, and through its gates we shall pass into the land of rest.

(2) *There was Unbelief.* It was as if he had felt that a word was not enough. As if there must be something more of human might and instrumentality. There was a too evident reliance upon his own share in the transaction, or on the mysterious power of the rod which had so often wrought great wonders. He thought too much of these, to the exclusion or dwarfing of God's eternal power. He did not realize how small an act on his part was sufficient to open the sluice gates of Omnipotence. A touch is enough to set Omnipotence in action.

It is very wonderful to hear God say to Moses, "Ye believed not in Me." Was not this the man by whose faith the plagues of Egypt had fallen on that unhappy land; and the Red Sea had cleft its waters; and the daily manna had spread the desert floor with food; and the people had marched for thirty-eight years unhurt by hostile arm? What had happened? Had the wanderings impaired that mighty soul, and robbed it of its olden strength, and shorn the locks of its might, and left it like any other? Surely, something of this sort must have happened! One act could only have wrought such havoc by being the symptom of unsuspected wrong beneath. Oaks do not fall beneath a single storm, unless they have become rotten at their heart.

Let us watch and pray, lest there be in any of us an evil heart of unbelief; lest we depart in our most secret thought from simple faith in the living God; lest beneath a fair exterior we yield our jewel of faith to the solicitation of some unholy passion. Let us especially set a watch at our strongest point. Just because we are so confident of being strong there, we are liable to leave it unguarded and unwatched, and therefore open to the foe. So shall we be saved from a fall that shall shut the gates of Canaan against us, and consign us to an unknown and untimely grave.

But how much there is of this reliance on the rod in all Christian endeavor! Some special method has been owned of God in times past, in the conversion of the unsaved, or in the edification of God's people, and we instantly regard it as a kind of fetish. We try to meet new conditions by bringing out the rod and using it as of yore. It is a profound mistake. God never repeats Himself. He suits novel instrumentalities to new emergencies. He puts new wine into new bottles. Where a rod was needful once, He sees that a word is better now. It is for us to consult Him, and to abide by his decision; doing precisely as He tells us, and when, and where.

(3) *There was the spoiling of the type.* "That Rock was Christ"; from whose heart, smitten in death on Calvary, the river of water of life has flowed to make glad the city of God, and to transform deserts into Edens. But death came to Him, and can come to Him but once. "Christ was once offered to bear the sins of many." "The death that He died, He died unto sin once, but the life that he liveth, He liveth unto God." "I am He that was dead; and behold, I am alive forevermore." These texts prove how important it was to keep clear and defined the fact of the death of Christ being a finished act, once for all. It is evident that for the completeness of the likeness between substance and shadow, the rock should have been stroked but once. Instead of that, it was smitten at the beginning and at the close of the desert march. But this was a misrepresentation of an eternal fact; and the perpetrator of the heedless act of iconoclasm must suffer the extreme penalty, even as Uzzah died for trying to steady the swaying ark.

But there was something even deeper than these things. There was an eternal fitness in the nature of the case in Moses not being permitted to lead the people into the land of rest. Moses represented the law. It came by him; and he therefore fitly stands before the gaze of the ages as the embodiment of that supreme law, whose eye does not wax dim or its force abate, under the wear and tear of time. But the law can never lead us into rest. It can conduct us to the very margin and threshold, but no further. Another must take us in, the true Joshua—Jesus, the Savior and Lover of men.

III. THE IRREVOCABLENESS OF THE DIVINE DECISIONS. Moses drank very deeply of the bitter cup of disappointment. And it seems to have been his constant prayer that God would reverse or mitigate his sentence. "Let me go over, I pray Thee, and see the good land that is beyond Jordan, that goodly mountain, and Lebanon" (Deut. 3:25). No poet could have painted that land with more glowing colors. He dipped his brush in rainbow tints as he spoke of that good land—that land of brooks and fountains and depths; that land of wheat and barley, of vines and pomegranate and figs; that land of oil, olives, and honey. And no patriot ever yearned for fatherland as Moses to tread that blessed soil. With all the earnestness that he had used to plead for the people he now pleaded for himself. But it was not to be. "The Lord was wroth, and said unto me, Let it suffice thee; speak no more unto Me of this matter." The sin was forgiven, but its consequences were allowed to work out to their sorrowful issue. There are experiences with us all in which God forgives our sin, but takes vengeance on our inventions. We reap as we have sown. We suffer where we have sinned.

At such times our prayer is not literally answered. By the voice of his Spirit, by a spiritual instinct, we become conscious that it is useless to pray further. Though we pray, not thrice, but three hundred times, the thorn is not taken away. But there is a sense in which the prayer is answered. Our suffering is a lesson warning men in all after time. We are permitted from Pisgah's height to scan the fair land we long for, and are then removed to a better. We have the answer given to us in the after time, as Moses, who had his prayer gloriously fulfilled when he stood with Christ on the Transfiguration Mount. And in the meanwhile we hear his voice saying, My grace is sufficient for thee; my strength is made perfect in weakness.

But oh that God would undertake the keeping of our souls! Else, when we least expect it, we may be overtaken by some sudden temptation; which befalling us in the middle, or towards the close of our career, may blight our hopes, tarnish our fair name, bring dishonor to Him, and rob our life of the worthy capstone of its edifice.

27
Preparing for Pisgah

And Moses said unto them, I am a hundred
and twenty years old this day; I can no more
go out and come in: also the Lord hath said
unto me, Thou shalt not go over this Jordan.
—Deuteronomy 31:2

J ust before the dark River through which Pilgrims pass to the
City of God, Bunyan places the land of Beulah, where the sun ever
shines, the birds sing, and every day the flowers appear on the
earth. The air is very sweet and pleasant. It is within sight of the City,
but it is beyond the reach of Giant Despair; and they who come
thither cannot so much as see the turrets of Doubting Castle. And in
some such blissful experience saintly men have sought to spend a
brief parenthesis between the press of life's business and their entrance into the welcome of Christ. But such was not the experience of
Moses. The last year of his life was as full of work as any that had ever
passed over his head.

There was, first, the conquest of Eastern Canaan. Dean Stanley speaks
of it as that mysterious eastern frontier of the Holy Land, so beautiful,
so romantic, so little known. Its original inhabitants had been expelled by the kindred tribes of Moab and Ammon, but they, in their
turn, had been dispossessed of a considerable portion of the territory
thus acquired, by the two Canaanite chiefs, Sihon and Og, whose
names occur so frequently in this narrative.

The attack of the Israelites was justified by the churlish refusal of Sihon to the request that they might march through his borders on their way to Jericho. He not only refused them passage, but gathered all his people together, and went out against Israel on the frontier line between his territory and the wilderness. The son which commemorated the victory lays special emphasis on the prowess of the slingers and archers of Israel, afterwards so renowned: "We have shot at them; Heshbon is perished." These words suggest the probable reason for the overthrow of this powerful monarch, under the providence of God. The sword followed on arrow or stone, so that the army was practically annihilated; nor further resistance was offered to the march of the victorious foe. The cities opened their gates; and this fertile region between the Arnon and the Jabbok, consisting of "a wide tableland, tossed about in wild confusion of undulating downs, clothed with rich grass, and in spring waving with great sheets of wheat and barley, came into possession of the chosen people.

But this was not all. North of this lay Bashan, which has been described by Canon Tristram and others as a rich and well-wooded country, abounding in noble forests of oak and of olive trees, interspersed with patches of corn in the open glades. It was and is the most picturesque and the most productive portion of the Holy Land. Og, its king, was renowned for his gigantic stature. According to Josephus' narrative, he was coming to the assistance of Sihon, when he heard of his defeat and death. But, undaunted, he set his army in array against the hosts of Israel. The battle took place at Edrei, which stood to guard the entrance of a remarkable mountain fastness; and it ended in the complete victory of Israel. The result is told in the strong, concise narrative of Moses. "They smote him, his sons, and all his people, until there was none left him remaining; and they possessed his land."

Nothing could have accounted for the marvelous victories, which gave Israel possession of these valuable tracts of country—with cities fenced with high walls, gates, and bars, together with a great many unwalled towns—but the interposition of God. He had said beforehand, "Fear not! I have delivered him into thy hand"; and so it befell. Immense swarms of hornets, which are common in Palestine, seemed to have visited the country at this juncture; so that the people were driven from their fortresses into the open plains, where they were less able to stand the assault of the Israelites.

Moses, at their urgent request, proceeded to allot this rich and beautiful territory to the Reubenites and Gadites and the half tribe of Manasseh, after receiving their solemn pledge to bear their share in the conquest of Western Palestine. "I commanded you," he said afterwards, "that ye shall pass armed before your brethren, the children of Israel, until the Lord give rest unto your brethren, as unto you."

Next came his last charge to the people. This was delivered in a series of farewell addresses, which are contained in chapters 1–30 of the Book of Deuteronomy. This book is to the four preceding ones much what the Gospel according to John is to the other three. It is full of the most pathetic and stirring appeals. Memory of the past, gratitude, fear, self-interest, are the chords made to vibrate to this master touch. Well may it be said of Moses that he loved the people; and in these pages we may trace the course of the molten lava which poured from his heart.

The key phrases of that remarkable book are: Keep diligently; Observe to do; and, The Lord shall choose. It abounds with exquisite descriptions of the Land of Promise, which may be spiritually applied to those rapturous experiences denoted by the phrase, The Rest of Faith. It is, indeed, as old Canaan was, a good land, a land of brooks of water, of fountains and depths springing out of valleys and hills. There we drink of the river of the water of life; there we eat the bread of life without scarceness, and lack nothing that we really need. The 28th chapter anticipates the Beatitudes of our Lord's Sermon on the Mount; and happy is he that can appropriate them in blissful experience, and go in to possess the land.

In our judgment the much-debated questioning of authorship is settled by the distinct affirmation of the New Testament. Take, for instance, the quotation of Deuteronomy 30:11–14 in Romans 10:6–10. The Apostle Paul distinctly speaks of Moses as having written these words.

Next came his anxiety about a successor. Moses spoke unto the Lord, saying, "Let the Lord, the God of the spirits of all flesh, set a man over the congregation, which may go out before them, and which may go in before them; which may lead them out, and bring them in, that the congregation of the Lord be not as sheep which have no shepherd." In answer to this request, he had been directed to take Joshua, the son of Nun, in whom was the Spirit, to bring him before Eleazar, the priest, and before all the congregation, and to give him a charge. This he seems to have done, but as death drew near he apparently gave him a second charge (compare Num. 27:16, 17, and Deut. 31:7, 8).

What a striking scene it must have been when, on his one-hundred-and-twentieth birthday, the aged lawgiver called unto Joshua, and said unto him in the sight of all Israel, "Be strong and of a good courage: for thou must go with this people unto the land which the Lord hath sworn unto their fathers to give them; and thou shalt cause them to inherit it. And the Lord, He it is that doth go before thee; He will be with thee; He will not fail thee, neither forsake thee; fear not, neither be dismayed." Immediately afterwards the pillar of cloud stood over the door of the Tabernacle, and Moses and Joshua were summoned to present themselves before God in its sacred precincts. There, in almost identical words to those which He had spoken by the lips of Moses, God gave Joshua his commission to bring the children of Israel into the land which He had sworn unto them, together with the promise that He would be with them.

His last acts were to arrange for the custody of the Law and the perpetuation of its reading. He did the first by depositing the book, in which he had recorded the Divine revelations made to him, in the side of the Ark of the Covenant. It was to be kept under the custody of the Levites; and passages were to be read from it at the end of every seven years, when all Israel appeared before God in the place which He should choose.

And as to the second, Moses put his exhortations and entreaties into two magnificent odes, the one dealing out warnings against apostasy, the other dwelling seriatim on the characteristics of the tribes, and giving them a parting blessing, after the fashion of the dying Jacob.

The thirty-second chapter of Deuteronomy is one of the sublimest human compositions on record. It was Moses' swan song. It is the store from which later Scripture writers draw plentifully, It has been called the Magna Charta of Prophecy. It is worthy to be compared to one only song else, the Song of the Lamb, with which it is combined by the harpers on the margin of the glassy sea: "They sing the song of Moses, the servant of God, and the song of the Lamb."

The repeated comparisons of God to a Rock; the lavish kindness with which He had treated his people since He first found them in a desert land; the comparison of the Eternal to a mother eagle in teaching its young to climb the unaccustomed steeps of air; the ingratitude with which his marvelous kindness had been requited; the dread fate to which their rebellion must expose them; the mercy with which their repentance would be greeted—all these are recorded in glowing, eloquent words, that stand forever as a witness of how stammering lips may speak when they have been touched with the live altar coal. Or take the closing verses of the Benediction on the tribes. The lonely glory of the God of Jeshurun, who rides on the heavens to help and save his people; the home which men may find in his eternal nature; the underpinning everlasting arms; the irresistible might with which He thrusts out the enemy from before the forward march of the soul He loves; the safe though isolated dwelling of Israel; the fertility of the soil and the generosity of the clouds; the blessedness of having Jehovah as the shield of help and the sword of excellency—all these features of the blessed life are delineated by the master hand of one who dipped his brush in the colors mixed by his own experience.

What glimpses we get of the inner life of this noble man! All that he wrought on earth was the outcome of the secret abiding of his soul in God. God was his home, his help, his stay. He was nothing: God was all. And all that he accomplished on the earth was due to that Mighty One indwelling, fulfilling, and working out through him, as his organ and instrument, his own consummate plans.

Thus Moses drew his life work to a close. Behind him, a long and glorious life, before, the ministry and worship of the heavenly sanctuary. Here, the Shekinah; there, the unveiled face. Here, the tent and pilgrim march; there, the everlasting rest. Here, the promised land, beheld from afar, but not entered; there, the goodly land beyond Jordan entered and possessed. What though it was a wrench to pass away, with the crowning stone not placed on the structure of his life; to depart and be with God was far better!

28
The Death of Moses

So Moses, the servant of the Lord, died there
in the land of Moab, according to the word
of the Lord. And He buried him in a valley
in the land of Moab, over against Beth-peor.
—Deuteronomy 34:5, 6

The Bible is the book of *life*. Its pages teem with biography; they contain but scant memorials of death. The only death they described at length is that of Him who in dying slew death. The very minuteness of the description there shows how unique and all-important it was. Men make more of death than of life as a gauge of character. A few pious sentences spoken then will go far to efface the memory of years of inconsistency. God makes most of life.

The records of Scripture find little room by dying testimonies, words, or experiences; while they abound in stories of the exploits and words of those who have stormed and suffered and wrought in life's arena. This may explain why, contrary to human custom and expectation, the death of the great Lawgiver is described with such brief simplicity.

But this simplicity is only equaled by the sublimity of the conception. After such a life it was meet that Moses should have a death and burial unparalleled in the story of mankind; and we do not wonder that poet, painter, and preacher, have found in that lonely death on Pisgah's summit a theme worthy of their noblest powers. We can but cull a few wild flowers as they caress that mountain brow; more we must leave to others. Moses' death casts a light on sin, and death, and dispensational truth.

I. ITS BEARING ON SIN. We cannot suppose that the sudden outburst of impetuous temper at Meribah—when his spirit was agitated by a fierce whirlwind of wrath, as a storm sweeping down some mountain rent on an inland lake—could remain long unforgiven. As far as the east is from the west, so far had that transgression been removed. But though the remission was complete, yet the result lingered in his life, and shut him out from an experience which should have been the crown of his career.

"The Lord hath put away thy sin," said Nathan to the royal transgressor, but "thy child shall die, and the sword shall not depart out of thy house." The dying chief was pardoned, but he suffered in his body the extreme penalty of his sin. The mistrust which hinders a man from accepting all the benefits of Christ's Ascension is put away, but nothing can compensate him for his loss. Never a word may be spoken about the evil courses that have wrecked the health and fortunes of the Prodigal, but though he sits at his father's board, he can never be in health or vigor or overflowing joy, as he might have been if he had never wandered forth.

Nor does sin only entail loss and sorrow on the transgressor; it robs mankind of much of the benefit which otherwise had accrued from his life. If it had not been for his want of faith and his passionate behavior, Moses had led his people across the Jordan, and served them for many an after year.

Let not the ease of pardon ever tempt thee to think lightly of sin, or to imagine that it leaves no traces on soul or life, because it is secure, through penitence and faith, of God's forgiving mercy. If one act of mistrustful anger laid Moses, the friend and servant of God, in a desert grave on the frontiers of the Land, what may it not do for thee?

II. ITS BEARING ON DEATH. *Its Loneliness.* That majestic spirit had ever lifted itself, like some unscaled peak, amid other men. Into its secrets no foot had intruded, no human eye had peered. Alone it wrought and suffered, and met God, and legislated for the people. But its loneliness was never more apparent than when, unattended even by Joshua, he passed up to die amid the solitudes of Nebo. Alone he trod the craggy steep; alone he gazed on the fair landscape; alone he laid down to die.

But in that loneliness there is a foreshadowing of the loneliness through which each of us must pass unless caught up to meet the Lord in the air. In that solemn hour human voices will fade away, beloved forms retire, familiar scenes dim to the sight. Silent and lonely, the spirit migrates to learn for itself the great secret. Happy the man who, anticipating the moment, can say: "Alone, yet not alone, my Savior is with me. He who went this way by Himself is now retreading at my side."

Its Method. We die, as Moses did, "by the word of the Lord." It is said in the Hebrew legend that one angel after another sought to take his life in vain. First, there came the one who had been his special instructor, but his courage failed him when he essayed to destroy the fabric on which he had spent so much pains. Then the angel of death was summoned to undertake the task. He eagerly approached him, but when he saw the wondrous luster of his face shining like the sun, and heard him recite the prodigies of his career, he, too, shrank back abashed.

And when these great angels had given up the work as surpassing their loftiest powers, Moses turned to the Almighty (so the legend runs) and said, "Thou, Lord of the Universe, who wast revealed unto me in the burning bush, remember that Thou didst carry me up into thy heaven, where I abode forty days and forty nights; have mercy upon me, and hand me not over into the power of the angel of death."

This, of course, is the picturesque form in which the love and reverence of after generations elaborated these wonderful words, which tell us that Moses died "by the word of the Lord." Some still further substituted "kiss" for "word"; so that it seemed as if the Almighty had kissed away the soul of his faithful servant, drawing it back to himself in a long, sweet, tender embrace.

Is not this the manner in which all saints die? Their deaths are precious to the Lord, and after the troubled day of life—agitated in its early morning by the trumpet calling to battle; fretted through an overcast noon by the pressure of its responsibilities and cares; lit in the evening by the rays of a stormy sunset, piercing through the cloud drift, the tired spirit sinks down upon the couch, which the hands of God had spread, and He bends over it to give its goodnight kiss, as in earliest days the mother had done to the wearied child. That embrace, however, is the threshold, not of a long night of insensibility, but of an awakening in the supernal light of the everlasting morning.

Its Sepulcher. We are told that "the Lord buried him in a valley in the land of Moab," in spite of the opposition of the Evil One, who contended with the archangel sent to secure that noble deserted shrine. What had the archfiend to do with it? Did he desire to make it vie with the temple of the living God, filching honors which the people would be only too glad to give? We know not, but his purpose was ignominiously frustrated. God cared for the dead body of his child. Not even the king of terrors could make it distasteful to the Father's love. Though in ruins, the temple was precious. And so even a band of angels was not permitted to perform the sacred work of interment. We are told that *He* buried him; as if the Almighty would not delegate the sacred office to any inferior hand. And is it not attributable of the love of God that through the love of friendly hearts the last rites are rendered to the bodies which Christ has purchased?

As we trust God to supply the needs of the body in life, so let us trust Him for its burial in death. He marks where the dust of each of his children mingles with its mother earth. When a grave is opened, his eye rests on it; and though no foot may ever tread its soil, no hand keep it decked with flowers, He never forgets it; and none will be overlooked when the archangel blows his trumpet over land and sea.

Its Purpose. We are told that "the children of Israel wept for Moses thirty days"; and if we connect this statement with the fact of the unknown grave, we shall be able to discern the Divine purpose in its concealment. We often underrate the living, and have to wait until they are removed from us to estimate them truly.

Few men have had greater claims on their fellows than Moses. He had sacrificed his high position in Pharaoh's court to bear his people as a nurse through the ailments of their childhood. He had enjoyed unparalleled opportunities of fellowship with God. He had wielded uncommon power: at the bidding of his faith winds had brought meat; rocks had gushed with water springs; the sea had parted and met; the desert floor had been strewn with food. Is it not more than likely that, if the Lord had not concealed his grave, the valley of Beth-peor would have become a second Mecca, trodden by the feet of pilgrims from all the world? It was best to make such idolatry impossible. The hidden grave forced the people to turn from earth to heaven.

Is not this God's policy with us? When Lazarus is dead, the sisters send for Jesus. When the gourd is blasted the pilgrim in the weary land turns to the shadow of the great Rock. When no place is found for the sole of her foot, the dove makes for the window of the air. When the supply fails from the rock cisterns, we are driven to the stream which flows from the throne of God. This is why your home is desolate, and your heart bereaved. It is for this that he who was to you what Moses was to the people has been removed.

> For e'en the cloud
> That spread above, and veiled love,
> Itself is love.

Its Vision. From the spot on which he stood, without any extraordinary gift of vision, his eye could range over an almost unequaled panorama. At his feet, the faraway tents of Israel; to the North, the rich pasture lands of Gilead, and Bashan, bounded by the desert haze on the one hand, and on the other by the Jordan valley, from the blue waters of the Lake of Galilee to the dark gorge of the Dead Sea. And beyond the river he could sweep over the fair land of Promise, from the snow-capped summits of Hermon and Lebanon to the uplands of Ephraim and Manasseh; with the infinite variety of cities perched on their pinnacles of rock, of cornfields and pasture lands, of oil, olives, figs, vines, and pomegranates. Immediately before him, looking West, was Jericho, in its green setting of palm trees, connected by the steep defile with Jerusalem, not far from which Bethlehem, on the ridge of the hills, gleamed as a jewel.

So to dying men still comes the vision of the goodly land beyond the Jordan. It is not far away—only just across the river. On fair days of vision, when some strong wind parts the veils of mist and smoke that too often dominate our spiritual atmosphere, it is clearly visible. But the vision is most often reserved for those who are waiting on the confines of the Land, ready for the signal to enter. They tell us that on that borderland they hear voices, and discern visions of beauty and splendor, of which heart had not conceived. Dr. Payson said, shortly before he died, "The Celestial City is full in my view. Its glories have been upon me; its breezes fan me; it odors are wafted to me; its sounds strike upon my ears; and its spirit is breathed into my heart." May God grant us the blessedness of dying on the hilltop with that vision in our gaze.

III. THE BEARING ON DISPENSATIONAL TRUTH. The Law came by Moses; and Moses stands on the plains of history as the embodiment; as he was also the vehicle, of the moral law, whether given from Sinai or written on the fleshy tablets of the human heart.

It was in perfect keeping with this conception that there was no decay in his natural vigor. His eye was as a falcon's, his step lithe and elastic, his bearing erect. He did not die of disease, or amid the decrepitude of old age; "he was not, because God took him." Time had only made him venerable, but not weak. And thus he represents God's holy law, which cannot grow outworn or weak, but always abides in its pristine and perfect strength, though it cannot bring us into God's rest.

Of that rest it is not possible to speak here. Canaan does not primarily represent the rest which awaits us on the other side of death, where the fret and chafe of life are over, but the rest which may be entered here and now, in which the soul is set free from the tyranny of self and corruption, and abides in the peace of God which passes all understanding. Then life becomes one blessed succession of trustful obedience to the will of God; then, too, we are satisfied with the abundant wealth stored up for us in God, and He makes us drink of the river of his pleasure. This is the goodly Land of promise, which can only be seen from afar by those who know nothing except what Moses can teach them, but may be entered by those who follow the Ark through the river of death to the self-life and forward to resurrection ground.